Economic Analysis of the Digital Economy

National Bureau of
Economic Research
Conference Report

Economic Analysis of the Digital Economy

Edited by **Avi Goldfarb, Shane M. Greenstein, and Catherine E. Tucker**

The University of Chicago Press

Chicago and London

AVI GOLDFARB is professor of marketing at the Rotman School of Management at the University of Toronto. SHANE M. GREENSTEIN is the Kellogg Chair in Information Technology and professor of management and strategy at the Kellogg School of Management at Northwestern University. CATHERINE E. TUCKER is the Mark Hyman Jr. Career Development Professor and associate professor of management science at the MIT Sloan School of Management. All three editors are research associates of the National Bureau of Economic Research.

The University of Chicago Press, Chicago 60637
The University of Chicago Press, Ltd., London
© 2015 by the National Bureau of Economic Research
All rights reserved. Published 2015.
Printed in the United States of America

24 23 22 21 20 19 18 17 16 15   1 2 3 4 5
ISBN-13: 978-0-226-20684-4 (cloth)
ISBN-13: 978-0-226-20698-1 (e-book)
DOI: 10.7208/chicago/9780226206981.001.0001

Library of Congress Cataloging-in-Publication Data

Economic analysis of the digital economy / edited by Avi Goldfarb, Shane M. Greenstein, and Catherine E. Tucker.
    pages cm — (National Bureau of Economic Research conference report)
    ISBN 978-0-226-20684-4 (cloth : alk. paper) —
ISBN 978-0-226-20698-1 (e-book) 1. Digital media—Economic aspects. 2. Digital media—Government policy. 3. Internet—Economic aspects. I. Goldfarb, Avi. II. Greenstein, Shane M. III. Tucker, Catherine (Catherine Elizabeth) IV. Series: National Bureau of Economic Research conference report.
    ZA4045.E26 2015
    302.23'1—dc23
                                                                    2014035487

♾ This paper meets the requirements of ANSI/NISO Z39.48-1992 (Permanence of Paper).

National Bureau of Economic Research

Officers

Martin B. Zimmerman, *chairman*
Karen N. Horn, *vice chairman*
James M. Poterba, *president and chief executive officer*
Robert Mednick, *treasurer*

Kelly Horak, *controller and assistant corporate secretary*
Alterra Milone, *corporate secretary*
Denis Healy, *assistant corporate secretary*

Directors at Large

Peter C. Aldrich
Elizabeth E. Bailey
John H. Biggs
John S. Clarkeson
Don R. Conlan
Kathleen B. Cooper
Charles H. Dallara
George C. Eads
Jessica P. Einhorn

Mohamed El-Erian
Linda Ewing
Jacob A. Frenkel
Judith M. Gueron
Robert S. Hamada
Peter Blair Henry
Karen N. Horn
John Lipsky
Laurence H. Meyer

Michael H. Moskow
Alicia H. Munnell
Robert T. Parry
James M. Poterba
John S. Reed
Marina v. N. Whitman
Martin B. Zimmerman

Directors by University Appointment

Jagdish Bhagwati, *Columbia*
Timothy Bresnahan, *Stanford*
Alan V. Deardorff, *Michigan*
Ray C. Fair, *Yale*
Edward Foster, *Minnesota*
John P. Gould, *Chicago*
Mark Grinblatt, *California, Los Angeles*
Bruce Hansen, *Wisconsin–Madison*

Benjamin Hermalin, *California, Berkeley*
Marjorie B. McElroy, *Duke*
Joel Mokyr, *Northwestern*
Andrew Postlewaite, *Pennsylvania*
Cecilia Rouse, *Princeton*
Richard L. Schmalensee, *Massachusetts Institute of Technology*
David B. Yoffie, *Harvard*

Directors by Appointment of Other Organizations

Jean-Paul Chavas, *Agricultural and Applied Economics Association*
Martin Gruber, *American Finance Association*
Ellen L. Hughes-Cromwick, *National Association for Business Economics*
Arthur Kennickell, *American Statistical Association*
William W. Lewis, *Committee for Economic Development*
Robert Mednick, *American Institute of Certified Public Accountants*

Alan L. Olmstead, *Economic History Association*
Peter L. Rousseau, *American Economic Association*
Gregor W. Smith, *Canadian Economics Association*
William Spriggs, *American Federation of Labor and Congress of Industrial Organizations*
Bart van Ark, *The Conference Board*

Directors Emeriti

George Akerlof
Glen G. Cain
Carl F. Christ
Franklin Fisher

George Hatsopoulos
Saul H. Hymans
Rudolph A. Oswald
Peter G. Peterson

Nathan Rosenberg
John J. Siegfried
Craig Swan

**Relation of the Directors to the
Work and Publications of the
National Bureau of Economic Research**

1. The object of the NBER is to ascertain and present to the economics profession, and to the public more generally, important economic facts and their interpretation in a scientific manner without policy recommendations. The Board of Directors is charged with the responsibility of ensuring that the work of the NBER is carried on in strict conformity with this object.

2. The President shall establish an internal review process to ensure that book manuscripts proposed for publication DO NOT contain policy recommendations. This shall apply both to the proceedings of conferences and to manuscripts by a single author or by one or more co-authors but shall not apply to authors of comments at NBER conferences who are not NBER affiliates.

3. No book manuscript reporting research shall be published by the NBER until the President has sent to each member of the Board a notice that a manuscript is recommended for publication and that in the President's opinion it is suitable for publication in accordance with the above principles of the NBER. Such notification will include a table of contents and an abstract or summary of the manuscript's content, a list of contributors if applicable, and a response form for use by Directors who desire a copy of the manuscript for review. Each manuscript shall contain a summary drawing attention to the nature and treatment of the problem studied and the main conclusions reached.

4. No volume shall be published until forty-five days have elapsed from the above notification of intention to publish it. During this period a copy shall be sent to any Director requesting it, and if any Director objects to publication on the grounds that the manuscript contains policy recommendations, the objection will be presented to the author(s) or editor(s). In case of dispute, all members of the Board shall be notified, and the President shall appoint an ad hoc committee of the Board to decide the matter; thirty days additional shall be granted for this purpose.

5. The President shall present annually to the Board a report describing the internal manuscript review process, any objections made by Directors before publication or by anyone after publication, any disputes about such matters, and how they were handled.

6. Publications of the NBER issued for informational purposes concerning the work of the Bureau, or issued to inform the public of the activities at the Bureau, including but not limited to the NBER Digest and Reporter, shall be consistent with the object stated in paragraph 1. They shall contain a specific disclaimer noting that they have not passed through the review procedures required in this resolution. The Executive Committee of the Board is charged with the review of all such publications from time to time.

7. NBER working papers and manuscripts distributed on the Bureau's web site are not deemed to be publications for the purpose of this resolution, but they shall be consistent with the object stated in paragraph 1. Working papers shall contain a specific disclaimer noting that they have not passed through the review procedures required in this resolution. The NBER's web site shall contain a similar disclaimer. The President shall establish an internal review process to ensure that the working papers and the web site do not contain policy recommendations, and shall report annually to the Board on this process and any concerns raised in connection with it.

8. Unless otherwise determined by the Board or exempted by the terms of paragraphs 6 and 7, a copy of this resolution shall be printed in each NBER publication as described in paragraph 2 above.

Contents

Acknowledgments	xi
Introduction Avi Goldfarb, Shane M. Greenstein, and Catherine E. Tucker	1

I. INTERNET SUPPLY AND DEMAND

1. Modularity and the Evolution of the Internet Timothy Simcoe *Comment*: Timothy F. Bresnahan	21
2. What Are We Not Doing When We Are Online? Scott Wallsten *Comment*: Chris Forman	55

II. DIGITIZATION, ECONOMIC FRICTIONS, AND NEW MARKETS

3. The Future of Prediction: How Google Searches Foreshadow Housing Prices and Sales Lynn Wu and Erik Brynjolfsson	89
4. Bayesian Variable Selection for Nowcasting Economic Time Series Steven L. Scott and Hal R. Varian	119

5. Searching for Physical and Digital Media: The Evolution of Platforms for Finding Books   137
   Michael R. Baye, Babur De los Santos, and Matthijs R. Wildenbeest
   Comment: Marc Rysman

6. Ideology and Online News   169
   Matthew Gentzkow and Jesse M. Shapiro

7. Measuring the Effects of Advertising: The Digital Frontier   191
   Randall Lewis, Justin M. Rao, and David H. Reiley

8. Digitization and the Contract Labor Market: A Research Agenda   219
   Ajay Agrawal, John Horton, Nicola Lacetera, and Elizabeth Lyons
   Comment: Christopher Stanton

9. Some Economics of Private Digital Currency   257
   Joshua S. Gans and Hanna Halaburda

III. GOVERNMENT POLICY AND DIGITIZATION

10. Estimation of Treatment Effects from Combined Data: Identification versus Data Security   279
    Tatiana Komarova, Denis Nekipelov, and Evgeny Yakovlev

11. Information Lost: Will the "Paradise" That Information Promises, to Both Consumer and Firm, Be "Lost" on Account of Data Breaches? The Epic is Playing Out   309
    Catherine L. Mann
    Comment: Amalia R. Miller

12. Copyright and the Profitability of Authorship: Evidence from Payments to Writers in the Romantic Period   357
    Megan MacGarvie and Petra Moser
    Comment: Koleman Strumpf

13. Understanding Media Markets in the Digital Age: Economics and Methodology   385
    Brett Danaher, Samita Dhanasobhon, Michael D. Smith, and Rahul Telang

14. **Digitization and the Quality of New Media Products: The Case of Music**   407
    Joel Waldfogel

15. **The Nature and Incidence of Software Piracy: Evidence from Windows**   443
    Susan Athey and Scott Stern
    Comment: Ashish Arora

    Contributors   481
    Author Index   485
    Subject Index   491

Acknowledgments

It almost goes without saying, but it is worth saying nonetheless: we are grateful to our authors and discussants for working with us on this project. This was a collective effort of many contributors, and we thank all of the participants. We also thank the Sloan Foundation for their support and encouragement. In addition to funding, Danny Goroff, Josh Greenberg, and Paul Joskow each provided the advice, criticism, and praise necessary to create a successful project. Josh Lerner, Scott Stern, Nick Bloom, and Jim Poterba enabled the creation of a digitization initiative at the NBER. The NBER provided the intellectual home to the project, and we are grateful for the infrastructure and environment conducive to creative economic thinking about the impact of digitization. The staff at the University of Chicago Press and Rob Shannon and Helena Fitz-Patrick at the NBER provided essential support without which this book would have been impossible to complete. We thank the Kellogg School of Management for hosting our preconference in Chicago and Ranna Rozenfeld for hosting our dinner. Finally, we thank Rachel, Ranna, and Alex, as well as all of our children, for their patience with us as this project developed.

Introduction

Avi Goldfarb, Shane M. Greenstein,
and Catherine E. Tucker

Research on the economics of digitization studies whether and how digital technology changes markets. Digital technology has led to a rapid decline in the cost of storage, computation, and transmission of data. As a consequence, economic activity is increasingly digital. The transformative nature of digital technology has implications for how we understand economic activity, how consumers behave, how firms develop competitive strategy, how entrepreneurs start new firms, and how governments should determine policy.

This volume explores the economic impact of digitization in a variety of contexts and also aims to set an agenda for future research in the economics of digitization. While no one volume can be comprehensive, the objective is to identify topics with promising areas of research. The chapters summarize and illustrate areas in which some research is already underway and warrant further exploration from economists.

Of the various technology drivers enabling the rise of digital technology, growth in digital communication—particularly the Internet—has played a central role. It is constructive to focus a volume around digital communi-

Avi Goldfarb is professor of marketing at the Rotman School of Management, University of Toronto, and a research associate of the National Bureau of Economic Research. Shane M. Greenstein is the Kellogg Chair of Information Technology and professor of management and strategy at the Kellogg School of Management, Northwestern University, and a research associate of the National Bureau of Economic Research. Catherine Tucker is the Mark Hyman Jr. Career Development Professor and associate professor of management science at the Sloan School of Management, Massachusetts Institute of Technology, and a research associate of the National Bureau of Economic Research.

For acknowledgments, sources of research support, and disclosure of the authors' material financial relationships, if any, please see http://www.nber.org/chapters/c12987.ack.

cation as a key driver of economic activity. In particular, digitization has some features that suggest that many well-studied economic models may not apply, suggesting a need for a better understanding of how digitization changes market outcomes.

The development of a nearly ubiquitous Internet has motivated many new questions. In particular, the Internet's deployment and adoption encouraged the growth of digital products and services, and many of these display very low marginal costs of production and distribution. Correspondingly, digital markets are often easy to enter. These features have motivated questions about how digitization has restructured economic activities across a broad array of the economy.

Similarly, low communication costs, even over long distances, also brought about economic restructuring by creating opportunities for new marketplaces. This motivates questions about how new marketplaces can overcome information asymmetries between buyers and sellers in different places, and reduce search costs for either type of participant in a market. Low communication costs also translate into low distribution costs for information services. That means that nonexcludable information services resemble public goods that can be consumed at enormous scales, by hundreds of millions of people, and perhaps by billions in the future. That has focused attention on the incentives to develop public goods and understand how these diffuse. It has also focused attention on the valuation issues that arise when businesses and households reallocate their time to unpriced goods.

While these features of digital markets and service do not generally require fundamentally new economic insight, they do require more than simply taking theoretical and empirical results from other markets and assuming the implications will be the same. For example, digital information can be stored easily and aggregated to improve measurement. This creates previously unseen challenges for privacy and security, and those issues are not salient in other economic analyses because they do not have to be. More broadly, many policies that have been settled for many years seem poorly adapted to digital markets. It is no secret that firms and governments have struggled to apply copyright, security, and antitrust regulations to the digital context, as the reasoning that supported specific policies came under pressure from piracy, or lost relevance in a new set of economic circumstances. General pressures to alter policies are coming from mismatches between historical institutions and the present circumstances, and these mismatches generate calls from private and public actors to make changes. These pressures will not disappear any time soon, nor will the calls for change. Economic research on digitization can inform the debate.

We do not think the economics of digitization is a new field. Rather, digitization research touches a variety of fields of economics including (but not limited to) industrial organization, economic history, applied econometrics, labor economics, tax policy, monetary economics, international economics, and industrial organization. Many of the key contributions to the economics of digitization have also found an intellectual home in these fields. What distinguishes research on the economics of digitization is an understanding of the role of digital technology. Research on the economics of digitization therefore has a consistent framing, even if the applications are diverse.

There are two complementary approaches to motivating new work. One characterizes the progress to date in addressing fundamental research questions, as a handbook might do (see, e.g., Peitz and Waldfogel 2012). The other approach, which this volume pursues, stresses different ways to address open research questions by providing extensive examples of how to frame, execute, and present research on the frontier. These are not mutually exclusive approaches, and many chapters in this book dedicate substantial attention to the prior literature before providing new analysis and ideas.

As might be expected, the scope of the book is quite broad, and drawing boundaries required several judgment calls. In general, the topics in the book emphasize the agenda of open questions and also tend to stress unsettled issues in public policy.

A few traits are shared by all the chapters. The topics are representative of many of the active frontiers of economic research today and are not slanted toward one subdiscipline's approach to the area. More affirmatively, the chapters illustrate that the economics of digitization draw from many fields of economics and matches the approach to the question. No chapter argues for any form of digitization exceptionalism—as if this research requires the economic equivalent of the invention of quantum mechanics, or a fundamental break from prior precedents in positive analysis or econometric methods. The Internet contains unique features that require additional data, as well as sensitivity to new circumstances, not a radical abandoning of prior economic lessons.

The volume's chapters take steps toward building a theoretically grounded and empirically relevant economic framework for analyzing the determinants and consequences of digitization. For example, several chapters examine questions about how digitization changes market structure and market conduct. These changes are especially evident in newspapers, music, movies, and other media. Relatedly, there are many broad questions arising in areas where copyright plays an important role. The application of copyright to online activity has altered both the incentives for innovation and creativity. The advent of piracy has altered the monetization of the products and services. Digitization has also altered the costs of collecting, retaining, and distributing personal information, which is an important development in itself. It is also consequential for the personalization of commerce, such as in targeted advertising.

Many chapters address policy issues related to digitization, including copyright law, privacy law, and efforts to restructure the delivery and access to digitized content and data. There also is a strong emphasis on developing unbiased approaches to economic measurement. Unbiased measurement can assess the extent of digitization and begin the long-term conversation toward understanding the private and social costs of digitization. As a consequence, this will improve understanding of the rate of return on investments in digitization by public and private organizations.

An astute reader will notice that some topics do not make it into the book. Perhaps most directly, all chapters focus on digitization enabled through the Internet rather than other consequences of digital technology such as increased automation in manufacturing and services or increased use of digital medical records. In addition, some relevant Internet-related topics do not appear. There is only a peripheral discussion about universal service for new communications technology such as broadband Internet access to homes in high-cost regions or low-income regions. It is an important topic, but the economic issues are not fundamentally unique to digitization and resemble universal service debates of the past. There is also limited coverage of many issues in the design of markets for search goods (e.g., keyword auctions) because there is already a robust conversation in many areas related to these services. Therefore, the book focuses attention on frontier questions that remain open, such as search and online matching in labor markets.

Finally, the volume also largely eschews the well-known debates about information technology (IT)'s productivity and what has become known as the Solow Paradox, often stated as "We see the IT everywhere except in the productivity statistics." Again, that is because the literature is large and robust. The contrast is, however, particularly instructive. This volume stresses vexing issues in measuring the value of digital services where the measurement issues are less widely appreciated by academic economists and where mainstream economic analysis could shed light.

The remainder of the introduction provides some detail. The first set of chapters discusses the basic supply and demand for Internet access. The next set of chapters discusses various ways in which digitization reduces economic frictions and creates new opportunities and challenges for business. The final set of chapters lays out some policy issues that these opportunities and challenges create. All the chapters received comments from discussants at a conference held in June 2013, in Park City, Utah. In some cases the discussants chose to make their commentary available and these are provided as well.

Internet Supply and Demand

The Internet is not a single piece of equipment with components from multiple suppliers. It is a multilayered network in which different participants operate different pieces. Sometimes these pieces are complements to one another, and sometimes substitutes. Many years ago, the "Internet" referred to the networking technology that enables computer networks to communicate. Over time it has come to also mean the combination of standards, networks, and web applications (such as streaming and file sharing) that have accumulated around the networking technology.

Internet technology has evolved through technological competition. Many firms possess in-house technical leadership that enables them to develop and sell components and services that are valuable to computer users. Firms that do not possess such capabilities can acquire them through the market by, for example, hiring a team of qualified engineers. Consequently, multiple firms can possess both the (expensive) assets and the (rare) employees with skills to reach the frontier and commercialize products near the technical frontier. Bresnahan and Greenstein (1999) call this feature of market structure "divided technical leadership," contrasting it with earlier eras in which a single firm could aspire to control the vast majority of inputs near the technical frontier. Therefore, one of the big open research questions is: What are the principles of competition in this area of divided technical leadership?

Computing market segments are typically defined by "platforms," which Bresnahan and Greenstein define as "a reconfigurable base of compatible components on which users build applications." Platforms are identified by a set of technical standards or by engineering specifications for compatible hardware and software. The emergence of platforms with many stakeholders (including firms, academics, and nonprofits) increased the importance of organizations that design standards and platforms, referred to as "standard-setting committees" (Mowery and Simcoe 2002; Simcoe 2012). The key standard-setting committees for the Internet such as the Internet Engineering Task Force (IETF), the Institute for Electrical and Electronics Engineers (IEEE), and the World Wide Web Consortium (W3C), made decisions that shaped much of the equipment that underlies the Internet, with the IETF shaping the infrastructure layer, the IEEE shaping local area network and wireless communications, and the W3C shaping the web-based software and applications layer.

The chapter by Simcoe (chapter 1) inquires whether modularity shaped technological competition and specialization. The chapter offers an empirical examination of the consequences of the Internet architecture using data from the IETF and W3C. Both organizations adopted modular architectures, which produced specialized division of labor in designing and operating protocols. The chapter analyzes citations between Internet standards as further evidence of this specialization. Such specialization is the key to avoiding diminishing marginal returns in scaling up these networks. Modularity helps these technologies adapt to new circumstances and heterogeneous applications, helping them deploy more widely. This particular approach arises frequently with digital technologies and, the chapter argues, warrants attention as a fundamental feature of the digital economy.

In his comments Timothy Bresnahan stresses that modularity should be distinguished from openness. The former is a partitioning of the technical architecture while the latter arises from the policies and actions of those involved with commercialization, typically making information available. Bresnahan stresses these two aspects of the Transmission Control Protocol/ Internet Protocol (TCP/IP) commercial experience and argues that these processes turned TCP/IP into what it is today. That leads Bresnahan to raise questions about platform governance and the evolution of general-purpose technologies. In his view, Simcoe's chapter illustrates a major unaddressed question in digitization economics, namely, why processes that depart from strict contractual approaches have had a successful historical record. Modularity's value, therefore, may depend on more than merely the specialization that it permits, but also the institutional processes that guide the specialists. In that sense, Bresnahan speculates that Simcoe has introduced the reader to a potentially rich new agenda.

Many fundamental questions remain open. Competition between platforms determines prices for customers deciding between platforms, and divided technical leadership shapes the supply of vendor services that build on top of a platform. How does such competition shape the division of returns within a platform? How do these two margins differ when a third type of participant, such as an advertiser, plays an important role in creating market value for the platform? If platforms differentiate in terms of their capabilities and approaches to generating revenue, does that alter the composition of returns to its participants? If platforms develop in collective organizations, what type of firm behavior shapes participation in standards committees? How do these incentives shape the direction of innovation in markets connecting multiple platforms? In practice, do most of the returns for new platform development go to existing asset holders in the economy or to entrepreneurial actors who create and exploit value opened by the technical frontier? These are rich areas for additional research, and some of the following chapters also touch on these questions.

In addition to understanding how the technology evolved, how the infrastructure was built, and how decentralized platforms develop standards, it is also important to understand demand for digital technology. Without an understanding of the value of the technology to users, it is difficult to tease out policy implications. Several recent studies have examined demand for services. For example, Greenstein and McDevitt (2011) examine the diffusion of broadband Internet and its associated consumer surplus by looking at revenue of Internet service providers over time. Rosston, Savage, and Waldman (2010) use survey data to estimate household demand.

Wallsten (chapter 2) examines the microbehavior comprising demand in household behavior. In particular, he examines what people do when they are online, which often involves many choices between priced and unpriced options, or among unpriced options. The chapter provides detailed insight into the debate about how the Internet has changed lives, particularly in households, where many of the changes involve the allocation of leisure time. This allocation will not necessarily show up in gross domestic product (GDP) statistics, thereby framing many open questions about valuing the changes. The chapter is also novel for its use of the American Time Use Survey from 2003 to 2011 to estimate the crowd-out effects. That data shows that time spent online and the share of the population engaged in online activities has been steadily increasing since 2000. At the margin, each minute of online leisure time is correlated with fewer minutes on all other types of leisure. The findings suggest that any valuation of these changes must account for both opportunity costs and new value created, both of which are hard to measure.

Chris Forman's discussion of Wallsten's chapter emphasizes a household's trade-off in terms of opportunity costs and links it to prior literature on the implications of online behavior on offline markets. The discussion suggests opportunities for future research to leverage differences across locations in order to understand how the relative value of the Internet varies with the availability of offline substitutes.

Many open questions remain. If Internet use changes the allocation of leisure time, then what about the converse? How do changes in leisure time (for example, over the life cycle) affect Internet use and demand for Internet access? Does wireless access and ubiquitous connectivity (for example, in transit) change the relative benefit of different types of Internet use? How do particular applications (e.g., social networks, online shopping) affect the adoption and usage intensity of wireless and wireline Internet by consumers and businesses? Will improvements in technology, such as speed and memory, change demand and spill over into other areas of economic activity? How do these changes in demand reshape the allocation of supply? Many of these issues arise in other chapters, especially where public policy shapes markets.

Digitization, Economic Frictions, and New Markets

Among the major themes in the literature on digitization is an assessment of how it changes economic transactions. In particular, the literature identifies a variety of economic frictions that are increased or decreased as a consequence of digitization.

Much of the literature on digitization has emphasized the impact of the cost of storage, computation, and transmission of data on the nature of economic activity. In particular, technology makes certain economic transactions easier, reducing several market frictions. This could lead to increased market efficiency and increased competition. At the same time, if the technology reduces some frictions but not others, it could distort market outcomes, helping some players and hurting others. Broadly, changes related to digitization have changed economic measurement, altered how some markets function, and provided an opportunity for new markets to arise.

The influx of data due to the reduced cost of collecting and storing information, combined with improvements in the tools for data analysis, has created new opportunities for firms and policymakers to measure the economy and predict future outcomes. The economics literature on the opportunities presented by data analysis of this kind is relatively sparse. Goldfarb and Tucker (2012) describe the opportunities from Internet data with respect to advertising; Einav and Levin (2013) describe the opportunities from Internet data for economics researchers; and Brynjolfsson, Hitt, and Kim (2011) document that companies that use data often tend to do better.

Two different chapters in this book emphasize the potential of Internet data to improve measurement. In the policy section, two other chapters emphasize the challenges created by ubiquitous data. Just as predicting the weather had profound consequences for much economic activity, such as agriculture, better measurement and prediction of a wide range of economic activity could generate profound economic gains for many participants in the economy. Wu and Brynjolfsson (chapter 3) highlight the potential of online data to predict business activity. They ask whether there is a simple but accurate way to use search data to predict market trends. They illustrate their method using the housing market. After showing the predictive power of their method, they suggest several directions for future work regarding the potential of detailed data to help consumers, businesses, and policymakers improve decision making.

Scott and Varian (chapter 4) also highlight the potential of online data to improve the information that goes into decision making. Rather than prediction, they emphasize "nowcasting," or the ability of online data in general (and search data in particular) to provide early signals of economic and political indicators. They develop an approach to deal with one of the main challenges in using online data for prediction: there are many more potential predictors than there are observations. Their method helps identify the key variables that are most useful for prediction. They demonstrate the usefulness of the method in generating early measures of consumer sentiment and of gun sales.

Together, chapters 4 and 5 demonstrate that online data has the potential to substantially improve the measurement of current economic activity and the ability to forecast future activity. These chapters represent early steps toward identifying (a) what types of economic activity are conducive to measurement with online data, (b) the specific data that is most useful for such measurement, and (c) the most effective methods for using digital data in economic measurement. However, as the chapters both note, there is still much work to be done, and open questions remain around refining these methods, developing new methods, and recognizing new opportunities.

The next three chapters discuss ways in which digitization has altered how markets function. Digital technology makes some activities easier, thereby changing the nature of some economic interactions. Perhaps the oldest and largest stream of research on the Internet and market frictions emphasized reduced search costs. This literature, still going strong, builds on an older theory literature in economics (e.g., Stigler 1961; Diamond 1971; Varian 1980) that examines how search costs affect prices. This older literature showed that prices and price dispersion should fall when search costs fall. Digitization of retail and marketing meant that consumers could easily compare prices across stores, so the empirical work on Internet pricing examined the impact on prices and price dispersion. Initially hypothesized by Bakos (1997), the first wave of this research empirically documented lower prices, but still substantial dispersion (Brynjolfsson and Smith 2000; Baye, Morgan, and Scholten 2004; Ellison and Ellison 2009).

Baye, De los Santos, and Wildenbeest (chapter 5) is a good example of the newest wave of this research, which collects data about online searches to examine the actual search process that consumers undertake when looking for a product online. They focus on the question of how consumers search for books and booksellers online. This is of itself an interesting topic, both because books have often been the focus of studies that explore the "long tail" and because there have been policy concerns about how the online sales of books has affected offline channels. The chapter asks whether most book searches have been conducted on proprietary systems such as Amazon's Kindle and Barnes & Noble's Nook rather than consumers searching on general search engines such as Google or Bing, meaning that search might be mismeasured in the literature. This question also emphasizes that the final stage of purchase is often controlled by a more familiar retail environment, and it raises questions about the growing importance of standards and platforms in the distribution of creative content.

As noted earlier, near-zero marginal costs of distribution for information goods might change where and how information goods get consumed. Geographic boundaries might be less important if information can travel long distances for free (Sunstein 2001; Sinai and Waldfogel 2004; Blum and Goldfarb 2006). A big open question concerns the incidence of the impact of low distribution costs. The benefits might vary by location, with locations with fewer offline options generating a larger benefit from digitization (Balasubramanian 1998; Forman, Ghose, and Goldfarb 2009; Goldfarb and Tucker 2011a).

Gentzkow and Shapiro (chapter 6) explore the potential of near-zero marginal costs of distribution to affect political participation and the nature of news consumption. In particular, they ask whether technology-driven reductions in the costs of news distribution, both within and across geographic boundaries, affect the diversity of media production and consumption. Digital media could increase the diversity of news consumption because it enables inexpensive access to a broad range of sources; digital media could decrease the diversity of news consumption because it may permit specialized outlets that serve niche tastes that are not viable when physical production costs are high or when demand is limited to a geographically localized market. This contribution addresses an important open question: Will digitization of news content exacerbate existing political divisions as consumers access only content that supports their existing political ideology? The work of these authors does not stoke the worst fears. Their findings suggest that those who have niche tastes in news are still obtaining the majority of their news content from mainstream sources.

For many pure information goods, online platforms link readers to advertisers. Given the challenges of protecting online information content from being shared (a topic we discuss below in the context of policy), advertising has become an important source of revenue for many providers of pure information goods. Because of this, it is important to understand how online advertising works in order to understand the opportunities and challenges faced by providers of digital information goods. Goldfarb and Tucker (2011b) emphasize that online advertising is better targeted and better measured because of the ease of data collection.

The study of online advertising continues to attract attention because this is the principal means for generating revenues in much of the Internet ecosystem. Most of the content on the Internet and many of the services (such as search or social networking) rely on advertising revenues for support. Lewis, Rao, and Reiley (chapter 7) discuss the methods used for measuring the effects of advertising. To do this, they draw on their previous and current work that has used multiple field experiments to try and measure how effective online display advertising is at converting eyeballs into actual incremental sales. They emphasize that an important challenge to the accurate measurement of advertising is the high noise-to-signal ratio. This chapter suggests that as clients become increasingly sophisticated about measurement, this revenue source may be called into question.

Many other markets have also be changed by digitization. Other promising areas of research include rating mechanisms and quality signals (e.g., Cabral and Hortaçsu 2010; Jin and Kato 2007; Mayzlin, Dover, and Chevalier 2014), niche products and superstar effects (e.g., Brynjolfsson, Hu, and Smith 2003; Fleder and Hosanagar 2009; Bar-Isaac, Caruana, and Cunat 2012), and skill-biased technical change and the organization of work (e.g., Autor 2001; Garicano and Heaton 2010).

Chapters 8 and 9 discuss examples of markets that have been enabled by digitization. Agrawal, Horton, Lacetera, and Lyons (chapter 8) examine online markets for contract labor, another area in which digitization reduces frictions. In particular, digitization makes it easier for an employer to hire someone for information-related work without ever meeting the employee in person. If the work can be described digitally, completed off site, and then sent back to the employer digitally (such as with computer programming), then there might be an opportunity for long-distance North-South trade in skilled labor. The key challenges relate to information asymmetries regarding the quality of the employee and the trustworthiness of the employer. The chapter frames a large agenda about the role of online platforms to reduce these information asymmetries, thereby changing the types of contract labor transactions that are feasible online. They lay out a clear research agenda around the key players, their incentives, and the potential welfare consequences of this market.

Stanton's discussion extends the agenda behind this finding. His discussion speculates on whether the digitization of labor relationships enables labor outsourcing to other countries even without a platform intermediary.

Chapter 8 also extends a fourth stream of research related to frictions and digitization, the potential for new markets and new business models that take advantage of the lower frictions. Many successful Internet firms provide platforms that facilitate exchange, including eBay, Monster, Prosper, Airbnb, and oDesk. This is another channel through which digitization has restructured the supply of services. New policies—for copyright, privacy, and identity protection, for example—directly shape firm incentives by shaping the laws that apply to these new business models. Several other chapters also touch on these themes.

Addressing an important policy issue for governments, Gans and Halaburda (chapter 9) discuss the potential of digitization to create markets for private currencies that support activities on a particular platform, seemingly bypassing state-sponsored monetary authorities. They focus on the viability of the market for private digital currencies with noncurrency-specific platforms and speculate on the potential for a privacy-oriented entity to launch a real currency to compete with government-backed currencies such as the dollar and the euro. They lay out a model in which a platform currency offers "enhancements" to people who spend time on the platform. People allocate time between working and using the platform. They ask whether platforms have incentives to allow users to exchange at full convertibility private digital currency for government-backed currency. Their analysis illustrates the broad open question about whether private currencies in support of a platform are likely to migrate beyond the platform.

Online labor markets and private currencies are just two examples of markets enabled by digitization. Other promising related research areas include markets for user-generated content and the provision of public goods (e.g., Zhang and Zhu 2011; Greenstein and Zhu 2012), online banking and finance (e.g., Agrawal, Catalini, and Goldfarb 2013; Rigbi 2013; Zhang and Liu 2012), and "the sharing economy" of hotels and car services (e.g., Fradkin 2013).

Thus, the chapters in this section give a summary of some of the impact of digitization on a variety of markets. This is a big and growing area of research and much remains to be done. As digital technology advances, new opportunities for markets (and new ideas for research) will continue to arise.

Government Policy and Digitization

Increasing digitization has implications for policy, but the literature on the impact of digitization on policy is still in its infancy. As hinted above, ubiquitous data yields new challenges to privacy and security that policymakers need to address (e.g., Goldfarb and Tucker 2012; Miller and Tucker 2011; Arora et al. 2010). Near-zero marginal costs of distribution and the nonrival nature of digital goods pose challenges to copyright policy (e.g., Rob and Waldfogel 2006; Oberholzer-Gee and Strumpf 2007). The ease with which digital goods can be transferred over long distances and across borders might affect tax policy (e.g., Goolsbee 2000), financial regulation (e.g., Agrawal, Catalini, and Goldfarb 2013), and trade policy (Blum and Goldfarb 2006).

Privacy and data security are an area where digitization has substantially changed the costs and benefits to various economic actors. The current policy structure was implemented in a different regime, when data sharing was costly and data security was not an everyday concern. It is important to assess whether such laws match with the needs of a digital era in which everyone is of sufficient interest (relative to costs) to warrant data tracking by firms and governments.

Komarova, Nekipelov, and Yakovlev (chapter 10) make an important contribution. They combine a technically rich approach to econometrics with the question of how researchers, and research bodies who share data with those researchers, can protect the security and privacy of the people in the data. This is important because, all too often, researchers are unable to make use of the increasing scale and detail of data sets collected by government bodies because access is restricted due to unspecified privacy and data security concerns. This means that potentially many important research questions are being left unanswered, or are being answered using less adequate data, because of our technical inability to share data without creating privacy concerns. The authors develop the notion of the risk of "statistical partial disclosure" to describe the situation where researchers are able to infer something sensitive about the individual by combining public and private data sources. They develop an example to emphasize that there is a risk to individual privacy due to researchers' ability to combine multiple anonymized data sets. However, beyond that, they also suggest that there are ways that data-gathering research bodies can minimize such risks by adjusting the privacy guarantee level.

Mann (chapter 11) looks at the question related to data security. She provides several frameworks for analyzing how the question of data breaches should be evaluated in economic terms. She argues that markets for data security are incomplete and suggests that a good market analog to consider is the market for pollution. This market similarly is characterized by negative economies of scale, asymmetric information, and systematic uncertainty.

She also provides useful data to calibrate just how large the problem of data breaches actually is, and why breaches tend to occur. Interestingly, despite policy emphasis on external threats such as hacking and fraud, most breaches occur because of carelessness on the part of the data curator. She emphasizes that typically the number of records involved in a data breach is surprisingly small, and that many data breaches stem from the medical sector, though the data breaches that involve the release of a Social Security number are often from retail. She concludes by emphasizing the complexity introduced into the issue by questions of international jurisdiction.

Miller's discussion of Mann's chapter provides a useful synthesis of other literature on this topic. She focuses on the extent to which traditional policy-making on data security issues can backfire if it distorts incentives. For example, emphasizing the need for encryption to firms can lead firms to focus only on external outsider threats to data and ignore internal threats to the security of data from employee fraud or incompetence. She also points to the difficulty of making policy recommendations about differences in US and EU approaches to data security when there is, so far, scant information about the relative perceived costs to firms and consumers of data breaches.

A second area of policy interest concerns intellectual property. The digitization process resembles the creation of a giant free photocopier that can duplicate any creative endeavor with little or no cost. Varian (2005) supplies a theoretical framework for thinking about this change from an economics perspective. Usually, the economic effect on copyright holders in the context of free copying is considered to be negative. However, Varian suggests an important counterargument. If the value a consumer puts on the right to copy is greater than the reduction in sales, a seller can increase profits by allowing that right. Varian also provides a detailed description of several business models that potentially address the greater difficulty of enforcing copyrights as digitization increases. These models span strategies based on balancing prices, selling complementary goods, selling subscriptions, personalization, and supporting the goods being sold through advertising. Empirical research has not reached the point of having established a set of accepted facts about the merits or demerits of these different strategies, which the earlier sociological and political science literature has discussed in broad terms (Castells 2003).

This volume provides a sample of the range of new thinking in this area and it complements existing work on the effect of the digitization of music downloads on copyright holders (e.g., Rob and Waldfogel 2006; Hong 2007; Oberholzer-Gee and Strumpf 2007). The four chapters on this topic all shed light on how business activity changes when the protection of intellectual property changes. Together these chapters demonstrate the importance of copyright policy for market outcomes.

MacGarvie and Moser (chapter 12) address an argument often made by proponents of stronger copyright terms. Due to the scarcity of data about the profitability of authorship under copyright, they go to historical events to discover whether a historical episode that increased copyright terms did, in fact, encourage creativity by increasing the profitability of authorship. Their historical study also encounters a setting with much shorter copyright lengths than our current copyright length of seventy years after the author's death. That is an advantage, since further extensions today—beyond seventy—may not have any effects on the profitability of authorship, whereas in their study further extensions could have major consequences. The chapter also introduces a new data set of publishers' payments to authors of British fiction between 1800 and 1830. These data indicate that payments to authors nearly doubled following an increase in the length of copyright in 1814.

Further exploring themes related to copyright's influence on the incentives to distribute creative works, this volume also includes a chapter by Danaher, Dhanasobhon, Smith, and Telang (chapter 13). It examines research opportunities related to the erosion of copyright caused by Internet file sharing. Digitization has created many new opportunities to empirically analyze open questions by leveraging new data sources. This chapter discusses methodological approaches to leverage the new data and natural experiments in digital markets to address these questions. The chapter closes with a specific proof-of-concept research study that analyzes the impact of legitimate streaming services on the demand for piracy.

Waldfogel (chapter 14) explores another side to these questions, namely, how copyright policy alters incentives to create music. Revenue for recorded music has collapsed since the explosion of file sharing, and yet, Waldfogel argues, the quality of new music has not suffered. He considers an explanation that stresses changes on the supply side, namely, that digitization has allowed a wider range of firms to bring far more music to market using lower-cost methods of production, distribution, and promotion. Prior to the supply change, record labels found it difficult to predict which albums would find commercial success. In that situation many released albums necessarily would fail, and, relatedly, many nascent but unpromoted albums might have been successful. After the change in supply conditions, the increasing number of products released would allow consumers to discover more appealing choices if they can sift through the offerings. The chapter argues that digitization is responsible for such a supply shift: specifically that Internet radio and a growing cadre of online music reviewers provide alternatives to radio airplay as means for new product discovery.

Despite a long history of piracy software markets, researchers have not been able to assemble informative data about the phenomenon, much less their causes. Athey and Stern (chapter 15) make a novel contribution by analyzing data that permits direct measurement of piracy for a specific product—Windows 7. They are able to use anonymized telemetry data to characterize the ways in which piracy occurs, the relative incidence of piracy across different economic and institutional environments, and the impact of enforcement efforts on choices to install pirated versus paid software. The chapter has several provocative new observations. For example, most piracy in this setting can be traced back to a small number of widely distributed "hacks" that are available through the Internet. Despite the availability of these hacks to any potential Internet user, they do not get used everywhere. The microeconomic and institutional environment appears to play a crucial role in fostering or discouraging piracy. Moreover, piracy tends to focus on the most "advanced" version of Windows (Windows Ultimate). The chapter lays out a broad agenda for this area of research.

These chapters all demonstrate the important role of copyright policy in digital markets. Copyright enforcement affects what is produced and what is consumed. Still, as should be evident from these chapters, many open policy questions remain.

Questions about the role of policy in determining copyright rules, privacy norms, and security practices arise in many markets for digital goods and services. Questions about the principles for redesigning these policies also remain elusive. We hope this book motivates further investigation into the economics underlying these policy issues.

Conclusions

The emerging research area of the economics of digitization improves our understanding of whether and how digital technology changes markets. Digitization enables outcomes that were not possible a few decades earlier. It not only reduces existing costs, but has also enabled the development of new services and processes that did not exist before because they were just too costly or merely technologically infeasible. The opportunities generated by digitization have also generated dramatic resource reallocation and restructuring of routines, market relationships, and patterns of the flow of goods and services. This in turn has led to a new set of policy questions and made several existing policy questions more vexing.

References

Agrawal, Ajay, Christian Catalini, and Avi Goldfarb. 2013. "Some Simple Economics of Crowdfunding." In *Innovation Policy and the Economy*, vol. 14, edited by Josh Lerner and Scott Stern, 63–97. Chicago: University of Chicago Press.
Arora, A., A. Nandkumar, C. Forman, and R. Telang. 2010. "Competition and Patching of Security Vulnerabilities: An Empirical Analysis." *Information Economics and Policy* 10:164–77.

Autor, David H. 2001. "Wiring the Labor Market." *Journal of Economic Perspectives* 15 (1): 25–40.
Bakos, J. 1997. "Reducing Buyer Search Costs: Implications for Electronic Marketplaces." *Management Science* 43 (12): 1676–92.
Balasubramanian, S. 1998. "Mail versus Mall: A Strategic Analysis of Competition between Direct Marketers and Conventional Retailers." *Marketing Science* 17 (3): 181–95.
Bar-Isaac, H., G. Caruana, and V. Cunat. 2012. "Search, Design, and Market Structure." *American Economic Review* 102 (2): 1140–60.
Baye, Michael, John Morgan, and Patrick Scholten. 2004. "Price Dispersion in the Small and in the Large: Evidence from an Internet Price Comparison Site." *Journal of Industrial Economics* 52 (4): 463–96.
Blum, Bernardo S., and Avi Goldfarb. 2006. "Does the Internet Defy the Law of Gravity?" *Journal of International Economics* 70 (2): 384–405.
Bresnahan, T., and S. Greenstein. 1999. "Technological Competition and the Structure of the Computing Industry." *Journal of Industrial Economics* 47 (1): 1–40.
Brynjolfsson, Erik, L. M. Hitt, and H. H. Kim. 2011. "Strength in Numbers: How Does Data-Driven Decision-Making Affect Firm Performance?" http://ssrn.com/abstract=1819486.
Brynjolfsson, Erik, Yu "Jeffrey" Hu, and Michael D. Smith. 2003. "Consumer Surplus in the Digital Economy: Estimating the Value of Increased Product Variety." *Management Science* 49 (11): 1580–96.
Brynjolfsson, Erik, and Michael Smith. 2000. "Frictionless Commerce? A Comparison of Internet and Conventional Retailers." *Management Science* 46 (4): 563–85.
Cabral, L., and A. Hortaçsu. 2010. "Dynamics of Seller Reputation: Theory and Evidence from eBay." *Journal of Industrial Economics* 58 (1): 54–78.
Castells, M. 2003. *The Internet Galaxy: Reflections on the Internet, Business, and Society*. Abingdon, UK: Taylor and Francis.
Diamond, P. 1971. "A Simple Model of Price Adjustment." *Journal of Economic Theory* 3:156–68.
Einav, Liran, and Jonathan D. Levin. 2013. "The Data Revolution and Economic Analysis." NBER Working Paper no. 19035, Cambridge, MA.
Ellison, G., and S. F. Ellison. 2009. "Search, Obfuscation, and Price Elasticities on the Internet." *Econometrica* 77 (2): 427–52.
Fleder, D., and K. Hosanagar. 2009. "Blockbuster Culture's Next Rise or Fall: The Impact of Recommender Systems on Sales Diversity." *Management Science* 55 (5): 697–712.
Forman, C., A. Ghose, and A. Goldfarb. 2009. "Competition between Local and Electronic Markets: How the Benefit of Buying Online Depends on Where You Live." *Management Science* 55 (1): 47–57.
Fradkin, Andrey. 2013. "Search Frictions and the Design of Online Marketplaces." Working Paper, Department of Economics, Stanford University.
Garicano, Luis, and Paul Heaton. 2010. "Information Technology, Organization, and Productivity in the Public Sector: Evidence from Police Departments." *Journal of Labor Economics* 28 (1): 167–201.
Goldfarb, Avi, and Catherine Tucker. 2011a. "Advertising Bans and the Substitutability of Online and Offline Advertising." *Journal of Marketing Research* 48 (2): 207–28.
———. 2011b. "Privacy Regulation and Online Advertising." *Management Science* 57 (1): 57–71.
———. 2012. "Privacy and Innovation." In *Innovation Policy and the Economy*, vol. 12, edited by J. Lerner and S. Stern, 65–89. Chicago: University of Chicago Press.

Goolsbee, A. 2000. "In a World without Borders: The Impact of Taxes on Internet Commerce." *Quarterly Journal of Economics* 115 (2): 561–76.

Greenstein, S., and R. McDevitt. 2011. "The Broadband Bonus: Estimating Broadband Internet's Economic Value." *Telecommunications Policy* 35:617–32.

Greenstein, S., and F. Zhu. 2012. "Is Wikipedia Biased?" American Economic Review 102 (3): 343–48.

Hong, Seung-Hyun. 2007. "The Recent Growth of the Internet and Changes in Household Level Demand for Entertainment." *Information Economics and Policy* 3–4:304–18.

Jin, G. Z., and A. Kato. 2007. "Dividing Online and Offline: A Case Study." *Review of Economic Studies* 74 (3): 981–1004.

Mayzlin, Dina, Yaniv Dover, and Judith Chevalier. 2014. "Promotional Reviews: An Empirical Investigation of Online Review Manipulation." *American Economic Review* 104 (8): 2421–55.

Miller, A., and C. Tucker. 2011. "Encryption and the Loss of Patient Data." *Journal of Policy Analysis and Management* 30 (3): 534–56.

Mowery, D., and T. Simcoe. 2002. "The Origins and Evolution of the Internet." In *Technological Innovation and Economic Performance*, edited by R. Nelson, B. Steil, and D. Victor, 229–64. Princeton, NJ: Princeton University Press.

Oberholzer-Gee, Felix, and Koleman Strumpf. 2007. "The Effect of File Sharing on Record Sales: An Empirical Analysis." *Journal of Political Economy* 115 (1): 1–42.

Peitz, Martin, and Joel Waldfogel. 2012. *The Oxford Handbook of the Digital Economy*. New York: Oxford University Press.

Rigbi, Oren. 2013. "The Effects of Usury laws: Evidence from the Online Loan Market." *Review of Economics and Statistics* 95 (4): 1238–48.

Rob, Rafael, and Joel Waldfogel. 2006. "Piracy on the High C's: Music Downloading, Sales Displacement, and Social Welfare in a Sample of College Students." *Journal of Law & Economics* 49 (1): 29–62.

Rosston, Gregory, Scott J. Savage, and Donald M. Waldman. 2010. "Household Demand for Broadband Internet in 2010." *The B.E. Journal of Economic Analysis & Policy* 10 (1): article 79.

Simcoe, T. 2012. "Standard Setting Committees: Consensus Governance for Shared Technology Platforms." *American Economic Review* 102 (1): 305–36.

Sinai, T., and J. Waldfogel. 2004. "Geography and the Internet: Is the Internet a Substitute or a Complement for Cities?" *Journal of Urban Economics* 56 (1): 1–24.

Stigler, George J. 1961. "The Economics of Information." *Journal of Political Economy* 69 (3): 213–25.

Sunstein, C. 2001. *Republic.com*. Princeton, NJ: Princeton University Press.

Varian, H. 1980. "A Model of Sales." *American Economic Review* 70:651–59.

———. 2005. "Copying and Copyright." *Journal of Economic Perspectives* 19 (2): 121–38.

Zhang, Juanjuan, and Peng Liu. 2012. "Rational Herding in Microloan Markets." *Management Science* 58 (5): 892–912.

Zhang, X., and F. Zhu. 2011. "Group Size and Incentives to Contribute: A Natural Experiment at Chinese Wikipedia." *American Economic Review* 101:1601–15.

I

Internet Supply and Demand

1
Modularity and the Evolution of the Internet

Timothy Simcoe

1.1 Introduction

The Internet is a global computer network comprised of many smaller networks, all of which use a common set of communications protocols. This network is important not only because it supports a tremendous amount of economic activity, but also as a critical component within a broader constellation of technologies that support the general-purpose activity of digital computing. Given its widespread use and complementary relationship to computing in general, the Internet is arguably a leading contemporary example of what some economists have called a general purpose technology (GPT).

The literature on GPTs highlights the importance of positive feedback between innovations in a GPT-producing sector and the process of "coinvention" (i.e., user experimentation and discovery) in various application sectors that build upon the GPT.[1] Much of this literature elaborates on the implications of coinvention for understanding GPT diffusion and the timing of associated productivity impacts.[2] However, the literature on GPTs is

---

Timothy Simcoe is associate professor of strategy and innovation at Boston University School of Management and a faculty research fellow of the National Bureau of Economic Research.

This research was funded by the NBER Digitization program with support from the Kauffman Foundation. Useful comments were provided by Tim Bresnahan, Shane Greenstein, Avi Goldfarb, Joachim Henkel, and Catherine Tucker. All errors are my own, and comments are welcome: tsimcoe@bu.edu. For acknowledgments, sources of research support, and disclosure of the author's material financial relationships, if any, please see http://www.nber.org/chapters/c13000.ack.

1. See Bresnahan (2010) for a recent review of this literature.
2. For a historical example, see Paul David (1990) on the role of coinvention in industrial electrification. For a contemporary quantitative application of these ideas, see Dranove et al.'s (2012) analysis of the productivity benefits from adopting health information technology.

less precise about how the supply of a GPT can or should be organized, or what prevents a GPT from encountering decreasing returns as it diffuses to application sectors with disparate needs and requirements.

This chapter provides an empirical case study of the Internet that demonstrates how a *modular* system architecture can have implications for industrial organization in the GPT-producing sector, and perhaps also prevent the onset of decreasing returns to GPT innovation. In this context, the term "architecture" refers to an allocation of computing tasks across various subsystems or components that might either be jointly or independently designed and produced. The term "modularity" refers to the level (and pattern) of technical interdependence among components. I emphasize voluntary cooperative standards development as the critical activity through which firms coordinate complementary innovative activities and create a modular system that facilitates a division of innovative labor. Data collected from the two main Internet standard-setting organizations (SSOs), the Internet Engineering Task Force (IETF), and World Wide Web Consortium (W3C), demonstrate the inherent modularity of the Internet architecture, along with the division of labor it enables. Examining citations to Internet standards provides evidence on the diffusion and commercial application of innovations within this system.

The chapter has two main points. First, architectural choices are multidimensional, and can play an essential role in the supply of digital goods. In particular, choices over modularity can shape trade-offs between generality and specialization among innovators and producers. Second, SSOs play a crucial role in designing modular systems, and can help firms internalize the benefits of coordinating innovation within a GPT-producing sector. While these points are quite general, it is not possible to show how they apply to all digital goods. Instead, I will focus on a very specific and important case, showing how modularity and SSOs played a key role in fostering design and deployment of the Internet.

The argument proceeds in three steps. First, after reviewing some general points about the economics of modularity and standards, I describe the IETF, the W3C, and the Transmission Control Protocol/Internet Protocol (TCP/IP) "protocol stack" that engineers use to characterize the Internet's architecture. Next, I use data from the IETF and W3C to illustrate the modularity of the system and the specialized division of labor in Internet standard setting. In this second step, I present results from two empirical analyses. The first analysis demonstrates the modular nature of the Internet by showing that citations among technical standards are highly concentrated within "layers" or modules in the Internet Protocol stack. The second analysis demonstrates that firms contributing to Internet standards development also specialize at particular layers in the protocol stack, suggesting that the technical modularity of the Internet architecture closely corresponds to the division of labor in standards production. The final step in the chapter's broader argument is to consider how components within a modular system evolve and are utilized through time. To illustrate how these ideas apply to the Internet, I return to citation analysis and show that intermodule citations between standards occur later than intramodule citations. Similarly, citations from patents (which I use as a proxy for commercial application of Internet standards) occur later than citations from other standards. These patterns suggest that modularity facilitates asynchronous coinvention and application of the core GPT, in contrast to the contemporaneous and tightly coupled design process that occur within layers.

1.1.1 Modularity in General

Modularity is a general strategy for designing complex systems. The components in a modular system interact with one another through a limited number of standardized interfaces.

Economists often associate modularity with increasing returns to a finer division of labor. For example, Adam Smith's famous description of the pin factory illustrates the idea that system-level performance is enhanced if specialization allows individual workers to become more proficient at each individual step in a production process. Limitations to such increasing returns in production may be imposed by the size of the market (Smith 1776; Stigler and Sherwin 1985) or through increasing costs of coordination, such as the cost of "modularizing" products and production processes (Becker and Murphy 1992). The same idea has been applied to innovation processes by modeling educational investments in reaching the "knowledge frontier" as a fixed investment in human capital that is complementary to similar investments made by other workers (Jones 2008). For both production and innovation, creating a modular division of labor is inherently a coordination problem, since the ex post value of investments in designing a module or acquiring specialized human capital necessarily depend upon choices and investments made by others.

A substantial literature on technology design describes alternative benefits to modularity that have received less attention from economists. Herb Simon (1962) emphasizes that modular design isolates technological interdependencies, leading to a more robust system, wherein the external effects of a design change or component failure are limited to other components within the same module. Thus, Simon highlights the idea that upgrades and repairs can be accomplished by swapping out a single module instead of rebuilding a system from scratch. Baldwin and Clark (2000) develop the idea that by minimizing "externalities" across the parts of a system, modularity multiplies the set of options available to component designers (since design constraints are specified ex ante through standardized interfaces, as opposed to being embedded in ad hoc interdependencies), and thereby facilitates decentralized search of the entire design space.

Economists often treat the modular division of labor as a more or less inevitable outcome of the search for productive efficiency, and focus on the potential limits to increasing returns through specialization. However, the literature on technology design is more engaged with trade-offs that arise when selecting between a modular and a tightly integrated design. For example, a tightly integrated or nondecomposable design may be required to achieve optimal performance. The fixed costs of defining components and interfaces could also exceed the expected benefits of a modular design that allow greater specialization and less costly ex post adaptation. Thus, modularity is not particularly useful for a disposable single-purpose design. A more subtle cost of modularity is the loss of flexibility at intensively utilized interfaces. In a sense, modular systems "build in" coordination costs, since modifying an interface technology typically requires a coordinated switch to some new standard.[3]

The virtues of modular design for GPTs may seem self-evident. A technology that will be used as a shared input across many different application sectors clearly benefits from an architecture that enables decentralized end-user customization and a method for upgrading "core" functionality without having to overhaul the installed base. However, this may not be so clear to designers at the outset, particularly if tight integration holds out the promise of rapid development or superior short-run performance. For example, during the initial diffusion of electricity, the city electric light company supplied generation, distribution, and even lights as part of an integrated system. Langlois (2002) describes how the original architects of the operating system for the IBM System 360 line of computers adopted a nondecomposable design, wherein "each programmer should see all the material."[4] Similarly, Bresnahan and Greenstein (1999) describe how divided technical leadership—which might be either a cause or a consequence of product modularity—did not emerge in computing until the personal computer era.

The evolution or choice of a modular architecture may also reflect expectations about the impact of modularity on the division of rents in the GPT-producing sector. For example, during the monopoly telecommunications era, AT&T had a long history of opposing third-party efforts to sell equipment that would attach to its network.[5] While the impact of compatibility on competition and the distribution of rents is a complex topic that goes beyond the scope of this chapter, the salient point is that the choice of a modular architecture—or at a lower level, the design of a specific interface—will

---

3. A substantial economics literature explores such dynamic coordination problems in technology adoption, starting from Arthur (1989), David (1985), and Farrell and Saloner (1986).
4. The quote comes from Brooks (1975).
5. Notable challenges to this arrangement occurred in the 1956 "Hush-a-Phone" court case (238 F.2d 266, D.C. Cir., 1956) and the Federal Communication Commission's 1968 Carterphone ruling (13 F.C.C.2d 420).

not necessarily reflect purely design considerations in a manner that weighs social costs and benefits.[6]

It is difficult to say what a less modular Internet would look like. Comparisons to the large closed systems of earlier eras (e.g., the IBM mainframe and the AT&T telecommunications network) suggest that there would be less innovation and commercialization by independent users of the network, in part because of the greater costs of achieving interoperability. However, centralized design and governance could also have benefits in areas such as improved security. Instead of pursuing this difficult counterfactual question, the remainder of this chapter will focus on documenting the modularity of the Internet architecture and showing how that modularity is related to the division of labor in standardization and the dynamics of complementary innovation.

1.1.2 Setting Standards

If the key social trade-off in selecting a modular design involves up-front fixed costs versus ex post flexibility, it is important to have a sense of what is being specified up front. Baldwin and Clark (2000) argue that a modular system partitions design information into visible design rules and hidden parameters. The visible rules consist of (a) an architecture that describes a set of modules and their functions, (b) interfaces that describe how the modules will work together, and (c) standards that can be used to test a module's performance and conformity to design rules. Broadly speaking, the benefits of modularity flow from hiding many design parameters in order to facilitate entry and lower the fixed costs of component innovation, while its costs come from having to specify and commit to those design rules before the market emerges.

The process of selecting globally visible design parameters is fundamentally a coordination problem, and there are several possible ways of dealing with it. Farrell and Simcoe (2012) discuss trade-offs among four broad paths to compatibility: decentralized technology adoption (or "standards wars"); voluntary consensus standard setting; taking cues from a dominant "platform leader" (such as a government agency or the monopoly supplier of a key input); and ex post efforts to achieve compatibility through converters and multihoming. In the GPT setting, each path to compatibility provides an alternative institutional environment for solving the fundamental contracting problem among GPT suppliers, potential inventors in various applications sectors, and consumers. That is, different modes of standardization imply alternative methods of distributing the ex post rents from complementary inventions, and one can hope that some combination of conscious

---

6. See Farrell (2007) on the general point and MacKie-Mason and Netz (2007) for one example of how designers could manipulate a specific interface.

choice and selection pressures pushes us toward a standardization process that promotes efficient ex ante investments in innovation.

While all four modes of standardization have played a role in the evolution of the Internet, this chapter will focus on consensus standardization for two reasons.[7] First, consensus standardization within SSOs (specifically, the IETF and W3C, as described below) is arguably the dominant mode of coordinating the design decisions and the supply of new interfaces on the modern Internet. And second, the institutions for Internet standard setting have remarkably transparent processes that provide a window onto the architecture of the underlying system, as well as the division of innovative labor among participants who collectively manage the shared technology platform. If one views the Internet as a general purpose technology, these standard-setting organizations may provide a forum where GPT-producers can interact with application-sector innovators in an effort to internalize the vertical (from GPT to application) and horizontal (among applications) externalities implied by complementarities in innovation across sectors, as modeled in Bresnahan and Trajtenberg (1995).

1.2 Internet Standardization

There are two main organizations that define standards and interfaces for the Internet: the Internet Engineering Task Force (IETF) and World Wide Web Consortium (W3C). This section describes how these two SSOs are organized and explains their relationship to the protocol stack that engineers use to describe the modular structure of the network.

1.2.1 History and Process

The IETF was established in 1986. However, the organization has roots that can be traced back to the earliest days of the Internet. For example, all of the IETF's official publications are called "Requests for Comments" (RFCs), making them part of a continuous series that dates back to the very first technical notes on packet-based computer networking.[8] Similarly, the first two chairs of the IETF's key governance committee, called the Internet Architecture Board (IAB), were David Clark of MIT and Vint Cerf, who worked on the original IP protocols with Clark before moving to the Defense Advanced Research Projects Agency (DARPA) and funding the

---

7. For example, Russell (2006) describes the standards war between TCP/IP and the OSI protocols. Simcoe (2012) analyzes the performance of the IETF as a voluntary SSO. Greenstein (1996) describes the NSF's role as a platform leader in the transition to a commercial Internet. Translators are expected to play a key role in the transition to IPv6, and smartphones are multihoming devices because they select between Wi-Fi (802.11) and cellular protocols to establish a physical layer network connection.

8. RFC 1 "Host Software" was published by Steve Crocker of UCLA in 1969 (http://www.rfc-editor.org/rfc/rfc1.txt). The first RFC editor, Jon Postel of UCLA, held the post from 1969 until his death in 1998.

initial deployment of the network. Thus, in many ways, the early IETF formalized a set of working relationships among academic, government, and commercial researchers who designed and managed the Advanced Research Projects Agency Network (ARPANET) and its successor, the National Science Foundation Network (NSFNET).

Starting in the early 1990s, the IETF evolved from its quasi-academic roots into a venue for coordinating critical design decisions for a commercially significant piece of shared computing infrastructure.[9] At present the organization has roughly 120 active technical working groups, and its meetings draw roughly 1,200 attendees from a wide range of equipment vendors, network operators, application developers, and academic researchers.[10]

The W3C was founded by Tim Berners-Lee in 1994 to develop standards for the rapidly growing World Wide Web, which he invented while working at the European Organization for Nuclear Research (CERN). Berners-Lee originally sought to standardize the core web protocols, such as the Hypertext Markup Language (HTML) and Hypertext Transfer Protocol (HTTP), through the IETF. However, he quickly grew frustrated with the pace of the IETF process, which required addressing every possible technical objection before declaring a consensus, and decided to establish a separate consortium, with support from CERN and MIT, that would promote faster standardization, in part through a more centralized organization structure (Berners-Lee and Fischetti 1999).

The IETF and W3C have many similar features and a few salient differences. Both SSOs are broadly open to interested participants. However, anyone can "join" the IETF merely by showing up at a meeting or participating on the relevant e-mail listserv. The W3C must approve new members, who are typically invited experts or engineers from dues-paying member companies. The fundamental organizational unit within both SSOs is the working group (WG), and the goal of working groups is to publish technical documents.

The IETF and W3C working groups publish two types of documents. The first type of document is what most engineers and economists would call a standard: it describes a set of visible design rules that implementations should comply with to ensure that independently designed products work together well. The IETF calls this type of document a standards-track RFC, and the W3C calls them Recommendations.[11] At both SSOs, new standards must be approved by consensus, which generally means a substantial supermajority, and in practice is determined by a WG chair, subject

---

9. Simcoe (2012) studies the rapid commercialization of the IETF during the 1990s, and provides evidence that it produced a measurable slowdown in the pace of standards development.
10. http://www.ietf.org/documents/IETF-Regional-Attendance-00.pdf.
11. Standard-track RFCs are further defined as proposed standards, draft standards, or Internet standards to reflect their maturity level. However, at any given time, much of the Internet runs on proposed standards.

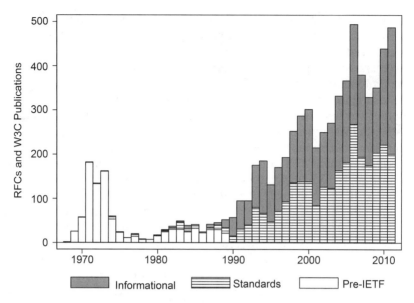

Fig. 1.1 Total RFCs and W3C publications (1969–2011)

Notes: Figure 1.1 plots a count of publications by the IETF and W3C. Pre-IETF publications refer to Request for Comments (RFCs) published prior to the formation of the IETF as a formal organization. Standards are standards-track RFCs published by IETF and W3C Recommendations. Informational publications are nonstandards-track IETF RFCs and W3C notes.

to formal appeal and review by the Internet Engineering Steering Group (IESG) or W3C director.[12]

The IETF and W3C working groups also publish documents that provide useful information without specifying design parameters. These informational publications are called nonstandards-track RFCs at the IETF and Notes at the W3C. They are typically used to disseminate ideas that are too preliminary or controversial to standardize, or information that complements new standards, such as "lessons learned" in the standardization process or proposed guidelines for implementation and deployment.

Figure 1.1 illustrates the annual volume of RFCs and W3C publications between 1969 and 2011. The chart shows a large volume of RFCs published during the early 1970s, followed by a dry spell of almost fifteen years, and then a steady increase in output beginning around 1990. This pattern coincides with a burst of inventive activity during the initial development of ARPANET, followed by a long period of experimentation with various

---

12. For an overview of standards-setting procedures at IETF, see RFC 2026 "The Internet Standards Process" (http://www.ietf.org/rfc/rfc2026.txt). The W3C procedures are described at http://www.w3.org/2005/10/Process-20051014/tr.

networking protocols—including a standards war between TCP/IP and various proprietary implementations of the open systems interconnection (OSI) protocol suite (Russell 2006). Finally, there is a second wave of sustained innovation associated with the emergence of TCP/IP as the de facto standard, commercialization of the Internet infrastructure and widespread adoption.

If we interpret the publication counts in figure 1.1 as a proxy for innovation investments, the pattern is remarkably consistent with a core feature of the literature on GPTs. In particular, there is a considerable time lag between the initial invention and the eventual sustained wave of complementary innovation that accompanies diffusion across various application sectors. There are multiple explanations for these adoption lags, which can reflect coordination delays such as the OSI versus TCP/IP standards war; the time required to develop and upgrade complementary inputs (e.g., routers, computers, browsers, and smartphones); or the gradual replacement of prior technology that is embedded in substantial capital investments. With respect to replacement effects, it is interesting to note that the share of IETF standards-track publications that upgrade or replace prior standards has averaged roughly 20 percent since 1990, when it becomes possible to calculate such statistics.

Another notable feature of figure 1.1 is the substantial volume of purely informational documents produced at IETF and W3C. This partly reflects the academic origins and affiliations of both SSOs, and highlights the relationship between standards development and collaborative research and development (R&D). It also illustrates how, at least for "open" standards, much of the information about how to implement a particular module or function is broadly available, even if it is nominally hidden behind the layer of abstraction provided by a standardized interface.

To provide a better sense of what is actually being counted in figure 1.1, table 1.1A lists some of the most important IETF standards, as measured by the number of times they have been cited in IETF and W3C publications, or as nonpatent prior art in a US patent in table 1.1B.

All of the documents listed in tables 1.1A and 1.1B are standards-track publications of the IETF.[13] Both tables contain a number of standards that one might expect to see on such a list, including Transmission Control Protocol (TCP) and Internet Protocol (IP), the core routing protocols that arguably define the Internet; the HTTP specification used to address resources on the Web; and the Session Initiation Protocol (SIP) used to control multimedia sessions, such as voice and video calls over IP networks.

Several differences between the two lists in tables 1.1A and 1.1B are also noteworthy. For example, table 1.1A shows that IETF and W3C publica-

---

13. I was not able to collect patent cites for W3C documents, and the W3C Recommendation that received the most SSO citations was a part of the XML protocol that received 100 cites.

Table 1.1A Most cited Internet standards (IETF and W3C citations)

Document	Year	IETF & W3C citations	Title
RFC 822	1982	346	Standard for the format of ARPA Internet text messages
RFC 3261	2002	341	SIP: Session Initiation Protocol
RFC 791	1981	328	Internet Protocol
RFC 2578	1999	281	Structure of Management Information Version 2 (SMIv2)
RFC 2616	1999	281	Hypertext Transfer Protocol—HTTP/1.1
RFC 793	1981	267	Transmission Control Protocol
RFC 2579	1999	262	Textual conventions for SMIv2
RFC 3986	2005	261	Uniform Resource Identifier (URI): Generic syntax
RFC 1035	1987	254	Domain names—implementation and specification
RFC 1034	1987	254	Domain names—concepts and facilities

Note: This list excludes the most cited IETF publication, RFC 2119 "Key Words for Use in RFCs to Indicate Requirement Levels," which is an informational document that provides a standard for writing IETF standards, and is therefore cited by nearly every standards-track RFC.

tions frequently cite the Structure of Management Information Version 2 (SMIv2) protocol, which defines a language and database used to manage individual "objects" in a larger communications network (e.g., switches or routers). On the other hand, table 1.1B shows that US patents are more likely to cite security standards and protocols for reserving network resources (e.g., Dynamic Host Configuration Protocol [DHCP] and Resource Reservation Protocol [RSVP]). These differences hint at the idea that citations from the IETF and W3C measure technical interdependencies or knowledge flows within the computer-networking sector, whereas patent cites measure complementary innovation linked to specific applications of the larger GPT.[14] I return to this idea below when examining diffusion.

1.2.2 The Protocol Stack

The protocol stack is a metaphor used by engineers to describe the multiple layers of abstraction in a packet-switched computer network. In principle, each layer handles a different set of tasks associated with networked communications (e.g., assigning addresses, routing and forwarding packets, session management, or congestion control). Engineers working at a particular layer need only be concerned with implementation details at that layer, since the functions or services provided by other layers are described in a set of standardized interfaces. Saltzer, Reed, and Clark (1984) provide

---

14. Examining citations to informational publications reinforces this interpretation: The nonstandards-track RFCs most cited by other RFCs describe IETF processes and procedures, whereas the nonstandards-track RFCs most cited by US patents describe technologies that were too preliminary or controversial to standardize, such as Network Address Translation (NAT) and Cisco's Hot-Standby Router Protocol (HSRP). On average, standards receive many more SSO and patent citations than informational publications.

Table 1.1B   Most cited Internet standards (US patent citations)

Document	Year	US Patent citations	Title
RFC 2543	1999	508	SIP: Session Initiation Protocol
RFC 791	1981	452	Internet Protocol
RFC 793	1981	416	Transmission Control Protocol
RFC 2002	1996	406	IP mobility support
RFC 3261	2002	371	SIP: Session Initiation Protocol
RFC 2131	1997	337	Dynamic Host Configuration Protocol
RFC 2205	1997	332	Resource ReSerVation Protocol (RSVP)—Version 1
RFC 1889	1996	299	RTP: A transport protocol for real-time applications
RFC 2401	1998	284	Security architecture for the Internet Protocol
RFC 768	1980	261	User Datagram Protocol

an early description of this modular or "end-to-end" network architecture that assigns complex application-layer tasks to "host" computers at the edge of the network, thereby allowing routers and switches to focus on efficiently forwarding undifferentiated packets from one device to another. In practical (but oversimplified) terms, the protocol stack allows application designers to ignore the details of transmitting a packet from one machine to another, and router manufacturers to ignore the contents of the packets they transmit.

The canonical TCP/IP protocol stack has five layers: applications, transport, Internet, link (or routing), and physical. The IETF and W3C focus on the four layers at the "top" of the stack, while various physical layer standards are developed by other SSOs, such as the IEEE (Ethernet and Wi-Fi/802.11b), or 3GPP (GSM and LTE). I treat the W3C as a distinct layer in this chapter, though most engineers would view the organization as a developer of application-layer protocols.[15]

In the management literature on modularity, the "mirroring hypothesis" posits that organizational boundaries will correspond to interfaces between modules. While the causality of this relationship has been argued in both directions (e.g., Henderson and Clark 1990; Sanchez and Mahoney 1996; Colfer and Baldwin 2010), the IETF and W3C clearly conform to the basic cross-sectional prediction that there will be a correlation between module and organizational boundaries. In particular, both organizations assign individual working groups to broad technical areas that correspond to distinct modules within the TCP/IP protocol stack.

For each layer, the IETF maintains a technical area comprised of several related working groups overseen by a pair of area directors who sit on the Internet Engineering Steering Group (IESG). In addition to the areas cor-

---

15. Within the W3C there are also several broad areas of work, including Web design and applications standards (HTML, CSS, Ajax, SVG), Web infrastructure standards (HTTP and URI) that are developed in coordination with IETF, XML standards, and standards for Web services (SOAP and WSDL).

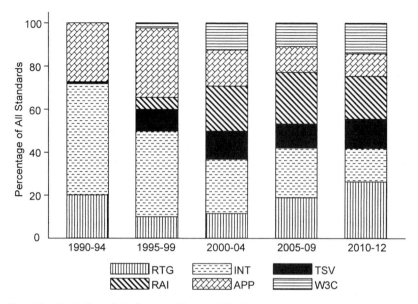

Fig. 1.2   Evolution of the Internet Protocol Stack

Notes: Figure 1.2 plots the share of all IETF and W3C standards-track publications associated with each layer in the Internet Protocol Stack, based on the author's calculations using data from IETF and W3C. The full layer names are: RTG = routing, INT = Internet, TSV = transport, RAI = real-time applications and infrastructure, APP = applications, and W3C = W3C. The figure excludes RFCs from the IETF operations and security areas, which are not generally treated as a "layer" within the protocol stack (see figure 1.3).

responding to layers in the traditional protocol stack, the IETF has created a real-time applications area to develop standards for voice, video, and other multimedia communications sessions. This new layer sits "between" application and transport-layer protocols. Finally, the IETF manages two technical areas—security and operations—that exist outside of the protocol stack and develop protocols that interact with each layer of the system.

Figure 1.2 illustrates the proportion of new IETF and W3C standards from each layer of the protocol stack over time. From 1990 to 1994, protocol development largely conformed to the traditional model of the TCP/IP stack. Between 1995 and 1999, the emergence of the Web was associated with an increased number of higher-level protocols, including the early IETF work on HTML/HTTP, and the first standards from the W3C and real-time applications and infrastructure layers. From 2000 to 2012 there is a balancing out of the share of new standards across the layers of the protocol stack. The resurgence of the routing layer between 2005 and 2012 was based on a combination of upgrades to legacy technology and the creation of new standards, such as label-switching protocols (MPLS) that allow IP networks to function more like a switched network that maintains a specific path between source and destination devices.

Figure 1.2 illustrates several points about the Internet's modular architecture that are linked to the literature on GPTs. If one views the Web as a technology that enables complementary inventions across a wide variety of application sectors (e.g., e-commerce, digital media, voice-over IP, online advertising, or cloud services), it is not surprising to see initial growth in application-layer protocol development, followed by the emergence of a new real-time layer, followed by a resurgence of lower-layer routing technology. This evolution is broadly consistent with the notion of positive feedback from application-sector innovations to extensions of the underlying GPT. Unfortunately, like most papers in the GPT literature, I lack detailed data on Internet-related inventive activity across the full range of application sectors, and I am therefore limited to making detailed observations about the innovation process where it directly touches the GPT. Nevertheless, if one reads the RFCs and W3C Recommendations, links to protocols developed by other SSOs to facilitate application sector innovation are readily apparent. Examples include standards for audio/video compression (ITU/H.264) and for specialized commercial applications of general-purpose W3C tools like the XML language.

Figure 1.2 also raises several questions that will be taken up in the remainder of the chapter. First, how modular is the Internet with respect to the protocol stack? In particular, do we observe that technical interdependencies are greater within than between layers? Is there a specialized division of labor in protocol development? Second, is it possible to preserve the modularity of the entire system when a new set of technologies and protocols is inserted in the middle of the stack, as with the real-time area? Finally, the dwindling share of protocol development at the Internet layer suggests that the network may be increasingly "locked in" to legacy protocols at its key interface. For example, the IETF has long promoted a transition to a set of next generation IP protocols (IPv6) developed in the 1990s, with little success. This raises the question of whether modularity and collective governance render technology platforms less capable of orchestrating "big push" technology transitions than alternative modes of platform governance, such as a dominant platform leader.

1.3 Internet Modularity

Whether the Internet is actually modular in the sense of hiding technical interdependencies and, if so, how that modularity relates to the division of innovative labor, are two separate questions. This section addresses them in turn.

1.3.1 Decomposability

Determining the degree of modularity of a technological system is fundamentally a measurement problem that requires answering two main questions: (1) how to identify interfaces or boundaries between modules, and

(2) how to identify interdependencies across modules. The TCP/IP protocol stack and associated technical areas within the IETF and W3C provide a natural way to group protocols into modules. I use citations among standards-track RFCs and W3C Recommendations to measure interdependencies. The resulting descriptive analysis is similar to the use of design structure matrices, as advocated by Baldwin and Clark (2000) and implemented in MacCormack, Baldwin, and Rusnak (2012), only using stack layers rather than source files to define modules, and citations rather than function calls to measure technical interdependencies.

Citations data were collected directly from the RFCs and W3C publications. Whether these citations are a valid proxy for technical interdependencies will, of course, depend on how authors use them. Officially, the IETF and W3C distinguish between normative and informative citations. Normative references "specify documents that must be read to understand or implement the technology in the new RFC, or whose technology must be present for the technology in the new RFC to work." Informative references provide additional background, but are not required to implement the technology described in a RFC or Recommendation.[16] Normative references are clearly an attractive measure of interdependency. Unfortunately, the distinction between normative and informative cites was not clear for many early RFCs, so I simply use all cites as a proxy. Nevertheless, even if we view informative cites as a measure of knowledge flows (as has become somewhat standard in the economic literature that relies on bibliometrics), the interpretation advanced below would remain apt, since a key benefit of modularity is the "hiding" of information within distinct modules or layers.

Figure 1.3 is a directed graph of citations among all standards produced by the IETF and W3C, with citing layers/technical areas arranged on the Y-axis and cited layers/areas arranged on the X-axis. Shading is based on each cell's decile in the cumulative citation distribution. Twenty-seven percent of all citations link two documents produced by the same working group, and I exclude these from the analysis.[17]

In a completely modular or decomposable system, all citations would be contained with the cells along the main diagonal. Figure 1.3 suggests that the Internet more closely resembles a nearly decomposable system, with the majority of technical interdependencies and information flows occurring either within a module or between a module and an adjacent layer in the protocol stack.[18] If we ignore the security and operations areas, 89 percent of all citations in figure 1.3 are on the main diagonal or an adjacent cell,

---

16. For the official IESG statement on citations, see http://www.ietf.org/iesg/statement/normative-informative.html.

17. Including within-WG citations would make the Internet architecture appear even more modular.

18. An alternative nonmodular and non-interdependent design configuration would be a hierarchy, with all cites either above or below the main diagonal.

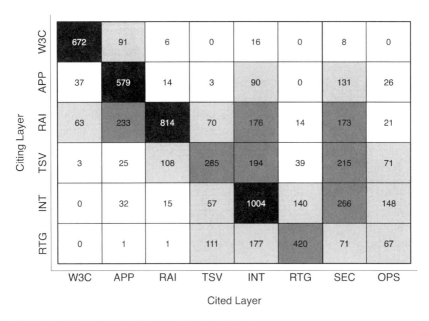

Fig. 1.3 Citations in the Internet Protocol Stack

Notes: Figure 1.3 is a matrix containing cumulative counts of citations from citing layer standards-track publications to cited layer standards-track publications based on the author's calculations using data from IETF and W3C. Layer names are: RTG = routing, INT = Internet, TSV = transport, RAI = real-time applications and infrastructure, APP = applications, W3C = W3C, SEC = security, and OPS = operations.

whereas a uniformly random citation probability would lead to just 44 percent of all citations on or adjacent to the main diagonal.

The exceptions to near-decomposability illustrated in figure 1.3 are also interesting. First, it is fairly obvious that security and operations protocols interface with all layers of the protocol stack: apparently there are some system attributes that are simply not amenable to modularization. While straightforward, this observation may have important implications for determining the point at which a GPT encounters decreasing returns to scale due to the costs of adapting a shared input to serve heterogeneous application sectors.

The second notable departure from near-decomposability in figure 1.3 is the relatively high number of interlayer citations to Internet layer protocols. This turns out to be a function of vintage effects. Controlling for publication-year effects in a Poisson regression framework reveals that Internet layer specifications are no more likely to receive between-layer citations than other standards.[19] Of course, the vintage effects themselves are inter-

---

19. These regression results are not reported here, but are available from the author upon request.

esting to the extent that they highlight potential "lock in" to early design choices made for an important interface, such as TCP/IP.

Finally, figure 1.3 shows that real-time and transport-layer protocols have a somewhat greater intermodule citation propensity than standards from other layers. Recall that these layers emerged later than the original applications, Internet, and routing areas (see figure 1.2). Thus, this observation suggests that when a new module is added to an existing system (perhaps to enable or complement coinvention in key application areas), it may be hard to preserve a modular architecture, particularly if that module is not located at the "edges" of the stack, as with the W3C.

1.3.2 Division of Labor

While figure 1.3 clearly illustrates the modular nature of the Internet's technical architecture, it does not reveal whether that modularity is associated with a specialized division of labor. This section will examine the division of labor among organizations involved in IETF standards development by examining their participation at various layers of the TCP/IP protocol stack.[20] The data for this analysis are extracted from actual RFCs by identifying all e-mail addresses in the section listing each author's contact information, and parsing those addresses to obtain an author's organizational affiliation.[21] The analysis is limited to the IETF, as it was not possible to reliably extract author information from W3C publications. On average, IETF RFCs have 2.3 authors with 1.9 unique institutional affiliations.

Because each RFC in this analysis is published by an IETF working group, I can use that WG to determine that document's layer in the protocol stack. In total, I use data from 3,433 RFCs published by 328 different WGs, and whose authors are affiliated with 1,299 unique organizations. Table 1.2 lists the fifteen organizations that participated (i.e., authored at least one standard) in the most working groups, along with the total number of standards-track RFCs published by that organization.

One way to assess whether there is a specialized division of labor in standards creation is to ask whether firms' RFCs are more concentrated within particular layers of the protocol stack than would occur under random assignment of RFCs to layers (where the exogenous assignment probabilities equal the observed marginal probabilities of an RFC occupying each layer in the stack). Comparing the actual distribution of RFCs across layers to a simulated distribution based on random choice reveals that organizations participating in the IETF are highly concentrated within particular

---

20. In principle, one might focus on specialization at the level of the individual participant. However, since many authors write a single RFC, aggregating to the firm level provides more variation in the scope of activities across modules.

21. In practice, this is a difficult exercise, and I combined the tools developed by Jari Arkko (http://www.arkko.com/tools/docstats.html) with my own software to extract and parse addresses.

Table 1.2   Major IETF participants

Sponsor	Unique WGs	Total standards
Cisco	122	590
Microsoft	65	130
Ericsson	42	147
IBM	40	102
Nortel	38	78
Sun	35	76
Nokia	31	83
Huawei	28	49
AT&T	27	50
Alcatel	26	64
Juniper	25	109
Motorola	24	42
MIT	24	42
Lucent	23	41
Intel	23	33

layers. Specifically, I compute the likelihood-based multinomial test statistic proposed by Greenstein and Rysman (2005) and find a value of –7.1 for the true data, as compared to a simulated value of –5.3 under the null hypothesis of random assignment.[22] The smaller value of the test statistic for the true data indicates agglomeration, and the test strongly rejects the null of random choice (SE = 0.17, p = 0.00).

To better understand this pattern of agglomeration in working group participation, it is helpful to consider a simplistic model of the decision to contribute to drafting an RFC. To that end, suppose that firm i must decide whether to draft an RFC for working group w in layer j. Each firm either participates in the working group or does not: $a_i = 0,1$. Let us further assume that *all* firms receive a gross public benefit B_w if working group w produces a new protocol. Firms that participate in the drafting process also receive a private benefit S_{iw} that varies across working groups, and incur a participation cost F_{ij} that varies across layers. In this toy model, public benefits flow from increasing the functionality of the network and growing the installed base of users. Private benefits could reflect a variety of idiosyncratic factors, such as intellectual property in the underlying technology or improved interoperability with proprietary complements. Participation costs are assumed constant within-layer to reflect the idea that there is a fixed cost to develop the technical expertise needed to innovate within a new module. If firms were all equally capable of innovating at any layer ($F_{ij} = F_{ik}$, for all $i, j \neq k$), there would be no specialized division of labor in standards production within this model.

22. Code for performing this test in Stata has been developed by the author and is available at http://econpapers.repec.org/software/bocbocode/s457205.htm.

To derive a firm's WG-participation decision, let Φ_w represent the endogenous probability that at least one other firm joins the working group. Thus, firm i's payoff from working group participation are $B_w + S_{iw} - F_{ij}$, while the expected benefits of not joining are ΦB_w. If all firms have private knowledge of S_{iw}, and make simultaneous WG participation decisions, the optimal rule is to join the committee if and only if $(1 - \Phi_w)B_w + S_{iw} > F_{ij}$.

While dramatically oversimplified, this model yields several useful insights. First, there is a trade-off between free riding and rent seeking in the decision to join a technical committee. While a more realistic model might allow for some dissipation of rents as more firms join a working group, the main point here is that firms derive private benefits from participation, and are likely to join when S_{iw} is larger. Likewise, when S_{iw} is small, there is an incentive to let others develop the standard, and that free-riding incentive increases with the probability (Φ) that at least one other firm staffs the committee. Moreover, because Φ depends on the strategies of other prospective standards developers, this model illustrates the main challenge for empirical estimation: firms' decisions to join a given WG are simultaneously determined.

To estimate this model of WG participation I treat S_{iw} as an unobserved stochastic term, treat B_w as an intercept or WG random effect, and replace Φ_w with the log of one plus the actual number of other WG participants.[23] I parameterize F_{ij} as a linear function of two dummy variables—prior RFC (this layer) and prior RFC (adjacent layer)—that measure prior participation in WGs at the same layer of the protocol stack, or at an adjacent layer conditional on the same-layer dummy being equal to zero. These two dummies for prior RFC publication at "nearby" locations in the protocol stack provide an alternative measure of the division of labor in protocol development that may be easier to interpret than the multinomial test statistic reported above.

The regression results presented below ignore the potential simultaneity of WG participation decisions. However, if the main strategic interaction involves a trade-off between free riding and rent seeking, the model suggests that firms will be increasingly dispersed across working groups when the public benefits of protocol development (B_w) are large relative to the private rents (S_{iw}). Conversely, if we observe a strong positive correlation among participation decisions, the model suggests that private benefits of exerting some influence over the standard are relatively large and/or positively correlated across firms. It is also possible to explore the rent-seeking hypothesis by exploiting the difference between standards and nonstandards-track RFCs, an idea developed in Simcoe (2012). Specifically, if the normative aspects of standards-track documents provide greater opportunities for rent seek-

---

23. An alternative approach would be to estimate the model as a static game of incomplete information following Bajari et al. (2010). However, I lack instrumental variables that produce plausibly exogenous variation in Φ_w, as required for that approach.

Table 1.3   Summary statistics

Variable	Mean	SD	Min.	Max.
Stds.—track WG participation	0.06	0.24	0	1
Nonstds.—track participation	0.05	0.22	0	1
Prior RFC (this layer)	0.34	0.47	0	1
Prior RFC (adjacent layer)	0.17	0.38	0	1
log(1 + other participants)	2.11	0.86	0	4.51

ing (e.g., because they specify how products will actually be implemented), there should be a stronger positive correlation among firms' WG participation decisions, leading to more agglomeration when "participation" is measured as standards-track RFC production than when it is measured as nonstandards-track RFC publication.

The data used for this exercise come from a balanced panel of 43 organizations and 328 WGs where each organization contributed to ten or more RFCs and is assumed to be at risk of participating in every WG.[24] Table 1.3 presents summary statistics for the estimation sample and table 1.4 presents coefficient estimates from a set of linear probability models.[25]

The first four columns in table 1.4 establish that there is a strong positive correlation between past experience at a particular layer of the protocol stack and subsequent decisions to join a new WG at the same layer. Having previously published a standards-track RFC in a WG in a given layer is associated with a 5 to 7 percentage-point increase in the probability of joining a new WG at the same layer. There is a smaller but still significant positive association between prior participation at an adjacent layer and joining a new WG. Both results are robust to adding fixed or random effects for the WG and focal firm. Given the baseline probability of standards-track entry is 6 percent, the "same layer" coefficient corresponds to a marginal effect of 100 percent, and is consistent with the earlier observation that participation in the IETF by individual firms is concentrated within layers.

The fifth column in table 1.4 shows that the number of other WG participants has a strong positive correlation with the focal firm's participation decision. A 1 standard deviation increase in participation by other organizations, or roughly doubling the size of a working group, produces a 5 percentage-point increase in the probability of joining and is therefore roughly equivalent to prior experience at the same layer. I interpret this as

---

24. Increasing the number of firms in the estimation sample mechanically reduces the magnitude of the coefficient estimates (since firms that draft fewer RFCs participate in fewer working groups, and therefore exhibit less variation in the outcome) but does not qualitatively alter the results.

25. The linear probability model coefficients are nearly identical to average marginal effects from a set of unreported logistic regressions.

Table 1.4   Linear probability models of IETF working group participation

	Stds.—track particip.					
Outcome	(1)	(2)	(3)	(4)	(5)	(6)
Prior RFC (this layer)	0.06	0.07	0.07	0.05	0.06	0.06
	[6.87]***	[11.98]***	[9.64]***	[6.25]***	[11.24]***	[11.19]***
Prior RFC (adjacent	0.02	0.02	0.02	0.01	0.02	0.01
layer)	[3.27]***	[3.12]***	[2.72]***	[1.54]	[3.49]***	[2.36]**
log(other WG					0.06	0.04
participants)					[23.70]***	[17.82]***
WG random effects	N	Y	N	N	N	N
WG fixed effects	N	N	Y	Y	N	N
Firm fixed effects	N	N	N	Y	N	N
Observations	14,104	14,104	14,104	14,104	14,104	14,104

Notes: Unit of analysis is a firm-WG. Robust standard errors clustered by WG (except random effects model). *T*-statistics in brackets.
***Significant at the 1 percent level.
**Significant at the 5 percent level.
*Significant at the 10 percent level.

evidence that private benefits from contributing to specification development are highly correlated across firms at the WG level, and that the costs of WG participation are low enough for these benefits to generally outweigh temptations to free ride when an organization perceives a WG to be important.

The last column in table 1.4 changes the outcome to an indicator for publishing a nonstandards-track RFC in a given WG. In this model, the partial correlation between a focal firm's participation decision and the number of other organizations in the WG falls by roughly one-third, to 0.04. A chi-square test rejects the hypothesis that the coefficient on log(other participants) is equal across the two models in columns (5) and (6) ($\chi^2(1) = 6.22$, $p = 0.01$). The stronger association among firms' WG participation decisions for standards-track RFCs than for nonstandards-track RFCs suggests that the benefits of exerting some influence over the standards process are large (relative to the participation costs and/or the public-good benefits of the standard) and positively correlated across firms.[26]

In summary, data from the IETF show that the division of labor in protocol development does conform to the boundaries established by the modular protocol stack. This specialized division of labor emerges through firms' decentralized decisions to participate in specification development in vari-

---

26. In unreported regressions, I allowed the standards/nonstandards difference to vary by layer, and found that standards was larger at all layers except applications and operations, with statistically significant differences for real-time, Internet, and routing and security.

ous working groups. The incentive to join a particular WG reflects both the standard economic story of amortizing sunk investments in developing expertise at a given layer, and idiosyncratic opportunities to obtain private benefits from shaping the standard. The results of a simple empirical exercise show that forces for agglomeration are strong, and suggests that incentives to participate for private benefit are typically stronger than free-riding incentives (perhaps because the fixed cost of joining a given committee are small). Moreover, firms' idiosyncratic opportunities to obtain private benefits from shaping a standard appear to be correlated across working groups, suggesting that participants know when a particular technical standard is likely to be important.

Finally, it is important to note that while this analysis focused on firms that produce at least ten RFCs in order to disentangle their motivations for working group participation, those forty-three firms are only a small part of the total population of 1,299 unique organizations that supplied an author on one or more RFCs. Large active organizations do a great deal of overall protocol development. However, the organizations that only contribute to one or two RFCs are also significant. By hiding many of the details of what happens within any given layer of the protocol stack, the Internet's modular architecture lowers the costs of entry and component innovation for this large group of small participants.

1.4 Diffusion across Modules and Sectors

The final step in this chapter's exploration of Internet modularity is to examine the distribution of citations to RFCs over time. As described above, lags in diffusion and coinvention occupy center stage in much of the literature on GPTs for two reasons: (1) they help explain the otherwise puzzling gap between the spread of seminal technologies and the appearance of macroeconomic productivity effects, and (2) they highlight the role of positive innovation externalities between and among application sectors and the GPT-producing sector.

Analyzing the age distribution of citations to standards can provide a window onto the diffusion and utilization of the underlying technology. However, it is important to keep in mind the limitations of citations as a proxy for standards utilization in the following analysis. In particular, we do not know whether any given citation represents a normative technical interdependency or an informative reference to the general knowledge embedded in an RFC. One might also wish to know whether citations come from implementers of the specification, or from producers of complements, who reference the interface in a "black box" fashion. While such fine-grained interpretation of citations between RFC are not possible in the data I use here, examining the origin and rate of citations does reveal some interesting patterns that hint at the role of modularity in the utilization of Internet standards.

1.4.1 Diffusion across Modules

I begin by examining citation flows across different modules and layers within the IETF and the TCP/IP protocol stack. If the level of technical interdependency between any two standards increases as we move inward from protocols in different layers, to protocols in the same layer, to protocols in the same working group, we should expect to see shorter citation lags. The intuition is straightforward: tightly coupled technologies need to be designed at the same time to avoid mistakes that emerge from unanticipated interactions. Two technologies that interact only through a stable interface need not be contemporaneously designed, since a well-specified interface defines a clear division of labor.[27]

To test the idea that innovations diffuse within and between modules at different rates, I created a panel of annual citations to standards-track RFCs for sixteen years following their publication. Citation dates are based on the publication year of the citing RFC. The econometric strategy is adapted from Rysman and Simcoe (2008). Specifically, I estimate a Poisson regression of citations to RFC i in citing year y that contains a complete set of age effects (where age equals citing year minus publication year) and a third order polynomial for citing years to control for time trends and truncation: $E[\text{Cites}_{iy}] = \exp\{\lambda_{age} + f(\text{Citing year})\}$.

To summarize these regression results, I set the citing year equal to 2000 and generate the predicted number of citations at each age. Dividing by the predicted cumulative cites over all sixteen years of RFC life yields a probability distribution that I call the citation-age profile. These probabilities are plotted and used to calculate a hypothetical mean citation age, along with its standard error (using the delta method).

Figure 1.4 illustrates the citation-age profile for standards-track RFCs using three different outcomes: citations originating in the same WG, citations originating in the same layer of the protocol stack, and citations from other layers of the protocol stack.[28] The pattern is consistent with the idea that more interconnected protocols are created closer together in time. Specifically, I find that the average age of citations within a working group is 3.5 years (SE = 0.75), compared to 6.7 years (SE = 0.56) for cites from the same layer and 8.9 years (SE = 0.59) for other layers.

The main lesson contained in figure 1.4 is that even within a GPT, innovations diffuse faster within than between modules. This pattern is arguably driven by the need for tightly interconnected aspects of the system to coordinate on design features simultaneously, whereas follow-on innovations can rely on the abstraction and information hiding provided by a well-defined

---

27. The costs of time shifting when the division of labor is nor clearly defined ex ante will be familiar to anyone who has worked on a poorly organized team project.
28. For this analysis, I exclude all cites originating in the security and operations layers (see figure 1.3).

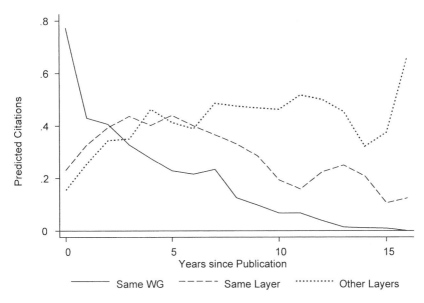

Fig. 1.4 Age profiles for RFC-to-RFC citations

interface. The importance of contemporaneous design for tightly coupled components may be compounded by the fact that many interface layers may need to be specified before a GPT becomes useful in specific application sectors. For example, in the case of electricity, the alternating versus direct current standards war preceded widespread agreement on standardized voltage requirements, which preceded the ubiquitous three-pronged outlet that works with most consumer devices (at least within the United States). While this accretion of interrelated interfaces is likely a general pattern, the Internet and digital technology seems particularly well suited to the use of a modular architecture to reduce the rate at which technical knowledge depreciates and to facilitate low-cost reuse and time shifting.

1.4.2 Diffusion across Sectors

To provide a sense of how the innovations embedded in Internet standards diffuse out into application sectors, I repeat the empirical exercise described above, only comparing citations among all RFCs to citations from US patents to RFCs. The citing year for a patent-to-RFC citation is based on the patent's application date. While there are many drawbacks to patent citations, there is also a substantial literature that argues for their usefulness as a measure of cumulative innovation based on the idea that each cite limits the scope of the inventor's monopoly and is therefore carefully assessed for its relevance to the claimed invention. For this chapter, the key assumption is simply that citing patents are more likely to reflect inventions that enable applications of the GPT than citations from other RFCs.

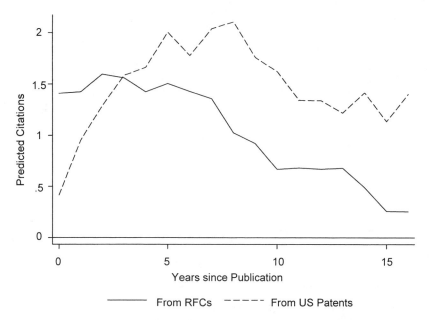

Fig. 1.5 Age profiles for RFC-to-RFC and US patent-to-RFC citations

Figure 1.5 graphs the age profiles for all RFC cites and all patent cites. The RFC age profile represents a cite-weighted average of the three lines in figure 1.4, and the average age of an RFC citation is 5.9 years (SE = 0.5). Patent citations clearly take longer to arrive, and are more persistent in later years than RFC cites. The average age of a US patent nonprior citation to an RFC is 8.2 years (SE = 0.51), which is quite close to the mean age for a citation from RFCs at other layers of the protocol stack.

At one level, the results illustrated in figures 1.4 and 1.5 are not especially surprising. However, these figures highlight the idea that a GPT evolves over time, partly in response to the complementarities between GPT-sector and application sector innovative activities. The citation lags illustrated in these figures are relatively short compared to the long delay between the invention of packet-switched networking and the emergence of the commercial Internet illustrated in figure 1.1. Nevertheless, it is likely that filing a patent represents only a first step in the process of developing application-sector-specific complementary innovations. Replacing embedded capital and changing organizational routines may also be critical, but are harder to measure, and presumably occur on a much longer time frame.

1.5 Conclusion

The chapter provides a case study of modularity and its economic consequences for the technical architecture of the Internet. It illustrates the modular design of the Internet architecture, the specialized division of innovative labor in Internet standards development, and the gradual diffusion of new ideas and technologies across interfaces within that system. These observations are limited to a single technology, albeit one that can plausibly claim to be a GPT with significant macroeconomic impacts.

At a broader level, this chapter suggests that modularity and specialization in the supply of a GPT may help explain its long-run trajectory. In the standard model of a GPT, the system-level trade-off between generality and specialization is overcome through "coinvention" within application sectors. These complementary innovations raise the returns to GPT innovation by expanding the installed base, and also by expanding the set of potential applications. A modular architecture facilitates the sort of decentralized experimentation and low-cost reusability required to sustain growth at the extensive margin, and delivers the familiar benefits of a specialized division of labor in GPT production.

Finally, this chapter highlights a variety of topics that can provide grist for future research on the economics of modularity, standard setting, and general-purpose technologies. For example, while modularity clearly facilitates an interfirm division of labor, even proprietary systems can utilize modular design principles. This raises a variety of questions about the interaction between modular design and "open" systems, such as the Internet, which are characterized by publicly accessible interfaces and particular forms of platform governance. The microeconomic foundations of coordination costs that limit the division of innovative labor within a modular system are another broad topic for future research. For example, we know little about whether or why the benefits of a modular product architecture are greater inside or outside the boundaries of a firm, or conversely, whether firm boundaries change in response to architectural decisions. Finally, in keeping with the theme of this volume, future research might ask whether there is something special about digital technology that renders it particularly amenable to the application of modular design principles. Answers to this final question will have important implications for our efforts to extrapolate lessons learned from studying digitization to other settings, such as life sciences or the energy sector.

References

Arthur, W. Brian. 1989. "Competing Technologies, Increasing Returns, and Lock-In by Historical Events." *Economic Journal* 97:642–65.

Bajari, P., H. Hong, J. Krainer, and D. Nekipelov. 2010. "Estimating Static Models of Strategic Interactions" *Journal of Business and Economic Statistics* 28 (4): 469–82.

Baldwin, C. Y., and K. B. Clark. 2000. *Design Rules: The Power of Modularity*, vol. 1. Boston: MIT Press.

Becker, G. S., and K. M. Murphy. 1992. "The Division-of-Labor, Coordination Costs and Knowledge." *Quarterly Journal of Economics* 107 (4): 1137–60.

Berners-Lee. T., and M. Fischetti. 1999. *Weaving the Web: The Original Design and Ultimate Destiny of the World Wide Web by its Inventor*. San Francisco: Harper.

Bresnahan, T. 2010. "General Purpose Technologies." In *Handbook of the Economics of Innovation*, vol. 2, edited by B. Hall and N. Rosenberg, 761–91. Amsterdam: Elsevier.

Bresnahan, T. F., and S. Greenstein. 1999. "Technological Competition and the Structure of the Computer Industry." *Journal of Industrial Economics* 47 (1): 1–40.

Bresnahan, T., and M. Trajtenberg. 1995. "General Purpose Technologies: Engines of Growth?" *Journal of Econometrics* 65:83.

Brooks, F. 1975. *The Mythical Man-Month*. Boston: Addison-Wesley.

Colfer, L., and C. Baldwin. 2010. "The Mirroring Hypothesis: Theory, Evidence and Exceptions." Working Paper no. 10–058, Harvard Business School, Harvard University.

David, Paul A. 1985. "Clio and the Economics of QWERTY." *American Economic Review* 77 (2): 332–37.

David, Paul A. 1990. "The Dynamo and the Computer: An Historical Perspective on the Modern Productivity Paradox." *American Economic Review Papers and Proceedings* 80 (2): 355–61.

Dranove, D., C. Forman, A. Goldfarb, and S. Greenstein. 2012. "The Trillion Dollar Conundrum: Complementarities and Health Information Technology." NBER Working Paper no. 18281, Cambridge, MA.

Farrell, J. 2007. "Should Competition Policy Favor Compatibility?" In *Standards and Public Policy*, edited by S. Greenstein and V. Stango. Cambridge: Cambridge University Press.

Farrell, J., and G. Saloner. 1986. "Installed Base and Compatibility—Innovation, Product Preannouncements, and Predation." *American Economic Review* 76 (5): 940–55.

Farrell, J., and T. Simcoe. 2012. "Four Paths to Compatibility." In *Oxford Handbook of the Digital Economy*, edited by M. Peitz and J. Waldfogel, 34–58. Oxford: Oxford University Press.

Greenstein, S. 1996. "Invisible Hand versus Invisible Advisors." In *Private Networks, Public Objectives*, edited by Eli Noam. Amsterdam: Elsevier.

Greenstein, S., and M. Rysman. 2005. "Testing for Agglomeration and Dispersion." *Economics Letters* 86 (3): 405–11.

Henderson, R., and K. B. Clark. 1990. "Architectural Innovation: The Reconfiguration of Existing Product Technologies and the Failure of Established Firms." *Administrative Science Quarterly* 35 (1): 9–30.

Jones, B. F. 2008. "The Knowledge Trap: Human Capital and Development Reconsidered." NBER Working Paper no. 14138, Cambridge, MA.

Langlois, R. 2002. "Modularity in Technology and Organization." *Journal of Economic Behavior & Organization* 49 (1): 19–37.

MacCormack, A., C. Baldwin, and J. Rusnak. 2012. "Exploring the Duality between Product and Organizational Architectures: A Test of the 'Mirroring' Hypothesis." *Research Policy* 41:1309–24.

MacKie-Mason, J., and J. Netz. 2007. "Manipulating Interface Standards as an Anticompetitive Strategy." In *Standards and Public Policy*, edited by S. Greenstein and V. Stango, 231–59. Cambridge: Cambridge University Press.

Russell, A. 2006. "'Rough Consensus and Running Code' and the Internet-OSI Standards War." *Annals of the History of Computing, IEEE* 28 (3): 48–61.

Rysman, M., and T. Simcoe. 2008. "Patents and the Performance of Voluntary Standard Setting Organizations." *Management Science* 54 (11): 1920–34.
Saltzer, J. H., D. P. Reed, and D. D. Clark. 1984. "End-to-End Arguments in System Design." *ACM Transactions on Computer Systems* 2 (4): 277–88.
Sanchez, R., and J. T. Mahoney. 1996. "Modularity, Flexibility, and Knowledge Management in Product and Organization Design." *Strategic Management Journal* 17:63–76.
Simcoe, T. 2012. "Standard Setting Committees: Consensus Governance for Shared Technology Platforms." *American Economic Review* 102 (1): 305–36.
Simon, H. A. 1962. "The Architecture of Complexity." *Proceedings of the American Philosophical Society* 106 (6): 467–82.
Smith, A. 1776. *Wealth of Nations*, vol. 10, Harvard Classics, edited by C. J. Bullock. New York: P. F. Collier & Son.
Stigler, G., and R. Sherwin. 1985. "The Extent of the Market." *Journal of Law and Economics* 28 (3): 555–85.

Comment   Timothy F. Bresnahan

In "Modularity and the Evolution of the Internet" Tim Simcoe brings valuable empirical evidence to bear on the structure and governance of the Internet's more technical, less customer-facing, layers. His main empirical results are about the Internet's protocol stack, that is, the structure of the technical layers' modular architecture and of the division of labor in invention of improvements.

To organize my discussion, I will follow Simcoe's main results. There are, however, three distinctions that I want to draw before proceeding: (1) modularity is not the same as openness; (2) one can say that an architecture is modular (or open), which is not the same as saying the process by which the architecture changes is modular (or open); and (3) the Internet, like most ICT platforms, includes both purely technical standards and de facto standards in customer-facing products.

1. Modularity is related to, but not the same as, openness. Modularity is an engineering design concept. A large, complex problem can be broken up into pieces, and engineers working on one piece need know only a small amount about all the other pieces. They *do* need to know how their piece can interact with the other pieces—for which they (ideally) need know only the information contained in the interface standards described in the IETF (and preceding) and W3C documents analyzed by Simcoe. In contrast, openness is an economic organization concept. It refers to the availability and control

Timothy F. Bresnahan is the Landau Professor in Technology and the Economy at Stanford University and a member of the board of directors of the National Bureau of Economic Research.

For acknowledgments, sources of research support, and disclosure of the author's material financial relationships, if any, please see http://www.nber.org/chapters/c13056.ack.

of information about interface standards and to the role of a platform sponsor as a gatekeeper. In a closed (or proprietary) architecture, a GPT sponsor controls certain interface standards, and access to information about those standards flows to other firms through contracting with the sponsor. The sponsor can compel others to contract either because it only has the interface information or because it controls access to distribution to customers or both. Modularity makes openness feasible, but many proprietary architectures are quite modular.

2. Modularity is most precisely used as a modifier of an architecture at a moment in time. Modularity in this sense means that the boundaries between layers exist and "local" inventive effort can proceed. An architecture can remain modular over time, however, either by respecting the old boundaries (a part of "backward compatibility") or by moving them in light of new technical or market developments. As we move to this dynamic viewpoint, an important element of openness is that outsiders can define new general-purpose layers and add them to the stack.

3. The Internet, like most multilayered GPTs, has both technical layers and user-facing layers among its general-purpose components. Simcoe focuses on technical layers and the interfaces between them. He does not focus on the commercial layers that connect the Internet to customers. Search, from Google or Microsoft, is an important general-purpose layer in the Internet for both users and advertisers. So, too, is product search inside Amazon or eBay or other storefronts, for both merchants and consumers. For a long time, the Internet index created by Yahoo appeared to be a general-purpose component. Other examples abound. The key point is that not all of the general components associated with the Internet fall within the organized standard setting of the IETF or the W3C. Some are, instead, set in markets or by dominant firms in some layer.

A Great Transformation as New Uses Are Found

Simcoe usefully notes that the time-series pattern of the count of Internet documents (RFCs and W3C publications) corresponds to the role of the Internet as a GPT, or more precisely, a GPT for which important applications were discovered after a lag. If we interpret the count of documents as an indicator of the amount of inventive activity, there is a burst of invention in the 1970s, comparatively less until the 1990s, and a steady growth from the mid-1990s through the present day. This corresponds broadly to the two main eras of the application of the Internet. From its invention until the commercialization of the Internet in the early 1990s, the Internet largely connected technical users in military and academic labs. While there was steady invention throughout this period, Simcoe shows that the architecture of the Internet, at least as measured by the count of documents, needed to be invented to support this technical-user era but, once invented, did not need radical expansion in capabilities.

The second main era in the application of the Internet is its widespread use for commercial and mass market electronic communication, commerce, and content, hereafter EC^3. The commercial portion of this begins in the early to mid-1990s, and, famously, the mass market part of this in the mid- to late 1990s. As Simcoe shows, the ongoing explosion in the range of applications of the Internet that began then and continues to the present has been associated with a dramatic expansion in the number of Internet documents. His interpretation, which is clearly right, is that the wider range of applications elicited new improvements in the general-purpose components. This pulls together a familiar and an unfamiliar aspect of GPT economics. Familiarly, important applications of a GPT can lag years behind its original invention. Less familiarly, new applications, particularly if they involve much larger demand for the GPT than earlier ones, can call for changes in the technical capabilities of the general-purpose components themselves.

Surprising Persistence of Openness

As Simcoe suggests, this transformation involves at least two surprising and very positive developments: commercialization without proprietization and expansion by outsiders. Both are related to modularity and openness.

Most commercial computing and communications platforms are proprietary.[1] The IBM 360 family was proprietary from the get-go, though an essential feature of the family was its modular architecture. The personal computer (PC) began as an open system, but is now the proprietary Microsoft Windows platform, even though there is a great deal of modularity in its architecture. The Oracle or SAP software platforms of the present are at once modular and proprietary. In each case, a single-firm GPT sponsor maintains control over the GPT and, in particular, either controls or commodifies supply of general-purpose layers. The Internet moved from being mostly a technical-uses GPT to being mostly a commercial-uses GPT without (yet) becoming a proprietary platform with a dominant sponsor firm, and with continued openness. This is a borderline miracle.

How the miracle of commercialization without proprietization was achieved is partly reflected in Simcoe's tables. Within the technical layers there continues to be an open architecture, and he shows this. Still, our best understanding of how and why this miracle occurred comes from detailed

---

1. As Bresnahan and Greenstein (1999) point out, this tendency is less marked for technical platforms such as minicomputers. Thus, the distinction between the technical layers of the Internet and the commercial GPTs running "on top of" them is economically important.

examinations of the important historical epochs at which there was a risk of some or all of the Internet becoming proprietary. Shane Greenstein (forthcoming) writes with compelling depth and understanding of the exit of the NSF from Internet funding, the "commercialization of the Internet." At that stage, it could easily have transited to being an IBM technology— only a very thoughtful exit by the NSF prevented this. Another moment when the Internet might have become proprietary was after Microsoft won the browser war. Faced with substantial scope diseconomies between the businesses offering Windows and the Internet (Bresnahan, Greenstein, and Henderson 2012), the firm ultimately focused on maintaining control of the Windows standard for mass market computing and chose not to use command of the browser to proprietize the Internet.

These important historical transitions illustrate an important theme about causation. The technical layers of the Internet stack studied by Simcoe have remained open and modular in part because of their governance, as Simcoe suggests. Equally important, however, has been the absence of a takeover of standards setting by the firm supplying a complementary commercial layer.

Outsider Innovation

The second surprising and very positive development is expansion of the set of open, modular, general-purpose layers of the Internet by outsiders. An important pair of examples is the World Wide Web (WWW) and the web browser. These inventions transformed the Internet into a mass medium. Today, if you ask most consumers what the Internet is, they will answer in terms of the WWW viewed through a browser. Both the WWW and the web browser were new layers in the stack. Economically, they are complements to the preexisting layers of the Internet.

The openness of the Internet architecture meant that the WWW could be invented without getting the permission of any suppliers of existing Internet components or engaging in contracts with them. Instead, the WWW could be defined in a way that it "runs on top of" the Internet; that is, that it interacts with the other layers through open interface standards. This is, as Shane Greenstein (forthcoming) has emphasized, an important element of open organization. In turn, the outsiders who invented and (some of whom) later commercialized the web browser did not need to get the permission of the inventors of the WWW or engage in contracts with them. This would have gone badly if it were required, since Tim Berners-Lee, inventor of the Web, strongly disapproved of the web browser once it became commercialized at Netscape. This is an important example of uncontrolled, uncontracted for, invention by outsiders permitted by open systems, for the series of events culminating in the commercialization of the web browser is one of the top ten economic growth innovations of the twentieth century.

Decomposability, Division of Labor, and Diffusion

Simcoe uses citations—from later Internet documents and from patents—to Internet documents to examine the structure of Internet innovation, both organizationally and technically, and the diffusion of new applications of the Internet. This is an extremely valuable undertaking and we can learn much from it. Of course, it also suffers from the difficulties of citations analysis generally.

Simcoe's analysis of the division of innovative labor seems to me to be a particularly successful deployment of citations methods. The Internet is largely modular in its different technical layers, and firms that work on a layer also tend to patent inventions that are related to that layer. As he points out, considerable gains have been made by having multiple firms inventing and supplying general-purpose components.

The study of the diffusion of new applications for the Internet is a difficult one, and particularly so from a technical-layer-centric perspective. This is, of course, not particularly a weakness of Simcoe's chapter. Data sets on new technologies generally emphasize the technical rather than application. One cautionary note, however, is what the measurable perspective of an "application" is here. Most of the "applications" studied by Simcoe are themselves GPTs, which connect to the Internet and to which, in turn, many specific applications are connected. This is not a small point. A list of things that are *not* applications from the perspective of the citations used in this chapter includes Google Search, Facebook social networking, and Apple media and applications sales in the iTunes store. My interpretation would be that there is no doubt that the enormous transformation of the uses of the Internet to the commercial realm and then to mass market EC^3 is behind these tables, but that it is less obvious that the timing or breadth of the spread of applications can be seen in these tables. A difficulty for patent citations is that patent policy is changing over the relevant time period, so that it is not obvious whether the quantitative growth lies in the breadth of applications or in the tendency to patent inventions. The Internet document citations difficulty is that they are, by their nature, from within the standardized GPT layers of the Internet, not from applications. Only insofar as new applications lead to a change in the GPT layers will an expansion of applications be reflected there.

The Framework

Ultimately, the most interesting thing about Simcoe's chapter is the perspective it takes on the analysis. We have two very different literatures on coordination between suppliers of general-purpose components and applications. These are sufficiently different, especially in their treatment of the optimal form of coordination, that much confusion has arisen.

The first literature, typically writing about "two-sided markets" or "platform economics," is concerned mostly with the coordination of production and prices.[2] The literature takes a contractual approach to the coordination of applications supply with platform (GPT) supply. To facilitate the contractual approach, the most common assumption is that the general-purpose components are supplied by a single firm. By that I mean each platform or GPT cluster has a single supplier of general-purpose components at its center, and that this firm contracts with, or offers incentives to, suppliers of applications. Sometimes there is competition to be (or to become) the dominant platform or GPT, so that there are competing central sponsors, each offering contracts or incentives to an atomless distribution of applications developers.

While the second literature, typically calling itself "GPT" or "Recombination,"[3] treats the same industries, it emphasizes very different phenomena and modeling elements. First, this literature is concerned with the problem of invention, especially repeated rounds of invention, much more than pricing and production. This arises because the practical GPT literature has had to deal with the phenomenon—so emphasized by Simcoe—of general-purpose components supplied by many firms. The "layered" architecture of systems like the Internet involves competition within each layer (rather than competition between whole systems), but complementary invention of improvements across layers. An important general point of this literature is that explicit contracts to coordinate innovation may be impossible so that "softer" governance structures such as the one described by Simcoe are optimal.

Why might the softer governance structures work? Are they optimal only because the governance structure we would really like, explicit contracts among complementary suppliers, is impossible? There are several important points to make here. The most important point concerns the possibility of unforeseen and perhaps unforeseeable change. Sometimes after a period of exploitation of a general-purpose technology, new demands or new inventions call for improvements in the general-purpose components. This is a moment at which not drawing too sharp a distinction between "applications" and general-purpose components can be valuable. A system that is open to the invention of new applications (in the strong sense that they do not need to contract with anyone) will have low barriers to entry. If an application is very widely used and itself becomes a general purpose input into new applications, then the platform is transformed.

In Simcoe's chapter, as in other studies, we see the value of uncoordinated (or only loosely coordinated) innovation for this kind of ex post flexibility.

2. See Jullien (2011) or Rysman (2009). An important exception is Tirole and Weyl (2010), which attempts to extend this framework to invention.
3. See Bresnahan and Trajtenberg (1995).

Modularity and openness permit flexible innovation ex post. They permit flexibility not only in reconfiguration of the platform's general-purpose components but also in allowing an ex post opportunity for multiple heterogeneous innovators to undertake differentiated efforts to improve the general-purpose components of the same GPT. Elsewhere (Bresnahan 2011) I have argued that it was the modularity and openness of the Internet that made it the winner in a multiway race to be the general-purpose technology underlying the enormous EC^3 breakthroughs of the last two decades. Simcoe offers us a fascinating glimpse into the workings of that modularity and openness underlying flexible improvements in the Internet's GPT components.

References

Bresnahan, T. 2011. "General Purpose Technologies." In *Handbook of the Economics of Innovation*, edited by Bronwyn Hall and Nathan Rosenberg. North Holland: Elsevier.

Bresnahan, T., and S. Greenstein. 1999. "Technological Competition and the Structure of the Computer Industry." *Journal of Industrial Economics* 47 (1): 1–40.

Bresnahan, T., S. Greenstein, and R. Henderson. 2012. "Schumpeterian Competition and Diseconomies of Scope: Illustrations from the Histories of Microsoft and IBM." In *The Rate and Direction of Inventive Activity Revisted*, edited by Josh Lerner and Scott Stern. Chicago: University of Chicago Press.

Bresnahan, T., and Manuel Trajtenberg. 1995. "General Purpose Technologies: 'Engines of Growth'?" *Journal of Econometrics* special issue 65 (1): 83–108.

Greenstein, S. Forthcoming. *Innovation from the Edges*. Princeton, NJ: Princeton University Press.

Jullien, B. 2011. "Competition in Multi-Sided Markets: Divide-and-Conquer." *American Economic Journal: Microeconomics* 3 (4): 1–35.

Rysman, M. 2009. "The Economics of Two-Sided Markets." *Journal of Economic Perspectives* 23:125–44.

Tirole, Jean, and Glen Weyl. 2010. "Materialistic Genius and Market Power: Uncovering the Best Innovations." IDEI Working Paper no. 629. Institut d'Économie Industrielle (IDEI), Toulouse, France.

2

What Are We Not Doing When We Are Online?

Scott Wallsten

2.1 Introduction

The Internet has transformed many aspects of how we live our lives, but the magnitude of its economic benefits is widely debated. Estimating the value of the Internet is difficult, in part, not just because many online activities do not require monetary payment, but also because these activities may crowd out other, offline, activities. That is, many of the activities we do online, like reading the news or chatting with friends, we also did long before the Internet existed. The economic value created by online activities, therefore, is the incremental value beyond the value created by the activities crowded out. Estimates of the value of the Internet to the economy that do not take into account these transfers will, therefore, overstate the Internet's economic contribution.

This observation is, of course, not unique to the Internet. In the 1960s Robert Fogel noted that the true contribution of railroads to economic growth was not the gross level of economic activity that could be attributed to them, but rather the value derived from railroads being better than previously existing long-haul transport such as ships on waterways (Fogel 1962,

---

Scott Wallsten is vice president for research and senior fellow at the Technology Policy Institute.

I thank Alexander Clark and Corwin Rhyan for outstanding research assistance and Avi Goldfarb, Chris Forman, Shane Greenstein, Thomas Lenard, Jeffrey Macher, Laura Martin, John Mayo, Gregory Rosston, Andrea Salvatore, Robert Shapiro, Amy Smorodin, Catherine Tucker, and members of the NBER Economics of Digitization Group for comments. I am especially grateful to Avi, Catherine, and Shane for including me in this fun project. I am responsible for all mistakes. For acknowledgments, sources of research support, and disclosure of the author's or authors' material financial relationships, if any, please see http://www.nber.org/chapters/c13001.ack.

1964). The true net economic benefit of the railroad was not small, but was much smaller than generally believed.

This chapter takes to heart Fogel's insight and attempts to estimate changes in leisure time spent online and the extent to which new online activities crowd out other activities. If people mostly do online what they used to do offline, then the benefits of time spent online are biased upward, potentially by a lot. In other words, if online time substitutes for offline time then that online time purely represents an economic transfer, with the net incremental benefit deriving from advantages of doing the activity online, but not from the time doing the activity, per se. By contrast, brand new online activities or those that complement offline activities do create new value, with activities crowded out representing the opportunity cost of that new activity.

Using the available data, this chapter does not evaluate which online activities substitute or complement offline activities. Instead, it estimates the opportunity cost of online leisure time. The analysis suggests that the opportunity cost of online leisure is less time spent on a variety of activities, including leisure, sleep, and work. Additionally, the effect is large enough that better understanding the value of this opportunity cost is a crucial issue in evaluating the effects of online innovation.

To my knowledge, no empirical research has investigated how leisure time online substitutes for or complements other leisure activities.[1] In this chapter I begin to answer that question using detailed data from the American Time Use Survey, which allows me to construct a person-level data set consisting of about 124,000 observations from 2003 to 2011.

I find that the share of Americans reporting leisure time online has been increasing steadily, and much of it crowds out other activity. On average, each minute of online leisure is associated with 0.29 fewer minutes on all other types of leisure, with about half of that coming from time spent watching TV and video, 0.05 minutes from (offline) socializing, 0.04 minutes from relaxing and thinking, and the balance from time spent at parties, attending cultural events, and listening to the radio. Each minute of online leisure is also correlated with 0.27 fewer minutes working, 0.12 fewer minutes sleeping, 0.10 fewer minutes in travel time, 0.07 fewer minutes in household activities, and 0.06 fewer minutes in educational activities, with the remaining time coming from sports, helping other people, eating and drinking, and religious activities.

Among the interesting findings by population groups, the crowd-out effect of online leisure on work decreases beyond age thirty, but remains fairly con-

---

1. One existing study tries to investigate the effects of information technology (IT) use using the same data I use in this chapter, though only from 2003 to 2007. The author finds no particular effect of IT use on other time spent on other activities, though the empirical test is simply whether IT users and nonusers spend significantly different amounts of time on various activities. See Robinson (2011).

stant with income. Online leisure has a large crowd-out effect on time spent on education among people age fifteen to nineteen, but the effect decreases steadily with age.

2.2 Existing Research on the Economic Value of the Internet

The value of the Internet is intrinsically difficult to estimate, in part, because it enables so many activities and, in part, because many of the most popular online activities are "free" in the sense that they have no direct monetary cost to consumers. Several tools exist for valuing nonmarket goods, such as contingent valuation surveys to revealed preference inferred by related market activities (Boardman et al. 1996). Those mechanisms have shortcomings. In principle, contingent valuation can tell you willingness to pay, but people often have no reason to respond truthfully to contingent valuation surveys. Measuring spending on relevant complements reveals how much people spend on an activity, but not how much they would be willing to spend.

Given those weaknesses, perhaps the most common approach to valuing time spent on activities outside of work is to value that time at the wage rate under the implicit assumption that the marginal minute always comes from work. Of course, that assumption may be problematic, as those who employ that approach readily admit. Nevertheless, it is a useful starting point.

Goolsbee and Klenow (2006) were among the first to apply this approach to the Internet. They estimated the consumer surplus of personal (i.e., nonwork) online time using the wage rate as the measure of time value and an imputed demand curve. They estimated a consumer surplus at about $3,000 per person. Setting aside the question of whether the wage rate is an accurate measure of the value of all leisure time, this approach provides an estimate of gross consumer surplus as it does not measure incremental benefits.

Brynjolfsson and Oh (2012) improves on Goolsbee and Klenow with newer survey data from 2003 to 2010 to measure the value of incremental time spent online. Although they also use the wage rate to estimate surplus, their estimates are smaller in magnitude because they focus on the increase in time spent online over this time period rather than the aggregate time spent online. Based on that approach, they estimate the increase in consumer surplus from the Internet to be about $33 billion, with about $21 billion coming from time spent using "free" online services.

Both Goolsbee and Klenow (2006) and Brynjolfsson and Oh (2012) almost certainly overestimate the true surplus created by the Internet, even setting aside the question of whether all leisure time should be valued at the wage rate. In particular, they neglect to factor in the extent to which consumers are simply doing some things online that they used to do offline and that new activities must, at least partially, come at the expense of activities they are no longer doing. Spending an hour reading the paper online shows up as a "free" activity, assuming no subscriber paywall, but is not intrinsically more valuable than the same hour spent reading the news on paper. Similarly, the net benefit of reading an electronic book on a Kindle, for example, does not include the time spent enjoying the book if it would have otherwise been read in dead-tree format. Instead, the net benefit is only the incremental value of reading an electronic, rather than paper, book.

To be sure, the online version of the newspaper must generate additional consumer surplus relative to the offline version or the newspaper industry would not be losing so many print readers, but not all time spent reading the paper online reflects the incremental value of the Internet. Additionally, at a price of zero the activity might attract more consumers than when the activity was paid, or consumers might read more electronic books than paper books because they prefer the format, or because e-books are so much easier to obtain. But even if lower prices increase consumption of a particular activity, the cost of that additional consumption is time no longer spent on another activity.

Activities that once required payment but became free, such as reading the news online, represent a transfer of surplus from producers to consumers, but not new total surplus. Of course, these transfers may have large economic effects as they can lead to radical transformations of entire industries, especially given that consumers spend about $340 billion annually on leisure activities.[2] Reallocating those $340 billion is sure to affect the industries that rely on it. Hence, we should expect to see vigorous fights between cable, Netflix, and content producers even if total surplus remains constant. Similarly, as Joel Waldfogel shows in this volume (chapter 14), the radical transformation in the music industry does not appear to have translated into radical changes in the amounts of music actually produced. That is, the Internet may have thrown the music industry into turmoil, but that appears to be largely because the Internet transferred large amounts of surplus to consumers rather than changing net economic surplus.

As the number and variety of activities we do online increases, it stands to reason that our Internet connections become more valuable to us. Greenstein and McDevitt (2009) estimate the incremental change in consumer surplus resulting from upgrading from dialup to broadband service based on changes in quantities of residential service and price indices. They estimate the increase in consumer surplus related to broadband to be between $4.8 billion and $6.7 billion.

2. See table 57 at http://www.bls.gov/cex/2009/aggregate/age.xls. The $340 billion estimate includes expenditures on entertainment, which includes "fees and admissions," "audio and visual equipment and services," "pets, toys, hobbies, and playground equipment," and "other entertainment supplies, equipment, and services." I added expenditures on reading to entertainment under the assumption that consumer expenditures on reading are likely to be primarily for leisure.

Rosston, Savage, and Waldman (2010) explicitly measure consumer willingness to pay for broadband and its various attributes using a discrete choice survey approach. They find that consumers were willing to pay about $80 per month for a fast, reliable broadband connection, up from about $46 per month since 2003. In both years the average connection price was about $40, implying that (household) consumer surplus increased from about $6 per month in 2003 to $40 per month in 2010. That change suggests an increase of about $430 per year in consumer surplus between 2003 and 2010. Translating this number into total consumer surplus is complicated by the question of who benefits from each broadband subscription and how to consider their value from the connection. That is, a household paid, on average, $40 per month for a connection, but does each household member value the connection at $80? Regardless of the answer to that question, Rosston, Savage, and Waldman's (2010) estimate is clearly well below Goolsbee and Klenow (2006).

In the remainder of the chapter I will build on this research by explicitly estimating the cost of online activities by investigating the extent to which online activities crowd out previous activities.

2.3 The American Time Use Survey, Leisure Time, and Computer Use

Starting in 2003, the US Bureau of Labor Statistics and the US Census began the American Time Use Survey (ATUS) as a way of providing "nationally representative estimates of how, where, and with whom Americans spend their time, and is the only federal survey providing data on the full range of nonmarket activities, from childcare to volunteering."[3]

Each year the survey includes about 13,000 people (except in 2003, when it included about 20,000) whose households had recently participated in the Current Population Survey (CPS).[4] From the relevant BLS files we constructed a 2.5 million-observation data set at the activity-person-year level for use in identifying the time of day in which people engage in particular activities, and a 124,000-observation, person-year-level data set for examining the crowd-out effect.

The ATUS has several advantages for estimating the extent to which online time may crowd out or stimulate additional time on other activities. First, each interview covers a full twenty-four-hour period, making it

---

3. http://www.bls.gov/tus/atussummary.pdf.
4. More specifically, BLS notes that "Households that have completed their final (8th) month of the Current Population Survey are eligible for the ATUS. From this eligible group, households are selected that represent a range of demographic characteristics. Then, one person age 15 or over is randomly chosen from the household to answer questions about his or her time use. This person is interviewed for the ATUS 2–5 months after his or her household's final CPS interview." See http://www.bls.gov/tus/atusfaqs.htm.

possible to study how time spent on one activity might affect time spent on another activity. Second, it is connected to the CPS, so it includes copious demographic information about the respondents.

Third, the survey focuses on activities, not generally on the tools used to conduct those activities. So, for example, reading a book is coded as "reading for personal interest" regardless of whether the words being read are of paper or electronic provenance.[5] As a result, the value of the time spent reading would not be mistakenly attributed to the Internet when using these data. Similarly, time spent watching videos online would be coded as watching TV, not computer leisure time.

The survey does, however, explicitly include some online activities already common when the survey began in 2003. In particular, time spent doing personal e-mail is a separate category from other types of written communication.[6] Online computer games, however, are simply included under games.

The ATUS coding rules therefore imply that any computer- or Internet-based personal activity that did not exist in 2003 as its own category would be included under "Computer use for leisure (excluding games)," which includes "computer use, unspecified" and "computer use, leisure (personal interest)."[7] For example, Facebook represents the largest single use of online time today, but ATUS has no specific entry for social media, and therefore Facebook would almost certainly appear under computer use for leisure.

This feature of the ATUS means that increases in computer use for leisure represent incremental changes in time people spend online and that it should be possible to determine the opportunity cost of that time—what people gave up in order to spend more time online. It is worth noting, however, that the ATUS does not code multitasking, which is a distinct disadvantage to this research to the extent that online behavior involves doing multiple activities simultaneously. In principle the survey asks whether the respondent is doing multiple activities at a given time, but only records the "primary" activity.

To reiterate, the ATUS does not make it possible to determine, say, how much time spent watching video has migrated from traditional television to online services like Netflix. It does, however, tell us how new online activities since 2003 have crowded out activities that existed at that time and—to extend the video example—how much those activities have crowded out (or in) time spent watching video delivered by any mechanism.

A significant disadvantage of the survey, however, is that as a survey,

5. More explicitly, reading for pleasure is activity code 120312: major activity code 12 (socializing, relaxing, and leisure), second-tier code 03 (relaxing and leisure), third-tier code 12 (reading for personal interest). http://www.bls.gov/tus/lexiconwex2011.pdf.
6. Code 020904, "household and personal e-mail and messages," which is different from code 020903 "household and personal mail and messages (not e-mail). See http://www.bls.gov/tus/lexiconwex2011.pdf, p.10. Inexplicably, however, any time spent doing volunteer work on a computer is its own category (150101) (http://www.bls.gov/tus/lexiconwex2011.pdf, p.44).
7. See http://www.bls.gov/tus/lexiconwex2011.pdf, p. 34.

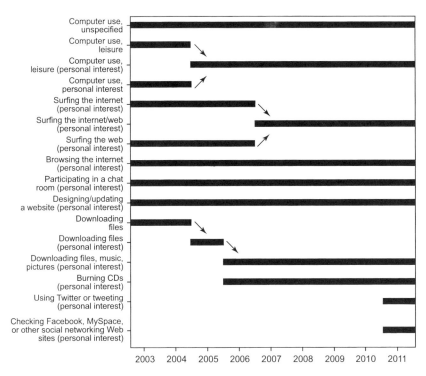

Fig. 2.1   Evolution of examples of "computer use for leisure" provided for ATUS coders

Source: "ATUS Single-Year Activity Coding Lexicons," 2003–2011, http://www.bls.gov/tus/lexicons.htm.

as discussed above, respondents have little reason to respond truthfully, especially about sensitive subjects. For example, would viewing pornography online be categorized under "computer use for leisure" (based on the "unspecified" example in the codebook), or under "personal/private activities" (also the "unspecified" example under this subcategory)?

2.3.1   "Computer Use for Leisure" is Online Time

The relevant ATUS category is time spent using a computer for leisure.[8] This measure explicitly excludes games, e-mail, and computer use for work and volunteer activities. While some computer leisure activities may not necessarily involve the Internet, nearly all of the many examples provided to interviewers under that heading involve online activities (figure 2.1). Addi-

---

8. Computer games are simply recorded as "leisure/playing games," and e-mail is coded as "household and personal e-mail and messages." Text messaging is recorded as "telephone calls." Bureau of Labor Statistics (2010).

Table 2.1   Top ten online activities by time spent on them

		Share of time			Position change
Rank	Category	May–11 (%)	Jun–10 (%)	Jun–09 (%)	'10–'11 (%)
1	Social networks	22.50	22.70	15.80	↔
2	Online games	9.80	10.20	9.30	↔
3	E-mail	7.60	8.50	11.50	↔
4	Portals	4.50	4.40	5.50	↔
5	Videos/movies[a]	4.40	3.90	3.50	↑1
6	Search	4.00	3.50	3.40	↑1
7	Instant messaging	3.30	4.40	4.70	↓2
8	Software manufacturers	3.20	3.30	3.30	↔
9	Classifieds/auctions	2.90	2.70	2.70	↑1
10	Current events and global news	2.60	—	—	↑1
	Multicategory entertainment	—	2.80	3.00	↓2
	Other[b]	35.10	34.30	37.30	

Source: Nielsen NetView (June 2009–2010) and Nielsen State of the Media: The Social Media Report (Q3 2011).

[a]Nielsen's videos/movies category refers to time spent on video-specific (e.g., YouTube, Bing Videos, Hulu) and movie-related websites (e.g., IMDB, MSN Movies, and Netflix). It does not include video streaming non–video-specific or movie-specific websites (e.g., streamed video on sports or news sites).

[b]Other refers to 74 remaining online categories for 2009–2010 and 75 remaining online categories for 2011 visited from PC/laptops.

tionally, while the measure is coded as "computer use for leisure," based on the coding instructions it also likely includes mobile device use.

Based on what the ATUS measure excludes and other sources of information detailing what online activities include, we can get a good idea of what people are probably spending their time doing. Nielsen identifies the top ten online activities (table 2.1). Of the top ten, the ATUS variable excludes online games, e-mail, and any Internet use for work, education, or volunteer activities. Based on this list, it is reasonable to conclude that the top leisure uses included in the ATUS variable are social networks, portals, and search.

2.3.2   How Do Americans Spend Their Time?

The *New York Times* produced an excellent representation of how Americans spend their time from the ATUS (figure 2.2). As the figure highlights, ATUS data track activities by time of day and activity, as well as by different population groupings due to coordination with the CPS. Each major activity in the figure can be broken down into a large number of smaller activities under that heading. The figure reveals the relatively large amount of time people spend engaged in leisure activities, including socializing and watching TV and movies.

The ATUS includes detailed data on how people spend their leisure time.

What Are We Not Doing When We Are Online? 63

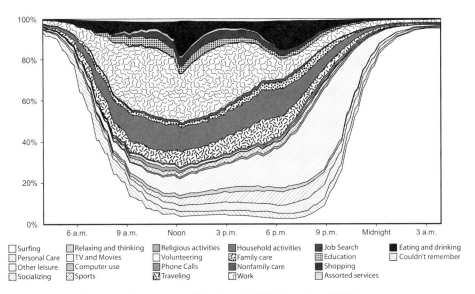

Fig. 2.2 How Americans spent their time in 2008, based on ATUS
Source: *New York Times* (2009). http://www.nytimes.com/interactive/2009/07/31/business/20080801-metrics-graphic.html.

The ATUS has seven broad categories of leisure, but I pull "computer use for leisure" out of the subcategories to yield eight categories of leisure. Figure 2.3 shows the share of time Americans spent on these leisure activities in 2011.

The total time Americans engage in leisure on average per day has remained relatively constant at about five hours, increasing from 295 minutes in 2003 to about 304 minutes in 2011, though it has ranged from 293 to 305 minutes during that time.

Figure 2.4 shows the average number of minutes spent per day using a computer for leisure activities. While the upward trend since 2008 is readily apparent, the data also show that, on average, at about thirteen minutes per day, leisure time online is a small share of the total five hours of daily leisure activities the average American enjoys.

This average is deceptively low, in part, not just because it does not include time spent doing e-mail, watching videos, and gaming, but also because it is calculated across the entire population, so is not representative of people who spend any time online. Figure 2.5 shows that the average is low primarily because a fairly small share of the population reports spending any leisure time online (other than doing e-mail and playing games). However, the figure shows that the share of the population who spend nongaming and non–e-mail leisure time online is increasing, and, on average, people who spend any leisure time online spend about 100 minutes a day—nearly one-third of their total daily leisure time.

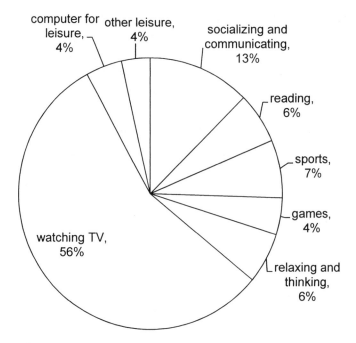

Fig. 2.3 Share of leisure time spent on various activities, 2011
Source: ATUS 2011 (author's derivation from raw data).
Note: Average total daily leisure time is about five hours.

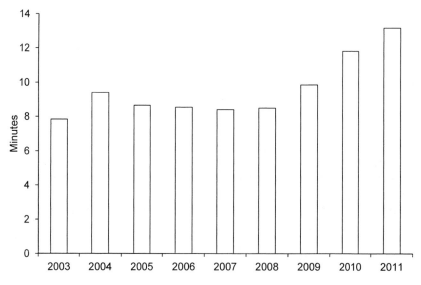

Fig. 2.4 Average minutes per day spent using computer for leisure

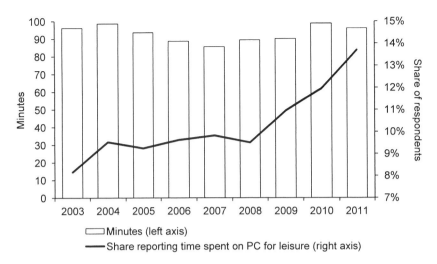

Fig. 2.5 Share of population using computer for leisure and average number of minutes per day among those who used a computer for leisure

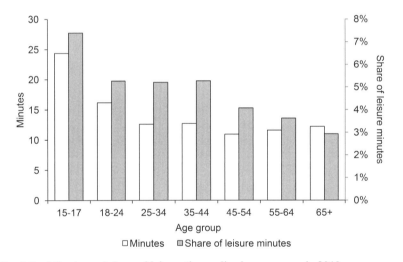

Fig. 2.6 Minutes and share of leisure time online by age group in 2010

2.3.3 Who Engages in Online Leisure?

Online leisure time differs across many demographics, including age and income. As most would expect, the amount of online leisure time decreases with age, more or less (figure 2.6). People between ages fifteen and seventeen spend the most time online, followed by eighteen- to twenty-four-year-olds. Perhaps somewhat surprisingly, the remaining age groups report spending similar amounts of time engaged in online leisure. However, because total

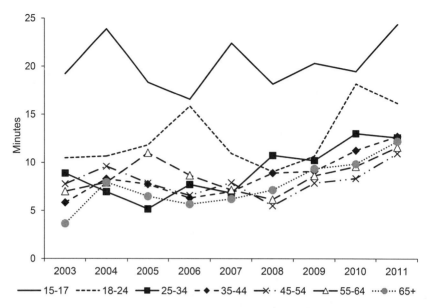

Fig. 2.7 Time spent using computer for leisure by age and year

leisure time increases with age, beginning with the group age thirty-five to forty-four, the share of leisure time spent online continues to decrease with age.

Perhaps not surprisingly given the trends discussed above, both the amount of leisure time spent online (figure 2.7) and the share of respondents reporting spending leisure time online is generally increasing over time (figure 2.8).

Leisure time also varies by income. Figure 2.9 shows average total leisure time excluding computer use and computer use for leisure by income. The figure shows that overall leisure time generally decreases with income. Computer use for leisure, on the other hand, appears to increase with income.

People with higher incomes, however, are more likely to have computer access at home, meaning average computer use by income is picking up the home Internet access effect.

Goldfarb and Prince (2008) investigated the question of online leisure by income in a paper investigating the digital divide. Based on survey data from 2001, they find that conditional on having Internet access, wealthier people spend less personal time online than poorer people. Their key instrument identifying Internet access is the presence of a teenager living in the house, which may make a household more likely to subscribe to the Internet but not more likely to spend personal time online except due to having Internet access.

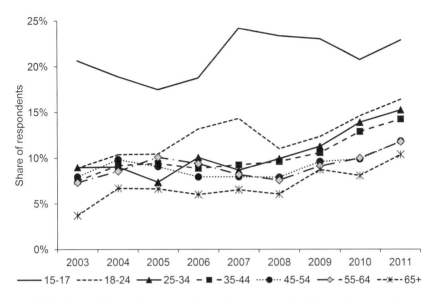

Fig. 2.8 Share of respondents reporting using computer for leisure by age and year

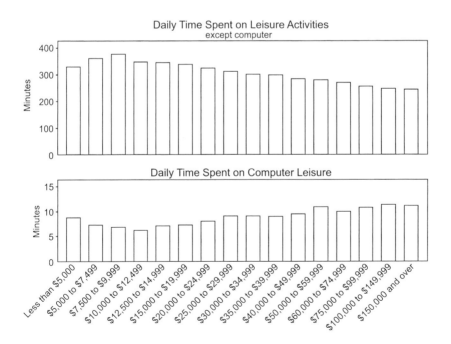

Fig. 2.9 Leisure time by income

With the ATUS data I can attempt to replicate their instrumental variables results using this more recent data. While I know the ages of all household members, the data do not indicate whether a household has Internet access. However, I can identify some households that have access. In particular, any ATUS respondent who spends any time at home involved in computer leisure, e-mail, or using a computer for volunteer work must have home Internet access. Following Goldfarb and Prince, I estimate the following two simultaneous equations using two-stage least squares:

(1) $\text{home Internet access}_i = f \begin{pmatrix} \text{income}_i, \text{education}_i, \text{age}_i, \text{sex}_i, \text{race}_i, \text{married}_i, \text{number of children} \\ \text{in household}_i, \text{Spanish-speaking only}_i, \text{labor force status}_i, \\ (\text{metro, suburban, rural})_i, \text{leisure excluding computer use}_i, \text{year}_t, \\ \text{survey day of week}_i, \text{teenager in house}_i \end{pmatrix}$

(2) $\text{computer use for leisure}_i = f(\mathbf{Z}, \overline{\text{home Internet access}_i})$,

where i indicates a respondent, and $\mathbf{Z}$ is the vector of independent variables included in the first equation. Note the absence of a t subscript—no individual appears more than once in the survey, so the data are a stacked cross section rather than a pure time series. "Labor force status" is a vector of dummy variables indicating whether the respondent is employed and working, employed but absent from work, employed but on layoff, unemployed and looking for work, or not in the labor force. I include year dummy variables to control for time trends. I include an indicator for the day of the week the survey took place since certain activities—leisure time especially—differs significantly across days. As mentioned, my indicator for home Internet access identifies only a portion of households that actually have Internet access. This method implies that only 17 percent of households had access in 2010 when the US Census estimated that more than 70 percent actually had access.[9] Nevertheless, in the first stage of this two-stage model the variable is useful in creating a propensity to have access for use in the second stage in that while the level is wrong, the fitted trend in growth in Internet access tracks actual growth in access reasonably well. The fitted propensity to have access increases by about 70 percent while actual home Internet access increased by about 78 percent during that same time period.[10]

Table 2.2 shows the (partial) results of estimating the set of equations above. The first column replicates Goldfarb and Prince. These results mirror theirs: conditional on home Internet access, computer leisure time decreases with income. In order to see whether computer leisure looks different from

---

9. See http://www.ntia.doc.gov/files/ntia/data/CPS2010Tables/t11_2.txt.
10. See http://www.pewinternet.org/Trend-Data-(Adults)/Internet-Adoption.aspx.

Table 2.2 Computer leisure as a function of income

Variable	Computer leisure	Computer as share of leisure	Variable	Computer leisure	Computer as share of leisure
$10k–$19.9k	0.00264	0.00124	Black	3.078***	0.0101***
	(0.00453)	(0.748)		(4.590)	(5.414)
$20k–$29k	–1.015	–0.00238	American Indian	1.176	0.00801**
	(–1.371)	(–1.134)		(0.829)	(1.975)
$30k–$49k	–2.352***	–0.00622**	Asian	2.250***	0.0122***
	(–2.621)	(–2.477)		(3.194)	(5.864)
$50k–$75k	–3.510***	–0.0101***	White	–2.314*	–0.00195
	(–3.079)	(–3.148)	American Indian	(–1.842)	(–0.545)
$75k–$99k	–3.993***	–0.0108***	White Asian	8.130***	0.0227***
	(–3.257)	(–3.155)		(3.112)	(3.026)
$100k–$149k	–4.690***	–0.0122***	White Asian	42.55***	0.450***
	(–3.530)	(–3.241)	Hawaiian	(4.270)	(15.62)
>= $150k	–4.701***	–0.0124***	Spanish only Hhld	0.906*	0.00177
	(–3.699)	(–3.447)		(1.741)	(1.254)
Age	–0.0244	–6.83e–05	Monday	–2.568***	0.00127
	(–1.355)	(–1.241)		(–5.955)	(0.875)
Male	4.164***	0.00661***	Tuesday	–3.292***	–0.000695
	(18.00)	(9.131)		(–7.548)	(–0.461)
Grade 6	3.459**	0.0119***	Wednesday	–4.565***	–0.00189
	(2.086)	(2.582)		(–9.920)	(–1.107)
Grades 7, 8, 9	2.044**	0.00827***	Thursday	–3.374***	–0.00289*
	(2.180)	(3.005)		(–7.596)	(–1.853)
High school, no diploma	3.450***	0.0100***	Friday	–0.781*	0.00240**
	(3.910)	(3.903)		(–1.758)	(1.975)
High school grad.	1.777**	0.00345	Saturday	0.217	0.00127
	(2.154)	(1.429)		(0.498)	(1.030)
Some college	0.0904	–0.00229	Constant	1.988	0.00500
	(0.144)	(–1.281)		(1.067)	(1.289)
Associate/vocational degree	–0.0462	–0.00250	Observations	110,819	106,869
	(–0.0563)	(–1.067)	R-squared	0.176	0.238
Bachelor's	–4.004***	–0.00969***			
Master's	–5.909***	–0.0163***			
	(–5.276)	(–5.321)			
Professional	–2.928**	–0.0116***			
	(–2.374)	(–3.292)			
Doctoral	–5.557***	–0.0116***			
	(–3.809)	(–2.820)			

Notes: Other variables included but not shown: year fixed effects; number of household children; urban, rural, suburban status; labor force status. (Abridged results of second stage only; full results, including first stage, in appendix at http://www.nber.org/data-appendix/c13001/appendix-tables.pdf.)
***Significant at the 1 percent level.
**Significant at the 5 percent level.
*Significant at the 10 percent level.

other types of leisure, I change the dependent variable to computer leisure as a share of total leisure (column [2]). These results are similar in that conditional on home Internet access, computer time as a share of total leisure time decreases with income, although the effect is fairly small in magnitude above $50,000 in annual family income.

I also find that computer use for leisure decreases with education, conditional on access, although the effect on computer use as a share of leisure is less straightforward. For example, online leisure as a share of total leisure is less for people with master's degrees than for people with doctorate degrees. By race, people who identify as "White-Asian-Hawaiian" spend the most time engaged in online leisure, followed by "White-Asian," "Black," and finally "White." Not surprisingly, the largest amount of online leisure takes place on Saturday and Sunday, followed closely by Friday. Wednesday appears to have the least online leisure.

As Goldfarb and Prince note, these results shed some light on the nature of the digital divide. In particular, while we know from census and other data that a significant gap remains on Internet access conditional on access, poorer people and minorities are more likely to engage in computer leisure than are rich people and white people. Goldfarb and Prince note that these results are consistent with poorer people having a lower opportunity cost of time. These results, using ATUS data, are also consistent with that hypothesis. However, because, as shown above, poorer people engage in more leisure time overall, the results also suggest that online leisure may not be so different from offline leisure, at least in terms of how people value it.

2.3.4 What Times Do People Engage in Online Leisure?

As discussed, to better understand the true costs (and benefits) of time spent online, it is important to figure out the source of the marginal minute online—What activities does it crowd out? It is reasonable to assume that much of it comes from other leisure activities, since leisure time has remained unchanged for so many years, but it need not necessarily come only from other leisure time. To begin to understand where online time comes from, we first look at it in the context of some other (major) activities throughout the day. Figure 2.10 shows how sleep, work, leisure (excluding computer time), and computer time for leisure are distributed throughout the day. Not surprisingly, most people who work begin in the morning and end in the evening, with many stopping mid-day, presumably for lunch. People begin heading to sleep en masse at 9:00 p.m. with nearly half the population over age fifteen asleep by 10:00 p.m. and almost everyone asleep at 3:00 a.m. Leisure time begins to increase as people wake up and increases steadily until around 5:00 p.m. when the slope increases and the share of people engaged in leisure peaks at about 8:45 p.m. before dropping off as people go to sleep.

Time engaged in computer leisure, a subcategory of leisure, tracks overall

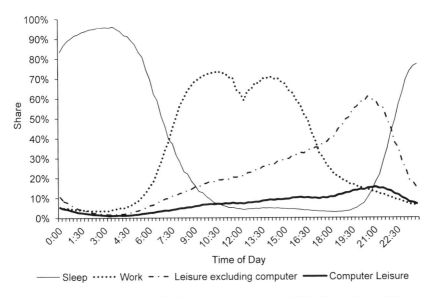

Fig. 2.10 Percentage of people who engage in major activities doing that activity throughout the day

leisure fairly well, but exhibits somewhat less variation. In particular, the peak in the evening is not as pronounced and continues later in the evening. This time distribution suggests that computer leisure may, in principle, crowd out not just other leisure activities, but also work, sleep, and other (smaller) categories. The next section investigates the extent to which online leisure crowds out these other categories.

2.4 What Does Online Leisure Crowd Out?

The ATUS has seventeen major categories of activities (plus one unknown category for activities that the interviewer was unable to code). Each of these major categories includes a large number of subcategories. The first step in exploring where online leisure time comes from is to investigate its effects at the level of these major categories. The second step will be investigating the effects within those categories.

2.4.1 Major Activity Categories

Figure 2.11 shows the average time spent on each of the eighteen major categories. Personal care, which includes sleep, represents the largest block of time, followed by leisure, work, and household activities.

To explore potential crowd-out effects, I begin by estimating eighteen versions of equation (3), once for each major activity category.

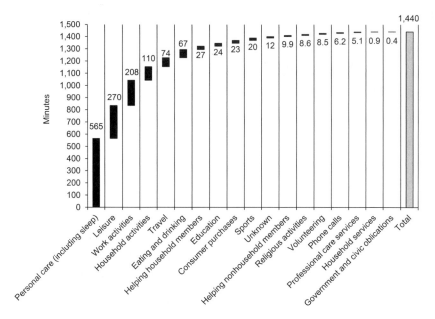

Fig. 2.11   Average time spent on daily activities, 2003–2011

major activity$_i$ =

$$(3) \quad f \begin{pmatrix} \text{computer leisure}_i, \text{income}_i, \text{education}_i, \text{age}_i, \text{sex}_i, \text{race}_i, \text{married}_i, \\ \text{number children in household}_i, \text{occupation}_i \\ \text{Spanish-speaking only}_i, \text{labor force status}_i, (\text{metro, suburban, rural})_i, \\ \text{year}_t, \text{survey day of week}_i \end{pmatrix}.$$

Table 2.3 shows the coefficient (and *t*-statistic) on the computer leisure variable from each of the eighteen regressions.[11] Figure 2.12 shows the results graphically. Perhaps not surprisingly, since computer use for leisure is a component of the major leisure category, computer use for leisure has the largest effect on other leisure. Each minute spent engaged in computer leisure represents almost 0.3 minutes less of doing some other type of leisure. Online leisure appears to have a relatively large effect on time spent at work as well, with each minute of online leisure correlated with about 0.27 minutes less time working. Each minute of online leisure is also correlated with 0.12 minutes of personal care. Most other activities also show a negative, though much smaller, correlation with online leisure.

Travel time, too, is negatively correlated with online leisure time. Avoided

---

11. The full regression results are in an online appendix at http://www.nber.org/data-appendix/c13001/appendix-tables.pdf.

Table 2.3 **Estimated crowd-out effects of computer leisure on major categories**

Leisure (excluding computer)	−0.293***
	(22.34)
Work activities	−0.268***
	(19.38)
Personal care (including sleep)	−0.121***
	(12.36)
Travel	−0.0969***
	(17.36)
Household activities	−0.0667***
	(7.149)
Education	−0.0574***
	(8.560)
Sports	−0.0397***
	(9.17)
Helping household members	−0.0368***
	(7.589)
Eating and drinking	−0.0254***
	(6.991)
Helping nonhousehold members	−0.0232***
	(6.763)
Religion	−0.0146***
	(5.758)
Unknown	−0.0141***
	(4.080)
Volunteer	−0.0120***
	(3.503)
Professional care and services	−0.00360*
	(1.896)
Household services	−0.00129
	(1.583)
Government and civic obligations	−0.000177
	(0.303)
Consumer purchases	0.00368
	(1.025)
Phone calls	0.0134***
	(7.433)

Note: Equation (3) shows the variables included in each regression. Full regression results in appendix at http://www.nber.org/data-appendix/c13001/appendix-tables.pdf.
***Significant at the 1 percent level.
**Significant at the 5 percent level.
* Significant at the 10 percent level.

travel time is generally considered a benefit, suggesting at least one area where the trade-off yields clear net benefits.

Phone calls are positively correlated with online leisure time, although the magnitude is small. It is conceivable that this result reflects identifying the type of person who tends to Skype. Calls made using Skype or similar VoIP services would likely be recorded as online leisure rather than phone calls

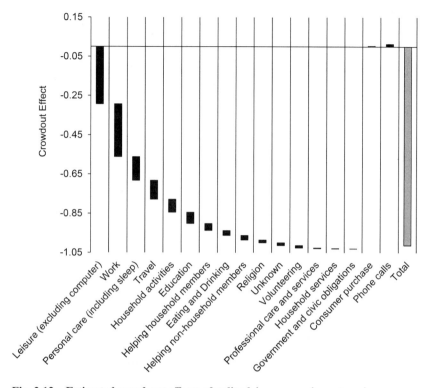

Fig. 2.12 Estimated crowd-out effects of online leisure on major categories

since phone calls are specifically time spent "talking on the telephone."[12] If people who are inclined to talk on the phone are also inclined to Skype, then perhaps the correlation is picking up like-minded people.

The analysis above controls for demographics, but any crowd-out (or crowd-in) effects may differ by those demographics, as well. Table 2.4 shows the abridged regression results by demographic group.

Men and women show few differences in terms of crowd-out effects, except for time spent helping household members. While online leisure time is not statistically significantly correlated with helping household members for men, each minute of online leisure is associated with 0.08 fewer minutes helping household members for women. This result, however, is at least partly because women spend more than 50 percent more time helping household members than men do.

Among race, black people show the biggest crowd-out correlation between online and other leisure, while Hispanic people show the smallest crowding out. Black, white, and Hispanic people show similar levels of crowding out

---

12. See http://www.bls.gov/tus/tu2011coderules.pdf, p.47.

Table 2.4 Crowd-out effect on selected major categories by demographics

Demographic	Leisure (other than online)	Work	Travel	Household activities	Education	Helping household members
Men	−0.307***	−0.258***	−0.0638***	−0.0668***	−0.0620***	−0.00833
Women	−0.283***	−0.264***	−0.0554***	−0.0642***	−0.0555***	−0.0724***
White	−0.274***	−0.273***	−0.0680***	−0.0732***	−0.0546***	−0.0418***
Black	−0.394***	−0.308***	−0.00453	−0.0348	−0.0450**	0.00511
Asian	−0.305***	−0.151**	−0.0589***	0.00178	−0.227***	−0.0195
Hispanic	−0.230***	−0.275***	−0.0590***	−0.174***	0.0177	−0.0709***
<$10k	−0.399***	−0.125***	−0.0180	−0.0686**	−0.0817***	−0.0175
$10k–$19k	−0.410***	−0.124***	−0.0255*	−0.151***	−0.0335	−0.0398***
$20k–$29k	−0.395***	−0.254***	−0.0287**	−0.0345	−0.0307*	−0.0581***
$30k–$49k	−0.218***	−0.297***	−0.0658***	−0.0997***	−0.0425***	−0.0282**
$50k–$74k	−0.267***	−0.262***	−0.0746***	−0.0725***	−0.0733***	−0.0482***
$75k–$99k	−0.209***	−0.383***	−0.0934***	−0.0134	−0.0892***	−0.0220*
$100k–$149k	−0.291***	−0.254***	−0.0600***	−0.0781***	−0.129***	−0.0186
$150k +	−0.220***	−0.297***	−0.0713***	−0.0229	−0.0774***	−0.00642
Age 15–19	−0.390***	−0.0871***	−0.0526***	−0.0377**	−0.295***	−0.00295
Age 20–24	−0.178***	−0.231***	−0.0651***	−0.0304	−0.118***	−0.0363*
Age 25–29	−0.223***	−0.326***	−0.0332*	−0.100***	−0.107***	−0.0268
Age 30–34	−0.209***	−0.375***	−0.0754***	−0.0906***	−0.0776***	−0.0887***
Age 35–39	−0.151***	−0.375***	−0.0722***	−0.0605**	−0.0255**	−0.0488**
Age 40–44	−0.221***	−0.331***	−0.0485***	−0.0531	−0.0314***	0.00239
Age 45–49	−0.233***	−0.315***	−0.0604***	−0.0934***	−0.0206*	−0.0156
Age 50–54	−0.268***	−0.326***	−0.0721***	−0.0436	−0.0155	−0.00327
Age 55–59	−0.282***	−0.294***	−0.0803***	−0.0837**	−0.00132	−0.00695
Age 60–64	−0.308***	−0.296***	−0.0793***	−0.0834**	0.000424	0.00246
Age 65–69	−0.412***	−0.146***	−0.0640***	−0.0877*	−0.00597	−0.00429
Age 70+	−0.471***	−0.0347*	−0.0464***	−0.134***	0.000160	−0.00708

Note: Each cell shows the coefficient on the "computer use for leisure" variable and its statistical significance in a regression in which the column heading is the dependent variable and regression includes only the observations in the group represented by the row heading. Thus, the table shows a single coefficient from each of 156 separate regressions. Each regression includes variables shown in equation (3). Full results available upon request.

***Significant at the 1 percent level.
**Significant at the 5 percent level.
*Significant at the 10 percent level.

on work, with Asians showing the smallest crowding out of work. Asians, however, show the most crowding out of online time on education, with each minute of online leisure correlated with 0.23 fewer minutes engaged in educational activities.

Perhaps the most striking result is how the correlation between online time and education differs by age. Figure 2.13 shows this information graphically. Among people age fifteen to nineteen, each minute of online leisure is correlated with 0.3 fewer minutes engaged in educational activities. The magni-

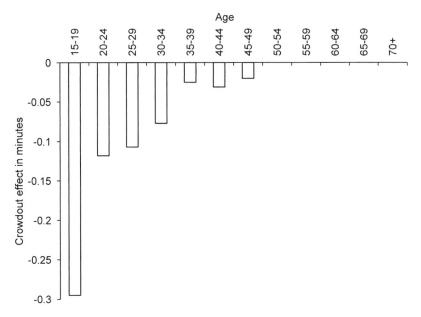

Fig. 2.13   Crowd-out effect on education by age

tude of the crowd-out correlation decreases quickly with age: 0.12 minutes for ages twenty to twenty-four, 0.03 minutes for ages forty-five to fifty-nine, and no statistically significant correlation beyond age fifty.

To some extent, the decreasing magnitude of the correlation with age has to do with the simple fact that the amount of time spent engaged in educational activities decreases sharply with age—much more sharply than the time spent in online leisure activities. This relationship, however, does not change markedly when estimating elasticities rather than levels: among the youngest group, each percent increase in time spent online is correlated with 0.06 percent less time spent in educational activities. The correlation becomes generally smaller in magnitude with age and statistically insignificant by age forty-five.

2.4.2   Activity Subcategories

As discussed above, each major category includes multiple subcategories (and even more sub-subcategories). To get a better idea of which specific activities online leisure might crowd out, I now estimate a set of similar regressions with the largest subcomponents of leisure as the dependent variable. Table 2.5 shows the coefficient its statistical significance for the online leisure variable for each regression.[13]

Online leisure has the strongest (in magnitude) negative correlation with

---

13. The full regression results are in the online appendix at http://www.nber.org/data-appendix/c13001/appendix-tables.pdf.

Table 2.5 Abridged regression results of online leisure on other types of leisure

Activities	Crowd out
TV and movies (nonreligious)	−0.12***
	(−10.39)
Socializing and communicating	−0.054***
	(−9.121)
Relaxing and thinking	−0.037***
	(−8.286)
Parties	−0.016***
	(−5.923)
Attending cultural events/institutions	−0.010***
	(−4.069)
Listening to the radio	−0.0044***
	(−3.637)
TV and movies (religious)	−0.0004
	(−0.628)
Other leisure	−0.0003
	(−0.591)
Waiting associated with leisure	−0.0002
	(−0.855)
Smoking/drugs	0.0002
	(0.357)
Writing	0.0005
	(0.918)
Listening to music (not radio)	0.0021
	(1.538)
Hobbies	0.0036**
	(1.994)

Note: Each entry shows the coefficient (and t-statistic) on the variable representing time engaged in online leisure in a regression in which the dependent variable is the row heading. Each regression includes the variables shown in equation (3). The t-statistics are in parentheses.
***Significant at the 1 percent level.
**Significant at the 5 percent level.
*Significant at the 10 percent level.

watching TV and movies. Each minute of online leisure is associated with 0.12 minutes less of watching video. Note that this result does not speak to the question of whether over-the-top (OTT) video like Netflix complements or substitutes for traditional TV.[14] Watching video online in any form—

---

14. How OTT affects traditional TV is, of course, an important question that will affect the video delivery industry. Israel and Katz (2010) argue that Nielsen surveys and other data suggest online video complements traditional video because people watch online video to "catch up with programming or if the TV itself is unavailable." Other data suggest the two are not complements. Subscription TV services lost a record number of subscribers in the second quarter of 2011 with estimates of the loss ranging from 380,000 to 450,000 (http://www.usatoday.com/money/media/2011-08-10-cable-satellite_n.htm). Liebowitz and Zentner (2012) examine econometrically the relationship between Internet penetration and TV watching, using data from 1997 to 2003. They find a small negative correlation between the two, suggesting that online video was substituting for TV watching, at least among younger people.

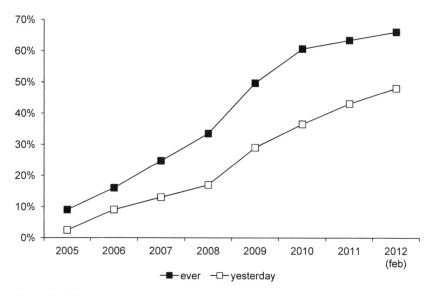

Fig. 2.14 Share of Internet users who use social networking sites
Source: Pew Internet and American Life Project. http://www.pewinternet.org/Static-Pages/Trend-Data-(Adults)/Usage-Over-Time.aspx.

including YouTube and Netflix—is coded as watching video, not computer leisure time. Thus, these results suggest that online activities not captured by the 2003-era list of leisure activities have a crowding-out effect on TV viewing. Given that Americans spend 2.75 hours per day watching TV (according to ATUS; more according to Nielsen), the crowd-out effect is small.

Nevertheless, the crowd-out effect on video suggests that the net effect of the Internet is less time watching all forms of video. If this result holds true, it means not only that OTT video competes with traditional video but that they are competing over a shrinking share of Americans' time.

The next-largest effect is on socializing and communicating. Each minute of online leisure time is correlated with 0.05 minutes less socializing in more traditional ways. Social media has become among the most popular online activities. Survey data from the Pew Internet and American Life Project show that by 2012 nearly 70 percent of all Internet users had engaged in social media online and almost half had done so the day prior to being surveyed. (figure 2.14). Given the ubiquity of social media, it is not surprising that scholars in various fields have investigated whether social networking strengthened or weakened other social ties, though there does not appear to be consensus on the answer.[15]

Previous studies have asked whether online social networking might crowd out other activities. Early studies, primarily during dial-up days, were incon-

---

15. See, for example, Wellman et al. (2001) and Valenzuela, Park, and Kee (2009).

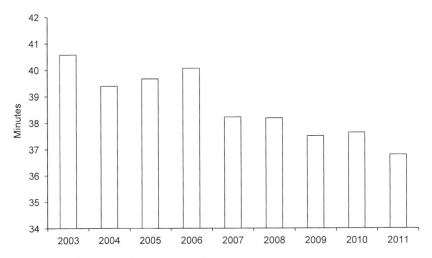

Fig. 2.15 Minutes per day spent socializing offline
Source: Derived from ATUS.

clusive (Wellman et al. 2001, 439), though the relevance of that research to today's activities is questionable, given the changes in the Internet, its ubiquity, and the growing variety of social networking applications. My results suggest a small crowding-out effect of online leisure on offline socializing. Data from the ATUS show generally declining levels of offline socializing since 2003 (figure 2.15).

My results also suggest that other offline leisure activities that involve interacting with other people are crowded out by online leisure: attending parties and cultural events and going to museums are all negatively correlated with online leisure. In short, these results based on ATUS data suggest that a cost of online activity is less time spent with other people.

Listening to the radio is also negatively and statistically significantly correlated, but the magnitude of the effect is quite small. Given the way the ATUS is coded, one might expect that if time spent listening to the radio is negatively correlated with online leisure that time spent listening to music but not on the radio would be positively correlated, not because listening to online streaming music would show up in the online leisure variable, but because people likely to engage in online leisure may also be likely to listen to streaming media. The coefficient is positive, but is not statistically significant.

Online leisure is statistically and positively correlated with one category of leisure, hobbies, although the magnitude is small. Each minute of online leisure is correlated with 0.004 minutes of doing hobbies. However, considering Americans spend, on average, only about two minutes a day on hobbies, the effect is not as small as it might seem based on the coefficient alone. A possible explanation for this effect is that the Internet has given people a way to find and interact with others who share their particular hobby interests. Similarly, the Internet is awash with instructional videos, product manuals, and other ways to get information about hobbies, and it is therefore not surprising to find a correlation between time spent doing hobbies and time online.

2.5 Conclusions

The amount of leisure time we spend online is increasing steadily as is the variety of activities available to do online. Translating this time into increased economic surplus is difficult, not just because many of these activities require no monetary payments, but because many online activities represent activities we already did but in a different form, and even brand new activities like social media come at the expense of activities we no longer do. Estimates of the value of online time that do not take these factors into account will overestimate the incremental economic surplus created by the Internet.

This chapter does not estimate the net change in surplus, but uses data from the American Time Use Survey to estimate the extent to which new online activities crowd out other, offline, activities. I find that online leisure does crowd out other activities. In particular, some incremental online leisure comes primarily from offline leisure, work time, and sleep. Online time is also correlated with less time traveling, which should count as a benefit. Online leisure is also associated with less time engaged in educational activities, especially among younger people. The crowd-out effect is sufficiently large that understanding the true economic effects of the Internet must take them into account.

This research is a small step forward in understanding the economic effects of the Internet. The data clearly show that time spent and the share of the population engaged in online leisure is increasing. The analyses suggest that new online activities come at least partly at the expense of less time doing other activities. Much, however, remains yet to be understood. While I control for a large number of relevant factors in the analyses, the relationships between online and offline time are correlations, meaning we cannot say definitively that an incremental minute translates into a tenth-of-a-minute less sleep. Perhaps, instead, when people suffer from bouts of insomnia they take to the Internet, either to look for insomnia cures or other ways of passing a sleepless night. Nevertheless, the analysis shows that online activities, even when free from monetary transactions, are not free from opportunity cost.

A next research step may be estimating the increase in economic surplus from new online activities net of the activities they replace, à la Robert Fogel's analyses of the true net economic effects of railroads. While such work is challenging, such an effort may be a worthwhile endeavor to counter much of the poorly informed hyperbole that routinely emanates from policymakers.

Appendix
Full Regression Results

See appendix tables 1 and 2 at http://www.nber.org/data-appendix/c13001/appendix-tables.pdf.

References

Boardman, Anthony, David Greenberg, Aidan Vining, and David Weimer. 1996. *Cost-Benefit Analysis: Concepts and Practice*. Upper Saddle River, NJ: Prentice Hall.

Brynjolfsson, Erik, and JooHee Oh. 2012. "The Attention Economy: Measuring the Value of Free Goods on the Internet." January. http://conference.nber.org/confer/2012/EoDs12/Brynjolfsson_Oh.pdf.

Fogel, Robert William. 1962. "A Quantitative Approach to the Study of Railroads in American Economic Growth: A Report of Some Preliminary Findings." *Journal of Economic History* 22 (2): 163–97.

———. 1964. *Railroads and Economic Growth: Essays in Econometric History*. Baltimore: Johns Hopkins Press.

Goldfarb, Avi, and Jeff Prince. 2008. "Internet Adoption and Usage Patterns Are Different: Implications for the Digital Divide." *Information Economics and Policy* 20 (1): 2–15.

Goolsbee, Austan, and Peter J. Klenow. 2006. "Valuing Consumer Products by the Time Spent Using Them: An Application to the Internet." *American Economic Review* 96 (2): 108–13.

Greenstein, Shane M., and Ryan McDevitt. 2009. "The Broadband Bonus: Accounting for Broadband Internet's Impact on US GDP." NBER Working Paper no. 14758, Cambridge, MA.

Israel, Mark, and Michael Katz. 2010. *The Comcast/NBCU Transaction and Online Video Distribution*. May 4, para. 30. http://ly.comcast.com/nbcutransaction/regulatoryinfo.html.

Liebowitz, Stan J., and Alejandro Zentner. 2012. "Clash of the Titans: Does Internet Use Reduce Television Viewing?" *Review of Economics and Statistics* 94 (1): 234–45.

Robinson, John. 2011. "IT, TV and Time Displacement: What Alexander Szalai Anticipated but Couldn't Know." *Social Indicators Research* 101 (2): 193–206. doi:10.1007/s11205-010-9653-0.

Rosston, Gregory, Scott Savage, and Donald Waldman. 2010. "Household Demand for Broadband Internet Service." *B.E. Journal of Economic Analysis and Policy* 10 (1): September 9. http://www.degruyter.com/view/j/bejeap.2010.10.1/bejeap.2010.10.1.2541/bejeap.2010.10.1.2541.xml?format=INT.

US Bureau of Labor Statistics. 2010. *American Time Use Survey (ATUS) Coding Rules.* 17, 47. http://www.bls.gov/tus/tu2010coderules.pdf.

Valenzuela, Sebastián, Namsu Park, and Kerk F. Kee. 2009. "Is There Social Capital in a Social Network Site? Facebook Use and College Students' Life Satisfaction, Trust, and Participation." *Journal of Computer-Mediated Communication* 14 (4): 875–901. doi:10.1111/j.1083-6101.2009.01474.x.

Wellman, Barry, Anabel Quan Haase, James Witte, and Keith Hampton. 2001. "Does the Internet Increase, Decrease, or Supplement Social Capital? Social Networks, Participation, and Community Commitment." *American Behavioral Scientist* 45 (3): 436–55.

Comment   Chris Forman

It was a pleasure for me to read and comment on this chapter, which highlights an important set of issues and also presents some interesting statistics using a data set that has not frequently been employed by the digitization community. Increasingly, researchers have access to fine-grained data that allow us to make precise statements about behavior online. This has allowed us to make advances in a great many areas related to economic activity that has been digitized, which are reflected in many of the other chapters in this volume. However, there have generally not been similar advances in data that allow us to measure behavior online and offline simultaneously. As a result, we know comparatively little about how our behavior online influences our behavior offline. This is particularly true for offline behavior that is not monetized and for which we have little means other than surveys to track what people are doing. It is therefore difficult to observe, for example, how use of online social platforms such as Facebook influence offline social interactions.

The chapter uses the American Time Use Survey (ATUS), a data set that was started in 2003 and that provides national estimates of how Americans spend their time. After documenting American time use online and offline, the main analysis of the chapter then examines how time spent on computer leisure—the chapter's primary measure of online activity—"crowds out" time spent offline. The ATUS is a repeated cross section, so the identification approach uses cross-sectional variation with time controls. There are an impressive array of regressions that study the association between computer leisure time and a wide variety of offline activities such as work, personal care, and travel, and leisure categories such as watching TV and movies, socializing and communicating, and relaxing and thinking. A nice feature

---

Chris Forman is the Brady Family Term Professor at the Scheller College of Business at the Georgia Institute of Technology.

For acknowledgments, sources of research support, and disclosure of the author's material financial relationships, if any, please see http://www.nber.org/chapters/c13024.ack.

of the data is that it uses survey panels from the Current Population Survey (CPS), which allow Wallsten to examine how his results vary according to a rich set of demographic factors.

The chapter makes an important point—that as you spend more time online, there are nonzero opportunity costs of foregone activity offline. This point may seem straightforward, but it sometimes receives little attention and its implications have not previously been measured across such a wide range of categories. There are two broad implications for this set of findings. First, as the author notes, welfare calculations that use time spent online and the opportunity cost of lost wages to measure the welfare benefits of online activity will, in general, be overestimates to the extent that they ignore the opportunity costs of foregone offline activity. Unfortunately, the ATUS may not be well suited toward making the appropriate adjustments to these welfare calculations for reasons related to its data collection methodology that I describe below.

Second, from the perspective of setting an agenda for digitization research, the study highlights the implications of online behavior for offline markets and encourages more work in this important area. To be sure, there has been important work in the digitization community and elsewhere that has studied user behavior in specific, relatively narrow contexts such as online and brick-and-mortar retail stores (e.g., Forman, Ghose, and Goldfarb 2009), online and offline newspapers (Gentzkow 2007), and many others. However, the chapter highlights three important gaps in our knowledge. First, online activity will have important implications for offline behavior that is frequently not monetized and so not easily measured, such as offline socializing and other types of leisure activities. Second, time spent online may crowd out a wide range of both related and unrelated offline activity. That is, time spent reading online newspapers may not only crowd out offline newspaper use but also time spent watching traditional TV and movies. Third, the chapter documents that the relationship between online and different offline categories of activity vary significantly with different demographic characteristics like gender, income, and age.

While these gaps in knowledge are significant, they are also difficult to address in large part because of an absence of data. While the ATUS are very helpful in getting first answers to some of these questions, they also have their limitations. The chapter is very clear about these limitations and also about what the analyses are able to tell us. Still, it is useful to document the specific challenges faced in an exercise like this because it may help future efforts in this area.

The primary explanatory variable is "computer use for leisure." This variable includes estimates for a range of online activities. However, many online activities that were popular by 2003 are not included in this variable. As the chapter documents, this is because the ATUS focuses on activities rather than the tools used to conduct those activities, so many traditional online activities are included in broader categories that include both online and offline behavior. For example, the time spent watching online videos is coded within the same category as that for watching traditional TV. As a result, one can think of the core explanatory variable as measuring the time spent on new online activities since 2003.

Since the variable represents only a subset of online activity, this limits our ability to use it for adjusting current estimates of the welfare gains from online activity for the opportunity costs of foregone offline economic activity. It also has important implications for how we view the regression results. A recent paper by Brynjolfsson and Oh (2012), using data from the Nielsen Three Screen Report, estimates that individuals spent about 13.8 hours per week on the Internet at home each week, or about 8.2 percent of total hours. In contrast, this chapter estimates that individuals spend thirteen minutes per day on computer leisure, or less than 1 percent of total time available during the day. The estimates of time spent online are similarly low compared to work on Internet use using data from Forrester Research over a much earlier period (2001) by Goldfarb and Prince (2008). This shows that the ATUS's measure of computer use for leisure may include only a fraction of total time spent online. To the extent that online activities included in computer leisure (e.g., online social networks) displace different activities than those that are included in other categories (e.g., online TV watching), the ATUS will provide an incomplete picture of how online behavior displaces offline activities.

The chapter candidly states that the results examining the implications of computer use for leisure for other activities cannot be view causally. The major challenge is that identification in the regression models comes from cross-sectional variation across ATUS respondents, so even with the extensive controls the relationships identified could reflect a causal relationship, reverse causality, or some other type of omitted variable bias. In future work, it might be useful to pursue other identification approaches. Prior work that has examined substitution between online and offline activities might provide some clues on how to do this. For example, one approach has been to use CPS data on computer use at work as an instrument for behavior online (Gentkow 2007). Another approach could be to combine individuals into cohorts and estimate pseudopanel models of how changes in time spent online influence offline behavior. This would, at a minimum, allow one to see whether the results continue to hold using a different source of variation in the data.

There are opportunities for future research using these data. The chapter shows there are considerable differences in the relationship between computer leisure time and offline activities based on demographic characteristics like age and income. These results are very interesting. However, more research could be done by exploiting geographic variation in the data. Offline leisure options differ widely by location; for example, the opportunities for sports or eating and drinking differ significantly for urban and rural areas. These differences in offline opportunities may affect value of an online connection (e.g., Sinai and Waldfogel 2004). One might similarly expect that the relationship between computer leisure use and offline activities would vary significantly based upon the offline options available. This would be an exciting area for future research.

References

Brynjolfsson, Erik, and JooHee Oh. 2012. "The Attention Economy: Measuring the Value of Free Goods on the Internet." Working Paper, Massachusetts Institute of Technology.

Forman, Chris, Anindya Ghose, and Avi Goldfarb. 2009. "Competition between Local and Electronic Markets: How the Benefit of Buying Online Depends on Where You Live." *Management Science* 55 (1): 47–57.

Gentzkow, Matthew. 2007. "Valuing New Goods in a Model with Complementarity: Online Newspapers." *American Economic Review* 97 (3): 713–44.

Goldfarb, Avi, and Jeff Prince. 2008. "Internet Adoption and Usage Patterns are Different: Implications for the Digital Divide." *Information Economics and Policy* 20 (1): 2–15.

Sinai, Todd, and Joel Waldfogel. 2004. "Geography and the Internet: Is the Internet a Substitute or Complement for Cities?" *Journal of Urban Economics* 56:1–24.

II

Digitization, Economic Frictions, and New Markets

3
The Future of Prediction
How Google Searches Foreshadow Housing Prices and Sales

Lynn Wu and Erik Brynjolfsson

> It's difficult to make predictions, especially about the future.
> —Attributed to Niels Bohr

3.1 Introduction

Traditional economic and business forecasting has relied on statistics gathered by government agencies, annual reports, and financial statements. Invariably, these are published after significant delay and are aggregated into a relatively small number of prespecified categories. This limits their usefulness for predictions, especially for addressing time-sensitive issues or novel questions. However, the widespread adoption of search engines and related information technologies facilitates the near-real-time collection of highly disaggregated data on literally hundreds of billions[1] of economic decisions. Recently, query technology has made it possible to obtain such information at nearly zero cost, virtually instantaneously and at a fine-grained level of disaggregation. Each time a consumer or business decision maker searches for a product via the Internet, valuable information is revealed about that individual's intentions to make a future economic transaction. In turn, knowledge of these intentions can be used to predict future demand and

---

Lynn Wu is assistant professor of operations and information management at The Wharton School, University of Pennsylvania. Erik Brynjolfsson is the Schussel Family Professor at the MIT Sloan School of Management, director of the MIT Center for Digital Business, and a research associate of the National Bureau of Economic Research.

We thank Karl Case, Avi Goldfarb, Andrea Meyer, Dana Meyer, Shachar Reichman, Lu Han, and Hal Varian as well as seminar participants at the NBER, MIT, the Workshop on Information Systems and Economics, and the International Conference on Information Systems for valuable comments on this research. The MIT Center for Digital Business provided generous funding. For acknowledgments, sources of research support, and disclosure of the authors' material financial relationships, if any, please see http://www.nber.org/chapters/c12994.ack.

1. Americans performed 14.3 billion Internet searches in March 2009, which is an annualized rate of over 170 billion searches per year. Worldwide searches grew by 41 percent between 2008 and 2009.

supply. This revolution in information and information technology is well underway, and it portends a concomitant revolution in our ability to make business predictions and, ultimately, a sea change in business and policy decision making. This new use of technology is not a mere difference in degree, but a fundamental transformation of how much is known about the present and what can be known about the future.

Assisting with predictions has always been a central contribution of social science research. In the past several decades, much of social science research has focused on ever more complex mathematical models for many types of important business and economic predictions. However, the latest recession has shown that none of the models was sophisticated enough to foresee the biggest economic downturn in our recent history (Krugman 2009). Perhaps instead of honing techniques to extract information out of noisy and error-prone data, social science research should focus on inventing tools to observe phenomenon at a higher resolution (Simon 1984). Search engine technology delivers such a tool by effectively aggregating consumers' digital traces and improving data quality by several orders of magnitude. This technology can transform the ways we solve the problem of predicting the future. By observing billions of consumers and business intentions as revealed by online search, researchers can significantly improve the accuracy, granularity, and timeliness of predictions about future economic activities.

In this chapter, we demonstrate how data on Internet queries could be used to make reliable predictions about changes in both market prices and sales volumes literally months before they actually change in the marketplace. We use the housing market as our case example. We started making housing market predictions in January of 2009 and showed they outperformed both the baseline model as well as those of experts like the National Association of Realtors. As of September 2011, almost three years after we released our first set of real estate predictions, search queries continue to provide a significant improvement in forecasting real estate trends and outperform predictions from the National Association of Realtors. This suggests the persistence of the economic value derived from search.

Economic predictions from search data can be applied to almost any market where Internet search often precedes the transaction, which is to say, an increasingly large share of the economy. Our techniques can be focused on particular regions or specific cities or the nation as a whole, and can look at broad or narrow product categories. Search not only precedes purchase decisions, but in many cases is a more "honest signal" (Pentland 2010) of actual interests and preferences because no bargaining, gaming, or strategic signaling is involved, in contrast to many market-based transactions or other types of data gathering such as surveys. As a result, consumers' digital traces can be compiled to reveal their likely underlying economic intentions and activities. Using aggregated query data collected from the Internet has the potential to make accurate predictions about areas as diverse as the eventual winners of standard wars or the potential success of product introductions.

3.2 The Real Estate Market

We use the real estate market to demonstrate how online search can be used to reveal the present economic activities and predict future economic trends. Studying the real estate market is especially important in the wake of the recent bursting of the real estate bubble that triggered an economic downturn in the United States and the rest of the world. In turn, the recovery of the housing market may signal the recovery of the economy as well. Economists, politicians, and investors alike pore over government data released every month to assess the current housing market and predict its recovery and, subsequently, the revival of economic growth. However, as noted above, government data arrives with a lag of months or more, delaying assessment of the current economic conditions. By analyzing consumers' interests, as revealed by their online behaviors, we are able to uncover trends before they appear in published data.

By using the Internet as a research tool, consumers can find critical information to make purchase decisions (Horrigan 2008; Brynjolfsson, Hu, and Rahman 2013). As the Web becomes ubiquitous, more shoppers are using the Internet to gather product information and refine their purchasing choices, especially for products that require a high level of financial commitment, such as buying a home. According to the 2012 Profile of Home Buyers and Sellers by the National Association of Realtors (NAR), 90 percent of home buyers used the Internet to search for a home in 2012 (NAR 2012). Similarly, a report written by the California Association of Realtors in 2008 shows that 63 percent of homebuyers find their real estate agent using a search engine (Appleton-Young 2008). To explore the link between search and actual sales, we analyze individual searches from eight years of data in the Google Web Search portal[2] to predict housing sales and housing prices. Using these fine-grained data on individual consumer behaviors, we built a comprehensive model to predict housing market trends.

We find evidence that queries submitted to Google's search engine are correlated with both the volume of housing sales as well as a house price index—specifically the Case-Shiller index—released by the Federal Housing Finance Agency. The Case-Shiller index is a popular housing index and is widely used in government reports. Search frequencies can reveal the current housing trends, but search is especially well suited for predicting the *future* unit sales of housing. Specifically, we find that a 1-percentage point increase in search frequency about real estate agents is associated with selling an additional 3,520 future quarterly housing sales in the average US state. We

---

2. See http://www.google.com/insights/search/#.

also compared our predictions with the prediction released by the NAR and our simple linear prediction model using search frequencies outperforms NAR's predictions by 23 percent.

Similarly, we also examine the relationship between housing prices and housing-related searches online. Using the house price index (HPI) from the Federal Housing Finance Agency,[3] we find a positive relationship between housing-related online queries and the future house price index, though the predictive power is not as strong as it is for home sales. Perhaps, predicting HPI is intrinsically more difficult than predicting sales volume because the effects of search volume on HPI are theoretically ambiguous. On one hand, if the search volume reflects changes in demand, as when potential buyers look for houses, then HPI will increase with searches. On the other hand, if the search volume reflects the supply side, as when sellers look at comparable homes and assess the market, then HPI might decrease with increased searches. Thus, aggregated search indices on general real estate categories may be well suited to predict sales volume but not as effective for predicting HPI. However, less aggregated and more fine-grained search categories could be created to differentiate the shifts on the demand side from the supply side.

We also find evidence that the total volume of houses sold is correlated with consumers' intention to purchase home appliances. We use the search frequency of home appliances to approximate consumers' interests (Moe and Fader 2004). We find that every thousand houses sold six months earlier are correlated with a 1.14 percentage point increase in the frequency of search terms that are related to home appliances. This highlights the linkages between home sales and other parts of the economy that complement home sales.

3.3 Literature Review

In the past decades, much of the social science research focused on refining increasingly complex mathematical models to predict social and economic trends. However, in recent years, the availability of fine-grained digital data opens up new options. Specifically, advances in information technologies such as the Internet search technologies, mobile phones, e-mail, and social media offer remarkably detailed records of human behaviors. Recently, researchers have started to take advantage of real-time data collected from these new technologies. For example, deploying sociometric badges to measure moment-to-moment interactions among a group of IT workers, Wu et al. (2008) uncovered new social network dynamics that are only possible

---

3. Historical HPI data can be downloaded at http://www.fhfa.gov/Default.aspx?Page=87.

by accessing accurate data at the microlevel. Lazer et al. (2009) provided various examples of how high-quality data produced by novel technologies are transforming the landscape of social network research. Similarly, firms have also used the massive amounts of data collected online to make predictions about consumer preferences, supplies, and demands for various goods, as well as basic operational parameters such as inventory level and turnover rate. The ability to collect and efficiently analyze the enormous amount of data made available by information technology has enabled firms such as Amazon, Caesar's Entertainment, and Capital One to hone their business strategies and to achieve significant gains in profitability and market shares (McAfee and Brynjolfsson 2012; Davenport 2006).

Our work follows a similar stream in demonstrating the power of using fine-grained data to predict underlying social and economic trends. Unlike previous research and businesses that have primarily used proprietary data, we leverage free and publicly available data from Google to accurately forecast economic trends. Research has shown that online behaviors can be used to reveal consumers' intentions and predict purchase outcomes (e.g., Kuruzovich et al. 2008). We believe that we can rely on digital traces left by trillions of online searches to reveal consumers' intentions and examine their power to predict underlying social and economic trends. The study of individual buying or selling decisions or transactions has been called nanoeconomics (Arrow 1987).

We believe that we are only at the beginning of the data revolution. Newer and more fine-grained data are becoming available every day from various search, social media, and microblogging platforms. These data are made available instantaneously, allowing consumers, business managers, researchers, and policymakers to tap into the pulse of economic activities as they are happening. However, predicting medium or longer-term trends, such as movements in the real estate market, could be easier because they are less prone to short-term manipulations, such as fake Twitter feeds that go viral quickly but die down shortly after they are revealed to be false.

Our methodologies are similar to a recent analysis of flu outbreaks using Google Flu Trends (Ginsberg et al. 2009) and also to parallel research by Choi and Varian (2009) where the authors also correlate housing trends in the United States using search frequencies. Similarly, Scott and Varian (chapter 4, this volume) applied Bayesian variable selection techniques to forecast some present economic trends such as the current consumer sentiment and the current gun sales. Whereas Choi and Varian (2009) and Scott and Varian (chapter 4, this volume) mainly focus on using search frequencies to reveal the current economic statistics, our work attempts to predict *future* economic trends, such as forecasting the price and quantity of houses sold in the future. Within the real estate setting, at least, we show that using search is especially beneficial for predicting the future when compared to existing models that do not use search data. Furthermore, our work also uses more fine-grained data at the state level, instead of at the level of the whole nation, to provide a more nuanced prediction of the real estate market, which often varies greatly depending on geographical location. In future work, we intend to expand the analysis to the metropolitan statistical areas and other products and services.

3.3.1 Economics of Real Estate

Our work also contributes to the literature on real estate economics. There are two general methodologies for forecasting real estate market trends. The first is technical analysis, similar to techniques used to predict stock market trends. The main assumption for this type of analysis is that the key statistical regularities of changes in housing market trends do not change. Price-trending behaviors might appear to exhibit short-term momentum, but also long-term reversion to the mean (e.g., Case and Shiller 1987, 1989). Glaeser and Gyourko (2006) found evidence of long-term mean reversion in housing prices. They found that, ceteris paribus, if regional prices go up by an extra dollar over one five-year period, they would also drop by thirty-two cents on average over the next five years. The second methodology for predicting housing market trends is to focus on the underlying economic fundamentals. Housing prices should depend on the cost of construction, interest rates available to finance housing purchases, regional income, and even the January temperature (Glaeser 2008). In principle, this suggests that regions with steady building costs and relatively stable income levels should have steady housing prices. However, these economic variables do not seem to fully capture housing price trends. For instance, Dallas is a region with steady fundamentals, but housing prices have been increasing despite the predictions of fundamental analysis.

Some dynamic housing demand models try to incorporate both approaches to predict housing trends (Glaeser and Gyourko 2006; Han 2010). Using dynamic rational expectations to model housing price, Glaeser and Gyourko (2006) detect a mean-reverting mechanism but they cannot explain serial correlation or price changes in most volatile markets. Glaeser (2008) suggests this may reflect sentiment or even "irrational exuberance" in some housing markets, generating a bigger boom and bust cycle than what is predicted by the model (Glaeser 2008).

With the ability to gather billions of search queries over time, Google Trends is essentially aggregating signals of decision makers' intentions to capture some of this overall level of "sentiment." This provides an opportunity to improve predictions in housing markets. Using very simple regression models, we demonstrate that Google search frequencies can be used as a reliable predictor for the underlying housing market trends both in the present and in the future.

3.4 Data Sources

3.4.1 Google Search Data

We collected the volume of Internet search queries related to real estate from Google Trends, which provides weekly and monthly reports on query statistics for various industries. It allows users to obtain a query index pertaining to a specific phrase, such as "housing price." Google Trends has also systematically captured online queries and categorized them into several predefined categories such as "computer and electronics," "finance and business," and "real estate." As Nielsen NetRatings has consistently placed Google to be the top search engine, which processed more than 66.7 percent of all the online queries in the world in December 2012 (comScore 2012), the volume of queries submitted to Google reflects a large fraction of Americans' interests over time.

Google Trends provides a search index for the volume of queries based on geographic locations and time. The search index is a compilation of all Internet queries submitted to Google's search engine since 2004. The index for each query phrase is not the absolute number of queries submitted. Instead, it reports a query index measured by query share, which is calculated as the search volume for the query in a given geographical location divided by the total number of queries in that region at a given point in time.[4] Thus, the reported index is always a number between 0 and 100. The reports on search indices are also much more finely grained than most government reports. Typically, Google calculates the query index on a weekly or a monthly basis, and the index can be disaggregated down to country, state/province, and city levels around the world. For example, in the United States, a query index can be calculated at the state level. A more detailed query index at the metropolitan statistical area (MSA) level can also be computed by specifying the appropriate subregions within a state. Figure 3.1 shows the overall interest in the search category "real estate" using online searches in the United States, using the quarterly averages of the search index. From the graph, interests in housing peaked in 2005 at the height of the recent real estate bubble and fell through 2009 amid the housing market collapse and the onset of the Great Recession.

Our analysis uses a predefined category in Google Trends, "real estate agencies" and "real estate listings" to approximate the overall interest for housing.[5] We also compiled our own sets of phrases related to vari-

---

4. For details, please refer to http://www.google.com/support/insights//bin/answer.py?answer=87285.
5. We explored various predefined categories on Google Trends: "apartments and residential rentals," "commercial and investment real estate," "property management," "property inspection and appraisals," "property development," "real estate agencies," "real estate listings," and "timeshares and vacation properties."

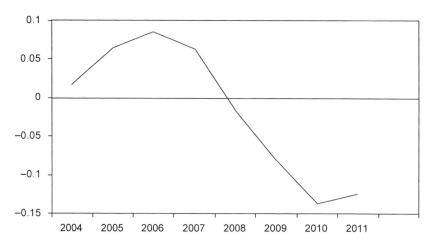

Fig. 3.1 Quarterly search index for "real estate" normalized to total search volume ranging from 0 to 100

ous housing-related transactions such as "housing sales," "home staging," and "home inspection." We hypothesized that these housing-related search indices are correlated with the underlying conditions of the US housing market. To test this hypothesis, we gathered housing market indicators such as the volume of houses sold and the house price index in each US state, all from publicly available sources.

3.4.2 Housing Market Indicators

We collected data on the volume of sales of existing single-family housing units from the National Association of Realtors for all fifty states in the United States and the District of Columbia from the first quarter of 2006 to the third quarter of 2011.[6] This date range coincides with published expert predictions from the National Association of Realtors (NAR). The NAR started publishing their predictions in 2005, but stopped publishing them after the third quarter of 2011. We also obtained the house price index (HPI) for the same period at the Federal Housing Finance Agency, which collects housing prices for nine Census Bureau divisions.[7] The Federal and Finance Agency has calculated the HPI for each state in the United States and the District of Columbia on a quarterly basis since 1975.[8] Because search engine data is only available after 2004 and data on NAR's prediction is only available before the third quarter of 2011, we were able to match the real estate market data with the Google Trend data from the first quarter of 2004 to the third quarter of 2011 for fifty states in the United States and the District of

---

6. See http://www.realtor.org/research.
7. See http://www.fhfa.gov.
8. See http://www.fhfa.gov/Default.aspx?Page=81.

Columbia. We use roughly half of the sample as training data and use the rest to test our prediction models.

As shown in figure 3.2, panel (a), the number of houses sold in the United States peaked at around 2005 and then declined precipitously soon after, reaching a historical low at the beginning of 2009, and has since recuperated slightly after 2011. The HPI also increased gradually and reached a peak in 2007, two years after the housing sales peak (figure 3.2, panel [b]), and began to fall shortly after. Comparing housing market indicators (figure 3.2) to their associated online search indices (figure 3.1) shows that they appear to be correlated. As shown in figure 3.1, housing-related search peaked in 2005 and gradually declined to its lowest point in early 2009, mirroring the volume of houses sold in figure 3.2, panel (a) and the HPI in figure 3.2, panel (b). This provides some evidence that the search indices are related to underlying housing trends and they could be used to predict both the contemporaneous and future housing market trends.

3.5 Empirical Methods

First, we show that search indices are highly correlated with the underlying housing trends. We use a simple seasonal autoregressive (AR) model to estimate the relationship between search indices and housing market indicators—the volume of housing sales and the house price index (HPI). A single class of explanatory variable is studied: search indices for housing-related queries for each state in the United States and the District of Columbia. In this chapter we primarily focus on a simple and consistent set of models to highlight the power of the new data, rather than the sophistication of our modeling techniques, although we found simple linear regression to perform just as well as or even better than more sophisticated nonlinear models. We first estimate the baseline model to predict the current housing sales using only home sales and HPI in the past. Then, we add the search indices to see if they improve predicting the contemporaneous home sales.

(1) $\text{HomeSales}_{it} = \alpha + \beta_1 \text{HomeSales}_{i,t-1} + \beta_2 \text{HPI}_{it,-1} + \beta_3 \text{Population}_{it}$
$+ \Sigma S_i + \Sigma R_j + \Sigma T_t + \varepsilon_{it}.$

(2) $\text{HomeSales}_{it} = \alpha + \beta_1 \text{HomeSales}_{i,t-1} + \beta_2 \text{HPI}_{i,t-1} + \beta_3 \text{SearchFreq}_{it}$
$+ \beta_4 \text{SearchFreq}_{i,t-1} + \beta_5 \text{Population}_{it} + \Sigma S_i + \Sigma R_j$
$+ \Sigma T_t + \varepsilon_{it}.$

We then examine whether housing-related search indices could forecast future home sales. We only use the past housing statistics to predict the future housing trends because the present housing sales and HPI are not available. Essentially, we are using a two-period lag to predict the future as opposed to a one-period lag to predict the present. Although the govern-

(a) Number of Existing Houses Sold Quarterly.

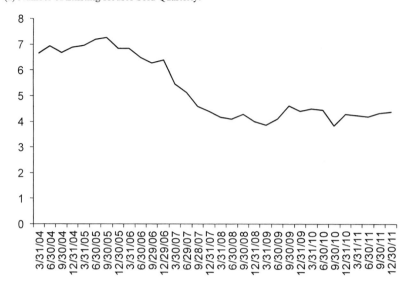

(b) Quarterly House Price Index

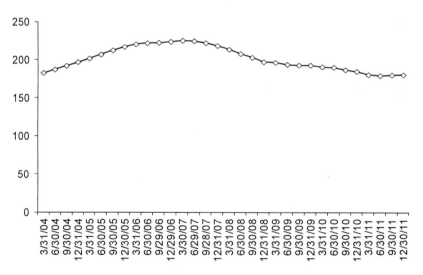

Fig. 3.2 Prices and volumes of existing houses sold in the United States
Note: Panel (a), number of existing houses sold quarterly; panel (b), quarterly house price index.

ment statistics are released with a lag, search frequencies on housing-related inquiries are available in real time and instantaneously down to the daily level. We can thus use both the present and the past search indices to predict future housing sales. Specifically, we use both one-period and two-period lags in the model because they are the most relevant for predictions. Third-order lags can sometimes improve predictions, but in general, higher-order lags fail to have much predictive power. Presumably, housing searches nine months or one year earlier are too early to predict the present and future housing trends because most of these searches likely have already resulted in purchase decisions.

(3) $\text{HomeSales}_{it+1} = \alpha + \beta_1 \text{HomeSales}_{i,t-1} + \beta_2 \text{HPI}_{i,t-1} + \beta_3 \text{SearchFreq}_{it}$
$+ \beta_4 \text{SearchFreq}_{i,t-1} + \beta_5 \text{SearchFreq}_{i,t-2}$
$+ \beta_6 \text{Population}_{it} + \Sigma S_i + \Sigma R_j + \Sigma T_t + \varepsilon_{it}.$

Similarly, we use the same approach to predict the current and future HPI. In the baseline model, we only use the past HPI and the past housing sales to predict the current HPI. We then incorporate the current and past search indices into the baseline model.

(4) $\text{HPI}_{it} = \alpha + \beta_1 \text{HPI}_{i,t-1} + \beta_2 \text{HomeSales}_{i,t-1} + \beta_3 \text{Population}_{it} + \Sigma S_i$
$+ \Sigma R_j + \Sigma T_t + \varepsilon_{it}$

(5) $\text{HPI}_{it} = \alpha + \beta_1 \text{HPI}_{i,t-1} + \beta_2 \text{HomeSales}_{i,t-1} + \beta_3 \text{SearchFreq}_{it}$
$+ \beta_4 \text{SearchFreq}_{i,t-1} + \beta_5 \text{Population}_{it} + \Sigma S_i + \Sigma R_j + \Sigma T_t + \varepsilon_{it}.$

Lastly, we predict the future HPI by adding the present and past search indices into the model. In addition to exploring various lags, we also explored nonlinear functions of the search indices to see if they improve model fit and predictions.

(6) $\text{HPI}_{it+1} = \alpha + \beta_1 \text{HomeSales}_{i,t-1} + \text{HPI}_{i,t-1} + \beta_2 \text{SearchFreq}_{it}$
$+ \beta_3 \text{SearchFreq}_{i,t-1} + \beta_5 \text{Population}_{it} + \Sigma S_i + \Sigma R_j + \Sigma T_t + \varepsilon_{it}.$

For all the models above, we apply state- and region-level dummies in order to control for any time-invariant influences, such as the demographics of a state/region, and any statewide/region-wide policies that may affect real estate purchase decisions. We then train these models using data between the first quarter of 2006 and the fourth quarter of 2008[9] to find a set of

---

9. We chose this period for training because it roughly divides the data in half. We also tested a tenfold cross-validation approach that randomly partitions the sample into ten equal sizes regardless of the timing of the data. Nine sets are then used to train the model and the tenth set is used to test the model. While we were able to improve the predictive accuracy using cross validation, we chose to train the model only using the past data because it is a more conservative estimate. It also reflects the reality that we should not know anything about the future in the training data to make predictions about the future.

search indices that best predict the present and future housing indicators. We then use these indices and their associated estimates to predict housing trends from the first quarter of 2009 to the third quarter of 2011. For each prediction, we calculate the mean absolute error (MAE)[10] to examine the accuracy of our predictions that use search indices when compared to the predictions from the baseline model, as well as from the National Association of Realtors. The mean absolute error is simply the deviation away from the actual value.

$$(7) \quad MAE = \frac{1}{N}\sum_{t=1}^{N}\left|\frac{y_t - \hat{y}_t}{y_t}\right|.$$

In addition to housing predictions, we also examine whether housing-related search queries can also spur future economic activities in complementary industries. For example, if consumers' intentions can be revealed through online search, we may also expect a surge in Internet queries about home appliances after observing a rise in home sales. Because new homeowners may plan to purchase appliances to furnish their property, tracking their online search behavior allows us to detect their intention to purchase home appliances. Accordingly, we correlate housing sales with the search index for home appliances. If search index for home appliance can translate into actual purchases, we would expect a rise in search frequencies for home appliances, spurred from home sales, to indicate a rise in their future demands as well.

$$(8) \quad \text{HomeApplianceSearch}_{it} = \alpha + \beta_1 \text{HomeSales}_{it} + \beta_2 \text{HomeSales}_{i,t-1} + \varepsilon_{it}.$$

3.6 Empirical Results

First, we compare predictions between the baseline model and the model that uses search indices. We used the model to predict the present home sales and HPI as well as the future home sales and HPI in the next quarter. Although our model can be used to predict even more fine-grained forecasts, such as monthly or even weekly housing trends, we chose to forecast at the quarterly level because the government only releases state-level housing sales and HPI every quarter. To calculate our predictions' accuracy, we aggregated the weekly search data into quarterly data. Furthermore, we also compare our predictions with the forecasts of quarterly housing sales released by the National Association of Realtors (NAR). The NAR does not predict

---

10. We also use other metrics such as the mean squared errors (MSE) to evaluate the accuracy of our predictions. The results do not qualitatively change when we use MSE. In fact, we find our improvements using MSE are even better than using MAE. Thus, we conservatively reported the MAE values.

Table 3.1 Linear regression to predict the present home sales using search frequency

Dependent var.	Quarterly sales					
	(0)	(1)	(2)	(3)	(4)	(5)
$Sales_{t-1}$	0.864***	0.864***	0.819***	0.842***	0.806***	
	(0.0125)	(0.0125)	(0.0142)	(0.0130)	(0.0144)	
HPI_{t-1}	−0.140***	−0.140***	−0.158***	−0.177***	−0.188***	
	(0.0175)	(0.0175)	(0.0175)	(0.0196)	(0.0195)	
Real estate agencies$_t$		16.55***	17.09***		13.41***	48.47***
		(2.450)	(3.424)		(3.523)	(6.415)
Real estate agencies$_{t-1}$			−0.780		1.170	33.04***
			(3.414)		(3.451)	(6.297)
Real estate listing$_t$				23.36***	18.41***	37.37***
				(4.797)	(4.917)	(9.007)
Real estate listing$_{t-1}$				−8.062	5.503	−13.16
				(4.831)	(4.876)	(8.728)
Obs.	1,561	1,561	1,561	1,561	1,561	1,561
Controls	Quarters, states, regions, population	Quarters, states, regions, population	Quarters, states, regions, population	Quarters, states, regions, population	Quarters, states, regions, population	Quarters, states, regions, population
States	51	51	51	51	51	51
Adjusted R^2	.973	.980	.981	.982	.983	.970

Note: Huber-White robust standard errors are shown in parentheses. Quarterly sales are in 1000s.
***Significant at the 1 percent level.
**Significant at the 5 percent level.
*Significant at the 10 percent level.

future HPI, and thus we cannot compare our model with the NAR's when predicting the future HPI.

3.6.1 Predicting Home Sales Using Online Search

Table 3.1 explores the relationship between housing sales and housing-related search indices that could support the use of search indices in predictions. All models in table 3.1 are based on a seasonal autoregressive (AR) model, which assumes that the sales in the future are related to sales in the past. We see a broad support for the AR model because the lagged sales are strongly correlated with the contemporary sales. We also applied a state-level, fixed-effect specification to eliminate influence from any time-invariant factors, and we use seasonality dummies to control for time-specific changes. In addition, we also included the state population and region dummies to improve the fit of the model. To capture online interests for purchasing real estate properties, we use a search index of a predefined category in Google Trends—"real estate listing"—that contains all queries pertaining to real estate listings and advertisements. We also use the "real estate agencies" category to approximate home buying activities. We assume people who are looking for real estate agents and real estate listings online are more likely to participate in a real estate transaction than those who search for other related queries such as property management.

First, we estimate the baseline model to predict the present home sales using only the past home sales and the past HPI. As shown in the baseline AR(1) model (model 0), the past home price and sales are highly correlated with the current home sales. We then examine various search indices related to the real estate market[11] and find two categories—"real estate agencies" and "real estate listings"—to best predict the contemporaneous sales. Overall, we find that the contemporaneous search indices for "real estate agencies" and "real estate listings" are statistically significantly correlated with the present home sales. As shown in Model 1, a 1-percentage point increase in the current search index for the category "real estate agencies" is associated with 16,550 additional sales for existing homes in the contemporaneous quarter. The average state-level home sales are 112,037 units per quarter, so 16,550 units of additional sales represent a 14.8 percent increase from the state average. Similarly, a 1-percentage point increase in the search index for the category "real estate listing" is correlated with 23,360 houses sold in the present quarter (Model 3). We explore the effect of using both the present and past search indices for "real estate listing" and "real estate agencies" in Model 4. The present search indices for both categories are again positively correlated with sales, but the past indices are not. However, the adjusted R^2 improved slightly if both the present and the past search indices are included. In Model 5, we only use the search indices, without lagged home sales and HPI, to predict housing sales, and the results are similar to what is shown in Model 4. This suggests that using online search frequencies alone can predict future sales. The adjusted R^2 was just slightly below the baseline model if the past sales and HPI were included. Overall, results in table 3.1 show that online search behaviors are highly correlated with the contemporaneous home sales.

To examine whether our model can actually predict the contemporaneous home sales, we generate a set of one-quarter-ahead predictions. We first create a training set using data from the first quarter of 2006 to the fourth quarter of 2008. Using these eleven quarters of data for fifty states and the District of Columbia, we select a set of features or variables that best predict the contemporaneous sales. We also experimented with various functional forms and the window of data to use that would give the best predictive results in the training set. We find a simple linear model with search terms to consistently provide superior prediction results. For predicting the present sales, using the previous eight quarters of data gives the best consistent

---

11. We also examined the following predefined categories on Google Trends: "apartments and residential rentals," "commercial and investment real estate," "property development," "property inspection and appraisals and property management," "real estate listings," "real estate agencies," and "timeshares and vacation properties."

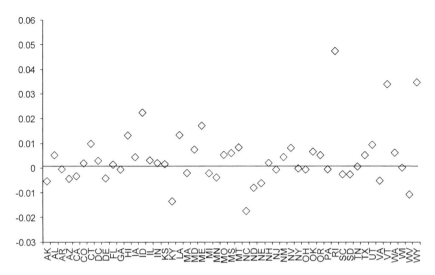

Fig. 3.3 The Y-axis indicates the average difference in MAE between the baseline model (equation [1]) and the model that uses search indices (equation [2])

Note: We use predictions from the first quarter of 2009 to the third quarter of 2011. When the dots are above the zero line, the baseline MAE is worse than the MAE from the model that uses search.

results.[12] In addition to using "real estate agencies" and "real estate listings," we also explored other predefined categories from Google Trends as well as our own set of search phrases. However, we find "real estate agencies" and "real estate listings" are the best features for predicting the present sales in the training set. Next, we use the best-predicted model and estimates to predict sales from the first quarter of 2009 to the third quarter of 2011. To gauge how accurate our predictions are compared to the actual real estate indicators, we use mean absolute error (MAE), as shown in equation (7).

The mean absolute error (MAE) using our model with search indices (equation [2]) is 0.170 (17 percent deviation from the actual value), compared to 0.174, the MAE of the baseline model. Simply adding search terms in the linear model provides a 2.3 percent improvement over the baseline and it is statistically significant at $p < 0.05$ percent (Model 0). We graphed the differences in MAE between the baseline model and the model that uses search indices in figure 3.3, specifically as MAE(baseline)—MAE(search). Dots above the zero line indicate that predictions are better with the added search indices than with the baseline model alone. As shown in figure 3.3, the MAE for the baseline is mostly worse than for our predictions that use

---

12. We also experimented with using the previous four, six, eight, twelve, twenty-four, and thirty-six quarters to predict the contemporaneous sales and, while there was little difference, using the previous eight quarters appears to produce the most accurate predictions.

search. While the improvement is relatively modest on average, the variation for the improvement among different states is large. In general, predictions using search indices are better for states that have a high volume of sales, possibly indicating that a high volume of sales is also indicative of having more real estate-related online searches. However, because search indices do not indicate the absolute number of searchers, it is difficult to ascertain if more online searches lead to better predictions. We find the correlation between sales and the MAE differences to be negative.

Next, we apply our methods to predict the future housing trends using available data today that include the past housing statistics and the present and past search indices. We only use the housing statistics from the previous quarter because when making a given prediction, the present housing statistics would not be available. Unlike housing statistics, which are always released with a lag, search indices are obtainable almost instantaneously, allowing us to incorporate virtually real-time search behaviors to predict future real estate trends.

We first use the training data to find the best statistical model to predict future sales. The best model we found is a linear prediction model using the past eight quarters of data. After experimenting with various housing-related search terms and predefined search categories from Google Trends, we find the best predictors are the current index for "real estate agencies" as well as its one-quarter and two-quarter lags. Interestingly, the "real estate listings" index no longer adds much predictive power if indices on "real estate agencies" are included. Using only the present and the past indices on "real estate agencies" as well as the past statistics on HPI and home sales, we predict the future home sales and plot the difference between the MAE of the baseline model and the MAE of our predictions in figure 3.4: MAE(baseline)—MAE(search). For most of the states, predictions using search indices outperform the baseline predictions, especially for states where the sales volume is high. For states with lower volumes of real estate transactions, adding search indices does not improve the predictions. Overall, the MAE for predictions using search indices is 0.172 (or 17.2 percent deviation from the true value) whereas the baseline MAE is 0.185. This is a 7.1 percent improvement over the baseline model and it is statistically significant at $p < 0.05$.

Interestingly, this result suggests that search indices are actually better at predicting the future home sales than they are at predicting contemporaneous sales (7.1 percent vs. 2.3 percent over the baseline). Perhaps future sales are more correlated with past search indices because buying and selling a house often takes more than a quarter. For example, while there are many factors affecting the duration of a sale, the average time to sell a home in the United States is ten months in 2011.[13] Thus, search activities on the Internet,

---

13. Statistics come from the Accredited Seller Agent Council. See http://www.realty101.com/what-is-the-average-time-to-sell-a-home.

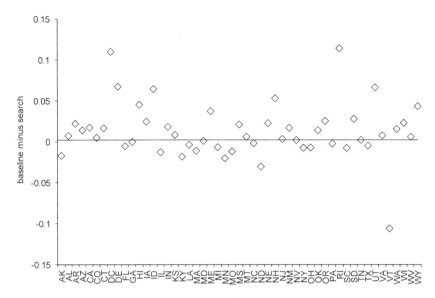

Fig. 3.4 MAE differences between the baseline model and predictions using search indices

at least from the seller side, can potentially forecast home sales ten months in the future. Another reason why using search to predict the future is better could be because the baseline model is not as good at predicting the future as it is with predicting the present. Using housing statistics from the previous quarter can well capture the trends in the contemporaneous quarter better than trends in the future. Thus, behavioral information such as the search indices could be relatively more valuable for these predictions than information provided by the two-period lags of home sales and HPI.

While we find that using search indices can improve prediction outcomes in comparison to the baseline model, it is important to also compare our model with real forecasts from experts in the field. Thus, we collected data from the National Association of Realtors, who release quarterly forecasts for US home sales. To predict home sales for the entire United States, we aggregated the state-level predictions that use search indices in each quarter. We compared NAR's forecasts with our predictions from the second quarter of 2009 to the third quarter of 2011, for a total of ten quarters. For predicting the present home sales, we find that our predictions have been slightly better than NAR's but the difference is not statistically significant. However, our predictions were considerably better than NAR for predicting future home sales. The MAE for the National Association of Realtor's forecast is 0.110 while the MAE for the model that uses search indices is 0.084, a 23.6 percent improvement over the estimates from real estate experts. Results are summarized in the table 3.2. This again shows the power of using search indices for predicting the future. Using a simple linear prediction model

Table 3.2   Comparing with predictions from the National Association of Realtors for home sales in the United States

MAE for sales$_{t+1}$	Obs.	Mean	Std. err.	Min.	Max.
Search	10	0.084	0.031	0.012	0.156
NAR	10	0.110	0.026	0.050	0.169
Diff.		23.6%		$p < 0.01$	

with search indices, we are able to outperform predictions from established experts in the field.

One concern is that NAR tends to overpredict the existing homes sales and that is why our predictions are superior. We tested this hypothesis and found that the NAR is indeed more likely to overpredict than to underpredict sales. On average, NAR overpredicted sales in twenty out of the twenty-two quarters from 2006 to 2011, and the error rate was 7.8 percent more than the actual sales.[14] By contrast, our predictions using search overestimated the US home sales in only six out of ten quarters with an average error of 2.4 percent. A reason for the overprediction in both NAR's model and our model could be attributed to the time period of the prediction. Between 2008 and 2010, the US real estate market experienced one of the biggest busts in recent history. In a more stable period, the overprediction could be less severe.

3.6.2   Predicting the House Price Index Using Online Search Data

In table 3.3, we explore the relationship between the housing-related search indices and HPI, which is calculated based on a modified version of the weighted-repeat sales (WRS) methodology proposed by Case and Shiller (1989). All models in table 3.3 use a fixed-effect specification on an AR model with region, population, and seasonality controls. Similar to table 3.1, the purpose of this table is to illustrate that search indices are correlated with HPI and could be used for predictions. As expected from the baseline AR model (Model 0), the lagged HPI and lagged sales are positively correlated with the present HPI. In Model 1, we estimate the correlation between the current search index for "real estate agencies" and the HPI and find that a 1-percentage point increase in the search index is associated with an increase of 5.986 points in HPI. However, the past search index on "real estate agencies" from the previous quarter does not have a statistically significant correlation to the present HPI (Model 2). Next, we introduce both the current and the past indices for "real estate listings" in Model 3. We find that the current search index for "real estate listings" is positively correlated with

---

14. The error rate is calculated as (actual sales–NAR prediction)/actual sales. This formulation uses the actual error as opposed to MAE that uses the absolute value of the error.

Table 3.3 Linear regression of HPI on the search index related to real estate and real estate agencies

	HPI$_t$					
Dependent var.	(0)	(1)	(2)	(3)	(4)	(5)
Sales$_{t-1}$	0.959***	0.952***	0.951***	0.952***	0.947***	
	(0.006)	(0.006)	(0.006)	(0.006)	(0.006)	
HPI$_{t-1}$	0.086***	0.700***	0.069***	0.081***	0.066***	
	(0.004)	(0.0052)	(0.005)	(0.004)	(0.005)	
Real estate agencies$_t$		5.986***	5.069***		3.520***	6.817
		(0.780)	(1.107)		(1.138)	(4.543)
Real estate agencies$_{t-1}$			1.268		2.361**	9.146**
			(1.088)		(1.104)	(4.414)
Real estate listing$_t$				8.951***	7.919***	16.82***
				(1.528)	(1.560)	(6.246)
Real estate listing$_{t-1}$				−5.116***	−4.989***	51.97***
				(1.514)	(1.523)	(5.945)
Obs.	1,561	1,561	1,561	1,561	1,561	1,561
Controls	Quarters, states, regions, population	Quarters, states, regions, population	Quarters, states, regions, population	Quarters, states, regions, population	Quarters, states, regions, population	Quarters, states, regions, population
States	51	51	51	51	51	51
Adjusted R^2	0.987	0.986	0.987	0.987	0.987	0.987

Note: Huber-White robust standard errors are shown in parentheses. Quarterly sales are in 1000s.
***Significant at the 1 percent level.
**Significant at the 5 percent level.
*Significant at the 10 percent level.

the contemporaneous HPI while its one-period lag is negatively correlated with HPI. Finally, we include the present and the past search indices for both "real estate listings" and "real estate agencies" in Model 4 and find that all search indices are correlated with the present HPI. The fit of the model also improves slightly. These results give us confidence that incorporating the present and past search indices from the two search categories can help predict the contemporaneous HPI.

Next, we predict the contemporaneous HPI from the first quarter of 2009 to the third quarter of 2011 after finding the best-fitted model from the training data set. Among various search terms and real estate-related categories, we continue to find the contemporaneous and the one-period lag of search indices on "real estate agencies" and "real estate listings" to best predict the present HPI. In contrast to using the previous eight quarters of data to predict home sales, we find that using data from the past four quarters can best predict the present HPI. Overall, we find that our predictive accuracy improves on the baseline model by 2.54 percent, which is comparable to the results on predicting the present home sales. We show the state-by-state

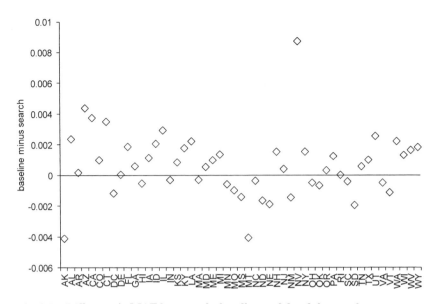

Fig. 3.5 Difference in MAE between the baseline model and the search-based model

scatter plot for the MAE difference between the baseline and the search indices model (figure 3.5). Again, dots above the zero line represent states where the prediction using search outperforms the baseline model, whereas the opposite is true for dots below the zero line.

Overall, using search, we are able to predict thirty-nine states better than the baseline model, but our predictions are particularly bad for a few states, such as Montana and South Dakota. These states tend to have fewer transactions on housing sales than other states. Similar to what we found for home sales, search indices help predictions the most for states where the sales volume is high.

Furthermore, predicting HPI may just be inherently more difficult than predicting home sales. Although home sales can increase when either the housing demand or supply changes, HPI would increase only when the demand for housing is increased without a corresponding increase in supply, and decrease when the supply is increased without a corresponding increase in demand. It is difficult to know whether the search queries in general categories such as "real estate agencies" or "real estate listings" are coming from the demand side or the supply side, and thus it is harder to predict HPI than the volume of home sales. For example, both sellers and buyers need real estate agents, so an increase in the search index related to real estate agencies could come from both the supply and the demand sides that can either increase or decrease home price. To address this issue, we tentatively aggregated some search terms relating to buyers' activities—such as home financing, mortgage, and home inspections—and also some search terms related to sellers' activities only, such as home staging. For example, home buyers are more likely to look for loans than sellers, whereas sellers are more likely to hire a staging company to make the property more appealing to the highest number of potential buyers. We would therefore expect that an increase in search frequencies related to financing and loans to shift the demand curve, while a similar increase for searches related to home staging is more likely to shift the supply curve for housing. We see some evidence that home financing is positively correlated with HPI, suggesting it may be shifting the demand outward. Currently, we have not found a set of queries that can consistently identify shifts in the supply curve. However, because of the fine-grained nature of the search terms, we are hopeful that indices can be created to precisely tease out a shift in the demand curve from a shift in the supply curve.

To explore how search indices can be used to predict future HPI in the next quarter, we use the training data to find the best features that can be used to predict the future HPI. In addition to using the present and past search indices of "real estate agencies" and "real estate listings," we also explored some nonlinear forms of the search indices, such as their quadratic terms. Overall, we find the best predictors continue to be the present and past indices for "real estate agencies" and "real estate listings." Interestingly, we find the quadratic terms of "real estate agencies" to also help with the predictive accuracy in the training set. Thus, we include these variables to predict the future HPI from the second quarter of 2009 to the third quarter of 2011. We plot the difference in MAE between the baseline model and the search model for each state of the United States in figure 3.6. For most states, predictions using search were better than the baseline model, though the variance among states is even higher than predicting the present HPI. We predicted eleven quarters for fifty states and the District of Columbia. The baseline MAE is 0.027 and the MAE for the model that uses search is 0.026, about a 2.96 percent improvement in accuracy and statistically significant at the $p = 0.01$ level. Unfortunately, the National Association of Realtors does not forecast HPI, at least from public-available sources, and thus we are not able to compare our HPI predictions with NAR's.

We summarize our results in table 3.4. Whereas using search frequencies can improve the accuracy of prediction for both the present and future home sales as well as HPI, it is actually more effective for predicting the future than predicting the present. Because a housing transaction that often takes months to more than a year to complete, search indices in the present can be particularly useful to forecast future housing indicators. Search frequency data are more effective for predicting sales volume than for predicting HPI, in part because of the difficulty of distinguishing supply and demand shifts, which influence home prices.

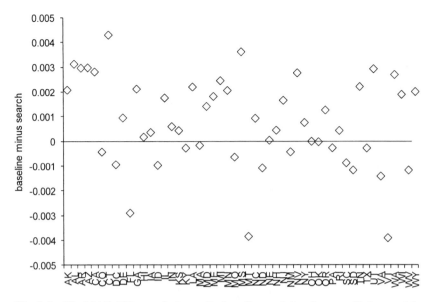

Fig. 3.6 The MAE difference between the baseline model and our prediction model

Table 3.4 Summary of MAE for predicting the present and the future housing trends

	Obs.	MAE search	MAE baseline	Improvement over baseline (%)
$Sales_t$	561	.170	.174	2.3**
HPI_t	561	.026	.027	2.45***
$Sales_{t+1}$	561	.172	.185	7.1**
HPI_{t+1}	561	.026	.027	2.96***

***Significant at the 1 percent level.
**Significant at the 5 percent level.
*Significant at the 10 percent level.

3.6.3 Predicting the Demand for Home Appliances

Lastly, we explore trends in home appliance sales. We expect that housing sales would spur interest in buying home appliances, increasing their demand in the future. To gauge the overall interest in home appliances, we use the search index for the "home appliance" category from Google Trends and show its relationship with home sales (table 3.5). We observe that the current home sales are not correlated with the contemporaneous search index for home appliances (Model 1, Model 4). But with a six-month lag, each one thousand houses previously sold is correlated with a 1.14 percentage point increase in the search index for home appliances. Because

Table 3.5 Linear regression on search terms related to home appliances and the volume of housing sales

| Dependent var. search terms related to home appliances | Search terms on home appliances (quarterly) ||||
| | Fixed effect ||||
	(1)	(2)	(3)	(4)
Home sale$_t$	−.054			0.188
	(.0001)			(0.0004)
Home sale$_{t-1}$		−.020		−0.627
		(.0001)		(0.393)
Home sale$_{t-2}$			.590**	1.140***
			(.3)	(0.427)
Obs.	254	203	152	152
Controls	Quarters	Quarters	Quarters	Quarters
States	51	51	51	51

Note: Huber-White robust standard errors are shown in parentheses.
***Significant at the 1 percent level.
**Significant at the 5 percent level.
*Significant at the 10 percent level.

buyers move into their new properties first before making major purchases (and often research such purchases), it is natural that the number of online searchers for home appliances would increase after a consumer has already bought a house. Thus, we may expect the online search for home appliances to lag behind housing sales. The actual demand for home appliances may rise after this increase in the appliance search index if some of the online searches translate into future sales. Similarly, we correlated the housing real estate-related search index with the home appliance search index and we find that they are also positively correlated. This highlights the linkages between home sales and other parts of the economy that may complement real estate purchases.

3.7 Implications

Twenty-five years ago, Herbert Simon (1984, 40) observed:

> In the physical sciences, when errors of measurement and other noise are found to be of the same order of magnitude as the phenomena under study, the response is not to try to squeeze more information out of the data by statistical means; it is instead to find techniques for observing the phenomena at a higher level of resolution. The corresponding strategy for economics is obvious: to secure new kinds of data at the micro level.

Today, advances in information technology in general, and in Internet search query data in particular, are making Simon's vision a reality. Who could have imagined that we would be observing literally billions of consumer and business intentions to buy or sell before the consumer sets foot in a store and transactions occur in the marketplace? Yet that is what search query data enables us to observe. Even more, we can do so at nearly zero cost, virtually instantaneously and at remarkably fine-grained levels of disaggregation. These data are increasingly available to ordinary consumers, business people, and researchers of all types.

We have found that analyzing online search data with relatively simple models can yield more accurate predictions about the housing market than were previously possible. If online search patterns can be construed as a broad indicator of interest within a group, they can also be used as a reliable predictor to forecast economic activities. By analyzing housing market trends, we find evidence that search indices add substantial power to predicting the underlying economic trends, and that predictions using search indices can outperform predictions from experts in the field, such as the National Association of Realtors. This supports the hypothesis that Web search can be used to predict present and future economic activities. For example, housing-related searches might be used to predict turning points in economic cycles.

Currently, we are able to make fairly accurate predictions using simple linear prediction models and a few predefined real estate categories in Google Trends. Because of the fine-grained nature of these data, they can be aggregated in many different ways to predict specific underlying economic shifts. For example, instead of using rough categories such as "real estate agencies" or "real estate listings," we can create our own sets of words specific for gauging changes in demand as well as changes in supply. Distinguishing the search indices of the supply side from those of the demand side can more accurately detect what is driving changes in the real estate market. Similarly, we can test more fine-grained predictions about the real estate market beyond sales and price. For example, search indices can be created to measure the interest of people buying homes as opposed to renting, or whether new construction activities are growing over time or not. Because of the fine-grain nature of individuals' search queries, it is possible to construct different types of indices and quickly test their validity in predicting various real estate trends and beyond.

Timely and accurate predictions about the housing market can benefit a wide array of industries, such as construction and home appliances, as well as individuals, such as homebuyers and sellers. Because buying a home is the single biggest expenditure and one of the biggest financial decisions for most people, obtaining accurate and timely information can help them make informed decisions and potentially save tens of thousands of dollars for the average family. Similarly, businesses that depend on the housing market can benefit from this simple use of Internet search data. Timely and accurate forecasts of housing demand would allow the construction industry to improve future plans for developments and thus reduce the probability of experiencing the housing boom and bust cycles. Accurate housing market forecasts can also help the home appliances industry to manage its inventory.

Currently, economists, managers, and investors primarily rely on housing data released from the government and trade groups such as the National Association of Realtors to understand the current housing market and forecast future market trends. However, government and trade group data are released with a delay and often with pending revisions. Furthermore, they do not provide fine-grained reports at the town level, which is the level needed for buyers and sellers to make informed decisions. With easy access to billions of online search frequencies, it is now possible to use a simple technology to cheaply collect timely, accurate, and fine-grained data about the housing market. Not only does Google Trends provide weekly reports on the volume of housing-related queries, it also offers a detailed regional analysis at country, state, and city levels. By leveraging microdata collected from Google Trends, investors and policymakers can obtain deeper insight about the housing market in order to make informed decisions.

3.7.1 Other Applications and Future Research

Not only can search data be used to provide better predictions about the housing market using Google Trends, but search data can also be used in many other contexts to predict future economic activities. Scott and Varian (chapter 4, this volume) demonstrate cases of using search indices from Google Trends for "nowcasting." Specifically, they used Bayesian variable selection methods to forecast the current consumer sentiment and the current gun sales. Similarly, Choi and Varian (2009) show that search engine data can be used to forecast other macroeconomic indicators such as retail, car sales, travel, and housing. In addition to predicting the present, we find that Google Trends can be used to predict the outcome of a standards war in the technology sector. We were able to track the progression of the standards war between HD-DVD and Blu-ray. Google Trends and search indices were prescient in predicting that Blu-ray would win in the end. Similarly, we can also use search frequency to predict the market share of an electronic product or an operating system such as Macintosh. Instead of paying a premium for industry reports, Google Trends can be used to predict if a particular technology would gain market shares.

It appears that predicting the future using search engine data can be much better than many existing models, especially for a market that does not change instantaneously, such as real estate and employment. Presumably, finding a job or a place to live often takes many months and thus the signals aggregated from search can be very helpful for predicting the future trends in real estate or the labor market.

Because of the fine-grained nature of the search queries, there are many ways to dissect the data for various prediction purposes. Furthermore, search data can be combined with other types of nanodata, such as various digital traces from digital and social media. Together, these data allow consumers, managers, researchers, and policymakers to tap into the pulse of economic activities to make more informed decisions.

Many other types of predictions are possible now using Google Trends. For example, instead of waiting for the government to release labor statistics every month, we can use Google Trends to predict the current unemployment rates by using search indices related to job search activities. As job search activities are increasingly done through the Internet, search queries could be far more powerful in predicting the unemployment rates than government surveys. Similarly, instead of waiting for industrial reports to become available, we can use Google Trends to predict sales such as automobiles sales. As purchasing a home, searching for a job, and buying a car can all incur significant search costs and consumers often conduct extensive research online before making purchase decisions, the digital trace left from the searching process can be tremendously valuable for making predictions. We expect research to validate many similar types of predictions in the future.

However, this approach also has important limitations. Precisely because search query data can be easily collected and used to make predictions, they are also prone to be manipulated. For example, searchbots could be used to generate irrelevant search queries to substantially change search indices and consequently influence many economic decision-making processes. Future work should also focus on how to detect data manipulations. Furthermore, when major search engines change their search algorithms or user interface, predictability of search queries could also change significantly. Because some search engines conduct frequent experiments and adjustments to their algorithms, a search query that works well for today's prediction may not work well tomorrow. Thus, it is important to monitor and update the set of keywords used in each search index for prediction purposes. An important focus for research is to improve the methods to generate search keywords and validate them over time. See, for example, the "crowd-squared" approach that draws on a set of users to suggest potential keywords (Brynjolfsson, Geva, and Reichman 2014). If search queries were to have important implications for making important policy and economic decisions, it is also important to ensure key stakeholders, such as the search engine providers, would not be able to manipulate the search data to their own benefits.

3.8 Conclusions, Limitations, and Future Work

Today, due to advances in IT and IT research, we are gaining the capability to observe microbehaviors online. Rather than rely on costly, time-consuming surveys and census data, predefined metrics and backward-looking financial reports, today's social science researchers can use query data to learn the intentions of buyers, sellers, employers, gamers, engineers, lovers, travelers, and all manner of other decision makers even before they execute their decisions. It is possible to accurately predict what will happen in the marketplace days, weeks, and even months in the future with this approach. Search technology has revolutionized many markets, and it is now revolutionizing our research.

This is an exploratory study investigating whether online search behavior from Google Search can predict underlying economic activities. Using housing sales data, we find evidence that search terms are correlated with future sales and prices in the housing market. This evidence lends credibility to the hypotheses that Web search can be used to predict future economic activities, for example, when the economy may recover from the recent recession. We are aware of the fact that Google search queries do not represent all the online housing search activities nor do they represent a demographically random sample of all home sellers and home buyers. Some consumers may bypass the search engine all together and go directly to certain websites, such as Realtor.org, when considering buying and selling a home. Others might have a long-standing relationship with a trusted realtor or do not use the Internet. Using Google Search alone would miss these types of consumers. However, despite missing some segments of the population, we can still predict the housing sales and housing price using only online search captured by Google, demonstrating the power of online queries in forecasting economic trends.

Ultimately, microdata collected using Google Trends may prove to be one of the most powerful tools for helping consumers, businesses, and government officials make accurate predictions about the future so that they can make effective and efficient decisions. This data distills the collective intelligence and unfiltered intentions of millions of people and businesses at a point in their decision-making process that precedes actual transactions. Because search is generally not strategic, it provides honest signals of decision-makers' intentions. The breadth of coverage, the level of disaggregation, and the speed of its availability is a radical break from the majority of earlier social science data. Even simple models can thus be used to make predictions that matter.

Of course, there are many obstacles yet to overcome and refinements to be made. For instance, paradoxically, as businesses and consumers come to rely on query data for their decision making, as we expect they will, there will be incentives for opposing parties to try to degrade the value of the data, perhaps by generating billions of false or misleading queries. This will in turn call for countermeasures and perhaps the golden age of simple models using these data will be brief. However, more than four years have passed since we first started using Google Trends to forecast real estate trends. We are encouraged to see that search indices continue to have the power to predict the future, as we have shown in this chapter. Informational value derived from search indices has not been absorbed into economic equilibria, as many have argued. Instead, its effect, at least for the real estate market, has persisted over time. Meanwhile, new types of nanodata have become available, such as Twitter feeds, social networking data, cell phone location data, and various other digital traces of consumers' daily lives. Along with search, detailed nanodata have continued to proliferate at a pace that has far outgrown our ability to manage and use these data appropriately. For example, a single simple hoax message—claiming that two bombs had exploded at the White House—using a single Twitter feed on April 23rd, 2013, seemingly caused the Dow Jones Industrial Average to drop by 145 points in less than five minutes. Perhaps the instantaneous connectivity of Twitter and the potential short-term nature of stock price fluctuations enable a fake Tweet to quickly go viral and affect the actions of many high-frequency traders. Consequently, the stock market erased $136 billion in equity in a matter of minutes. However, this type of gaming is less likely to happen for markets that are not prone to change so quickly, such as home buying and selling. Because selling a home can take months to complete, a swing in search indices on housing queries in an hour or a day would not make a significant impact on the predictions of future real estate trends. These types of hacking are often quickly discovered using tests for statistical anomalies, making long-term manipulation more difficult. Future research should investigate what types of markets search and other forms of digital trace are most useful for predictions and what types of markets are susceptible to gaming. We have so far identified that the rate of market changes may play a role, but many other factors could also be at play.

Ultimately, the availability of various digital traces[15] has grown so quickly over the years that they have outpaced our ability to understand and use them effectively. It is thus important for future research to investigate how to integrate and use them in a meaningful fashion to understand underlying consumer sentiments and economic consequences. Through improved understanding, we may be able to better distinguish malicious and faulty information from the true economic signals, although it may also be a cat-and-mouse game where malicious attack will always happen on strategic tools that can affect decision making. Through these explorations we will also have a better understanding of which types of markets can benefit from the use of nanodata in predictions and which types of markets are less predictable. Perhaps some markets require higher data quality or are more prone to manipulation, such as the stock market. Markets might vary in the horizon of predictability, depending on the lag between the digital trace presaging the transaction and the transaction itself. There might be some predictions that will always be difficult to do regardless of how fine-grained

---

15. The antecedents of economic activity have always existed in the form of the daily conversations and wanderings of consumers over the economic landscape. What has changed is the cost of unobtrusive observation of these antecedents.

data have become. However, as more nanodata and methods become more widely used, we can only conclude that the future of prediction is far brighter than it was only a few years ago.

References

Appleton-Young, L. 2008. "State of the California Housing Market 2008–2009." Technical Report, California Association of Realtors.
Arrow, K. 1987. "Chapter Reflections on Essays" In *Arrow and the Foundations of the Theory of Economic Policy*, edited by G. R. Feiwel, pages 727–34. New York: New York University Press.
Brynjolfsson, E., T. Geva, and S. Reichman. 2014. "Crowd-Squared: A New Method for Improving Predictions by Crowd-Sourcing Google Trends Keyword Selection." Working Paper, Center for Digital Business, Massachusetts Institute of Technology.
Brynjolfsson, E., Y. J. Hu, and M. S. Rahman. 2013. "Competing in the Age of Omnichannel Retailing." *MIT Sloan Management Review* 54 (4). http://sloanreview.mit.edu/article/competing-in-the-age-of-omnichannel-retailing/.
Case, K. E., and R. J. Shiller. 1987. "Prices of Single-Family Real Estate Prices." *New England Economic Review* 1:45–56.
———. 1989. "The Efficiency of the Market for Single-Family Homes." *American Economic Review* 79 (1): 125–37.
Choi, H., and H. R. Varian. 2009. "Predicting the Present with Google Trends." Google Research Blog. http://static.googleusercontent.com/media/www.google.com/en/us/googleblogs/pdfs/google_predicting_the_present.pdf.
comScore. 2012. "qSearch: A Comprehensive View of the Search Landscape." Technical Report, comScore. https://www.comscore.com/Products/Audience-Analytics/qSearch.
Davenport, T. H. 2006. "Competing on Analytics." *Harvard Business Review* 84 (1): 98.
Ginsberg, J., M. H. Mohebbi, R. S. Patel, L. Brammer, M. S. Smolinski, and L. Brilliant. 2009. "Detecting Influenza Epidemics Using Search Engine Query Data." *Nature* 457 (7232): 1012–14.
Glaeser, E. L. 2008. "Housing Prices in the Three Americas." *New York Times*, September 30.
Glaeser, E. L., and J. Gyourko. 2006. "Housing Dynamics." NBER Working Paper no. 12787, Cambridge, MA.
Han, L. 2010. "The Effects of Price Risk on Housing Demand: Empirical Evidence from US Markets." *Review of Financial Studies* 2 3(11): 3889–928.
Horrigan, J. B. 2008. "The Internet and Consumer Choice: Online Americans Use Different Search and Purchase Strategies for Different Goods." Technical Report, Pew Internet and American Life Project.
Krugman, P. 2009. "How Did Economists Get It So Wrong?" *New York Times Magazine*, September 2, MM36.
Kuruzovich, J., S. Viswanathan, R. Agarwal, S. Gosain, and S. Weitzman. 2008. "Marketspace or Marketplace? Online Information Search and Channel Outcomes in Auto Retailing." *Information Systems Research* 19 (2): 182–201.
Lazer, D., A. Pentland, L. Adamic, S. Aral, A.-L. Barábasi, D. Brewer, N. Christa-

kis, N. Contractor, J. Fowler, M. Gutmann, T. Jebara, G. King, M. Macy, D. Roy, and M. Van Alstyne. 2009. "Computational Social Science." *Science* 323 (5915): 721–23.

McAfee, A., and E. Brynjolfsson. 2012. "Big Data: The Management Revolution." *Harvard Business Review* 90 (10): 60–66.

Moe, W. W., and P. S. Fader. 2004. "Dynamic Conversion Behavior at E-Commerce Sites." *Management Science* 50 (3): 326–35.

National Association of Realtors (NAR) Research Staff. 2012. "Profile of Home Buyers and Sellers 2012." Technical Report, National Association of Realtors.

Pentland, A. S. 2010. *Honest Signals*. Cambridge, MA: MIT Press.

Simon, H. A. 1984. "On the Behavioral and Rational Foundations of Economic Dynamics." *Journal of Economic Behavior and Organization* 5 (1): 35–55.

Wu, L., B. Waber, S. Aral, E. Brynjolfsson, and A. S. Pentland. 2008. "Mining Face-to-face Interaction Networks using Sociometric Badges: Predicting Productivity in an IT Configuration Task." International Conference on Information Systems 2008 Proceedings, 127.

4
Bayesian Variable Selection for Nowcasting Economic Time Series

Steven L. Scott and Hal R. Varian

4.1 Introduction

Computers are now in the middle of many economic transactions. The details of these "computer-mediated transactions" can be captured in databases and used in subsequent analyses (Varian 2010). However, such databases can contain vast amounts of data, so it is normally necessary to do some sort of data reduction.

Our motivating example for this work is Google Trends, a system that produces an index of search activity on queries entered into Google. A related system, Google Correlate, produces an index of queries that are correlated with a time series entered by a user. There are many uses for these data, but in this chapter we focus on how to use the data to make short-run forecasts of economic metrics.

Choi and Varian (2009a, 2009b, 2011, 2012) described how to use search engine data to forecast contemporaneous values of macroeconomic indicators. This type of contemporaneous forecasting, or "nowcasting," is of particular interest to central banks, and there have been several subsequent research studies from researches at these institutions. See, for example, Arola and Galan (2012), McLaren and Shanbhoge (2011), Hellerstein and Middeldorp (2012), Suhoy (2009), and Carrière-Swallow and Labbé (2011). Choi and Varian (2012) contains several other references to work in this area. Wu and Brynjolfsson (chapter 3, this volume) describe an application of Google Trends data to the real estate market using cross-state data.

Steven L. Scott is a statistician at Google, Inc. Hal R. Varian is the chief economist at Google, Inc. and emeritus professor at the University of California at Berkeley.

For acknowledgments, sources of research support, and disclosure of the authors' material financial relationships, if any, please see http://www.nber.org/chapters/c12995.ack.

In these studies, the researchers selected predictors using their judgment of relevance to the particular prediction problem. For example, it seems natural that search engine queries in the "vehicle shopping" category would be good candidates for forecasting automobile sales while queries such as "file for unemployment" would be useful in forecasting initial claims for unemployment benefits.

One difficulty with using human judgment is that it does not easily scale to models where the number of possible predictors exceeds the number of observations—the so-called "fat regression" problem. For example, the Google Trends service provides data for millions of search queries and hundreds of search categories extending back to January 1, 2004. Even if we restrict ourselves to using only category data, we have several hundred possible predictors and about 100 months of data. In this chapter we describe a scalable approach to time series prediction for fat regressions of this sort.

4.2 Approaches to Variable Selection

Castle, Qin, and Reed (2009) and Castle, Fawcett, and Hendry (2010) describe and compare twenty-one techniques for variable selection for time-series forecasting. These techniques fall into four major categories:

- Significance testing (forward and backward stepwise regression, Gets)
- Information criteria (AIC, BIC)
- Principle component and factor models (e.g., Stock and Watson 2010)
- Lasso, ridge regression, and other penalized regression models (e.g., Hastie, Tibshirani, and Friedman 2009)

Our approach combines three statistical methods into an integrated system we call Bayesian Structural Time Series, or BSTS for short. The three methods are:

- a "basic structural model" for trend and seasonality, estimated using Kalman filters;
- spike and slab regression for variable selection; and
- Bayesian model averaging over the best performing models for the final forecast.

We briefly review each of these methods and describe how they fit into our framework.

4.2.1 Structural Time Series and the Kalman Filter

Harvey (1991), Durbin and Koopman (2001), Petris, Petrone, and Campagnoli (2009) and many others have advocated the use of Kalman filters for time series forecasting. The "basic structural model" decomposes the time series into four components: a level, a local trend, seasonal effects, and an error term. The model described here drops the seasonal effect for simplicity and adds a regression component; it is then called a "local linear trend model with regressors."

This model is a stochastic generalization of the classic constant-trend regression model

$$y_t = \mu + bt + \beta x_t + e_t.$$

In this classic model the level (μ) and trend (b) parameters are constant, (x_t) is a vector of contemporaneous regressors, β is a vector of regression coefficients, and e_t is an error term.

In a local linear trend model each of these structural components is stochastic. In particular, the level and slope terms each follow a random walk model.

(1) $\quad y_t = \mu_t + z_t + v_t \qquad v_t \sim N(0,V)$

(2) $\quad \mu_t = \mu_{t-1} + b_{t-1} + w_{1t} \qquad w_{1t} \sim N(0,W_1)$

(3) $\quad b_t = b_{t-1} + w_{2t} \qquad w_{2t} \sim N(0,W_2)$

(4) $\quad z_t = \beta x_t$

The unknown parameters to be estimated in this system are the variance terms (V, W_1, W_2) and the regression coefficients, β.

If we drop the trend and regression coefficients by setting $b_t = 0$ and $\beta = 0$, the "local trend model" becomes the "local level" model. When $V = 0$, the local level model is a random walk, so the best forecast of y_{t+1} is y_t. When $W_1 = 0$, the local level model is a constant mean model, so the best forecast of y_{t+1} is the average of all previously observed values of y_t. Hence, the local level model has two popular time series models as special cases.

It is easy to add a seasonal component to the local linear trend model, in which case it is referred to as the "basic structural model." In the appendix we describe a general structural time series model that contains these and other models in the literature as special cases.

It is also possible to allow for time-varying regression coefficients by simply including them as another set of state variables. In practice, one would want to limit this to just a few coefficients, particularly when dealing with small sample sizes.

4.2.2 Spike-and-Slab Variable Selection

The spike-and-slab approach to model selection was developed by George and McCulloch (1997) and Madigan and Raftery (1994).

Let γ denote a vector of zeros and ones that indicates whether or not a particular regressor is included in a regression. More precisely, γ is a vector the same length as β, where $\gamma_i = 1$ indicates $\beta_i \neq 0$ and $\gamma_i = 0$ indicates $\beta_i = 0$. Let β_γ indicate the subset of β for which $\gamma_i = 1$, and let σ^2 be the residual variance from the regression model.

A spike-and-slab prior for the joint distribution of $(\beta, \gamma, \sigma^{-2})$ can be factored in the usual way.

(5) $$p(\beta, \gamma, \sigma^{-2}) = p(\beta_\gamma | \gamma, \sigma^{-2}) p(\sigma^{-2} | \gamma) p(\gamma).$$

There are several ways to specify functional forms for these prior distributions. Here, we describe a particularly convenient choice.

The "spike" part of a spike-and-slab prior refers to the point mass at zero, for which we assume a Bernoulli distribution for each i, so that the prior is a product of Bernoulli's:

(1) $$\gamma \sim \prod_i \pi_i^{\gamma_i}(1 - \pi_i)^{1-\gamma_i}.$$

When detailed prior information is unavailable, it is convenient to set all π_i equal to the same number, π. Alternatively, the researcher might expect that on average only k out of K possible coefficients are nonzero. In this case it is natural to set $\pi = k/K$. In our particular application, where we will use Google Trends categories as predictors, we may have prior beliefs about which categories are likely to be relevant.

More complex choices of $p(\gamma)$ can be made as well. For example, a non-Bernoulli model could be used to encode rules such as the hierarchical principle (no high order interactions without lower order interactions). The MCMC methods described below are robust to the specific choice of the prior.

The "slab" component is a prior for the values of the nonzero coefficients, conditional on knowledge of which coefficients are nonzero. Let b be a vector of prior guesses for regression coefficients, let Ω^{-1} be a prior precision matrix, and let Ω_γ^{-1} denote rows and columns of Ω^{-1} for which $\gamma_i = 1$. A conditionally conjugate "slab" prior is:

(7) $$\beta_\gamma | \gamma, \sigma^2 \sim \mathcal{N}(b_\gamma, \sigma^2(\Omega_\gamma^{-1})^{-1}), \quad \frac{1}{\sigma^2} \sim \Gamma\left(\frac{df}{2}, \frac{ss}{2}\right).$$

It is conventional to assume $b = 0$ (with the possible exception of the intercept term) and $\Omega^{-1} \propto X^T X$, in which case equation (7) is known as Zellner's g-prior (Chipman et al. 2001). Because $X^T X / \sigma^2$ is the total Fisher information in the full data, it is reasonable to parametrize $\Omega^{-1} = \kappa(X^T X)/n$, the average information available from κ observations.

One issue with Zellner's g-prior is that when the design matrix contains truly redundant predictors (as is the case when the number of possible predictors exceeds the number of observations), then $X^T X$ is rank deficient, which means that for some values of γ, $p(\beta, \sigma | \gamma)$ is improper. We can restore propriety by averaging $X^T X$ with its diagonal, so that

$$\Omega^{-1} = \frac{\kappa}{n}[w X^T X + (1 - w)\text{diag}(X^T X)].$$

The final values that need to be chosen are *df* and *ss*. These can be elicited by asking the modeler for the R^2 statistic he expects to obtain from the regression, and the weight he would like to assign to that guess, measured in terms of the equivalent number of observations. The *df* parameter is the equivalent number of observations, and $ss = df(1 - R^2)s_y^2$.

Software implementing the spike-and-slab prior can make reasonable default choices for expected model size, κ, expected R^2, and *df*, thereby giving the modeler the option either to accept the defaults, or to provide his own inputs.

4.2.3 Bayesian Model Averaging

Bayesian inference with spike-and-slab priors is an effective way to implement Bayesian model averaging over the space of time series regression models. As described below, we estimate the model by sampling from the posterior distribution of the parameters in the model. Each draw of parameters from the posterior can be combined with the available data to yield a forecast of y_{t+1} for that particular draw. Repeating these draws many times gives us an estimate of the posterior distribution of the forecast y_{t+1}.

This approach is motivated by the Madigan and Raftery (1994) proof that averaging over an ensemble of models does no worse than using the best single model in the ensemble. See Volinsky (2012) for links to tools and applications of Bayesian model averaging.

4.3 Estimating the Model

The Kalman filter, spike-and-slab regression, and model averaging all have natural Bayesian interpretations and tend to play well together. The basic parameters we need to estimate are γ (which variables are in the regression), β (the regression coefficients), and the variances of the error terms (V, W_1, W_2, W_3).

As the appendix describes in detail, we specify priors for each of these parameters and then sample from the posterior distribution using Markov Chain Monte Carlo (MCMC) techniques. There are a number of attractive short cuts available that make this sampling process quite efficient. These are described in more detail in the appendix and in a companion paper, Scott and Varian (2014).

These techniques yield a sample from the posterior distribution for the parameters that can then be used to construct a posterior distribution for forecasts of time series of interest.

4.4 Fun with Priors

We have already indicated that it is possible to use an informative prior to describe beliefs about the expected number of predictors. It is also possible to use a prior in the regression to indicate likely relationships. For example, one might expect that automobile purchases are likely to be correlated with automotive-related queries.

A less obvious example involves using data-based priors for estimating the state and observation variances, (V, W_1, W_2, W_3). Even though the Google Trends data only goes back to January 2004, economic time series are often much longer. One can estimate posterior distribution of the parameters in the univariate Kalman filter using the long series, then use this posterior distribution as the prior distribution for the shorter series where the Google Trends data are available.

4.5 Nowcasting Consumer Sentiment

To illustrate the use of BSTS for nowcasting, we examine the University of Michigan monthly survey of Consumer Sentiment from January 2004 to April 2012. We focus on "nowcasting" since we expect that queries at time t could be related to sentiment at time t but are not necessarily predictive of sentiment in the more distant future.

Our data from Google Trends starts at January 2004, and our sample ends in April 2012, giving us 100 observations. For predictors, we use 151 categories from Google Trends that have some connection with economics. These potential predictors were chosen from the roughly 300 query categories using the authors' judgment.

Our problem is to find a good set of predictors for 100 observations chosen from a set of 151 possible predictors. This qualifies as a mildly obese, if not truly fat, regression.

The Consumer Sentiment index is not highly seasonal, but many of the potential predictors are seasonal, so we first deseasonalize the data by using the R command **stl**. We then detrend the predictors by regressing each predictor on a simple time trend. A visual inspection of the time series of the predictors indicated that these techniques were sufficient to "whiten" the data.

We then applied the BSTS estimation procedure described earlier. Figure 4.1 shows the inclusion probability for the top five predictors. A white bar indicates that the predictor has a positive relationship with consumer sentiment and a black bar indicates a negative relationship. The length of the bar measures the proportion of the estimated models in which that predictor was present.

The top predictor is financial planning, which is included in almost all of the models explored. The top queries in this category in the United States can be found on the Google Trends web page. They are "schwab," "401k," "charles schwab," "ira," "smith barney," "fidelity 401k," "john hancock," "403b," "401k withdrawl," and "roth ira."

The second most probable predictor is investing, which tends to have a

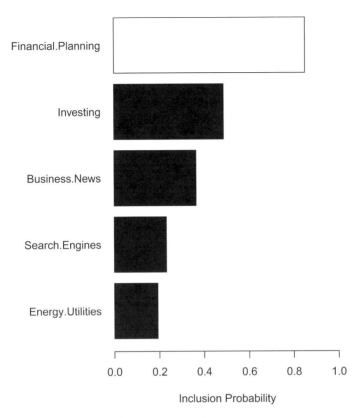

Fig. 4.1 Top five predictors for consumer sentiment
Note: Bars show the probability of inclusion. Shading indicates the sign of the coefficient.

negative relationship with confidence. The top queries in this category are "stock," "gold," "fidelity," "stocks," "stock market," "silver," "gold price," "mutual," "scottrade," and "finance."

The inclusion of the energy category is likely due to gasoline prices, which are known to have a negative relationship with consumer sentiment in the United States. We have no explanation for the search engine inclusion, though a visual inspection of the series shows that it does change direction at about the time the recession started. We speculate that the financial crisis influenced queries relating to economic conditions, which were classified as being related to both business news and search engines.

Figure 4.2 shows the posterior distribution of the one-step-ahead forecast along with the actual observations.

Note that the regression parameters are estimated using the entire sample of data, but the forecasts for period t are made using the value of consumer sentiment at $t-1$ and the observed query categories at time t (for the included categories).

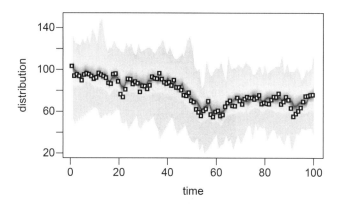

Fig. 4.2 Posterior distribution of forecast and the observations

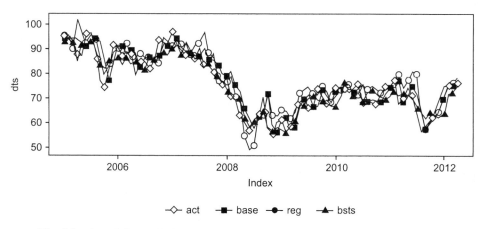

Fig. 4.3 Actual, base AR(1), regression, and BSTS one-step-ahead predictions

The model predicts reasonably well with a mean absolute one-step-ahead prediction error of about 4.5 percent. A naive AR(1) model has a mean absolute one-step-ahead prediction error of 5.2 percent, indicating an improvement of about 14 percent. See figure 4.3 for a time series plot of the actual, AR(1), and BSTS one-step-ahead predictions.

As we have seen, the BSTS system can decompose the forecast into the trend and regression components. The trend component is basically the univariate Kalman filter forecast, while the regression component uses the predictors from the query categories. Figure 4.4 illustrates the contribution of each state variable and regressor to the fit. The faint line in each panel is the previous fit.

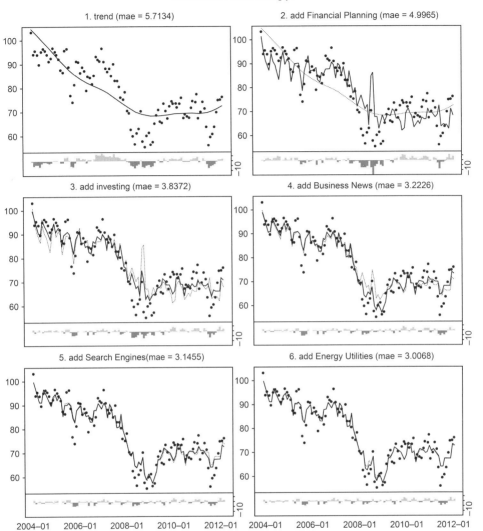

Fig. 4.4 Decomposition of forecast for consumer sentiment using Google Trends data

Note: Variables are ordered by probability of inclusion, mean absolute error is given in title, and residuals are shown at the bottom of each panel.

4.6 Nowcasting Gun Sales

The National Instant Criminal Background Check (NICS) is a service offered by the FBI to federal firearms licensees that can quickly determine whether a prospective buyer is eligible to buy firearms or explosives. A monthly report on the number of checks conducted is available on the Web.[1]

We downloaded the NICS data and fed it to Google Correlate, which produced 100 queries that were highly correlated with this series. The first ten were "stack on," "bread," "44 mag," "buckeye outdoors," "mossberg," "g star," "ruger 44," "baking," ".308," and "savage 22." Most of these queries are related to weapons; the exceptions (bread and baking) have to do with the fact that hunting season starts at about the same time as Thanksgiving in many states.

We used BSTS to find the best predictors from this set for the NICS background check data. Since the data was highly seasonal, we used both a local linear trend and seasonal state variables. The best predictor by far was "gun stores" which, interestingly, only ranked 36th on the list of correlates. The in-sample MAE of the simple model using only trend + seasonal was 0.34, but adding "gun stores" cut the MAE to 0.15, a substantial reduction. Figure 4.5 shows how adding trend, seasonal, and query data improves the in-sample fit.

We also ran BSTS using all 585 verticals produced by Google Trends to fit the 107 observations of monthly NICS data. The two most probable predictors are shown in table 4.1. The category "Recreation::Outdoors::Hunting: and:Shooting" is by far the most probable predictor. The forecast decomposition is shown in figure 4.6, which indicates a substantial contribution by the regression component.

4.7 Summary

We have described a Bayesian approach to variable selection for time series that combines Kalman filtering, spike-and-slab regressions, and model averaging. Although the system was developed for nowcasting using Google Trends data, there are many other possible applications.

For example, Brodersen et al. (2013) describe how to use BSTS to estimate ad effectiveness. The basic idea is to build a BSTS model that predicts website visits using trend, seasonal, and regression components. When an ad campaign is initiated, this model can be used to predict the counterfactual—what would have happened in the absence of the campaign. The difference between the actual and the counterfactual is the causal effect of the ad campaign.

We have focused on nowcasting since, in most cases, the action taken by

---

1. http://www.fbi.gov/about-us/cjis/nics/reports/080112_1998_2012_Monthly_Yearly_Totals.pdf.

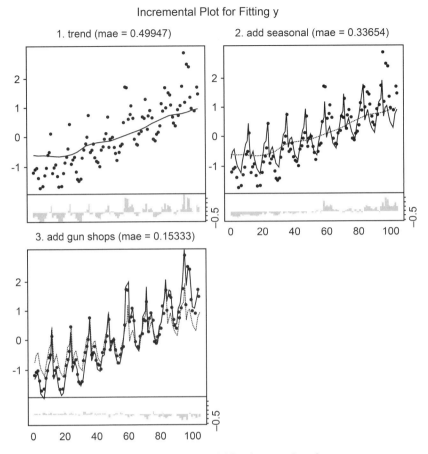

Fig. 4.5 Decomposition of forecast for NICS using correlate data

Note: Variables are ordered by probability of inclusion, mean absolute error is given in the title, and residuals are shown at the bottom of each panel.

Table 4.1 Google Trends predictors for NICS checks

Category	Mean	Inc. prob.
Recreation::outdoors::hunting:and:shooting	1,056,208	0.97
Travel::adventure:travel	−84,467	0.09

individuals is contemporaneous with the related queries. But in some cases, such as vacation planning or housing purchases, the relevant queries may precede the actions by several months. In such cases queries may help in longer-term forecasting. (See, e.g., Choi and Liu 2011.)

As more and more data becomes available the problem of "fat regressions" will arise in many other contexts and we anticipate there will be considerable interest in model selection. Given the widespread availability of "big data" it

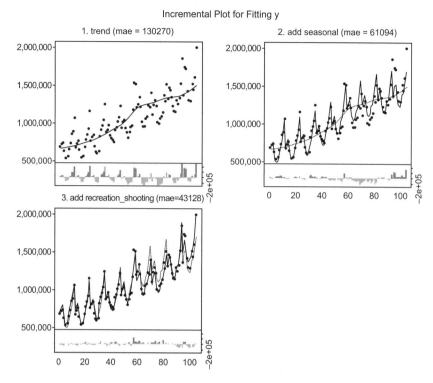

Fig. 4.6 Decomposition of forecast for NICS using Google Trends data
Note: Variables are ordered by probability of inclusion, mean absolute error is given in the title, and residuals are shown at the bottom of each panel.

seems strange that so much attention is paid to sampling uncertainty when the real issue in most cases is model uncertainty. We believe that Bayesian methods such as those we have described allow for better ways to describe model uncertainty. (See Varian [2014] for further discussion.)

It is widely recognized that averaging many small models tends to give better out-of-sample forecasting performance than using a single complex model. Bayesian methods give a principled way to perform such averaging which should, in turn, lead to better forecasts.

Appendix

Structural Time Series Models

Here we describe our Bayesian Structural Time Series model. More detail can be found in Scott and Varian (2014). We focus on structural time series models of the standard form

$$y_t = Z_t^T \alpha_t + \epsilon_t \qquad \epsilon_t \sim \mathcal{N}(0, H_t)$$
(8)
$$\alpha_{t+1} = T_t \alpha_t + R_t \eta_t \qquad \eta_t \sim \mathcal{N}(0, Q_t).$$

Here y_t is time series to be modeled and the vector α_t is a latent variable indicating the state of the model; it contains any trend, seasonal, or other components deemed necessary by the modeler.

Z_t is a vector of coefficients applied to the state variables, ϵ_t is a normally distributed error term with mean zero, and H_t is its variance. Each state component contributes to the block diagonal transition matrix T_t, the rectangular block diagonal residual matrix R_t, and the observation vector Z_t. The error term η_t has covariance matrix Q_t.

The model matrices (Z, T, R, H, Q) can be used to construct the Kalman filter, which can then be used to forecast future values $y_{t+\tau}$ from current observations ($y_1, \cdots, y_t$). One attractive feature of the Kalman filter is that it has a natural Bayesian interpretation and can easily be combined with the variable selection and model averaging techniques we have chosen.

Regression

Regressors can be included in a structural time series model in either a static framework (where the regression coefficients are fixed) or dynamic framework (where the regression coefficients can change over time).

In a dynamic regression the coefficients are a component of the state vector, which evolve over time according to some stochastic process. In a static regression, by contrast, the coefficients are fixed, unknown parameters. A convenient way to include a static regression component in the model is to set $\alpha_t = 1$, $t_t = 1$, $q_t = 0$, and $z_t = \beta' x_t$. This specification adds $\beta' x_t$ to the contributions of the other state components in a computationally efficient way because it only adds one additional state to the model. A small dimension is helpful because the Kalman recursions are quadratic in the dimension of the state space.

Estimating the Model Using Markov Chain Monte Carlo

We estimate the posterior distribution of the model parameters using Markov Chain Monte Carlo. Let θ denote the collection of model parameters (β, σ, ψ) where ψ is the collection of all model parameters associated with state components other than the static regression. Then the complete data posterior distribution is:

(9)
$$p(\theta, \alpha | y) \propto p(\theta) p(\alpha_0) \prod_{t=1}^{n} p(y_t | \alpha_t, \theta) p(\alpha_t | \alpha_{t-1}, \theta).$$

In order to sample from the posterior distribution we use an efficient Gibbs sampling algorithm that alternates between draws of $p(\alpha | \theta, y)$ and $p(\theta | \alpha, y)$, which produces a sequence $(\theta, \alpha)_0, (\theta, \alpha)_1, \cdots$ from a Markov chain with stationary distribution $p(\theta | \alpha, y)$.

The key point is that, conditional on α, the time series and regression components of the model are independent. Thus the draw from $p(\theta|\alpha, y)$ decomposes into several independent draws from the different conditional posterior distributions of the state components. In particular, $p(\psi, \beta, \sigma^{-2}|\alpha, y) = p(\psi|\alpha, y)p(\beta, \sigma^{-2}|\alpha, y)$.

Sampling α

The idea of using Kalman filtering to sample the state in a linear Gaussian structural time series model was independently proposed by Carter and Kohn (1994) and Frühwirth-Schnatter (1994). Various improvements to the early algorithms have been made by de Jong and Shepard (1995), Rue (2001), and others. We use the method proposed by Durbin and Koopman (2002), who observed that the variance of $p(\alpha|\theta, y)$ does not depend on the numerical value of y. Durbin and Koopman (2001) describe a fast smoothing method for computing $E(\alpha|y, \theta)$ using the Kalman filter.

Thus one may simulate a fake data set $(y^*, \alpha^*) \sim p(y, \alpha|\theta)$ by simply iterating equation (8). Then the fast mean smoother can be used to subtract the conditional mean $E(\alpha^*|\theta, y^*)$ from α^*, which is now mean zero with the correct variance. A second fast smoother can be used to add in $E(\alpha|y, \theta)$, yielding a draw of α with the correct moments. Because $p(\alpha|y, \theta)$ is Gaussian, the correct moments imply the correct distribution.

Sampling θ

Many of the usual models for state components are simple random walks, whose variance parameters are trivial to sample conditional on α. For example, consider the state variables for the local linear trend model described in equation (4):

$$\mu_{t+1} = \mu_t + \delta_t + \eta_{0t}$$

$$\delta_{t+1} = \delta_t + \eta_{1t}$$

where η_0 and η_1 are independent Gaussian error terms with variances ψ_0^2 and ψ_1^2. With independent Gamma priors on $\psi_0^{-2} \sim \Gamma(df_0/2, ss_0/2)$ and $\psi_1^{-2} \sim \Gamma(df_1/2, ss_1/2)$, their full conditional is the product of two independent Gamma distributions

$$p(\psi_0^{-2}, \psi_1^{-2}|\alpha) = \Gamma\left(\frac{df_0 + n - 1}{2}, \frac{SS_0}{2}\right)\Gamma\left(\frac{df_1 + n - 1}{2}, \frac{SS_1}{2}\right),$$

where $SS_0 = ss_0 + \sum_{t=2}^{n}(\mu_t - \mu_{t-1} - \delta_{t-1})^2$ and $SS_1 = ss_1 + \sum_{t=2}^{n}(\delta_t - \delta_{t-1})^2$. These complete data sufficient statistics are observed given α, so drawing ψ_0^{-2} and ψ_1^{-2} from their full conditional distribution is trivial. Most of the traditional state models can be handled similarly, including the seasonal component of the BSM and dynamic regression coefficients.

The full conditional for (β, σ^{-2}) is likewise independent of the other state components, with $\tilde{y}_t = y_t - Z_t^T\alpha_t + \beta^T x_t \sim \mathcal{N}(\beta^t x_t, \sigma^2)$. Thus, by subtracting the contributions from the other state components from each y_t we are left with a standard spike-and-slab regression. The posterior distribution can be simulated efficiently by drawing from $p(\gamma|\alpha, y)$ using a sequence of Gibbs sampling steps, and then drawing from the well-known closed form $p(\beta_\gamma, \sigma^{-2}|\gamma, \alpha, y)$. This technique is known as "stochastic search variable selection" (George and McCulloch 1997). There have been many suggested improvements to the SSVS algorithm (notably Ghosh and Clyde 2011), but we have obtained satisfactory results with the basic algorithm.

The conditional posteriors for β_γ and σ^{-2} can be found in standard texts (e.g., Gelman et al. 2002). They are:

(10) $\quad p(\beta|y,\alpha,\gamma,\sigma^{-2}) = \mathcal{N}(\tilde{\beta}_\gamma, \sigma^2 V_\gamma)$, and $p(\sigma^{-2}|y,\alpha,\gamma) = \Gamma\left(\dfrac{df+n}{2}, \dfrac{ss+\tilde{S}}{2}\right)$

where the complete data sufficient statistics are $V_\gamma^{-1} = X^T X_\gamma + \Omega_\gamma^{-1}$, $\tilde{\beta}_\gamma = V_\gamma(X^T \tilde{y}_\gamma + \Omega_\gamma^{-1} b_\gamma)$, and $\tilde{S} = \sum_{t=1}^{n}(\tilde{y}_t - x_t^T \tilde{\beta}_\gamma)^2 + (\tilde{\beta}_\gamma - b_\gamma)^T \Omega_\gamma^{-1}(\tilde{\beta}_\gamma - b_\gamma)$. The distribution for $p(\gamma|\alpha, y)$ can be shown to be

(11) $\quad\quad\quad\quad p(\gamma|y,\alpha) \propto \dfrac{|\Omega_\gamma^{-1}|^{-1/2}}{|V_\gamma^{-1}|^{-1/2}} \tilde{S}^{-(df+n)/2}.$

Let $|\gamma|$ denote the number of included components. Under Zellner's g-prior it is easy to see that

$$\frac{|\Omega_\gamma^{-1}|}{|V_\gamma|} = \left(\frac{\kappa/n}{1+\kappa/n}\right)^{|\gamma|}$$

is decreasing in $|\gamma|$. It is true in general that $|\Omega_\gamma^{-1}| \leq |\Omega_\gamma^{-1} + X^T X_\gamma|$, which implies that $p(\gamma|y, \alpha)$ prefers models with few predictors and small residual variation.

Equation (11) can be used in a Gibbs sampling algorithm that draws each γ_i given γ_{-i} (the elements of γ other than γ_i). Each full conditional distribution is proportional to equation (11), and γ_i can only assume two possible values. Notice that $p(\gamma|y, \alpha)$ only requires matrix computations for those variables that are actually included in the model. Thus if the model is sparse, the Gibbs sampler involves many inexpensive decompositions of small matrices, which makes SSVS computationally tractable even for problems with a relatively large number of predictors.

References

Arola, Concha, and Enrique Galan. 2012. "Tracking the Future on the Web: Construction of Leading Indicators Using Internet Searches." Technical Report, Bank of Spain. http://www.bde.es/webbde/SES/Secciones/Publicaciones/Publicaciones Seriadas/DocumentosOcasionales/12/Fich/do1203e.pdf.

Brodersen, Kay, Fabian Gallusser, Jim Koehler, Nicolas Remy, and Steven L. Scott. 2013. "Inferring Causal Impact Using Bayesian Structural Time-series Models." Technical Report, Google, Inc. http://research.google.com/pubs/pub41854.html.

Carrière-Swallow, Yan, and Felipe Labbé. 2011. "Nowcasting with Google Trends in an Emerging Market." *Journal of Forecasting* 32 (4): 289–98. doi: 10.1002/for.1252.

Carter, Chris K., and Robert Kohn. 1994. "On Gibbs Sampling for State Space Models." *Biometrika* 81 (3): 541–53.

Castle, Jennifer L., Nicholas W. P. Fawcett, and David F. Hendry. 2010. "Evaluating Automatic Model Selection." Technical Report no. 474, Department of Economics, University of Oxford. http://economics.ouls.ox.ac.uk/14734/1/paper474.pdf.

Castle, Jennifer L., Xiaochuan Qin, and W. Robert Reed. 2009. "How to Pick the Best Regression Equation: A Review and Comparison of Model Selection Algorithms." Technical Report no. 13/2009, Department of Economics, University of Canterbury. http://www.econ.canterbury.ac.nz/RePEc/cbt/econwp/0913.pdf.

Chipman, Hugh, Edward I. George, Robert E. McCulloch, Merlise Clyde, Dean P. Foster, and Rober A. Stine. 2001. "The Practical Implementation of Bayesian Model Selection." In *Lecture Notes-Monograph Series*, vol. 38, 65–134. Beachwood, OH: Institute of Mathematical Statistics.

Choi, Hyunyoung, and Paul Liu. 2011. "Reading Tea Leaves in the Tourism Industry: A Case Study in the Gulf Oil Spill. Technical Report, Google, Inc. http://www.google.com/url?q=http%3A%2F%2Fwww.google.com%2Fgoogleblogs%2Fpdfs%2Fgoogle_gulf_tourism_march2011.pdf.

Choi, Hyunyoung, and Hal Varian. 2009a. "Predicting Initial Claims for Unemployment Insurance Using Google Trends." Technical report, Google, Inc. http://research.google.com/archive/papers/initialclaimsUS.pdf.

———. 2009b. "Predicting the Present with Google Trends." Technical report, Google, Inc. http://google.com/googleblogs/pdfs/google_predicting_the_present.pdf.

———. 2011. "Using Search Engine Data for Nowcasting–An Illustration." In *Actes des Rencontrees Économiques*, pages 535–38. Recontres Économiques d'Aix-en-Provence, Le Cercle des économistes. Aix-en-Provence, France. http://www.lecercledeseconomistes.asso.fr/IMG/pdf/Actes_Rencontres_Economiques_d_Aix-en-Provence_2011.pdf.

———. 2012. "Predicting the Present with Google Trends." *Economic Record* 88, 2–9. http://onlinelibrary.wiley.com/doi/10.1111/j.1475-4932.2012.00809.x/pdf.

de Jong, Piet, and Neil Shepard. 1995. "The Simulation Smoother for Time Series Models." *Biometrika*, 82 (2): 339–50.

Durbin, James, and Siem Jan Koopman. 2001. *Time Series Analysis by State Space Methods*. Oxford: Oxford University Press.

———. 2002. "A Simple and Efficient Simulation Smoother for State Space Time Series Analysis." *Biometrika* 89 (3): 603–16.

Frühwirth-Schnatter, Sylvia. 1994. "Data Augmentation and Dynamic Linear Models. *Journal of Time Series Analysis* 15 (2): 183–202.

Gelman, Andrew, John B. Carlin, Hal S. Stern, and Donald B. Rubin. 2002. *Bayesian Data Analysis*, 2nd ed. Boca Raton, FL: Chapman and Hall/CRC.

George, Edward I., and Robert E. McCulloch. 1997. "Approaches for Bayesian Variable Selection." *Statistica Sinica* 7: 339–73. http://www3.stat.sinica.edu.tw/statistica/oldpdf/A7n26.pdf.

Ghosh, Joyee, and Merlise A. Clyde. 2011. "Rao-Blackwellization for Bayesian Variable Selection and Model Averaging in Linear and Binary Regression: A Novel Data Augmentation Approach." *Journal of the American Statistical Association* 106 (495): 1041–52.

Harvey, Andrew. 1991. *Forecasting, Structural Time Series Models and the Kalman Filter*. Cambridge: Cambridge University Press.

Hastie, Trevor, Robert Tibshirani, and Jerome Friedman. 2009. *The Elements of Statistical Learning*, 2nd ed. New York: Springer Science+Business Media.

Hellerstein, Rebecca, and Menno Middeldorp. 2012. "Forecasting with Internet Search Data." Liberty Street Economics Blog of the Federal Reserve Bank of New York, January 4. http://libertystreeteconomics.newyorkfed.org/2012/01/forecasting-with-internet-search-data.html.

Madigan, David M., and Adrian E. Raftery. 1994. "Model Selection and Accounting for Model Uncertainty in Graphical Models Using Occam's Window. *Journal of the American Statistical Association* 89:1335–46.

McLaren, Nick, and Rachana Shanbhoge. 2011. "Using Internet Search Data as Economic Indicators." Bank of England Quarterly Bulletin, June. http://www.bankofengland.co.uk/publications/quarterlybulletin/qb110206.pdf.

Petris, Giovanni, Sonia Petrone, and Patrizia Campagnoli. 2009. *Dynamic Linear Models with R*. New York: Springer Science+Business Media.

Rue, Håvard. 2001. "Fast Sampling of Gaussian Markov Random Fields." *Journal of the Royal Statistical Society*: Series B (Statistical Methodology) 63 (2): 325–38.

Scott, Steven L., and Hal R. Varian. 2014. "Predicting the Present with Bayesian Structural Time Series." *International Journal of Mathematical Modelling and Numerical Optimisation* 5 (1/2): 4–23.

Stock, James. and Mark Watson. 2010. "Dynamic Factor Models." In *Oxford Handbook of Economic Forecasting*, edited by M. Clements and D. Hendry. Oxford: Oxford University Press.

Suhoy, Tanya. 2009. "Query Indices and a 2008 Downturn: Israeli Data." Technical Report, Bank of Israel. http://www.bankisrael.gov.il/deptdata/mehkar/papers/dp0906e.pdf.

Varian, Hal R. 2010. "Computer Mediated Transactions." *American Economic Review Papers & Proceedings* 100 (2): 1–10.

———. 2014. "Big Data: New Tricks for Econometrics." *Journal of Economic Perspectives* 28 (2): 3–28.

Volinksy, Chris. 2012. "Bayesian Model Averaging Home Page." Technical Report, Bell Labs. http://www2.research.att.com/~volinsky/bma.html.

5 Searching for Physical and Digital Media
The Evolution of Platforms for Finding Books

Michael R. Baye, Babur De los Santos, and Matthijs R. Wildenbeest

5.1 Introduction

The Internet has had a profound impact on the way people shop; online sales in the United States were $213 billion in 2012, accounting for 8 percent of all retail sales.[1] The Internet and digitization have had an even greater impact on sales of media products, thanks in part to changes in the way people search for, acquire, and consume these products. Online sales of books accounted for about 44 percent of all US book sales in 2012, with e-books accounting for 11 percent of total book sales.[2] Digital sales of music accounted for over half of the industry's 2012 total sales.[3]

This chapter focuses on how the Internet and digitization are changing the way consumers obtain information about media products such as books, music, and movies. Less than two decades ago, a consumer looking for a

---

Michael R. Baye is the Bert Elwert Professor of Business and a professor of business economics and public policy at the Kelley School of Business, Indiana University. Babur De los Santos is assistant professor of business economics and public policy at the Kelley School of Business, Indiana University. Matthijs R. Wildenbeest is associate professor of business economics and public policy at the Kelley School of Business, Indiana University.

We thank two anonymous referees, as well as Avi Goldfarb, Shane Greenstein, Marc Rysman, Catherine Tucker, Hal Varian, and seminar participants at the NBER Economics of Digitization conference for valuable comments. We also thank Susan Kayser, I. K. Kim, Joowon Kim, Yoojin Lee, and Sarah Zeng for research assistance. Funding for the data and research assistance related to this research was made possible by a grant from Google to Indiana University. The views expressed in this chapter are those of the authors and do not necessarily reflect the views of Indiana University or Google. For acknowledgments, sources of research support, and disclosure of the authors' material financial relationships, if any, please see http://www.nber.org/chapters/c12989.ack.

1. Figures from Forrester Research, March 2013.
2. Figures from *Publishers Weekly*, May 2013.
3. Figures from Nielsen, January 2013.

book, CD, or DVD had to spend considerable time searching among sellers of these physical products. Given search technologies at the time (e.g., using a telephone to call different sellers or traveling from one physical store to another), the typical consumer limited purchase decisions to retailers proximate to his or her domicile. The Internet and digitization have reduced consumers' costs of obtaining information, thus making it easier for consumers to identify and purchase media that best match their preferences.

Leading media platforms (e.g., Netflix, Amazon, and iTunes) now provide users with recommendations for specific media titles based on sophisticated algorithms that account for a given user's preferences as well as the ratings provided by other users. Consumers also receive recommendations through social networks such as Facebook; "friends" can indicate whether they "liked" a particular song, movie, or book. Many of these recommendation systems operate in real-time and use purchase patterns of consumers with similar profiles to identify products consumers would be otherwise unaware of.

Additionally, advances in search technologies have made it easier for consumers to directly access information that is relevant for their purchase decisions. Consumers can easily search for product information by using a general search engine (e.g., Google), a price comparison site (e.g., Book-Finder), as well as by navigating to a specific retailer's site and conducting a search on its platform (e.g., Amazon and iTunes). These changes in search technologies allow consumers to find a greater breadth of products and make the long tail more accessible; it is now easier to find rare and obscure books, music, and movies. And thanks to digitization, consumers can now view samples of book pages, listen to sample music tracks, and watch scenes from movies through a plethora of devices connected to the Internet. In short, finding the "right" product now takes less effort, and it is easier to compare the prices different sellers charge for that product.

This chapter is motivated by more recent changes in the way consumers search for media products. Until recently, most online product searches for media were conducted using browser-based platforms. Increasingly, however, searches for digital media take place on closed platforms that sell music and video content (e.g., iTunes) or books (e.g., the Amazon Kindle and Barnes & Noble Nook). This shift is more mature in the music industry; digital content accounted for 37 percent of music sales in 2012—more than three times the share of digital books among total book sales.

Because digital books are still in their infancy, the remainder of this chapter focuses on the impact of the Internet and digitization on the book industry. Our goal is to provide readers with a glimpse of how searches for books are likely to evolve over the next decade and to highlight some of the challenges and questions that researchers working in this area are likely to encounter in the years to come. Nonetheless, many of the issues that we discuss are relevant for media such as music and videos, as well as nonmedia products that consumers may search for and purchase online. We highlight a number of data limitations and technical challenges associated with identifying product and product-related searches on browser-based platforms (e.g., search engines, price comparison sites, and retail websites), as well as closed systems (e.g., applications, or apps, on smartphones and tablets such as the iPad, and platforms such as the Kindle and Nook). Finally, we provide some preliminary evidence that searchers are shifting toward new and evolving search platforms and away from browser-based platforms (such as search engines) to find books.

As alluded to above, the book industry is a useful one to examine because it has already felt significant changes as a result of the Internet and is likely to experience additional changes over the next decade as a result of digitization. Even though e-books are still in their infancy, this technology allows consumers to locate, purchase, and read books virtually anywhere. The challenge for researchers over the next decade is that this activity increasingly occurs on closed systems where search activity is not readily observable by those "outside" of the platform.

Our chapter is related to a vast literature on consumer search behavior that began with Stigler's (1961) seminal article on the economics of information. Subsequent literature has focused on explaining price dispersion as an equilibrium phenomenon—particularly in online markets where informational frictions are very modest.[4] The more recent literature is decidedly empirical and examines how industry characteristics, such as search costs, impact levels of price dispersion. For instance, at the beginning of the millennium a large number of studies examined the effects of the Internet on prices and price dispersion.[5] Several of these studies focused specifically on the online book industry. Clay, Krishnan, and Wolff (2001) examined prices at online bookstores and found that heightened competition among sellers led to lower prices and less price dispersion. Moreover, they established heterogeneity in firm-level behavior. Brynjolfsson, Hu, and Smith (2003) quantify the economic impact of increased variety at online bookstores (and the ability of consumers to identify books in the long tail). Their estimates indicate that online markets for books increased consumer welfare by as much as $1 billion for the year 2000. Chevalier and Goolsbee (2003) show how to use sales rank data to obtain elasticity estimates for Amazon and Barnes & Noble, and find that demand is much more price elastic for Barnes & Noble than Amazon. Chevalier and Mayzlin (2006) study the effect of consumer reviews on sales at amazon.com and barnesandnoble.com. Hong and Shum (2006) develop techniques to estimate search costs using only price data and apply their methods to books sold online. Forman, Ghose,

---

4. See Baye, Morgan, and Scholten (2006) for a survey.
5. See Baye, De los Santos, and Wildenbeest (2013) for an overview of the evolution of product search in both offline and online markets.

and Goldfarb (2009) provide powerful evidence that online and offline markets for books are linked: when a physical book store opens, consumers near the area purchase fewer books online. De los Santos (2012) and De los Santos, Hortaçsu, and Wildenbeest (2012) use data on browsing behavior and book purchases to estimate search costs.

The remainder of this chapter is organized as follows. The next section provides a brief overview of the book industry and highlights some of the more important changes that have occurred over the past twenty years. Section 5.3 provides a data-driven look at how consumers use different browser-based platforms (such as websites of booksellers, price comparison sites, and search engines) to locate books and booksellers. Section 5.4 investigates how search intensity changes throughout the life cycle of a book and provides preliminary evidence that searches for book titles on general search engines are beginning to decline. Specifically, consumers appear to be shifting away from general search engines and are increasingly using retailer sites and closed systems to find books. Section 5.5 provides a look at differences in the prices of digital and physical books. It also examines how these prices evolved before, during, and after the Antitrust Division of the Department of Justice filed suit against Apple and book publishers regarding their use of agency contracts. We conclude in section 5.6 by briefly describing several additional agenda items for research programs.

5.2 Overview of the Book Industry and Description of Data Sets

The book industry has seen many changes throughout the past twenty years. The most significant change, to date, has been the move from selling physical books in traditional brick-and-mortar bookstores to selling physical books online. Books were one of the first products that were successfully sold online. One of the earliest and largest online retailers, Amazon, started as an online bookstore in July 1995. Barnesandnoble.com was launched in May 1997. Many startups followed, and existing brick-and-mortar bookstores began creating an online presence. Most of these online bookstores (retailers such as 1bookstreet, A1books, and Fatbrain) no longer exist; many went bankrupt during the collapse of the Internet bubble shortly after the new millennium began. Borders, which was one of the largest brick-and-mortar bookstores in the United States, went bankrupt in 2011. Today, the retail book industry consists of Amazon, Barnes & Noble, and smaller bookstores as well as mass merchants (such as Walmart), which typically have thinner offerings of titles.

A more recent change in the book industry is the shift toward electronic books, or e-books. Although e-books have been around since at least 1971, when Michael Hart made the Declaration of Independence electronically available as part of Project Gutenberg, the release of the Sony LIBRIé e-book reader in 2004 in Japan (the United States followed in 2006 with

Table 5.1   US print and e-book sales, 2006–2009

	Trade print		E-books		Total
Year	($ in millions)	(%)	($ in millions)	(%)	($ in millions)
2006	11,123	99.5	54	0.5	11,177
2007	11,384	99.4	67	0.6	11,451
2008	10,831	99.0	113	1.0	10,944
2009	10,711	97.2	313	2.8	11,024

Source: Mintel/American Association of Publishers. E-book sales exclude educational and professional books.

the release of the Sony PRS-500) marked the beginning of the recent surge in popularity of e-books.[6] The Sony LIBRIé was the first commercially available device to use E Ink technology, which dramatically improved the reading experience and required less battery power than existing e-readers at the time. Amazon released its E Ink technology-based Kindle in November 2007. Barnes & Noble followed in November 2009 with the release of the Nook. At the end of June 2012, Amazon led the market for devices used for reading e-books, with an overall market share of 55 percent (with its Kindle and Kindle Fire), followed by Nook (14 percent). Today, Sony's e-book readers have 1 percent of the market.[7] The definition of an e-reader is increasingly blurred by the presence of devices such as tablets, smartphones, desktops, and laptops with applications for reading e-books. Indeed, after having seen dramatic growth since 2006, the sales of traditional e-readers are expected to decline in 2012, with consumers shifting toward tablets.[8]

The sales of e-books have grown alongside the increasing popularity of e-readers. By July 2010, Amazon was selling more Kindle books than hardcover books, and since April 2011 it is selling more Kindle books than hardcover and paperback books combined (excluding free e-books).[9] However, as shown in table 5.1, e-books accounted for a very modest share of overall industry sales between 2006 and 2009. Between 2009 and 2012, however, sales of e-books grew from 2.8 percent to 11 percent of total industry sales.

Most e-readers support the open ePub format (Amazon's Kindle, which supports the proprietary AZW format, is a notable exception). In theory, this means consumers can buy an e-book at one of the bookstores that supports the ePub format and read it on a different e-reader. However, bookstores use Digital Rights Management (DRM) to protect the content of the e-books,

6. See Manley and Holley (2012) for an overview of the history of e-books.
7. Estimates from Bowker Market Research.
8. See http://news.cnet.com/8301–1035_3–57558710–94/rip-e-book-readers-rise-of-tablets-drives-e-reader-drop/.
9. See http://phx.corporate-ir.net/phoenix.zhtml?c=176060&p=irol-newsArticle&ID=1565581.

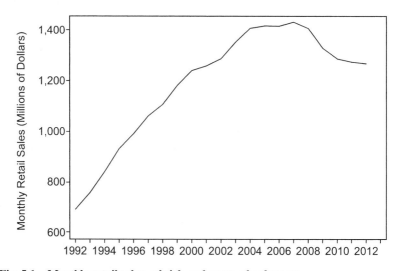

Fig. 5.1 Monthly retail sales at brick-and-mortar bookstores
Source: Monthly Retail Trade Survey for NAICS 451211 (bookstores), US Census Bureau.

and different bookstores do not necessarily use the same DRM standard. Even though there are ways to get around this (for instance, by stripping the DRM), for most consumers this is difficult to do. This means that in practice the e-book market has many characteristics of a two-sided market, with publishers on one side of the market, readers on the other side, and bookstores and e-readers as intermediaries.[10]

The rise of e-books is likely to significantly impact the way consumers search for books. Buyers of e-books are less likely to use web browsers to find and purchase books, as it is often more convenient to search within the device that is used to read e-books. Moreover, the lack of interchangeability due to DRM makes it less beneficial for consumers to compare prices across bookstores or platforms, resulting in fewer retailers being visited. Unfortunately, we do not observe consumer search patterns within most of the (closed) platforms, and future researchers are likely to increasingly experience this problem not only for searches for books, but searches for any product that take place through a closed device or mobile device app. Our challenge here is to attempt to tease out—from available data on browser-based searches—evidence of shifts toward searches on platforms or devices for which search data are unavailable. Thus, the remainder of this chapter focuses exclusively on browser-based searches.

These developments—the move toward selling books online as well as the transition to e-books—have significantly impacted the sales of books at traditional brick-and-mortar stores. Figure 5.1 shows that average

---

10. See Rysman (2009) for a discussion of the economics of two-sided markets.

Table 5.2 Revenue of leading bookstores, 2005–2009

	Revenue ($ in millions)					Change (%)
	2005	2006	2007	2008	2009	
Bookstore chains						
Barnes & Noble	5,103	5,261	5,411	5,122	5,596	9.7
Borders	4,031	4,063	3,775	3,242	2,791	–30.8
Books-A-Million	504	521	536	515	509	1.0
Online bookstores						
Amazon.com	3,046	3,582	4,630	5,350	5,964	95.8
Barnesandnoble.com	440	433	477	466	525	19.4
Borders.com	—	—	—	46	60	—
Booksamillion.com	28	26	27	25	24	–13.8

Source: Simba information, from company reports. Figures for Amazon.com are for US books, music, and video/DVD segment only. Until 2008 Borders.com was powered by Amazon.com.

monthly sales at brick-and-mortar bookstores roughly doubled between 1992 and 2007. Since 2007, however, sales at traditional bookstores have been in decline. This decline in the sales of physical books coincides with two events, making it difficult to separately identify the cause of the decline. One event was a recession, which according to the National Bureau of Economic Research (NBER) started in December 2007 and ended in June 2009. The other event was Amazon's introduction of the Kindle e-book reader in November 2007. While we view the cause of this decline as an interesting and open question, the data in table 5.2 suggest that the post-2007 decline in sales at traditional bookstores may, in part, be due to a shift toward e-books and the online channel more generally.

The analysis in the remainder of this chapter relies on four different data sets. The first data set is assembled using data from comScore Search Planner and contains information on the most popular search terms that are used at the main general search engines to reach specific websites for the period between February 2010 and February 2013.[11] Search Planner uses the comScore panel, which contains all online browsing activity of around two million US users. Our second data set, comScore qSearch, also uses the comScore panel and contains monthly data (between January 2011 and February 2013) on search volume and search intensity at over 200 online properties.[12] The third data set uses relative search volume data from Google Trends for the period 2004–2013. Our final data set contains prices for printed and

---

11. For a more detailed description of these data, see Baye, De los Santos, and Wildenbeest (2012).
12. For a more detailed description of these data, see Baye, De los Santos, and Wildenbeest (2013).

digital books for a large number of titles sold at the major bookstores for 2012. These data were obtained using a scraper written in Java.[13]
With this brief background, we now turn to search.

5.3 Searching for Books and Booksellers

There are numerous ways consumers can use the Internet to search for books or a bookseller. Consumers can use a general search engine such as Google, Yahoo, or Bing to search for a specific book title, author name, or other book-related search term. When using a search engine, search results typically appear as links that can be clicked, which redirect the user to a specific (often external) website. Most of the general search engines display both paid and nonpaid (organic) results; paid results typically appear on top of the search results page as well as on the side.

An alternative way to search is by using a price comparison site to identify sellers of a particular book. Price comparison sites are intermediaries that provide consumers with price information as well as other product information.[14] Most price comparison sites are free for consumers to use, while retailers pay fees. Typically, these fees are paid each time a searcher clicks a link at the price comparison site that directs the user to the retailer's site. Most comparison sites allow users to either browse or use a search box to search. Consumers searching for books can choose among many different comparison sites, ranging from general price comparison sites such as Nextag and Bing Shopper to book-specific comparison sites such as BooksPrice or BookFinder. The more book-oriented price comparison sites typically allow users to search by ISBN as well as title or author name.

A third option is to go directly to a bookseller's (or other retailer's) website and conduct a search within its site. Most online bookstores allow consumers to search by title, author name, or ISBN. Online bookstores such as Amazon and Barnes & Noble also provide links to bestselling books on their web pages, allowing consumers to explore product offerings without having to use the search box. In addition, suggestions based on previous purchases or items previously viewed are displayed to help consumers find the right book. Some online booksellers also allow third-party sellers to sell books on their websites (e.g., Amazon Marketplace and Barnes & Noble Marketplace), which allows consumers to do a price comparison without having to leave the site.

As we noted earlier, an increasingly attractive fourth option—especially for those searching for e-books—is to conduct a search on a closed device

13. For a more detailed description of these data, see De los Santos and Wildenbeest (2014).
14. See Moraga-González and Wildenbeest (2012) for a discussion on comparison sites and their implications for price competition.

such as Amazon's Kindle or the Barnes & Noble Nook. Recall that these search data are not readily available to researchers.

The remainder of this section examines the relative importance of the first three types of book searches and highlights a number of obstacles that make it difficult to precisely measure the share of book searches that are conducted on different search platforms. Later, we will attempt to use the data that are available to examine whether recent trends in general search engine use suggest that consumers are indeed shifting to closed search platforms, for which detailed search data are presently unavailable.

5.3.1 Book-Related Searches on General Search Engines

We first turn to the issue of measuring the number of book-related searches on the main general search engines (Google, Bing, Yahoo, and Ask). For this we use comScore's Search Planner data, which is based on the browsing activity of two million US users that are part of the comScore panel. As part of this data we observe the most popular search terms used at the main general search engines to reach a specific site. To illustrate the nature of the data, table 5.3 shows the top twenty-five search terms on Google that resulted in organic traffic to Barnes & Noble.[15] The number one search phrase is "barnes and noble," which generated 376,678 clicks to this site. Notice that several other top twenty-five search terms in table 5.3 are variations or misspellings of the site name or URL (e.g., "barnes and nobles," "barnes," "bn," and "www.bn.com"). This suggests that searchers may frequently use general search engines as a shortcut for typing in the URL of the site they wish to visit, and then conduct actual searches for books at the site. Also notice that the list of top twenty-five search terms includes competitors (e.g., "amazon"). Farther down the list we begin seeing terms related to specific books (e.g., the 20th ranked search term is "the vow book").

Table 5.3 also illustrates a weakness of the Search Planner data: for privacy and other reasons, comScore sometimes reports "***" and "name name" rather than the actual search phrase. This is the case for the fourth and sixth ranked search terms in table 5.3, and as a consequence, one cannot precisely determine the nature of these searches. For purposes of the analysis that follows, these terms are ignored. This is not ideal, since these unknown (and hence excluded) searches may refer to an author or ISBN number.

In order to get a better picture of the nature of search terms leading users from search engines to bookstores, we examined the entire list of search terms resulting in traffic to Amazon and Barnes & Noble (2,053 and 180

---

15. In September 2011, Barnes & Noble acquired Borders's intellectual property, including Borders's domain name. Borders.com now redirects to barnesandnoble.com, explaining the relatively large number of Borders's related search terms in table 5.3.

Table 5.3   Top twenty-five search terms on Google leading users to Barnes & Noble

Rank	Search phrase	No. organic clicks
1	barnes and noble	376,678
2	borders bookstore	82,689
3	borders book store	52,006
4	***	27,699
5	barnes and noble locations	21,666
6	name name	20,675
7	barnes and nobles	19,800
8	amazon	19,748
9	barnesandnoble	17,785
10	nook	13,483
11	facebook	10,680
12	barnes & noble	9,900
13	nook tablet	9,775
14	barnes	8,623
15	borders.com	7,465
16	google	7,163
17	bn.com	7,118
18	books	6,923
19	borders	6,382
20	the vow book	6,199
21	name fire	5,143
22	bn	4,819
23	nook color update	4,564
24	gmail	4,383
25	www.bn.com	4,179

Source: comScore Search Planner data from February 2012. Search phrases are ranked by the total number of organic clicks on Google.

search terms, respectively), and grouped them into five categories: (1) site name, which includes the name or URL (including misspellings) of the site; (2) nonbook, which includes products other than books; (3) book, which includes physical as well as e-books; (4) e-reader, which includes searches for e-reader-related hardware or software; and (5) other bookstore, which includes names and URLs of other bookstores (including misspellings). The results are displayed in figure 5.2, panels (a) and (b), and provide a breakdown of the observed search terms consumers entered at the main search engines that resulted in clicks to Amazon and Barnes & Noble, respectively.

Several features of figure 5.2 are worth noting. First, the overwhelming majority of searches at the main search engines leading users to Amazon or Barnes & Noble were navigational searches, that is, search terms that only include the name or URL of the retailer. This means that most of the traffic Amazon and Barnes & Noble receive from the main search engines is from consumers using search engines instead of the address bar to navigate. Pre-

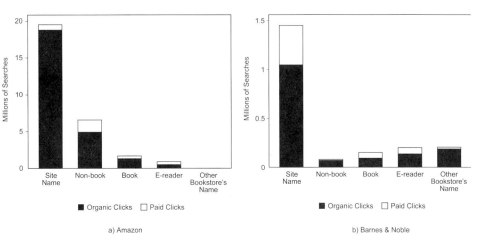

Fig. 5.2 Search terms in main search engines leading users to Amazon and Barnes & Noble
Source: comScore Search Planner, February 2012.

sumably, users conduct specific searches for books once they land on these booksellers' sites.

Second, notice in figure 5.2, panel (a), that searches that are not book related generate more traffic to Amazon than book-related searches. This is consistent with the fact that Amazon is now a mass merchant that sells many products other than books. Figure 5.2, panel (b), shows that book-related search terms generate far more traffic to Barnes & Noble than search terms that are not book related. This is consistent with the fact that Barnes & Noble specializes in books. Finally, figure 5.2 reveals that searches for e-readers and other bookstores are more important for Barnes & Noble than for Amazon in generating traffic to its site. The key takeaway from figure 5.2 is that navigational searches account for much of the traffic that Amazon and Barnes & Noble obtain from general search engines.

We conclude this section with a caveat that is related to another drawback of the Search Planner data used in our analysis: comScore reports search terms leading users to a particular site only if the number of clicks exceeds a certain threshold. Thus, while we do observe the most popular search terms generating traffic to a specific bookstore, we do not observe the more obscure searches taking place on general search engines. For instance, for Amazon we only observe the search terms corresponding to 24 percent of total click volume. Brynjolfsson, Hu, and Simester (2011) have shown that Internet markets have increased the importance of niche markets in terms of sales. This long-tail phenomenon suggests that a portion of the unobserved searches may include searches for book titles and other more obscure book-

Table 5.4   Percentage of incoming visits to bookstores from search engines and other platforms

	Amazon (%)	Barnes & Noble (%)	eCampus (%)	Powell's (%)	Books-A-Million (%)
Direct logins	27.8	16.0	1.9	3.0	10.0
Google	40.2	31.7	17.9	20.8	45.9
Yahoo	5.9	4.9	6.3	3.5	1.9
Bing	15.1	5.8	1.3	2.9	0.0
Other search	2.9	3.3	0.0	0.0	1.9
Other bookstores	3.9	38.3	72.6	69.9	40.4
Price comparison	4.1	0.1	0.0	0.0	0.0

Source: comScore Search Planner data from August 2012.

related search terms. If this is the case, figure 5.2 may understate the relative importance of book-related searches on search engines. The importance of the long tail for book sales and searches remains an open question.

5.3.2   Incoming and Outgoing Traffic

Search engines are not the only way consumers reach a bookseller's site. Consumers may directly visit the site, be referred from another site (such as a price comparison site), and so on. Likewise, consumers that visit a bookseller's site may simply be gathering information before visiting another site to compare prices or make a purchase. This section examines these patterns of incoming and outgoing traffic.

How Searchers Reach Booksellers

To better understand how searchers actually reach the websites of different online booksellers, we analyze incoming traffic to five of the leading online bookstores in the United States (Amazon, Barnes & Noble, Books-A-Million, eCampus, and Powell's). In addition to observing the most popular search terms for these retailers, comScore's Search Planner data allows us to observe which sites get clicks for specific searches conducted at the main search engines as well as the source of incoming and the destination of outgoing traffic for each site.

The results summarized in table 5.4 show the percentages of visitors to these online bookstores in August 2012, categorized by the most important referring sites or platforms. For example, 27.8 percent of Amazon's traffic is due to direct logins, that is, consumers directly navigating to its site. Amazon received 40.2 percent of its traffic through Google, 5.9 percent through Yahoo, and 15.1 percent through Bing. As shown in figure 5.2, panel (a), most of this traffic stemmed from navigational searches, which are effectively a shortcut for direct logins. Finally, 3.9 percent of Amazon's traffic originated at another bookstore while 4.1 percent came from a price comparison site.

Table 5.5 Percentage of outgoing visits from bookstores to search engines and other platforms

	Amazon (%)	Barnes & Noble (%)	eCampus (%)	Powell's (%)	Books-A-Million (%)
Logoff	43.0	31.4	5.7	29.8	27.9
Google	28.4	21.5	11.1	44.8	21.1
Yahoo	3.7	2.8	1.6	2.0	0.0
Bing	13.7	3.4	2.1	8.5	7.5
Other search	4.2	1.9	0.0	0.0	0.0
Other bookstores	4.2	38.7	79.5	14.8	43.5
Price comparison	2.9	0.3	0.0	0.0	0.0

Source: comScore Search Planner data from August 2012.

More broadly, table 5.4 shows that there is considerable heterogeneity in the sources of traffic for different booksellers. Amazon and Barnes & Noble receive much more traffic through direct logins than eCampus, Powell's, and Books-A-Million. This may stem from the fact that Amazon and Barnes & Noble are better-known brands; see Baye, De los Santos, and Wildenbeest (forthcoming). Powell's and Books-A-Million rely more heavily on general search engines to receive traffic, while referrals from other bookstores are relatively important for Barnes & Noble, eCampus, and Books-A-Million.[16] Finally, Amazon receives a far greater share of its traffic from price comparison sites than do the other booksellers.

What Searchers Do After Visiting a Bookseller

To identify what happens after having visited an online bookseller, we analyze the outgoing traffic from the bookstores using comScore's Search Planner data. The results are summarized in table 5.5, using data from August 2012 for Amazon, Barnes & Noble, eCampus, Powell's, and Books-A-Million.

First, note that a searcher that terminates his or her search activity after visiting a bookseller is more likely to have consummated a purchase than is a searcher that does not terminate but instead visits another bookseller or a price comparison site. Table 5.5 shows that 43 percent of users that visited Amazon terminated their search by logging off; this share is much lower for the other bookstores, especially for eCampus, which was 5.7 percent.

Second, note that consumers that choose to leave one bookstore and visit another bookstore may be doing so because the book was not in stock or was

---

16. The other bookstores category includes abebooks.com, alibris.com, amazon.com, audible.com, barnesandnoble.com, biggerbooks.com, bkstr.com, bncollege.com, bookbyte.com, booksamillion.com, campusbookrentals.com, christianbook.com, ebooks.com, ecampus.com, half.com, kobobooks.com, powells.com, and textbooks.com.

priced above their reservation price. Table 5.5 shows that only 4.2 percent of visitors to Amazon chose to visit another bookstore after searching there. This is significantly lower than for the other bookstores in our sample; for example, 79.5 percent of eCampus visitors chose to search another bookstore immediately after visiting the site.

Finally, consumers may visit a bookseller with the intent of free riding on the general information, reviews, or recommendations it provides, and then leave the bookseller's site to search for the best available price. As shown in table 5.5, 2.9 percent of Amazon visitors directly visit a price comparison site after viewing pages at Amazon. Visits to price comparison sites comprise a negligible share of outgoing traffic for the other booksellers in our sample.

5.3.3 Search Activity on Book-Oriented Platforms

As discussed earlier, general search engines are not the only way consumers can search for books. Consumers can search the websites of booksellers and other retailers, as well price comparison sites. In light of the fact that major booksellers receive a considerable share of their traffic from direct logins and navigational searches, one would expect the number of searches on these sites to be substantial. Unfortunately, comScore does not provide information about the keywords used for searches "inside" these retailers. Nonetheless, limited information is available through the qSearch database.

The qSearch data are based on the comScore panel, which contains all of the browsing activity of about two million users in the United States. It contains monthly data on searches conducted by consumers on the Internet.[17] These searches include searches through traditional search boxes as well as toolbars and widgets. The qSearch database includes the actual search volume and search intensity at over 200 online properties, including Amazon, Barnes & Noble, and several other book-oriented platforms. Unlike Search Planner, the data indicate the total number of searches on each site rather than a breakdown of searches by keyword. Thus, one cannot distinguish between searches for books versus other products with the qSearch data.

Table 5.6 provides a snapshot (February 2012) of the total number of searches conducted on the five largest book-oriented sites that are tracked by the qSearch database. Amazon processed the majority of searches among the bookstores, having almost ten times as many searches as the number two bookstore, Barnes & Noble. In terms of total searches, a smaller number of searches were conducted on the price comparison site (BookFinder). The

---

17. According to comScore's qSearch documentation, a search is defined as: (1) a user interaction where the user is presented with a search result page that contains results that match the consumer's search intent; (2) the search result page allows the user to refine or change the search parameters; and (3) the search can be initiated from a drop down menu or by clicking a link, as long as the first two rules are satisfied.

Table 5.6   Number of searches on book-oriented platforms

	Searches (×1,000)	Searches (%)	Search visits (×1,000)	Search visits (%)	Searches per search visit
Bookstores					
Amazon	326,658	26.22	150,643	26.22	2.17
Barnes & Noble	37,205	2.99	10,620	2.99	3.50
AbeBooks	1,659	0.13	561	0.13	2.96
Other book sites					
Google Book Search	10,124	0.81	4,719	0.81	2.15
Price comparison sites					
BookFinder	692	0.06	220	0.06	3.15

Source: comScore qSearch, February 2012.

level of search activity is even more skewed toward Amazon when one measures searches using search visits.[18]

Figure 5.3 shows the evolution of searches between January 2011 and February 2013 for these book-oriented qSearch properties. The graph shows that, especially for Amazon and Barnes & Noble, there is seasonality in searches during the holiday shopping season, with searches increasing sharply near the end of the calendar year. Searches at Barnes & Noble appear to have peaked near the end of 2011, while searches at Amazon have generally increased, with the exception of the most recent few months.

We emphasize that the qSearch data displayed in figure 5.3 does not indicate how many of the searches at these book-oriented platforms are, in fact, book related. While this is not so much an issue for sites that specialize in books (such as Barnes & Noble, BookFinder, and Google Book Search), it is clearly an issue for Amazon. While Amazon began its life as an online bookstore, it has evolved into a mass merchant where over 53 percent of its 2009 revenues derived from products outside the book category. And today, Amazon is itself a platform that services thousands of Amazon Marketplace sellers. Similarly, these data do not permit us to measure book-related searches at retailers such as Walmart or on platforms such as eBay (which received more than twice as many searches as Amazon in February 2012).

5.4 The Dynamics of Book-Related Searches

This section provides a look at how searches for books on search engines evolve during a window around the release date of the book and also explores

---

18. According to comScore's qSearch documentation, a search visit is a session in which a user conducted one or more searches. If searches are conducted at different points during the day, with more than thirty minutes of search inactivity at the site, they count as multiple search visits.

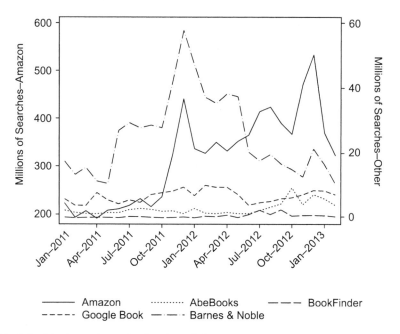

Fig. 5.3 Total searches at book-oriented sites
Source: comScore qSearch, January 2011–February 2013.
Note: Amazon scaled on left, all others on right.

how the shifts toward other platforms have impacted book-related searches at the main search engines.

5.4.1 Combining Data from comScore and Google Trends

Since our comScore database only contains information about searches for specific book-related keywords on a monthly basis for the 2010–2012 period, our strategy is to combine these data with data from Google Trends to create a data set that runs from 2004 through 2013.[19]

For a given search term, Google Trends provides a measure of the number of searches for that term between 2004 and 2013. The measure is relative: the maximum number of searches within the period is normalized to 100. To illustrate, figure 5.4 displays search volume reported by Google Trends for the term "Amazon."[20] The bars represent monthly search "volume," whereas the curve gives the seasonally adjusted trend. The figure shows search volume has been rising for the term "Amazon," with the growth in

---

19. Choi and Varian (2012) describe how Google Trends data can help to predict economic time series of interest. Google Trends data has been used in epidemiology to detect influenza epidemics (Ginsberg et al. 2009) and in economics to predict the unemployment rate (D'Amuri and Marcucci 2010) and inflation (Guzmán 2011).
20. We limit search volume to the United States only.

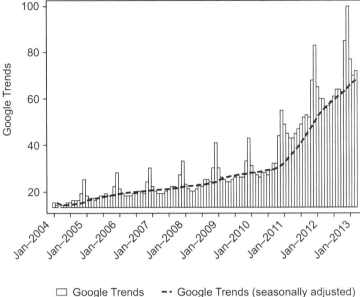

Fig. 5.4 Google Trends for the term "Amazon"
Source: Google Trends, January 2004–March 2013.

search volume accelerating after July 2010. Figure 5.5 displays the relative search volume over time for "Amazon" and "Barnes and Noble" in a single graph. The number of search queries for Barnes & Noble was relatively stable up to 2010, after which searches went up quickly. However, searches at Barnes & Noble peaked near the end of 2011, whereas the search volume for Amazon kept growing.

Since the Google Trends measure of search is relative, the relative position of the two lines in figure 5.5 is uninformative: it would be erroneous to infer that Barnes & Noble had more navigational searches than Amazon for the 2004–2012 period. Our strategy for overcoming this limitation is to use information about the actual number of searches for a given search term in comScore to convert the Google Trends index into historical data on the numbers of searches for that search term.[21]

Figure 5.6 provides one example of the utility of combining Google Trends and comScore data. This graph shows the evolution of searches

---

21. Google Trends allows a comparison of up to five search terms. Nevertheless, the relative search volume of more than five search terms can be obtained by running multiple Google Trends comparisons, with each comparison having at least one search term that is common across all comparisons. Nonetheless, the comScore (or similar) data is still needed to pin down the level of searches. Also notice that searches according to the comScore data by definition lead to a click to a bookstore, whereas a search according to Google Trends may not result in a click.

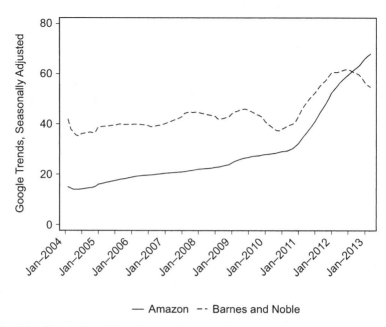

Fig. 5.5 Google Trends for the terms "Amazon" and "Barnes and Noble"
Source: Google Trends, January 2004–March 2013.

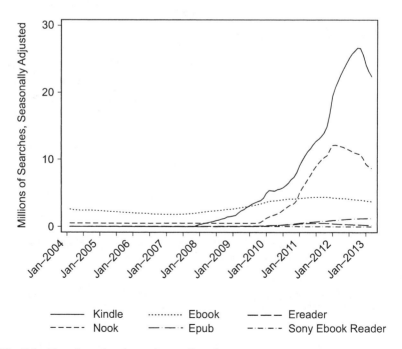

Fig. 5.6 E-reader-related searches on Google
Source: Google Trends and comScore Search Planner.

for six terms related to e-readers: "kindle," "nook," "e-book," "ereader," and "sony ebook reader." By combining the data, we not only obtain a time series dating back to 2004, but the resulting numbers of searches are cardinal so the different graphs may be compared. Figure 5.6 illustrates that searches for "kindle" took off in January 2008, and the number of searches for the Kindle has exceeded that for the Nook every year since. Notice that the recent decline in searches for these two e-readers is consistent with our earlier remarks regarding the projected decline in post-2012 e-reader sales as consumers switch to tablets and other devices.

5.4.2   Searches for Specific Titles

We are now in a position to take a deeper dive into searches for books on search engines and to examine how search patterns are evolving over time. We use the Search Planner data for a sample of 735 books to study how the number of clicks on Google changes throughout a book's life cycle. Our sample includes titles released in every year since 2003, but roughly half of the sample is composed of books released in 2012. The search queries we use to obtain the clicks on Google are the exact titles of the book in our sample. In addition to clicks, we observe book characteristics such as ISBN, list price, publisher, date of publication, format (hardcover or paperback), number of pages, edition (e.g., first or reprint), dimension, and weight. Moreover, for 2012 we have daily observations of a book's price as well as availability at each of the leading online bookstores.[22] For Amazon we also observe a book's customer rating, number of customer reviews, and sales rank. Most books in our sample are first editions; the vast majority are *New York Times* bestsellers that came out during 2011 and 2012.

The Search Planner data has two limitations. The first limitation is that we only observe clicks for the period between February 2010 and February 2013. The second is that we only observe clicks if they exceed a certain threshold. To deal with these two matters, we supplement the Search Planner data with Google Trends data, as discussed above. For each book in our sample we use Google Trends to capture the volume of search queries that users enter into Google when searching for the title of a book.[23] Since Google Trends only gives a relative measure of search volume, we convert the index to actual levels of search volume by setting the maximum value of the index during the period between February 2010 and February 2013 equal to the corresponding clicks according to Search Planner.

Figure 5.7 gives an example for the book *The End of Illness* by David B. Agus, which was released on January 17, 2012. The number of searches on Google for this title is relatively high shortly after release, but within a few months declines to a relatively low level. Also shown in this graph is Ama-

---

22. These are amazon.com, barnesandnoble.com, booksamillion.com, walmart.com, powells.com, and ecampus.com. See section 5.5 for a more detailed description of the price data.

23. We use exact phrases (exact words in quotes), for example, "Gone girl" instead of Gone girl. We limit search volume to the United States only.

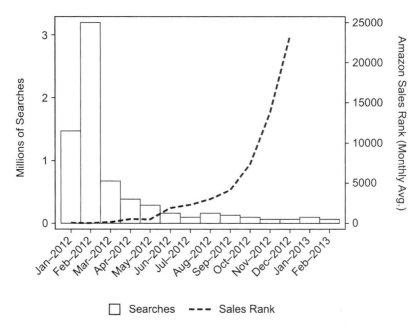

Fig. 5.7 Google searches for *The End of Illness*
Source: comScore Search Planner.

zon's sales rank for this title, which shows a reverse pattern. This illustrates that sales rank is actually inversely related to the number of searches. It is an open question whether this is a result of lags in Amazon's construction of sales rank or whether this means that, during the life cycle of a book, consumers increasingly visit Amazon's site directly to purchase the book rather than using a general search engine.

The pattern for this particular title is fairly representative of the other titles in our sample. In particular, we ran a linear regression of the total number of searches for each book title in our sample on a constant and a set of dummies that represent months since release. The underlying regression results for various specifications are shown in table 5.7. For the specification in column (1), which includes book fixed effects to control for heterogeneity among books, most of the month-since-release coefficients are significantly different from zero at conventional levels. Figure 5.8 plots the predicted values of each of the dummies using the parameter estimates for specification (1). This figure shows that the patterns of search observed around the release window for *The End of Illness* (see figure 5.7) is typical of newly released books: search activity tends to be high in the first few months, but then quickly drops to significantly lower levels.

Column (2) of table 5.7 is a specification that includes book characteristics rather than book fixed effects. Although this reduces the fit of the model and

Table 5.7 Regression results

	(1)		(2)		(3)	
Months before release						
2 months	−0.696	(0.188)***	−0.688	(0.281)**	−0.765	(0.282)***
1 month	−0.734	(0.188)***	−0.732	(0.281)***	−0.771	(0.281)***
Months after release						
1 month	−0.299	(0.188)	−0.297	(0.281)	−0.257	(0.281)
2 months	−0.426	(0.188)**	−0.424	(0.281)	−0.342	(0.282)
3 months	−0.540	(0.188)***	−0.537	(0.281)*	−0.413	(0.282)
4 months	−0.503	(0.188)***	−0.499	(0.281)*	−0.329	(0.284)
5 months	−0.540	(0.191)***	−0.515	(0.285)*	−0.311	(0.288)
6 months	−0.654	(0.195)***	−0.628	(0.291)**	−0.391	(0.296)
7 months	−0.681	(0.199)***	−0.581	(0.297)*	−0.318	(0.303)
8 months	−0.692	(0.202)***	−0.580	(0.301)*	−0.280	(0.308)
9 months	−0.725	(0.205)***	−0.612	(0.306)**	−0.277	(0.315)
10 months	−0.747	(0.209)***	−0.613	(0.312)**	−0.248	(0.323)
11 months	−0.798	(0.216)***	−0.600	(0.321)*	−0.212	(0.333)
12 months	−0.719	(0.221)***	−0.510	(0.328)	−0.095	(0.342)
First edition indicator			−0.813	(0.200)***	−0.820	(0.202)***
Format						
Mass market paperback			1.228	(0.249)***	1.467	(0.255)***
Paperback			0.757	(0.208)***	0.736	(0.208)***
Other			0.256	(0.365)	0.660	(0.377)*
Pages			−0.005	(0.000)***	−0.005	(0.001)***
Weight			0.097	(0.007)***	0.099	(0.007)***
Time index					0.094	(0.024)***
Time index squared					−0.001	(0.000)***
Constant	1.398	(0.133)***	1.049	(0.297)***	−1.344	(0.913)
Book indicators	Yes		No		No	
Publisher indicators	No		No		Yes	
Observations	10,615		10,585		10,585	
R-squared	0.664		0.213		0.214	

Notes: Dependent variable: number of searches for a specific book title. Standard errors in parentheses.
***Significant at the 1 percent level.
**Significant at the 5 percent level.
*Significant at the 10 percent level.

the significance of some of the months-since-release dummies, the magnitude of the coefficients is similar to that in the first specification. Most book characteristic variables have parameter estimates that are significantly different from zero. There is less search for first edition books than for books in later editions. This may stem from the fact that later editions are only published if the book is popular. There are more searches for paperbacks than hardcover books in our sample, and again this may reflect the fact that paperbacks are targeted to the masses and therefore result in more searches. The final column of table 5.7 adds a linear and quadratic time trend to control for possible changes in search behavior between 2004 and 2013. Both

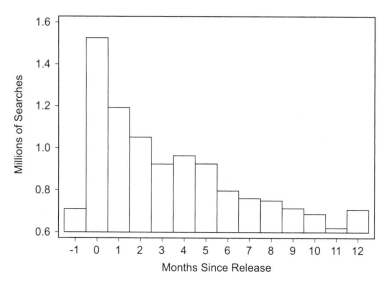

Fig. 5.8 Predicted searches for book titles on Google

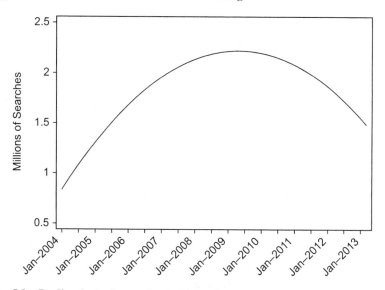

Fig. 5.9 Predicted searches per book title on Google, 2004–2013

coefficients are highly significant, suggesting that (controlling for changes in search behavior around release windows, edition, format, and so on) the number of book searches at search engines is evolving.

To more clearly see the implied evolution of searches for books over time, figure 5.9 plots the number of searches predicted by the model for each year in our sample. This plot shows that searches per book on Google increased between 2003 and 2007, but since then have declined. This predicted pattern is consistent with our view that searchers are shifting away from using general search engines to find books and are increasingly (1) visiting online bookstores (such as Amazon and Barnes & Noble) to conduct searches, and (2) searching within closed systems (e.g., Kindle or Nook) to purchase books. Thus, while we cannot directly measure book-related searches within these alternative search platforms, the observable data from search engines is consistent with this hypothesis.

We conclude by noting that the pattern in figure 5.9 is also consistent with the trend in average monthly retail sales for brick-and-mortar bookstores, as shown in figure 5.1, and may reflect the same structural changes in the book industry that have led to a decline in the sales of physical books at traditional bookstores. For instance, the decline coincides with the increasing popularity of e-readers shown earlier in figure 5.6, the general shift toward e-books, and the rising prominence of Amazon as a platform for searching for books and other products.

5.5 Book Prices

Another open question is how changes in search technologies and behavior have impacted the prices of physical and digital books. A priori, it is not clear how these prices should evolve over time. In the short run, intermediaries may use penetration pricing in an attempt to induce consumers to switch from buying printed books to e-books. Once the market is more mature, and a sufficient number of consumers is locked into a specific platform, firms may find it optimal to increase prices. Sales of physical and digital books are also likely to be related. Hu and Smith (2013) use a natural experiment to analyze the effect of e-book availability on sales of physical books and find that delayed e-book availability results in a large decrease in total e-book sales.

We analyze book prices using a large data set of daily prices collected using a scraper written in Java. The data set contains daily price information throughout 2012 for physical books as well as e-books sold at Amazon, Barnes & Noble, and Books-A-Million, physical books sold at eCampus, Powell's Books, and Walmart, and e-books sold at Kobo and Google. In addition to prices, we observe availability and several book characteristics such as the publisher, format (hardcover or paperback), edition, number of pages, weight, and dimension.

Figure 5.10 shows the kernel estimates of the price densities for hardcover books, paperbacks, and e-books. The prices used are average prices across books within format and across bookstores, so the variation reflects changes over time. E-books are on average less expensive than hardcover books, but slightly more expensive than paperbacks.

The relationship between publishers and retailers complicates the anal-

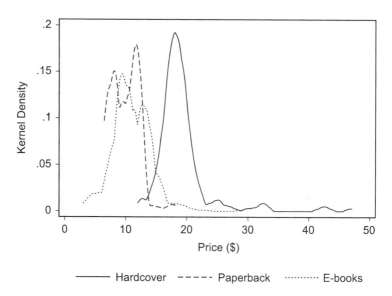

Fig. 5.10 Price distributions for hardcover, paperback, and digital books
Note: Data truncated at $50.

ysis of prices for e-books. Traditionally, books were sold using a wholesale model: a publisher sells a book to a retailer at a wholesale price, which is typically half the list price for the book. The retailer is then free to sell the book at whatever price it wants. Initially this model was used by all players for selling e-books as well. However, to foster e-book sales, Amazon began heavily discounting popular e-books, selling them for $9.99—a price that is below the wholesale price of many physical books. Publishers, fearing that e-books would cannibalize sales of printed books and that consumers would grow accustomed to low e-book prices, were concerned about the low e-book prices. When Apple launched its iBookstore in April 2010, five of the "big six" publishers (HarperCollins, Hachette, Macmillan, Penguin, and Simon & Schuster) adopted Apple's newly developed agency model. Under the agency model the retailer receives a fixed percentage of the book's sale price (typically 30 percent). Moreover, under the agency model, the retail price is no longer set by the retailer but set by the publisher. Other online bookstores reached similar agreements with the publishers. As a reaction to these developments, the Department of Justice sued Apple and the five publishers on April 12, 2012, alleging that they conspired to fix the prices of e-books.

Table 5.8 provides descriptive statistics for the prices of books in our sample. The table makes a distinction between e-books that are sold under the agency model and those that are sold under the wholesale model. Average prices are generally higher for the agency model e-books and show less variation.

Figure 5.11 plots the average prices of paperbacks, e-books sold under

Table 5.8 Descriptive statistics for book prices

Bookstore	Hardcovers Mean ($)	Std. dev.	Paperbacks Mean ($)	Std. dev.	E-books (agency) Mean ($)	Std. dev.	E-books (wholesale) Mean ($)	Std. dev.
Both formats								
Amazon	16.3	5.7	9.9	6.3	11.2	2.7	8.6	7.5
Barnes & Noble	16.8	6.0	10.5	7.1	11.3	2.6	10.2	5.0
Books-A-Million	16.7	6.6	10.2	9.7	11.4	2.5	9.9	4.2
Physical books only								
eCampus	21.9	4.9	10.5	9.0				
Powell's	27.0	7.1	12.9	4.2				
Walmart	16.2	3.6	9.0	7.3				
E-books only								
Kobo					11.1	2.6	11.0	6.6
Google					11.1	3.4	9.8	8.1

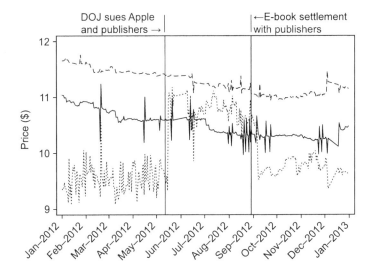

Fig. 5.11 **Average book prices by book format**

the agency model, and e-books sold under the wholesale model across bookstores.[24] Even though the DOJ reached a settlement with three of the publishers in April 2012 (HarperCollins, Hachette, and Macmillan), and as part of the settlement e-book retailers are allowed to discount e-book titles, prices for e-books sold under the wholesale model increased shortly after the

24. Since we do not have sales data, average prices are not weighted by sales.

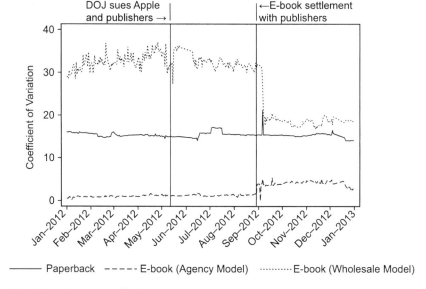

Fig. 5.12 Average coefficient of variation by book format

lawsuit was announced. The steep decline in e-book prices sold under the wholesale model a few months later coincides with the final approval of the settlement between the DOJ and the three publishers, with HarperCollins books starting to be discounted on Amazon soon after (Hachette and Simon & Schuster discounting began in December 2012).

One might wonder whether the evolution of search has impacted the degree of price dispersion for books. One standard measure of dispersion is the coefficient of variation—the ratio of the standard deviation in the prices different sellers charge for a given book divided by the average price sellers charge for that book. Since this measure is homogeneous of degree zero in the level of prices, one can average these coefficients of variation across all books in our sample to obtain a useful summary statistic for the level of price dispersion. Figure 5.12 plots the average coefficient of variation over time for the three book formats in our sample. Notice that the coefficient of variation is highest for e-books sold under the wholesale model, lower for paperback books, and lowest for e-books sold under the agency model. Additionally, note that the coefficient of variation for e-books sold under the wholesale model declined significantly after the e-book settlement, while the coefficient of variation for e-books sold under the agency model increased slightly. In contrast, the coefficient of variation for paperbacks was relatively stable throughout the entire period.

The underlying reason for these changes in prices and levels of price dispersion remains an open question. We note that the two remaining publishers (Macmillan and Penguin) settled in early 2013, so this event is unlikely to be the driver of the patterns observed in figures 5.11 and 5.12.

5.6 Concluding Remarks

Our initial look at the evolution of platforms through which consumers search for, purchase, and read books highlights a number of issues that should be on the agenda of those interested in digital media and other products sold online. There are a variety of different platforms where consumers can search for books, including online bookstores (such as Barnes & Noble), mass merchants (Amazon), and price comparison sites (BookFinder). While data suggest that consumers are increasingly conducting searches on closed systems (such as e-readers) and retailer platforms (such as Amazon), measurement of these trends is difficult. In contrast to these platforms, data on the types of searches conducted on search engines is readily available.

While Amazon and Barnes & Noble get significant numbers of visits from those conducting searches on Google and Bing, most of the observed searches are navigational ones—situations in which users query a search engine as a shortcut for navigating to the site of the bookseller where actual product searches are performed. Navigational searches to these top booksellers have steadily increased since 2004. The number of browser-based searches on book-related platforms such as Amazon, Barnes & Noble, BookFinder, and Google Books is sizable, but it is an open question whether browser-based searches on these platforms will continue to grow. Indeed, our preliminary analysis of searches for book titles on Google suggests a declining trend in book searches since 2007. While these patterns are consistent with shifts toward nonbrowser searches on closed platforms, including smartphone and tablet apps, additional research is required to reach any definitive conclusions.

Another open agenda item is the importance of the long tail for product searches in general, and more specifically for book searches. The search terms corresponding to long-tail searches at the major search engines are not observed in comScore data because of low search volume; we do not observe niche searches, which presumably take place in the long tail. Additional research will be needed to analyze the long tail.

An interesting new area of research has emerged relating to e-books. We have identified several new developments with respect to pricing strategies of publishers and booksellers and have provided some preliminary findings on how some of these developments have influenced book prices. More research will be needed on how different selling formats (e.g., the agency and wholesale models) affect pricing more generally, from both a theoretical and empirical point of view.[25]

Finally, note that we have completely sidestepped the first-order question of what consumers are seeking when they conduct searches for books, digital media, or (more broadly) other products. More bluntly, this chapter

---

25. Johnson (2013) and Abhishek, Jerath, and Zhang (2013) develop theoretical models that are geared toward a comparison of the different selling formats in the book industry.

says nothing about whether consumers are searching for information about the best book to read or information about the best prices available. Future research that unpacks these and other motives for search would be a valuable addition to the literature.

References

Abhishek, Vibhanshu, Kinshuk Jerath, and Z. John Zhang. 2013. "Agency Selling or Reselling? Channel Structures in Electronic Retailing." Working Paper, Carnegie Mellon University.
Baye, Michael R., Babur De los Santos, and Matthijs R. Wildenbeest. 2012. "What's in a Name? Measuring Prominence, and Its Impact on Organic Traffic from Search Engines." Working Paper no. 2012-09, Kelley School of Business, Indiana University. http://dx.doi.org/10.2139/ssrn.2191051.
———. 2013. "The Evolution of Product Search." *Journal of Law, Economics & Policy* 9 (2): 201–21.
———. Forthcoming. "Search Engine Optimization: What Drives Organic Traffic to Retail Sites?" *Journal of Economics and Management Strategy*.
Baye, Michael R., John Morgan, and Patrick Scholten. 2006. "Information, Search, and Price Dispersion." In *Handbook in Economics and Information Systems*, edited by T. Hendershott. Amsterdam: Elsevier.
Brynjolfsson, Erik, Yu (Jeffrey) Hu, and Michael D. Smith. 2003. "Consumer Surplus in the Digital Economy: Estimating the Value of Increased Product Variety at Online Booksellers." *Management Science* 49 (11): 1580–96.
———. 2011. "Goodbye Pareto Principle, Hello Long Tail: The Effect of Search Costs on the Concentration of Product Sales." *Management Science* 57 (8): 1373–86.
Chevalier, Judith, and Austan Goolsbee. 2003. "Measuring Prices and Price Competition Online: Amazon.com and BarnesandNoble.com." *Quantitative Marketing and Economics* 1 (2): 203–22.
Chevalier, Judith A., and Dina Mayzlin. 2006. "The Effect of Word of Mouth on Sales: Online Book Reviews." *Journal of Marketing Research* 43 (3): 345–54.
Choi, Hyunyoung, and Hal Varian. 2012. "Predicting the Present with Google Trends." *Economic Record* 88 (s1): 2–9.
Clay, Karen, Ramayya Krishnan, and Eric Wolff. 2001. "Prices and Price Dispersion on the Web: Evidence from the Online Book Industry." *Journal of Industrial Economics* 49 (4): 521–39.
D'Amuri, Francesco, and Juri Marcucci. 2010. "Google It! Forecasting the US Unemployment Rate with Google Job Search Index." Working Paper no. 18732, Munich Personal RePEc Archive.
De los Santos, Babur. 2012. "Consumer Search on the Internet." Working Paper no. 08-15, NET Institute. http://dx.doi.org/10.2139/ssrn.1285773.
De los Santos, Babur, Ali Hortaçsu, and Matthijs R. Wildenbeest. 2012. "Testing Model of Consumer Search Using Data on Web Browsing and Purchasing Behavior." *American Economic Review* 102 (6): 2955–80.
De los Santos, Babur, and Matthijs R. Wildenbeest. 2014. "E-book Pricing and Vertical Restraints." Working Paper, Indiana University.

Forman, Chris, Anindya Ghose, and Avi Goldfarb. 2009. "Competition between Local and Electronic Markets: How the Benefit of Buying Online Depends on Where You Live." *Management Science* 55 (1): 47–57.

Ginsberg, Jeremy, Matthew H. Mohebbi, Rajan S. Patel, Lynnette Brammer, Mark S. Smolinski, and Larry Brilliant. 2009. "Detecting Influenza Epidemics Using Search Engine Query Data." *Nature* 457 (7232): 1012–14.

Guzmán, Giselle. 2011. "Internet Search Behavior as an Economic Forecasting Tool: The Case of Inflation Expectations." *Journal of Economic & Social Measurement* 36 (3): 119–67.

Hong, Han, and Matthew Shum. 2006. "Using Price Distributions to Estimate Search Costs." *RAND Journal of Economics* 37 (2): 257–75.

Hu, Yu (Jeffrey), and Michael D. Smith. 2013. "The Impact of e-Book Distribution on Print Sales: Analysis of a Natural Experiment." Working Paper, Carnegie Mellon University.

Johnson, Justin. 2013. "The Agency and Wholesale Models in Electronic Content Markets." Working Paper, Cornell University.

Manley, Laura, and Robert P. Holley. 2012. "History of the e-Book: The Changing Face of Books." *Technical Services Quarterly* 29 (4): 292–311.

Moraga-González, José Luis, and Matthijs R. Wildenbeest. 2012. "Comparison Sites." In *Handbook of the Digital Economy*, edited by Martin Peitz and Joel Waldfogel, 224–53. Oxford: Oxford University Press.

Rysman, Marc. 2009. "The Economics of Two-Sided Markets." *Journal of Economic Perspectives* 23 (3): 125–43.

Stigler, George. 1961. "The Economics of Information." *Journal of Political Economy* 69 (3): 213–25.

Comment   Marc Rysman

The book publishing industry has provided one of the most visible and tangible digital transformations of market. Most of the focus has been on the production, distribution, and ownership rights in the context of digital e-books, or on how online booksellers compare to offline booksellers. However, little attention has been paid to how consumers find the books that they ultimately buy. Browsing bookstores, asking store employees for suggestions, and waiting for reviews in your local newspaper has been replaced by online opinions, suggestion engines, and immediate access to an enormous number of outlets that review books. Even in the case where a consumer already knows the book they want and they merely have to locate the book, digitization has important implications. It is much easier to search across a broad set of sellers on the Internet—indeed, shopping websites specifically facilitates this activity. The chapter by Baye, De Los Santos, and Wildenbeest

---

Marc Rysman is professor of economics at Boston University.

For acknowledgments, sources of research support, and disclosure of the author's material financial relationships, if any, please see http://www.nber.org/chapters/c13126.ack.

fills an important void, providing one of the first looks with detailed data at the nature of the consumer search process for books.

As the authors point out, one of the important contributions of the chapter is outlining the kinds of limitations in data that we can expect as research moves forward on these issues. Their own data collection is impressive, but leaves them asking for more. They use comScore's Search Planner and qSearch databases, which follows the Internet activity of about two million survey participants. They show several interesting facts. Amazon receives 50 percent of its traffic from Google and 20 percent from people directly entering the Amazon URL in their browser. For the traffic from search engines, a large percentage of searches that lead to Amazon and Barnes & Noble websites start with searches for those websites in particular, rather than a search for a book title for which those websites would appear. However, the authors see search terms that are used infrequently that add up to a substantial portion—75 percent—of the traffic from search engines that arrives at Amazon.

While the comScore data covers only 2010–2012, the authors provide a creative method to extend the data back to 2004. Google Trends provides a relative measure of search intensity over this time, which the authors pin down to an absolute level for the 2010–2012 time period using their comScore data. They show a surprising result: search intensity starts high upon the introduction of a new book and then falls off within a few weeks, whereas the Amazon sales rank climbs just as search intensity is dropping off. Thus, the relationship between sales and search is more complicated than one might imagine. Interestingly, searches for books on Google have declined since 2007, while searches that start with the Amazon website have increased. Thus, book search appears to be shifting to book-selling websites such as Amazon, as well as to alternative systems such as the Kindle store.

The chapter identifies several interesting areas for future research such as search from tablets, search within platforms such as amazon.com or from within a Kindle, and also, distinguishing how much search is meant to learn about which book to purchase versus determining the best price for a book that has already been decided upon. I wish to point out several more areas that should prove fruitful. Book search provides a fascinating and complex example of competition between platforms. Amazon.com, barnesandnoble.com and the other bookseller websites constitute platforms in the sense that they match readers to books. Although these websites largely follow a one-sided model in the sense that they purchase books wholesale and then retail the books to consumers, there are still important elements of platform competition in this market. In particular, book publishers sell to multiple venues and make a number of strategic choices along these lines, as the Apple antitrust case makes clear.

An important result in the literature on platform competitions is that competition between platforms is governed by whether agents multihome, that is, use multiple platforms, or single home. Most books are available on a variety of platforms, but consumer search is unclear. In this light, the result that consumers increasingly search for books within bookseller platforms rather than the broader Google website is particularly interesting. A further question would be whether consumers typically navigate to multiple bookseller sites before making their purchase, or do they go to a single one, which represents true single homing. This has implications for pricing because when a platform has a set of devoted single-homing consumers, it can extract large rents from the firms that want to reach those consumers. In this case, it would take the form of low wholesale prices for books or other terms that are attractive to the website. Can we see a change in these terms as the market moves toward single homing?

One widely acknowledged feature of the Internet is that it facilitates the service of the "long tail." While much of the focus on the long tail has emphasized the wholesaling cost of low-demand products, it is also easier for consumers with esoteric tastes to search for low-demand products. An implication that these authors may be in a position to study is whether we see a change in the supply of esoteric products. That is, is there an increased provision of goods with relatively low expected market shares in the light of new search and distribution technologies?

Finally, the authors have added to their remarkable data set by collecting prices. This naturally opens up several new avenues for research. For instance, can we sort out the relationship between the level of search and the level of price dispersion? Each one could have a causal effect on the other, and providing empirical analyses of this topic has implications for a wide swath of literature that engages with search behavior.

6
Ideology and Online News

Matthew Gentzkow and Jesse M. Shapiro

6.1 Introduction

The news media are a fundamental democratic institution. Access to the news affects political participation (Gentzkow, Sinkinson, and Shapiro 2011), and the portrayal of the news affects how voters vote (DellaVigna and Kaplan 2007). Digital news is still in its infancy, with digital platforms accounting for only 8 percent of time spent consuming news in the United States (Edmonds 2013). Yet it seems inevitable that this share will climb as new technologies develop and diffuse. If this march of technology will transform the Fourth Estate, it may thereby transform democratic politics.

Key to understanding how the rise of digital media will affect politics is understanding how it will affect the breadth and depth of sources from which Americans get their news. These effects are theoretically ambiguous

---

Matthew Gentzkow is the Richard O. Ryan Professor of Economics and Neubauer Family Faculty Fellow at the University of Chicago Booth School of Business and a research associate of the National Bureau of Economic Research. Jesse M. Shapiro is the Chookaszian Family Professor of Economics at the University of Chicago Booth School of Business and a research associate of the National Bureau of Economic Research.

We are grateful to the project organizers, Shane Greenstein, Avi Goldfarb, and Catherine Tucker, and to the participants for helpful comments during the preparation of the chapter. We are especially grateful to Ben Jones for an outstanding discussion. Wharton Research Data Services (WRDS) was used in preparing this chapter. This service and the data available thereon constitute valuable intellectual property and trade secrets of WRDS and/or its third-party suppliers. This research benefited from funding by the National Science Foundation, the Alfred P. Sloan Foundation, and the Initiative on Global Markets, the George J. Stigler Center for the Study of the Economy and the State, the Ewing Marion Kauffman Foundation, the Centel Foundation/Robert P. Reuss Faculty Research Fund, the Neubauer Family Foundation and the Kathryn C. Gould Research Fund, all at the University of Chicago Booth School of Business. For acknowledgments, sources of research support, and disclosure of the authors' material financial relationships, if any, please see http://www.nber.org/chapters/c12993.ack.

(Mullainathan and Shleifer 2005). On the one hand, the Internet enables inexpensive access to a tremendous range of sources. On the other hand, inexpensive customization may permit highly specialized outlets that serve niche tastes and create echo chambers of self-confirming ideological banter (Sunstein 2001).

In this chapter we formulate an estimable economic model of the production and consumption of online news. We estimate the demand side of the model using a combination of microdata and aggregate moments from a panel of Internet users. We evaluate the fit of the model to key features of the data and use it to explore predictions for the supply of news.

Our model is designed to parsimoniously capture important empirical features of online news consumption. In the model, sites are endowed with two attributes: an ideology and an overall quality. Households are likewise endowed with an overall taste for news and with an ideology. Households choose news sites based on the ideological match between the site and the household. News sites face fixed costs of content that depend on quality and possibly on ideology. News site revenue is from advertising, and advertising revenue depends on audience metrics.

We estimate the demand portion of the model using panel microdata on a sample of Internet users from comScore. For each user we observe total visits to a set of five news sites in 2008. For identification we supplement these data with the overall share conservative on each site, as measured through a separate comScore survey. The demand model fits many aggregate moments well, though it predicts more cross-visiting between news outlets than is present in the data.

We then turn to our supply model. We show that the economics of advertising competition may lead to an important incentive to differentiate ideologically. For a benchmark model of advertising competition, we compute (in the spirit of Gentzkow and Shapiro [2010]) the extent to which different news sites are close to their optimal ideological position given the positions of other sites.

The model we present in this chapter complements the descriptive analysis in Gentzkow and Shapiro (2011). In that paper, which we describe in more detail later in the chapter, we use data on the size and ideological composition of online news to construct a measure of ideological segregation for the Internet and to compare the Internet to other media and to nonmedia domains in which political interaction takes place. We find that the extent of ideological segregation online is low both in absolute terms and in comparison to other domains of interaction.

The value of the model is that it permits evaluation of counterfactual changes in tastes or technology that by definition cannot be envisioned by descriptive statistics alone. Although we do not undertake such calculations here, the model could, in principle, be used to calculate how the configuration of the market and the consumption of news will change as fixed costs fall or as news domains subdivide into more specialized or customized outlets. Because the model incorporates the advertising market, it can also confront changes in the online advertising market and predict how these will change the mix of products on offer.

The model may also provide a window into the underlying motivations of online news consumers. Where our model fails to fit the facts, there is room for additional modeling to more accurately capture the structure of consumer preferences.

The remainder of the chapter is as follows. Section 6.2 provides background on broader issues surrounding digitization and the consumption of political news. Section 6.3 summarizes our data and the descriptive evidence in Gentzkow and Shapiro (2011). Section 6.4 presents our model. Section 6.5 discusses our estimation strategy and presents our results. Section 6.6 concludes with an agenda for future work.

6.2 Digitization and Political News

There is good evidence of rising elite polarization in the United States. Roll call voting records in the US Congress show a widening gap between the parties since the 1970s (McCarty, Poole, and Rosenthal 2006). Though the evidence for a rise in polarization among nonelites is weaker (Fiorina and Abrams 2008), there are important patterns in the data that suggest strengthening party identification among at least some groups of voters (Prior 2013).

A possible explanation for these patterns comes from widening media choice. The rise of cable television, and the subsequent rise of the Internet, proliferate options that may change how citizens obtain the news. Prior (2005) shows that expanding media choice reduces political engagement among those seeking entertainment but increases it among those seeking information. Prior (2013) reviews evidence on other channels by which the media may influence political polarization.

A central theme in the literature on media and polarization is selective exposure. With many choices, it is easier for an individual with a strong ideological predisposition to consume like-minded news. This can reduce the moderating influence of mainstream media and can result in an ideologically pigeonholed society (Sunstein 2001).

The logic for this type of effect is as follows. Imagine the news is differentiated only horizontally and that news outlets are arrayed on a unit line segment from left to right, along which citizens are uniformly distributed. Suppose that there are J news outlets, equally spaced along the line, and each citizen consumes news from the outlet closest to her. In a world with $J = 1$ news outlet, everyone sees the same news, and the news outlet optimally caters to a broad audience. In a world with $J = 2$, those on the extreme right share an outlet with those on the moderate right, and similarly for the left. So, right-wingers see right-wing news, but extreme right-wingers may not get extreme right-wing news. In a world with $J = 3$, those close to the center (right or left) share an outlet and those on the wings get dedicated outlets, though perhaps not yet fringe outlets. As J rises, news outlets serve narrower audiences, and so presumably serve them with narrower content. Mullainathan and Shleifer (2005) formalize this type of logic in a model with much richer economic forces.

The logic of this prediction is strongest in a model with purely horizontal differentiation and each citizen consuming news from a single outlet. Both the addition of vertical attributes and the option to visit multiple outlets complicate the picture. To see why, step away from the news domain and consider another: the market for DVDs. When DVDs were rented via brick-and-mortar shops, catalogs were often limited to the top films of the day. The advent of rental services like Netflix meant that choice expanded tremendously because inventory costs fell by orders of magnitude (Anderson 2006). Obscure films were now widely available.

But expanding choice did not polarize the movie rental market. Data from Quickflix (an Australian DVD-by-mail service) show that those renting movies from the bottom decile by popularity devote only 8 percent of their rentals to movies in that group, and over a third to movies in the top decile by popularity. Subscribers who rent at least one movie from the least popular decile rent more than twice as many movies total as those who rent at least one from the most popular decile (Elberse 2008).

Put differently, those with niche tastes are still highly engaged with mainstream content, a finding that resonates with evidence from other domains such as cable television (Webster and Ksiazek 2012). Some watch ESPN and some watch the Food Network. Both groups meet at CBS.

In Gentzkow and Shapiro (2011), we show that something similar is at work in online news. The Internet makes sites with extreme content available. But the visitors to these sites get the majority of their news elsewhere, and as a result, patterns of viewership are not well approximated by the simple horizontal model that we sketch above.

There are two reasons. First, in the purely horizontal model, an extreme liberal consumes news from the most liberal news outlet and no other outlet. In practice, she might combine reading from a progressive blog with reading of a middle-of-the-road website like cnn.com. Second, in the purely horizontal model, all outlets are equally good. In practice, they are not, and since quality is primarily a fixed cost, quality is highest where the market is largest, which is in the middle of the road. There are websites that spin the news from a neo–Nazi perspective, but even accounting for the perspective the overall quality and timeliness of their coverage is poor.

In this chapter we will review the evidence in Gentzkow and Shapiro (2011) and complement it with a model that can rationalize patterns of online news consumption. Though we focus on the news, the model we present may also be useful in understanding consumption in other media domains that have undergone transformative increases in product variety.

6.3 Data and Descriptive Evidence

In this section we describe our data sources and we summarize the descriptive evidence in Gentzkow and Shapiro (2011) regarding the ideological segregation of online news. Portions of this section are excerpted from Gentzkow and Shapiro (2011).

6.3.1 Data Sources

Our data on Internet news consumption come from comScore. We construct a universe of 119 national political news and opinion websites for which it is possible to measure both the size and ideology of the audience (Gentzkow and Shapiro 2011).

We measure site size using the average daily unique visitors to each site over the twelve months in 2009 from comScore Media Metrix. Media Metrix data come from comScore's panel of over one million US-resident Internet users. Panelists install software on their computers to permit monitoring of their browsing behavior, and comScore uses a passive method to distinguish multiple users of the same machine.

We measure site ideology using data from comScore Plan Metrix. Plan Metrix data come from a survey distributed electronically to approximately 12,000 comScore panelists. The survey asks panelists the question "In terms of your political outlook, do you think of yourself as very conservative, somewhat conservative, middle of the road, somewhat liberal, or very liberal?" The average number of daily unique visitors in each category is reported by comScore for each site for each month. We average these figures over the twelve months in 2009.

We also use comScore microdata on the browsing behavior of a subset of panelists obtained from Wharton Research Data Services (WRDS). The data include 50,000–100,000 machines per year and contain the domain name of each site visited.

Relative to the site-level aggregates, the microdata have two important limitations. First, because the comScore microdata are defined at the domain level (e.g., yahoo.com), we cannot distinguish news content on subpages of large sites such as aol.com and yahoo.com. Sites such as Yahoo! News and AOL News are therefore excluded from the microdata sample. Second, the microdata do not distinguish between multiple users of the same machine.

In this chapter, we use a subset of the data for structural estimation. We focus on five sites: foxnews.com, nytimes.com, huffingtonpost.com, drudgereport.com, and cnn.com. We use the 2008 comScore microdata panel and we limit to machines that visit the universe of news sites in Gentzkow and Shapiro (2011) no more than 100 times total throughout the year.

6.3.2 Descriptive Features of Online News Consumption

In Gentzkow and Shapiro (2011) we use data on the news consumption habits of a panel of Internet users to evaluate whether news online constitutes an "echo chamber" in which people hear only their own views. To do this, we measure the ideological segregation of online news using an approach borrowed from the literature on racial segregation.

For each news outlet, we define the *share conservative*: the share of users who report their political outlook as "conservative" among those who report being either "conservative" or "liberal." We then define each individual's *conservative exposure* to be the average share conservative on the outlets she visits. For example, if the only outlet an individual visits is nytimes.com, her exposure is defined as the share conservative on nytimes.com. If she visits both nytimes.com and foxnews.com, her exposure is the average of the conservative shares on these two sites. Next, we define the *isolation index* (White 1986; Cutler, Glaeser, and Vigdor 1999) as the difference in the average conservative exposure of conservatives minus the average conservative exposure of liberals. If conservatives only visit foxnews.com and liberals only visit nytimes.com, the isolation index will be equal to 100 percentage points. If both conservatives and liberals get all their news from cnn.com, the two groups will have the same conservative exposure, and the isolation index will be equal to zero.

We find that news consumption online is far from perfectly segregated. The average Internet news consumer's exposure to conservatives is 57 percent. (Excluding self-described moderates, about two-thirds of the US population self-describes as conservative.) The average conservative's exposure is 60.6 percent, similar to a person who gets all her news from usatoday.com. The average liberal's exposure is 53.1 percent, similar to a person who gets all her news from cnn.com. The isolation index for the Internet is 7.5 percentage points, the difference between the average conservative's exposure and the average liberal's exposure.

News consumers with extremely high or low exposure are rare. A consumer who got news exclusively from nytimes.com would have a more liberal news diet than 95 percent of Internet news users, and a consumer who got news exclusively from foxnews.com would have a more conservative news diet than 99 percent of Internet news users.

The isolation index we estimate for the Internet is higher than that of broadcast television news (1.8), cable television news (3.3), magazines (4.7), and local newspapers (4.8), and lower than that of national newspapers (10.4). We estimate that eliminating the Internet would reduce the ideological segregation of news and opinion consumption across all media from 5.1 to 4.1.

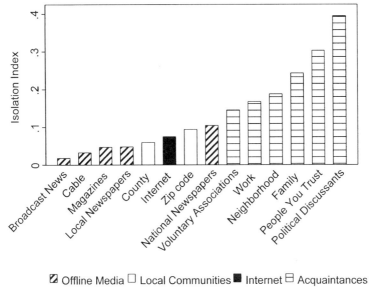

Fig. 6.1 Ideological segregation across domains
Sources: Internet data are from 2009 comScore Media Metrix and Plan Metrix. County, zip code, and offline media data are from the 2007 and 2008 Mediamark Research and Intelligence Surveys of the American Consumer. Voluntary associations, work, neighborhood, family, and "people you trust" data are from the 2006 General Social Survey. Political discussants data are from the 1992 Cross-National Election Study. The figure is reprinted from Gentzkow and Shapiro (2011).

Online segregation is somewhat higher than that of a social network where individuals matched randomly within counties (5.9), and lower than that of a network where individuals matched randomly within zip codes (9.4). It is significantly lower than the segregation of actual networks formed through voluntary associations (14.5), work (16.8), neighborhoods (18.7), or family (24.3). The Internet is also far less segregated than networks of trusted friends (30.3) and political discussants (39.4).

Figure 6.1 shows the relative segregation of different domains graphically.

6.4 Model

The facts we describe above suggest the elements of a satisfactory model of the production and consumption of news online.

News outlets differ in two dimensions: a vertical or quality dimension, and a horizontal or ideology dimension. Accounting for quality variation is critical because most online news consumption is concentrated among a very small number of outlets. In Gentzkow and Shapiro (2011) we report that the top twenty sites account for nearly 80 percent of the daily visits to news outlets online. Accounting for variation in ideology is critical because it is an important driver of demand. For example, 78 percent of visitors to drudgereport.com are conservative as against 22 percent for huffingtonpost.com. Accounting for ideology is also important because many of the concerns about the effects of the Internet relate to its effects on the ideological composition of the news diet.

News consumers differ in two ways as well: their overall taste for consuming news online, and their ideology. We have already stressed the importance of modeling ideology. As we document below, there is enormous heterogeneity across households in the amount of online news consumed, suggesting significant heterogeneity in the overall taste for news (or equivalently in the value of the outside option).

News outlets, especially those with no offline presence, primarily compete for advertising revenue. The growing literature on platform competition with multihoming (Armstrong 2002; Ambrus and Reisinger 2006; Anderson, Foros, and Kind 2010; Athey, Calvano, and Gans 2013) shows that two outlets compete in the market for advertising to the extent that they have audience in common. Therefore, a news outlet's revenue will increase to the extent that the outlet garners a greater audience, and especially to the extent that its audience does not overlap with the audience of other outlets. The importance of audience overlap in determining advertising revenue also suggests that a good model should allow for significant multihoming by consumers.

News outlets face costs of news production. Improving along the vertical or quality dimension requires payment of fixed costs that do not depend on the size of the audience (Berry and Waldfogel 2010). The costs of varying along the horizontal or ideology dimension are less clear; we will think of these costs as negligible for the purposes of discussion.

In this model, only a small number of outlets will want to make large investments in quality (Shaked and Sutton 1987), and those that do will want to appeal to the widest possible audience. This helps explain the dominance of a small number of relatively centrist sites. Moreover, the incentive to operate outlets on the ideological fringe depends greatly on whether fringe outlets attract unique audience. To the extent that their audience mostly overlaps with that of the major sites, they will obtain vanishingly small revenues in a model in which only unique audience pays.

6.4.1 Model of Demand

Setup and Notation

There is a set of news outlets $\{1, \ldots, J\}$ indexed by j and a set of consumers $\{1, \ldots, I\}$ indexed by i. Each consumer has T_i occasions to consume news online. At each occasion $t \in \{1, \ldots, T_i\}$ each consumer must choose one news outlet. We can think of an occasion as a unit of time—a minute, say—that is small enough so that it is impractical to visit multiple outlets on the same occasion. Let $y_{it} \in \{1, ..., J\}$ denote consumer i's choice at occasion t.

Each consumer i has a time-constant ideology τ_i, and ideologies are distributed i.i.d. across consumers with known pdf $\phi(\ )$.[1] Each consumer i has a taste for news μ_i, with μ_i distributed i.i.d. $Gamma(\theta, \theta)$ conditional on τ_i.

Conditional on τ_i and μ_i, the number of occasions to consume news T_i is distributed across consumers as $Pois(\lambda_i)$, where

(1) $$\log(\lambda_i) = \log f(\tau_i) + \log(\mu_i).$$

Conditional on τ_i, this defines a negative binomial count model (Greene 2012).[2] We include $f(\tau_i)$ in the arrival probability to capture the possibility that taste for news is correlated with ideology.

A site j is characterized by a quality α_j and an ideology γ_j, where higher values represent higher quality or more right-wing ideology. The utility to consumer i from visiting site j on occasion t is

(2) $$u_{ijt} = \alpha_j - (\tau_i - \gamma_j)^2 + \varepsilon_{ijt},$$

where ε_{ijt} is a type-I extreme value error, drawn independently across consumers, outlets, and occasions, and independently of μ_i and τ_i. On each occasion, a consumer chooses the site that maximizes her utility:

(3) $$y_{it} = j \Leftrightarrow u_{ijt} \geq u_{ij't} \ \forall \ j' \neq j.$$

Choice Probabilities

Let $\pi_j(\tau) \equiv \Pr(y_{it} = j | \tau_i = \tau)$ denote the probability that a household with ideology τ chooses to visit site j on a given occasion, conditional on choosing to consume news. Then:

(4) $$\pi_j(\tau) = \frac{\exp(\alpha_j - (\tau - \gamma_j)^2)}{\sum_{j'=1}^{J} \exp(\alpha_{j'} - (\tau - \gamma_{j'})^2)}.$$

Let $\pi(\tau) = (\pi_1(\tau), ..., \pi_J(\tau))$ denote the vector of πs.

Likelihood

An econometrician observes the sequence $\{y_{it}\}_{t=1}^{T_i}$ for each consumer i. Let $K_{ij} = \sum_{t=1}^{T_i} 1_{y_{it}=j}$ denote the number of visits to site j made by consumer i. Let $\mathbf{K_i} = \{K_{ij}\}_{j=1}^{J}$ denote the vector of visit counts for consumer i.

Let

$$B(\tau_i, T_i) = \frac{\Gamma(\theta + T_i)}{\Gamma(T_i + 1)\Gamma(\theta)} \left(\frac{f(\tau_i)}{f(\tau_i) + \theta} \right)^{T_i} \left(\frac{\theta}{f(\tau_i) + \theta} \right)^{\theta}$$

---

1. In estimation we will assume that τ is standard normal. The assumption that the pdf $\phi(\ )$ is known is necessary in order to pin down the scale of outlet ideology. In the normal case, an equivalent alternative would be to normalize the scale of outlet ideology and allow the standard deviation of τ to be a model parameter.
2. Formally, $T_i | \tau_i \sim NB\{\theta, f(\tau_i)/[f(\tau_i) + \theta]\}$.

denote the negative binomial probability that a household with ideology τ_i has T_i occasions to consume news.

Let $Multinomial(\mathbf{K_i}, T_i, \pi(\tau_i))$ denote the probability of visit counts $\mathbf{K_i}$ given T_i occasions and ideology τ_i.

The conditional likelihood for household i given ideology τ_i is then

$$L(T_i, \mathbf{K_i} | \tau_i) = B(\tau_i, T_i) \, Multinomial(\mathbf{K_i}, T_i, \pi(\tau_i)).$$

The unconditional likelihood for household i is

(5) $$L(T_i, \mathbf{K_i}) = \int_{-\infty}^{\infty} L(T_i, \mathbf{K_i} | \tau_i) \phi(\tau_i) d\tau_i.$$

The unconditional log likelihood of the data is

(6) $$\ln(L) = \sum_{i=1}^{I} \ln L(T_i, \mathbf{K_i}).$$

Here we make explicit the dependence on T_i just for emphasis; T_i is just the sum of the elements of the vector $\mathbf{K_i}$.

The parameters of the likelihood, which we have suppressed in the notation above, are θ, $\{\alpha_j, \gamma_j\}_{j=1}^{J}$, and any parameters of the function $f(\ )$.

Constraints

Let $c_i = 1_{\tau_i > \tau_0}$ be an indicator for whether a household reports being conservative, where τ_0 is a cutoff.

With some abuse of notation, let

(7) $$c_j = \frac{\sum_{i=1}^{I} c_i K_{ij}}{\sum_{i=1}^{I} K_{ij}}$$

denote the share of visitors to site j who are conservative.

The econometrician observes $\{c_j\}_{j=1}^{J}$. The econometrician can therefore impose the following J constraints:

(8) $$c_j = \frac{\int_{\tau_0}^{\infty} \pi_j(\tau) f(\tau) \phi(\tau) d\tau}{\int_{-\infty}^{\infty} \pi_j(\tau) f(\tau) \phi(\tau) d\tau}.$$

These constraints are necessary to identify τ_0 and the γ_j's in a sample of households whose ideology is unknown.

6.4.2 Model of Supply of Online News

Setup and Notation

We define several summaries of the number of visits to site j. Let V_j denote the total number of visitors to site j. Let S_j denote the fraction of consumers who visit site j at least once. Let X_j denote the fraction of consumers who visit site j and no other site.

Write the operating profits of outlet j as

$$\Pi_j = a(V_j, S_j, X_j) - g(\alpha_j, \gamma_j),$$

where $a(V_j, S_j, X_j)$ is annual advertising revenue and $g(\alpha_j, \gamma_j)$ is the annual cost of content production.

The function $a(\ )$ allows for several possible advertising technologies. The case where $a(V_j, S_j, X_j) = \tilde{a}V_j$ for some constant $\tilde{a}$ corresponds to a constant per-viewer advertising rate. The case where $a(V_j, S_j, X_j) = \tilde{a}S_j$ exhibits strong diminishing returns to additional impressions to the same viewer on the same site. The case where $a(V_j, S_j, X_j) = \tilde{a}X_j$ exhibits strong diminishing returns to additional impressions both across and between sites. This last form of diminishing returns is especially interesting in light of the theoretical literature on multihoming (Armstrong 2002; Ambrus and Reisinger 2006; Anderson, Foros, and Kind 2010; Athey, Calvano, and Gans 2013).

The function $g(\alpha_j, \gamma_j)$ is similarly abstract. A convenient starting point is that $g(\alpha_j, \gamma_j) = g(\alpha_j)$ strictly increasing in α_j. Such an assumption implies that it is costly to produce quality but free to locate anywhere on the ideological spectrum for a given quality.

Audience Metrics

Using our demand model it is possible to derive simple expressions for the various audience metrics that we define above.

The number of visits to site j by the average consumer is given by

(9) $$V_j = \int_{-\infty}^{\infty} \sum_{T=0}^{\infty} \pi_j(\tau) T \Pr(T|\tau) \phi(\tau) d\tau = \int_{-\infty}^{\infty} \pi_j(\tau) f(\tau) \phi(\tau) d\tau.$$

The derivation uses the fact that $E(T|\tau) = f(\tau)$.

The share of consumers who ever visit site j is given by

(10) $$S_j = \int_{-\infty}^{\infty} \sum_{T=0}^{\infty} (1 - (1 - \pi_j(\tau))^T) \Pr(T|\tau) \phi(\tau) d\tau = 1 - \int_{-\infty}^{\infty} \left(\frac{\theta}{f(\tau)\pi_j(\tau) + \theta} \right)^{\theta} \phi(\tau) d\tau.$$

To derive the second expression from the first, observe that

$$\sum_{T=0}^{\infty} (1 - \pi_j(\tau))^T \Pr(T|\tau) = E_{T|\tau}((1 - \pi_j(\tau))^T) = E_{T|\tau}(\exp(T \ln(1 - \pi_j(\tau))))$$

$$= \left(\frac{\theta}{f(\tau)\pi_j(\tau) + \theta} \right)^{\theta},$$

where the last step follows from the moment-generating function of the negative binomial.

The share of consumers who visit site j and no other site is given by

$$X_j = \int_{-\infty}^{\infty} \sum_{T=1}^{\infty} (\pi_j(\tau))^T \Pr(T|\tau) \phi(\tau) d\tau$$

(11)
$$= \int_{-\infty}^{\infty} \left(\left(\frac{\theta}{f(\tau)(1 - \pi_j(\tau)) + \theta} \right)^\theta - \left(\frac{\theta}{f(\tau) + \theta} \right)^\theta \right) \phi(\tau) d\tau.$$

The derivation here is analogous to that for S_j, but begins by noting that

$$\sum_{T=1}^{\infty} (\pi_j(\tau))^T \Pr(T|\tau) = E_{T|\tau}((\pi_j(\tau))^T) - \Pr(T = 0|\tau).$$

Equilibrium Choice of Attributes

Given the set of outlets, we suppose that attributes $\{\alpha_j, \gamma_j\}_{j=1}^J$ are a Nash equilibrium of a game in which all outlets simultaneously choose attributes. The first-order conditions are that

(12)
$$\frac{\partial \Pi_j}{\partial \alpha_j} = \frac{\partial \Pi_j}{\partial \gamma_j} = 0 \forall j.$$

The first-order conditions are a useful starting point for empirical work, because the game we have specified will in general have many equilibria. (For example, any set of attributes that constitutes an equilibrium is also an equilibrium under a relabeling of the outlets.)

Coupled with an estimate of demand, the first-order conditions have substantial empirical content. Consider, for example, the case in which $\Pi_j = \tilde{a} V_j - g(\alpha_j)$ for some constant $\tilde{a}$. Then the model implies that

$$g'(\alpha_j) = \tilde{a} \frac{\partial V_j}{\partial \alpha_j} \forall j.$$

An estimate of the demand model implies a value for $\partial V_j / \partial \alpha_j$ and the constant $\tilde{a}$ may be approximated from aggregate data. By plotting $g'(\alpha_j)$ against α_j for all outlets j one can trace out the shape of the cost function for quality. The model also implies that

(13)
$$0 = \frac{\partial V_j}{\partial \gamma_j} \forall j.$$

That is, since we have assumed that ideology can be chosen freely, each outlet must be at the visit-maximizing ideology. This is a version of Gentzkow and Shapiro's (2010) test for the optimality of print newspapers' choice of slant.

Equilibrium Number of Outlets

If news outlets are substitutes in demand then, in general, the profits of all outlets will decline in the number of outlets. A natural way to define the equilibrium number of outlets is then the number of outlets such that the next entering outlet would be unprofitable. For such a number to exist there must be a sunk entry cost. Suppose that this cost is uniform across potential entrants. Then the sunk cost can be bounded above by the operating profit of the least profitable outlet and below by the operating profit that the $J + 1$st outlet would earn if it were to enter and choose the optimal position given the positions of the existing J outlets.

6.5 Estimation and Results

6.5.1 Empirical Strategy and Identification

Our demand estimator solves the following problem:

$$\text{(14)} \qquad \min_{\tau_0, \theta, f(\cdot), \{\alpha_j, \gamma_j\}_{j=1}^J} \ln(L)$$

$$\text{(15)} \qquad s.t. \quad c_j = \frac{\int_{\tau_0}^{\infty} \pi_j(\tau) f(\tau) \phi(\tau) d\tau}{\int_{-\infty}^{\infty} \pi_j(\tau) f(\tau) \phi(\tau) d\tau} \forall j.$$

subject to a normalization of the location of the αs and γs.

Our data include panel microdata on individual households, but to develop intuition for model identification it is useful to imagine data that consist only of the shares c_j and the market shares of each site. Consider the problem of identifying τ_0 and $\{\alpha_j, \gamma_j\}_{j=1}^J$ taking as given the parameters governing the number of sites visited by each household.

There are J conservative shares c_j and $J - 1$ market shares (these must sum to one): $2J - 1$ empirical objects that can vary separately.

Up to an appropriate normalization, there are $J - 1$ qualities α_j, $J - 1$ site ideologies γ_j, and one reporting cutoff τ_0: $2J - 1$ parameters.

We assume that $\tau \sim N(0, 1)$. We parameterize $f(\tau) = \kappa$ for some constant κ. This allows us to factor the likelihood into two components: the likelihood for the count model of total visits and the likelihood for the logit model of outlet choice. We exploit this factoring to estimate the model via two-step maximum likelihood, first fitting the count model to the total number of visits T_i, then fitting the logit choice model to each household's individual sequence of visits. In the second step we limit attention to consumers who make fifteen or fewer visits to the five sites in our sample. Appendix table 6A.1 presents Monte Carlo evidence on the performance of our estimator.

6.5.2 Demand Estimates

Table 6.1 presents estimates of model parameters and their standard errors. We normalize γ so that it has a visit-weighted mean of zero. We normalize α so that it is equal to zero for the least-visited site. Estimates are in general very precise; this precision is somewhat overstated as we do not incorporate uncertainty in the constraints in equation (15).

We explore several dimensions of model fit.

Table 6.1   Model parameters

γ		
	CNN	−0.0127
		(0.00058)
	Drudge Report	0.7229
		(0.0000)
	Fox News	0.5320
		(0.00015)
	Huffington Post	−0.3645
		(0.00082)
	New York Times	−0.2156
		(0.00072)
α		
	CNN	4.3252
		(0.0488)
	Drudge Report	0
		(.)
	Fox News	2.7345
		(0.0475)
	Huffington Post	1.8632
		(0.0547)
	New York Times	3.6381
		(0.0502)
θ		0.3132
		(0.0000)
κ		3.0259
		(0.0000)
$Pr(\tau > \tau_0)$		0.5431
		(0.00087)

Notes: The table presents the estimated parameters of the model presented in section 6.4. Estimates use 2008 comScore data for five sites. Estimation is by two-step maximum likelihood, estimating (θ, κ) in the first step and the remaining parameters in the second step. We normalize γ to have a visit-weighted mean of zero across all sites, and α to take value zero for the least-visited site. Asymptotic standard errors are in parentheses.

Figure 6.2 shows that the negative binomial model provides a good fit to the distribution of total visits across machines in our panel.

Table 6.2 shows that the model provides a good fit to the overall size and ideological composition of the sites.

Table 6.3 shows that the model does an adequate job of replicating the distribution of conservative exposure in the data.

Table 6.4 shows that the model predicts far more cross-visiting than is observed in the data.

6.5.3 Supply Estimates

We focus on the supply model's implications for sites' choice of ideology. To get a feel for how the model works, we begin with the incentives of a hypothetical news site. Consider a world with $J = 2$ and $\alpha_1 = \alpha_2 = 0$. Suppose

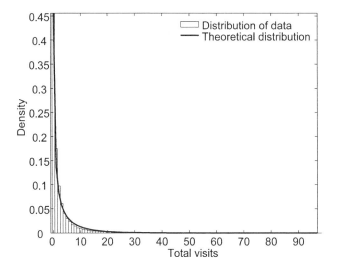

Fig. 6.2 Fit of model to total visit counts

Note: Plot shows total visits to the five sites in our sample in 2008 for each machine in the panel and the density predicted from our estimated model.

Table 6.2   Model fit to size and ideology of news outlets

	Share of total visits		Conservative share of site visits	
	Data	Simulation	Data	Simulation
CNN	0.5297	0.5348	0.5504	0.5604
Drudge Report	0.0113	0.0101	0.9266	0.9270
Fox News	0.1401	0.1339	0.8669	0.8731
Huffington Post	0.0483	0.0488	0.3008	0.3079
New York Times	0.2707	0.2724	0.4027	0.4080

Notes: The table presents, for each site, the share of total visits that each site receives, and the share of visits to each site from conservative consumers, along with analogues from a single simulation at the estimated parameters.

that site 1 chooses $\gamma_1 = 0$. Should site 2 stick to the center as well or move out to the extremes?

Figure 6.3 plots our three audience size metrics—average visits V_j, share ever visiting S_j, and share visiting exclusively X_j—as a function of site 2's choice of γ_2. We find that site 2 maximizes visits and the share ever visiting by being centrist. In the case of a site maximizing exclusive visits, it is optimal to be slightly to the right or to the left of the center. Moving away from the center attracts viewers who are not attracted to site 1, and hence who are more likely to visit site 2 exclusively.

Figure 6.4 explores the incentive to differentiate ideologically in the con-

Table 6.3 Model fit to conservative exposure

	Conservative exposure of households visiting at least one site						
	Percentile						
	5th	25th	50th	75th	95th	Mean	Standard deviation
Data	0.4027	0.4256	0.5504	0.5504	0.8669	0.5387	0.1360
Simulation	0.4080	0.4842	0.5604	0.5805	0.8213	0.5516	0.1155

Notes: The table presents statistics of the distribution of conservative exposure in the data and in a single simulation at the estimated model parameters. A consumer's conservative exposure is the visit-weighted average share conservative across the sites visited by the consumer.

Table 6.4 Model fit to cross-visiting patterns

		Also visiting site:				
Share of visitors to site:		CNN	Drudge Report	Fox News	Huffington Post	*New York Times*
CNN	Data	—	0.0087	0.1635	0.0711	0.3027
	Simulation	—	0.0406	0.3254	0.1781	0.5667
Drudge Report	Data	0.4131	—	0.2278	0.0656	0.2857
	Simulation	0.8495	—	0.6905	0.1153	0.5133
Fox News	Data	0.4774	0.0140	—	0.0826	0.2996
	Simulation	0.8019	0.0814	—	0.1485	0.5684
Huffington Post	Data	0.4640	0.0090	0.1847	—	0.3556
	Simulation	0.8442	0.0261	0.2857	—	0.7363
New York Times	Data	0.4472	0.0089	0.1516	0.0805	—
	Simulation	0.7896	0.0342	0.3213	0.2164	—

Notes: For each site, the table shows the share of visitors to that site who also visit each of the other sites, both for the empirical data and for a single simulation at the estimated parameters.

text of the five sites in our data. We take the αs as given at their estimated values. For each site j, we plot our audience size metrics as a function of γ_j, taking as given the estimated γs for the other sites. The plot also shows the estimated position $\hat{\gamma}_j$ for each site.

Whether a given site would increase its audience by moving closer to or further from the center depends on the audience metric of interest. Most sites would get more households to visit at least once by moving to the center. But most would get more exclusive visitors by moving further from the center. Most sites would also increase total visits by becoming more ideologically extreme.

6.6 Discussion and Conclusions

We propose a model of the demand and supply of online news designed to capture key descriptive features of the market. We estimate the model on

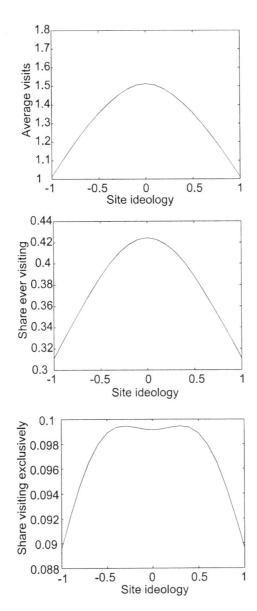

Fig. 6.3 Audience size and ideology: Hypothetical news site

Notes: The figure shows objects computed from our model using the values of the parameters θ and κ in table 6.1. In each plot we assume that $J = 2$, that $\alpha_1 = \alpha_2 = 0$, and that $\gamma_1 = 0$, and we plot measures of the size of the audience for outlet $j = 2$ as a function of its ideology γ_2. "Average visits" is the number of visits V_2 made by the average consumer to site 2 across all consumers. "Share ever visiting" is the share of consumers S_2 who visit site 2 at least once. "Share visiting exclusively" is the share of consumers X_2 who visit site 2 and only site 2. See text for formal definitions. Audience size metrics are approximated using Gaussian quadrature.

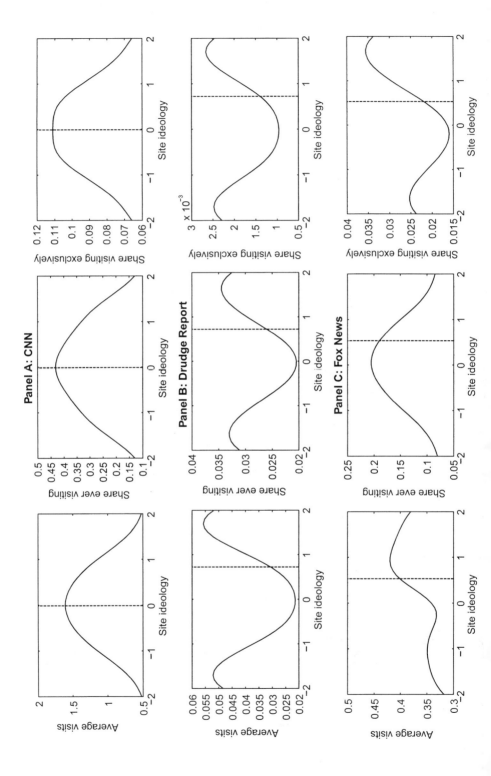

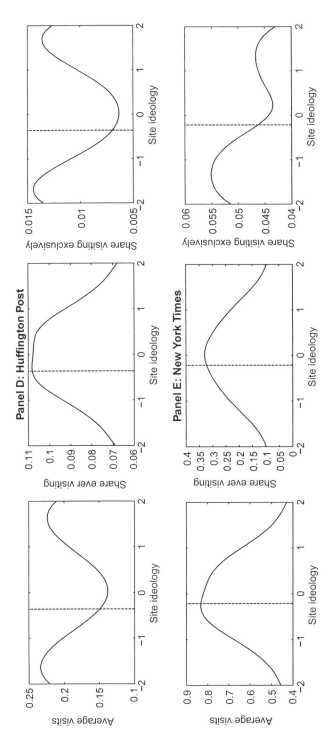

Fig. 6.4 Audience size and ideology: Actual news sites

Notes: Panel A, CNN; panel B, Drudge Report; panel C, Fox News; panel D, Huffington Post; and panel E, *New York Times*. The figure shows objects computed from our model using the values of the parameters γ, α, θ, and κ in table 6.1. In each plot we show measures of the size of the audience for outlet j as a function of its ideology $γ_j$, holding constant all other parameters. "Average visits" is the number of visits V_j made by the average consumer to site j across all consumers. "Share ever visiting" is the share of consumers S_j who visit site j at least once. "Share visiting exclusively" is the share of consumers X_j who visit site j and only site j. See text for formal definitions. Audience size metrics are approximated using Gaussian quadrature. The dashed line indicates the site's estimated ideology $\hat{γ}_j$.

data from a panel of Internet users and explore its fit to consumer behavior. We then study the model's implications for the supply of news.

We stop short of a full equilibrium model of the supply of news, but we believe such a model can be estimated with the primitives we propose. A proposed strategy is as follows. From our demand model, it is possible to calculate how much each outlet would gain in terms of audience from increasing its quality. Using a model of equilibrium advertising rates, one can translate this audience gain into a revenue gain. Conditions for a static equilibrium imply that the gain in revenue must equal the cost of additional content. By performing this exercise for a large set of sites, it is in principle possible to trace out the marginal cost of quality at different points in the quality distribution, and hence to recover the shape of the cost function for quality. A similar exercise could, in principle, yield a cost function for ideology.

Given cost functions and a notion of equilibrium, the model implies a set of equilibrium positions for news outlets under various assumptions. For example, it would be possible to contemplate changes in the value of online audience to advertisers, or changes in fixed costs or other elements of the news production technology. The model will imply a mapping from these primitives to features of consumer demand such as the extent of ideological segregation.

Stepping further back, it may also be interesting to explore how well the same model can perform in rationalizing patterns of demand in other domains. As we note in section 6.2, many of the descriptive features of news consumption are reminiscent of other domains such as DVD-by-mail rental patterns. Though the conditions of supply likely differ greatly across domains, common features in demand may suggest a similar underlying model of consumer behavior.

Finally, it is important to note that we focus on the supply and demand for news but not its impact on political beliefs or behavior. As technology evolves it will be important to accumulate theory and evidence on how media platforms change politics.

Appendix

Table 6A.1 Monte Carlo experiments

Parameter	Baseline estimate	Average estimate across simulations	Asymptotic standard errors	Bootstrap standard errors
γ				
CNN	−0.0127	−0.0127	0.0006	0.0000
Drudge Report	0.7229	0.7230	0.0000	0.0003
Fox News	0.5320	0.5321	0.0002	0.0002
Huffington Post	−0.3645	−0.3645	0.0008	0.0001
New York Times	−0.2156	−0.2157	0.0007	0.0001
α				
CNN	4.3252	4.3264	0.0488	0.0267
Drudge Report	0.0000	0.0000	0.0000	0.0000
Fox News	2.7345	2.7389	0.0475	0.0237
Huffington Post	1.8632	1.8663	0.0547	0.0303
New York Times	3.6381	3.6393	0.0502	0.0249
θ	0.3132	0.3132	0.0000	0.0000
κ	3.0259	3.0259	0.0000	0.0000
$Pr(\tau > \tau_0)$	0.5431	0.5432	0.0009	0.0003

Notes: The table reports the results of Monte Carlo experiments in which we first simulate ten data sets from our model at the parameter values shown in the first column, then reestimate our model on each simulated data set with the starting parameters set at the estimated values.

References

Ambrus, Attila, and Markus Reisinger. 2006. "Exclusive vs. Overlapping Viewers in Media Markets." Working Paper, Harvard University.
Anderson, Chris. 2006. *The Long Tail: Why the Future of Business is Selling Less of More.* New York: Hyperion.
Anderson, Simon P., Øystein Foros, and Hans Jarle Kind. 2010. "Hotelling Competition with Multi-Purchasing: Time Magazine, Newsweek, or Both?" CESifo Working Paper no. 3096, CESifo Group Munich.
Armstrong, Mark. 2002. "Competition in Two-Sided Markets." Working Paper, Nuffield College.
Athey, Susan, Emilio Calvano, and Joshua S. Gans. 2013. "The Impact of the Internet on Advertising Markets for News Media." Working Paper no. 2180851, Rotman School of Management, University of Toronto.
Berry, Steven, and Joel Waldfogel. 2010. "Product Quality and Market Size." *Journal of Industrial Economics* 58 (1): 1–31.
Cutler, David M., Edward L. Glaeser, and Jacob L. Vigdor. 1999. "The Rise and Decline of the American Ghetto." *Journal of Political Economy* 107 (3): 455–506.
DellaVigna, Stefano, and Ethan Kaplan. 2007. "The Fox News Effect: Media Bias and Voting." *Quarterly Journal of Economics* 122 (3): 1187–234.
Edmonds, Rick. 2013. "New Research Finds 92 Percent of Time Spent on News Consumption is Still on Legacy Platforms." Poynter Institute for Media Stud-

ies. http://www.poynter.org/latest-news/business-news/the-biz-blog/212550/new-research-finds-92-percent-of-news-consumption-is-still-on-legacy-platforms/.

Elberse, Anita. 2008. "Should You Invest in the Long Tail?" *Harvard Business Review* 86 (7): 88–96.

Fiorina, Morris P., and Samuel J. Abrams. 2008. "Political Polarization in the American Public." *Annual Review of Political Science* 11:563–88.

Gentzkow, Matthew, and Jesse M. Shapiro. 2010. "What Drives Media Slant? Evidence from US Daily Newspapers." *Econometrica* 78 (1): 35–71.

———. 2011. "Ideological Segregation Online and Offline." *Quarterly Journal of Economics* 126 (4): 1799–839.

Gentzkow, Matthew, Michael Sinkinson, and Jesse M. Shapiro. 2011. "The Effect of Newspaper Entry and Exit on Electoral Politics." *American Economic Review* 101 (7): 2980–3018.

Greene, William H. 2012. *Econometric Analysis*. New York: Prentice Hall.

McCarty, Nolan, Keith T. Poole, and Howard Rosenthal. 2006. *Polarized America: The Dance of Ideology and Unequal Riches*. Cambridge, MA: MIT Press.

Mullainathan, Sendhil, and Andrei Shleifer. 2005. "The Market for News." *American Economic Review* 95 (4): 1031–53.

Prior, Markus. 2005. "News vs. Entertainment: How Increasing Media Choice Widens Gaps in Political Knowledge and Turnout." *American Journal of Political Science* 49 (3): 577–92.

———. 2013. "Media and Political Polarization." *Annual Review of Political Science* 16:101–27.

Shaked, Avner, and John Sutton. 1987. "Product Differentiation and Industrial Structure." *Journal of Industrial Economics* 36 (2): 131–46.

Sunstein, Cass R. 2001. *Republic.com*. Princeton, N.J.: Princeton University Press.

Webster, James G., and Thomas B. Ksiazek. 2012. "The Dynamics of Audience Fragmentation: Public Attention in an Age of Digital Media." *Journal of Communication* 62:39–56.

White, Michael J. 1986. "Segregation and Diversity Measures in Population Distribution." *Population Index* 52 (2): 198–221.

7
Measuring the Effects of Advertising
The Digital Frontier

Randall Lewis, Justin M. Rao, and David H. Reiley

7.1 Introduction

In the United States, advertising is a $200 billion industry, annually. We all consume "free" services—those monetized by consumer attention to advertising—such as network television, e-mail, social networking, and a vast array of online content. Yet despite representing a relatively stable 2 percent of gross domestic product (GDP) since World War I and subsidizing activities that comprise most of Americans' leisure time (Bureau of Labor Statistics 2010), advertising remains poorly understood by economists. This is primarily because offline data have typically been insufficient for a firm (or researcher) to measure the true impact of advertising on consumer purchasing behavior. Theories of advertising (Demsetz 1982; Kessides 1986; Becker and Murphy 1993) that have important implications for competition are even harder to empirically validate. The digital era offers an unprecedented opportunity to bridge this informational divide. These advances, both realized and potential, can be attributed to two key factors: (1) individual-level data on ad delivery and subsequent purchasing behavior can be linked and made available to advertisers at low cost; and (2) ad delivery can be randomized at the individual level, generating exogenous variation essential to

---

Randall Lewis is an economic research scientist at Google, Inc. Justin M. Rao is an economic researcher at Microsoft Research. David H. Reiley is a research scientist at Google, Inc.

Much of this work was done when all the authors were at Yahoo! Research. We thank Garrett Johnson, Dan Nguyen, Sergiy Matusevych, Iwan Sakran, Taylor Schreiner, Valter Sciarillo, Christine Turner, Michael Schwarz, Preston McAfee, and numerous other colleagues for their assistance and support in carrying out the research. For acknowledgments, sources of research support, and disclosure of the authors' material financial relationships, if any, please see http://www.nber.org/chapters/c12991.ack.

identifying causal effects.[1] In this chapter we explore the dramatic improvement in the empirical measurements of the returns to advertising, highlight fundamental challenges that currently remain, and look to what solutions we think the future will bring.

Digital advertising has led to standard reporting of precise quantitative data for advertising campaigns, most notably the click-through rate (CTR). Of course, the CTR of an ad is only an intermediate proxy for the real outcome of interest to the advertiser: increased purchases by consumers, both in the present and future.[2] Despite these limitations, intermediate metrics such as the CTR have proved to be enormously useful dependent variables in automated targeting algorithms that match ads with consumers and contexts (Pandey and Olston 2006; Gonen and Pavlov 2007). Related intermediate metrics come from "purchasing intent" surveys paired with randomized exposure to a firm's advertising. Cross-experiment analysis of such surveys has provided estimates of the relative value of targeted (versus untargeted) advertising (Goldfarb and Tucker 2011b), contextual relevance and ad intrusiveness (Goldfarb and Tucker 2011a), and has informed the debate on privacy (Tucker 2012).

The advances in both academic understanding and business best-practice attributable to these intermediate metrics should not be understated. But while general insights on how ad features impact users can guide advertising spend and CTR maximizing algorithms can make spending more efficient, a firm is presumably interested in measuring the overall returns on advertising investment: dollars of sales causally linked to the campaign versus dollars spent. An overreliance on intermediate metrics can draw attention away from the true underlying goal, and research has shown it can lead to highly suboptimal spending decisions (Blake, Nosko, and Tadelis 2014).

Along with deficiencies in intermediate metrics, endogeneity of advertising exposure is the other key challenge in measuring advertising returns. Traditional econometric measurements typically rely on aggregate data fraught with identification problems due to the targeted nature of advertising (Bagwell 2007).[3] Yet despite the ability to run very large randomized control trials made possible by digital delivery and measurement, we have discovered a number of conceptual flaws in standard industry data collection and anal-

1. There have been experimental approaches to measuring advertising effectiveness in the past, see most notably the split-cable experiments of Lodish et al. (1995), but these were typically conducted as small pilots and not using the normal ad delivery pipeline.
2. Toward these ends, advertisers use browser cookies and click beacons to obtain a "conversion rate," the ratio of transactions attributed to the campaign to ad exposures. This measure seems ideal, but the attribution step is critical and current methods of assigning attribution have serious flaws, which we discuss in detail.
3. The split cable TV experiments reported in Lodish et al. (1995) are a notable exception. The sample sizes in these experiments, run in a small US town, were far smaller than online experiments, and the authors did not report per experiment confidence intervals, rather they used cross-experiment techniques to understand what factors tended to influence consumers (for a follow-up analysis, see Hu, Lodish, and Krieger [2007]).

ysis methods used to measure the effects of advertising. In other words, the deluge of data on advertising exposures, clicks, and other associated outcomes have not necessarily created greater understanding of the basic causal effects of advertising, much less an understanding of more subtle questions such as the relative effectiveness of different types of consumer targeting, ad creatives, cross-channel effects, or frequency of exposure. The voluminous data, it seems to us, have not only created opportunity for intelligent algorithmic advances, but also mistaken inference under the guise of "big data."

First, many models assume that if you do not click on the ad, then the ad has no effect on your behavior. Here we discuss work by coauthors Lewis and Reiley that showed online ads can drive offline sales, which are typically not measured in conversion or click rates; omitting these nonclick-based sales leads to underestimating the total effects of advertising. Linking online and offline sales requires a dedicated experimental infrastructure and third-party data merging that have only recently become possible.

Second, many models assume that if you do click on an ad and subsequently purchase, that conversion must have been *due to that ad*. This assumption seems particularly suspect in cases, such as search advertising, where the advertising is deliberately targeted at those consumers most likely to purchase the advertised product and temporally targeted to arrive when a consumer is performing a task related to the advertised good. Research has shown, for example, that a person searching for "ebay shoes" is very likely to purchase shoes on eBay regardless of the intensity of advertising (Blake, Nosko, and Tadelis 2014). While this is an extreme example, Blake, Nosko, and Tadelis (2014) also show that the problem arises generally, and measuring the degree to which advertising crowds out "organic conversions" is difficult to measure precisely. Näive approaches effectively assume this problem away, but since only "marginal clicks" are valuable and all clicks count toward the CTR, these methods will always overstate the causal effect on users who clicked the ad.

Third, more sophisticated models that do compare exposed to unexposed users to establish a baseline purchase rate typically rely on natural, endogenous advertising exposure and can easily generate biased estimates due to unobserved heterogeneity (Lewis, Rao, and Reiley 2011). This occurs when the pseudo-control group does not capture important characteristics of the treated group, such as purchase intent or browsing intensity, which we show can easily be correlated with purchases whether advertising is present or not. Using data from twenty-five large experiments run at Yahoo! (Lewis and Rao 2013), we have found that the standard deviation of purchases is typically ten times the mean. With such a noisy dependent variable, even a tiny amount of endogeneity can severely bias estimates. Beyond inducing bias in coefficient estimates, these specification errors also give rise to an overprecision problem. Because advertising typically explains only a very small fraction of the variance in consumer transaction behavior, even cleanly designed experiments typically require over a million subjects in order to be able to measure economically meaningful effects with any statistical precision (but even experiments with one million subjects can have surprisingly weak power, depending on the variance in sales).

Since experiments are generally considered the gold standard for precision[4] (treatment is exogenous and independent across individuals), we should be suspicious if observational methods claim to offer higher precision. Further, with nonexperimental methods, omitted heterogeneity or selection bias (so long as it can generate a partial R-squared of 0.00005 or greater) can induce bias that swamps plausible estimates of advertising effectiveness. Thus, if an advertiser does not use an experiment to evaluate advertising effectiveness, she has to have a level of confidence in her model that, frankly speaking, we find unreasonable given the obvious selection effects due to ad targeting and synchronization of advertising with product launches (e.g., new iPad release) and demand shocks (e.g., holiday shopping season).

Experimental work on measuring the dollar returns to advertising has given us a deeper appreciation for the limits of current data and methods. For example, we show that seemingly simple "cross-channel" complementarity measures are exceedingly difficult to reliably estimate. Here we present evidence taken from Lewis and Nguyen (2013) that display advertising can increase keyword searches for the advertised brand. Some clicks on sponsored links are incorrectly attributed entirely to the search ad, but while the directional impact on searches can be documented, we cannot tell if search ads perform better or worse in terms of the conversion rate when paired with display advertising. A similar experimental design at a much larger scale could answer this sort of question, but advertising to over five to ten million individuals may be out of reach[5] for most advertisers. These findings are confirmed by similar work on online advertising spillovers (Rutz and Bucklin 2011; Papadimitriou et al. 2011).

So while some questions are answerable with feasible (at least for some market participants) scale, we believe other questions are still outside the statistical power of current experimental infrastructure and methods. The most prominent example is the long-run effects of advertising. Essentially any analysis of the impact of advertising has to make a judgment call on which time periods to use in the analysis. Often this is the "campaign window" or the campaign window plus a chosen interval of time (typically one to four weeks). These thresholds are almost certainly "wrong" because any impact that occurs after the cutoff should count in the return on investment (ROI) calculation. We explain why practitioners typically choose relatively short impact windows. The intuition is that the longer the time window

---

4. Not all experiments are created equal and methodologies to use preexperiment data to enhance power as well as postexperiment trimming have advanced considerably in the digital era (Deng, Kohavi, and Walker 2013).
5. Pun intended.

under study, the lower the signal-to-noise ratio in the data (presuming the ad gets less impactful over time): point estimates of the cumulative effect tend to increase with longer time horizons, but standard errors of the effect increase by even more. This leads to an estimation "impossibility" analogous to the well-known "curse of dimensionality."

In the next two sections we shift our gaze further into the future. First, we discuss how computational methods have increased advertising effectiveness through automated targeting and bidding. With automated targeting, the conversation is usefully shifted from "who to hit" to "what should I get." Currently, the key parameters of the automated system such as the valuation of actions such as clicks or conversions, the budget of the campaign and the duration, must still be entered by a human. Indeed, these are the exact parameters that we have argued are very difficult to estimate. However, there is no major technical barrier to incorporating controlled randomization—on the fly experimentation—into the core algorithm. By constantly incorporating experimentation, an informative prior could be developed and returns could be more precisely estimated (which would then govern bid, budget, and so forth). To unlock the full potential of this class of algorithms, ad exchanges would have to provide data to participants on the outcomes of auctions in which the bidder intentionally lost. Currently, outcome tracking is only possible if you win the auction, meaning today this type of experimentation is limited to temporal and geography-based identification, severely limiting power. In our final section we extend the discussion on how advances in ad delivery, measurement, and infrastructure are creating opportunities to advance the science of advertising. We discuss how the provision of these features and data relates to the incentives facing the advertising platform. In the final section we present concluding remarks.

7.2 Selection and Power

In today's dollars, the average American is exposed to about $500 worth of advertising per year.[6] To break even, the universe of advertisers needs to net about $1.35 in *marginal profits* per person per day. Given the gross margins of firms that advertise, our educated guess is that this roughly corresponds to about four to six dollars in incremental sales per day.

When an advertiser enters this fray, it must compete for consumers' attention. The cost per person of a typical campaign is quite low. Online "display" (banners, rectangular units, etc.) campaigns that deliver a few ads per day to a targeted individual cost about one to two cents per person per day. Televi-

---

6. Mean GDP per American is approximately $50,000 in 2011, but median household income is also approximately $50,000. The average household size is approximately 2.5, implying an individual's share of median household income is roughly $20,000. Thus, while 2 percent of GDP actually implies a per capita expenditure of $1,000, we use $500 as a round and conservative figure that is more representative of the average American's ad exposure.

sion ads delivered once per person per day are only a bit more expensive. Note that even an aggressive campaign will typically only garner a small percentage of an individual's daily advertising exposure. We see many ads per day and presumably only a minority of them are relevant enough to a given person to impact his behavior.

The relatively modest average impact per person makes it difficult to assess costeffectiveness. What complicates matters further is that individual-level sales are quite volatile for many advertisers. An extreme example is automobiles—the sales impact is either tens of thousands of dollars or zero.[7] While not as extreme, many other heavily advertised categories, including consumer electronics, clothing and apparel, jewelry, air travel, banking, and financial planning also have volatile consumption patterns.[8] Exceptions to this class are single goods sold through direct conversion channels. Here we summarize work presented in Lewis and Rao (2013), which used twenty-five large advertising field experiments to quantify how individual expenditure volatility impacts the power of advertising effectiveness (hereafter, adfx) experiments. In general, the signal-to-noise ratio is much lower than we typically encounter in economics.

We now introduce some formal notation to clarify the argument. Consider an outcome variable y (sales), an indicator variable x equal to 1 if the person was exposed to the advertising, and a regression estimate, $\hat{\beta}$, of the average difference between the exposed (E) and unexposed (U) groups. In an experiment, exposure is exogenous—determined by a flip of the proverbial coin. In an observational study, one would also condition on covariates W, which could include individual fixed effects, and the following notation would use $y|W$. All the following results go through with the usual "conditional upon" caveat. We consider a regression of y on x, whose coefficient $\hat{\beta}$ will give us a measure of the average dollar impact of the advertising per consumer.

We use standard notation for the sample means and variances of the sales of the exposed and unexposed groups, the difference in means between those groups, and the estimated standard error of that difference in means. We assume for simplicity that the exposed and unexposed samples are the same size ($N_E = N_U = N$) as well as equal variances ($\sigma_E = \sigma_U = \sigma$) to simplify the formulas:

(1) $$\bar{y}_E \equiv \frac{1}{N_E}\sum_{i\in E} y_i, \bar{y}_U \equiv \frac{1}{N_U}\sum_{i\in U} y_i$$

(2) $$\hat{\sigma}_E^2 \equiv \frac{1}{N_E - 1}\sum_{i\in E}(y_i - \bar{y}_E)^2, \hat{\sigma}_U^2 \equiv \frac{1}{N_U - 1}\sum_{i\in U}(y_i - \bar{y}_U)^2$$

---

7. The marginal profit impact is large, but clearly smaller, as it is the gross margin times the sales impact.
8. For a bank, the consumption pattern once you sign up might be predictable, but the bank is making money from consumer switching, which is "all or nothing."

(3) $$\Delta \bar{y} \equiv \bar{y}_E = \bar{y}_U$$

(4) $$\hat{\sigma}_{\Delta \bar{y}} \equiv \sqrt{\frac{\hat{\sigma}_E^2}{N_E} + \frac{\hat{\sigma}_U^2}{N_U}} = \sqrt{\frac{2}{N}} \cdot \hat{\sigma}.$$

We focus on two familiar econometric statistics. The first is the R^2 of the regression of y on x, which gives the fraction of the variance in sales explained by the advertising (or, in the model with covariates, the partial R^2 after first partialing out covariates—for more explanation, see Lovell [2008]):

(5) $$R^2 = \frac{\sum_{i \in U}(\bar{y}_U - \bar{y})^2 + \sum_{i \in E}(\bar{y}_E - \bar{y})^2}{\sum_i (y_i - \bar{y})^2} = \frac{2N[(1/2)\Delta \bar{y}]^2}{2N\hat{\sigma}^2} = \frac{1}{4}\left(\frac{\Delta \bar{y}}{\hat{\sigma}}\right)^2.$$

Second is the t-statistic for testing the hypothesis that the advertising had no impact:

(6) $$t_{\Delta \bar{y}} = \frac{\Delta \bar{y}}{\hat{\sigma}_{\Delta \bar{y}}} = \sqrt{\frac{N}{2}} \left(\frac{\Delta \bar{y}}{\hat{\sigma}}\right).$$

In both cases, we have related a standard regression statistic to the ratio between the average impact on sales and the standard deviation of sales between consumers.

In the following hypothetical example, we calibrate values using approximately median values from nineteen retail sales experiments run at Yahoo!. For expositional ease, we will discuss it as if it is a single experiment. The campaign goal is a 5 percent increase in sales during the two weeks of the campaign, which we will use as our "impact period" of interest. During this period, customers of this advertiser make purchases with a mean of $7 and a standard deviation of $75.[9] The campaign costs $0.14 per customer, which amounts to delivering 20–100 display ads at a price of $1–$5 CPM,[10] and the gross margin (markup over cost of goods sold, as a fraction of price) is assumed to be about 50 percent.[11] A 5 percent increase in sales equals $0.35 per person, netting profits of $0.175 per person. Hence, the goal for this campaign is to deliver a 25 percent return on investment (ROI): $0.175/$0.14 = 1.25.[12]

The estimation challenge facing the advertiser in this example is to detect a $0.35 difference in sales between the treatment and control groups amid

---

9. Based on data-sharing arrangements between Yahoo! and a number of advertisers spanning the range from discount to high-end retailers, the standard deviation of sales is typically about ten times the mean. Customers purchase goods relatively infrequently, but when they do, the purchases tend to be quite large relative to the mean.
10. CPM is the standard for impression-based pricing for online display advertising. It stands for "cost per mille" or "cost per thousand"; M is the Roman numeral for 1,000.
11. We base this assumption on our conversations with retailers and our knowledge of the industry.
12. For calibration purposes, note that if the gross margin were 40 percent instead of 50 percent, this would imply a 0 percent ROI.

the noise of a $75 standard deviation in sales. The ratio is very low: 0.0047. From our derivation above, this implies an R^2 of:

$$(7) \qquad R^2 = \frac{1}{4} \cdot \left(\frac{\$0.35}{\$75}\right)^2 = 0.0000054.$$

That is, even for a *successful* campaign with a *relatively large* ROI, we expect an R^2 of only 0.0000054. This will require a very large N to identify any influence at all of the advertising, let alone give a precise confidence interval. Suppose we had two million unique users evenly split between test and control in a fully randomized experiment. With a true ROI of 25 percent and a ratio of 0.0047 between impact size and standard deviation of sales, the expected t-stat is 3.30, using the above formula. This corresponds to a test with power of about 95 percent at the 10 percent (5 percent one-sided) significance level, as the normally distributed t-statistic should be less than the critical value of 1.65 about 5 percent of the time given the true effect is a 25 percent ROI. With 200,000 unique customers, the expected t-statistic is 1.04, indicating the test is hopelessly underpowered to reliably detect an economically relevant impact: under the alternative hypothesis of a healthy 25 percent ROI, we fail to reject the null 74 percent of the time.[13]

The low $R^2 = 0.0000054$ for the treatment variable x in our hypothetical randomized trial has serious implications for observational studies, such as regression with controls, difference-in-differences, and propensity score matching. A very small amount of endogeneity would *severely bias* estimates of advertising effectiveness. An omitted variable, misspecified functional form, or slight amount of correlation between browsing behavior and sales behavior generating R^2 on the order of 0.0001 is a *full order of magnitude* larger than the true treatment effect. Compare this to a classic economic example such as the Mincer wage/schooling regression (Mincer 1962), in which the endogeneity is roughly 1/8 the treatment effect (Card 1999). For observational studies, it is always important to ask, "What is the partial R^2 of the treatment variable?" If it is very small, as in the case of advertising effectiveness, clean identification becomes paramount, as a small amount of bias can easily translate into an economically large impact on the coefficient estimates.

Our view has not yet been widely adopted, however, as evidenced by the following quotation from the president of comScore, a large data provider for online advertising:

> Measuring the online sales impact of an online ad or a paid-search campaign—in which a company pays to have its link appear at the top of a page of search results—is straightforward: We determine who has viewed

---

13. Note that when a low-powered test does, in fact, correctly reject the null, the point estimates conditional on rejecting will be significantly larger than the alternatively hypothesized ROI. See Gelman and Carlin (2013) regarding this "exaggeration factor."

the ad, then compare online purchases made by those who have and those who have not seen it. (Abraham 2008)

The argument we have made shows that simply comparing exposed to unexposed can lead to bias that is many orders of magnitude larger than the true size of the effect. Indeed, this methodology led the author to report as much as a 300 percent improvement in outcomes for the exposed group, which seems surprisingly high (it would imply, for instance, that advertisers are grossly underadvertising). Since all ads have some form of targeting,[14] endogeneity is always a concern. For example, most display advertising aims to reach people likely to be interested in the advertised product, where such interest is inferred using demographics or past online behavior of that consumer. Similarly, search advertising targets consumers who express interest in a good at a particular point in time, where the interest is inferred from their search query (and potentially past browsing behavior). In these cases, comparing exposed to unexposed is precisely the *wrong* thing to do. By creating exogenous exposure, the first generation of advertising experiments have been a step in the right direction. Experiments are ideal—necessary, in fact—for solid identification.

Unfortunately, for many advertised products the volatility of sales means that even experiments with millions of unique users can still be underpowered to answer basic questions such as "Can we reject the null hypothesis that the campaign had zero influence on consumers' purchasing behavior?" Measuring sales impact, even in the short run, turns out to be much more difficult than one might have thought. The ability to randomize ad delivery on an individual level and link it to data on customer-level purchasing behavior has opened up new doors in measuring advertising effectiveness, but the task is still by no means easy. In the remainder of the chapter we discuss these challenges. The next section focuses on using the right metrics to evaluate advertising.

7.3 The Evolution of Advertising Metrics

The click-through-rate, or CTR, has become ubiquitous in the analysis and decision making surrounding online advertising. It is easy to understand why: clicks are cleanly defined, easily measurable, and occur relatively frequently. An obvious but intuitively appealing characteristic is that an ad click cannot occur in the absence of an ad. If one runs 100,000 ads and gets a 0.2 percent CTR (a typical rate for a display ad or a low-ranked search ad), it is tempting to conclude the ad caused 200 new website visits. The assump-

---

14. "Untargeted" advertising usually has implicit audience targeting based on where the ads are shown or implicit complementary targeting due to other advertisers purchasing targeted inventory and leaving the remnant inventory to be claimed by advertisers purchasing "untargeted" advertising inventory.

tion may well be true for new or little-known brands. But for well-known advertisers, there are important ways that consumers might navigate to the site in the absence of an ad, such as browsing directly to the site by typing the name in the URL window of the browser or finding it in organic (that is, not paid or "sponsored") search results on a topic like "car rental." It is a mistake to assume that *all* of those 200 visits would not have occurred in the absence of the ad—that is, those clicks may be crowding out visits that would have happened via other means (Kumar and Yildiz 2011; Chan et al. 2010).

The overcounting problem is surmountable with randomized trials where the control group is used to estimate the "baseline arrival rate." For example, a sponsored search ad could be turned off during random times of the day and the firm could measure arrivals from the search engine for when the ad is running and when it is not (this approach is used in Blake, Nosko, and Tadelis [2014]).[15] A deeper problem with the CTR is what it misses. First, it does little for "brand advertisers"—firms that are not trying to generate immediate online sales, but rather to promote awareness and goodwill for the brand. To assess their spend, brand advertisers have traditionally relied on surveys that attempt to measure whether a campaign raised the opinion of the firm in the minds of their target consumers (Goldfarb and Tucker 2011b). Linking the surveys to future purchasing behavior adds another layer of complexity, both because the time frame from exposure to sale is longer (something we will discuss in more detail in section 7.5) and because it requires a reliable link from hypothetical responses to actual behavior, which can be fraught with what is known as "hypothetical bias" (Dickie, Fisher, and Gerking 1987; Murphy et al. 2005). One common approach to neutralize hypothetical bias is to use the surveys to make relative comparisons between campaigns.

For advertisers that sell goods both online and in brick-and-mortar stores the click (or online conversions) can be a poor proxy for overall ROI. Lewis and Reiley (2013a) show that for a major retailer, the *majority* of the sales impact comes offline. Johnson, Lewis, and Reiley (2013) link the offline impact to consumers who lived in close physical proximity to one of the retailer's locations. These studies indicate purely online measurements can induce a large negative bias in measuring the returns to advertising. For firms that do business on- and offline it is essential to develop the infrastructure to link online ad exposure to offline sales.

An alternative to the click is the further downstream outcome measure known as a "customer acquisition" (which itself might be considered a short-term proxy for the net-present-discounted value of a customer). Advertisers can now run "cost per acquisition" (CPA) advertising on many

---

15. Despite the simplicity of their design, Blake, Nosko, and Tadelis (2014) estimate that their employer, eBay, had been wasting tens of millions of dollars a year.

ad exchanges.[16] An acquisition, or conversion, is defined as a successful transaction that has a "qualifying connection" to the advertisement. On the surface, focusing on conversions seems more attractive than clicks because it is a step closer to sales. Unfortunately, this benefit brings with it what is known as the "attribution problem": which ad gets "credit" for a given sale? Suppose a consumer views and clicks a given ad, but does not purchase on the same day. Over the next few days, she sees a host of other ads for the product (which is likely, given a practice known as "retargeting") and then purchases the good. Which ad should get credit for the purchase?

Ad exchanges tend to use a set of rules to solve these problems from an accounting perspective. Common rules include requiring a click for credit or only counting the "last click" (so if a consumer clicks a retargeted ad, that ad gets credit). Requiring a click seems to make sense and is enormously practical as it means a record of all viewers that see the ad but do not click need not be saved.[17] However, requiring a click errs in assuming that ads can only have an impact through clicks, which is empirically not true (Lewis, Reiley, and Schreiner 2012). The "last click" rule also has intuitive appeal. The reasoning goes as follows: had the last click not occurred, the sale would not have happened. Even if this were true, which we doubt, the first click or ad view might have led to web search or other activity, including the behavioral markers used for retargeting, which made the last click possible. The causal attribution problem is typically solved by ad hoc rules set by the ad exchange or publisher such as "the first ad and the last ad viewed before purchase each get 40 percent of the credit, while the intermediate ad views share the remaining 20 percent of the credit for the purchase."[18] A proliferation of such rules gives practitioners lots of choices, but none of them necessarily gives an unbiased measurement of the performance of their ad spending. In the end, such complicated payment rules might make the click more attractive after all.

The attribution problem is also present in the question of complementaries between display and search advertising. Recent work has shown that display ads causally influence search behavior (Lewis and Nguyen 2013). The authors demonstrate this by comparing the search behavior of users exposed to the campaign ad to users who would have been served the campaign ad but were randomly served a placebo. Brand-related keywords were significantly more prevalent in the treatment group as compared to the control. The attribution problem has received more attention in online advertising because of the popularity of cost-per-acquisition and cost-per-click payment mechanisms, but it applies to offline settings as well. How do we

16. But not the major search engines, as of August 2013.
17. A CTR of ≈ 0.2 percent meaning, storage, and processing costs of only clicks involves only 1/500 of the total ad exposure logs.
18. Source: https://support.google.com/analytics/bin/answer.py?hl=en\&answer=1665189.

know, for example, whether an online ad was more responsible for an online conversion than was the television ad that same user saw? Nearly every online campaign occurs contemporaneously with a firm's offline advertising through media such as billboards and television because large advertisers are continuously advertising across many media.[19] Directly modeling the full matrix of first-order interactions is well beyond the current state of the art. Indeed in every paper we know of evaluating online advertising, the interactions with offline spending is ignored.

Our discussion thus far has indicated that the evolution of advertising metrics has brought forth new challenges linking these metrics to the causal impact on sales. However, one way in which intermediate metrics have proved unambiguously useful for advertisers is providing relatively quick feedback on targeting strategies allowing for algorithmic adjustments to the ad-serving plan. For instance, while it may be unreasonable to assume that the click captures all relevant effects of the ad, it may very natural to assume that within a given class of advertisements run by a firm a higher CTR is always preferred to a lower one. If so, bandit algorithms can be applied to improve the efficiency of advertising spend and give relative comparisons of campaign effectiveness, allowing one to prioritize better performing advertisements (Pandey and Olston 2006; Gonen and Pavlov 2007). We discuss these advances in more detail in section 7.7.

7.4 A Case Study of a Large-Scale Advertising Experiment

To get a better idea of how large advertising experiments are actually run, in this section we present a case study taken from Lewis and Reiley (2013a) (herein "LR"). Lewis and Reiley ran a large-scale experiment for a major North American retailer. The advance the paper makes is linking existing customers in the retailer's sales records, for both online and brick-and-mortar sales, to a unique online user identifier, in this case the customer's Yahoo! username.

The experiment was conducted as follows. The match yielded a sample of 1,577,256 individuals who matched on name and either e-mail or postal address. The campaign was targeted only to existing customers of the retailers as determined by the match. Of these matched users, LR assigned 81 percent to a treatment group who subsequently viewed two advertising campaigns promoting the retailer when logged into Yahoo's services. The remaining 19 percent were assigned to the control group and prevented from seeing any of the retailer's ads from this campaign on the Yahoo! network of sites. The simple randomization was designed to make the treatment-control assignment independent of all other relevant variables.

---

19. Lewis and Reiley (2013b) show that Super Bowl commercials cause viewers to search for brand-related content across a wide spectrum of advertisers.

Table 7.1   Summary statistics for the campaigns

	Campaign 1	Campaign 2	Both campaigns
Time period covered	Early fall '07	Late fall '07	
Length of campaign	14 days	10 days	
Number of ads displayed	32,272,816	9,664,332	41,937,148
Number of users shown ads	814,052	721,378	867,839
Treatment group viewing ads	63.7%	56.5%	67.9%
Mean ad views per viewer	39.6	13.4	48.3

Source: Lewis and Reiley (2013a).

The treatment group of 1.3 million Yahoo! users was exposed to two different advertising campaigns over the course of two months in fall 2007, separated by approximately one month. Table 7.1 gives summary statistics for the campaigns, which delivered 32 million and 10 million impressions, respectively. The two campaigns exposed ads to a total of 868,000 users in the 1.3-million-person treatment group. These individuals viewed an average of forty-eight ad impressions per person.

The experiment indicated an increase in sales of nearly 5 percent relative to the control group during the campaign, a point estimate that would translate to an extremely profitable campaign (with the retailer receiving nearly a 100 percent rate of return on the advertising spending). However, purchases had sufficiently high variance (due in part to 95 percent of consumers making zero purchases in a given week) to render the point estimate not statistically significantly different from zero at the 5 percent level. Controlling for available covariates (age, gender, state of residence) did not meaningfully reduce standard errors. This is a good example of how economically important effects of advertising can be statistically very difficult to detect, even with a million-person sample size. Just as we saw in section 7.2, we see here that the effects of advertising are so diffuse, explaining such a small fraction of the overall variance in sales, that the statistical power can be quite low. For this experiment, power calculations show that assuming the alternative hypothesis that the ad broke even is true, the probability of rejecting the null hypothesis of zero effect of advertising is only 21 percent.

The second important result of this initial study was a demonstration of the biases inherent in using cross-sectional econometric techniques when there is endogenous advertising exposure. This is important because these techniques are often employed by quantitative marketing experts in industry. Abraham (2008), for example, advocates comparing the purchases of exposed users to unexposed users, despite the fact that this exposure is endogenously determined by user characteristics and browsing behavior, which might easily be correlated with shopping behavior. To expose the biases in these methods, LR temporarily "discarded" their control group and compared the levels of purchases between exposed and (endogenously) unexposed parts of the treatment group. The estimated effects of advertising were three times as large as in the experiment, and with the opposite sign! This erroneous result would also have been deemed highly statistically significant. The consumers who browsed Yahoo! more intensely during this time period (and hence were more likely to see ads) tended to buy less, on average, at the retailer, regardless of whether they saw the ads or not (this makes sense, because as we will see most of the ad effect occurred offline). The control group's baseline purchases prior to the ad campaign showed the same pattern. Without an experiment an analyst would have had no way of realizing the extent of the endogeneity bias (in this case, four times as large as the true causal effect size) and may have come to a strikingly wrong conclusion.

Observing the consistent differences between exposed and unexposed groups over time motivated LR to employ a difference-in-differences estimator. Assuming that any unobserved heterogeneity was constant over time allowed LR to take advantage of both exogenous and endogenous sources of variation in advertising exposure, which turned out to reduce standard errors to the point where the effects were statistically significant at the 5 percent level. The point estimate was approximately the same as (though slightly higher than) the straight experimental estimate, providing a nice specification check. With this estimator, LR also demonstrated that the effects of the advertising were persistent for weeks after the end of the campaign, that the effects were significant for in-store as well as online sales (with 93 percent of the effect occurring offline), and that the effects were significant even for those consumers who merely viewed but never clicked the online ads (with an estimated 78 percent of the effect coming from nonclicking viewers). In a companion paper (Lewis and Reiley, forthcoming), the authors also showed that the effects were particularly strong for the older consumers in the sample—sufficiently strong to be statistically significant even with the simple (less efficient) experimental estimator.

In a follow-up study, Johnson, Lewis, and Reiley ([2013], henceforth JLR) improved on some of the weaknesses of the design of the original LR experiment. First, JLR ran "control ads" (advertising one of Yahoo!'s own services) to the control group, allowing them to record which control-group members would have been exposed to the ad campaign if they had been in the treatment group. This allowed them to exclude from their analysis those users (in both treatment and control groups) who were not exposed to the ads and therefore contributed noise but no signal to the statistics. Second, JLR convinced the advertiser to run equal-sized treatment and control groups, which improved statistical power relative to the LR article's 81:19 split. Third, JLR obtained more detailed data on purchases: two years of precampaign sales data on each individual helped to explain some of the variance in purchases, and disaggregated daily data during the campaign allowed them to exclude any purchases that took place before the first ad delivery to a given customer (which, therefore, could not have been caused by the ads, so including those purchases merely contributed noise to the estimates). The more precise estimates in this study corroborate the results of LR, showing point estimates of a profitable 5 percent increase in advertising, which are statistically significant at the 5 percent level, though the confidence intervals remain quite wide.

7.5 Activity Bias

In the preceding sections, we have presented this argument on an abstract level, arguing that the since the partial R^2 of advertising, even for a successful campaign, is so low (on the order of 0.00001 or less), the likelihood of omitted factors not accounting for this much variation is unlikely, especially since ads are targeted across time and people. In this section we show that our argument is not just theoretical. Here we identify a bias that we believe is present in most online ad serving; in past work, we gave it the name "activity bias" (Lewis, Rao, and Reiley 2011). Activity bias is a form of selection bias based on the following two features of online consumer behavior: (1) since one has to be browsing online to see ads, those browsing more actively on a given day are more likely to see your ad; and (2) active browsers tend to do more of *everything online*, including buying goods, clicking links, and signing up for services. Any of the selection mechanisms that lead to their exposure to the advertising are highly correlated with other online activities. Indeed, many of the selection mechanisms that lead to their exposure to the advertising, such as retargeting[20] and behavioral targeting, are highly correlated with other online activities. Hence, we see that ad exposure is highly and noncausally correlated with many online activities, making most panel and time-series methods subject to bias. In a nonexperimental study, the unexposed group, as compared to the group exposed to an ad, typically failed to see the ad for one or both of the following reasons: the unexposed users browsed less actively or the user did not qualify for the targeting of the campaign. When the former fails, we have activity bias. When the latter fails, we have classic selection bias.

In our 2011 paper, we explored three empirical examples demonstrating the importance of activity bias in different types of web browsing. The first application investigates the causal effects of display ads on users' search queries. In figure 7.1 we plot the time series of the number of searches by exposed users for a set of keywords deemed to be brand-relevant for a firm. The figure shows results for a time period that includes a one-day-display advertising campaign for a national brand on www.yahoo.com.

The campaign excluded a randomized experimental control group, though for the moment we ignore the control group and focus on the sort

20. For a discussion and empirical analysis of retargeting see Lambrecht and Tucker (2013).

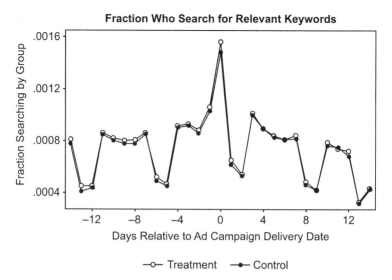

Fig. 7.1 Brand keyword search patterns over time
Source: Lewis, Rao, and Reiley (2011).

of observational data typically available to advertisers (the treatment group, those that saw the firm's advertisements). The x-axis displays days relative to the campaign date, which is labeled as Day 0. One can easily see that on the date of the ad, ad viewers were much more likely to conduct a brand-relevant search than on days prior or following. The advertising appears to *double* baseline search volume. Is this evidence of a wildly successful ad? Actually, no. Examining the control group, we see almost the same trend. Brand-relevant keyword searches also spike for those who saw a totally irrelevant ad. What is going on? The control group is, by design of the experiment, just as active online as the treatment group, searching for more of *everything*, not just the brand-relevant keywords of interest. The time series also shows that search volume is positively serially correlated over time and shows striking day-of-week effects—both could hinder observational methods. The true treatment-control difference is a statistically significant, but far more modest, 5.1 percent. Without an experiment, we would have no way of knowing the baseline "activity-related increase" that we infer from the control group. Indeed, we might have been tempted to conclude the ad was wildly successful.

Our second application involves correlation of activity not just across a publisher and search engine, but across very different domains. We ran a marketing study to evaluate the effectiveness of a video advertisement promoting the Yahoo! network of sites. We recruited subjects on Amazon Mechanical Turk, showed them the video, and gave them a Yahoo! cookie so we could track their future behavior. Using the cookie we could see if the

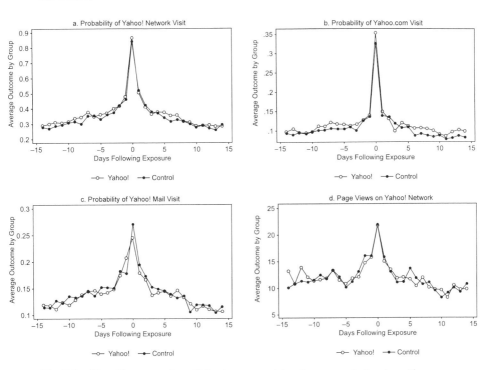

Fig. 7.2 The effect on various Yahoo! usage metric of exposure to treatment/control ads

Source: Lewis, Rao, and Reiley (2011).

Note: Panels A, B, and C: probability of at least one visit to the Yahoo! network, Yahoo.com, and Yahoo! mail, respectively. Panel D: total page views on the Yahoo! network.

ad really generated more Yahoo! activity. The control group saw a political ad totally unrelated to Yahoo! products and services. Again, we ignore the control group to begin. Figure 7.2 has the same format as figure 7.1 Day 0 on the x-axis labels the day an individual saw the video ad (with the actual calendar date depending on the day the subject participated in the study).

Examining the treatment group, we can see that on the day of and the days following ad exposure, subjects were much more likely to visit a Yahoo! site as compared to their baseline propensity, indicating a large apparent lift in engagement. However, data on the control group reveals the magnitude of activity bias—a very similar spike in activity on Yahoo! occurs on the day of placebo exposure as well. Both groups also show some evidence of positive serial correlation in browsing across days: being active today makes it more likely that you will be active tomorrow as compared to several days from now. People evidently do not engage in the same online activities (such as visiting Yahoo! and visiting Amazon Mechanical Turk) every day, but they engage in somewhat bursty activity that is contemporaneously correlated across sites. Online activity leads to ad exposure, which mechanically tends to occur on the same days as outcome measures we hope to affect with advertising. In the absence of a control group, we can easily make errors in causal inference due to activity bias. In this particular case, the true causal effect of the ad was estimated to be small and not statistically significant—given the cost of running a video ad, it was probably not worth showing, but the biased estimates would have led us to a wrong conclusion in this regard.

The third application again involves multiple websites. This time the outcome measure was filling out a new account sign-up form at an online brokerage advertised on Yahoo! Finance. Again, our results show that even those who were randomly selected to see irrelevant placebo ads were much more likely to sign up on the day they saw the (placebo) ad than on some other day. We refer the reader to our original paper for the details, stating here that the results are very similar to the ones we have just presented (the now familiar mountain-shaped graphs are again present). With activity bias it seems that one could erroneously "show" that nearly any browsing behavior is caused by nearly any other browsing behavior! We hope that our results will cause industry researchers to be more cautious in their conclusions. Activity bias is a real form of bias that limits the reliability of observational methods.

In the absence of an experiment, researchers may be able to use some other cross-validation technique in order to check the robustness of causal effects. For example, one could measure the effect of movie advertisements on searches for the seemingly irrelevant query "car rental." Similarly, one could check whether (placebo) ad views of a Toyota ad on the *New York Times* website on May 29 causes the same effect on Netflix subscriptions that day as did the actual Netflix ad on the *New York Times* website on May 30. Differences in differences using such pseudo-control groups will likely give better estimates of true causal effects than simple time-series or cross-sectional studies, though, of course, a randomized experiment is superior if it is available (Lewis, Rao, and Reiley 2011).[21]

Is activity bias a new phenomenon that is unique to the online domain? While it is not obvious that offline behavior is as bursty and as contemporaneously correlated as online behavior, before our study we did not think these patterns were obvious in online behavior either (and scanning industry white papers, one will see that many others still do not find it obvious!). We believe the importance of activity bias in the offline domain is an open question. It is not difficult to come up with examples in which offline advertising exposure could spuriously correlate with dependent variables of interest. Billboards undoubtedly "cause" car accidents. Ads near hospitals "cause" illness. Restaurant ads near malls probably "cause" food consumption in

---

21. In some cases, even such placebo tests may fail as the qualifications for seeing the ad may be intrinsically correlated with the desired outcome, as may be the case for remarketing and other forms of targeting, which account for search activity and browsing behavior.

general. Exposure to ads in the supermarket saver are likely correlated with consumption of unadvertised products, and so forth. The superior quality of data (and experiments) available in online advertising has laid bare the presence of activity bias in this domain. We believe the level of activity bias in other domains is an interesting, open question.

7.6 Measuring the Long-Run Returns to Advertising

Any study of advertising effectiveness invariably has to specify the window of time to be included in the study. While effects of advertising could in principle last a long time, in practice one must pick a cut-off date. From a business perspective, making decisions quickly is an asset worth trading decision accuracy for at the margin. But can patient scholars (or firms) hope to measure the long-run effects of advertising? Here we address the statistical challenges of this question. The answer, unfortunately, is rather negative. As one moves further and further from the campaign date, the cumulative magnitude of the sales impact tends to increase. (This is not guaranteed, as ads could simply shift purchases forward in time, so a short time window could measure a positive effect while a long time window gives a zero effect. But in practice, we have so far noticed point estimates of cumulative effects to be increasing in the time window we have studied.) However, the amount of noise in the estimate tends to increase faster than the increase in the signal (treatment effect) itself because in the additional data the control and treatment groups look increasingly similar, making long-run studies less statistically feasible than short-run ones. In the remainder of this section we formalize and calibrate this argument.

We again employ the treatment versus control t-statistic indexed by little t for time. For concreteness, let time be denominated in weeks. For notational simplicity, we will assume constant variance in the outcome over time, no covariance in outcomes over time,[22] constant variance across exposed and unexposed groups, and balanced group sizes. We will consider the long-term effects by examining a cumulative t-statistic (against the null of no effect) for T weeks rather than a separate statistic for each week. We write the cumulative t-statistic for T weeks as:

$$(8) \quad t_{\Delta \bar{y}_t} = \sqrt{\frac{N}{2}} \left(\frac{\sum_{t=1}^{T} \Delta_{\bar{y}_t}}{\sqrt{T} \hat{\sigma}} \right).$$

At first glance, this t-statistic appears to be a typical $O(\sqrt{T})$ asymptotic rate with the numerator being a sum over T ad effects and the denominator grow-

---

22. This assumption is clearly false: individual heterogeneity and habitual purchase behavior result in serial correlation in purchasing behavior. However, as we are considering the analysis over time, if we assume a panel structure with fixed effect or other residual-variance absorbing techniques to account for the source of this heterogeneity, this assumption should not be a first-order concern.

ing at a $\sqrt{T}$ rate. This is where economics comes to bear. Since $\Delta_{\bar{y}t}$ represents the impact of a given advertising campaign during and following the campaign (since $t = 1$ indexes the first week of the campaign), $\Delta_{\bar{y}t} \geq 0$. But the effect of the ad each week cannot be a constant—if it were, the effect of the campaign would be infinite. Thus, it is generally modeled to be decreasing over time.

With a decreasing ad effect, we should still be able to use all of the extra data we gather following the campaign to obtain more statistically significant effects, right? Wrong. Consider the condition necessary for an additional week to increase the t-statistic:

$$t_{\Delta\bar{y}T} < t_{\Delta\bar{y}T+1}$$

$$\frac{\sum_{t=1}^{T}\Delta_{\bar{y}t}}{\sqrt{T}} < \frac{\sum_{t=1}^{T+1}\Delta_{\bar{y}t}}{\sqrt{T+1}}.$$

Some additional algebra leads us to

$$1 + \frac{1}{T} < \left(1 + \frac{\Delta_{\bar{y}T+1}}{\sum_{t=1}^{T}\Delta_{\bar{y}t}}\right)^2,$$

which approximately implies

(9) $$\frac{1}{2} \cdot \frac{1}{T}\sum_{t=1}^{t}\Delta_{\bar{y}t} < \Delta_{\bar{y}T+1}.$$

This last expression says, "If the next week's expected effect is less than one-half the average effect over all previous weeks, then adding it in will only reduce precision." Thus, the marginal week can easily cloud the previous weeks, as its signal-to-noise ratio is not sufficiently large enough to warrant its inclusion.[23] If the expected impact of the campaign following exposure decays rapidly (although not necessarily all the way to zero), it is likely that including additional weeks beyond the campaign weeks will decrease the statistical precision.

Suppose that you were just content with the lower bound of the confidence interval increasing in expectation. A similar calculation, under similar assumptions, shows that the lower bound of a 95 percent confidence interval will increase if and only if

(10) $$1.96(\sqrt{T+1} - \sqrt{T}) < \frac{\Delta_{\bar{y}T+1}}{\hat{\sigma}/\sqrt{N}}$$

where the right-hand expression is the marginal expected t-statistic of the $T + 1^{th}$ week.

---

23. Note that this expression is completely general for independent random draws under any marginal indexing or ordering. In the identically distributed case, though, the expected mean for the marginal draw is equal to all inframarginal draws, so the inequality always holds.

We can summarize these insights by returning to our formula for the *t*-statistic:

$$t_{\Delta \bar{y} T} = \sqrt{\frac{N}{2}} \left(\frac{\sum_{t=1}^{T} \Delta_{\bar{y}t}}{\sqrt{T} \sigma} \right).$$

Since the denominator is growing at $O(\sqrt{T})$, in order for the *t*-statistic to grow, the numerator must grow at a faster rate. In the limit we know this cannot be, as the total impact of the advertising would diverge faster than even the harmonic series.[24]

Now, ex ante it is hard to know when the trade-off turns against you. The effect may decay slower than the harmonic series initially and then move toward zero quite quickly. Of course, if we knew the pattern of decay, we would have answered the question the whole exercise is asking! So in the end, the practitioner must make a judgment call. While choosing longer time frames for advertising effectiveness analyses should capture more of the cumulative effect (assuming that it is generally positive), including additional weeks may just cloud the picture by adding more noise than ad impact. Measuring the effects of advertising inherently involves this sort of "judgment call"—an unsatisfying step in the estimation process for any empirical scientist. But the step is necessary since, as we have shown, estimating the long-run effect of advertising is a losing proposition—the noise eventually overwhelms the signal. The question is "when," and right now our judgment call is to use one to four weeks, but this is far from the final word.

7.7 Advances in Computational Advertising

In traditional media, targeting is typically a human-controlled process of determining the demographic groups most likely to consume the product. Readers may be familiar with Nielsen ratings for television, which break down to viewership by demographic categories. Campaigns often have "reach goals" for specific demographics a firm is interested in advertising to and marketing representatives use a portfolio of media outlets to meet these goals.

Online advertising opens up the possibilities for automated approaches to targeting because online ad delivery systems both gather information about specific users and make real-time, ad-serving decisions. "Computational advertising" is described by one of the founders of the field, Andrei Broder, as "a principled way to find the best match between a given user in a given context and a suitable advertisement" (Broder 2008). In traditional media, you have to specify who you want to advertise to. With computational adver-

---

24. We note that an asset with infinite (nominal) returns is not implausible per se (a consol does this), but we do find infinite effects of advertising implausible. The harmonic series is $\Sigma(1/t)$ whereas the requisite series for an increasing *t*-statistic would be $\approx \Sigma(1/\sqrt{t})$, which diverges much more quickly.

tising, you instead specify outcome metrics—an end-goal supported by the system—and the system's algorithms determine how to achieve that goal most efficiently. The end goal could be online sign-ups, clicks to a sales page, and so on. The end goals a system can support is limited by the bidding rules and data feedback supported by the advertising exchange. Some supported goals, such as conversions, might exhibit slow learning because the success rate is so low (1 in 300,000 would not be uncommon for account sign-ups, for instance).

While the details of these systems are well beyond the scope of this chapter, we will give the flavor of how they work. Which display ad to show can be modeled as a multiarmed bandit problem. The possible ads are the "arms" and a user-ad pair is a "pull of the arm." Papers in this literature adapt classic machine learning tools to the ad-serving context (see, for instance, Pandey, Chakrabarti, and Agarwal [2007]). A complimentary approach (which borrows from search advertising technology) is to view the advertisement as a document that must be retrieved and matched to the content page the ad is served on (which can be thought of as the query in search terminology; Rusmevichientong and Williamson 2006; Cary et al. [2007]).

We view (the current incarnation of) computational advertising primarily as automated targeting and local bid adjustment (to equalize CTR across campaigns, for instance). It helps to *locally* optimize ad spend by minimizing costs for given a campaign goal. By using an end goal, such as clicks or sign-ups, combined with a budget, these systems reduce the need to set targeting dimensions (reduces, not eliminates, because one might still set priors for the learning system, which might matter a lot in slow-to-learn tasks) and funnels spend to better performing inventory. Focusing on end goals also helps shift the conversation from "Who should get ads?" to "What do we want to get from our ad spending?" Practitioners should be cautious, however, that the system does not conflate "the audience most likely to convert" to the "audience that delivers the most *additional* conversions." To see the difference, imagine a customer that would buy anyway, but finds it convenient to click on an ad if he sees one. Paying for this conversion is a total waste of money. In our experience, some automated systems fail to draw this distinction and in doing so "order anticipate" by advertising to people likely to make a future purchase anyway. A natural solution is to integrate computational advertising with experimental platforms to provide randomization in order to measure incremental conversions. The technical infrastructure to make this possible would require advertisers to express a demand for reliable information.

Computational advertising is providing advances in advertising science. It can improve efficiency in the market by providing a better match of advertisements to consumers, thereby creating value, but current systems do not solve all the challenges we have laid out thus far, such as how much of a given action should be attributed to a given ad. For instance, suppose an online brokerage calculates that it nets $100 in profit from every account sign-up. Should it specify $100 as a maximum bid on an automated system and then "set it and forget it?" Presumably the brokerage is advertising heavily on TV and other media, including other online media that was not the "last click." Bidding $100 effectively says all this other spending gets zero credit—the firm would overadvertise using this rule. Of course, this is just the attribution problem reframed from the advertiser's perspective.

Thus, it is our opinion that many of the difficulties we have discussed about globally optimizing ad spending apply to *the current incarnation* of computational advertising as well. Perhaps the next revolution in advertising science will be in core algorithms to conduct automated experiments to measure incremental conversions and self-govern bids based on the experimental feedback. To our knowledge, there are no major technical barriers to this sort of pervasive experimentation and it has been applied fruitfully to infer causality in other online settings (Li et al. 2010). The challenge is that unlike ranking in search or recommendation of a news story, the response rate on a profitable ad is very low, on the order of 1/100–1/1000 for clicks on a display ad and an order of magnitude smaller for purchases, meaning feedback typically has low informational content. A second challenge is that the advertising exchange would have to facilitate the use of this technology by providing data on auctions the advertiser did not win (due to randomly entering a bid of 0 to experiment, for instance), which interacts with privacy concerns and platform incentives in interesting ways. Current practice does not provide this level of feedback, and we discuss workarounds firms currently use further on.

7.8 Moving Forward

Digital measurement has opened up many doors in measuring advertising effectiveness, but many challenges persist. In this section we look toward the future and discuss how we think many of the existing challenges will be overcome. Overall, we expect the advances to mainly come from better experimentation infrastructure to generate high-quality data at scale.

Experimental infrastructure has the potential to drastically reduce the cost of experimentation. The first generation of field experiments we ran at Yahoo! randomly selected a relatively small sample of users targeted by the campaign to see an unrelated advertisement. The problem was that an unrelated ad had to be entered into the booking system and run for the users that were randomized into the control group. The booking system was set up so that a firm could run multiple "creatives" (different versions of the ad) and the firm for whom we ran the experiment did not want to let another retailer get the traffic, because the competitor would benefit from the targeting dimensions set up by the retailer (including, for instance, past purchasing behavior).[25] The solution was to use charity ads for the control group. But this meant that either the advertiser had to pay for the control ads or Yahoo! had to donate them—both options came at a cost that increased linearly in the size of the control group, meaning that first generation experiments had relatively small control groups.

A small control group not only hurts power but also makes experimentation less useful as an evaluative tool. An experiment with 90 percent of subjects in the treatment group and 10 percent in the control has the same power as one with 10 percent in the treatment and 90 percent control. If control ads are free, then an advertiser could run nine of the latter for the cost of one of the former.[26] For control ads to be free, the ad server needs to be able to serve the "next ad in line" every time a user is randomized into the control group. Technologically, this requires a short-serving latency between the request to the ad server, the randomization, and the request for the replacement ad. The replacement ads are known as "ghost ads"—ads that naturally qualified to be served to a given user targeted by the campaign under study but not associated with the advertiser. Ghost ads make exploration and evaluation cheaper. Small treatment groups limit cost and allow advertisers to hone copy early in a campaign, while free control subjects help evaluate the campaign ex post.

Major online publishers are developing similar experimentation platforms. As experiments become cheaper and easier to run, advertisers will be able to form more precise beliefs on effectiveness than has heretofore been possible and further integrate experimentation into computational advertising platforms. These systems could incorporate an informative prior, which would help combat the power concerns we detailed earlier.

Another experimentation technology that improves power is the preexperiment matching of users. To see how this works, consider an experiment with subjects spread across treatment and control fifty-fifty. A standard experiment would simply flip a coin each time a user arrived at the website and show the ad corresponding to the outcome of the flip. Matching works as follows: Specify a set of attributes you care about such as recent sales levels and linear time trend. Form pairs of users by minimizing some objective function that defines the distance between two nodes in the graph of users. Then for each pair, flip a coin to determine experimental grouping. By

---

25. The treatment/control comparison would also provide the answer to a different question of advertising effectiveness.

26. Note that the statistical gains from such a change in experimental design are threefold. Further altering the design, assuming constant returns to scale from advertising (Lewis 2010; Johnson, Lewis, and Reiley 2012), by concentrating the 90 percent treatment group's ad impressions all within a smaller 10 percent treatment group expects an impact that is nine times as large, resulting in the equivalent ad effectiveness insights from running 81 of the 90 percent/10 percent experiments, producing confidence intervals of the ROI that are nine times more precise at no additional advertising cost.

construction, the specified metrics should be almost exactly equal between the two groups. For evaluating a noisy variable such as sales, guaranteeing the preperiod sales were the same can be useful. The treatment assignment is still totally exogenous, so all our normal intuition on how experiments identify causal effects goes through. Recent work has demonstrated that these techniques can double the power of experiments in many relevant settings (Deng, Kohavi, and Walker 2013).

These experimentation technologies create great potential for the next generation of computational advertising algorithms that we discussed in the last section. Automated experimentation would not be possible without the ability to deliver "non-ads" for free, record the interaction, and provide this feedback to nonwinning bidders. Of course, major publishers and exchanges will have to facilitate this capability, currently an advertiser bidding on an exchange only gets data on the impression (and what happens to the user) only when it wins the auction. Temporally (or geographic) based experiments offer something of a workaround, but can severely damage power (Nosko, and Tadelis 2014). As to whether this capability becomes standard practice for ad exchanges will presumably depend on advertiser demand, market power by major ad exchanges, and privacy legislation.

The future is also looking up for evaluating television advertising and associated "cross media" interaction effects (Joo et al. 2013). More people are viewing TV through devices like the Xbox and through services like Google TV, both of which link users to ads in systems similar to major web publishers. Furthermore, these users often have identifiers that can link television, sponsored search, and display ads for a single individual. Never before in the history of advertising has this been possible. The ability to measure cross-channel effects with the reliability of randomized experiments opens the door to many new questions for academics and many new strategies for advertisers. As more forms of advertising become measurable on an individual level, our ability to provide reliable estimates of advertising effectiveness will expand as well. The advances so far have already set a new state of the art in measurement, and we expect the trend to continue.

7.9 Concluding Remarks

The science of measuring advertising effectiveness has evolved considerably due to new digital data sources and experimentation platforms. We view experimentation on the individual level with the ad delivery linked to purchasing behavior as a true game changer offered by digital media as compared to traditional counterparts. Whether in search or display, new advertisers can gather feedback that is immune from the biases that plague observational methods. Another important advance is computational advertising. Computational advertising helps solve the targeting problem and usefully shifts the conversation from "who to hit" to "what do I get." Yet neither of these advances has yet to solve all the measurement problems in advertising science. Experiments are noisy and computational advertising still relies on humans to enter the key parameters, such as valuations of clicks or conversions, that govern spend. The future holds promise, but depends on economic incentives that at this point are hard to predict.

Moving forward, experimentation and data collection technology is evolving alongside new forms of ad serving and computational advertising systems. Questions such as the cross-derivative of certain media on the effectiveness of other media will be in play in the coming years. Measuring the effectiveness of media, such as television, that were previously not technologically feasible because randomizing delivery was not possible at scale, will also greatly expand knowledge on advertising effectiveness. This will in turn allow firms to more accurately guide their advertising expenditure. Our view, however, is that challenges such as measuring the long-run effects of advertising and the impact of brand advertising appear to be out of reach for at least the next five to ten years, if not longer. We await new developments in advertising science at the digital frontier to facilitate the answers to these and new questions.

References

Abraham, M. 2008. "The Off-Line Impact of Online Ads." *Harvard Business Review* 86 (4): 28.
Bagwell, K. 2007. "The Economic Analysis of Advertising." In *Handbook of Industrial Organization*, vol. 3, edited by M. Armstrong and R. Porter. Amsterdam: North Holland.
Becker, G. S., and K. M. Murphy. 1993. "A Simple Theory of Advertising as a Good or Bad." *Quarterly Journal of Economics* 108 (4): 941–64.
Blake, T., C. Nosko, and S. Tadelis. 2014. "Consumer Heterogeneity and Paid Search Effectiveness: A Large Scale Field Experiment." NBER Working Paper no. 20171, Cambridge, MA.
Broder, A. 2008. "Computational Advertising and Recommender Systems." In *Proceedings of the 2008 ACM Conference on Recommender Systems*, 1–2. Association for Computing Machinery.
Bureau of Labor Statistics. 2010. *American Time Use Survey*. http://www.bls.gov/tus/charts/leisure.htm.
Card, D. 1999. "The Causal Effect of Education on Earnings." In *Handbook of Labor Economics*, vol. 3, edited by O. C. Ashenfelter and D. Card, 1801–63. Amsterdam: North Holland.
Cary, M., A. Das, B. Edelman, I. Giotis, K. Heimerl, A. Karlin, C. Mathieu, and M. Schwarz. 2007. "Greedy Bidding Strategies for Keyword Auctions." In *Proceedings of the 8th ACM conference on Electronic Commerce*, 262–71. Association for Computing Machinery.
Chan, D., R. Ge, O. Gershony, T. Hesterberg, and D. Lambert. 2010. "Evaluating Online Ad Campaigns in a Pipeline: Causal Models at Scale." In *Proceedings of*

the *16th ACM SIGKDD International Conference on Knowledge Discovery and Data Mining*, 7–16. Association for Computing Machinery.

Demsetz, H. 1982. "Barriers to Entry." *American Economic Review* 72 (1): 47–57.

Deng, A., Y. Xu, R. Kohavi, and T. Walker. 2013. "Improving the Sensitivity of Online Controlled Experiments by Utilizing Pre-Experiment Data." In *Proceedings of the sixth ACM International Conference on Web Search and Data Mining*, 123–32. Association for Computer Machinery.

Dickie, M., A. Fisher, and S. Gerking. 1987. "Market Transactions and Hypothetical Demand Data: A Comparative Study." *Journal of the American Statistical Association* 82 (397): 69–75.

Gelman, A., and J. Carlin. 2013. "Beyond Power Calculations to a Broader Design Analysis, Prospective or Retrospective, Using External Information." Working Paper, Columbia University.

Goldfarb, A., and C. Tucker. 2011a. "Online Display Advertising: Targeting and Obtrusiveness." *Marketing Science* 30 (3): 389–404.

———. 2011b. "Search Engine Advertising: Channel Substitution When Pricing Ads to Context." *Management Science* 57 (3): 458–70.

Gonen, R., and E. Pavlov. 2007. "An Incentive-Compatible Multi-Armed Bandit Mechanism." In *Proceedings of the 26th Annual ACM Symposium on Principles of Distributed Computing*, 362–3. Association for Computing Machines.

Hu, Y., L. M. Lodish, and A. M. Krieger. 2007. "An Analysis of Real World TV Advertising Tests: A 15-Year Update." *Journal of Advertising Research* 47 (3): 341.

Johnson, G., R. A. Lewis, and D. H. Reiley. 2012. "Location, Location, Location: Geo-Targeting Increases Effectiveness of Online Display Advertising." Unpublished manuscript.

———. 2013. "Add More Ads? Experimentally Measuring Incremental Purchases Due to Increased Frequency of Online Display Advertising." Working Paper, Rochester University.

Joo, M., K. C. Wilbur, B. Cowgill, and Y. Zhu. 2013. "Television Advertising and Online Search." *Management Science* 60 (1): 56–73.

Kessides, I. N. 1986. "Advertising, Sunk Costs, and Barriers to Entry." *Review of Economics and Statistics* 68 (1): 84–95.

Kumar, D., and T. Yildiz. 2011. "Measuring Online Ad Effectiveness." In *12th ACM Conference on Electronic Commerce*. Association for Computing Machines.

Lambrecht, A., and C. Tucker. 2013. "When Does Retargeting Work? Information Specificity in Online Advertising." *Journal of Marketing Research* 50 (5): 561–76.

Lewis, R. 2010. "Where's the Wear-Out?" Online Display Ads and the Impact of Frequency." PhD diss., Massachusetts Institute of Technology.

Lewis, R. A., and D. T. Nguyen. 2013. "A Samsung Ad and the iPad: Display Advertising's Spillovers to Online Search." Unpublished manuscript.

Lewis, R. A., and J. M. Rao. 2013. "On the Near-Impossibility of Measuring the Returns to Advertising." Unpublished manuscript.

Lewis, R., J. Rao, and D. Reiley. 2011. "Here, There, and Everywhere: Correlated Online Behaviors Can Lead to Overestimates of the Effects of Advertising." In *Proceedings of the 20th International Conference on World Wide Web*, 157–66. Association for Computing Machines.

Lewis, R. A., and D. H. Reiley. Forthcoming. "Advertising Effectively Influences Older Users: A Yahoo! Experiment Measuring Retail Sales." *Review of Industrial Organization*.

———. 2013a. "Online Advertising and Offline Sales: Measuring the Effects of Retail Advertising via a Controlled Experiment on Yahoo!" Unpublished manuscript.

———. 2013b. "Super Bowl Advertising Causes Down-to-the-Minute Online Search Behavior." In *Proceedings of the 14th ACM Conference on Electronic Commerce*. Association for Computing Machines.

Lewis, R., D. Reiley, and T. Schreiner. 2012. "Ad Attributes and Attribution: Large-Scale Field Experiments Measure Online Customer Acquisition." Unpublished manuscript.

Li, L., W. Chu, J. Langford, and R. E. Schapire. 2010. "A Contextual-Bandit Approach to Personalized News Article Recommendation." In *Proceedings of the 19th International Conference on World Wide Web*, 661–70. Association for Computing Machines.

Lodish, L., M. Abraham, S. Kalmenson, J. Livelsberger, B. Lubetkin, B. Richardson, and M. Stevens. 1995. "How TV Advertising Works: A Meta-Analysis of 389 Real World Split Cable TV Advertising Experiments." *Journal of Marketing Research* 32 (2): 125–39.

Lovell, M. 2008. "A Simple Proof of the FWL Theorem." *Journal of Economic Education* 39 (1): 88–91.

Mincer, J. 1962. "On-the-Job Training: Costs, Returns, and Some Implications." *Journal of Political Economy* 70 (5): 50–79.

Murphy, J., P. Allen, T. Stevens, and D. Weatherhead. 2005. "A Meta-Analysis of Hypothetical Bias in Stated Preference Valuation." *Environmental and Resource Economics* 30 (3): 313–25.

Pandey, S., D. Chakrabarti, and D. Agarwal. 2007. "Multi-Armed Bandit Problems with Dependent Arms." In *Proceedings of the 24th International Conference on Machine Learning*, 721–8. Association for Computing Machines.

Pandey, S., and C. Olston. 2006. "Handling Advertisements of Unknown Quality in Search Advertising." In *Advances in Neural Information Processing Systems*, edited by M. Jordan, Y. LeCun, and S. Solla, 1065–72. Cambridge, MA: MIT Press.

Papadimitriou, P., H. Garcia-Molina, P. Krishnamurthy, R. A. Lewis, and D. H. Reiley. 2011. "Display Advertising Impact: Search Lift and Social Influence." In *Proceedings of the 17th ACM SIGKDD International Conference on Knowledge Discovery and Data Mining*, 1019–27. Association for Computing Machines.

Rusmevichientong, P., and D. Williamson. 2006. "An Adaptive Algorithm for Selecting Profitable Keywords for Search-Based Advertising Services." In *Proceedings of the 7th ACM Conference on Electronic Commerce*, 260–69. Association for Computing Machines.

Rutz, O. J., and R. E. Bucklin. 2011. "From Generic to Branded: A Model of Spillover in Paid Search Advertising." *Journal of Marketing Research* 48 (1): 87–102.

Tucker, C. E. 2012. "The Economics of Advertising and Privacy." *International Journal of Industrial Organization* 30 (3): 326–29.

8
Digitization and the Contract Labor Market
A Research Agenda

Ajay Agrawal, John Horton, Nicola Lacetera, and Elizabeth Lyons

8.1 Introduction

We begin this chapter on the digitization of the market for contract labor with three observations. First, this market is growing rapidly in terms of the number and variety of participants and transactions. Second, in contrast to the highly localized exchange of services typical in the traditional offline market for contract work, the online market is dominated by long distance north-south (as defined below) trade. Third, the online platforms that facilitate trade in this market introduce seemingly small informational frictions that have significant effects on outcomes. We describe each of these market features in turn.

The growth of online markets for contract labor has been fast and steady. According to Horton (2010), workers in this market earned about $700 million by 2009, and Vanham (2012) estimated this market to be worth $1 billion annually by the end of 2012. Additional details from oDesk, the largest online marketplace for contract labor in terms of earnings, provide further insight into the growth of this market. The number of employers billing on

---

Ajay Agrawal is the Peter Munk Professor of Entrepreneurship at the Rotman School of Management of the University of Toronto and a research associate of the National Bureau of Economic Research. John Horton is an economist and assistant professor in the Information Systems Group at New York University's Stern School of Business. Nicola Lacetera is assistant professor of management at the University of Toronto and a faculty research fellow of the National Bureau of Economic Research. Elizabeth Lyons is assistant professor at UC San Diego.

This research was funded by the Centre for Innovation and Entrepreneurship at the Rotman School of Management and the Social Sciences and Humanities Research Council of Canada. We thank Shane Greenstein, Catherine Tucker, Avi Goldfarb, and participants at the NBER preconference meeting at Northwestern University for valuable feedback. Errors remain our own. For acknowledgments, sources of research support, and disclosure of the authors' material financial relationships, if any, please see http://www.nber.org/chapters/c12988.ack.

the site per quarter increased by over 800 percent between 2009 and 2013 (figure 8.1), and the number of working contractors per quarter increased by approximately 1,000 percent over the same period (figure 8.3). In pecuniary terms, the quarterly wage bill on oDesk increased by approximately 900 percent, from $10,000,000 to almost $100,000,000 over the same four-year period (figure 8.2).

North-south exchange dominates the pattern of trade in these markets (e.g., relative to north-north, south-south, and south-north). In other words, employers are predominantly from high-income countries[1] and contractors are mainly from lower-income countries. We classify countries as "high income" using the 2012 World Bank list of high-income countries. We classify the remaining countries as "lower income." In figure 8.1 we illustrate that not only are there more employers on oDesk from high- compared to lower-income countries, but the number from high-income countries is also growing at a faster rate. Similarly, the wage bill per quarter is significantly greater and growing faster for employers from high- versus lower-income countries (figure 8.2). While the contrast is not quite as extreme on the contractor side of the market (a significant number of contractors are from high-income countries), there were approximately three times as many lower- versus high-income contractors in 2009 and that difference increased to five times by 2013 (figure 8.3). This does not simply reflect a growing volume of small jobs performed by contractors from lower-income countries. In figure 8.4 we illustrate that the wage bill reflects a similar pattern in terms of contractors from high- versus lower-income countries.

A number of studies examine how seemingly small information frictions may significantly influence matching outcomes in online markets for contract labor. Perhaps the most dramatic finding is the one reported by Pallais (2012). In this study, Pallais conducts a field experiment where she "treats" 952 randomly selected contractors by hiring them and then providing feedback on their performance. Then she compares the subsequent employment performance of these treated contractors with a set of 2,815 other contractors (controls) who applied for her posted jobs but whom she did not hire and therefore did not post information on. She reports that, for those with no prior work experience on oDesk, the subsequent income of treated contractors almost triples relative to the income of control contractors over the following two-month period. She then takes a number of steps to provide further evidence that the observed increase in employment performance is due to the information she posted to the platform about the contractor (i.e., rating and feedback), rather than due to other explanations such as human capital accumulation by the contractor due to the experience of doing the job. The reason this result is so dramatic is because the treatment is so small:

---

1. We define high-income countries according to the World Bank classification available at http://data.worldbank.org/income-level/HIC.

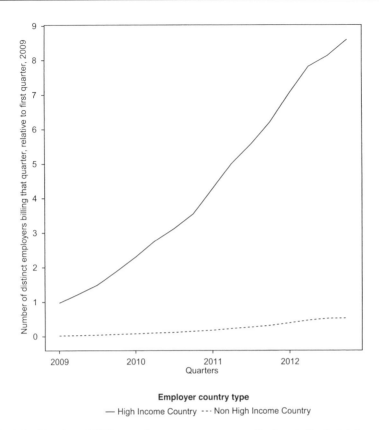

Fig. 8.1 Number of billing employers per quarter on oDesk, relative to total number of employers in first quarter of 2009, by employer country income level

Notes: This figure uses data collected from oDesk to show the relative number of billing employers per quarter, by country income status. We use the 2012 World Bank list of high-income countries for our country classification. The base quarter is the first quarter (i.e., January, February, and March) for 2009. Although the count looks like it is exactly 1 for HIC in 2009, it is slightly below—there were a small but nonzero number of employers from lower-income countries during that quarter.

the job is only a ten-hour data entry task, the rating is only a single score out of five, and the feedback is only a single sentence: "It was a pleasure working with (x)." In fact, for inexperienced workers, the marginal effect of a more detailed comment that specifies data entry speed, accuracy, following of directions, and timely task completion is not statistically distinct from zero. In other words, the trebling of income is caused by minimal information provided by the employer based on a remarkably small job. Although the observed effect is based on low-wage, data-entry specialists who propose wages of $3 per hour or less, the effect of such a seemingly small amount of information is striking. It points to an important market friction present in this online setting. The author draws a welfare implication from her find-

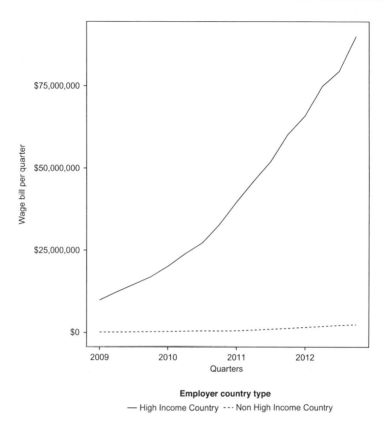

Fig. 8.2 Quarterly wage bill on oDesk by employer country income level
Notes: This figure uses data collected from oDesk to show the quarterly wage bill by the employer's country's income status. We use the 2012 World Bank list of high-income countries for our country classification.

ing: "Under plausible assumptions, the experiment's market-level benefits exceeded its cost, suggesting that some experimental workers had been inefficiently unemployed."

Similar information frictions are reported in other studies in this market setting. Stanton and Thomas (2012) estimate the effect of information from intermediaries on contractor employment. They find that inexperienced contractors affiliated with an intermediary have substantially higher jobfinding probabilities (almost double) and wages (15 percent) at the beginning of their careers on oDesk. Agrawal, Lacetera, and Lyons (2013) examine the relative role of information about experience on oDesk for contractors from high- versus low-income countries. They find that information about platform-based work experience disproportionately benefits contractors from low-income countries (approximately 40 percent premium). In a related study, Mill (2011) finds that once an employer on Freelancer has

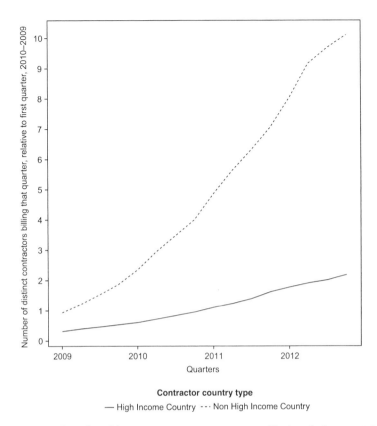

Fig. 8.3 Number of working contractors per quarter on oDesk, relative to total number of contractors in first quarter of 2009, by contractor country income level
Notes: This figure uses data collected from oDesk to show the relative number of working contractors per quarter, by country income status. We use the 2012 World Bank list of high-income countries for our country classification. The base quarter is the first quarter (i.e., January, February, and March) for 2009.

a good experience with a contractor from a particular country, then the employer is more likely to hire someone else from that country. Also related, Ghani, Kerr, and Stanton (2012) report that members of the Indian diaspora hiring on oDesk are more likely to hire workers in India than are other employers. Finally, Horton (2012) finds that recommendations increase the likelihood of a hire in job categories with fewer qualified candidates. In each of these cases, seemingly small amounts of information have significant effects on employment outcomes, suggesting that information frictions play an important role in the matching process online.

With these three market features in mind—rapid growth, north-south trade, and sensitivity to information-based frictions—we turn to analyzing the basic economics of online markets for contract labor in section 8.2. In

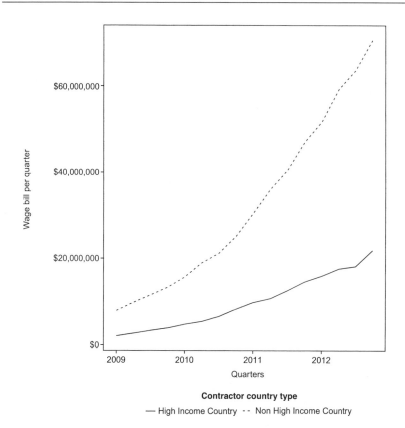

Fig. 8.4 Contractor quarterly earnings on oDesk by contractor country income level

Notes: This figure uses data collected from oDesk to show the quarterly wage bill, by the contractor's country's income status. We use the 2012 World Bank list of high-income countries for our country classification.

doing so, we consider the characteristics of both the demand and supply sides, stressing the incentives that lead employers as well as contractors to utilize this channel. The main trade-off that we consider is between the reduction in search, communication, monitoring, and transportation costs on the one hand and the potential for new sources of information-related frictions to arise on the other. We then describe the role that online contract labor platforms play in facilitating matches between demand and supply and in addressing some of these trade-offs. Again, we use evidence from oDesk to provide an in-depth illustration.

Drawing on these insights regarding the basic economic properties of online markets for contract labor, we outline a research agenda predicated on three lines of inquiry. These include: (1) distributional effects, (2) market design, and (3) welfare. We describe each in turn.

In section 8.3 we ask: How will the digitization of this market influence the distribution of economic activity? We consider distribution along three dimensions. First, we contemplate the distribution of work across geographies. Will digitization shift the distribution of contract work toward lower-income countries? Second, we question the distribution of income within and across countries. Will digitization further accentuate income inequality by amplifying superstar-type distributions, whereby only a small fraction of contractors capture a large fraction of rents (although some of these individuals may be in lower-income countries)? Finally, we raise the question of outsourcing. Will digitization lead to a shift in the distribution of work across firm boundaries, constricting the boundary of the firm due to a lowering cost of contracting out discrete jobs? The answers to these lines of inquiry regarding distribution-related effects of digitization will have important implications for understanding the effect of digitization on the overall organization of work, and thus implications for social welfare.

Next, in section 8.4 we raise this question: How might market design features influence matching in the digital setting? We describe above the impact of ratings and feedback, a market design feature common across most platforms. In the digital setting, platforms can add or change market features at reasonably low cost. However, the ease with which they can be added, deleted, or changed belies the influence they may have on matching outcomes. While contracting platforms employ many interesting market design features, we focus our discussion on five: (1) performance feedback (e.g., ratings); (2) machine-aided recommendations (for employers and contractors); (3) the allocation of visibility; (4) pricing to reduce congestion; and (5) job category specification. Although platforms in the online contract labor market do not have the match-setting power that is typically analyzed in the market design literature (i.e., directly matching trading partners in settings such as kidney exchanges and medical student-hospital matching), they do influence which matches are ultimately formed and under what terms. Thus, as market design features evolve, so will the types of matches they facilitate.

Finally, in section 8.5 we ask: How will the digitization of this market affect social welfare? In particular, we specify two channels through which digitization may generate efficiency gains: (1) better matching, and (2) better production. With regard to matching, the shift from local to global search along with the utilization of market design features enabled by the digitization of relevant information may lead to efficiency gains. With regard to production, a reduction in coordination costs that enables more flexibility in terms of the location and timing (asynchronous) of work as well as a finer division of labor due to the feasibility of contracting out smaller jobs, which enables more specialization, may lead to efficiency gains. At the same time, however, new frictions may lead to new forms of welfare losses.

We conclude by outlining three primary challenges to this research agenda. First, offline data for this sector is costly to obtain but is required to estimate the causal effect of digitization on changes in distributional properties (geography, income, firm boundaries) and welfare effects. Second, the economic salience of particular market design features may be fleeting since the market is evolving quickly and subject to rapid technological change. Finally, data ownership is concentrated among a few platforms that seem interested in engaging with the research community but have interests that are not fully aligned. Despite these challenges, this research agenda identifies opportunities to shed light on questions that are of first-order importance from both a scholarly and economic relevancy perspective.

8.2 The Economics of Online Contract Labor Markets

Like other digitized markets, the most salient features of online labor markets are the potential for a large number of transactions and services to be provided by suppliers who may be geographically distant from buyers. What are the implications for the demand and supply of services in this context? Who supplies labor online? What entities search for online services and what are the trade-offs they face? What institutions contribute to clearing these markets? To address these questions, we begin by discussing how oDesk works. This will frame the ensuing discussion on labor supply, labor demand, and market-making platforms.

8.2.1 Work Process on oDesk

To post jobs on oDesk, employers have to register on the site by giving their contact details and information on their company, including name, owner, and location. Once registered, employers are free to post as many jobs as they like. Job postings include a description of the task, the location of the employer, and the type of contract being offered. oDesk supports two contract types—hourly wage and fixed price. Beyond the different payment structures, the contracts have different implications for monitoring and duration specifications. Specifically, when posting an hourly wage job, employers have to specify the expected number of hours per week and the number of weeks required to complete the job. They stipulate a limit on the number of hours per week a contractor can work. When posting a fixed-price job, employers have to specify the budget and deadline. Employers can make job postings public (so that any contractor can apply to them) or private (so that only contractors they invite can apply to them).

To be hired on oDesk, workers similarly must register on the site by giving their contact details, name, and location as well as by setting up a profile page. Profile pages are meant to advertise contractors to potential employers and can include a description of skills, education, work experience outside of oDesk, oDesk-administered test scores, certifications, whether or not they belong to an agency, and oDesk-specific work histories and feedback scores. Once they have set up their profile pages, contractors can apply to jobs by submitting cover letters and bids to job postings. A bid indicates the amount a contractor is willing to be paid to work on a job.

Employers have the option to interview and negotiate over bids with applicants before hiring and to hire as many contractors as they like. Once hired, contractors complete tasks remotely. Contractors submit their work to employers online and are paid via oDesk. Employers have the option to give contractors bonuses and can also reimburse expenses through oDesk.

After each job, employers give contractors a rating out of five based on six criteria: skills, quality, availability, deadlines, communication, and cooperation. Each contractor also has an overall feedback score, which is a job-size-weighted average of the individual scores. Contractors can provide their employers feedback scores based on the same criteria; employers have a similarly constructed overall score. oDesk provides this service in exchange for 10 percent of every transaction made on the site.

In addition to oDesk, Elance, Freelancer, and Guru are among the largest online contract labor markets. Elance and Guru were both launched in 1999, followed by oDesk in 2005 and Freelancer in 2009. These sites are similar in that they allow employers to find and hire short-term workers by registering on the platform and posting jobs to attract applicants. Similarly, they all allow registered contract workers from around the world to apply for jobs posted on the sites by bidding on them and to advertise themselves to employers with profile pages. These platforms earn revenue by charging a percentage of each transaction or member fees to workers and, in some cases, both. In addition to providing a (virtual) place for demand and supply to meet and for the market to clear, these platforms have evolved over time toward addressing some of the key challenges of labor markets in general and online labor markets in particular.

While the other major platforms in the industry share several features with oDesk, they differ on certain dimensions. The primary variations lie in the services they provide participants. For instance, some support contractor employment agencies while others do not, some offer guaranteed payment for hourly wage contracts while others do not, and at least one of the major platforms does not have a virtual office application. Perhaps the most significant difference concerns Freelancer, which supports both traditional hiring and crowdsourcing. Given that crowdsourcing has different implications for matching and production, findings from research based on traditional hiring may not generalize to crowdsourcing settings.

8.2.2 Labor Supply

What are the incentives for individuals to supply labor online? One of the most important benefits to having access to online contract labor markets, especially for individuals participating from lower-income countries who are more constrained in terms of opportunities, is that these marketplaces dramatically increase the pool of available jobs. In addition to increasing the number of opportunities, they also increase the likelihood that contractors will find suitable matches for their skills and preferences.

Contractors also benefit from an increase in flexibility in this market setting. For the most part, these transactions are contract based: workers are not employees and therefore have more control over their schedules and how they allocate time between the provision of these services and other activities (e.g., another job, family, leisure, etc.; *The Economist* [2010]). In a survey of workers on oDesk, more than 80 percent state that the flexibility and freedom associated with working on the site is a major benefit of online work. Evidence also shows that the flexibility provided by telecommunication contributes to a significant increase in female labor force participation (Dettling 2011). Thus, these online marketplaces may induce women previously out of the labor market to enter. Especially for contractors in the developing world, who make up the vast majority of workers, easier access to job opportunities from entities in higher-income countries might also imply higher earnings.

Some of the characteristics leading to benefits in participating in these markets may also be sources of costs and risks for contractors. In particular, the contractual nature of these labor relations might lead to more uncertainty about the duration and conditions of a work relationship. The dramatic increase in participation in these markets and the typical profile of participants as relatively highly educated suggest that, on balance, these markets represent viable and appealing opportunities for a large set of individuals.

8.2.3 Demand for Contract Labor

The online market for contract labor offers several benefits to employers relative to traditional offline markets. It lowers the cost of search, communication, and transportation, which benefits trade in various services, such as data entry, translation, and software development. This also enables access to a broader pool of prospective workers with potentially more suitable skills, and possibly at more competitive wage rates. Although oDesk has a range of organization types and sizes that use the platform, the access to a large and diverse pool of contract workers provided by these platforms is particularly unique for small, entrepreneurial ventures. For instance, in a survey of employers using oDesk, more than half consider themselves start-ups.

However, the relative lack of face-to-face interactions might make it difficult for employers to extract high-bandwidth information (Autor 2001). Furthermore, the increased heterogeneity of applicants make comparisons among them more challenging; for instance, comparing seemingly similar school degrees or job experiences of applicants from different countries may be problematic, particularly for novice recruiters. In addition to hidden-quality problems, an obvious issue for prospective employers is the difficulty in monitoring and verifying effort from a distance and through an Internet-mediated transaction.

8.2.4 Market-Making Platforms

Consistent with other two-sided markets, intermediaries in online markets take actions to ensure the participation of both suppliers and buyers (Armstrong 2006; Rysman 2009). As mentioned above, a key challenge in online contract labor transactions arises from the limited access to high-bandwidth information about both applicants and employers (Autor 2001). Online contract labor platforms are increasingly providing features that attempt to solve these information problems.[2] First, platforms provide a verification and standardization device for some of this information; for example, although offline work experiences and educational attainments cannot be easily compared across individuals, especially if they come from very different institutional and cultural contexts, employers can more easily compare work experience accumulated by contractors on the platform (i.e., the number of jobs, duration, types, as well as performance as expressed by the rating given by the employers and workers). This information is available in online contract labor markets on contractor profiles, and platforms generally do not allow contractors to delete or block this information from their profiles, thus reducing selectivity issues and increasing the reliability of these signals. Platforms also offer the possibility for applicants to perform standardized tests that offer some easy-to-assess quality measures for prospective employers. Moreover, some platforms support contractor agencies or companies. Contractors in an agency can cooperate to apply for and complete jobs on the site. Some evidence illustrates that agencies help reduce information asymmetries (Stanton and Thomas 2012).

In addition to providing quality information, online contract labor platforms also help solve challenges relative to the observability and verifiability of effort, on both the worker's and employer's sides, through various mechanisms. Direct monitoring is available on some platforms through virtual office applications.[3] Contractors who perform their work while logged into these virtual offices are monitored through regular screen shots and activity logs. To provide incentives for contractors to accept this degree of monitoring, some platforms guarantee contractor payment for hourly wage work only if it is performed while logged into the virtual office. Along with direct monitoring, workers' ratings represent a potentially powerful reputational mechanism for aligning their objectives with employer objectives.

---

2. Dellarocas (2006) provides a review of reputation systems designed to solve information problems in online markets.
3. Evidence shows that strict monitoring is important for the success of working from home. Bloom et al. (2013) study a Chinese travel agency that decided to try having some employees work from home. The study finds significant gains from working from home in terms of worker productivity and satisfaction. This may be partially a result of the firm's careful monitoring of telecommuting workers. Dutcher and Jabs Saral (2012) highlight the difficulties that may arise if telecommuting workers are not properly monitored by showing experimental evidence that nontelecommuting workers perceive that their telecommuting counterparts are shirkers.

Likewise, and as in other online markets, moral hazard issues can arise on the part of employers (see, for instance, Resnick and Zeckhauser [2002] and Cabral and Hortacsu [2010] for a discussion of moral hazard in online markets). For example, employers could refuse to pay for work performed outside virtual offices or to reimburse expenses. However, contract workers can rate their experience with an employer on most platforms, thus reducing concerns about the risk of exploitative behavior and reneging on previous agreements. Furthermore, both employers and contractors can file disputes if they feel they have been unjustly charged or underpaid. Platforms act as mediators in these disputes and ultimately decide how they should be resolved.

8.3 Digitization and the Distribution of Work

Keeping in mind the incentives and frictions facing employers and contractors that we described above, we turn to contemplating how the digitization of this market may influence the distribution of work. We consider and describe in turn distributional effects along three dimensions: geography, contractor income, and firm boundaries.

8.3.1 Geographic Distribution

The reduction in search, communication, and monitoring costs brought by the digitization of contract labor markets raises the possibility of improving employer-contractor matching and thus enhancing gains from trade. A consequence of this is a potential impact on the geographic distribution of work. Perhaps the most immediate and dramatic gains are those based on cross-region wage variation. Indeed, the dramatic growth in activity on oDesk seems to be primarily of this nature. Specifically, employers in high-income countries hire contractors from low-income countries, even for small jobs that were previously infeasible offline due to transaction costs. As reported in figure 8.1, not only were there more than ten times as many employers from high- compared to lower-income countries by late 2012, but the growth rate of employers from high-income countries was much higher than that from lower-income countries. The gap was even greater when expressed in terms of the wage bill rather than the number of employees (figure 8.2). Conversely, by 2013, approximately 4.5 times as many contractors were from lower- compared to high-income countries (figure 8.3). The trends so far suggest that the spread will continue to increase over time since the number of contractors from lower-income countries is growing at a faster rate. Figure 8.4 confirms this trend also exists in terms of the total monthly wage bill, not just the number of contractors, despite the fact that, as one might expect, wages are higher for contractors in more developed countries.

Although access to lower-cost labor is one reason for recruiting distant contractors, employers report other reasons as well. In a survey of its users

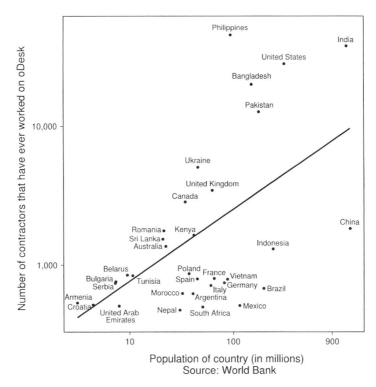

Fig. 8.5 Number of contractors per country on oDesk versus country population, on a log-log scale

Notes: This figure uses data collected from oDesk to show the count of contractors who have ever worked on oDesk by country versus the 2012 World Bank estimate of that country's population. Both axes are log-log scale. We only include countries with 500 or more ever-active contractors.

conducted by oDesk, 76 percent indicated that "remote is less expensive" was a primary reason they were interested in using the platform. However, 46 percent selected "can get work done faster remotely," 31 percent selected "difficult to find local talent," and 21 percent selected "no room/equipment." Thus, in addition to the reduced cost of accessing lower-wage workers, enhanced matching seems to benefit from gains on multiple dimensions.

Countries vary in terms of their level of participation in online contract labor markets. For example, on oDesk approximately ten times as many contractors are from the Ukraine as from Spain, even though the two countries are similar in size (populations in 2013: Ukraine 45 million and in Spain 47 million. However, Spain's economy is approximately ten times larger: 1.4 trillion USD compared to 0.165 trillion USD for the Ukraine). We illustrate this in figure 8.5, where we plot the number of contractors on oDesk per country against population. Nations such as Mexico, Brazil, and China appear to

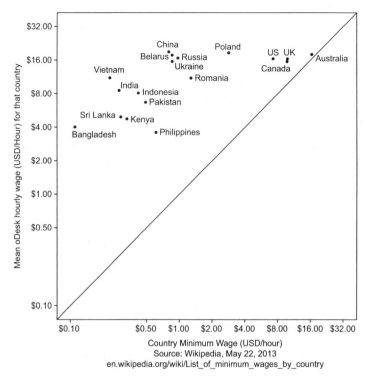

Fig. 8.6 Contractor mean hourly wage on oDesk by country, relative to that country's estimated local minimum wage

Notes: This figure uses data collected from oDesk to compare the mean hourly wage (log scale). To estimate hourly wages, we restrict our attention to hourly contracts in the first half of 2013. Harmonized minimum wage data is difficult to acquire. As a proxy, we use the Wikipedia estimates, as of May 2013.

be underusers (participation below what their population would predict), whereas the Philippines, Bangladesh, and India appear to be overusers.

The variation in usage of this digital marketplace may simply reflect offline employment opportunities. oDesk contractors from Bangladesh and the Philippines, for example, earn significantly more than local minimum wages, perhaps partly explaining their disproportionate use of the platform. However, contractors from China also earn significantly above the local minimum wage on average, yet underuse the platform relative to other nations. Furthermore, contractors from several countries, like Australia, earn only slightly more than the local minimum wage, on average, and yet seem to be overusers (see figure 8.6). This variation reflects the relative benefits and costs, including opportunity costs, faced by the labor force in each country. Factors such as proficiency in English (the language used on the site), Internet access, and education levels all affect the returns to engaging with a

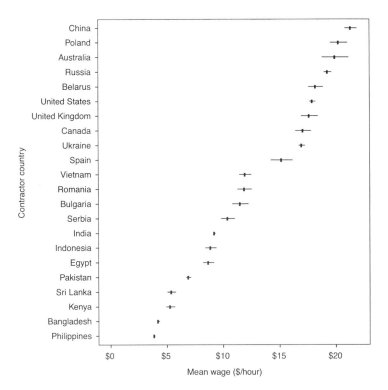

Fig. 8.7   Contractor mean hourly wages on oDesk by country

Notes: We estimate hourly wages using a sample of all hourly contracts in the first half of 2013. We exclude observations of less than 10 cents and more than 100 dollars, as these observations are more likely to not be true hourly wages but rather individuals using the time-tracking software provided by oDesk or approximating a fixed-price contract of some kind with a high hourly wage. For each wage estimate we include a 95 percent confidence interval. Note that for high-population countries like India and the Philippines, these confidence intervals are so narrow that they appear to be point estimates.

digitized labor market platform such as this. As these online markets grow, they will provide researchers with useful data to better understand offline employment opportunities (particularly where reliable government data is sparse) and the relative returns to different forms of education in a global work environment. In addition, they will provide a setting for further analysis on the extent to which geographic, language, cultural, and other forms of distance influence flows of trade in labor.

The different composition of online contract workers across countries may also explain the unexpectedly high average wages received by contractors in certain countries, such as China, Poland, and Russia, as reported in figure 8.7. Contractors from these three countries in particular are primarily concentrated in software development, information systems, and web development, which offer higher wages on average than most other types of

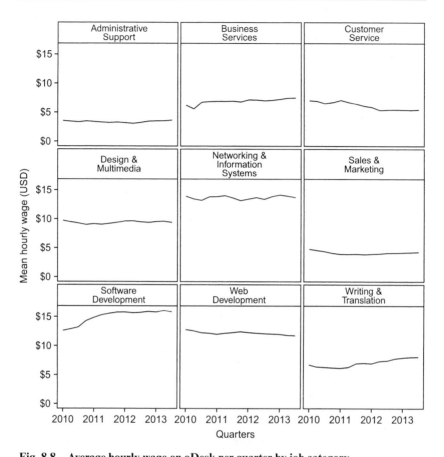

Fig. 8.8 Average hourly wage on oDesk per quarter by job category

Notes: This figure uses oDesk data to show the mean hourly wages per quarter in each of the main oDesk categories of work.

work on oDesk: by 2013, the average wage in software development ($16) was approximately double that of writing and translation ($8) and more than triple that of administrative support ($4), as well as customer support ($5) and sales and marketing ($5). (See figure 8.8.) Furthermore, the quarterly spend in software development and web development is significantly greater than in any other category (figure 8.9). We plot the concentration of total contractor wage bill by country over time in figure 8.10. Russia and Ukraine stand out as especially concentrated in only a few sectors (software development in particular).[4] In contrast, contractors from the United States

---

4. This is consistent with the geographic distribution of work on Kaggle, an online data science competition platform, where software programmers are disproportionately located in Eastern Europe.

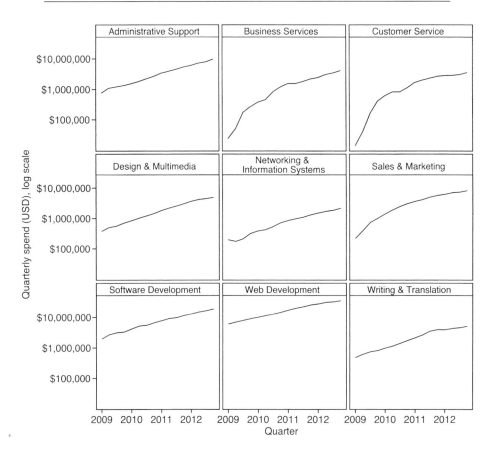

Fig. 8.9 Quarterly wage bill per job category on oDesk (log scale)
Notes: This figure uses oDesk data to show the total quarterly wage bill by job category.

and the Philippines do work across many categories. This variation in the geographic distribution of work by category likely reflects language, education, and offline work opportunities. That said, figure 8.11 indicates that software is one of the least concentrated sectors in terms of the distribution of total wages across countries.

8.3.2 Income Distribution

The digitization of contract labor markets may affect the distribution of income across workers. However, the direction of this effect is ambiguous. On the one hand, digitization could amplify income inequality by way of the superstar effect (Rosen 1981), whereby the shift to lower search costs enables employers to identify and contract for the best workers (or workers supplying the best value) in a global rather than local context such that the distribution of the total wage bill skews further toward a minority of

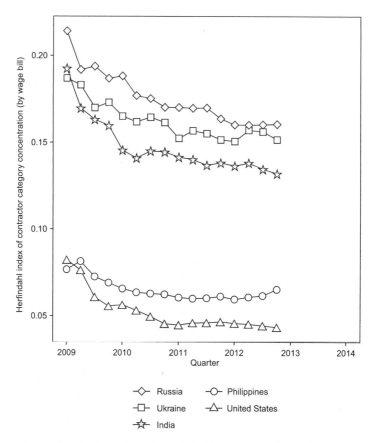

Fig. 8.10 Contractor job category concentration on oDesk by contractor country over time

Notes: This figure uses oDesk data to compute a quarterly Herfindahl for a select number of oDesk contractor countries. We compute the index by treating oDesk job categories as "firms" and contractor countries as "industries." To compute this measure, for each quarter we estimate the share of dollars earned by contractors from a particular country in each category. We then report the sum of the square of these shares. The higher the index, the more concentrated workers from that country. For example, if an index is near 1, it would mean that nearly all workers from that country work in a single category.

contractors. On the other hand, digitization could reduce inequality due to more information leading to less mainstream skills in the "long tail" being more efficiently matched (Anderson 2006).

Researchers report evidence of both types of effects resulting from digitization. For example, Tucker and Zhang (2007) find that when consumers on a wedding vendor website are able to see the popularity of a given vendor, sales concentrate around the more popular vendors. This suggests that online feedback systems have the potential to increase skewness. Elberse and Oberholzer-Gee (2008) find similar support for video sales. In other

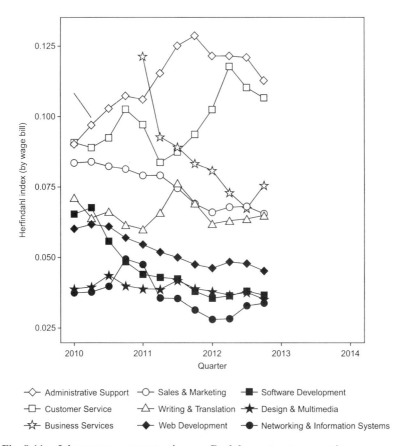

Fig. 8.11 Job category concentration on oDesk by contractor, over time

Notes: This figure uses oDesk data to compute a quarterly Herfindahl for each job category, treating each country as a "firm" and each category as an "industry." To compute this measure, for each quarter we estimate the share of dollars within a category earned by contractors from each country. We then report the sum of the square of these shares. The higher the index, the more that particular category is dominated by workers from a particular country. For example, if an index is near 1, it would mean that nearly all work in that category is completed by workers from a single country.

cases, the reverse is true. Zentner, Smith, and Kaya (2013) show that online video rentals are less concentrated around blockbusters than physical rentals, Peltier and Moreau (2012) show that online book sales in France are less concentrated around superstars than offline, and Brynjolfsson, Hu, and Simester (2011) find that Internet sales for women's clothing are less concentrated than catalog sales. All of these papers identify search cost differences as a core explanation for the results.

Superstar and long-tail effects are not necessarily mutually exclusive, and both, in fact, may be at work in the context of online markets for contract labor. This is because they are influenced by related but distinct characteristics of the services traded in this market. Vertical differentiation (quality) drives the superstar effect, whereas horizontal differentiation (variety) drives the long-tail effect (Bar-Isaac, Caruana, and Cuñat 2012). Therefore, subject to demand constraints, they may coexist. The superstar effect will result in increased income inequality as employers tend toward the highest quality (or best value) contractors based on a global rather than local search. Thus, income will shift from contractors supplying the best value locally to those supplying the best value globally. Increased demand will drive up the wages of the highest-quality workers, mainly in cases where the spread is greatest between local and global wages (i.e., low-income countries). The superstar effect may be exacerbated due to information asymmetries and features of the market.

At the same time, horizontally differentiated contractors (e.g., those who specialize in less common areas) whose offline wages are lower due to limited local demand for their expertise may particularly benefit from digitization since the shift from local to global matching may disproportionately increase the demand for their skills relative to the supply. For example, a software developer in Malaysia who learns to program in a new cutting-edge language (e.g., django) may benefit from digitization, since by connecting to the global market that contractor will likely face a greater increase in demand for that skill than an increase in competition for supplying that skill.

In summary, digitization may shift the income distribution in a manner that benefits contractors with skills that are vertically differentiated (i.e., higher quality), horizontally differentiated (i.e., scarce), or lower cost (due to fewer local offline opportunities) at the expense of those with skills that are neither differentiated nor low cost (i.e., mediocre quality, common skills, in high- or middle-income countries). The net effect of such a shift is ambiguous, both at the country level and the individual level. At the country level, although the immediate effect of digitization may be to decrease income inequality as the total wage bill shifts from high- to low-income countries due to expanded search for skills and lower wage rates in low-income countries, the resulting increase in productivity of firms in high-income countries may further increase offline wages there, offsetting the effect of offshoring. At the individual level, while digitization will favor the highly skilled relative to the less skilled, particularly in high-income countries, the services provided by a contractor have increasing marginal costs, unlike products with low marginal costs such as music, books, and software. Therefore, enhanced matching and constrained supply may at least partially offset increased competition and thus temper the extent to which digitization amplifies the skewness of income distribution at the individual level.

Information asymmetries may also affect income distribution. The available evidence shows that even small amounts of (employer- or platform-provided) information have a large effect on future employment prospects

(Pallais 2012; Agrawal, Lacetera, and Lyons 2013). On the one hand, this may increase the skewness of income distribution because contractors who obtain a small lead early on, in terms of online work experience with a positive public employer review, may experience subsequent gains and benefit from increasing returns (at least in the short term). On the other hand, to the extent that online markets facilitate low-cost trials for employers to test working with novice contractors and then publicize their quality, the digitization of this market may decrease skew through the increased public revelation of contractor quality. The fact that a small amount of verified work experience online is associated with a disproportionate increase in winning subsequent jobs for contractors in low-income countries (Agrawal, Lacetera, and Lyons 2013) seems consistent with this latter view.

8.3.3 Boundaries of the Firm

How will the digitization of this marketplace influence the boundary of the firm? Economic theory suggests that because digitization lowers transaction costs (search, communication, and monitoring), the returns to contracting in the market increase relative to performing these services in-house. For example, Grossman and Rossi-Hansberg (2008) model the tension between the benefits (lower cost of labor) and costs (coordination and monitoring) of offshoring to examine precisely the effects of a decline in the cost of offshoring, focusing on the productivity effect of increased offshoring. Similarly, Antras and Helpman (2004) present a model of north-south trade where final-goods firms choose whether to vertically integrate into the production of intermediate goods or to outsource them. Their model offers an explanation for variation in firm boundary decisions (in equilibrium, some firms outsource while others do not, and those that do vary in their outsourcing location choice) based on the variation in firms' productivity levels. Although the authors do not focus on the effect of falling transaction costs associated with outsourcing per se, the influence of this on firm boundaries is a natural implication of their model.

Several studies report empirical evidence that digitization is associated with a contraction in the boundary of the firm. For example, Abramovsky and Griffith (2006) report that more ICT-intensive firms purchase a greater amount of services on the market (rather than vertically integrating) and are more likely to purchase offshore, Brynjolfsson et al. (1994) report that investment in IT is correlated with a subsequent decrease in firm size, and Hitt (1999) shows that an increase in IT use is correlated with a decrease in vertical integration.

A recent survey conducted by oDesk of its users sheds further light on the relationship between digitization and firm boundary decisions. Two of the survey questions offer insight on how employers perceive the online platform relative to alternatives for performing contracted work. One of the survey questions asks: "If there had not been an appropriate oDesk contractor available for this project, then what would you most likely have done?" Of the 6,912 respondents, only 15 percent indicated they would have turned to a local hire, whereas 22 percent replied they would have worked extra hours, 9 percent replied they would have delayed or canceled the project, and 50 percent indicated that they would have used some other remote source. Although there is room for alternative interpretations of these responses (for example, "other remote sources" could refer to other online contract labor platforms such that the results underrepresent the fraction who would hire locally in the absence of any online platforms), one possible explanation is that the digitization of this marketplace directly affected the boundary of the firm in only a minority (15 percent) of the cases. A second oDesk survey question asks: "Thinking about the last time that you hired a contractor through oDesk, what alternatives did you consider?" In this case, respondents were able to select more than one option. Again, only 15 percent selected "hiring an employee," whereas 58 percent selected "doing it myself." Shifting from local to distant contractors appears to be a more significant economic effect from the digitization of this market than contraction in the boundary of the firm. Indeed, 40 percent of respondents indicated that a "local contractor" was an alternative they considered when they last hired a contractor through oDesk.

It is important to note that the majority of oDesk users are small businesses (90 percent of 7,098 survey respondents indicated that their business had 10 employees or less, with an overall average firm size of 2.6 employees). This raises the question of how the effect of digitizing this marketplace may vary across firm size. For example, do small firms benefit disproportionately from digitization? We cannot draw this conclusion simply from observing a high fraction of small-firm users. First, the 90 percent small-firm user population may just reflect the distribution of firm sizes in the economy (interestingly, respondents reveal that 68 percent are part-time businesses, 69 percent are home-based businesses, and the average firm age is 2.7 years). Second, the survey sample distribution may not reflect the population distribution. Perhaps small firms are more likely to respond to the survey. Still, one might conjecture that small firms are more likely to hire contract workers since large firms are better able to aggregate tasks into full-time jobs and thus avoid the contracting and discontinuity costs associated with task-based hiring.

8.4 Market Design

Platforms in online contract labor markets do not have the match-setting power typical in other contexts that the market design literature has considered (e.g., Roth and Peranson 1999; Roth 2002; Milgrom 2011) because, unlike kidney exchanges and medical student and hospital-matching systems, they are not centralized. However, an inability to set matches explicitly does not imply an inability to influence which matches are ultimately formed and under what terms. The position of the platform vis-á-vis the marketplace is more like that of a government that sets policies to encourage efficient market outcomes without dictating trades. The platform decides how often and in what context participants are exposed to each other, what information is collected by parties, and how this information is displayed. Platforms also set policies about what trades are permissible, how entry is gained, what contracts and prices are allowed, and so on. The platform may also make recommendations and set defaults. A few market-design decisions in this softer matchmaking environment are worth considering to explore how these features affect matching.

First, platforms are in the position to provide standardized and verified information. For example, because oDesk does not permit contractors to delete ratings or comments provided by employers after a job is completed, this information is possibly distinct from what contractors might include in their resumes, and thus valuable to potential future employers. In the introduction above, we describe two studies that report findings indicating that online work history information has a significant influence on subsequent matching outcomes (Pallais 2012; Agrawal, Lacetera, and Lyons 2013). Furthermore, platforms can provide additional tools for contractors and employers to reveal standardized and verified information about themselves. For example, oDesk provides a series of standardized tests that contractors are able to take so that they may post their scores in order to communicate their proficiency in a specific domain.

Given that wading through too much information is costly for a potential employer, does a simple overall performance score convey an optimal amount of information? Would a more detailed scoring system enhance matching? Pallais (2012) reports that detailed feedback had no effect on subsequent outcomes, relative to simple feedback, for inexperienced contractors. However, for experienced contractors, the extra detail did make a difference. Furthermore, the Pallais result may underestimate the effect of a more detailed rating system since her feedback was conveyed via text rather than, for example, a simple ranking on five dimensions. Given the apparently high sensitivity to ratings and feedback, further research into market design features that address this particular type of information friction seems a fruitful direction for future research.

Second, because contractors have many decisions to make (such as what jobs to apply for, what wage to bid, what skills to learn), as do employers (who to hire, whether to use a fixed or variable fee contract, when to offer a bonus and how much), the digitized nature of these platforms, just like in other online markets, will likely lead to the development of algorithmic assistance with decision making. These recommendation systems will augment human decision making by, for example, reducing the search costs of market participants. One potential problem with recommending applicants is crowd out. Recommending one worker presumably puts another worker at a disadvantage. However, Horton (2012) shows that the quantity and quality of matches can be improved via algorithmic recommendations to employers about candidates to recruit for their openings, without significant crowd-out effects.

Aside from the obvious recommendations about who to trade with and at what terms, the platform can also make other kinds of recommendations. It can, for example, advise parties of best practices in how to manage a working relationship, such as suggesting more communication, periodic raises, and performance evaluations. One interesting challenge of recommender systems is the trade-off between learning and recommending; recommender systems rely on natural decision making to explore the space of alternatives to train models, but sufficiently good recommender systems that save their users substantial costs are likely to displace natural decision making. So, maintaining some natural decision making will eventually be costly, at least to some users.

Another area where algorithmic recommendations might particularly influence matching is in helping individuals make good decisions about the accumulation of human capital, particularly around which skills to learn. Traditionally, such decisions are made a small number of times by relatively uninformed individuals who receive one-time feedback about their choices. In offline markets, decisions about human capital investments are difficult to observe. Online, these choices are more visible and measurable. On platforms like oDesk, an enormous amount of information illustrates which combination of skills command higher wages in any particular domain. This enables recommender systems to distill which skills are most valuable to learn given a contractor's existing capabilities; the system further learns by observing how contractors perform via experimentation.

Third, how should contract labor sites allocate visibility? Which applicants should be listed at the top versus the bottom on an employer's screen? The large size and value of the search engine optimization (SEO) market provides some indication of the importance of visibility. Should allocation preserve assortativity (e.g., contractors with higher feedback ratings or hours worked are given more visibility)? Should each worker be given at least some visibility? If visibility is auctioned off, what would be the efficiency and distributional properties of such an allocation? While this topic has received much attention from researchers in the private sector at companies like Google and eBay concerning other markets, it remains an open question in the context of the market for contract labor. Yet, this issue is important. Market design decisions concerning the allocation of visibility will surely influence matching outcomes, which in turn will influence both distribution and welfare effects. Moreover, visibility relates to congestion, which we discuss next.

Fourth, platforms may need to control congestion due to the fact that posting (and applying for) a job is almost costless. The low cost of applications may lead to an everyone-applies-to-everything equilibrium in which each application also carries virtually no signal value. This was partly the motivation for introducing the American Economic Association (AEA) signaling mechanism (Coles et al. 2010), in which job market participants are given two (and only two) signals to send to schools. The school's knowledge of the scarcity of signals makes those signals informative. Accordingly, platforms may consider job application quotas. However, as described above, this strategy might penalize new entrants with low probabilities of being hired (Pallais 2012). It also ignores employer heterogeneity, with some employers preferring many applicants and others few. Another potentially interesting approach is to allow the employer to decide the cost of applying. These are additional areas for research that reflect the peculiarities of this market.

A fifth interesting market-design feature is the creation of submarkets and categories that are often defined through some combination of geography and time to coordinate activities and thus create a sufficiently thick market (e.g., the creation of industrial districts for specific sectors). The platform must attempt to define at some level of detail the various services being supplied and then organize the market accordingly. In the language of machine learning, there is both a clustering task (finding the meaningful groups of jobs/contractors based on historical data) and a labeling task (being able to assign a new job to one of the identified clusters based on that job's attributes).

The five market features we describe above represent only a fraction of those that may be important for influencing the matching of employers and contractors as well as the way in which work is managed and produced online. The unique feature of this line of inquiry, relative to the one described above concerning distribution and the one below concerning social welfare, is that this research can be performed without offline data. That is because online features can be compared against each other with respect to the behavior they elicit from users. So-called "A/B testing," which refers to controlled randomized experiments that allow for identifying causal relationships between variations in market design features and subsequent user behavior, has already become a standard industry practice for determining the relative performance of competing market design features. That is likely the reason that the majority of research concerning online markets for contract labor relate to this line of inquiry, whereas there is very little so far on the other topics.

8.5 Social Welfare

Two immediate consequences of digitization in this market may have important welfare implications. First, digitization may lead to better matching because the pool of prospective workers and employers increases dramatically due to the decline in costs associated with distance. Second, digitization may lead to efficiency gains from production due to lower coordination costs. We discuss both lines of inquiry below.

8.5.1 Matching Made Easier?

The ease of access to online contract labor markets, due to the development of platforms such as oDesk, Freelancer, Elance, and Guru, has the potential to considerably increase the pool of both job seekers and employers and to reduce search costs. Matching models, particularly as applied to labor markets, predict that this will lead to efficiency gains due to lower search costs and a lower likelihood of mismatches (Petrongolo and Pissarides 2001; Wheeler 2001).

However, opposite forces are also at play. While information technologies reduce the role of distance for search and execution of work, they also lead to a more heterogeneous pool of both workers and employers. In addition, the absence of personal interactions typical of offline and more localized labor markets precludes access to soft or high-bandwidth information about both job seekers and prospective employers (Autor 2001). This introduces uncertainty that, in turn, may lead to an overall reduction in the quality of workers (Akerlof 1970) and/or to search frictions (Stigler 1962). These search frictions could be exacerbated if quality is difficult to determine (Wilde 1981), which is quite possible because of the diverse labor pool.

Although theories of search and matching specific to online labor markets have not yet been developed, a growing body of evidence, described above, points to the presence of these informational problems and the ways in which they are addressed in online contract labor platforms (Horton 2012; Pallais 2012; Stanton and Thomas 2012). A common pattern to a number of these studies is to look at the presence of preferences for certain geographic locations of workers as a way to alleviate uncertainty about workers' quality (Mill 2011; Ghani, Kerr, and Stanton 2012; Agrawal, Lacetera, and Lyons 2013). An implication here is that online contract labor platforms contribute to the alleviation of informational asymmetries by providing verifiable, standardized information (such as previous experience on the same platform) for all workers, regardless of their origin.

The broadening of the pool of workers and employers and, at least potentially, the increased likelihood of good matches, is also likely to have implications for wages and income distribution. The fact that in online contract labor markets the number of workers outweighs the number of employers in every job category suggests that while many workers may be left unemployed, employers have a relatively good chance of finding a worker who meets their criteria, with wages driven down (Petrongolo and Pissarides 2006). However, because worker backgrounds may vary more than in traditional labor markets, a relatively small number of workers may meet the job requirements. As a result, wage offers could be higher than expected. This suggests that in job categories with many qualified workers, the wages will be lower than in those with few qualified workers relative to the number of job postings. As the market evolves, wage differences between job types should begin to disappear.

8.5.2 Efficiency Gains from Production?

Digitization may lead to efficiency gains in production due to lower coordination costs that enhance, for example, contractor flexibility, discretization of work into smaller jobs enabling more specialization, and remote team work. For instance, Dettling (2011) reports that flexibility provided by IT contributes to an increase in the female labor force participation. More broadly, digitization may enable efficiency gains in production through lowering the cost of outsourcing.

Of course, outsourcing and offshoring predates the development of online contract labor markets. Of particular relevance here are theories of service outsourcing and offshoring (e.g., Bhagwati, Panagariya, and Srinivasan 2004; Francois and Hoekman 2010). Combined, these theories predict that the gains to service outsourcing are potentially significant. However, they focus on relatively long arm's-length contracts between relatively large firms rather than on the short contracts between small organizations and individuals, typical of online markets.

Outsourcing services to online contract labor markets is also likely to lead to geographically dispersed production, even within narrowly defined tasks. For example, work teams may be composed of individuals who are not necessarily colocated. Lazear (1999) argues that cultural diversity in work teams is costly and should only occur when skill complementarities exist between teammates to offset these costs. It may be harder to meet these conditions in very diverse online labor markets than it is in more traditional labor markets. Two recent studies based on online labor markets focus on task completion and the effects of team organization, communication structure, incentives, and motivation on performance. Lyons (2013) provides field experimental evidence on how nationally diverse communication impacts online team production and finds that nationally homogeneous teams benefit from working together but that diverse teams perform better when members work independently of one another. Related to the topic of online labor market partnerships, Horton (2011) uses survey data from the crowdsourcing site Mechanical Turk to show that workers believe employers on the site are more fair and honest than offline employers.

8.6 Conclusion

We identify three broad lines of inquiry as central to the digitization research agenda. All three focus on the effect of digitizing the market for contract labor. The first concerns welfare effects, the second distribution effects, and the third user behavior effects. All three are set in the context of the market for contract labor, but have broader implications for digitization in other settings.

Access to data will pose a challenge to fully addressing these questions. In contrast to data from online platforms that collect information on hiring (as well as pre- and posthiring) transactions at a granular level and at low cost, it is costly to obtain even a basic level of offline contracting data. Yet, to fully address the first and third lines of inquiry outlined above, offline data is required to estimate the causal effect of digitization on changes in distributional properties (geography, income, firm boundaries) and welfare. This is likely why most of the first wave of studies concerning the digitization of this market focuses on market design-related subjects (e.g., experience, agencies, ratings) since these questions only require observing within platform variation in user behavior and do not require linking these data to nonplatform participants.

While the second line of inquiry concerning market design, information frictions, and user behavior is largely spared from the requirement to link with offline data, the greatest challenge to this research in the short and medium term will likely be the rapid evolution of the industry. As illustrated above, the industry is growing rapidly. In addition, complementary technologies, such as those associated with mobile and social, are changing rapidly. As such, market design features that seem salient today may be less relevant relative to other features in the future. For example, monitoring technologies such as workrooms with screen shots were only recently introduced and are already standard practice across many platforms. Furthermore, they are likely to be replaced soon with better technology such as streaming screen video. While the ultimate goal of research of this type is obtaining a deeper understanding of human behavior rather than of a particular market design feature, the economic salience of the feature is often important for generalizability and yet may be fleeting due to the rapid pace of change in this setting. Still, insight into user response to informational frictions is an important contribution.

Whereas the distribution and welfare lines of inquiry are most likely to be led by scholars and policymakers, the market design-related research will almost surely include important contributions from industry since this issue is of first-order importance for product development and competition. This has already been the case with oDesk (Horton 2010, 2012) as well as with other market design issues on platforms such as Google (Varian 2007; Choi and Varian 2012), eBay (Blake, Nosko, and Tadelis 2014), and Yahoo (Ghosh and McAfee 2011; Lewis and Reiley 2011). Industry interest coupled with their access to high-quality data may significantly accelerate progress on this research frontier. At the same time, the competitive implications of market design insights may inhibit the dissemination of this type of research, and thus the overall impact of industry interest in this subject on the rate and direction of progress on this part of the agenda is ambiguous.

Given the role that platforms play as the central collectors of data in these markets, they will influence the direction of research on all three lines if inquiry through their decisions regarding providing researchers with access to their data. Early signs are promising for the research community since many of the most prominent platforms have established chief economists or similar types of research-friendly leadership positions and encourage employees to participate in the academic community by publishing their research and participating at conferences and other scholarly events.

Given the rapid growth rate of the online market for contract labor, this research agenda is economically important. The welfare-related line of inquiry will help us better understand the potential private and social benefits due to the digitization of this sector of the economy. The distribution-related line of inquiry will shed light on how the benefits of digitization may be allocated across countries and individuals as well as its impact on the structure of the firm. Finally, the market design-related line of inquiry will provide further insight into the importance of particular information frictions and human behavior in the digital world as we explore user reactions to platform features, many of which are common across sectors outside of contract employment. Overall, these insights will be of great interest to scholars, policymakers, and industry participants alike.

References

Abramovsky, Laura, and Rachel Griffith. 2006. "Outsourcing and Offshoring of Business Services: How Important is ICT?" *Journal of the European Economic Association* 4 (2–3): 594–601.

Agrawal, Ajay, Nicola Lacetera, and Elizabeth Lyons. 2013. "Does Information Help or Hinder Job Applicants from Less Developed Countries in Online Markets?" NBER Working Paper no. 18720, Cambridge, MA.

Akerlof, George A. 1970. "The Market for 'Lemons': Quality Uncertainty and the Market Mechanism." *Quarterly Journal of Economics* 84 (3): 488–500.

Anderson, Chris. 2006. *The Long Tail: How Endless Choice is Creating Unlimited Demand.* London: Random House Business Books.

Antras, Pol, and Elhanan Helpman. 2004. "Global Sourcing." *Journal of Political Economy* 112 (3): 552–80.

Armstrong, Mark. 2006. "Competition in Two-Sided Markets." *RAND Journal of Economics* 37 (3): 668–91.

Autor, David H. 2001. "Wiring the Labor Market." *Journal of Economic Perspectives* 15 (1): 25–40.

Bar-Isaac, Heski, Guillermo Caruana, and Vicente Cuñat. 2012. "Information Gathering Externalities for a Multi-Attribute Good." *Journal of Industrial Economics* 60 (1): 162–85.

Bhagwati, Jagdish, Arvind Panagariya, and T. N. Srinivasan. 2004. "The Muddles over Outsourcing." *Journal of Economic Perspectives* 18 (4): 93–114.

Blake, Thomas, Chris Nosko, and Steven Tadelis. 2014. "Consumer Heterogeneity and Paid Search Effectiveness: A Large Scale Field Experiment." NBER Working Paper no. 20171, Cambridge, MA.

Bloom, Nicholas, James Liang, John Roberts, and Zhichun Jenny Ying. 2013. "Does Working from Home Work? Evidence from a Chinese Experiment." NBER Working Paper no. 18871, Cambridge, MA.

Brynjolfsson, Eric, Thomas W. Malone, Vijay Gurbaxani, and Ajit Kambi. 1994. "Does Information Technology Lead to Smaller Firms?" *Management Science* 40 (12): 1628–44.

Brynjolfsson, Eric, Yu Hu, and Duncan Simester. 2011. "Goodbye Pareto Principle, Hello Long Tail: The Effect of Search Costs on the Concentration of Product Sales." *Management Science* 57 (8): 1373–86.

Cabral, Luis, and Ali Hortacsu. 2010. "The Dynamics of Seller Reputation: Evidence from eBay." *Journal of Industrial Economics* 58 (1): 54–78.

Choi, Hyunyoung, and Hal Varian. 2012. "Predicting the Present with Google Trends." *Economic Record* 88 (s1): 2–9.

Coles, Peter, John Cawley, Phillip B. Levine, Muriel Niederle, Alvin E. Roth, and John J. Siegfried. 2010. "The Job Market for New Economists: A Market Design Perspective." *Journal of Economic Perspectives* 24 (4): 187–206.

Dellarocas, Chrysanthos. 2006. "Reputation Mechanisms." In *Handbook on Economics and Information Systems*, edited by T. Hendershott, 629–60. Bingley, United Kingdom: Emerald Publishing Group.

Dettling, Lisa L. 2011. "Opting Back In: Home Internet Use and Female Labor Supply." Unpublished manuscript, University of Maryland. http://artsci.wustl.edu/~gradconf/LisaDettling.pdf.

Dutcher, E. Glenn, and Krista Jabs Saral. 2012. "Does Team Telecommuting Affect Productivity? An Experiment." MPRA Paper no. 41594, University Library of Munich.

Elberse, Anita, and Felix Oberholzer-Gee. 2008. "Superstars and Underdogs: An Examination of the Long-Tail Phenomenon in Video Sales." MSI Reports, Working Paper Series no. 4, Marketing Science Institute.

Francois, Joseph, and Bernard Hoekman. 2010. "Services Trade and Policy." *Journal of Economic Literature* 48 (3): 642–92.

Ghani, Ejaz, William R. Kerr, and Christopher T. Stanton. 2012. "Diasporas and Outsourcing: Evidence from oDesk and India." NBER Working Paper no. 18474, Cambridge, MA.

Ghosh, Arpita, and Preston McAfee. 2011. "Incentivizing High-Quality User-Generated Content." *Proceedings of the 20th International Conference on World Wide Web*, 137–46. Association for Computing Machines.

Grossman, Gene M., and Esteban Rossi-Hansberg. 2008. "Trading Tasks: A Simple Theory of Offshoring." *American Economic Review* 98 (5): 1978–97.

Hitt, Lorin M. 1999. "Information Technology and Firm Boundaries: Evidence from Panel Data." *Information Systems Research* 10 (2): 134–49.

Horton, John J. 2010. "Online Labor Markets." *Internet and Network Economics* 6484:515–22.

———. 2011. "The Condition of the Turking Class: Are Online Employers Fair and Honest?" *Economic Letters* 111 (1): 10–12.

———. 2012. "Computer-Mediated Matchmaking: Facilitating Employer Search and Screening." Working Paper, oDesk Research and Harvard University. http://sole-jole.org/13473.pdf.

Lazear, Edward P. 1999. "Globalisation and the Market for Team-Mates." *Economic Journal* 109 (454): 15–40.
Lewis, Randall A., and David Reiley. 2011. "Does Retail Advertising Work? Measuring the Effects of Advertising on Sales via a Controlled Experiment on Yahoo!" CCP Working Paper no. 11-9, Centre for Competition Policy. http://www.uea.ac.uk/documents/107435/107587/ccp_11_9.pdf.
Lyons, Elizabeth. 2013. "Multinational Teams: Experimental Evidence from the Field." Working Paper, University of California, San Diego. www.irps.uscd.edu/assets/001/505697.pdf.
Milgrom, Paul. 2011. "Critical Issues in the Practice of Market Design." *Economic Inquiry* 49 (2): 311–20.
Mill, Roy. 2011. "Hiring and Learning in Online Global Labor Markets." NET Working Paper no. 11-17, Networks, Electronic Commerce, and Telecommunications Institute.
Pallais, Amanda. 2012. "Inefficient Hiring in Entry-Level Labor Markets." NBER Working Paper no. 18917, Cambridge, MA.
Peltier, Stephanie, and Francois Moreau. 2012. "Internet and the 'Long Tail versus Superstar Effect' Debate: Evidence from the French Book Market." *Applied Economics Letters* 19 (8): 711–15.
Petrongolo, Barbara, and Christopher A. Pissarides. 2001. "Looking into the Black Box: A Survey of the Matching Function." *Journal of Economic Literature* 39 (2): 390–431.
———. 2006. "Scale Effects in Markets with Search." *Economic Journal* 11 (508): 21–44.
Resnick, Paul, and Richard Zeckhauser. 2002. "Trust among Strangers in Internet Transacations: Empirical Analysis of eBay's Reputation System." *Advances in Applied Microeconomics* 11:127–57.
Rosen, Sherwin. 1981. "The Economics of Superstars." *American Economic Review* 71 (5): 845–58.
Roth, Alvin E. 2002. "The Economist as Engineer: Game Theory, Experimentation, and Computation as Tools for Design Economics." *Econometrica* 70 (4): 1341–78.
Roth, Alvin E., and Elliott Peranson. 1999. "The Redesign of the Matching Market for American Physicians: Some Engineering Aspects of Economic Design." *American Economic Review* 89 (4): 748–80.
Rysman, Marc. 2009. "The Economics of Two-Sided Markets." *Journal of Economic Perspectives* 23 (3): 125–43.
Stanton, Christopher T., and Catherine Thomas. 2012. "Landing the First Job: The Value of Intermediaries in Online Hiring." Working Paper, University of Utah.
Stigler, George J. 1962. "Information in the Labor Market." *Journal of Political Economy* 70 (5): 94–105.
The Economist. 2010. "Work in the Digital Age: A Clouded Future." May 13.
Tucker, Catherine, and Juanjuan Zhang. 2007. "Long Tail or Steep Tail? A Field Investigation into How Online Popularity Information Affects the Distribution of Customer Choices." Working Paper no. 39811, Sloan School of Management, Massachusetts Institute of Technology.
Vanham, Peter. 2012. "Virtual Working Takes Off in EMs." *Financial Times*, May 23.
Varian, Hal R. 2007. "Position Auctions." *International Journal of Industrial Organization* 25 (6): 1163–78.
Wheeler, Christopher H. 2001. "Search, Sorting, and Urban Agglomeration." *Journal of Labor Economics* 19 (4): 879–99.
Wilde, Louis L. 1981. "Information Costs, Duration of Search, and Turnover: Theory and Applications." *Journal of Political Economy* 89 (6): 1122–41.

Zentner, Alejandro, Michael D. Smith, and Cuneyd Kaya. 2013. "How Video Rental Patterns Change as Consumers Move Online." *Management Science* 59 (11): 2622–34.

Comment   Christopher Stanton

Introduction

Online platforms for contract labor, made possible by digitization, are rapidly growing. The chapter by Ajay Agrawal, John Horton, Nicola Lacetera, and Elizabeth Lyons provides clear guidance for a research agenda on the operation of these platforms and the resulting implications for trade in labor services, firm boundaries, productivity, and the income distribution. While digitization and its implications for labor markets is a broad topic, the authors' main focus is transactions through platforms, and the chapter is filled with interesting stylized facts and descriptive statistics about oDesk, the largest of these platforms. The presentation of this data is potentially quite useful for understanding trends in trade in labor services.

The growth of contract labor platforms represents a potential shift in how trade in services is conducted. This observation leads to important questions, some of which are beginning to be addressed in the literature: What is the extent of matching frictions (Pallais 2011)? How will platforms or institutions evolve to reduce frictions (Horton 2012; Stanton and Thomas 2011)? How will matching frictions across countries affect the contract labor market and the distribution of trade flows (Agrawal, Lacetera, and Lyons 2012; Ghani, Kerr, and Stanton 2012; Mill 2011)?

The literature to date has focused almost exclusively on matching, information frictions, and the operations of individual platforms. This is likely because these questions can be addressed with data from one platform. The authors' rightly call for additional research about the consequences of online labor markets for productivity, income inequality, and firm boundaries, and the chapter provides guidance for future work. Some specific topics of inquiry are: How will contract labor markets affect the north-south income distribution? How will matching and productivity change? How will the boundaries of firms change? How will management practices evolve to accommodate remote labor? The authors highlight that answering some of these new questions will require combining data from online markets

---

Christopher Stanton is assistant professor of finance at the University of Utah and a faculty research fellow of the National Bureau of Economic Research.

Special thanks are due to Catherine Thomas for providing helpful suggestions after a careful reading of this draft. For acknowledgments, sources of research support, and disclosure of the author's material financial relationships, if any, please see http://www.nber.org/chapters/c13023.ack.

with data from offline markets, or organization-level data, as well as well-grounded theoretical frameworks.

In this discussion, I focus on a big picture issue: what can be learned from contract labor platforms about trade in services more generally? First, what is the market, and what do we potentially miss when focusing on platforms? Second, information frictions on platforms seem prevalent. Are these frictions a long-run problem for the services trade and for these markets? Third, when are transactions through platforms versus other avenues for trade most likely, and what is the role of management and team production? After addressing these questions, I conclude that although data from platforms may not be entirely representative, studying platforms can enhance our understanding of trade in services.

What is the Market?

The markets under study currently involve relatively short-term labor transactions conducted at a distance. At this time, activity through platforms like oDesk constitutes a small fraction of total trade in labor services. Service imports into the United States totaled about $400 billion in 2012 according to the Bureau of Economic Analysis (BEA), and transactions through platforms represented less than 1 percent of this amount. Just several decades ago, it would have been inconceivable to send a core business function to India, but now information technology (IT) is routinely outsourced abroad. Firms and individuals have the choice of many possible paths to find outsourcing partners: through platforms like oDesk, through word-of-mouth references or other sources like Google, or through established, large firms like Infosys.

While the revenue numbers from oDesk look small in light of total service imports, platforms like oDesk are important for two reasons. First, many economists care about operational aspects of online platforms and competition between platforms, and studying the oDesk environment and resulting transactions between buyers and sellers may provide insight about platform economics. Second, economists care about understanding trade, and global trade in services has been increasingly made possible by digitization. Unfortunately, representative transaction-level data on services trade is nearly impossible to obtain. In contrast, data from individual platforms is often incredibly detailed and granular. This prompts the first main question: For economists who care about trade, and particularly trade in services, is it possible to generalize findings from contract labor platforms like oDesk?

First, it is helpful to ask how the information structure on oDesk compares to other markets for trade in services. While oDesk is a labor market with some unique features, and information frictions have a measurable impact on market quality, it is important to keep in mind that other markets exhibit significant information frictions as well. There is a substantial literature highlighting the importance of information frictions in the traditional labor market.[1] The literature on contract labor markets has likely focused on the role of information because it is possible for the econometrician to isolate changes in employers' information sets; however, there is no study that compares information frictions in online labor markets versus the traditional labor market. In fact, buyers of labor services on oDesk observe a tremendous amount of data about potential suppliers/workers and the platform facilities preemployment information exchange between potential trading partners. The original papers in this area seemed to view oDesk as a laboratory to understand information frictions in more general contexts. Given the information provided to market participants on the platform, we might even think information frictions in this setting provide a lower bound on the frictions in other settings.

Second, we want to understand whether transactions through platforms look representative of other service imports. At least on the size dimension, contracts sourced through platforms seem small in dollar value, hours of required work, and complexity compared to contracts made through other channels. The average job on oDesk is relatively short term, lasting a few hundred hours, and involves either individual work or the work of a small team. By contrast, projects sent abroad through traditional outsourcing-specialty firms tend to be much larger in complexity and involve much larger teams. In 2012, Infosys disclosed over $7 billion in revenue in its filings with the SEC, over seven times the total revenue flowing through online platforms. Tata Consultancy and Wipro, two other large outsourcing specialists, each have over 100,000 employees; both firms employ more workers than the number of full-time equivalent workers on oDesk. As I discuss below, a number of factors suggest that the average project size contracted through platforms is likely to remain small. It seems, then, that the generalizability of insights from these markets to larger organizations remains an open question.

Information and Matching Frictions: Features of Nascent Markets or Long-Term Hurdles?

The second main question is: Will the information frictions that have been documented become less relevant as these platforms mature?[2] The authors note that many of these issues may be fleeting as market operators make

---

1. For a few recent examples, Kahn (2013) shows that asymmetric information between employers is reduced for workers in occupations that require outside-of-the-firm communication, and DeVaro and Waldman (2012) study the effect of the arrival of a public signal—promotions—on outcomes in the labor market. Other literature studies how existing workers may provide information about new recruits, both online and offline (see, for example, Burks et al. 2013; Pallais and Sands 2013).
2. For a related discussion on the maturation of Internet job search, see Kuhn and Mansour (2013).

changes to market design. Except for John Horton's (2012) recent research on algorithmic matching recommendations, there has been very little experimentation to assess how platform features may reduce the inefficiencies arising from incomplete information. When I began working with oDesk data several years ago, I observed a substantial effect of past feedback on workers' wages and hiring probabilities. This suggested that employers required verifiable information about worker ability, conscientiousness, or some other quality beyond the details in a resume or through an interview. I proposed that new workers could be allowed to post a bond or guarantee a certain number of hours of work, but these features were never implemented. Bond posting is prevalent in procurement contracting, but no platform like oDesk has done something analogous.[3] While bond posting may be far from ideal because of holdup problems or administrative overhead, the point of the example is to illustrate that we have a very limited amount of observable variation in market characteristics and it is possible that a better-designed market would alleviate some of the information frictions that now exist.

It may also be possible that market participants learn to overcome information frictions. My work with Catherine Thomas on the evolution of small intermediaries suggests that platform environments are far from stationary: we provide evidence that participants have found ways to reduce market inefficiencies. Small intermediary organizations did not exist on oDesk initially, but as the market evolved, experienced workers began to share their "brand" with other workers, and oDesk built infrastructure to formally accommodate this arrangement. The entrance of intermediaries that branded novice workers had a substantially positive effect on new workers who were able to affiliate with an intermediary (Stanton and Thomas 2011). Market participants, either platform operators or workers and employers themselves, seem likely to figure out solutions that mitigate the long-run effects of information frictions.

Managerial Inputs and Tasks through Platforms

As platforms mature, they are likely to gain an increasing share of the low-skilled tasks that are easy to send abroad. This motivates the third question: Is the outsourcing of highly specialized tasks likely to migrate to platforms in the future, and how will management practices evolve to accommodate such a shift?

How substitutable are individual workers hired on a platform like oDesk for workers hired through a traditional labor market or traditional outsourcing firm? An online worker might be equally or more skilled than a local hire, but if coordination across workers is harder to achieve over platforms, pro-

---

3. Platforms for innovation contests may contain some features analogous to the bonding example.

ductivity will be limited. The importance of management practices has been documented in other settings (Bloom and Van Reenen 2007), but we know very little about how employers on platforms organize work practices. It is also theoretically appealing to consider whether it is possible for technically demanding projects to be conducted via arms-length contracting. Many of the firms that hire on oDesk are start-ups, and a generalist start-up founder may not be the ideal manager to oversee a specialized IT project. The literature on efficient hierarchies suggests that a manager should be able to solve the problems that a worker may face (Garicano 2000). This suggests a role for skilled management and hierarchies, which are perhaps harder to organize via a platform than via traditional labor markets or firms like Infosys.

The coordination problems in bringing teams together may also be especially hard for very practical reasons like scheduling and communications differences.[4] Scheduling may be difficult because many contractors juggle multiple simultaneous projects. In addition, communication between team members in multinational cooperative environments may be challenging. Efficient hierarchies and the difficulty of forming teams suggests that platforms are likely to grow rapidly for handling relatively low-skilled tasks, but extremely high-skilled trade in labor services will probably continue to flow through established firms (or firms that are started by the most skilled workers). The fact that firms like Infosys have experience in handling large projects while providing managerial value added provides one reason why arms-length contracting through platforms may make up a small value-weighted share of future trade in services. Ultimately, the nature of production and whether employers can adopt efficient management practices while utilizing online workers will determine how trade in services is conducted.

Conclusion

Agrawal, Horton, Lacetera, and Lyons have provided an intuitive guide for anyone interested in the economics of online contract labor markets. Although the data available from these markets has some limitations, they provide some of the best available transaction-level data for understanding international trade in services. The authors highlight important research questions for the future.

References

Agrawal, Ajay, Nicola Lacetera, and Elizabeth Lyons. 2012. "How Do Online Platforms Flatten Markets for Contract Labor?" Working Paper, University of Toronto.
Bloom, Nicholas, and John Van Reenen. 2007. "Measuring and Explaining Man-

---

4. See Lyons (2013).

agement Practices across Firms and Countries." *Quarterly Journal of Economics* 122 (4): 1351–1408.

Burks, Stephen, Bo Cowgill, Mitchell Hoffman, and Michael Housman. 2013. "'You'd Be Perfect for This': The Value of Hiring through Referrals." IZA Discussion Paper no. 7382, Institute for the Study of Labor.

DeVaro, Jed, and Michael Waldman. 2012. "The Signaling Role of Promotions: Further Theory and Empirical Evidence." *Journal of Labor Economics* 30 (1): 91–147.

Garicano, Luis. 2000. "Hierarchies and the Organization of Knowledge in Production." *Journal of Political Economy* 108 (5): 874–904.

Ghani, Ejaz, William R. Kerr, and Christopher Stanton. 2012. "Diasporas and Outsourcing: Evidence from oDesk and India." NBER Working Paper no. 18474, Cambridge, MA.

Horton, John. 2012. "Computer-Mediated Matchmaking: Facilitating Employer Search and Screening." Working Paper, New York University.

Kahn, Lisa. 2013. "Asymmetric Information between Employers." *American Economic Journal: Applied Economics* 5 (4): 165–205.

Kuhn, Peter, and Hani Mansour. 2013. "Is Internet Job Search Still Ineffective?" IZA Discussion Paper no. 5955, Institute for the Study of Labor.

Lyons, Elizabeth. 2013. "Multinational Teams: Experimental Evidence from the Field." Working Paper, University of Toronto.

Mill, Roy. 2011. "Hiring and Learning in Online Global Labor Markets." NET Working Paper no. 11-17, Networks, Electronic Commerce, and Telecommunications Institute.

Pallais, Amanda. 2012. "Inefficient Hiring in Entry-Level Labor Markets." NBER Working Paper no. 18917, Cambridge, MA.

Pallais, Amanda, and Emily Sands. 2013. "Why the Referential Treatment? Evidence from Field Experiments on Referrals." Working Paper, Harvard University.

Stanton, Christopher, and Catherine Thomas. 2011. "Landing the First Job: The Value of Intermediaries in Online Hiring." Working Paper, University of Utah.

9   Some Economics of Private Digital Currency

Joshua S. Gans and Hanna Halaburda

9.1   Introduction

As digitization has progressed, there has been an increase in *private digital currencies*. These are virtual goods that have the characteristics of money, offering a unit of account, a medium of exchange and a store of value, introduced by companies. Examples include Facebook Credits, Microsoft Points, or Amazon Coins. They are digital in the sense that they have no physical counterpart; specifically, they are not a claim on real assets. Moreover, they are often "issued" by companies whose activities focus on social networking, video games, or sales of applications for tablets. In this analysis we ask why companies would find issuing those private digital currencies beneficial, and what strategic considerations are related to such currencies.

It is important to distinguish between private digital currencies and *digitization of state-issued currencies*. The latter are digitized transactions that involve the execution of a contractual promise to transfer actual currency between two accounts (i.e., from one owner to another owner). This has been extensively studied in the literature on payments systems and, specifically, the contractual terms and standards that govern the settlement of

---

Joshua S. Gans is professor of strategic management and holder of the Jeffrey S. Skoll Chair of Technical Innovation and Entrepreneurship at the Rotman School of Management, University of Toronto, and a research associate of the National Bureau of Economic Research. Hanna Halaburda is an economist at the Bank of Canada and a senior research associate at CESifo.

The views here are those of the authors and no responsibility for them should be attributed to the Bank of Canada. We thank participants at the NBER Economics of Digitization conference and Warren Weber and Glen Weyl for helpful comments on an earlier draft of this chapter. Please send any comments to joshua.gans@gmail.com. For acknowledgments, sources of research support, and disclosure of the authors' material financial relationships, if any, please see http://www.nber.org/chapters/c12992.ack.

interaccount transfers of currency.[1] In effect, this is a digital layer to a set of activities that were previously performed nondigitally. In this case, however, digitization plays a straightforward role of reducing transaction costs associated with payments including the carrying of physical money, the storage and protection of that money, and the provision of short-term liquidity, as most naturally seen with credit and charge cards. Since this has been extensively studied, we will not concern ourselves with such digitization here.

However, both analyses of digitized money transfer systems and private digital currencies are closely related to economic research on platforms. A platform is a business, mechanism, or institution that brings together two or more distinct parties (or more generally, groups) for their eventual mutual gain. Economic research on platforms has been spurred by payments systems literature, such as the analysis of credit card associations, particularly their pricing and competitive elements.[2] The platforms literature is related to the issue of private digital currencies in a few ways. First, one can argue that currencies themselves are intrinsically platforms, and that coexisting multiple currencies should be analyzed as platform competition. Second, there have been a number of companies whose primary purpose is the transfer and storage of money; for example, PayPal, M-Pesa, Bitcoin, or Liberty Exchange. Some of them use private digital currencies (Bitcoin, Liberty Exchange), while others do not (PayPal, M-Pesa). But what is interesting is that, for the most part, private digital currencies have been set up in association with noncurrency-specific platforms. Historically, currencies were chosen from among existing commodities. Modern technology gives platforms unprecedented flexibility in *designing* the attributes of their currencies. In this analysis, we will focus exclusively on these.

Consider the example of Linden dollars. These were set up as a currency inside the game Second Life. Participants could earn Linden dollars by trading with other players for virtual goods. Players could bring more Linden dollars to the game by "buying in" with state-issued currency, for example, US dollars. Moreover, Linden dollars earned in the game could be converted back into US dollars. Thus, there was the potential for some individuals to earn more US dollars than they put in. This gave rise to calls for some taxation of those earnings as income but, in reality, the underlying principle was no different from that of casino chips.

Other platform-specific currencies did not have the full convertibility of Linden dollars. Game console makers (Nintendo and Microsoft) required players to pay for points that could be used to purchase games. However, once points were paid for, they could not be converted back. In Microsoft's case, consumers also needed points to purchase songs on their Zune portable music players. Nintendo has since phased out the points system, and Microsoft has been criticized for using points that may obscure the true

---

1. See Rochet and Tirole (2002) and Gans and King (2003).
2. See Rochet and Tirole (2003), Armstrong (2006), and Weyl (2010).

purchase value for some consumers. By contrast, Sony asked for prepayment of funds to download games to its console, but did not have an alternate unit of account, while Apple allowed consumers to purchase songs and games directly on their iOS platform. It is likely that these systems were set up in response to fees and logistical difficulties related to credit card payments (e.g., for small transactions, those fees could be a burden to merchants). Over time, this became less of an issue, as the volume of transactions rose, allowing merchants to bundle smaller consumer transactions into larger ones and save on those payment costs.

While these platform-specific currencies could be seen as moves to improve transactional efficiency subject to existing constraints, others that have evolved appear to be more tightly linked with the overall functioning of the platform. For instance, in the online multiplayer game World of Warcraft (WoW), players can perform activities and earn WoW Gold that allows them to buy improved weaponary, among other things. While this might seem like a currency akin to Monopoly money, WoW Gold can be expanded in supply by the activities of players. For this reason, players are prohibited from trading WoW Gold outside of the game. This, however, has not prevented a black market from arising, leading to "Gold farming" by players in countries with low market wages. In other cases, such as FarmVille, this outside trading has been alleviated by allowing players to purchase more "FV dollars" in the game (by which the platform may earn additional revenue). But, unlike Linden dollars, neither WoW Gold nor FV dollars can be converted back into state-issued currency.

In this chapter, we focus on these digital currencies that are platform-specific and can be exchanged "inwardly" for state-issued currency.[3] In section 9.2, we will discuss in more detail the case of Facebook Credits that have this feature. We focus on them because commentators in 2011 saw them as a threat to traditional currencies. "Could a gigantic nonsovereign like Facebook someday launch a real currency to compete with the dollar, euro, yen and the like?" Matthew Yglesias (2012). As for the payments, economist David Evans (2012) stated:

> Social game companies could pay developers around the world in Facebook Credits and small businesspeople could accept Facebook Credits because they could use them to buy other things that they need or reward customers with them. In some countries (especially those with national debts that are greater than their GDPs) Facebook Credits could become a safer currency than the national currency.

In other words, there was concern that Facebook Credits could become a currency, like the 2013 attention-getter, Bitcoin, which involved full convertibility.

---

3. There are currencies that feature the alternative approach: they can be earned via activity only and then converted into real goods and services; for instance, airline and other loyalty points schemes.

These predictions have raised issues as to whether such platform-specific currencies should be subject to additional regulation and oversight. However, in our opinion, first it would be useful to understand whether such expansion of the role of platform-specific credits would be in the interests of platform owners. Specifically, would it be worthwhile for a currency such as Facebook Credits to move from limited convertibility to full convertibility? If the answer is no, as we will argue below, then it would appear that the concerns being raised are potentially overblown.

This chapter is organized as follows. In the next section, we detail our motivating case of Facebook Credits. While now discontinued, these capture clearly all of the elements of the debates regarding platform-specific currencies. Section 9.3 then considers a model of platforms and how different attributes of a platform-specific currency can influence platform business models. Our goal here is not to model any one platform in particular, but to give a framework for some suggested forces that will impact any platform-specific currency choices. Future work, tailored to specific platforms, would likely yield richer results. Section 9.4 considers some issues associated with regulation. Since these are fast moving and involve deeper issues of monetary economics rather than digitization per se, we merely note some of these. A final section offers some thoughts as to future research directions.

9.2 Motivating Case: Facebook Credits

In the middle of 2009 the most popular social networking site, Facebook, introduced its virtual currency—Facebook Credits (FB Credits). In 2011, Facebook announced that game developers on its platform would be required to process payments solely through Facebook Credits.[4] However, the next year, Facebook decided to phase out Credits, since they were a confusing proposition to consumers who also had to purchase points or other currency-like instruments within Facebook games. Nonetheless, the case is instructive because it represents a clear instance of platform-sponsored currencies that, upon their introduction, led many to believe that these could become a significant payment instrument.

To recount this, even before the 2011 announcement, as noted above, many commentators expressed concern that FB Credits could become global currency, and perhaps take over state-issued currency. As early as 2009, predictions were made that "Facebook could rival PayPal by creating a virtual currency and making it usable for financial transactions, essentially making Facebook Credits the currency of the web."[5] And with 1 billion

---

4. "Facebook Sets July, 1, 2011 Deadline to Make Credits Sole Canvas Game Payment Option," Inside Facebook. Retrieved December 4, 2012. (http://www.insidefacebook.com/2011/01/24/facebook-sets-july-1-2011-deadline-to-make-credits-sole-canvas-game-payment-option/).

5. http://mashable.com/2009/12/15/facebook-credits-currency/.

users,[6] this currency would be more popular than most state currencies. After the 2011 announcement, those voices became more frequent.[7] It may have been one of the factors leading the European Central Bank to investigate virtual currencies in 2012.[8]

Facebook equipped its Credits with limited functionality. One could buy Credits (i.e., exchange state-issued currency for FB Credits) at the rate 50 FB Credits for US $5, with quantity discounts.[9] FB Credits could be spent in any Facebook application that accepts them.[10] It is also important to note that buying FB Credits was not the only way of obtaining them. A user could *earn* the Credits if they tested a new game or took a survey.

However, the users could not transfer FB Credits between each other. They also could not exchange FB Credits back for state-issued currency. This severely limited functionality of FB Credits as a means of payment. Clearly, with such limited functionality, FB Credits could not really become a global currency rivaling state-issued currencies. Internet pundits, however, claimed that it was only a matter of time, and soon Facebook would turn Credits into a functional currency by allowing interuser transfers and exchanging the FB Credits back into the state-issued currency.[11]

In this chapter, we claim that it would not be beneficial for Facebook to equip FB Credits with those additional attributes. Facebook's main source of revenue is advertising, which is linked directly to the activity of the users on the platform. Therefore, Facebook's objective is to increase the activity of its users. Limiting functionality and allowing for both "buying" and "earning" are features that maximize activity on the platform. Users spend FB Credits to enhance their platform experience, which increases their utility from using the platform and leads to more activity. With buying and earning, both time-poor and time-rich users obtain the Credits. If Facebook were to allow for reverse exchange (i.e., exchanging FB Credits to state currency), the time-rich users would sell the Credits they earned without increasing their activity on the platform. Allowing a transfer of FB Credits between users opens a way for the exchange of FB Credits into state-issued currency to bypass the platform: users can transfer FB Credits and pay each other outside the platform for the acquired Credits, as has happened with WoW

6. http://newsroom.fb.com/News/457/One-Billion-People-on-Facebook.
7. See, for example, http://emergentbydesign.com/2011/04/04/the-bank-of-facebook-currency-identity-reputation/ and http://www.slate.com/articles/business/cashless_society/2012/02/facebook_credits_how_the_social_network_s_currency_could_compete_with_dollars_and_euros_.html.
8. See "Virtual Currency Schemes," European Central Bank, October 2012. http://www.ecb.europa.eu/pub/pdf/other/virtualcurrencyschemes201210en.pdf.
9. For example, for $10 there is a 5 percent bonus, and one receives 105 Credits.
10. The applications were required to use FB Credits between July 2011 and June 2012. Before and after that period, use of FB Credits was voluntary.
11. See, for example, http://www.slate.com/articles/business/cashless_society/2012/02/facebook_credits_how_the_social_ network_s_currency_could_compete_with_dollars_and_euros_.html.

Gold. Thus, current functionality of FB Credits is optimal for Facebook's objective.

9.3 The Model

Consider an environment with one platform and two users, A and B.[12]

9.3.1 Users

Each user i can spend some time x_i using the platform, which yields utility $v(x_i, x_j)$. To account for consumption complementarity between the two users, the utility of i depends on that user's own consumption (x_i) as well as the consumption of the other user (x_j). The utility of an agent increases as the agent spends more time on the platform (but the rate of increase is declining). Due to complementarity, the agent's utility and marginal utility also increases when the other agent spends more time on the platform; that is, $[\partial v(x_i, x_j)]/(\partial x_i > 0)$, $[\partial^2 v(x_i, x_j)]/\partial x_i^2 < 0$, $[\partial v(x_i, x_j)]/\partial x_j > 0$, and $[\partial^2 v(x_i, x_j)]/(\partial x_i \partial x_j) > 0$.

Each user has total time Z available. The time can be spent either using the platform or working. When working, the user can earn wage w per unit of time. The total amount of money earned allows the user to consume a *numeraire* good (i.e., a composite of goods and services consumed outside of the platform), which adds to the user's utility. Both users are the same, with the exception of the wage—user A earns a higher wage than user $B (w_A > w_B)$. Hence, if user i spends n_i time to earn the numeraire, then he can consume $n_i w_i$ of the numeraire.

Each user aims to maximize his or her utility given the time constraint:

$$\max_{x_i, n_i} v(x_i, x_j) + n_i w_i$$

such that $x_i + n_i \leq Z$.

The constraint binds in the optimum, so $n_i = Z - x_i$, and the utility maximization problem simplifies to $\max_{x_i} v(x_i, x_j) + (Z - x_i) w_i$.

In the interior solution,[13] the optimal usage $\hat{x}_i$ is given by

---

12. The model can be easily extended to A and B denoting types of users with an arbitrary number of agents in each type. The qualitative results stay the same, but the notation is more complicated.

13. Corner solutions may happen for very high and very low w's. When w_i is low enough that $\{[\partial v(\hat{x}_i, x_j)] / \partial x_i\}|_{x_i = Z} > w_i$, then the user spends all of his or her time using the platform, $\hat{x}_i = Z$. Notice that, in such a case, increasing x_j does not change $\hat{x}_i$, but decreasing x_j may decrease $\hat{x}_i$ below Z if the derivative decreases to $\{[\partial v(\hat{x}_i, x_j)] / \partial x_i\}|_{x_i = Z} < w_i$. Similarly, when w_i is high enough that $\{[\partial v(\hat{x}_i, x_j)] / \partial x_i\}|_{x_i = 0} < w_i$, then the agent spends no time using the platform, $\hat{x}_i = 0$. Decreasing x_j will not change i's consumption decision. But increasing x_j may induce i to set positive $\hat{x}_i > 0$, in the case when the increase in x_j increases the derivative to $\{[\partial v(\hat{x}_i, x_j)] / \partial x_i\}|_{x_i = 0} > w_i$.

(1)
$$\frac{\partial v(\hat{x}_i, x_j)}{\partial x_i} = w_i.$$

Since $[\partial^2 v(x_i, x_j)]/\partial x_i^2 < 0$, $w_A > w_B$ implies $\hat{x}_A < \hat{x}_B$. That is, the user earning the higher wage is choosing to spend less time on the platform.

EXAMPLE. Suppose that $v(x_i, x_j) = x_i^\alpha x_j^{1-\alpha}$, for $\alpha > 1/2$. Combining the first-order conditions, we get

$$\frac{w_A}{w_B} = \left(\frac{\hat{x}_B}{\hat{x}_A}\right)^{2(1-\alpha)}.$$

Then, $w_A > w_B$ implies that $\hat{x}_A < \hat{x}_B$. Moreover, there are multiple equilibria possible. Any combination of x_A and x_B such that $w_A/w_B = (\hat{x}_B/\hat{x}_A)^{2(1-\alpha)}$ and $x_B \leq Z$ constitutes an equilibrium. Multiplicity of equilibria is not surprising, given the consumption complementarity.

9.3.2 The Platform

We assume that the platform's revenue directly depends on the usage, $r(x_A + x_B)$ where $r > 0$ is the revenue, say from advertising, related to the total level of activity on the platform, $x_A + x_B$. Higher level of activity induces higher revenue. For now, we assume that this is the only source of the platform's revenue. Under this assumption, the platform aims at maximizing the total usage, $x_A + x_B$. Later in the analysis, we allow other sources of revenue, for example, the sale of platform-specific currency. In that latter case, the platform's optimal decisions do not necessarily maximize total usage. Notice that, due to consumption complementarity, there may exist multiple equilibria with different total usage.

EXAMPLE (CONTINUED). Given multiplicity of equilibria, the platform's usage depends on the equilibrium played. In our example, the largest usage that may be obtained in an equilibrium is for $\hat{x}_B = Z$ and $\hat{x}_A = Z(w_B/w_A)^{1/[2(1-\alpha)]}$. The smallest one is arbitrarily close to 0, when $\hat{x}_B = \varepsilon \neq 0$ and $\hat{x}_A = \varepsilon(w_B/w_A)^{1/[2(1-\alpha)]}$.

9.3.3 Enhancing the Platform: "Buying" and "Earning"

Suppose that now the platform allows the users to acquire options, e_i, that enhance the value of platform usage. For example, this may be additional options in a game. The enhancement increases the usage utility; that is, for the same level of usage, $v(x_i, e'_i, x_j) > v(x_i, e_i, x_j)$ for $e'_i > e_i$. Moreover, we assume that $[\partial v(x_i, e'_i, x_j)]/\partial x_i > [\partial v(x_i, e_i, x_j)]/\partial x_i$, $[\partial v(x'_i, e_i, x_j)]/\partial e_i > [\partial v(x_i, e_i, x_j)]/\partial e_i$ for $x'_i > x_i$ and $[\partial v(x_i, e_i, x_j)]/\partial e_i \to \infty$ as $e_i \to 0$.[14] The enhancement may be obtained by "buying" it, or by "earning" it (e.g., through testing functionality or simply by playing the game more intensively). Specifically, we assume that

---

14. This is on top of the usual second-order conditions: $[\partial^2 v(x_i, e_i, x_j)]/\partial x_i^2 < 0$ and $[\partial^2 v(x_i, e_i, x_j)]/\partial e_i^2 < 0$.

$e_i = \gamma y_i + \phi t_i$, where y_i are the units of the numeraire (buying) and t_i are in units of time (earning).

User i's utility in the environment with the enhancement is

(2) $$v(x_i, e_i(t_i, y_i), x_j) + (Z - x_i - t_i)w_i - y_i,$$

which the user maximizes by choosing x_i, t_i, and y_i subject to the constraints that $y_i \leq (Z - x_i - t_i)w_i$ and $Z \geq x_i + t_i$. For a solution interior in all three variables, the first-order conditions are

(3) $$\text{w.r.t. } x_i : \quad \frac{\partial v(x_i, e_i, x_j)}{\partial x_i} = w_i$$

(4) $$\text{w.r.t. } t_i : \quad \frac{\partial v(x_i, e_i, x_j)}{\partial e_i}\phi = w_i$$

(5) $$\text{w.r.t. } y_i : \quad \frac{\partial v(x_i, e_i, x_j)}{\partial e_i}\gamma = 1.$$

Notice, however, that t_i and y_i are perfect substitutes in achieving e_i. Therefore, each user chooses only one way of obtaining e_i, whichever is cheapest. Buying a unit of e_i costs the user $1/\gamma$, while earning it costs w_i/ϕ.

If $w_i < \phi/\gamma$, then user i only earns the enhancement, and $y_i = 0$. Then, the two relevant first-order conditions are

(6) $$\frac{\partial v(x_i, e_i, x_j)}{\partial x_i} = w_i \text{ and } \frac{\partial v(x_i, e_i, x_j)}{\partial e_i}\phi = w_i.$$

When $w_i > \phi/\gamma$, then user i only buys, that is, $t_i = 0$. Then, the two relevant first-order conditions are

(7) $$\frac{\partial v(x_i, e_i, x_j)}{\partial x_i} = w_i \text{ and } \frac{\partial v(x_i, e_i, x_j)}{\partial e_i}\gamma = 1.$$

For exogenously given w's, ϕ, and γ, we assume here that Z is large enough that solutions on the relevant parameters (x_i and t_i, or x_i and y_i) are interior. For an interior x_i, we can prove the following result.

LEMMA 1. *Holding e_i and x_j fixed, a user i with lower w_i optimally chooses higher usage, x_i.*

PROOF. Since Z is large enough for x_i to be interior for both users, $[\partial v(x_i, e_i, x_j)]/\partial x_i = w_i$. With $w_A > w_B$, for the same e_i and x_j, the derivative is higher for the higher-wage user. And since $\partial^2 v(x_i, \cdot)/\partial x_i^2 < 0$, the derivative is higher for smaller usage x_i. Hence $x_A < x_B$ if e_i and x_j are unchanged.

Given that users have different wages, in equilibrium it will not be the case that e_i and x_j are the same for both users. With the higher usage x_i, the marginal benefit of enhancement is higher. Thus, users with lower w_i choose larger e_i, which further increases their optimal usage.

LEMMA 2. *The low-wage user acquires more enhancements and has higher usage in equilibrium.*

PROOF: We conduct this proof in two steps. In the first one, we show that the low-wage user acquires more enhancements for a fixed x_i and x_j. In the second step, we combine the result of the first step and Lemma 1 to complete the proof for the equilibrium outcome.

When both w_A and w_B are greater—or both lower—than ϕ/γ, we find that the low-wage user acquires more enhancement directly from the second-order conditions (for a fixed x_i and x_j). The interesting case is when $w_A > \phi/\gamma > w_B$. In this case, the first-order conditions are $(\partial v/\partial e_B)\phi = w_B$ and $(\partial v/\partial e_A)\gamma = 1$. Those conditions imply that $\partial v/\partial e_B = w_B/\phi$ and $\partial v/\partial e_A = 1/\gamma$. And since $\phi/\gamma > w_B \Leftrightarrow 1/\gamma > w_B/\phi$, then $\partial v/\partial e_A > \partial v/\partial e_B$. Therefore, if faced with the same x_i and x_j, $e_A < e_B$.

In the second step of the proof, notice, from Lemma 1, that we know that $x_A < x_B$ for the same e_i and x_j. Moreover, because own consumption has a larger effect on utility than x_j, it is still true that $x_A(x_B) < x_B(x_A)$ for the same e_i. Moreover, from the previous step of this proof, given x_i and x_j, $e_A < e_B$ reinforces the fact that in equilibrium $x_A^* < x_B^*$ (i.e., $x_B(e) - x_A(e) < x_B^*(e_B^*) - x_A^*(e_A^*)$).

Notice that usage increases more when both ways of procuring e_i are available. Because users choose the cheapest way, they choose more e_i than they would if only one way of procurement was allowed. Higher e_i leads to higher x_i. Moreover, due to consumption complementarities, it further increases the consumption of the other user, x_j. Therefore, by allowing users to both earn and buy an enhancement of the platform usage (e.g., Facebook Credits), the platform increases usage, as compared to allowing for only one type of enhancement procurement.

PROPOSITION 1. *When the platform allows for both earning and buying of the enhancement, the direct usage, $x_A + x_B$, (weakly) increases by more than when the platform allows for only one type of enhancement procurement (only buying or only earning).*

The increase is weak because if both users are choosing the same means of obtaining the enhancement, and the only option is the optimal option, then adding a new option does not strictly improve usage. The following proof focuses on the interesting case where improvement is strict.

PROOF. Let $w_A > \phi/\gamma > w_B$. Suppose that only option buy is available. Both $i = A, B$ choose their enhancement investment and usage based on equation (7). Let B's optimal choices in this case be $\hat{x}_B$ and $\hat{e}_B$.

When it becomes possible to earn, user B prefers to go for the new option, and chooses enhancement $\hat{\hat{e}}_B$ according to condition (6). Since $w_B/\phi < 1/\gamma$, then $[\partial v(\hat{x}_B, \hat{e}_B, x_A)]/\partial e_B > [\partial v(\hat{x}_B, \hat{\hat{e}}_B, x_A)]/\partial e_B$, which implies $\hat{\hat{e}}_B(\hat{x}_B) > \hat{e}_B(\hat{x}_B)$. But then, also, $\hat{\hat{x}}_B > \hat{x}_B$. So, in equilibrium $\hat{\hat{e}}_B$ and $\hat{\hat{x}}_B > \hat{x}_B$. Given the complementarity in users' activity, increasing x_B also increases x_A. Thus, allowing for earning of platform enhancement along with buying increases total platform usage by increasing both x_B and x_A.

In a similar way, we can also show that starting from earning only, and then allowing buying as well, increases total platform usage by increasing both x_A and x_B.

It is useful to consider the relevance of this proposition for digital currency. For instance, Facebook Credits represent a unit of account. It could have been that, like Microsoft and Nintendo, these credits were solely bought. In this way, they would merely be a way of converting real currency into on-platform payments. However, to the extent that some users of the platform are income or wealth constrained, this would reduce their use of enhancements. Complementarity among users would then imply a reduction in overall activity on the platform. Instead, by offering a means of earning enhancements, the platform provides an alternative pathway for income-constrained users. Of course, this may be strengthened if such earning was itself platform activity—as sometimes occurs—but we have supressed that effect here. Later, in section 9.3.5, we also discuss how Proposition 1 may sometimes fail if the platform has different objectives than maximizing total usage.

The proposition also demonstrates that allowing "inward convertibility" from real currency onto the platform encourages more usage from income-rich users. Once again, complementarity among users leads to more overall usage from convertibility. Thus, while World of Warcraft may officially prohibit "Gold farming," there is a sense in which it increases platform usage. Of course, it could be imagined that digital currencies associated with platforms could go further and allow outward convertibility—the reverse exchange back into state-issued currency. It is this feature that would put those currencies on a path to competing with state-issued currencies. We examine this option next.

9.3.4 Reverse Exchange

In this section, we show that if the platform were to allow for the reverse exchange of earned credits into state-issued currency, it would decrease platform usage.

PROPOSITION 2. *If the platform allows for the reverse exchange of e_i into y_i at any positive rate, it lowers platform usage.*

PROOF. Suppose that user i can spend t_i to get $e_i = \phi t_i$, but then can convert it back into cash at a rate of μ: $y_i = e_i/\mu = \phi t_i/\mu$. Then, the effective wage of user i is $y_i/t_i = \phi/\mu$. If the platform puts no restrictions on this exchange, it allows all agents with outside wage $w_i < \phi/\mu$ to achieve the effective wage of $\hat{w} = \phi/\mu$. But, from the previous results, we know that increasing the wage lowers the equilibrium usage x_i, and also lowers how much of e_i is actually used by the agent on the enhancement, (as the agent may redeem[15] part or all of e_i for y_i).

The proof here does not take into account the fact that reverse exchange would be costly for the platform. In other words, it is unambiguously detrimental to the platform. Thus, as long as the goal of the platform is to maximize direct activity ($x_A + x_B$), platforms have no incentive to allow for outward convertibility or reverse exchange. In other words, despite the concern of commentators, platforms that utilize digital currencies for within platform transactions have no incentive to move toward full convertibility.

It is worth considering the assumption that drives this strong result. Here we have assumed that platform activity—including the incentive to purchase an enhancement—is solely driven by utility earned within the platform. Specifically, the enhancement increases the marginal utility from activity and is reduced if currency is redeemed outside of the platform. However, it could be the case that by earning the enhancement, activity is increased even if the currency earned is redeemed rather than spent within the game. In this case, the incentive to earn that currency increases activity and could be enhanced by allowing convertibility. This may be part of the rationale for allowing full convertibility of Linden dollars in the game Second Life.

9.3.5 Optimal Choice of γ and ϕ

Until now, we have taken γ and ϕ as given. Typically, however, the platform sets γ and ϕ. Each user's choice of whether to earn or purchase an enhancement depends on the prices, $1/\gamma$ and $1/\phi$, and their relationship to the user's wage. The prices chosen by a platform depend on its precise objective. Thus far, we have focused on the impact of various platform choices on $x_A + x_B$, direct platform usage. This would be relevant if the platform's only source of revenue was, say, advertising, related to platform usage. In this case, the platform would aim to set both γ and ϕ as high as possible while still assuring that, regardless of how a user chooses to obtain the enhancement, each does so. In effect, the enhancement would be so ubiquitous that it would be an integral part of the platform, and there would be few interesting questions regarding currencies.

In some cases, the platform may also earn the same advertising revenue from users' activity while earning an enhancement. In this case, the platform would aim to maximize $r(x_A + x_B + t_A + t_B)$. The platform may then benefit from users engaging in a variety of activities (depending on the nature of $v(.)$), but, regardless, it would want ϕ to be as high as possible while still assuring that all users earn the enhancement. For γ, the platform faces a trade-off. Decreasing γ can induce high-wage types to switch their activity

---

15. Since part or all of the enhancement is redeemed, it does not enter as e_i into $v(x_i, e_i, x_j)$.

toward earning the enhancement, which directly increases t_A. However, this involves some substitution away from x_A which, depending upon $v(.)$, may lead to a reduction in activity by B. Thus, it is not possible to characterize this price in the general case, as the optimal price will depend on the particular functional forms.

Of course, the purchases of enhancements can also represent an alternative revenue stream for the platform. In this case, it would be reasonable to consider the platform as maximizing $r(x_A + x_B) + (y_A + y_B)$ or $r(x_A + x_B + t_A + t_B) + (y_A + y_B)$. Depending on the level of r, the platform may prefer to withdraw the possibility of earning an enhancement and force all agents to buy it. In such a case, Proposition 1 may fail. Regardless of whether Proposition 1 holds or fails, the platform will set the prices so that each user's time constraint is binding and focused on the platform, either through activity or income. That is, for users buying an enhancement, $t_i = 0$ and $y_i = (Z - x_i)w_i$, while for a user earning the enhancement, $y_i = 0$ and $t_i = Z - x_i$.

This allows us to identify the first-order conditions for users. For users earning the enhancement, it is

$$(8) \qquad \left.\frac{\partial v(x_i, e_i, x_j)}{\partial x_i}\right|_{e_i=\phi(Z-x_i)} = \phi \left.\frac{\partial v(x_i, e_i, x_j)}{\partial e_i}\right|_{e_i=\phi(Z-x_i)}.$$

Notice that this condition is independent of w_i. Thus, the optimal usage schedule for those earning the enhancement is independent of wage. That is, if both high-wage and low-wage agents decide to earn the enhancement, they would earn the same e_i and consume the same x_i. For a user buying the enhancement, the first-order condition yields

$$(9) \qquad \left.\frac{\partial v(x_i, e_i, x_j)}{\partial x_i}\right|_{e_i=\gamma(Z-x_i)w_i} = w_i\gamma \left.\frac{\partial v(x_i, e_i, x_j)}{\partial e_i}\right|_{e_i=\gamma(Z-x_i)w_i}.$$

Thus, users who buy the enhancement will differ in their usage levels, depending on the wage. This suggests that allowing users to buy enhancements can be useful when it is optimal to exploit their differential usage rather than ignore it. Of course, a precise characterization is not possible in the general case. For our running example, however, we can provide a more precise conclusion.

EXAMPLE (CONTINUED). Suppose that, in our example, the platform introduces the enhancement and now $v(x_i, e_i, x_j) = x_i^\alpha x_j^{1-\alpha} e_i^\beta$. Moreover, $e_i = \gamma y_i + \phi t_i$. Then, user i's utility is $x_i^\alpha x_j^{1-\alpha}(\gamma y_i + \phi t_i)^\beta + (Z - x_i - t_i)w_i - y_i$. For $w_i < \phi/\gamma$, that is, $y_i = 0$:

$$\begin{cases} \alpha x_i^{\alpha-1} x_j^{1-\alpha}(\phi t_i)^\beta = w_i \\ \phi\beta x_i^\alpha x_j^{1-\alpha}(\phi t_i)^{\beta-1} = w_i \end{cases} \Rightarrow t_i = \frac{\beta}{\alpha} x_i.$$

Using $t_i = (\beta/\alpha)x_i$, the first-order condition yields $x_i^{\alpha+\beta-1} = w_i/(\phi^\beta \alpha^{1-\beta}\beta^\beta x_j^{1-\alpha})$ if the solution is interior, that is, when $t_i < Z - x_i$. When ϕ is large enough (i.e., $\phi > (\alpha/\beta)\{[w_i(\alpha+\beta)^{\alpha+\beta-1}]/[x_j^{1-\alpha}(\alpha Z)^{\alpha+\beta-1}\alpha]\}^{1/\beta}$), so that $t_i = Z - x_i$, the user's problem becomes $\max_{x_i} x_i^\alpha x_j^{1-\alpha}(\phi(Z - x_i))^\beta$. The optimal usage is then $x_i = \alpha Z/(\alpha+\beta)$ and $t_i = \beta Z/(\alpha+\beta)$. Notice that it does not depend on ϕ once the time constraint is binding.

For $w_i > \phi/\gamma$, that is, $t_i = 0$,

$$\begin{cases} \alpha x_i^{\alpha-1} x_j^{1-\alpha}(\gamma y_i)^\beta = w_i \\ \gamma \beta x_i^\alpha x_j^{1-\alpha}(\gamma y_i)^{\beta-1} = 1 \end{cases} \Rightarrow y_i = \frac{\beta}{\alpha} x_i w_i.$$

And further it yields $x_i^{\alpha+\beta-1} = w_i^{1-\beta}/(\gamma^\beta \alpha^{1-\beta}\beta^\beta x_j^{1-\alpha})$ for the interior solution. The corner solution, which arises when γ is sufficiently large, is $x_i = \alpha Z/(\alpha+\beta)$ and $y_i = [\beta Z/(\alpha+\beta)]w_i$.

Depending on the wages and "prices" (γ and ϕ), there are three situations possible: both agents earn the enhancement, both buy it, or one buys and the other earns. We analyze each case in turn (for the interior solution).

1. When both agents earn the enhancement, then any consumption patterns in equilibrium must satisfy $(x_B/x_A)^{2(1-\alpha)-\beta} = w_A/w_B$. Together with the formula for x_i derived above, it yields

$$x_i^\beta = \left(\frac{w_j}{w_i}\right)^{(1-\alpha)/[2(1-\alpha)-\beta]} \frac{w_i}{\alpha^{1-\beta}\beta^\beta \phi^\beta}.$$

This is a complicated formula, but it uniquely characterizes x_i with respect to the exogenous parameters.

2. When both agents buy the enhancement, then in any equilibrium it must be that $(x_B/x_A)^{2(1-\alpha)-\beta} = (w_A/w_B)^{1-\beta}$. Then,

$$x_i^\beta = \left(\frac{w_j}{w_i}\right)^{[(1-\beta)(1-\alpha)]/[2(1-\alpha)-\beta]} \frac{w_i^{1-\beta}}{\alpha^{1-\beta}\beta^\beta \phi^\beta}.$$

3. When agent A buys the enhancement, while agent B earns, then in any equilibrium it must be that $(x_A/x_B)^{2(1-\alpha)-\beta} = (w_B/w_A^{1-\beta})(\gamma/\phi)^\beta$. And then,

$$x_A^\beta = \left(\frac{w_B}{w_A^{1-\beta}}\right)^{(1-\alpha)/[2(1-\alpha)-\beta]} \left(\frac{\gamma}{\phi}\right)^{[\beta(1-\alpha)]/[2(1-\alpha)-\beta]} \frac{w_A^{1-\beta}}{\gamma^\beta \alpha^{1-\beta}\beta^\beta}$$

$$x_B^\beta = \left(\frac{w_A^{1-\beta}}{w_B}\right)^{(1-\alpha)/[2(1-\alpha)-\beta]} \left(\frac{\phi}{\gamma}\right)^{[\beta(1-\alpha)]/[2(1-\alpha)-\beta]} \frac{w_B}{\phi^\beta \alpha^{1-\beta}\beta^\beta}.$$

Notice that, in all three cases, introducing the enhancement eliminates multiplicity of equilibria, since now x_A and x_B are uniquely characterized by the exogenous parameters.

Now consider the platform setting prices ϕ and γ to maximize its objective. We consider four possible objective functions for the platform:

1. $\max r(x_A + x_B)$: The platform is indifferent on whether to buy or earn. Whether γ is so high that both buy, ϕ so high that both earn, or one buys and one earns, the platform can always achieve the global maximum of $x_A = x_B = \alpha Z/(\alpha + \beta)$.

2. $\max r(x_A + x_B) + (y_A + y_B)$: The platform raises γ so that not only do both users buy the enhancement, but both reach the corner consumption schedule. The platform reaches the global maximum of $x_A = x_B = \alpha Z/(\alpha + \beta)$ and $y_i = [\beta Z/(\alpha + \beta)] w_i, i = A, B$.

3. $\max r(x_A + x_B + t_A + t_B)$: The platform raises ϕ so that not only do both users earn the enhancement, but both reach the corner consumption schedule. The platform reaches the global maximum of $x_A = x_B = \alpha Z/(\alpha + \beta)$ and $t_A = t_B = \beta Z/(\alpha + \beta)$ earning $2Z$. If the platform were to set ϕ lower so that $w_B < \phi/\gamma < w_A$, then $t_A = 0$ and $x_A = \alpha Z/(\alpha + \beta)$. Thus, the platform would earn $Z[1 + \alpha/(\alpha + \beta)] < 2Z$.

4. $\max r(x_A + x_B + t_A + t_B) + (y_A + y_B)$: Optimal prices (and optimal users' consumption schedule) depend on w_i's and r. The interesting case is when $w_B < r < w_A$. Then the platform is strictly better off by setting the prices such that user A buys and user B earns the enhancement with consumption achieving a global maximum, $x_A = x_B = \alpha Z/(\alpha + \beta)$, $t_B = \beta Z/(\alpha + \beta)$ and $y_A = [\beta Z/(\alpha + \beta)] w_A$.

9.3.6 Summary

For a platform whose main source of revenue is advertising (e.g., Facebook), its objective is to increase the activity of its users (e.g., the use of social games). When activity on the platform is more valuable for a user when other users increase their activity (e.g., from the social component), there is complementarity in activity on the platform. A platform can provide an enhancement of user experience to encourage more activity (e.g., buying special versions of crops for your farm in FarmVille, which have a higher yield than regular crops). Higher activity by one user increases the utility—and activity—of other users, due to the complementarity. For this reason, if two users acquire the enhancement, the increase in activity is larger than double the increase of activity resulting from a single user's enhancement. Therefore, it is optimal for the platform to encourage all users to acquire the enhancement. But some users may find the monetary cost too high, for example, if they have a low wage. Then, the platform gains if it allows for both *buying* and *earning* the enhancement. High-wage users will prefer to spend money rather than time, while low-wage users can spend time instead of money. Both types will acquire the enhancement and increase activity on the platform.

This reflects the policies of many social networks and also some gaming platforms. Of particular significance is Proposition 2, which prevents platform-specific currencies from being traded back for state-issued currency. This provides a strong result that such platforms are not interested in introducing currencies that would directly compete with existing state-issued currencies. That said, for a platform such as Facebook, there is a flow of money back through developer payments: that is, a developer writes a game that induces people to purchase enhancements. The developer then receives part of the revenue that Facebook receives when Credits are purchased. Nonetheless, this is really just an extension of the platform notion, where the game itself is the platform of interest. Indeed, in mid-2012, Facebook announced that it would phase out Credits by the end of 2013 and rely only on state-issued currencies. The users often needed to further convert Facebook Credits into currencies within apps and games, for example, zCoins in Zynga's games. Users and developers were against this additional layer of complication and wanted a direct link to state-issued currencies. This is consistent with the model, in that, for Facebook's core activity, literally the activity or news feed, all features were available to all users. It could still earn essentially "referral" fees for revenue generated by others on its platform, but for its core activity, a currency would perform no additional role.

By contrast, it is easy to imagine that app developers such as Zynga introduced their own currencies for exactly the same reason as in our main model: to increase activity on their "app platform." Just as Facebook Credits once bought or earned cannot be exchanged back into cash, so zCoins—once bought or earned—cannot be exchanged back into state-issued currency (or indeed Facebook Credits when they were available). This policy is driven by Zynga's objective to maximize activity on its *own* platform. This may, however, conflict with Facebook's objective to increase activity on the Facebook platform, possibly across different apps. A richer model would be required to explore issues arising from interlocking platforms.

A distinct argument lies behind Amazon Coins, introduced in the beginning of 2013. Amazon announced that it would give away "millions of US dollars worth" of Amazon Coins to customers, starting in May 2013. Like all other introductions of digital currencies, this attracted the usual concern about the threat to state-issued currencies. "But in the long term what [central banks] should perhaps be most worried about is losing their monopoly on issuing money," wrote the *Wall Street Journal*. "A new breed of virtual currencies are starting to emerge—and some of the giants of the web industry such as Amazon.com Inc. are edging into the market."[16]

However, Amazon Coins is simply a subsidy to buyers to participate in the platform (Kindle Fire), with the purpose of starting and accelerating any indirect network effects benefiting Amazon's app platform. When Kindle Fire users purchase Amazon Coins, they receive an effective discount on

16. *Wall Street Journal*, Market Watch. http://articles.marketwatch.com/2013-02-13/commentary/37064080_1_currency-war-bitcoin-central-banks.

apps (from 5 to 10 percent, depending on how many Coins are purchased), something that was a feature of Facebook Credits as well. Due to uncertainty about the quality of apps, a subsidy to users is more effective than a subsidy to the developers, since users will "vote" with their Coins for the best apps. At the same time, introducing Amazon Coins is potentially more convenient than subsidizing via cash, since it ensures that the subsidy is spent on the Amazon app platform, and not on other services on Amazon or outside.

9.4 Regulatory Issues

Our analysis of platform-specific currencies shows that voices calling for specific regulation of them overstate their case, since the purpose of those currencies is a natural complement to the business models associated with platforms such as Facebook or Amazon. To maximally benefit the platform, the use of currencies needs to be restricted. Thus, it is not in the interest of the platforms to provide fully functional currencies that could compete with state currencies.

In our analysis, however, we have not considered Bitcoin, which is a fully convertible, purely digital currency not associated with a given platform. It is explicitly designed to compete with state currencies. In March 2013, the US government for the first time imposed regulations on online currencies.[17] Virtual currencies are to be regulated by the US Treasury, since the Financial Crimes Enforcement Network (FinCEN) decided they fall under the anti-money-laundering laws.[18] According to the new rules, transactions worth more than $10,000 need to be reported by companies involved in issuing or exchanging online currencies. The rules do not single out Bitcoin, but apply to all "online currencies." This clarification of FinCEN laws was issued after evidence emerged that Bitcoin is used for illegal activity (e.g., Silk Road). Illegal activity is a concern because the anonymity of Bitcoin allows for untraceable trades.

There may be other reasons to regulate online currencies that apply to both anonymous and account-based currencies. The European Central Bank released a report at the end of 2012 analyzing whether virtual currency schemes can affect price stability, financial stability, or payment stability.[19] The report distinguishes between closed virtual currency schemes (i.e., used only within games or apps, akin to virtual Monopoly money) and virtual currency schemes that interact with state currencies (i.e., can be used to purchase real goods and services, or even directly converted to state curren-

---

17. http://finance.fortune.cnn.com/tag/facebook-credits/.
18. http://www.newscientist.com/article/mg21729103.300-us-to-regulate-bitcoin-currency-at-its-alltime-high.html.
19. http://www.ecb.europa.eu/pub/pdf/other/virtualcurrencyschemes201210en.pdf. The report focused specifically on case studies of Bitcoin and Linden dollars, but the conclusions were more general.

cies).[20] Closed virtual currency schemes are not a concern in the view of the report, since only virtual currency that interacts with the real economy can affect price stability, financial stability, and payment stability. However, the report also concluded that, currently, virtual currency that interacts with state currencies poses no risks, since such money creation is at a low level. Moreover, the interaction of Linden dollars, Bitcoin, and similar schemes with the real economy is low because those currencies are used infrequently, by a small group of users, and—most importantly—their use is dispersed geographically, across many state currencies, hence the impact on any one state currency is negligible.

In the case of Q-coin, used only in China, the impact could be significant enough for the central bank to step in and regulate the use of virtual currencies. A social networking site, Tencent QQ, introduced Q-coin to allow for virtual payments. This was not a platform-sponsored currency as we have modeled above, but instead a substitute for state-sponsored currency. Indeed, Q-coins are purchased with Chinese state currency. Thus, while Q-coin was intended for the purchase of virtual goods and services provided by Tencent, users quickly started transferring Q-coin as peer-to-peer payments, and merchants started accepting Q-coin as well.[21] As the amount of Q-coins traded in one year reached several billion yuan, the Chinese authorities stepped in with regulation. In June 2009, the Chinese government banned exchanging virtual currencies for real goods and services, in order to "limit the possible impact on the real financial system."[22]

9.5 Future Directions

This chapter has considered the economics of pure digital currencies and demonstrated that, in most cases, private currencies issued in support of a platform are unlikely to have implications that extend beyond the platform. Of course, our approach has been theoretical, but it does provide a framework to examine digital currencies as a lens for understanding platform strategy.

What is of broader future concern is the emergence of digital currencies that compete with state-issued currency. For this, the gap in economic knowledge arises from an imperfect set of frameworks for analyzing money and its uses per se, let alone whether they are real or virtual. That said, considering our exploration of these issues, we speculate here that platform

---

20. The European Central Bank report also acknowledges that virtual currency schemes "can have positive aspects in terms of financial innovation and the provision of additional payment alternatives for consumers" (47). However, the position of a central bank is to protect state currencies from the risks the virtual currencies may pose.
21. http://voices.yahoo.com/a-virtual-currency-qq-coin-has-taken-real-value-278944.html.
22. http://english.mofcom.gov.cn/aarticle/newsrelease/commonnews/200906/20090606364208.html.

economics may actually have a role in assisting a broader understanding of monetary economics.

Any currency can be viewed as a platform, where people need to "join" by believing in its value, that is, they join by accepting it. Transactions occur only between people who accept the currency and have joined the platform. Currencies also exhibit network effects: the more people accept it, the more value there is to accepting it.

If we were to consider any other technology platform instead of currency, the concerns expressed by regulators (e.g., in the European Central Bank report) would be akin to protecting the market power of an incumbent against innovative entrants. We know from the technology literature that such protection usually leads to loss of efficiency because new entrants can come up with ways to better and more cheaply serve the market, and perhaps also to expand the market.

Is there a good reason for such protection? The nineteenth and early twentieth century in North America saw a period of so-called "free banking," where private banks were allowed, under some initial conditions, to issue their own currency. That is, the state did not have a monopoly on issuing currency. However, throughout this period, regulatory interventions increased, and in the early twentieth century it became common practice to delegalize issuing currency by anyone except the state (Frankel 1998).

Issuing currency is profitable, since the issuer gains seigniorage. Thus, one reason for the state to institute a monopoly would be the incentive to capture the whole seigniorage profit—to the detriment of innovation. However, economic historians[23] point to other factors leading to the increasingly stricter regulation and eventual monopolization of currency. One such factor is frequent bank failures. In a competitive environment, firms often fail and new ones enter. Prior to the early twentieth century in North America, however, bank failures left customers with bank notes redeemable for only a fraction of their nominal value, and sometimes not redeemable at all (i.e., worthless).

This undermined financial stability and the public's trust in paper currency overall. Lack of trust sometimes resulted in bank runs, which led to more bank failures. The trust issues were also reflected in exchange rates between currencies from different issuers. Some private bank notes circulated at a discount (i.e., a $1 bank note was considered worth less than the nominal $1) when there were doubts about the bank's solvency. Another reason for lower trust was counterfeiting, which is, of course, also a concern with state-issued currency. But with multiple issuers the number and variety of notes in circulation is larger, and it is harder for the public to keep track of genuine features.

Since the notes were only redeemable at the issuing bank and banks were typically local, the acceptance of some notes would be geographically

---

23. See, for example, Rockoff (1974) or Smith (1990).

restricted. Farther away from the issuing bank's location, the notes would be accepted at a discount, if they were accepted at all. Both of these factors—lack of trust and varying exchange rates—created difficulties for trade. At times, it even created worries that the trade could collapse altogether.

But how do those well-known factors compare to the analyses in the technology literature? We know that the presence of network effects often creates multiple equilibria—either lots of people join the platform because they expect lots of other people to join, or no one joins because they do not expect others to join. Similar equilibria can be seen in currency usage. Trust in the currency helps to coordinate better equilibrium where people generally adopt paper currency. Another parallel in the technology literature is compatibility. Having multiple networks with limited or no compatibility lowers efficiency as compared to one single network, since under limited compatibility the network effects cannot be realized to their full value.

This brings out a well-known tension: On the one hand, the presence of multiple competing platforms creates inefficiency by limiting the extent of network effects (when compatibility is limited), and presents the risk of coordination failure when users will not join at all. On the other hand, a single, well-established dominant platform overcomes the issue of coordination and renders compatibility irrelevant while stifling innovation and possibly extracting monopoly profit from the users. In issuing currency, since the twentieth century states have traditionally considered one single network as the better side of this trade-off. Whether it is still a valid conclusion with respect to online currencies is a question for future research.

References

Armstrong, M. 2006. "Competition in Two-Sided Markets." *RAND Journal of Economics* 37 (3): 668–91.
Evans, D. S. 2012. "Facebook Credits: Do Payments Firms Need to Worry?" PYMNTS.com, February 28. http://www.pymnts.com/briefing-room/commerce-3-0/facebook-commerce-2/Facebook-Credits-Do-Payments-Firms-Need-to-Worry-2/.
Frankel, A. S. 1998. "Monopoly and Competition in the Supply and Exchange of Money." *Antitrust Law Journal* 66 (2): 313–61.
Gans, J. S., and S. P. King. 2003. "The Neutrality of Interchange Fees in Payments Systems." *B.E. Journal of Economic Analysis and Policy* 3 (1). doi:10.2202/1538-0653.1069.
Rochet, J-C., and J. Tirole. 2002. "Cooperation among Competitors: Some Economics of Payment Card Associations." *RAND Journal of Economics* 33 (4): 549–70.
———. 2003. "Platform Competition in Two-Sided Markets." *Journal of the European Economic Association* 1 (4): 990–1029.
Rockoff, H. 1974. "The Free Banking Era: A Reexamination." *Journal of Money, Credit and Banking* 6 (2): 141–67.

Smith, V. C. 1990. *The Rationale of Central Banking and the Free Banking Alternative*. Indianapolis: Liberty Fund.
Weyl, E. G. 2010. "A Price Theory of Multi-Sided Platforms." *American Economic Review* 100 (4): 1642–72.
Yglesias, M. 2012. "Social Cash: Could Facebook Credits Ever Compete with Dollars and Euros?" *Slate*, February 29. http://www.slate.com/articles/business/cashless_society/2012/02/facebook_credits_how_the_social_network_s_currency_could_compete_with_dollars_and_euros_.html.

Government Policy and Digitization

10
Estimation of Treatment Effects from Combined Data
Identification versus Data Security

Tatiana Komarova, Denis Nekipelov, and Evgeny Yakovlev

10.1 Introduction

In policy analysis and decision making, it is instrumental in many areas to have access to individual data that may be considered sensitive or damaging when released publicly. For instance, a statistical analysis of the data from clinical studies that can include the information on the health status of their participants is crucial to study the effectiveness of medical procedures and treatments. In the financial industry, a statistical analysis of individual decisions combined with financial information, credit scores, and demographic data allows banks to evaluate risks associated with loans and mortgages. The resulting estimated statistical model will reflect the characteristics of individuals whose information was used in estimation. The policies based on this statistical model will also reflect the underlying individual data. The reality of the modern world is that the amount of publicly available (or searchable) individual information that comes from search traffic, social networks, and personal online file depositories (such as photo collections) is increasing on a daily basis. Thus, some of the variables in the data sets used

---

Tatiana Komarova is assistant professor of economics at the London School of Economics and Political Science. Denis Nekipelov is assistant professor of economics at the University of California, Berkeley. Evgeny Yakovlev is assistant professor at the New Economic School in Moscow, Russia.

We appreciate helpful comments from Philip Haile, Michael Jansson, Phillip Leslie, Aureo de Paula, Martin Pesendorfer, James Powell, Pasquale Schiraldi, John Sutton, and Elie Tamer. We also thank participants of the 2013 NBER conference "Economics of Digitization: An Agenda" for their feedback. For acknowledgments, sources of research support, and disclosure of the authors' material financial relationships, if any, please see http://www.nber.org/chapters/c12998.ack.

for policy analysis may be publicly observable.[1] Frequently, various bits of information regarding the same individual are contained in several separate data sets. Individual names or labels are most frequently absent from available data (either for the purposes of data anonymization or as an artifact of the data collection methodology). Each individual data set in this case may not pose a direct security threat to individuals. For instance, a collection of online search logs will not reveal any individual information unless one can attach the names of other identifying information to the generic identifiers attached to each unique user. However, if one can combine information from multiple sources, the combined array of data may pose a direct security threat to some or all individuals contained in the data. For instance, one data set may be a registry of HIV patients in which the names and locations of the patients are removed. Another data set may be the address book that contains names and addresses of people in a given area. Both these data sets individually do not disclose any sensitive information regarding concrete individuals. A combined data set will essentially attach names and addresses to the anonymous labels of patients in the registry and, thus, will disclose some sensitive individual information.

The path to digitization in a variety of markets with the simultaneous availability of the data from sources like social networks makes this scenario quite realistic. Clearly, from a policy perspective the prevention of a further increase in the availaility of such multiple sources is unrealistic. As a result, a feasible solution seems to be aimed at assuring some degree of anonymization as a possible security measure. At the same time, inferences and conclusions based on such multiple sources may be vital for making accurate policy decisions. Thus, a key agenda item in the design of methods and techniques for secure data storage and release is in finding a trade-off between keeping the data informative for policy-relevant statistical models and, at the same time, preventing an adversary from the reconstruction of sensitive information in the combined data set.

In this chapter we explore one question in this agenda. Our aim is to learn how one can evaluate the treatment effect when the treatment status of an individual may present sensitive information while the individual demographic characteristics are either publicly observable or may be inferred from some publicly observable characteristics. In such cases we are concerned with the *risk of disclosing sensitive individual information*. The questions that we address are, first, whether the point identification of treatment effects from the combined public and sensitive data is compatible with formal restrictions on the risk of the so-called partial disclosure. Second, we want to investigate how the public release of the estimated statistical model can lead to an increased risk of such a disclosure.

1. Reportedly, many businesses indeed rely on the combined data. See, for example, Wright (2010) and Bradley et al. (2010), among others.

In our empirical application we provide a concrete example of the analysis of treatment effects and propensity scores from two "anonymized" data sets. The data that we use come from the Russian Longitudinal Monitoring Survey (RLMS) that combines several questionnaires collected on a yearly basis. The respondents are surveyed on a variety of topics from employment to health. However, for anonymization purposes any identifying location information is removed from the data making it impossible to verify where exactly each respondent is located.

Due to the vast Soviet heritage, most people in Russia live in large apartment developments that include several blocks of multistory (usually five floors and up) apartment buildings connected together with common infrastructure, shops, schools, and medical facilities. With such a setup in place the life of each family becomes very visible to most of the neighbors. Our specific question of interest is the potential impact of the dominant religious affiliation in the neighborhood on the decision of parents to get their children checked up by a doctor in a given year as well as the decision of the parents to vaccinate their child with the age-prescribed vaccine.

Such an analysis is impossible without neighborhood identifiers. Neighborhood identifiers are made available to selected researchers upon a special agreement with the data curator (University of North Carolina and the Higher School of Economics in Moscow). This allows us to construct the benchmark where the neighborhood identification is known. Then we consider a realistic scenario where such an identification needs to be restored from the data. Using a record linkage technique adopted from the data mining literature, we reconstruct neighborhood affiliation using the individual demographic data. Our data linkage technique relies on observing data entries with infrequent attribute values. Accurate links for these entries may disclose individual location and then lead to the name disclosure based on the combination of the location and demographic data. We note that the goal of our work is not to demonstrate the vulnerability of anonymized personal data but to demonstrate a synthetic situation that reflects the component of the actual data-driven decision making and to show the privacy versus identification trade-off that arises in that situation. Further, we analyze how the estimates of the empirical model will be affected by the constraints on partial disclosure. We find that any such limitation leads to a loss of point identification in the model of interest. In other words, we find that there is a clear-cut trade-off between the restrictions imposed on partial disclosure and the point identification of the model using individual-level data.

Our analysis combines ideas from the data mining literature with those from the literature on statistical disclosure limitations, as well as the literature on model identification with corrupted or contaminated data. We provide a new approach to model identification from combined data sets as a limit in the sequence of statistical experiments.

A situation when the chosen data combination procedure provides a link between at least one data entry in the data set with sensitive information (such as consumer choices, medical treatment, etc.) and auxiliary individual information from another data set with the probability exceeding the selected confidence threshold presents a case of a successful linkage attack and the so-called *individual disclosure*. The optimal structure of such attacks as well as the requirements in relation to the data release have been studied in the computer science literature. The structure of linkage attacks is based on the optimal record linkage results that have long been used in the analysis of databases and data mining. To some extent, these results were used in econometrics for combining data sets as described in Ridder and Moffitt (2007). In record linkage, one provides a (possibly) probabilistic rule that can match the records from one data set with the records from the other data set in an effort to link the data entries corresponding to the same individual. In several striking examples, computer scientists have shown that the simple removal of personal information such as names and Social Security numbers does not protect the data from individual disclosure. Sweeney (2002b) identified the medical records of William Weld, then governor of Massachusetts, by linking voter registration records to "anonymized" Massachusetts Group Insurance Commission (GIC) medical encounter data, which retained the birth date, sex, and zip code of the patient. Recent "depersonalized" data released for the Netflix prize challenge turned out to lead to a substantial privacy breach. As shown in Narayanan and Shmatikov (2008), using auxiliary information one can detect the identities of several Netflix users from the movie selection information and other data stored by Netflix.

Modern medical databases pose even larger threats to individual disclosure. A dramatic example of a large individual-level database is the data from genome-wide association studies (GWAS). The GWAS are devoted to an in-depth analysis of genetic origins of human health conditions and receptiveness to diseases, among other things. A common practice of such studies was to publish the data on the minor allele frequencies. The analysis of such data allows researchers to demonstrate the evidence of a genetic origin of the studied condition. However, there is a publicly available single nucleotide polymorphism (SNP) data set from the HapMap NIH project that consists of SNP data from four populations with about sixty individuals each. Homer et al. (2008) demonstrated that they could infer the presence of an individual with a known genotype in a mix of DNA samples from the reported averages of the minor allele frequencies using the HapMap data. To create the privacy breach, one can take an individual DNA sequence and then compare the nucleotide sequence of this individual with the reported averages of minor allele frequencies in the HapMap population and in the studied subsample. Provided that the entire list of reported allele frequencies can be very long, individual disclosure may occur with an extremely high probability. As a result, if a particular study is devoted to the analysis of a particular health condition or a disease, the discovery that a particular individual belongs to the studied subsample means that this individual has that condition or that disease.

Samarati and Sweeney (1998), Sweeney (2002a, 2002b), LeFevre, DeWitt, and Ramakrishnan (2005), Aggarwal et al. (2005), LeFevre, DeWitt, and Ramakrishnan (2006), and Ciriani et al. (2007) developed and implemented the so-called k-anonymity approach to address the threats of linkage attacks. Intuitively, a database provides k-anonymity, for some number k, if every way of singling an individual out of the database returns records for at least k individuals. In other words, anyone whose information is stored in the database can be "confused" with k others. Several operational prototypes for maintaining k-anonymity have been offered for practical use. The data combination procedure will then respect the required boundary on the individual disclosure (disclosure of identities) risk if it only uses the links with at least k possible matches.

A different solution has been offered in the literature on synthetic data. Duncan and Lambert (1986), Duncan and Mukherjee (1991), Duncan and Pearson (1991), Fienberg (1994, 2001), Duncan et al. (2001), and Abowd and Woodcock (2001) show that synthetic data may be a useful tool in the analysis of particular distributional properties of the data such as tabulations, while guaranteeing a certain value for the measure of the individual disclosure risk (for instance, the probability of "singling out" some proportion of the population from the data). An interesting feature of the synthetic data is that they can be robust against stronger requirements for the risk of disclosure. Dwork and Nissim (2004) and Dwork (2006) introduced the notion of differential privacy that provides a probabilistic disclosure risk guarantee against the privacy breach associated with an arbitrary auxiliary data set. Abowd and Vilhuber (2008) demonstrate a striking result that the release of synthetic data is robust to differential privacy. As a result, one can use the synthetic data to enforce the constraints on the risk of disclosure by replacing the actual consumer data with the synthetic consumer data for a combination with an auxiliary individual data source.

In our chapter we focus on the threat of *partial disclosure*. Partial disclosure occurs if the released information such as statistical estimates obtained from the combined data sample reveals with high enough probability some sensitive characteristics of a group of individuals. We provide a formal definition of partial disclosure and show that generally one can control the risk of this disclosure, so the bounds on the partial disclosure risk are practically enforceable.

Although our identification approach is new, to understand the impact of the bounds on the individual disclosure risk we use ideas from the literature on partial identification of models with contaminated or corrupted data. Manski (2003), Horowitz et al. (2003), Horowitz and Manski (2006), and Magnac and Maurin (2008) have understood that many data modifications such as top-coding suppression of attributes and stratification lead to the loss of point identification of parameters of interest. Consideration of the general setup in Molinari (2008) allows one to assess the impact of some data anonymization as a general misclassification problem. In this chapter we find the approach to the identification of the parameters of interest by constructing sets compatible with the chosen data combination procedure extremely useful. As we show in this chapter, the sizes of such identified sets for the propensity scores and the average treatment effect are directly proportional to the pessimistic measure of the partial disclosure risk. This is a powerful result that essentially states that there is a direct conflict between the informativeness of the data used in the consumer behavioral model and the security of individual data. An increase in the complexity and nonlinearity of the model can further worsen the trade-off.

In the chapter we associate the ability of a third party to recover sensitive information about consumers from the reported statistical estimates based on the combined data with the risk of partial disclosure. We argue that the estimated model *may itself be disclosive*. As a result, if this model is used to make (observable) policy decisions, some confidential information about consumers may become discoverable. Existing real-world examples of linkage attacks on the consumer data using the observable firm policies have been constructed for online advertising. In particular, Korolova (2010) gives examples of privacy breaches through micro ad targeting on Facebook.com. Facebook does not give advertisers direct access to user data. Instead, the advertiser interface allows them to create targeted advertising campaigns with a very granular set of targets. In other words, one can create a set of targets that will isolate a very small group of Facebook users (based on the location, friends, and likes). Korolova shows that certain users may be perfectly isolated from other users with a particularly detailed list of targets. Then, one can recover the "hidden" consumer attributes, such as age or sexual orientation, by constructing differential advertising campaigns such that a different version of the ad will be shown to the user depending on the value of the private attribute. Then the advertiser's tools allow the advertiser to observe which version of the ad was shown to the Facebook user.

When a company "customizes" its policy regarding individual users, for example, when a PPO gives its customers personalized recommendations regarding their daily routines and exercise or hospitals reassign specialty doctors based on the number of patients in need of specific procedures, then the observed policy results may disclose individual information. In other words, the disclosure may occur even when the company had no intention of disclosing customer information.

Security of individual data is not synonymous to privacy, as privacy may have subjective value for consumers (see Acquisti [2004]). Privacy is a complicated concept that frequently cannot be expressed as a formal guarantee against intruders' attacks. Considering personal information as a "good" valued by consumers leads to important insights in the economics of privacy. As seen in Varian (2009), this approach allowed the researchers to analyze the release of private data in the context of the trade-off between the network effects created by the data release and the utility loss associated with this release. The network effect can be associated with the loss of competitive advantage of the owner of personal data, as discussed in Taylor (2004), Acquisti and Varian (2005), and Calzolari and Pavan (2006). Consider the setting where firms obtain a comparative advantage due to the possibility of offering prices that are based on past consumer behavior. Here, the subjective individual perception of privacy is important. This is clearly shown in both the lab experiments in Gross and Acquisti (2005), Acquisti and Grossklags (2008), as well as in the real-world environment in Acquisti, Friedman, and Telang (2006), Miller and Tucker (2009), and Goldfarb and Tucker (2010). Given all these findings, we believe that the disclosure protection plays a central role in the privacy discourse, as privacy protection is impossible without the data protection.

The rest of the chapter is organized as follows. Section 10.2 describes the analyzed treatment effects models, the availability of the data, and gives a description of data combination procedures employed in the chapter. Section 10.3 provides a notion of the identified values compatible with the data combination procedure for the propensity score and the average treatment effect. It looks at the properties of these values as the sizes of available data sets go to infinity. Section 10.4 introduces formal notions of partial disclosure and partial disclosure guarantees. It discusses the trade-off between the point identification of the true model parameters and partial disclosure limitations. Section 10.5 provides an empirical illustration.

10.2 Model Setup

In many practical settings the treatment status of an individual in the analyzed sample is a very sensitive piece of information, much more sensitive than the treatment outcome and/or the individual's demographics. For instance, in the evaluation of the effect of a particular drug, one may be concerned with the interference of this drug with other medications. Many anti-inflammatory medications may interfere with standard HIV treatments. To determine the effect of the interference one would evaluate how the HIV treatment status influences the effect of the studied anti-inflammatory drug. The fact that a particular person participates in the study of the anti-inflammatory drug does not necessarily present a very sensitive piece of information. However, the information that a particular person receives HIV treatment medications may be damaging.

We consider the problem of estimating the propensity score and the average treatment effect in cases when the treatment status is a sensitive (and potentially harmful) piece of information. Suppose that the response of an individual to the treatment is characterized by two potential outcomes $Y_1, Y_0 \in \mathcal{Y} \subset \mathbb{R}$, and the treatment status is characterized by $D \in \{0,1\}$. Outcome Y_1 corresponds to the individuals receiving the treatment and Y_0 corresponds to the nontreated individuals. Each individual is also characterized by the vector of individual-specific covariates $X \in \mathcal{X} \subset \mathbb{R}^p$ such as the demographic characteristics, income, and location.

Individuals are also described by vectors V and W containing a combination of real-valued and string-valued variables (such as Social Security numbers, names, addresses, etc.) that identify the individual but do not interfere with the treatment outcome. The realizations of V belong to the product space $\mathcal{V} = \mathcal{S}^* \times \mathbb{R}^v$, where $\mathcal{S}^*$ is a finite space of arbitrary (nonnumeric) nature. $\mathcal{S}^*$, for instance, may be the space of combinations of all human names and dates of birth (where we impose some "reasonable" bound on the length of the name, e.g., thirty characters). The string combination {*'John','Smith', '01/01/1990'*} is an example of a point in this space. Each string in this combination can be converted into the digital binary format. Then the countability and finiteness of the space $\mathcal{S}^*$ will follow from the countability of the set of all binary numbers of fixed length. We also assume that the space $\mathcal{V}$ is endowed with the distance. There are numerous examples of definitions of a distance over strings (e.g., see Wilson et al. 2006). We can then define the norm in $\mathcal{S}^*$ as the distance between the given point in $\mathcal{S}$ and a "generic" point corresponding to the most commonly observed set of attributes. We define the norm in $\mathcal{V}$ as the weighted sum of the defined norm in $\mathcal{S}$ and the standard Euclidean norm in $\mathbb{R}^v$ and denote it $\| \|_v$. Similarly, we assume that W takes values in $\mathcal{W} = \mathcal{S}^{**} \times \mathbb{R}^w$, where $\mathcal{S}^{**}$ is also a finite space. The norm in $\mathcal{W}$ is defined as a weighted norm and denoted as $\| \|_w$. Spaces $\mathcal{S}^*$ and $\mathcal{S}^{**}$ may have common subspaces. For instance, they both may contain the first names of individuals. However, we do not require that such common elements indeed exist.

Random variables V and W are then defined by the probability space with a σ-finite probability measure defined on Borel subsets of $\mathcal{V}$ and $\mathcal{W}$.

We assume that the data-generating process creates N_y i.i.d. draws from the joint distribution of the random vector (Y, D, X, V, W). These draws form the (infeasible) "master" sample $\{y_i, d_i, x_i, v_i, w_i\}_{i=1}^{N_y}$. However, because either all the variables in this vector are not collected simultaneously or some of the variables are intentionally deleted, the data on the treatment status (treatment outcome) and individual-specific covariates are not contained in the same sample. One sample, containing N_y observations is the i.i.d. sample $\{x_i, v_i\}_{i=1}^{N_y}$ is in the *public domain*. In other words, individual researchers or research organizations can get access to this data set. The second data set is a subset of $N \leq N_y$ observations from the "master" data set and contains information regarding the treatment-related variables $\{y_j, d_j, w_j\}_{j=1}^{N}$.[2] This

---

2. Our analysis applies to other frameworks of split data sets. For instance, we could consider the case when x and y are contained in the same data subset, while d is observed only in the other data subset. We could also consider cases when some of the variables in x (but not all of them) are observed together with d. This is the situation we deal with in our empirical illustration. The important requirement in our analysis is that some of the relevant variables in x are not observed together with d.

data set is *private* in the sense that it is only available to the data curator (e.g., the hospital network) and cannot be acquired by external researchers or general public. We consider the case when, even for the data curator, there is no direct link between the private and the public data sets. In other words, the variables in v_i and w_j do not provide immediate links between the two data sets. In our example of the HIV treatment status, we could consider cases where the data on the HIV treatment (or testing) are partially or fully anonymized (due to the requests by the patients) and there are only very few data attributes that allow the data curator to link the two data sets.

We impose the following assumptions on the elements of the model:

ASSUMPTION 1.

(a) The treatment outcomes satisfy the conditional unconfoundedness, that is, $(Y_1, Y_0) \perp D | X = x$.

(b) At least one element of X has a continuous distribution with the density strictly positive on its support.

We consider the propensity score $P(x) = E[D|X = x]$ and suppose that for some specified $0 < \delta < 1$ the knowledge that the propensity score exceeds $(1 - \delta)$—that is,

$$P(x) > 1 - \delta,$$

constitutes sensitive information. The next assumption states that there is a part of the population with the propensity score above the sensitivity threshold.

ASSUMPTION 2.

$$Pr(x : P(x) > 1 - \delta) > 0.$$

$\bar{P}$ will denote the average propensity score over the distribution of all individuals:

$$\bar{P} = E[P(x)].$$

We leave distributions of potential outcomes Y_1 and Y_0 conditional on X nonparametric with the observed outcome determined by

$$Y = DY_1 + (1 - D)Y_0.$$

In addition to the propensity score, we are interested in the value of the conditional average treatment effect

$$t_{ATE}(x) = E[Y_1 - Y_0 | X = x],$$

or the average treatment effect conditional on individuals in a group described by some set of covariates $\mathcal{X}_0$:

$$t_{ATE}(\mathcal{X}_0) = E[Y_1 - Y_0 | X \in \mathcal{X}_0],$$

as well as overall average treatment effect (ATE)

$$t_{ATE} = E[Y_1 - Y_0].$$

In this chapter we focus on the propensity score and the overall average treatment effect.

The evaluation of the propensity score and the treatment effects requires us to observe the treatment status and the outcome together with the covariates. A consistent estimator for the average treatment effect t_{ATE} could be constructed then by, first, evaluating the propensity score and then estimating the overall effect via the propensity score weighting:

$$(2.1) \qquad t_{ATE} = E\left[\frac{DY}{P(X)} - \frac{(1-D)Y}{1-P(X)}\right].$$

In our case, however, the treatment and its outcome are not observed together with the covariates. To deal with this challenge, we will use the information contained in the identifying vectors V and W to connect the information from the two split data sets and provide estimates for the propensity score and the ATE.

Provided that the data curator is interested in correctly estimating the treatment effect (to further use the findings to make potentially observable policy decisions, for example, by putting a warning label on the package of the studied drug), we assume that she will construct the linkage procedure that will correctly combine the two data sets with high probability.

We consider a two-step procedure that first uses the similarity of information contained in the identifiers and covariates to provide the links between the two data sets. Then, the effect of interest will be estimated from the reconstructed joint data set. To establish similarity between the two data sets, the researcher constructs vector-valued variables that exploit the numerical and string information contained in the variables. We assume that the researcher constructs variables $Z^d = Z^d(D, Y, W)$ and $Z^x = Z^x(X, V)$ (individual identifiers) that both belong to the space $\mathcal{Z} = \mathcal{S} \times \mathbb{R}^z$. The space $\mathcal{S}$ is a finite set of arbitrary nature such as a set of strings, corresponding to the string information contained in $\mathcal{S}^*$ and $\mathcal{S}^{**}$. We choose a distance in $\mathcal{S}$ constructed using one of commonly used distances defined on the strings $d_S(\cdot, \cdot)$. Then the distance in $\mathcal{Z}$ is defined as a weighted combination of d_S and the standard Euclidean distance $d_z(Z^x, Z^d) = (\omega_s d_S(z_s^x, z_s^d)^2 + \omega_z \|z_z^x - z_z^d\|^2)^{1/2}$, where $Z^x = (z_s^x, z_z^x)$ and $\omega_s, \omega_d > 0$.

Then we define the "null" element in $\mathcal{S}$ as the observed set of attributes that has the most number of components shared with the other observed sets of attributes and denote it 0_S. Then the norm in $\mathcal{Z}$ is defined as the distance from the null element: $\|Z\|_z = (\omega_s d_S(z_s, 0_S)^2 + \omega_s \|z_z\|^2)^{1/2}$.

The construction of the variables Z^d and Z^x may exploit the fact that W and V can contain overlapping components, such as individuals' first names and the dates of birth. Then the corresponding components of the identifiers can be set equal to those characteristics. However, the identifiers may also include a more remote similarity of the individual characteristics. For instance, V may contain the name of an individual and W may contain the race (but not contain the name). Then we can make one component of Z^d to take values from 0 to 4 corresponding to the individual in the private data set either having the race not recorded, or being black, white, Hispanic, or Asian.

Then, using the public data set we can construct a component of Z^x that will correspond to the guess regarding the race of an individual based on his name. This guess can be based on some simple classification rule, for example, whether the individual's name belongs to the list of top 500 Hispanic names in the US Census or if the name belongs to the top 500 names in a country that is dominated by a particular nationality. This classifier, for instance, will classify the name "Vladimir Putin" as the name of a white individual giving Z^x value 2, and it will classify the name "Kim Jong Il" as the name of an Asian individual giving Z^x value 4.

When the set of numeric and string characteristics used for combining two data sets is sufficiently large or it contains some potentially "hard to replicate" information such as the individual's full name, then if such a match occurs it very likely singles out the data of one person. We formalize this idea by expecting that if the identifiers take infrequent values (we model this situation as the case of identifiers having large norms), then the fact that the values of Z^d and Z^x are close implies that with high probability the two corresponding observations belong to the same individual. This probability is higher the more infrequent are the values of Z^d and Z^x. Our maintained assumptions regarding the distributions of constructed identifiers are listed below.

ASSUMPTION 3. We fix some $\bar{\alpha} \in (0,1)$ such that for any $\alpha \in (0,\bar{\alpha})$:
(a) (Proximity of identifiers) $Pr(d_z(Z^x, Z^d) < \alpha | X = x, D = d, Y = y, \|Z^d\|_z > 1/\alpha) \geq 1 - \alpha$.
(b) (Nonzero probability of extreme values)

$$\lim_{\alpha \to 0} Pr\left(\|Z^d\|_z > \frac{1}{\alpha} \bigg| D = d, Y = y\right) / \phi(\alpha) = 1$$

$$\lim_{\alpha \to 0} Pr\left(\|Z^x\|_z > \frac{1}{\alpha} \bigg| X = x\right) / \psi(\alpha) = 1$$

for some nondecreasing and positive functions $\phi(\cdot)$ and $\psi(\cdot)$.
(c) (Redundancy of identifiers in the combined data) There exists a sufficiently large M such that for all $\|Z^d\|_z \geq M$ and all $\|Z^x\|_z \geq M$

$$f(Y | D = d, X = x, Z^d = z^d, Z^x = z^x) = f(Y | D = d, X = x).$$

Assumption 3(a) reflects the idea that more reliable matches are provided by the pairs of identifiers whose values are infrequent. In other words, if, for example, in both public and private data sets collected in Durham, NC, we found observations with an attribute "Denis Nekipelov," we expect them to belong to the same individual with a higher probability than if we found two attribute values "Jane Doe." Thus, the treatment status can be recovered more reliably for more unique individuals. We emphasize that infrequency of a particular identifier does not mean that the corresponding observation is an "outlier." In fact, if both public and private data sets contain very detailed individual information such as a combination of the full name and the address, most attribute values will be unique.

Assumption 3(b) requires that there are a sufficient number of observations with infrequent attribute values. This fact can actually be established empirically in each of the observed subsets and, thus, this assumption is testable.

Assumption 3(c) is the most important one for identification purposes. It implies that even for the extreme values of the identifiers and the observed covariates, the identifiers only served the purpose of data labels as soon as the "master" data set is recovered. There are two distinct arguments that allow us to use this assumption. First, in cases where the identifiers are high dimensional, infrequent attribute combinations do not have to correspond to unusual values of the variables. If both data sets contain, for instance, first and last names along with the dates of birth and the last four digits of the Social Security number of individuals, then a particular combination of all attributes can be can be extremely rare, even for individuals with common names. Second, even if the identifiers can contain model relevant information (e.g., we expect the restaurant choice of an individual labeled as "Vladimir Putin" to be different than the choice of an individual labeled as "Kim Jong Il"), we expect that information to be absorbed in the covariates. In other words, if the gender and the nationality of an individual may be information relevant for the model, than we include that information into the covariates.

We continue our analysis with the discussion of identification of the model from the combined data set.

In the remainder of the chapter we suppose that Assumptions 1–3 hold.

10.3 Identification of the Treatment Effect from the Combined Data

Provided that the variables are not contained in the same data set, the identification of the treatment effect parameter becomes impossible without having some approximation to the distribution of the data in the master sample. A way to link the observations in two data sets is to use the identifiers that we described in the previous section. The identifiers, on the other hand, are individual-level variables. Even though the data-generating process is characterized by the distribution over strings, such as names, we only recover the master data set correctly if we link the data of one concrete "John

Smith" in the two data sets. This means that the data combination is intrinsically a finite sample procedure. We represent the data combination procedure by the deterministic data combination rule $\mathcal{D}^N$ that for each pair of identifiers z_j^d and z_i^x returns a binary outcome

$$M_{ij} = \mathcal{D}^N(z_i^x, z_j^d),$$

which labels two observations as a match ($M_{ij} = 1$) if we think they belong to the same individual, and labels them as a nonmatch ($M_{ij} = 0$) if we think that the observations are unlikely to belong to the same individual or are simply uncertain about this. Although we can potentially consider many nonlinear data combination rules, in this chapter we focus on the set of data combination rules that are generated by our Assumption 3 (a). In particular, for some prespecified $\bar{\alpha} \in (0,1)$ we consider the data combination rule

$$\mathcal{D}^N = 1\{d_z(z_i^x, z_j^d) < \alpha_N, \|z_i^x\| > 1/\alpha_N\},$$

generated by a Cauchy sequence α_N such that $0 < \alpha_N < \bar{\alpha}$ and $\lim_{N\to\infty} \alpha_N = 0$. The goal of this sequence is to construct the set of thresholds that would isolate in the limit all of the infrequent observations. To guarantee that, such a sequence would have to satisfy the following two conditions. For infrequent observations, the probability of the correct match would be approaching one, as the probability of observing two identifiers taking very close values for two different individuals would be very small (proportional to the square of the probability of observing the infrequent attribute values). On the other hand, the conditional probability that the values of identifiers are close for a particular individual with infrequent values of the attributes would be of a larger order of magnitude (proportional to the probability of observing the attribute value). Thus, an appropriately scaled sequence of thresholds would be able to single out correct matches.

Let m_{ij} be the indicator of the event that the observation i from the public data set and the observation j from the private data set belong to the same individual. Given that we can make incorrect matches, M_{ij} is not necessarily equal to m_{ij}. However, we would want these two variables to be highly correlated, meaning that the data combination procedure that we use is good.

With our data combination procedure we will form the reconstructed master data set by taking the pairs of all observations from the public and the private data sets that we indicated as matches ($M_{ij} = 1$) and discard all other observations. We can consider more complicated rules for reconstructing the master sample. In particular, we can create multiple copies of the master sample by varying the threshold α_N and then we combine the information from those samples by downweighting the data sets that were constructed with higher threshold values.

The reconstructed master data set will have a small sample distribution, characterizing the joint distribution of outcomes and the covariates for all observations that are identified as matches by the decision rule $\mathcal{D}^N$. We use $f_{\alpha_N}^N(y_i|d_j, x_i, z_i^x, z_j^d)$ to denote the conditional density of the outcome distribution with the decision rule applied to samples of size N. Provided that the decision rule does not perfectly identify the information from the same individual, density $f_{\alpha_N}^N(\cdot)$ will be a mixture of the "correct" distribution with the distribution of outcomes that were incorrectly identified as matches:

$$f_{\alpha_N}^N(y_j|d_j, x_i, z_i^x) = f_{Y|D,X}(y_j|d_j, x_i)Pr(m_{ij} = 1|\mathcal{D}^N(z_i^x, z_j^d) = 1)$$

$$+ f_{Y|D}(y_j|d_j)Pr(m_{ij} = 0|\mathcal{D}^N(z_i^x, z_j^d) = 1),$$

where we used the fact that identifiers are redundant once a correct match was made, as well as the fact that in the i.i.d. sample the observations have to be independent. Thus, if an incorrect match was made, the outcome should not be correlated with the treatment. By $E_{\alpha_N}^N[\cdot|d_j]$ we denote the conditional expectation with respect to the density product $f_{\alpha_N}^N(\cdot|d_j, x_i, z_i^x)f(x_i, z_i^x)$.

We can also introduce the propensity score implied by the finite sample distribution, which we denote $P_{\alpha_N}^N(\cdot)$. The finite sample propensity score is characterized by the mixture distribution combining the correct propensity score and the average propensity score

$$P_{\alpha_N}^N(x) = P(x)Pr(m_{ij} = 1|x_i = x, \mathcal{D}^N(z_i^x, z_j^d) = 1)$$

$$+ \bar{P}Pr(m_{ij} = 0|x_i = x, \mathcal{D}^N(z_i^x, z_j^d) = 1).$$

We can extend our data combination method by choosing sequences α_N depending on the value of x. Then the value of $Pr(m_{ij} = 0|x_i = x, \mathcal{D}^N(z_i^x, z_j^d) = 1)$ even in the limit will depend on x. We allow for such situations. In fact, later in the chapter we make use of this opportunity to choose differences threshold sequences for different values of x. To stress that we permit the threshold sequences to depend on x we denote a sequence of thresholds chosen for x as $\alpha_{N,x}$ (instead of α_N).

In the beginning of this section, we indicated that the estimation that requires combining the data based on the string-valued identifiers is an intrinsically finite sample procedure. As a result, we suggest the analysis of identification of this model as the limit of a sequence of data combination procedures. We allow for situations when the data curator could want to use several sequences $\alpha_{N,x}$ for some x and denote the collection of such sequences as $C_{0,x}$.

DEFINITION 1. *By $\mathcal{P}^N$ we denote the set of all functions $p : \mathcal{X} \mapsto [0,1]$ that correspond to the set of finite sample propensity scores for all sequences $\alpha_{N,x}$ in $C_{0,x}$:*

$$\mathcal{P}^N = \bigcup_{\{\alpha_{N,x}\} \in C_{0,x}} \{P_{\alpha_{N,x}}^N(\cdot)\}.$$

We call $\mathcal{P}^N$ **the N-identified set for the propensity score compatible with the data combination procedure with a threshold decision rule**.

By $\mathcal{T}^N$ we denote the subset of $\mathbb{R}$ that corresponds to the set of treatment effects calculated as equation (2.1) for all sequences $\alpha_{N,x}$ in $C_{0,x}$ using the corresponding to $\alpha_{N,x}$ propensity score $P_{\alpha_{N,x}}^N(\cdot)$:

$$\mathcal{T}^N = \bigcup_{\{\alpha_{N,x}\} \in C_{0,x}} E_{\alpha_{N,x}}^N \left[\frac{D_j Y_j}{P_{\alpha_{N,x}}^N(X_i)} - \frac{(1-D_j)Y_j}{1 - P_{\alpha_{N,x}}^N(X_i)} \right].$$

We call $\mathcal{T}^N$ the **N-identified set for the average treatment effect compatible with the data combination procedure with a threshold decision rule**.

Definition 2 below characterizes the identified set compatible with the data combination procedure as the set of all limits of the estimated treatment effects and the propensity scores under all possible threshold sequences that are bounded and converge to zero. Provided that the reconstructed master sample depends on the sample size, the set of treatment effect parameters that are compatible with the data combination procedure applied to random split samples of size N will depend on N. Provided that the small sample distribution in the sample of size N will always be a mixture of the correct joint distribution and the marginal outcome distribution for the outcomes that are misidentified as matches, the only way to attain the point identification is in the limit. Thus, we consider the concept of parameter identification in terms of the limiting behavior of the identified sets compatible with the data combination procedure constructed from the finite sample distributions as the sample size N approaches infinity.

DEFINITION 2.

*(a) We call $\mathcal{P}^\infty$ the **identified set for the propensity score under the threshold decision rules** if $\mathcal{P}^\infty$ is the set of all partial pointwise limits of sequences of propensities score functions from the N-identified sets $\mathcal{P}^N$. That is, function $f(\cdot) \in \mathcal{P}^\infty$ if and only if for any x in the support of X,*

$$f(x) = \lim_{N_k \to \infty} f_{N_k}(x),$$

for some $f_{N_k}(\cdot) \in \mathcal{P}^{N_k}$.

*(b) Similarly, we call $\mathcal{T}^\infty$ the **identified set for the average treatment effect under the decision threshold rules** if $\mathcal{T}^\infty$ is the set of all partial limits of sequences of ATEs from the N-identified sets $\mathcal{T}^N$. That is, $t \in \mathcal{T}^\infty$ if*

$$t = \lim_{N_k \to \infty} t_{N_k},$$

for some $t_{N_k} \in \mathcal{T}^{N_k}$.

(c) The propensity score is point identified from the combined data if $\mathcal{P}^\infty = \{P(\cdot)\}$. Otherwise, it is identified only up to a set compatible with the decision threshold rules.

(d) The average treatment effect parameter is point identified from the combined data if the identified set is a singleton $\mathcal{T}^\infty = \{t_{ATE}\}$. Otherwise, it is identified only up to a set compatible with the decision threshold rules.

Our next idea will be based on the characterization of the sets for the average treatment effect parameter and the propensity score identified under the given threshold decision rule under Assumption 3. We start our analysis with the following lemma, that follows directly from the combination of Assumptions 3(b) and (c).

LEMMA 1. *Under Assumption 3 the propensity score can be point identified from the observations with infrequent attribute values as follows:*

$$P(x) = E\left[D \mid X = x, d_z(Z^x, Z^d) < \alpha_{N,x}, \|Z^x\|_z > \frac{1}{\alpha_{N,x}}\right].$$

Also, the average treatment effect can be point identified from the observations with infrequent attribute values as follows:

$$t_{ATE} = E\left[\frac{DY}{P(X)} - \frac{(1-D)Y}{1-P(X)} \,\Big|\, d_z(Z^x, Z^d) < \alpha_{N,x}, \|Z^x\|_z > \frac{1}{\alpha_{N,x}}\right].$$

This lemma states that if we are able to correctly reconstruct the master data set only for the observations with infrequent values of the attributes, those observations are sufficient for correct identification of the components of interest. Two elements are crucial for these results. First, we need Assumption 3(c) to establish redundancy of identifiers for matches constructed for observations with infrequent values of those identifiers. Second, we need Assumption 3(b) to guarantee that there is a nonzero probability of observing individuals with those infrequent values of identifiers.

The biggest challenge in our analysis is to determine which Cauchy sequences have appropriate behavior to isolate the infrequent attribute values as $N \to \infty$ and guarantee that the probability of a mismatch, conditional on the observation being in the reconstructed master sample, approaches zero. We do so by an appropriate inversion of the probability of misidentifying a pair of observations as a match. We can provide the general result that delivers a fixed probability of a mismatch in the limiting reconstructed master sample.

PROPOSITION 1. *Suppose that for $x \in \mathcal{X}$ the chosen sequence $\{\alpha_{N,x}\} \in C_{0,x}$ satisfies*

$$Pr(m_{ij} = 0 \mid x_i = x, \mathcal{D}^N(Z_i^y, Z_j^d) = 1) \to \gamma(x)$$

for some $\gamma(x) \in [0,1]$ as $N \to \infty$. Then

(3.2) $P_{\alpha_{N,x}}^N(x) = E_{\alpha_{N,x}}^N[D_j \mid X_i = x] \to (1-\gamma(x))P(x) + \gamma(x)\bar{P},$

and

$$T_{\alpha_{N,x}}^N = E_{\alpha_{N,x}}^N \left[\frac{D_j Y_j}{P_{\alpha_{N,x}}^N(X_i)} - \frac{(1-D_j)Y_j}{1-P_{\alpha_{N,x}}^N(X_i)} \right] \to t_{ATE}$$

(3.3)
$$+ E\left[(E[Y_1] - E[Y|X, D=1]\bar{P}) \frac{\gamma(X)}{(1-\gamma(X))P(X) + \gamma(X)\bar{P}} \right]$$

$$- E\left[(E[Y_0] - E[Y|X, D=0])(1-\bar{P}) \frac{\gamma(X)}{1-(1-\gamma(X))P(X) - \gamma(X)\bar{P}} \right].$$

Proposition 1 states that if one controls the mismatch probability in the combined data set, then the propensity score recovered through such a procedure is a convex combination of the true propensity score and the expected fraction $\bar{P}$ of treated individuals. Thus, the propensity score recovered through the data combination procedure will be biased toward the expected fraction of treated individuals. Also, the resulting identified average treatment effect will be a sum of the true ATE and a nontrivial term. In other words, the presence of mismatched observations in the "limiting" reconstructed master data set biases the estimated ATE toward zero.

The formulated theorem is based on the premise that a sequence in $C_{0,x}$ that leads to the limiting probability of an incorrect match equal to $\gamma(x)$ exists. The proof of existence of fundamental sequences satisfying this property is given in Komarova, Nekipelov, and Yakovlev (2011). These sequences are determined from the behavior of functions $\phi(\cdot)$ and $\psi(\cdot)$. The result in that paper demonstrates that for each $\gamma(x) \in [0,1]$ we can find a Cauchy sequence that leads to the limiting mismatch probability equal to $\gamma(x)$.

Our next goal is to use one particular sequence that will make the mismatch probability approach zero in the limit.

THEOREM 1. *(Point identification of the propensity score and the ATE).* Suppose that for each $x \in \mathcal{X}$ the chosen sequence $\{\alpha_{N,x}\} \in C_{0,x}$ satisfies

$$\lim_{N \to \infty} Pr(m_{ij} = 0 | x_i = x, \mathcal{D}^N(Z_i^y, Z_j^d) = 1) = 0.$$

Then

$$P_{\alpha_{N,x}}^N(\cdot) \to P(\cdot)$$

pointwise everywhere on $\mathcal{X}$ and

$$T_{\alpha_{N,x}}^N \to t_{ATE}$$

as $N \to \infty$.

In other words, the propensity score and the treatment effect are point identified.

10.4 Inference of the Propensity Score and the Average Treatment Effect with Limited Partial Disclosure

The calculations of the propensity score and the treatment effect require the data curator to have a technique that would combine the two data sets with the available observation-identifying information. Our approach to data combination described above is based on constructing the threshold decision rule that identifies the observations as "a match" corresponding to the data on a single individual if the observed individual attributes are close in terms of the chosen distance. With this approach we can construct the sequences of thresholds that would lead to very high probabilities of correct matches for a part of the population that allows us to point identify the propensity score and the treatment-effect parameter.

If we provide a high-quality match, then we have a reliable link between the public information regarding the individual and this individual's treatment status. The release of the reconstructed master data set would then constitute an evident threat to the individual's privacy. However, even if the reconstructed master data set is not public, the release of the estimated propensity score and/or the value of the treatment effect itself *may pose a direct threat to the security of individual data*. To measure the risk of such a disclosure in the possible linkage attacks, we use a measure based on the notion of disclosure in Lambert (1993). We provide a formal definition for this measure.

Partial disclosure can occur if the released information that was obtained from the data may potentially reveal some sensitive characteristics of individual. In our case, the information we are concerned with are the propensity score and the treatment effect. In particular, in our case the sensitive characteristic of an individual is her treatment status, or how an individual with given characteristics is likely to receive a treatment.

Below we provide a formal definition of the risk of partial disclosure for the propensity score. The definition takes as given the following two parameters. One parameter is $1 - \delta$ and it characterizes the sensitivity level of the information about the propensity score. Namely, the information that the propensity score of an individual is above $1 - \delta$ is considered to be damaging. The other parameter is denoted as $\underline{v}$ and represents a tolerance level—specifically, $\underline{v}$ is the upper bound on the proportion of individuals for whom the damaging information that $P(x) > 1 - \delta$ may be revealed.

Another important component of our definition of partial disclosure is how much information about the data combination procedure is revealed to the public by the data curator. We denote this information as $\mathcal{I}$. For instance, if the data curator reveals that $Pr(m_{ij} = 0 | x_i = x, \mathcal{D}^N(Z_i^y, Z_j^d) = 1) \to \gamma(x)$ for some $\gamma(x)$, then the public can determine that in the limit the released propensity score for an individual with characteristics x has the form $(1 - \gamma(x))P(x) + \gamma(x)\bar{P}$. If, in addition, the data curator releases the value of

$Pr(m_{ij} = 0 | x_i = x, \mathcal{D}^N(Z_i^y, Z_j^d) = 1)$ or the value of $\gamma(x)$, then the public can pin down the true propensity score $P(x)^3$ and, thus, obtain potentially damaging information if this propensity score is above $1 - \delta$.

DEFINITION 3. *Let $\mathcal{I}$ be the information about the data combination procedure released to the public by the data curator. Let $\delta \in (0,1)$ and $\underline{v} \in [0,1]$. Given $\mathcal{I}$, we say that a $(1 - \delta, \underline{v})$ bound guarantee is given for the risk of partial disclosure, if the proportion of individuals in the private data set for whom the public can determine with certainty that $P(x) > 1 - \delta$ does not exceed $\underline{v}$. The value of $\underline{v}$ is called the bound on the risk of partial disclosure.*

Setting $\underline{v}$ at $\underline{v} = 0$ means that we want to protect *all* the individuals in the private data set.

The idea behind our definition of partial disclosure is that one can use the released values of $P_{\alpha_{N,x}}^N$ (or $\lim_{N \to \infty} P_{\alpha_{N,x}}^N$) from the model to determine whether the probability of the positive treatment status exceeds the given threshold. If this is possible to determine with a high confidence level for some individuals, then this individual is identified as the one with "the high risk" of the positive treatment status. Such information can be extremely damaging.

In the following theorem we demonstrate that the release of the true propensity score is not compatible with a low disclosure risk.

THEOREM 2. *Suppose that*

(4.4) $\quad \lim_{N \to \infty} Pr(m_{ij} = 0 | x_i = x, \mathcal{D}^N(Z_i^x, Z_j^d) = 1) = 0$ for $x \in \mathcal{X}$.

If the data curator releases information (4.4), then for sufficiently large N the release of the propensity score $P_{\alpha_{N,x}}^N$ (or its limit) is not compatible with the bound on the risk of partial disclosure $\underline{v}$ for sufficiently small $\underline{v}$.

The formal result of Theorem 2 relies on Assumption 2, and Theorem 1 and is based on two elements. First, using the threshold decision rule we were able to construct the sequence of combined data sets where the finite-sample distribution of covariates approaches the true distribution. Second, from the estimated distribution we could improve our knowledge of the treatment status of individuals in the data. For some individuals the probability of the positive treatment status may be very high.

This result forces us to think about ways to avoid the situations where potentially very sensitive information may be learned about some individuals. The bound guarantee on the risk of partial disclosure essentially requires the data curator to keep a given proportion of incorrect matches in the data sets of any size. As discussed in Proposition 1, a fixed proportion of the incorrect matches leads to the calculated propensity score to be biased toward the proportion of treated individuals in the population, and also causes bias in the average treatment effect.

---

3. Note that the value $\bar{P}$ is known from the public data set.

THEOREM 3. *Suppose the value of $\bar{P}$ is publicly available, and $\bar{P} < 1 - \delta$. A $(1 - \delta, 0)$ bound guarantee for the risk of partial disclosure can be achieved if the data curator chooses $\alpha_N(x)$ in such a way that*

$$\gamma(x) = \lim_{N \to \infty} Pr(m_{ij} = 0 | x_i = x, \mathcal{D}^N(Z_i^x, Z_j^d) = 1) > 0 \text{ for all } x \in \mathcal{X}$$

and for individuals with $P(x) > 1 - \delta$ the value of $\gamma(x)$ is chosen large enough to guarantee that

$$\lim_{N \to \infty} P_{\alpha_N, x}^N = (1 - \gamma(x))P(x) + \gamma(x)\bar{P} < 1 - \delta.$$

We assume that the data curator provides information that the data were matched with an error and the matching error does not approach 0 as $N \to \infty$ but does not provide the values of $Pr(m_{ij} = 0 | x_i = x, \mathcal{D}^N(Z_i^x, Z_j^d) = 1)$ or $\gamma(x)$. In this case, the behavior of the released propensity score and the treatment effect is as described in equations (3.2) and (3.3), and thus, the true propensity score and the true treatment effect are not identified.

Note that in the framework of Theorem 3 for individuals with small $P(x)$ the data curator may want to choose a very small $\gamma(x) > 0$ whereas for individuals with large $P(x)$ the bias toward $\bar{P}$ has to be large enough.

REMARK 1. Continue to assume that $\bar{P} < 1 - \delta$. Note that if the released propensity score for an individual with x is strictly less than $\bar{P}$, then the public will be able to conclude that the true propensity score for this individual is strictly less than $\bar{P}$. If the released propensity score for an individual with x is strictly greater than $\bar{P}$, then the public will be able to conclude that the true propensity score for this individual is strictly greater than $\bar{P}$ but, under conditions of Theorem 3, will not know whether $P(x) > 1 - \delta$. If the released propensity score for an individual with x is equal to $\bar{P}$, then the public is unable to make any nontrivial conclusions about $P(x)$—that is, $P(x)$ can be any value from $[0, 1]$.

We can consider other approaches the data curator may exploit regarding the release of the propensity score values and the information provided with this release. For instance, for some individuals with $P(x) < 1 - \delta$ she may choose $\gamma(x) = 0$ and provide information that *for some individuals* the data were matched without an error in the limit, but for the other individuals the matching error is strictly positive and does not approach 0 as $N \to \infty$ (given that she does not specify the values of $Pr(m_{ij} = 0 | x_i = x, \mathcal{D}^N(Z_i^x, Z_j^d) = 1)$ or $\gamma(x)$). In this case, the result of Theorem 3 continues to hold.

The next theorem gives a result on privacy protection when the data curator releases more information.

THEOREM 4. *Suppose the value of $\bar{P}$ is publicly available, and $\bar{P} < 1 - \delta$. A $(1 - \delta, 0)$ bound guarantee for the risk of partial disclosure can be achieved if the data curator chooses $\alpha_N(x)$ in such a way that*

$$Pr(m_{ij} = 0 | x_i = x, \mathcal{D}^N(Z_i^x, Z_j^d) = 1) \geq \bar{\gamma} \text{ for all } x \in \mathcal{X}$$

for all N, and for individuals with $P(x) > 1 - \delta$ the value of $Pr(m_{ij} = 0 | x_i = x, \mathcal{D}^N(Z_i^x, Z_j^d) = 1)$ is chosen large enough to guarantee that

$$P_{\alpha_{N,x}}^N = (1 - Pr(m_{ij} = 0 | x_i = x, \mathcal{D}^N(Z_i^x, Z_j^d) = 1))P(x)$$
$$+ Pr(m_{ij} = 0 | x_i = x, \mathcal{D}^N(Z_i^x, Z_j^d) = 1)\bar{P} < 1 - \delta$$

for all N. We assume that the data curator provides information that the data were matched with an error and the matching error is greater or equal than the known $\bar{\gamma}$ but does not provide the values of $Pr(m_{ij} = 0 | x_i = x, \mathcal{D}^N(Z_i^x, Z_j^d) = 1)$ or $\gamma(x)$. In this case, the behavior of the released propensity score and the treatment effect is as described in equations (3.2) and (3.3), and thus, the true propensity score and the true treatment effect are not identified.

To summarize, the fact that we want to impose a bound on the risk of disclosure leads us to the loss of the point identification of the true propensity score and the true average treatment effect. This means that the point identification of the econometric model from the combined data set is incompatible with the security of individual information. If the publicly observed policy is based on the combination of the nonpublic treatment status and the public information regarding the individual, then the treatment status of any individual cannot be learned from this policy only if it is based on a biased estimate for the propensity score and a biased treatment effect.

The next theorem considers the case when $\bar{P} > 1 - \delta$. It shows that in this case *any* release of point estimates of the propensity score from the treatment effect evaluation is not compatible with a low disclosure risk.

THEOREM 5. *Suppose the value of $\bar{P}$ is publicly available, and $\bar{P} > 1 - \delta$. Then the released propensity score will reveal all the individuals with $P(x) > 1 - \delta$ even if the data are combined with a positive (even very large) error. Let*

$$p^* = Pr(x : P(x) > 1 - \delta),$$

that is, p^* is the proportion of individuals with the damaging information about the propensity score. Then a $(1 - \delta, \underline{v})$ bound guarantee cannot be attained for the risk of partial disclosure if $\underline{v} \leq p^*$.

In the framework of Theorem 5 the release (or publicly observable use) of the propensity score is blatantly nonsecure. In other words, there will exist a sufficient number of individuals for whom we can learn their high propensity scores. To protect their privacy, *no* propensity scores should be released.

10.5 Does a Religious Affiliation Affect a Parent's Decision on Childhood Vaccination and Medical Checkups?

To illustrate our theoretical analysis, we want to bring our results to the real data.

Even though in the main body of this chapter we do not develop a formal theory of the statistical estimation of $P^N_{\alpha_{N,x}}(\cdot)$ or the true propensity score $P(\cdot)$ in a finite sample, in this section we want to illustrate an empirical procedure one could implement in practice.

The data come from the Russian Longitudinal Monitoring survey (RLMS).[4] The RLMS is a nationally representative annual survey that covers more than 4,000 households (the number of children varies between 1,900 and 3,682), from 1992 until 2011. The survey gathers information on a very broad set of questions, including demographic and household characteristics, health, religion, and so on. The survey covers 33 Russian regions—31 oblasts (krays, republics), and also Moscow and St. Petersburg. Islam is the dominant religion in two regions, and Orthodox Christianity is the dominant religion in the rest.

We combine our data from two parts of the RLMS—the survey for adults and the survey for children. The question that we want to answer can be informally stated as follows: Does the religion of family members affect the probability of a child getting regular medical checkups or to be vaccinated against tuberculosis? More specifically, we analyze whether (1) religious (Muslim or Orthodox Christian) families have their children seen by doctors or have their children vaccinated against tuberculosis with lower probability; and (2) families from neighborhoods with high percentages of religious people have their children seen by doctors with lower probability.

From the data set for children we extract the following individual characteristics for a child: the indicator for whether the child had a medical checkup in the last twelve (or three) months, the indicator for whether the child was vaccinated against tuberculosis, the indicator for whether the child lives in a city, and the child's age. We also have the following information on the child's family: the share of Orthodox Christian family members, the share of Muslim family members,[5] and the share of family members with a college degree. From other publicly available data sets we obtain the following information for the child's region: the share of Muslims and the gross regional product per capita. The summary statistics of all these variables are presented in table 10.1.

Our analysis focuses on the propensity scores that represent the probabil-

---

4. This survey is conducted by the Carolina Population Center at the University of Carolina at Chapel Hill, and by the Higher School of Economics in Moscow. Official Source name: "Russia Longitudinal Monitoring Survey, RLMS-HSE," conducted by Higher School of Economics and ZAO "Demoscope" together with Carolina Population Center, University of North Carolina at Chapel Hill and the Institute of Sociology RAS. (RLMS-HSE websites: http://www.cpc.unc.edu/projects/rlms-hse, http://www.hse.ru/org/hse/rlms).

5. Variables for the shares of Muslims and Orthodox Christians in a family are constructed based on the following definition of a Muslim (Orthodox Christian). We say that a person is a Muslim (Orthodox Christian) if the person (a) says that she believes in God, and (b) says that she is a Muslim (Orthodox Christian). There are people in the survey who said, for example, that they are Muslims, but at the same time said that they are not believers. We consider such people nonbelievers.

Table 10.1 Summary statistics of various variables for a child

Variable	Obs.	Mean	Std. Dev.	Min.	Max.
Child: Medical checkup in last 12 months?	33,924	0.69	0.46	0	1
Child: Medical checkup in last 3 months?	62,316	0.45	0.50	0	1
Child: Vaccinated (tuberculosis)?	49,464	0.96	0.19	0	1
Child: I (lives in a city)	73,100	0.38	0.49	0	1
Child: Age	73,100	7.19	4.09	0	18
Family: Share of Orthodox Christians	59,142	0.22	0.35	0	1
Family: Share of Muslims	59,142	0.06	0.23	0	1
Family: Share of those with college degree	66,314	0.26	0.37	0	1
Region: Share of Muslims	73,100	0.09	0.17	0	0.71
Region: Log group per capita	71,466	10.96	1.38	7.04	13.50

ity of the child getting regular checkups (being vaccinated against tuberculosis). In our model, the following information is considered to be sensitive: propensity scores are below a given threshold; the variable of the share of Orthodox Christian (or Muslim) family members has a negative marginal effect on the propensity score; the variable of the share of Orthodox Christians (or Muslims) in the child's neighborhood has a negative marginal effect on the propensity score.

The RLMS data set has a clustered structure as people are surveyed within small neighborhoods with a population of around 300 people (so-called census district; see Yakovlev [2012]). Thus, it is possible to construct characteristics of neighborhoods—in particular, on the shares of Orthodox Christians (or Muslims) in neighborhoods—by using the religion variable from the RLMS data set for adults[6] if one has information on neighborhood labels. Due to a vast Soviet heritage, the majority of people in Russia live in large communal developments that combine several multistory apartment buildings. These developments have common infrastructure, shops, and schools. High concentration in a relatively small area makes the life of each family very visible to all the neighbors. The neighborhoods are defined precisely by such developments. Neighborhood labels were publicly available till 2009 but then were deleted by the RLMS staff due to the privacy concerns.[7] In our study, we exploit the RLMS survey data from 1994 until 2009 because the neighborhood identifiers were publicly available in those years and, thus, one was able to consider the child's neighborhood and then use the religious affiliation variable from the adult data set to construct the data for religion in that particular neighborhood, and use the income variable from the adult data set to calculate the average logarithm of income

---

6. Thus, the variable for the shares of Muslims and Orthodox Christians in a neighborhood is constructed using the same principle as in the case of families.

7. Fortunately, we happened to have the data on neighborhood identifiers.

Table 10.2   Summary statistics of neighborhood characteristics

Variable	Obs.	Mean	Std. Dev.	Min.	Max.
Neighborhood: Share of Muslims	53,800	0.06	0.20	0	1
Neighborhood: Share of Orthodox	53,800	0.23	0.18	0	1
Neighborhood: Log(income)	58,578	6.25	1.86	0	10.9

in that particular neighborhood. The summary statistics of neighborhood characteristics are presented in table 10.2.

In order to answer the posed questions, we estimate the following probit regression

$Pr(D_{it} = 1) = \Phi(\alpha_1 share\ of\ Muslims\ in\ family_{it}$

$+ \alpha_2 share\ of\ Orthodox\ Christians\ in\ family_{it}$

$+ \beta_1 share\ of\ Muslims\ in\ neighborhood_{it}$

$+ \beta_2 share\ of\ Orthodox\ Christians\ in\ neighborhood_{it} + \gamma' q_{it})$,

where D_{it} stands for the indicator of whether a child had a medical checkup within the last twelve (or three) months, or the indicator of whether a child has a vaccination against tuberculosis. The set of controls q_{it} contains child's characteristics of (age, I(live in city)), regional characteristics such as the GRP per capita and the share of Muslims in the region, family characteristics such as family income and the share of family members with a college degree, neighborhood characteristics (average income in neighborhood), and the year fixed effects. For notational simplicity, we write $Pr(D_{it} = 1)$ instead of $Pr(D_{it} = 1|religious\ characteristics_{it}, q_{it})$.

The estimation results are presented in table 10.3. Columns (2) and (4) in the table show the evidence that a higher percentage of Muslims in the family is associated with a lower chance of the child being regularly seen by a doctor. This holds for the sample of all children and for the subsample of children with health problems. Also, when the sample of all children is considered, a higher percentage of Muslims in the neighborhood has a negative marginal effect on the probability of the child being vaccinated against tuberculosis as well as being regularly seen by a doctor. The variables for the shares of Orthodox Christians are not significant.

The discussion below considers the sample of all children. The first two graphs in figure 10.1 are for the case when the dependent variable is the indicator for a checkup within the last twelve months. The last two graphs in that figure are for the case when the dependent variable is the indicator for a vaccination against tuberculosis. The large dot in the first graph in figure 10.1 shows the pair (–0.3416, –0.3314) of estimated coefficients for the share of Muslims in the family and the share of Muslims in the neighborhood from

Table 10.3   **Probit regression estimation**

	Sample: All children		Sample: Children with health problems
	Medical checkup in last 12 months?	Vaccinated against tuberculosis?	Medical checkup in last 3 months?
Child: Age	–0.0423	0.0685	–0.0438
	[0.0032]***	[0.0047]***	[0.0067]***
Child: I (live in city)	0.1704	–0.2062	0.0601
	[0.0313]***	[0.0441]***	[0.0543]
Family: Share of Muslims	–0.3314	–0.1506	–0.4193
	[0.1127]***	[0.1686]	[0.2515]*
Family: Share of Orthodox Christians	0.0478	–0.0936	–0.0244
	[0.0394]	[0.0604]	[0.0711]
Family: Average log(income)	0.0602	–0.0169	0.0437
	[0.0151]***	[0.0211]	[0.0303]
Family: Share of those with a college degree	0.0741	0.0296	0.1561
	[0.0367]**	[0.0571]	[0.0651]**
Region: Share of Muslims	–0.0129	–0.3195	0.2551
	[0.1421]	[0.2062]	[0.3075]
Region: Log GRP per capita	0.1838	–0.0412	–0.0858
	[0.0308]***	[0.0463]	[0.0544]
Neighborhood: Share of Muslims	–0.3416	–0.429	–0.4922
	[0.1757]*	[0.2319]*	[0.4512]
Neighborhood: Share of Orthodox	–0.105	–0.0169	–0.1603
	[0.0840]	[0.1272]	[0.1603]
Year fixed effects	yes	yes	yes
Constant	–2.0794	1.9472	–3.9003
	[0.3701]***	[0.4039]***	[103.6494]
Observations	10,780	17,413	2,902

***Significant at the 1 percent level.
**Significant at the 5 percent level.
*Significant at the 10 percent level.

column (2) in table 10.3. The large dot in the second graph in figure 10.1 shows the pair (–0.105, –0.3314) of estimated coefficients for the share of Orthodox Christians in the neighborhood and the share of Muslims in the neighborhood, respectively, from column (2) in table 10.3. The large dot in the third graph in figure 10.1 shows the pair (–0.1506, –0.429) of estimated coefficients for the share of Muslims in the family and the share of Muslims in the neighborhood from column (3) in table 10.3. The large dot in the fourth graph in figure 10.1 shows the pair (–0.105, –0.429) of estimated coefficients for the share of Orthodox Christians in the neighborhood and the share of Muslims in the neighborhood, respectively, from column (3) in table 10.3.

Finally, we analyze how the estimates of our parameters would change if

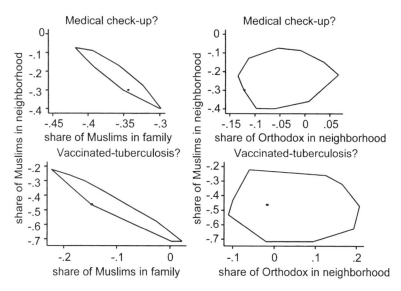

Fig. 10.1 Sets of estimates from 1,000 data sets combined using neighborhoods. Contour sets are for the cases of 2-anonymity

we enforce a bound on the risk of partial disclosure and consider the bound of 0.5—that is, $Pr(m_{ij} = 0 | \mathcal{D}^N(Z_i^x, Z_j^d) = 1) \geq \bar{\gamma}$, where $\bar{\gamma} = 0.5$. This is the case of attaining 2-anonymity.

In order to attain 2-anonymity we conduct the following exercise. For every child in our sample we create two possible neighborhoods—one neighborhood is the true one, and the other one is drawn randomly from the empirical distribution of neighborhoods in the corresponding region. Such empirical distributions can be easily obtained from the publicly available data in RLMS. As a result, for every child we have two possible sets of values of neighborhood characteristics.

Then, ideally we would like to simulate all possible combined data sets but the number of these data sets is of exponential complexity, namely, of the rate 2^n. Instead of considering all possible combined data sets, we randomly simulate only 1,000 such data sets. For each simulated combined data set we conduct the probit estimation. Thus, we end up with a 1,000 different sets of estimated coefficients (as well as the propensity scores). The contour sets in the graphs in figure 10.1 are the convex hulls of the obtained estimates. Namely, the contour set in the first graph in figure 10.1 is the convex hull of the 1,000 pairs of estimated coefficients for the share of Muslims in the family and the share of Muslims in the neighborhood, respectively. The contour set in the second graph in figure 10.1 is the convex hull of the 1,000 pairs of estimated coefficients for the share of Orthodox Christians in the neighborhood and the share of Muslims in the neighborhood, respectively. Similarly for the other two graphs.

As can be seen, in the analysis of the probability of a medical checkup in the last twelve months, all the 1,000 coefficients corresponding to variables of the share of Muslims in the family and the share of Muslims in the neighborhood are negative.[8] If the data curator thinks that the release of these sets of estimates is not satisfactory with regard to partial disclosure guarantees, then she should increase the guarantee level by, for instance, attaining 3-anonymity.

As for the case of the probability of being vaccinated against tuberculosis, among the 1,000 coefficients corresponding to the share of Muslims in the family, there are some positive ones, even though all the 1,000 coefficients corresponding to the share of Muslims in the neighborhood are negative.[9] Again, the data curator may want to increase the guarantee level.

10.6 Conclusion

In this chapter we analyze how the combination of data from multiple anonymized sources can lead to the serious threats of the disclosure of individual information. While the anonymized data sets by themselves may pose no direct threat, such a threat may arise in the combined data. The main question that we address is whether statistical inference based on the information from all these data sets is possible without the risk of disclosure. We introduce the notion of *statistical partial disclosure* to characterize a situation when data combination allows an adversary to identify a certain individual characteristic with a small probability of misidentification. We focus our analysis on the estimation of treatment effects where the treatment status of an individual is sensitive and, thus, the possibility of the statistical recovery of this treatment status may be highly undesirable. We show that a variety of techniques from data mining literature can be used for reconstruction of the combined data sets with little to no auxiliary information. We also demonstrate that the point identification of the statistical model for the average treatment effects is incompatible with bounds imposed on the risk of statistical partial disclosure imposed to protect individual information. We illustrate our findings in the empirical study of the impact of religious affiliation of parents on the probability of a child's medical checkups and vaccination from tuberculosis using the individual-level data from Russia.

Statistical partial disclosure is becoming of central importance in the "big data" world. While many consumer companies have been routinely collecting private consumer data, the modern data-driven business paradigm calls for using these data in business decisions. A common example is the online ad-targeting technology where the consumer is exposed to the ads based on

---

8. These variables are significant in each of 1,000 cases (even though the confidence intervals are not depicted in the graphs).
9. The variable of the share of Muslims in the neighborhood is significant in each of 1,000 cases.

the past consumer behavior and the known consumer characteristics. The ad delivery is based on the estimator that would be used to predict the consumer click on the ad based on the historical behavior of the given consumer and other consumers similar in some sense to the consumer of interest. *Forbes* magazine published a story explaining how Target uses credit card information to identify the repeated purchases from the same customer, and using a variety of sources identifies the set of demographic characteristics. Then, based on the collected demographic information and the sets of products that the consumers purchased in the past, Target was able to identify the sets of purchased products that most likely lead to a customer (a female) being pregnant. Based on this prediction, Target sent out coupons for the baby section in the store. *Forbes* then proceeds with the anecdotal story of when Target customer service got a call from an angry father of a teenager stating that his daughter got the coupon. A week later the father called Target back with an apology, as his daughter had indeed turned out to be pregnant.

With further advancement in econometric and machine-learning methods, similar stories will emerge in a large variety of settings, from medical services (where people already get customized automatic medical advice based on their reported lifestyle, eating, and exercise habits) to real estate (where companies like Zillow give the homeowners automated recommendations for the timing of the house sale and purchase). We argue that confidentiality restrictions can go hand in hand with the big data tools to provide technologies that are both aimed at higher consumer welfare (leading to better consumer targeting) and provide formal privacy guarantees. We have studied some of these technologies in this chapter.

References

Abowd, J., and L. Vilhuber. 2008. "How Protective Are Synthetic Data?" *Privacy in Statistical Databases* 5262:239–46.
Abowd, J., and S.Woodcock. 2001. "Disclosure Limitation in Longitudinal Linked Data." In *Confidentiality, Disclosure, and Data Access: Theory and Practical Applications for Statistical Agencies*, edited by P. Doyle, J. Lane, L. Zayatz, and J. Theeuwes, 215–77. Amsterdam: North Holland.
Acquisti, A. 2004. "Privacy and Security of Personal Information." In *Economics of Information Security*, vol. 12, edited by L. Jean Camp and Stephen Lewis, 179–86. New York: Springer Science+Business Media.
Acquisti, A., A. Friedman, and R. Telang. 2006. "Is There a Cost to Privacy Breaches? An Event Study." *Proceedings of the Twenty-Seventh International Conference on Information Systems.* doi: 10.1.1.73.2942&rep=rep1&type=pdf.
Acquisti, A., and J. Grossklags. 2008. "What Can Behavioral Economics Teach Us about Privacy?" In *Digital Privacy: Theory, Technologies, and Practices*, edited by A. Acquisti, S. Gritzalis, S. DiVimercati, and C. Lambrinoudakis, 363–79. Boca Raton, FL: Auerbach Publications, Taylor & Francis Group.

Acquisti, A., and H. Varian. 2005. "Conditioning Prices on Purchase History." *Marketing Science* 33:367–81.
Aggarwal, G., T. Feder, K. Kenthapadi, R. Motwani, R. Panigrahy, D. Thomas, and A. Zhu. 2005. "Approximation Algorithms for k-anonymity." *Journal of Privacy Technology*, Paper no. 2005112001.
Bradley, C., L. Penberthy, K. Devers, and D. Holden. 2010. "Health Services Research and Data Linkages: Issues, Methods, and Directions for the Future." *Health Services Research* 45 (5, pt. 2): 1468–88.
Calzolari, G., and A. Pavan. 2006. "On the Optimality of Privacy in Sequential Contracting." *Journal of Economic Theory* 130 (1): 168–204.
Ciriani, V., S. di Vimercati, S. Foresti, and P. Samarati. 2007. "k-Anonymity." In *Secure Data Management in Decentralized Systems*, vol. 33, edited by T. Yu and S. Jajodia. Berlin: Springer-Verlag.
Duncan, G., S. Fienberg, R. Krishnan, R. Padman, and S. Roehrig. 2001. "Disclosure Limitation Methods and Information Loss for Tabular Data." In *Confidentiality, Disclosure and Data Access: Theory and Practical Applications for Statistical Agencies*, edited by P. Doyle, 135–66. Amsterdam: North Holland.
Duncan, G., and D. Lambert. 1986. "Disclosure-Limited Data Dissemination." *Journal of the American Statistical Association* 81 (393): 10–18.
Duncan, G., and S. Mukherjee. 1991. "Microdata Disclosure Limitation in Statistical Databases: Query Size and Random Sample Query Control." In *Proceedings of IEEE Symposium on Security and Privacy*, 278–87.
Duncan, G., and R. Pearson. 1991. "Enhancing Access to Microdata While Protecting Confidentiality: Prospects for the Future." *Statistical Science* 6 (3): 219–32.
Dwork, C. 2006. "Differential Privacy." In *Automata, Languages and Programming*, edited by M. Bugliesi, B. Preneel, V. Sassone, and I. Wegener, 1–12. Berlin: Springer-Verlag.
Dwork, C., and K. Nissim. 2004. "Privacy-Preserving Data Mining on Vertically Partitioned Databases." In *Advances in Cryptology–CRYPTO 2004*, edited by M. Franklin, 134–38. New York: Springer.
Fienberg, S. 1994. "Conflicts between the Needs for Access to Statistical Information and Demands for Confidentiality." *Journal of Official Statistics* 10:115.
———. 2001. "Statistical Perspectives on Confidentiality and Data Access in Public Health." *Statistics in Medicine* 20 (9–10): 1347–56.
Goldfarb, A., and C. Tucker. 2010. "Online Display Advertising: Targeting and Obtrusiveness." *Marketing Science* 30 (3): 389–404.
Gross, R., and A. Acquisti. 2005. "Information Revelation and Privacy in Online Social Networks." In *Proceedings of the 2005 ACM Workshop on Privacy in the Electronic Society*, edited by V. Atluri, S. di Vimercati, and R. Dingledine, 71–80. New York: Association for Computing Machinery.
Homer, N., S. Szelinger, M. Redman, D. Duggan, W. Tembe, J. Muehling, J. Pearson, D. Stephan, S. Nelson, and D. Craig. 2008. "Resolving Individuals Contributing Trace Amounts of DNA to Highly Complex Mixtures Using High-Density SNP Genotyping Microarrays." *PLoS Genetics* 4 (8): e1000167.
Horowitz, J., and C. Manski. 2006. "Identification and Estimation of Statistical Functionals Using Incomplete Data." *Journal of Econometrics* 132 (2): 445–59.
Horowitz, J., C. Manski, M. Ponomareva, and J. Stoye. 2003. "Computation of Bounds on Population Parameters When the Data are Incomplete." *Reliable Computing* 9 (6): 419–40.
Komarova, T., D. Nekipelov, and E. Yakovlev. 2011. "Identification, Data Combination and the Risk of Disclosure." CeMMAP Working Paper no. CWP39/11, Centre for Microdata Methods and Practice, Institute for Fiscal Studies.

Korolova, A. 2010. "Privacy Violations Using Microtargeted Ads: A Case Study." In *IEEE International Workshop on Privacy Aspects of Data Mining (PADM'2010)*, 474–82, Washington, DC. doi:10.1109/ICDMW.2010.137.

Lambert, D. 1993. "Measures of Disclosure Risk and Harm." *Journal of Official Statistics* 9:313.

LeFevre, K., D. DeWitt, and R. Ramakrishnan. 2005. "Incognito: Efficient Full-Domain k-Anonymity." In *Proceedings of the 2005 ACM SIGMOD International Conference on Management of Data*, edited by Fatma Ozcan, 49–60. Association for Computing Machinery.

———. 2006. "Mondrian Multidimensional k-anonymity." In ICDE'06 Proceedings of the 22nd International Conference on Data Engineering, 25. Institute of Electronics and Electronic Engineers.

Magnac, T., and E. Maurin. 2008. "Partial Identification in Monotone Binary Models: Discrete Regressors and Interval Data." *Review of Economic Studies* 75 (3): 835–64.

Manski, C. 2003. *Partial Identification of Probability Distributions*. Berlin: Springer-Verlag.

Miller, A., and C. Tucker. 2009. "Privacy Protection and Technology Diffusion: The Case of Electronic Medical Records." *Management Science* 55 (7): 1077–93.

Molinari, F. 2008. "Partial Identification of Probability Distributions with Misclassified Data." *Journal of Econometrics* 144 (1): 81–117.

Narayanan, A., and V. Shmatikov. 2008. "Robust De-Anonymization of Large Sparse Datasets." In *SP 2008 IEEE Symposium on Security and Privacy*, 111–125. Institute of Electronics and Electrical Engineers.

Ridder, G., and R. Moffitt. 2007. "The Econometrics of Data Combination." *Handbook of Econometrics* 6 (6b): 5469–547.

Samarati, P., and L. Sweeney. 1998. "Protecting Privacy When Disclosing Information: k-Anonymity and Its Enforcement through Generalization and Suppression." Technical Report SRI-CSL-98-04, Computer Science Laboratory, SRI International.

Sweeney, L. 2002a. "Achieving k-Anonymity Privacy Protection Using Generalization and Suppression." *International Journal of Uncertainty Fuzziness and Knowledge-Based Systems* 10 (5): 571–88.

———. 2002b. "k-Anonymity: A Model for Protecting Privacy." *International Journal of Uncertainty Fuzziness and Knowledge-Based Systems* 10 (5): 557–70.

Taylor, C. 2004. "Consumer Privacy and the Market for Customer Information." *RAND Journal of Economics* 35 (4): 631–50.

Varian, H. 2009. "Economic Aspects of Personal Privacy." In *Internet Policy and Economics*, edited by W. H. Lehr and L. M. Pupillo, 101–09. New York: Springer Science+Business Media.

Wilson, A., T. Graves, M. Hamada, and C. Reese. 2006. "Advances in Data Combination, Analysis and Collection for System Reliability Assessment." *Statistical Science* 21 (4): 514–31.

Wright, G. 2010. "Probabilistic Record Linkage in SAS®." Working Paper, Kaiser Permanente, Oakland, CA.

Yakovlev, E. 2012. "Peers and Alcohol: Evidence from Russia." CEFIR Working Paper no. 182, Center for Economic and Financial Research.

11
Information Lost
Will the "Paradise" That Information Promises, to Both Consumer and Firm, Be "Lost" on Account of Data Breaches? The Epic is Playing Out

Catherine L. Mann

11.1 Introduction

The expanding scope of Internet use yields a widening array of firms with access to ever expanding databases of information on individuals' search, transactions, and preferences. This information translates into consumers' ease of transacting, range of complementary purchases, targeted news and advertising, and other directed goods, services, and information, all of which increase customer value—but also raise the probability and consequences of information loss. Similarly, firms have unprecedented windows into customer behavior and preferences with which they can improve products, segment markets, and, therefore, enhance profits—but also raise the probability of losing or abusing information. The Digitization Agenda can help frame and balance the benefits to firms and consumers of information gained with the risk and costs of information lost, particularly in the context of increasingly global flows of information and transactions.

A first priority is a conceptual framework. Three key elements in the structure of the information marketplace influence the valuation and balancing of benefits and costs. First, information exhibits economies of scale and scope, which challenges the ability of the market to efficiently price information. Second, participants in the information marketplace are not atomistic, rather they are asymmetric in terms of market power, which affects the incidence and distribution of benefits and costs. Third, information loss

---

Catherine L. Mann is the Barbara '54 and Richard M. Rosenberg Professor of Global Finance at Brandeis University.

Excellent research assistance from Alok Mistry, who experienced his own data breach (stolen laptop) during the course of this project. For acknowledgments, sources of research support, and disclosure of the author's material financial relationships, if any, please see http://www.nber.org/chapters/c12990.ack.

is a probabilistic event, but with unknown distribution, which challenges the valuation of benefits and, particularly, costs. A final element is that the information marketplace is global, populated by heterogeneous firms and consumers, and by policymakers who differ in their policy responses to the imperfections in the marketplace.

A second requirement is empirical analysis of the frameworks. Mandated disclosure in the United States of data breaches was the watershed enabling this study and its references. Without disclosure, it is impossible to investigate the risks and potential costs of information loss against the benefits of information collection and aggregation. Disclosure helps reveal to consumers, firms, and policymakers the nature of data loss, and may change incentives and affect the incidence and balancing of costs and benefits. However, disclosure can be along a spectrum from every incident being announced to everyone to only critical incidents being communicated to a few. In fact, there is no globally consistent approach to disclosure, nor even to the notion of disclosure at all, so the window into the empirical valuation of costs and benefits of the information marketplace is narrow.

Even so, evidence on how disclosure works is starting to emerge. If the market response to disclosure is sufficient to apportion and balance costs and benefits, then, in principle, no policy intervention into the marketplace is needed. So far, this does not appear to be the case. More information on the nature of data breaches, on incidence of benefits and costs, of market participant response, and on evidence of the efficacy of policy intervention should help prioritize the Digitization Agenda.

This chapter proceeds along the following path. The next section reviews various conceptual frameworks with which we can analyze the structure of the information marketplace. Section 11.3 presents evidence on the extent and nature of information lost. What are the trends? Size of loss, sector of loss, source of loss, cost of loss, market value of information, and so on, including in the global context. Section 11.4 addresses market and policy responses to information loss, and reviews legislative and legal strategies that could complement market discipline. Particular attention is given to the challenges of cross-border information flows, including differences in attitudes and priorities toward data security. Section 11.5 concludes with priorities for the Digitization Agenda.

11.2 Frameworks for Analyzing the Information Marketplace and Data Breaches

That consumers gain from using the Internet is clear from increased competition and reduced prices (Morton 2006), greater variety (Goolsbee and Klenow 2006), and faster access to a wider range of public information (Greenstein and McDevitt 2011; Yan, Jeon, and Kim 2013). Wallsten (chapter 2, this volume) continues the work of valuing the consumer benefits of using the Internet. Yet, with rapidly changing technology and social interaction, it is hard to pin down exactly how large the increase in consumer surplus might be, so there is much more work to do.

Using the Internet generates the information that is the basic building block of the marketplace for information. A conceptual framework for the incidence and balance of costs and benefits of information in this marketplace includes the valuing of consumer gain from using the Internet, but it is a more complex framework with more players. For simplicity, suppose the information marketplace is populated by originators of information (say consumers, as they reveal their preferences through search and transactions); intermediaries of the information (say, firms that transmit data, and those that collect, aggregate, and retain information); and final users (say, firms that call on the aggregated data to improve products). How should we model the interactions between the information and the three players? Is the information atomistic or are there economies and scale and scope in aggregation of the information into a database? Are the players atomistic and equally numerous, or do they differ in concentration and market power in their economic relationships? What about the nature of uncertainty? Answering these questions helps to determine to what extent the information marketplace is "classic" in the Adam Smith sense and "complete" in the Arrow-Debreu sense, or whether it is a market with imperfections.

Various authors have taken up the challenge of modeling the information marketplace, some explicitly in the context of data breaches. The several papers reviewed below are put into the context of a general framework that focuses on a market structure that includes economies of scale and scope in data aggregation, multiple nonatomistic players, and in an environment of uncertainty over the nature and probability of data breaches and consequences. In this kind of market structure it is challenging to value the cost and incidence of a data breach. Further challenges are that the basic building blocks of information may be valued differently across geographies and cultures. When information can flow across borders, these differences (and policymakers' responses) may create arbitrage opportunities.

11.2.1 Complete Markets: The Benchmark Market Structure

The purpose of outlining the characteristics of the perfectly competitive marketplace—the Adam Smith marketplace—is to provide a benchmark against which the structure of the global information marketplace can be assessed. If the environment for undertaking information-rich activities is characterized by perfect competition, then Adam Smith's invisible hand— whereby each acting in his own self-interest—achieves the highest economic well-being for all players.

In Adam Smith's market, one-off transactions generate unique prices for each transaction. In this classic marketplace, buyers, intermediaries, and sellers are all atomistic. There are no databases with a history of a specific buyer's transactions or those of buyers of similar characteristics that create correlations between transactions across time or across individuals. No information is retained, so no information can be lost. Balancing the benefits of information exchange with the potential cost of information lost is not an issue.

An extension of Adam Smith's market allows for transactions across time, proximity, currency, and uncertainty. In the so-called Arrow-Debreu "complete" market (Arrow and Debreu 1954), economic instruments exist for all possible transactions that the set of market participants can undertake with each other. A complete market accommodates all dimensions of a transaction through time, space, and under uncertainty and yields a unique and market-determined price for that transaction in a frictionless world.

Whereas these transactions may be correlated and/or uncertain, the correlations of transactions (such as interest rates and exchange rates) and uncertainties (probability of default) are fully known (in the complete market), and therefore will be efficiently embodied in the relevant prices. In a complete-markets framework, both private and social optimum outcome can be achieved because there is a perfect (complete) and frictionless match between transactions and atomistic market participants over all possible states-of-nature and time. With full information about correlation and uncertainty, prices will fully reflect benefits of information exchange, which can then be balanced against the potential cost of information lost. There are no market imperfections.

11.2.2 The Information Marketplace: Violating the Complete-Markets Framework

In a number of ways the information marketplace violates key assumptions of the complete-markets framework, which makes pricing information difficult, and opens up for consideration the topics of market imperfections and problems of ranking the second best. More specifically, without accurate prices, the benefit-cost calculation surrounding information exchange as against information lost through a data breach will be very challenging.

The first violation is the assumption that transactions are one-off or uncorrelated as in Adam Smith's work. In fact, information is characterized by economies of scale and scope. That is, the value of information over a series of transactions for an individual is greater than the sum of the individual transactions because of the correlations across the individual's behavior; for example, the information marketplace is characterized by economies of scale. The value of information aggregated over many individuals is greater than the sum of any individual's set because of the correlations across individuals; the information marketplace is characterized by economies of scope.

Even if each unique piece of information had a uniquely matched price, there would be an incomplete mapping between the value of that morsel of information by itself, its value in one database, and its value if two (or N) databases are merged together.[1] Databases, which are the product of the information marketplace, are characterized by economies of scale and scope so that the pricing of information is imperfect, unless there is full information about all the correlations among each morsel of data. Because the information marketplace and its players are evolving rapidly with technology and Internet use, it is clear that the correlations needed for the complete-markets framework cannot be known in sufficient detail or timeliness to incorporate them into the information price.

The second challenge that the information marketplace brings to the complete-markets framework is the nature of uncertainty. Uncertainty enters the information marketplace through the possible misuse of information. A complete markets set-up could, in theory, price insurance that pays off in the case of a data breach, but since such price determination in the information marketplace is, in practice, nearly impossible, an actuarially fair price for insurance is also extremely difficult.

The information marketplace exhibits two types of uncertainty that are difficult to price. First, and most challenging, is the potential correlation over time of information lost. A data breach today cannot be valued with certainty because the value of the information lost today is a function of all possible data breaches in the future. Future data breaches matter for today's valuation of information lost because of the unknown relationship between the information lost in today's breach with the information lost in a future breach. Economies of scale and scope in information in the future affect valuation in the present.

The second type of uncertainty is that information lost may not be information abused. The cost of information lost should differ depending on whether the lost information is used maliciously or not. The two uncertainties together make valuing information lost quite difficult. The insurance contracts, which are key instruments in the complete-market framework, are not likely to exist.[2]

The third violation of the assumptions that underpin the complete-markets benchmark model is that the players are not atomistic. Recall that the information marketplace has consumers (originators of information), intermediaries (transmitters and aggregators), and firms (that use information to improve products). Consumers are numerous. Firms are numerous. Transmitters and aggregators are concentrated and have several types

---

1. Another way to think about why there are economies of scope in information in databases is to consider the analogy from financial markets: there are diversification gains associated with merging two not-identical financial portfolios.

2. According to a *Financial Times* article (April 23, 2014), AIG is offering a "first of its kind" insurance product to protect firms against cyber attacks on the "Internet of things" that yield product liability and bodily harm (Alloway 2014). In these cases (product liability and bodily harm) the consequences of a data breach are seen at the time of the incident.

of market power that will affect the price and value of information and therefore influence cost-benefit calculations associated with information exchange, information security, and information loss. Moreover, the degree of market power and the rules under which the intermediaries operate vary substantially across countries and policy environments.

These violations of the complete-markets framework offer jumping-off points for research. The following selected papers focus on modeling the information marketplace. Some papers specifically address how to model the cost-benefit calculation in the case of information lost.[3]

11.2.3 Applying the Pollution Model to Information Flows

Pollution seems like a good analogy for the information marketplace: pollution has (negative) economies of scale, asymmetric market position of participants (upstream-downstream), and uncertainties as to costs and benefits of exposure and remediation. Hirsch (2006) uses the pollution model and focuses on the negative economies of scale. He presumes that collecting and aggregating personal information generates negative externalities. "There is a growing sense that the digital age is causing unprecedented damage to privacy . . . digital economy businesses often do not bear the cost of the harms that they inflict" (9).

Just as pollution is an outcome of production, so too is information aggregation an externality of "production" (search and transaction on the Internet). In the pollution model of the information marketplace, no data breach is necessary to generate harm. Aggregation alone departs from the complete-markets framework. With the economy of scale inherent in information aggregation, there will be a price wedge between the valuation of information by the consumer and by intermediaries and firms in the marketplace.

Hirsch continues with the pollution analogy and reviews the evolution of policy strategy from "command and control" compliance (quantities) to "second-generation" (prices) or "outcome-oriented" policy whereby the regulated entities find their own cost-effective strategy to achieve the legislated goal. Tang, Hu, and Smith (2007) take these strategies to the information marketplace. They model information collection looking through the lens of consumer preferences for trust. Standardized regulation does not map into the heterogeneity of consumer preferences for trust (with some consumers being too regulated, others not enough) so overall economic well-being is reduced by such an approach. In contrast, they find that under circumstances of clarity and credibility, self-regulation can achieve a nuanced strategy that meets the heterogeneous preferences in the marketplace. On the other hand, Ioannidis, Pym, and Williams (2013) argue that "information

---

3. The literature addressed in this chapter focuses on the benefits of information exchange and the costs of information lost. Other research focuses more specifically on the topic of privacy. For more on modeling privacy, see US Dept of Commerce, NTIA chapter compendium of articles; Roberds and Schreft (2009), Anderson (2006), and references therein.

stewardship" internalizes the social costs of data loss (much as a corporate social responsibility policy might internalize the firm's approach to its pollution or as an environmental group might publicize polluting behavior). With the prodding of such an information steward, firms internalize some of the costs of data loss and therefore undertake higher investments in information security than they would have. Ioannidis, Pym, and Williams find by using their model that social welfare is enhanced.

Whereas environmental economics offers a model for the information marketplace, the analogy is stretched because consumers and firms do gain from information aggregation, and it is hard to imagine anyone actually gaining from downstream pollution. Moreover, although the pollution model allows for market power and uncertainty, so far researchers have not put all three elements of economies of scale/scope, market power, and uncertainty together in the context of the information marketplace.

11.2.4 Too Much Information: Trade-Offs with Limits to Rationality

Full information and frictionless markets are key in the complete-market framework. Acquisti (2010) starts by arguing that the information marketplace is all about trade-offs. "In choosing the balance between sharing or hiding one's personal information (and in choosing the balance between exploiting or protecting individuals' data), both individuals and organizations face complex, sometimes intangible, and often ambiguous trade-offs. . . . But trade-offs are the natural realm of economics"(3).

But then, he notes that limited consumer rationality and transactions costs make calculating these trade-offs difficult. Both of these issues affect the pricing of information, as well as the distribution of benefits and costs of information aggregation and potentially of its loss. If consumers do not know the value of their information, they cannot calculate the trade-off between allowing collection and aggregation against the possible cost of a data breach. These issues depart from the complete-markets model and are Acquisti's (2010) jumping-off point for his modeling of the cost-benefit calculations. How significant are these departures in the information marketplace from the complete-markets framework?

Researchers have attempted to calculate the value of the aggregation of one's own information. Conjoint analysis by Hann et al. (2002) finds that consumers trade their information for about $40–$50 of product value. Convenience is often cited as a rationale for allowing the aggregation of one's own personal information, as in online banking (Lichtenstein and Williamson 2006). Another way to value personal information is to calculate the cost to firms of the inability to use individual and aggregate personal information to target advertising (Goldfarb and Tucker 2010). The empirical work on value of information to the consumer suggests that limited rationality is an important problem.

Policymakers and businesses differ in their response to the limited rationality of consumers. The European Union (EU) Privacy Directive is at one extreme, disallowing the collection and retention of personal information on the grounds that consumers do not know what they are giving up, and strengthening this approach in early 2014 with the "right to be forgotten." Other policy approaches require active consent (opt-in) or more transparency (e.g., this website uses cookies . . . click here for our cookie policy). Some firms are finding a market opportunity in responding to the limited rationality problem. Incorporated into the website are easy-to-use tools that allow customers to edit the information stream associated with their search and transactions activity and thereby improve the accuracy and targeting of their own information.[4]

However, the presence of economies of scale and scope in information aggregation, as well as the nature of uncertainty regarding data breaches, means that the analysis of the balancing of the benefits from information transmitted against the potential cost of information lost is more complex than just the limited rationality of individuals.

11.2.5 Multiple Players, Market Power, and the Role for Disclosure

Much of the literature that addresses the benefit of information aggregation versus cost when information is lost uses a two-player framework—so-called data subjects (such as customers that provide the information) and so-called data holders (such as a firm that aggregates customer data to create customized products). In fact, there is a third player in the information marketplace—the intermediaries—through which information "transits" and/or "rests." Examples range from Visa, Amazon, and Google to less familiar companies such as ChoicePoint or Acxiom.

Atomistic interaction among market players is an important underpinning of the complete-markets framework, but is clearly violated in the information marketplace. In particular, intermediaries are very highly concentrated: Google accounts for about 70 percent of all search,[5] collecting and retaining all that information; Visa accounts for about three-quarters of all US card transactions, creating a thick financial and purchase trail;[6] and Amazon accounts for 15 percent of all US online sales and is ranked fifteenth among all retail companies, collecting reams of data along the way.[7] On the other hand, there are billions of consumers and merchants that use Google and Visa and shop with Amazon. Virtually none of them interact with an intermediary such as ChoicePoint or Acxiom, although their information rests there. The differential interactions and differential concentra-

---

4. Singer (2013).
5. Multiple sources as of April, May, and June 2013.
6. http://www.forbes.com/sites/greatspeculations/2013/05/03/visa-and-mastercard-battle-for-share-in-global-shift-to-plastic/.
7. http://www.prnewswire.com/news-releases/amazoncom-captures-28-of-top-online-retailer-sales-205427331.html.

tions are important for the valuation of information and magnitude and incidence of costs in the case of a data breach.

Considering interactions and concentration, Romanosky and Acquisti (2009) use a systems control strategy to map alternative legislative approaches to reducing harm from information loss. Two of the three approaches draw from accident legislation: First, ex ante "safety regulation" (e.g., seat belts) in the context of the information marketplace would include promulgation and adherence by intermediaries to, say, Payment Card Industry Data Security Standards. But these authors argue that ex ante standards focus on inputs (encryption) rather than outcomes (harm), so they are not efficient. Second, ex post liability law (e.g., legal suits) could include fines for negligence in the protection of information. But, ex post litigation may be ineffective because courts have been unwilling to award damages based on the probability of some future harm coming as a consequence of a data breach (see the evolving legal landscape in section 11.4).

A third approach is disclosure of data breaches. Disclosure of data breaches is a key ingredient to calculating costs and benefits of providing and protecting information, and of apportioning responsibility and costs in the case of a data breach. Romanosky and Acquisti note that consumer cognitive bias (misperception of risk) and costs of disclosing the data breach itself (disclosing what to whom; see discussion that follows) are important caveats for the effectiveness of disclosure.

Romanosky and Acqusiti use their framework to outline an empirical example of where cognitive bias and disclosure costs are less significant because of the concentrated market structure of intermediaries. Specifically, they analyze the relationship between credit card-issuing institutions and firms that hold (and lose) credit card data. They argue that information disclosure has promoted the internalization of the costs of remediation by the data holders (and losers), which increases the incentives for the adequate protection of personal information even when the individual who has provided that information cannot demand such protection.

Why does disclosure help align (some of the) private interests? First, a sufficient number of data breaches have occurred such that these costs have begun to be quantified (to be discussed in sections 11.3 and 11.4). Second, the number of affected intermediaries (card issuers in this case) is sufficiently small that they have market power to demand remediation (or impose punishment) from the other concentrated intermediary, the data aggregators/holders. Third, the chain of causation between information loss and required remediation is revealed because of data-breach disclosure laws. The disclosure laws along with quantification of costs, as well as the small number of players, promote the transfer of remediation costs from the card issuers to the database aggregators, those who actually lost the information. Thus, at least some of the cost of the data breach was internalized in this example.

However, the costs of information loss borne by individual card holders were not transferred to those firms where the data breach occurred. The market power of individuals was insignificant, and in a transactions sense, the individuals were distant from the data aggregators/holders. Individuals can change card issuers, but they have no power to affect the relationship between their card issuer and what firm aggregates the transactions of that card. Thus, the cost of the data breach incurred by individuals was not internalized by the intermediaries, and the individuals had no market power to affect such an internalization. Unlike the atomistic players in the complete-market framework, the information marketplace has disparities in concentration and market power that affect the distribution of costs of a data breach, as well as the price and willingness to pay for techniques to avoid such a breach. (See more on disclosure in sections 11.3 and 11.4.)[8]

11.2.6 The Probability Distribution of Data Breaches

The third key underpinning of the complete-markets framework is the pricing of uncertainty. For a number of reasons, it is challenging to estimate, and therefore price, the uncertainty of incurring and then the uncertain consequences of a data breach. Nevertheless, in the face of costly data breaches (see section 11.3) firms increasingly are turning to risk modeling for the decision to invest in information technology security.

The shape of the probability distribution of data breach events is crucial to calculate both the costs of a breach and benefits of undertaking security investments. Assuming that data breaches follow a normal distribution will yield a different calculation than if data breaches are characterized by "fat tails" or extreme outlier distributions. Thomas et al. (2013) consider alternative probability distributions in a theoretical model of investment in information security.

An analogy comes from the market for foreign exchange and the financial instruments that are priced and used in that market. Suppose a firm wants to put a floor on the value in the home currency of the revenue stream earned abroad in the foreign currency. In a complete-markets framework, the firm could buy an option that will pay off when the home-to-foreign currency exchange rate reaches a particular value. In a complete-markets framework, the probability distribution of exchange rate movements is fully known. The option would be priced exactly so as to make the firm indifferent to buying it or not (and on the sell side, the seller indifferent to selling the option or not.) The factor inducing one firm to buy the option and the other to sell the option is differences in risk appetite, among other factors.

---

8. The massive Target data breach in the fall of 2013 opened a new front in the market power relationships. Although Target credit card transactions were the locus of the data breach, the company argued that chip-and-pin technology would have significantly altered the likelihood of the data breach. Since credit card companies have not generally supported chip-and-pin in the United States (despite this being the technology used in Europe), Target diverted some of the blame to the credit card companies.

But, suppose the probability distribution is not accurately parameterized. For example, suppose that exchange rate fluctuations are assumed to follow a normal distribution, but the true distribution has fat tails. The probability of the foreign currency depreciation that triggers the option will be underestimated relative to its value under the true probability distribution. The firm will not buy the option, and it will experience an uncompensated loss. On the other hand, if the firm assumes the extreme outlier distribution is correct, when the true distribution is normal, then the firm will buy too expensive an option, given the very small likelihood of the extreme event.

In the information market place there is a similar problem of deriving the correct probability distribution of a data breach. Information on the probability of incurring a data breach is limited, and incurring a data breach is not identical to the probability of data abuse. Without knowing the correct probability distribution, too much investment in information security or too little are equally possible. Moreover, whether the correct market player is the target of the security effort remains unclear. For example, Anderson et al. (2012) point out that one automated spammer accounted for about one-third of global spam in 2010 and profited $2.7 million. But the 2010 worldwide spending on preventing spam exceeded $1 billion. So neither the level of spending nor the target appeared to have been optimal.

The challenges to optimizing investment in data security run deeper because of the economies of scale and scope in the information and the differential market power of the players. Does the cost-benefit calculation for information security differ as to many small breaches (say, the normal distribution) compared to a rare but large data breach (the "black swan" event, from Taleb 2007, 2010). Is a large data breach more likely to lead to abuse of data, or less likely? The hypothesis of economies of scale and scope in information suggests that large data breaches, experienced over time, accumulate to enhance potential abuse of all revealed information, whether abused before or not. Differential market power has already been seen to shift the burden of costs of a data breach; it could similarly shift the burden of responsibility to invest in information security. Free riding and moral hazard are other aspects of differential market power that cause the information marketplace to deviate from the complete-markets framework.

11.2.7 Information Marketplace: Challenges to Pricing and Balancing Benefits and Costs

In sum, the information marketplace violates the classic complete-markets framework in three ways. First, information is characterized by economies of scale and scope, so it is difficult to price and value. Moreover, the benefits of aggregation increases, but so may the cost in the case where information is lost. Second, the various market players are not atomistic. The relationships between the originators of information—the intermediaries that transmit, aggregate, and hold information—and the users of the aggregated data to enhance products are characterized by differential market power. The differential market power affects the distribution of both benefits of information and the potential costs when information is lost. Finally, there is substantial uncertainty about the probability distribution describing both the data breach event and potential abuse of information that is exposed, so it is hard to value information lost. Collectively, these departures from the complete-markets framework point to potential inefficiencies in market pricing and in participant behavior. Whether such inefficiencies suggest policymaker intervention requires more analysis.

11.3 Trends in Information Lost

The literature and framework presented in section 11.2 pointed to a variety of data needs: how to value information that incorporates economies of scale and scope, the nature of the market-power relationships between different market actors, and the parameters of the probability distributions of information lost and/or misused. All of this is needed to evaluate whether the information marketplace is efficiently balancing the value of information aggregated against the costs of information lost.

Against this variety of data needs, this section presents evidence on only the extent and nature of information lost. What are the trends: size of loss, sector of loss, source of loss, cost of loss, market value of information, probability of abuse given a breach, and so on, including in the global context.

The raw data come from several sources including: the Privacy Rights Clearinghouse and Open Security Foundation, which draw from public news sources; a number of consulting firms that employ industry surveys such as the Ponemon Institute, Symantec, Verizon, Javelin Strategy and Research, KPMG Europe; and the Federal Trade Commission and the Department of Justice, which draw on the consumer fraud online report database. Only some of the raw data are available for research use; most is proprietary, and this chapter draws on the public sources. Access by researchers to proprietary data would be quite valuable.

11.3.1 How Much Information is Lost? And by What Means?

Privacy Rights Clearinghouse (PRC) data for 2005 to 2012[9] show that after a notable drop in data breaches in 2009, during the depths of the recession, data breaches are on the increase again.[10] (The number of records lost in each breach, which is a different measure of information lost, will be discussed below.) The PRC disaggregates breaches into various types: losing paper documents or losing computers (static desktop or portable);

---

9. www.privacyrights.org/data-breach.
10. The California disclosure law (discussed in section 11.4) passed in 2003. The jump in breaches from 2005 to 2006 is more likely a consequence of more widespread reporting of data breach announcements and collection into the database than it is an actual dramatic jump.

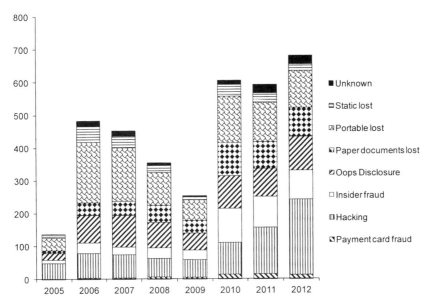

Fig. 11.1 Data breach, total number and by method
Source: Privacy Rights Clearinghouse.

inadvertent disclosure (such as using "cc" instead of "bcc" in an e-mail list); and various types of fraud (by an insider employee, by an outsider hacker, through payment card).[11] The first three types of information lost are more by mistake, although the disclosed information could still be misused. The three types of fraud are presumed to have some malicious intent.

Hacking dominates, and insider fraud is the increasingly important source of data breaches. But a surprising number of data breaches still take place the "old-fashioned way" by losing paper documents or laptops and through unintended disclosure. (See figure 11.1.)

Whereas the announcement of a breach indicates that information has been compromised, the actual number of records involved in each breach could be a better measure of potential cost of the breach in that a record represents granular information about an individual. Not all breach disclosures reveal how many records were lost in the breach. In fact only about half of the announcements include that information. (See more discussion of breaches that reveal Social Security numbers below.)

For the breach disclosures that reveal the number of records lost over the 2005–2012 period, the histogram of records lost per breach shows that the most frequent breach is small, involving 1–10,000 records. There is some reduction in breaches with medium-sized losses (100,000–500,000 records

---

11. Open Society Foundation also uses this classification scheme.

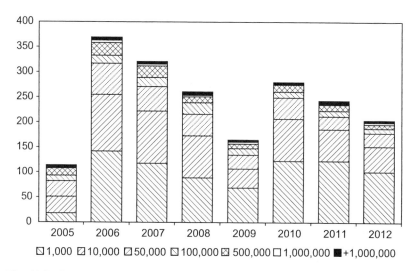

Fig. 11.2 Records per breach, all sectors
Source: Privacy Rights Clearinghouse.

lost), but little progress in stemming breaches of either small or huge size. In particular huge breaches (1,000,000 and up), though infrequent, have not been controlled (witness the enormous 2013 Target breach). This histogram of breaches offers an insight to the probability distribution of a breach event. A cross-tabulation of the type of breach with the size of the breach could help target investment in information security. However, not known is whether huge breaches are more likely to lead to information abuse, or whether data from small breaches are more likely to be misused. (See figure 11.2.)

11.3.2 What Kind of Information is Lost?

Revealing a Social Security number (SSN) during a data breach generates far greater concern and potential for costly information loss compared to a data breach that compromises other types of personal information (see evidence in section 11.4). Based on the PRC data, there is a mixed picture of whether more or less high-value information is being lost. In part, this mixed picture appears to be because reporting of SSN losses is increasingly incomplete.

Over the time period the number of breaches that reveal SNN has increased, but as a share of all data breaches those that reveal SSN has declined. The number of reported records where the SSN was compromised declined from a peak in 2007, although not in trend fashion. So, this suggests that SSN breaches are becoming less prevalent, perhaps because of enhanced security. (See figure 11.3.)

On the other hand, recall that not all breach announcements reveal the

Information Lost and Data Breaches 323

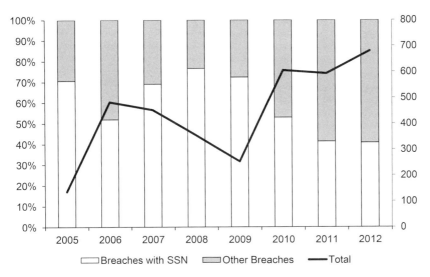

Fig. 11.3 Breaches with SSN

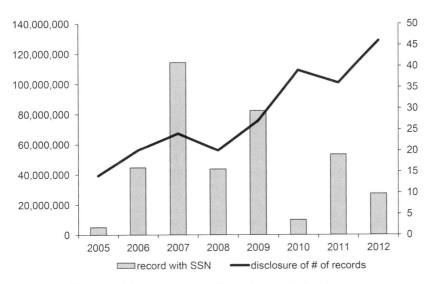

Fig. 11.4 SSN records lost, percentage of breaches not disclosing number of records

number of records lost. For breaches that compromise SSN, the share of those breaches that *do not disclose* the number of SSN-related records lost has *increased* over time (figure 11.4). Considering a sectoral decomposition of data breach announcements, the business-other (BSO) category is the largest sector that does not disclose whether SSN records have been compromised. Sectors that are perhaps under greater scrutiny, such as medical

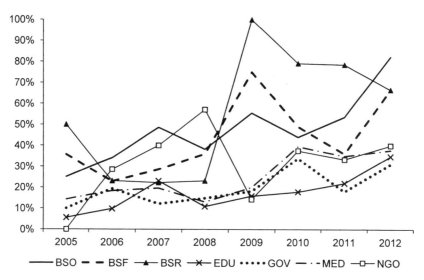

Fig. 11.5 Undisclosed number of records with SSN breaches (percentage of total breaches with SSN)

(MED), financial (BSF), and retail (BSR) appear to disclose more information. (See figure 11.5.)

In sum, interpreting the data on SSN breaches and required disclosure requires more analysis. Required disclosure may have led to security investment and thus fewer SSN-related breaches. Or, required disclosure may just have prompted less transparency in public reporting.

11.3.3 Is There Differentiation by Sector?

Looking behind the averages, are there differences by sector? Which sectors are the most prone to data breaches, by what means, and does the size of breach and information revealed differ by sector? The PRC data can be aggregated into business sectors (finance, retail, medical, other), government, education, and NGO.[12]

Data breaches in the medical sector are about double any other sector, with a huge increase in the last couple of years. This could be a fact, a function of disclosure, or a function of disclosure and reporting. In contrast to the aggregated data, the main source of data breach in the medical sector is lost paper documents and lost laptops. But, insider fraud has a rising role.

---

12. More granular data, including firm identifiers, can be obtained directly from the PRC website. The Open Security Foundation did have a public online database (until 2007, see it used in the Karagodsky and Mann [2011] reference), but it now is behind a permission wall. Efforts to obtain access were not successful. These two sources both draw from public announcements of data breaches. Cursory analysis comparing the two databases for overlapping years shows similarity, but they are not identical.

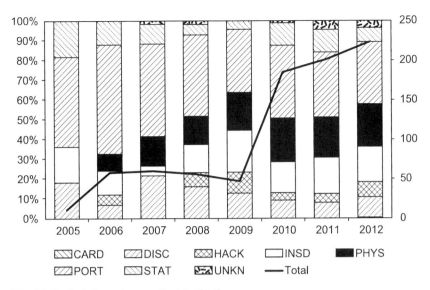

Fig. 11.6 Data breaches, medical institutions

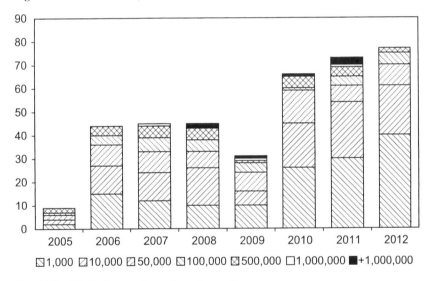

Fig. 11.7 Medical, records per breach over time

(Recall that for the aggregated data, outsider hacking appears the greatest threat.) The vast majority of data breaches for medical institutions are small breaches –1,000 to 10,000 records lost—but a lot of these data breaches reveal SSN. However, when the number of records lost with SSN is considered relative to other sectors, the medical sector is not the largest problem sector. (See figures 11.6, 11.7, and 11.8.)

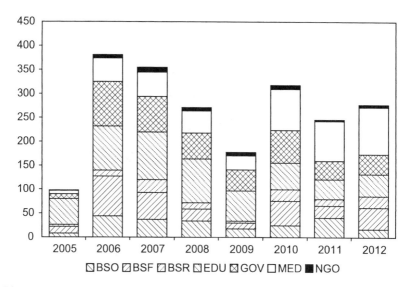

Fig. 11.8 Number of breaches with SSN by sector

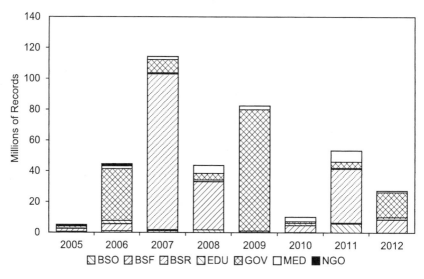

Fig. 11.9 Records with SSN by industry

The chart (fig. 11.9) on records lost that compromise SSN reveals that retail is another sector that has a lot of data breaches. As shown in figures 11.10 and 11.11, the vast majority of data breaches in retail are by hackers. The number of records lost per breach is generally very small, and the number of breaches that reveal SSN is generally quite small. But, when the retail sector experiences a big exposure (2007 and 2011, and Target in 2013,

Information Lost and Data Breaches 327

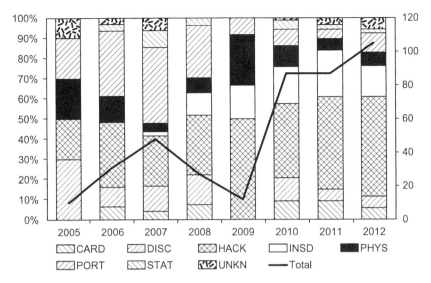

Fig. 11.10 Data breaches, retail

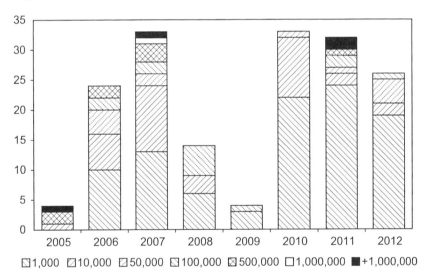

Fig. 11.11 Retail, records per breach over time

not yet in the data set), the loss of records with SSN is enormous. The chart also reveals that 2009, which was the low point for overall breaches, was low because of the low number of small retail breaches. The Great Recession hit consumer spending and small business retailing relatively hard. So, the relationship between macroeconomic activity and data breaches may warrant further analysis. (See figures 11.10 and 11.11.)

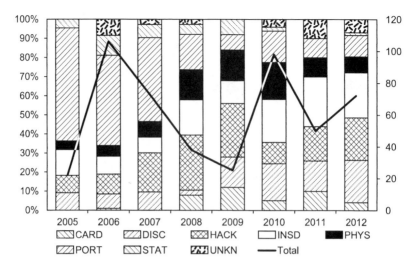

Fig. 11.12 Data breaches, finance/insurance

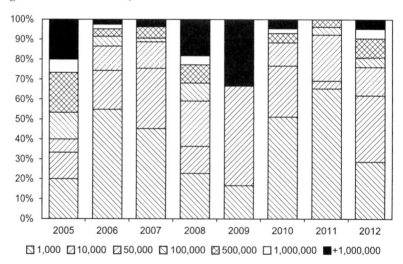

Fig. 11.13 Financial, records per breach over time

A third sector of particular interest is financial and insurance institutions. The number of data breaches appears to be under control. However, the origin of the breach through insiders is a significantly greater share than in other sectors, and both hackers and unintended disclosures are also large. Very large breaches occur nearly every year, along with mid-size breaches, and these breaches often contain SSN. (See figures 11.12 and 11.13.)

Government and educational institutions lose data both from hacking and from unintended disclosure. The bulk of the losses in the education

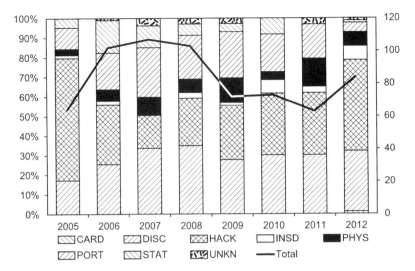

Fig. 11.14 Data breaches, educational institutions

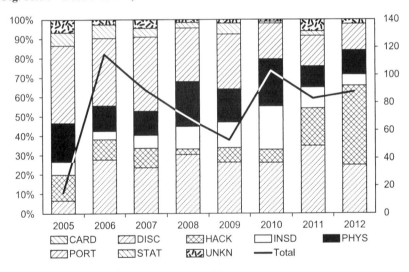

Fig. 11.15 Data breaches, government entities

sector are small, but the government has experienced some very large losses, and with a large number of records containing the SSN. (See figures 11.14, 11.15, 11.16, and 11.17.)

In sum, the sectoral decomposition of the data suggests that a one-size-fits-all approach to evaluating the costs of data breaches or the approach to data security is not appropriate. The sectors differ in terms of how data are lost and which size breach is most prevalent.

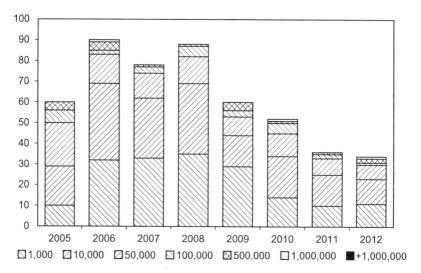

Fig. 11.16 Educational institutions, records per breach (2005–2012)

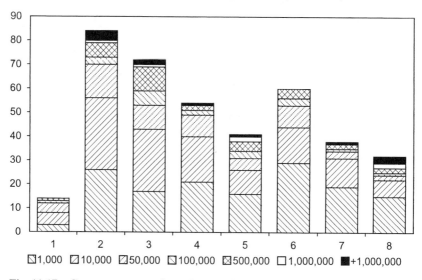

Fig. 11.17 Government, records per breach (2005–2012)

11.3.4 Cross-Border Data Breaches

Cross-border data breaches have two dimensions. A US institution or consumer may lose information to foreign perpetrators or a US institution, when it incurs a data breach, may expose the personal information of a foreign person or firm. What are the characteristics of these cross-border breaches? The picture is quite murky. First, only the United States has, since 2003, required public announcement. So a time series of public

Table 11.1 Geographical origin of external information lost, percent of incidents

	2007	2008	2009	2010	2011		2012
America-North	23	15	19	19	20	United States	16
America-South	3	6	n/a	<1		Colombia	1
						Brazil	1
Asia-east	12	18	18	3	2	China	2*
Asia-north/central	9	n/r	n/r	0	n/r		
Asia-south/southeast	14	3	2	6	1		
Europe-East, Russia, Turkey	24	22	21	65	67	Romania	28
						Russia	5
						Armenia	1
						Bulgaria	7
Europe-west/south/north	9	3	10	2	4	Germany	1
						Netherland	1
Middle East	5	n/a	5	n/a	n/a		
Africa	1	1	2	4	1		
unknown	n/r	n/r	31	n/r	10		

Source: Verizon (2014), Data Breach Investigations Report.
* External threats from China: 30 percent of threats; only 2 percent focused on financial (as opposed to industrial) information. The focus of this section of the chapter is not on industrial espionage.
n/r = not reported.

and reported disclosure is, at present, only available for US firms. When US firms incur a data breach, further information about the cross-border incident is obtained through firm surveys by consultancies such as Verizon or Ponemon/Symantec. Data on consumers' exposed information is self-reported to the US Federal Trade Commission or by other survey. In short, data on international breaches is spotty and incomplete.

Verizon reports that about 20 percent of incidents are US hackers compromising the data of US firms. However, Verizon reports a significant rise in the Central-Eastern European (CEE) countries as origin of compromise, which it reports as organized crime targeting smaller US firms using point-of-sale or other skimming-type devices (this is consistent with the prevalence in the PRC data on small breaches in the retail sector). Note, however, the very large share of incidents where the origin of the data breach cannot be determined. (See table 11.1.)

With regard to specific countries in CEE, Bulgaria and Romania (especially singled out in the 2012 Verizon report) joined the European Union (EU) in 2007. At that point, these countries should have been brought under the umbrella of the EU Directives on Privacy (1998), Privacy and Electronic Communications (2003), and Data Retention (2006). So, it is perhaps a surprise that so much threat activity emanates from these countries. However, another point to consider is that the EU has focused security strategies on data-in-transit, not data-at-rest. This is because the EU Directives

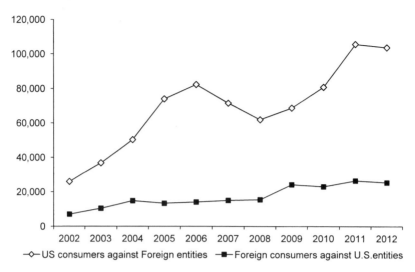

Fig. 11.18 Cross-border fraud complaints, number
Source: FTC: Consumer Sentinel Network.

stringently limit data retention. In contrast, the US security emphasis is on data-at-rest. It is possible that the different security focus of US versus EU methods exposes weakness in the US data-in-transit protocols that can be exploited by forum shoppers who have different knowledge sets. (See more discussion of Directives below.) Sullivan (2010) and MacCarthy (2010) discuss security and gaps in approach in the global payment card industry.[13]

The KPMG reporting on data breaches in the United Kingdom presents a quite different picture. The United States remains the largest source of global incidents (about 50 percent of the incidents in January–June 2012), but that is down from 75 percent of the incidents taking the KPMG data for 2008–June 2012. The KPMG does not even report separately the CEE region or any of its countries. The United Kingdom originates about 10 percent of incidents, which is not a country that Verizon examines separately. Whether the origin of breaches is indeed so different depending on who is surveyed, or whether the reporting is so uneven across countries, is an obvious question.

Considering just consumers, rather than a survey of firms as from the previous sources, the FTC reports that cross-border consumer fraud continues to be dominated by US consumers reporting to the US FTC. Cross-border consumer complaints (e.g., foreign consumers complaining about US firms) account for about 13 percent of all fraud complaints and that percentage has not changed over time. (See figure 11.18.)

---

13. The focus of discussion of chip-and-pin technology in the context of the Target data breach supports this hypothesis of technology forum shopping by hackers.

In sum, in the United States, much information is lost the old-fashioned way (e.g., lost laptops and paperwork and unintended disclosure). But, information lost via cross-border hacking is increasingly important in all sectors, with insider-originated losses particularly notable in finance. Many more data breaches occur with small numbers of records lost, but in any given year, the largest breaches with a huge number of records and high proportion of SSN can occur in any sector. So, should the focus of security protection be on the numerous small breaches or the very few disastrous breaches? Finally, sectoral variation and variation in the size of the breach and in how information is lost may be relevant when considering the role for a domestic focus versus a global emphasis on information security. These are all ripe issues for the Digitization Agenda.

11.4 Market Discipline versus Nonmarket Regulatory and Legal Discipline

This section reviews evidence on strategies to discipline market actors to internalize the costs of data breaches and balance the benefits of information aggregation against the costs when information is lost. If market discipline is sufficiently robust, regulatory intervention or private legal action may not be necessary.

A key problem, noted in the frameworks (section 11.2), is that there are multiple actors. Whether or not a firm will take action to reduce the probability or type of data breach depends not only on whether the market punishes the right firm, but also on how and who bears the burdens of lost information. For example, the costs of notification and of ameliorating a data breach (e.g., issuing new credit cards) could be the main channel for market discipline. Similarly, fines imposed within the self-regulatory hierarchy (e.g., between merchants, card issuers, and payment processors) offer a disciplining device, as do fines levied by a regulatory agency (such as the Federal Trade Commission). Finally, legal suits brought by those suffering the information loss could be sufficiently threatening, or actually costly enough, to encourage firms to enhance their data security or design their information systems differently, although the international nature of theft adds another dimension to the legal challenge.

Data on the costs of breaches is an integral part of the analysis—but how to measure costs, and costs borne by whom? Should the focus be on costs to prevent or costs to remediate? How might market actors respond when information is lost? If the company is customer-facing, such as a retail firm, sales might drop as customers buy from competitors. If the company is a financial intermediary, such as a payment processor, it may be shunned or fined by other parts of the payment chain. If the company is a technology firm, corporate governance of its own activities may be questioned. If the company is in the health-care sector, its reputation may suffer. How costly are these market responses to the announcement of a data breach, and how costly relative to the costs of enhanced security?

11.4.1 The Role for Disclosure

The disciplinary mechanisms noted above all require that a data breach be acknowledged. But, to whom the data breach should be disclosed—those whose data are compromised or an intermediary whose responsibility it is to safeguard the data, or to a government entity (or other) that can force remediation—is less clear. As noted in the frameworks (section 11.2), individuals are, by definition, atomistic. So, the individual may lack market power to discipline whomever lost the data. Moreover, with cognitive bias and limited rationality, disclosure to individuals may not yield the right incentives to protect one's own information, nor improve the outcome if data are lost. Intermediaries are fewer in number, but this market position may reduce the incentive to prevent or remediate a data breach, disclosed or not. With layers of intermediaries, moral hazard is another issue as one intermediary may free ride off the security approach of another. Disclosure to a government entity that can press for remediation and induce investment to avoid future losses might be socially optimal, as in the case of the information steward modeled above.

A US state law, first introduced in 2003 in California as Senate Bill 1386, mandates that organizations that maintain personal information about individuals must make a public announcement if the security of the information has been compromised. The legislation further stipulates that the organization responsible for the breach must notify each individual for whom it maintained information—this is a direct cost rather than simply an indirect cost of, say, loss of reputation. The law forced every firm doing business in California to comply. By 2007, forty-six of the US states had adopted similar versions of a breach-disclosure law, although to date there is no federal legislation governing most personal data.[14]

The US approach of such broad-based disclosure to individuals is unique around the world.[15] Among other countries, only the United Kingdom has legislated disclosure, but the disclosure is to a governmental agency. Similarly, Japan requires disclosure to a governmental agency, but the scope of incidents that must be disclosed has been narrowed on account of excessive information flooding the agency. Australia is considering whether a specific disclosure law is necessary or whether existing law addresses disclosure. The European Union's approach heretofore under the 2003 Directive on Privacy

---

14. There is federal legislation protecting children (COPPA), health (HIPPA), and financial data (Grahm-Leach-Bliley Act) but generalized personal information is not protected. At the state level there is a patchwork of legislation that protects some information in some states—for example, databases with drivers' license information are in the public domain in some states, but not in other states. For a complete review of US data security legislation, see Stevens (2012).

15. See Global Privacy Alliance (2009) for a comprehensive review.

and Electronic Communications has not required disclosure of information loss. But the promulgated and evolving General Data Protection Directive will require disclosure of material breaches to a supragovernmental unit (European Commission 2012).

Does disclosure even work to reduce the incidence of data breaches, and at what cost? There is relatively little research on whether disclosure itself works to reduce data breaches.[16] Romanosky, Telang, and Acquisti (2011) find that US breach disclosure rules reduce identity (ID) theft by about 6 percent. On the other hand, Romanosky, Acquisti, and Sharp (2010) consider the optimality of US-style disclosure. Considering parameters of cost to disclose, response of consumers to disclosure, consumer harm, and reduced rates of data breach, they find that US-style disclosure is probably too costly relative to the gains.

There is evidence that consumer-limited rationality is a problem. Survey evidence from Ponemon Institute (2012) indicates that 85 percent of consumers are very concerned about data breaches. Comparing 2012 with 2005, twice as many consumers recall receiving a notification of a data breach (25 percent vs. 12 percent). But, about 60 percent thought that the communication informing them of the breach was "junk mail." So, data security has salience, but people do not necessarily respond to disclosure as expected. Retzer (2008) argues that broad-based disclosure rules desensitizes the recipient to the announcement, which works counter to the role that disclosure should play as a disciplining device.

Even so, firms need to be aware that loss of trust could matter. Nearly 90 percent in the Ponemon Institute study said they had or might discontinue their relationship with the firm over a data breach (Target lost customers, revenues, and profits and its CEO stepped down). Consumers have reason to punish firms that lose their data. Around one-quarter of consumers who received a data-breach notification experienced identity theft. Consumers whose SSNs were compromised were five times more likely to experience identity theft. The average out-of-pocket consumer costs of a data breach ranged from $400 to $700 (2005–2012; Javelin Strategy and Research 2013). This is substantially higher than the per-record costs that businesses bear, as will be discussed below.

11.4.2 Trends in Business Costs: Lost Business and Remediation

If cleaning up after a data breach is sufficiently costly to a business, then presumably that business will undertake action to improve information security. Calculations suggest that the loss to a business of a data breach coming from customer turnover and reputational loss can be the relatively more important cost of a data breach, particularly in the United States. On

---

16. There is much more research (discussed next) on whether disclosure punishes firms, which presumably is the first step needed for firms to receive the signal to safeguard data.

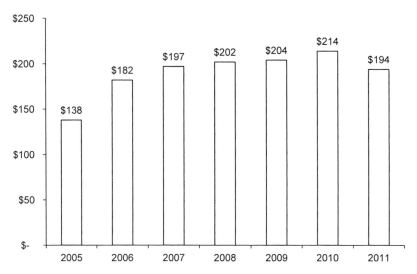

Fig. 11.19 Per record cost of data breaches, average all sectors
Source: Ponemon Institute (2012).

the other hand, remediation costs (customer notification, assistance, audits) are increasingly important (Ponemon Institute 2012).[17] There is substantial variation across sectors in the cost per record loss. Financial and health care were two sectors that had a high prevalence of fraud and a high prevalence of SSN losses. The higher costs of remediation could be due to these factors. (See figures 11.19 and 11.20.)

Comparing the business costs of losing data across countries reveals some interesting observations. There is substantial variation in cost per record lost, and also substantial variation in the components of the cost per record lost as disaggregated into detection, notification, postbreach costs, and lost business costs. However, these costs do not seem to depend on level of income of the economy and vary substantially across countries within the same jurisdiction (e.g., the EU). Therefore, the cost of a data breach to a business appears to be related to its sector and its customers, which would create a variable landscape of incentives to invest in information security.

First, consider the comparison across countries of overall cost per record lost. Countries that have a lower per capita income (India) have a lower average cost of records lost. This reflects lower domestic costs in general (which is consistent with the Balassa-Samuelson effect). On the other hand, countries

---

17. The cost per record lost as presented by the Ponemon Institute is calculated only for breaches of 100,000 records or less. Against these costs, it is possible for a firm to assess the benefits of engaging in better information security. For example, Symantec now offers an online calculator for potential risk of information loss: http://eval.symantec.com/flashdemos/campaigns/small_business/roi/.

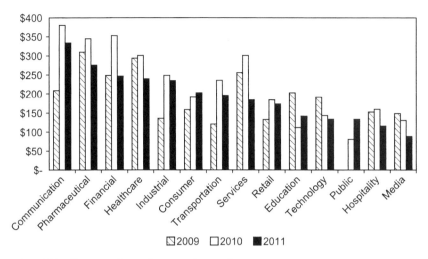

Fig. 11.20 Per record cost (by sector) over time
Source: Ponemon Institute (2012).

with similar regulatory environments (Germany, France, and Italy in the EU) have significant variation in the cost per record lost. These differences in cost, despite the same regulatory environment, could be due to different sectoral distribution of firms, or could reflect heterogeneity in consumer attitudes and response to data breaches.

Comparing sectoral variation across countries, it is not the case that countries with high costs (Germany) or low costs (India) have the highest or lowest cost in all sectors. For example, costs in the communication sector in Germany are quite low, but costs in the communication sector in India are rather high. Considering particular sectors across all countries, costs in the financial sector are highest among sectors (although not in India). But otherwise there is not a clear pattern where costs in certain sectors are always highest or lowest. (See table 11.2.)

Next, consider a decomposition of what types of costs are incurred by a data breach (as opposed to cost per record lost). In all countries the notification cost is the smallest component (although largest in dollar terms in the United States, which makes sense given the California law), and the lost business cost (from customer churn, etc.) is the largest, and relatively larger for the United States, which may also be consistent with the US disclosure law. On the other hand, detection of a breach is relatively larger for other countries compared to the United States, suggesting that the California disclosure law may, over time, have made detection by US firms more a matter of course (and therefore less expensive) rather than a special one-off event.

Using data variation over location, sector, and decomposition of costs would be a valuable research project for the Digitization Agenda. This

Table 11.2 Per record by sector (2011)

	Germany ($)	India ($)	United Kingdom ($)	Australia ($)	France ($)	Italy (%)	Japan ($)	United States ($)
Services	344.92	64.77	135.59	125.99	176.87	104.28	195.39	185.00
Industrial	318.18	38.43	103.24	134.92	111.63	101.60	n/a	235.00
Hospitality	290.11	148.20	147.92	99.21	145.05	90.91	n/a	116.00
Financial	275.40	40.57	158.71	199.40	218.85	147.06	365.88	247.00
Consumer	203.21	52.64	147.92	164.68	189.84	70.86	105.08	203.00
Retail	149.73	31.53	92.45	84.33	100.80	52.14	96.45	174.00
Technology	147.06	64.00	92.45	169.64	195.45	188.50	328.51	134.00
Public sector	129.68	23.70	95.53	101.19	75.94	62.83	84.18	134.00
Communications	89.57	140.40	n/a	n/a	128.61	89.57	124.96	334.00
Pharmaceutical	n/a	n/a	184.90	n/a	n/a	131.02	150.26	276.00
Overall (not average of sectors)	195.19	42.85	121.73	136.90	163.10	104.28	132.77	194.00
Exchange rate (2011)	0.748	49.124	0.649	1.008	0.748	0.748	82.931	

Source: Ponemon Institute (2012).

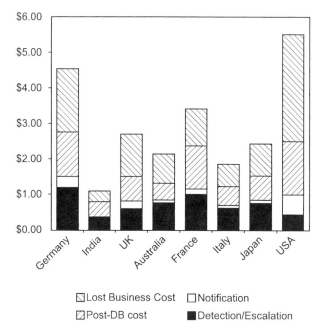

Fig. 11.21 Costs per breach by type of cost, in millions (2011)
Source: Ponemon Institute (2012).

research project would best be engaged with the detailed firm-level data that underpins the publicly available databases. (See figure 11.21.)

11.4.3 Market Value of Stolen Information

Another approach to measuring the value of information lost through a data breach is to go directly to the market. How much is stolen data worth? Getting this information in a systematic way is difficult. Snapshots of value in the market show very large ranges of value of stolen data and it is hard to map the valuation of stolen data to the sectors that have experienced data breaches. As a point of comparison, however, the value of "bank account credentials" at anywhere from $30 to $850 could be compared to the business cost per record lost of $250 in the financial sector (US data). Against the value of credit card information (worth 50 cents to 30 dollars on the open market), the business cost per record lost in retail is $174. If we consider just the business cost, perhaps the most efficient response is to just pay the thieves. But, recall that the consumer cost was multiples of the business cost. (See table 11.3.)

11.4.4 Discipline by Equity Market

The direct cost of a data breach is not the only way in which market discipline can work. A number of studies investigate whether the stock market

Table 11.3   Value of data (multiple Internet sources accessed early 2013)

	2007		2008		2009	
	Low ($)	High ($)	Low ($)	High ($)	Low ($)	High ($)
Credit card information	0.45	12.50	0.60	30.00	0.85	30.00
Bank account credentials	20.00	725.00	10.00	1,000.00	15.00	850.00
Full identities	6.50	15.00	0.70	60.00	0.70	20.00
E-mail accounts	2.50	35.00	0.10	100.00	1.00	20.00

"punishes" firms that lose customer data. (See appendix table 11A.1.) These papers use the same methodology—cumulative abnormal returns (CAR)—but differ somewhat in the time horizon over which they calculate the normal return as well as the window over which they calculate the CAR. They differ in the measure of the market against which to assess the abnormal return. There also can be a difference in terms of whether to measure losses as a percent of stock market value or in dollars. On balance, the stock market discipline appears limited as a strategy for aligning private incentives when it comes to increasing the security of information against data breaches.

The predominant conclusion is that there is a negative, short-term, statistically significant effect of a breach disclosure announcement on the equity market price of the announcing firm. The conclusion appears only when SSN are lost. Campbell (et al. 2003) sums up the findings: "we do not find a significant market reaction when we examine security breaches that are not related to confidentiality. In contrast, we find a highly significant negative reaction for those breaches that relate to violations of confidentiality" (445). Considering sector-specific comparators, rather than the broad market indicators as in Karagodsky and Mann (2011), relatively larger CAR losses are associated with data loss by banks and by health-care firms when SSN are lost and when data are lost or stolen through an intrusion by a hacker. This is consistent with the higher per-record cost for these sectors as noted earlier.

Are these results economically large compared with what it might cost to put into place security systems and procedures to avoid information loss? Karagodsky and Mann evaluate the dollar losses for four representative firms, one from each sector (bank, retail, computers, and health), by using the findings on CAR and calculating the cumulative decrease in the firms' value thirty days following the breach announcement event. The cumulative dollar loss ranged from $170,000 (JPMorgan Chase and Gap) to $1 billion (IBM) and $7.5 billion (Pfizer). This calculation depends not only on the loss per share, but also the number of shares outstanding. Firms with more shares outstanding experience a larger dollar loss, and the loss can be quite large. Whether such dollar losses are large enough to incentivize firms to increase information security depends on the cost of those systems and procedures, a topic beyond the bounds of this chapter, but which is critical to the cost-benefit analysis.[18]

11.4.5 Policy Intervention: Standardization amid Globalization

A back-of-the envelope calculation suggests that the macroeconomic business cost of information lost in the United States in 2011 was $40 billon, and triple that if consumer costs are added.[19] Is this large or small in a $14 trillion economy? Seems small. But, considering just the business costs, it is relatively larger when the reference is net business investment in equipment and software of $107 billion (US Department of Commerce, Bureau of Economic Analysis, NIPA table 5.2.5). The distribution of these costs across sector and size of firm is key for whether the market discipline will work. But for policymakers, the macroeconomic size may be the most relevant for considering intervention.

Policy intervention has many possible faces; two are standardized regulations and enforcement through fines. A key question is, who should be the policy target? The numerous consumers and customer-facing firms, or the relatively few intermediaries that transmit and/or aggregate information? The market-power analysis already suggests and data confirm that the cost to remediate a data breach per consumer exceeds most per business-related costs.

Oussayef (2008) and Orr (2012) suggest that the focus should be on the consumer—the originator but also ultimate user of information value, and the point of greatest cost of loss according to the data. A response to the consumer's limited rationality would be to standardize communications with them and, for example, standardize privacy policies. But, generally, this is not the direction that regulation or the market is going.

Another approach would be to standardize regulations for the relatively fewer intermediaries. However, countries differ in the focus for security (data-in-transit vs. data-at-rest) as noted earlier. How do firms that operate in both the United States and the EU address this problem? The US-EU Safe Harbor Agreement (discussed in more detail in Mann, Eckert, and Knight [2000]) remains the operational agreement governing cross-border information flows between the United States and Europe. US firms operating within the Safe Harbor Agreement self-certify as to their informa-

---

18. Research on security costs include: Brecht and Nowey 2012, and Demetz and Bachlechner 2012.

19. Assumes $200 per record lost and 200 million records lost. Fifty million reported records lost with SSN, grossed up by two (about half of breaches reveal SSN) and grossed up again by two (about half of SSN breaches disclose the number of records). Assuming the consumer costs of $400 (low end of the Javelin estimate) triples the total.

tion security arrangements and submit an enforcement policy to the US Department of Commerce.[20] Fundamentally, the Safe Harbor remains a self-regulatory mechanism that rests uncomfortably against the mandate-oriented approach of the EU Directives.[21]

Within the EU, the issue of standardization is emerging with still-evolving EU General Data Protection Regulation. As currently promulgated, this regulation would address information security both within the EU and between EU firms and firms in other countries. It would harmonize regulations for all members. Presumably, this may cause some standards to be loosened (in Germany, for example) and others to be tightened. It would extend these rules to all foreign companies processing data for EU citizens and EU firms could not transmit data to countries with insufficient protection.[22] Disclosure of data breaches would be within twenty-four hours, which is quite a switch from no disclosure now. Fines for data breaches could be up to 2 percent of global revenue, which is potentially huge. Disclosure to whom, assigning blame for a breach, and enforcement are also issues that remain in discussion.

In another cross-border policy discussion, the Federal Deposit Insurance Corporation (FDIC) (2004) considered the implications of "offshoring" financial activities to third parties in foreign countries. It noted that, while the Gramm-Leach-Bliley Act affirmed that US data-protection rules covered personal information regardless of its geographic location, it also noted that it can be difficult in practice to ensure the extraterritorial application of US rules. In particular, fragmentation and global information flows mean that US firms may not have (or may choose not to have) full transparency over the location of their information. Third party breaches can yield large and broad-based thefts.[23]

Within the United States, the Federal Trade Commission has been playing a more active role. The legal grounding for FTC jurisdiction is contract law. The FTC argues that firms that lose data are breaking the terms of service based on their privacy statement. Fines can be large: $800,000 fine for Spokeo under the Fair Credit Report Law.[24] But these fines do not always work to change behavior; for example, Wyndham has been fined three

20. US Department of Commerce, National Telecommunications and Information Agency. http://www.ntia.doc.gov/page/chapter-1-theory-markets-and-privacy.
21. For more on the market versus mandate approach to international data, see Mann (2001) and Mann and Orejas (2003).
22. At present, data transit is allowed to Argentina, Canada, Iceland, Norway, the United States under the Safe Harbor, and to various important financial centers—Switzerland, Lichtenstein, the Isle of Man, and Guernsey.
23. *New York Times*, "In Hours, Thieves Took $45 Million in A.T.M. Scheme," May 9, 2013. http://nyti.ms/ZKTw5H.
24. Edward Wyatt, "U.S. Penalized Online Company in Sale of Personal Data," *New York Times*, June 12, 2012. http://www.nytimes.com/2012/06/13/technology/ftc-levies-first-fine-over-internet-data.html.

times.²⁵ Another strategy is the mandated audit: many years and a big price tag could change the balance between which is more costly, to protect data or to experience a breach and incur both immediate and long-lived audit costs. A caveat to the firm's decision based on possible FTC punishment is that the advocacy of the FTC has a political dimension to it.

Finally, the issue of cross-border regulation of information comes up in global trade negotiations. The World Trade Organization General Agreement on Trade in Services (WTO GATS) is a positive list approach to trade negotiations. This is as opposed to the negative list approach whereby trade flows between countries are assumed to be unburdened by regulations, tariffs, and quotas, except for specific derogations (the negative list). (This is the so-called most favored nation principle, embraced in the WTO-precursor of the General Agreement on Tariffs and Trade [GATT].) The positive list approach implies that regulatory and tax treatment of bilateral data flows must be individually negotiated, thus creating the potential for a complex web of jurisdictions and regulatory guidelines.

11.4.6 Legal Recourse: Evolving Notion of "Standing"

The role of the legal profession is evolving, and may play a more important role in firms' decisions to invest in data security.[26] Initially, and still true in general today, courts have found that data breach cases have no standing because the link between a data breach and any future potential harmful use of that data cannot be proved ex ante. Simply losing data (as in losing property) is not sufficient grounds for a case, since in the United States there is no right to privacy. The costs of information loss have heretofore been hard to quantify as well (although this is changing, as per data above). Without threat of legal action, there is reduced incentive for firms to improve data protection.[27]

However, research suggests that the legal approach may be beginning to have traction as a disciplining device in the cases of breaches of financial

---

25. "The Federal Trade Commission filed suit against global hospitality company Wyndham Worldwide Corporation and three of its subsidiaries for alleged data security failures that led to three data breaches at Wyndham hotels in less than two years. The FTC alleges that these failures led to fraudulent charges on consumers' accounts, millions of dollars in fraud loss." http://www.ftc.gov/opa/2012/06/wyndham.shtm.

"In response, Parsippany, N.J.-based Wyndham moved to dismiss the complaint . . . saying . . . that the FTC 'singled out' Wyndham in 'unprecedented litigation.' . . . that the commission has neither the expertise nor the statutory authority to establish data security standards for the private sector." http://www.scmagazine.com/wyndham-hotels-challenges-ftc-security-suit-over-breaches/article/258559/.

26. See Fryer, Moore, and Chown (2013) and Bamberger and Mulligan (2011) for an extensive review of theory and practice.

27. A potential new direction is to focus on "industry standards": If a firm experiencing a data breach did not employ "industry standards," the courts are more likely to find against the firm, especially if data are used inappropriately, as in the case of RockYou, Inc (http://www.ftc.gov/enforcement/cases-proceedings/1023120/rockyou-inc).

and medical information. Romanosky, Hoffman, and Acquisti (2012) find a 3.5 times greater probability that a firm will be sued when financial data are involved. Settlement is 30 percent more frequent when there is allegation of financial loss, even higher for compromised medical information and if a class action lawsuit is a threat.

More generally, the risk of class action suits appears to be increasingly important to legal consultants. Poneman indicates that legal defense costs have risen steadily, from accounting for 6 percent of costs (2006) to 15 percent of costs in 2011 (Gibson Dunn 2012; Ponemon Institute, 2012). Increased legal costs and threats of legal costs increase incentives for firms to protect data and to avoid becoming embroiled in a case, even if the case would not go against them. But these potential legal costs also cause firms to push back against disclosure, particularly of the magnitude and sensitivity of information lost. Finally, whether potential legal costs will yield the right balance for information security investment is very unclear.

11.4.7 Challenges Facing an Expanding Insurance Market

The frameworks (section 11.2) pointed out the difficulties of creating insurance markets and products. Key information on the probability and costs of a data breach are not well known (although the latter is becoming clearer). Moreover, with the patchwork of regulations (across states and countries), it is not clear what circumstances would trigger an insurance policy payout, and what business or consumer costs in the event are covered or not.

Nevertheless, rising appreciation of the costs of data breaches is creating an expanding business opportunity for business insurers such as Marsh, Liberty Mutual, Hartford, Munich Re, and Chubb, among others. Individual-facing providers such as LifeLock and Experian's ProtectMyID are also on the rise.

11.4.8 Increased Information Security: The Costs

Given the costs of a data breach, it is not surprising that firms are investigating whether the benefits of investing in information security are greater than the costs of incurring a data breach. A full review of this literature is beyond the scope of this chapter. There are theoretical articles and practitioner analysis, and many firms whose business it is to sell information security solutions.[28] As part of the firm's decision, it is not just the investment cost, but also considerations of organizational behavioral in information security management (Kwon and Johnson 2012).

Moreover, the public good nature of the Internet can promote free riding, such that an increased expenditure on security by a firm may not improve

---

28. Selected research includes Aurora et al. 2004; Gordon and Loeb 2006; Bojanc and Jerman-Blazic 2007; Carty, Pimont, and Schmid 2012.

its overall security if other firms do not also improve security. August and Tunca (2011) examine this question in the context of a theoretical model when patches for known security flaws are installed at different speeds. See also Arora et al (2006) and Arora, Nandkumar, and Telang (2006).

Once information security is institutionalized, will investment costs decline? An important consideration is whether the investment in information security is against the "normal" intrusion or the "black swan" event. Do security investments differ for these two types of event? Is there a ratcheting up of security, even if the threat remains the same?

From a standpoint of organizational behavior, security professionals will want to ensure that the rare event never happens on their watch. But, if the way in which a rare event takes place changes with the technology frontier, it may imply an ever-increasing security budget. Neuhaus and Plattner (2012) address this issue in the narrow context of software security patches. But the principle needs broader recognition.

To get at the topic of whether data breaches generate media attention, I created a Google Alert using the term "data breach." I classified the media sources into "business," "general," and "security professional." Examining the outcome of the Google Alert for 300 days (from late June 2012 to late April 2013) yielded the following observations. There was at least one article every day. On average, there were one to two articles in the business press, with a single spike over the 300 days at five articles. The general press averaged about two articles per day, with several days spiking to seven articles. In media directed to security professionals, the average daily article count was three, and on more than twenty-five days the number of articles was six, seven, or eight articles. Thus, it appears that there is a lot of communication among security professionals about data breaches. A further analysis of this Alert could reveal whether the articles are about best practices (which could reduce incidence of data breaches) or about threats (which could increase investment in security).

11.5 Considerations for the Digital Agenda

11.5.1 Conceptual Framework

There are three characteristics of the information marketplace that pose challenges to the pricing of information and the balancing of costs and benefits of securing data: (1) information economies of scale and scope, (2) differential market power among participants, and (3) unknown probability distributions of data breaches and abuse of information.

The conceptual challenge is to put all three elements into a model. Probably the most difficult is to combine the economies of scale/scope and the probability function because the cost-benefit calculation regarding today's data breach is a function of all future possible data breaches. Numerical simulation models are one possible approach, but these need parameterization using data.

11.5.2 Data Needs and Analysis

An increasing amount of data is becoming available on the costs of data breaches to businesses and consumers. More analysis of these data as to the relationships between sectors, types of data lost, various costs associated with data loss, and nationality of perpetrator and victim of data loss is beginning to become possible. Research will be fruitful, but depends on access to a wide range of what often is proprietary data. Ensuring wider availability of these data would enhance research.

However, key variables are not known. What is the probability of a data breach? The "dog that didn't bark" (that is, transactions or databases that were not compromised) would seem to be greater than those that are compromised, but we do not know. Getting a handle on the probability of a data breach by sector, size of firm, or national jurisdiction is key for starting to evaluate and balance the costs of protecting data against the costs of intrusion. In addition, understanding the relationship between data lost and data abused is important. Most data appear to be lost the old-fashioned way, not stolen. Is the likelihood of abuse low or even zero for that kind of data breach? In this regard, the large but infrequent malicious data breaches would seem to be more costly than the small but frequent breaches, but more analysis of data breaches by size, sector, and type of breach is needed.

The relationships between costs and probabilities are not known. For example, the cost of investing in data security and how that affects the probability of a data breach would be useful. A second cost (more appropriately thought of as a lost benefit) is associated with limits on aggregating data (which is one outcome of the EU Directives); do these affect the probability of a breach? Investing against the infrequent but disastrous event may be inefficient, particularly in a rapidly changing technological environment.

11.5.3 International Jurisdiction

The information marketplace and many firms are global, but policy jurisdictions and consumers are still local. Countries differ in their emphasis on information security and data-in-transit versus data-at-rest, and these differences can create exploitable gaps for hackers (but also opportunities for security solutions). Considering ways to reduce international arbitrage offers an area for research in the political, economic, and technological spheres.

Countries also differ in their approach to information aggregation, protection, and breach disclosure. These differences are not likely to be overcome, since deep-seated cultural values play some role. More work is needed on the value of information, the value of protection, and the costs of a breach both within and across international borders.

Appendix

Table 11A.1 Summary of literature review of equity market effect of data breach

Author	Days to calculate market model	Market index	Interval for CAR calculation	No. events in the data set	Time period covered	Mean CAR % loss by window (reported if significant)
Campbell et al. (2003)	121	NYSE AMEX NASDAQ	−1 to +1	43	1997–2000	−0.02
Acquisti, Freidman, and Telang (2006)	92	NYSE NASDAQ	0 to +1 0 to +2 0 to +5 0 to +10	79	2000–2006	−0.58 −0.46 0.21 1.3
Cavusoglu, Mishra, and Raghunathan (2004)	160	NASDAQ	2 days Day 0 Day +1	78	1996–2001	Not significant −0.0086 −0.0123 (check magnitudes)
Kannan, Rees, and Sridhar (2007)	50	SIC codes control group S&P 500 index	−1 to +2 −1 to +7 −1 to +29	72	1997–2003	−0.65 −.4 2.22
Gatzlaff and McCullough (2010)	245	Value-weighted S&P500 index	Day 0 0 to 1 0 to x in one day increments to 0 to +35	77	2004–2006	−0.57 −0.84 avg.: −0.74
Karagodsky and Mann (2011)		NYSE, NASDQ, Ken French Sectors 1. banks 2. health 3. technology 4. retail 5. insurance 6. brokers	Day +1 Day −1 to +7 Day −1 to +7			−0.7 range: 1–1.3 1.2 2.5 no loss 1 no loss no loss

References

Acquisti, Alessandro. 2010. "The Economics of Personal Data and the Economics of Privacy." Working Paper, Heinz College, Carnegie Mellon University.

Acquisti, Alessandro, Allan Friedman, and Rahul Telang. 2006. "Understanding the Impact of Privacy Breaches." 35th Research Conference on Communication, Information and Internet Policy, Telecommunications Policy Research Conference.

Alloway, Tracy. 2014. "AIG Offers Insurance against Cyber Injury." *Financial Times*, April 23.

Anderson, Horace E. 2006. "The Privacy Gambit: Toward a Game-Theoretic Approach to International Data Protection." Pace University Law Faculty Publications, Pace University Law School. http://www.researchgate.net/publication/31873523_The_Privacy_Gambit_Toward_a_Game_Theoretic_Approach_to_International_Data_Protection.

Anderson, Ross, Chris Barton, Rainer Bohme, Richard Clayton, Michel J. G. van Eeten, Michael Levi, Tyler Moore, and Stefan Savage. 2012. "Measuring the Cost of Cybercrime." Conference Paper, Workshop on the Economics of Information Security.

Arora, Ashish, Christopher M. Forman, Anand Nandkumar, and Rahul Telang. 2006. "Competitive and Strategic Effects in the Timing of Patch Release." Working Paper, Carnegie Mellon University.

Arora, Ashish, Dennis Hall, C. Ariel Pinto, Dwayne Ramsey, and Rahul Telang. 2004. "An ounce of prevention vs. a pound of cure: How can we measure the value of IT security solutions?" Lawrence Berkeley National Laboratory.

Arora, Ashish, Anand Nandkumar, Rahul Telang. 2006. "Does Information Security Attack Frequency Increase with Vulnerability Disclosure? An Empirical Analysis." Working Paper, Carnegie Mellon University.

Arrow, Kenneth J., and Gerard Debreu. 1954. "Existence of an Equilibrium for a Competitive Economy." *Econometrica* 22:265–90. doi:10.2307/1907353.

August, Terrence, and Tunay I. Tunca. 2011. "Who Should be Responsible for Software Security? A Comparative Analysis of Liability Policies in Network Environments." *Management Science* 57 (5): 934–59.

Bamberger, Kenneth A., and Deirdre K. Mulligan. 2011. "Privacy on the Books and On the Ground." *Stanford Law Review* 63 (247): 247–315.

Bojanc, Rok, and Borka Jerman-Blažič, 2008. "Towards a standard approach for quantifying an ICT security investment." *Computer Standards & Interfaces* 30 (4), 216–222.

Brecht, Matthias, and Thomas Nowey. 2012. "A Closer Look at Information Security Costs." Working Paper, Workshop on the Economics of Information Security.

Campbell, K., L. A. Gordon, M. P. Loeb, and L. Zhou. 2003. "The Economic Cost of Publicly Announced Information Security Breaches: Empirical Evidence from the Stock Market." *Journal of Computer Security* 11 (3): 431–48.

Carty, Matt, Vincent Pimont, and David W. Schmid. 2012. "Measuring the Value of Information Security Investments." IT@Intel White Paper, Intel IT Best Practices Information Security, January. http://www.intel.com/content/www/us/en/it-management/intel-it-best-practices/information-security-investments-paper.html.

Cavusoglu, Huseyin, Birendra Mishra, and Srinivasan Raghunathan. 2004. "The Effect of Internet Security Breach Announcements on Market Value: Capital Market Reactions for Breached Firms and Internet Security Developers." *International Journal of Electronic Commerce* 9 (1): 69–104.

Data Loss Database-Open Source (DLDOS), Open Security Foundation public database. http://attrition.org/dataloss/dldos.html. (As for first quarter 2012, this database is no longer available for immediate download.)

Demetz, Lukas, and Daniel Bachlechner. 2012. "To Invest or Not To Invest: Assessing the Economic Viability of a Policy and Security Configuration Management Tool." Working Paper, Workshop on the Economics of Information Security.

European Commission. 2012. "Proposal for a Regulation of the European Parliament and of the Council on the Protection of Individuals with Regard to the Processing of Personal Data and on the Free Movement of Such Data (General Data Protection Regulation)." http://ec.europa.eu/justice/data protection/document/review2012/com_2012_11_en.pdf.

Federal Deposit Insurance Corporation. 2004. "Offshore Outsourcing of Data Services by Insured Institutions and Associated Consumer Privacy Risks." June. https://www.fdic.gov/regulations/examinations/offshore/.

Fryer, Huw, Roksana Moore, and Tim Chown. 2013. "On the Viability of Using Liability to Incentivise Internet Security." Working Paper, Workshop on the Economic of Information Security.

Gatzlaff, Kevin M., and Kathleen A. McCullough. 2010. "The Effect of Data Breaches on Shareholder Wealth." *Risk Management and Insurance Review* 13 (1): 61–83.

Gibson Dunn. 2012. "2011 Year-End Data Privacy and Security Update." February 7. http://gibsondunn.com/publications/pages/2011YearEndDataPrivacy-SecurityUpdate.aspx.

Global Privacy Alliance. 2009. "Breach Notification Legislation Key Elements to Consider." August. http://ec.europa.eu/justice/news/consulting_public/0003/contributions/organisations_not_registered/the_global_privacy_alliance_en.pdf.

Goldfarb, Avi, and Catherine E. Tucker. 2010. "Privacy Regulation and Online Advertising." doi: http://ssrn.com/abstract=1600259.

Gordon, Lawrence A., and Martin P. Loeb. 2002. "The Economics of Information Security Investment." *ACM Transactions on Information and System Security* 5 (4) 438–57.

Greenstein, Shane, and Ryan McDevitt. 2011. "The Global Broadband Bonus: Broadband Internet's Impact on Seven Countries." In *The Linked World: How ICT Is Transforming Societies, Cultures, and Economies*, edited by The Conference Board.

Hann, Il-Horn, Kai-Lung, Hui, Tom S. Lee, and I. P. L. Png. 2002. "Online Information Privacy: Measuring the Cost-Benefit Trade-Off." Twenty-Third International Conference on Information Systems. http://www.comp.nus.edu.sg/~ipng/research/privacy_icis.pdf.

Hirsch, Dennis D. 2006. "Protecting the Inner Environment: What Privacy Legislation Can Learn from Environmental Law." *Georgia Law Review* 41 (1): 1–62.

Ioannidis, Christos, David Pym, and Julian Williams. 2013. "Sustainability in Information Stewardship: Time Preferences, Externalities, and Social Co-Ordination." Working Paper, Workshop for the Economics of Information Security.

Javelin Strategy and Research. 2013. "Data Breaches Lead to Identity Fraud." http://www.slideshare.net/JavelinStrategy/data-breach-fraudcostsjavelin.

Kannan, Karthik, Jackie Rees, and Sanjay Sridhar. 2007. "Market Reactions to Information Security Breach Announcements: An Empirical Analysis." *International Journal of Electronic Commerce* 12 (1): 69–91.

Karagodsky, Igor and, Catherine L. Mann. 2011. "Do Equity Market Punish Firms that Lose Customer Data?" Unpublished manuscript.

Kwon, Juhee, and M. Eric Johnson. 2012. "Security Resources, Capabilties and Cultural Values: Links to Security Performance and Compliance." Working Paper, Workshop on the Economics of Information Security.

Lichtenstein, Sharman, and Kirsty Williamson. 2006. "Understanding Consumer Adoption of Internet Banking: An Interpretive Study in the Australian Banking Context." *Journal of Electronic Commerce Research* 7 (2),50-66.

MacCarthy, Mark. 2010. "Information Security Policy in the US Retail Payments Industry." Working Paper, Workshop on the Economics of Information Security.

Mann, Catherine L. 2001. "International Internet Governance: Oh, What A Tangled Web We Could Weave!" *Georgetown Journal of International Affairs* 2 (Summer/Fall). http://journal.georgetown.edu/past-issues/2-2-bioalert/.

Mann, Catherine L., Sue E. Eckert, and Sarah Cleeland Knight. 2000. *Global Electronic Commerce: A Policy Primer*. Washington, DC: Institute for International Economics.

Mann, Catherine L., and Diana Orejas. 2003. "Can the NAFTA Partners Forge a Global Approach to Internet Governance?" In *North-American Linkages*, edited by Richard G. Harris. Ottawa, ON: Industry Canada.

Morton, Fiona Scott. 2006. "Consumer Benefit from Use of the Internet." In *Innovation Policy and the Economy*, vol. 6, edited by Adam B. Jaffe, Josh Lerner, and Scott Stern. Cambridge, MA: MIT Press.

Neuhaus, Stephan, and Bernard Plattner. 2012. "Software Security Economics: Theory and Practice." Working Paper, Workshop on the Economics of Information Security.

Orr, Madolyn. 2012. "Foxes Guarding the Henhouse: An Assessment of Current Self-Regulatory Approaches to Protecting Consumer Privacy Interests in Online Behavioral Advertising." Working Paper, Federal Trade Commission. www.ftc.gov/os/comments/privacyreportframework/00231–57343.pdf.

Oussayef, Karim Z. 2008. "Selective Privacy: Facilitating Market-Based Solutions to Data Breaches by Standardizing Internet Privacy Policies." *Boston University Journal of Science and Technology Law* 14 (1): 104–31.

Ponemon Institute. 2012. "Consumer Study on Data Breach Notification." Sponsored by Experian Data Breach Resolution, June. http://www.experian.com/innovation/business-resources/ponemon-notification-study.jsp.

Retzer, Karin. 2008. "Data Breach Notification: The Changing Landscape in the EU." *Computer Law Review International* 9 (2): 39–42.

Roberds, William, and Stacey Schreft. 2009. "Data Breaches and Identity Theft." *Journal of Monetary Economics* 56:918–29.

Romanosky, Sasha, and Alessandro Acquisti. 2009. "Privacy Costs and Personal Data Protection: Economic and Legal Perspectives." *Berkeley Technology Law Journal* 24 (3): 1061–101.

Romanosky, Sasha, Alessandro Acquisti, and Richard Sharp. 2010. "Data Breaches and Identity Theft: When is Mandatory Disclosure Optimal?" Telecommunications Policy Research Conference. http://ssrn.com/abstract=1989594.

Romanosky, Sasha, David A. Hoffman, and Alessandro Acquisti. 2012. "Empirical Analysis of Data Breach Litigation." Legal Studies Research Paper no. 2012-30, Beasley School of Law, Temple University. http://dx.doi.org/10.2139/ssrn.1986461.

Romanosky, Sasha, Rahul Telang, and Alessandro Acquisti. 2011. "Do Data Breach Disclosure Laws Reduce Identity Theft?" *Journal of Policy Analysis and Management* 30 (2): 256–86.

Singer, Natasha. 2013. "If My Data Is an Open Book, Why Can't I Read It?" *New York Times*, May 25.

Stevens, Gina. 2012. "Data Security Breach Notification Laws." CRS Report for Congress R42475, Congressional Research Service. http://fas.org/sgp/crs/misc/R42475.pdf.

Sullivan, Richard J. 2010. "The Changing Nature of the US Card Payment Fraud: Issues for Industry and Public Policy." Working Paper, Workshop on the Economics of Information Security.
Taleb, Nassim Nicholas. 2001. *Fooled by Randomness: The Hidden Role of Chance in Life and in the Markets.* New York: Random House.
———. 2010. *The Black Swan: The Impact of the Highly Improbable*, 2nd ed. New York: Random House.
Tang, Zhulei, Yu (Jeffrey) Hu, and Michel D. Smith. 2007. "Gaining Trust through Online Privacy Protection: Self-Regulation, Mandatory Standards, or Caveat Emptor." *Journal of Management Information Systems* 24 (4): 153–73.
Thomas, Russell Cameron, Marcin Antkiewicz, Patrick Florer, Suzanne Widup, and Matthew Woodyard. 2013. "How Bad Is It? A Branching Activity Model to Estimate the Impact of Information Security Breaches." Working Paper, Workshop on the Economics of Information Security.
Yan Chen, Grace YoungJoo Jeon, and Yong-Mi Kim. 2013. "A Day without a Search Engine: An Experimental Study of Online and Offline Searches." Working Paper, University of Michigan.
Verizon. 2014. Data Breach Investigations Report. http://www.verizonenterprise.com/DBIR/.

Comment   Amalia R. Miller

As more personal information about consumers is collected, stored, and transmitted by businesses in electronic form, the chances increase that records will be lost. Data breach incidents caused by malicious hacking or theft, or even by accidental equipment loss, can harm the consumers whose information is breached. In the wrong hands, personal information about consumers, such as their Social Security numbers, Internet search and browsing histories, insurance claims, financial transactions, and purchases can be used to harass, embarrass, impersonate, or steal from them.

This chapter argues that data loss is an important concern to be addressed in the digitization research agenda. Mann points in particular to the facts that data breaches at firms remain regular occurrences and that reported cases of breaches affect millions of individual records each year. Even if these breached records comprise only a small fraction of the total amount of data collected, consumer concerns about data breaches can have broader effects. For example, as their actual or perceived risk of data loss increases, consumers may engage in costly behaviors to protect themselves and become less willing to share their personal information with firms. Similarly, firms

---

Amalia R. Miller is associate professor of economics at the University of Virginia and a research associate of the National Bureau of Economic Research.

For acknowledgments, sources of research support, and disclosure of the author's material financial relationships, if any, please see http://www.nber.org/chapters/c13025.ack.

incur costs in protecting the digital information in their care about consumers. This is true for measures aimed at reducing the likelihood of successful breaches, such as data encryption, use of passwords, locks and physical security around computer equipment and storage devices, and security training and procedure for employees. It is also true for measures that reduce the harm from breach incidents (and the appeal of the data to potential thieves), such as collecting less, storing less, aggregating less, and transmitting less data.

This chapter represents an initial attempt to set out an agenda for economic policy research on the issue of data security that considers the tension between the costs of data breaches and of security efforts to prevent them. The chapter first proposes some possible frameworks for assessing the trade-offs and presents some arguments for government intervention. It then reports summary tabulations on disclosed data breach incidents in the United States or affecting US consumers in an empirical section. Finally, a section on policy approaches discusses data security regulations adopted in the United States and elsewhere. In this comment, I summarize the key contributions of each section and suggest some additional topics and issues for consideration in future research on the economics of data security.

The central theme of the framework section is that there are several potential market imperfections that would lead to underinvestment in data security by firms that possess private information on individuals. In particular, firms may not internalize the benefits of their investments in data protection because of incomplete markets for data safety. One reason may be that property rights are not clearly defined for data that is created, collected, and maintained by private companies, but that is *about* particular individuals (who can be harmed by its dissemination). Even with clear property rights, there are information asymmetries between consumers and firms when it comes to data protection, and without policy intervention it could be impossible for consumers to discover what steps are being taken to protect their information or when their information is lost or stolen. As Mann points out in the chapter, the inherent difficulties in assessing the risks of and harms from data disclosure may also prevent markets for data protection from developing because of high transactions costs in devising appropriate contracts. Hence, an agency problem can arise between consumers whose information is being collected and the firms that are entrusted with that information leading to insufficient investment in data protection.

The framework section also discusses the possibility that consumers are either uninformed about risks or not completely rational (or capable of understanding information about risks and rare events) as further reasons for underinvestment in security. The idea is not that consumers want more protection than they are able to obtain from firms but, rather, that they want less than they should want. While the arguments are reasonable, and it is possible that consumers should care more about security than they do (or that they do care more than they show in their behavior), it is worth noting that this general type of argument based on irrationality or limited rationality could also lead to the opposite prediction. Consumers could easily overreact to small risks and demand too much costly data protection.

Although not discussed in the chapter, it may also be interesting to consider how the availability of insurance coverage that protects firms from the financial costs of data breach incidents (either as part of their casualty and property policy or as a separate plan) affects their decisions to invest in data security. Such coverage will typically dampen incentives for firms to invest in data protection, though the effects will be limited if coverage is incomplete (for example, because business loss and reputation effects are excluded) or if premiums are based on past claims experience. The effect could even be reversed in part if large insurers use their data on breach claims to provide incentives and useful guidance to firms about effective investments in data security.

Another issue that merits some attention is the possibility of externalities between firms from investments in data security. Negative spillovers will occur if the risk of theft increases after other firms make their data more secure. This spillover can lead to overinvestment in data security if companies feel compelled to match or escalate beyond the security levels of their competitors. However, if security protections reduce the value of data theft and are not visible to potential thieves, there may instead be positive externalities, comparable to those found in Ayres and Levitt's (1998) study of the LoJack device on auto theft.

In addition to outlining possible market imperfections that apply to data security, this section presents two separate discussions of the types of public policy responses used to address data security. In the first, presented in relation to Hirsch's (2006) pollution metaphor for the risk of data spills as an externality from greater data aggregation, command-and-control process regulation is contrasted with policies that target the outcomes of interest. Because security technologies and threats can evolve quickly, and firms may have better information about the costs and effects of different investments than regulators do, Hirsch argues the first approach, mandating specific data protection polices, is unlikely to be effective. There is some confirmation of this in the empirical finding in Miller and Tucker (2011) that state laws promoting the adoption of data encryption technologies led to an overall *increase* in incidents of data loss (driven by cases of internal fraud and loss of computer equipment). The second discussion of policy in the framework section takes a more legal approach. The options presented are the ones discussed in the policy section of the chapter: (1) mandated data security requirements, (2) government fines or penalties for data loss, and (3) mandated disclosure of data loss.

The empirical section of the chapter provides an overview of some of the recent trends in data breach incidents by economic sector, number of records breached, content of breached data (including SSN or not), and source of the breach (such as computer hackers, paper document loss, computer loss, and insider fraud). While it is hard to infer much from this limited information, a few points are worth noting. Most interesting is that a large share of data loss incidents are not coming from hackers, but are instead a result of insider fraud, accidental loss, or unintentional disclosure. Second, there are differences across sectors in the numbers and content of breaches and trends over time. The trends generally show relatively stable numbers of breaches between 2005 and 2012 (the number of breaches is highest in 2006) and declines in the share of reported breaches with SSN data. However, as Mann points out, it is hard to know if this reflects a decline in actual incidents or worse reporting. Although the framework in the previous section and discussion in most of the chapter is focused on the private sector, the data section also includes summary information on data breaches in the government sector. In theory, comparing public and private sector breaches could provide information about the role of incentives or market imperfections, but that is not possible without a better understanding of the incentives in the public sector and differences in the types of information collected in each sector.

The evidence in this section is necessarily constrained by the limited information available about data breach incidents. As Mann acknowledges in the chapter, in order for the evidence to be useful to inform public policy, more information is needed. First, a major limitation is that researchers only know about publically disclosed (or discovered) incidents. The requirements for disclosure, as discussed in the chapter, are not comprehensive, which means that many incidents do not need to be disclosed to the public. Furthermore, even when disclosure is required, it is unknown how well firms comply with the requirements. It is also impossible to compute risks or rates of information loss from data on breaches alone. We need to know how to scale for the amount of data collected, which is surely increasing over the time period.

The next section discusses existing public policies addressing data security. Building on the second discussion of policy approaches in the framework section, the chapter expands the discussion of the relative benefits of disclosure requirements and subsequent "market discipline" compared to rules that mandate security protections or impose penalties for data breaches.

In describing the policy environment, Mann contrasts the approaches taken in the United States and the European Union (EU). European policy has tended to favor global requirements for privacy and security protection measures on data holders, often specifying technology, staffing, and procedures for data collection, use, and transfers. These rules include strict limits on what information can be collected or shared and how long it can be stored, as well as requirements to obtain consent for different actions. US policy on data security is more heterogeneous, varying at the state level and according to the type of information. The main policy lever applied in the United States is the requirement that data breach incidents be disclosed publically and to affected consumers. There are federal disclosure requirements for certain types of information (breaches affecting children or including financial or health information) and broader disclosure rules in many states.

After distinguishing between the typical US and European approaches to data security policy (process regulation versus disclosure rules), the chapter notes recent convergence in the area disclosure rules. The EU and several other counties are now implementing or considering imposing these requirements. Interestingly, the EU disclosure rules will be more demanding than those in the United States (greater coverage and shorter time frame) and will be applied along with regulatory fines for data breaches. It is also worth noting that some US state and federal rules do mandate specific security procedures, such as data encryption or consent requirements for exchange, and other rules require that standards for "reasonable protection" be met without explicitly listing them or include incentives for the adoption of certain security technologies in the form of relief from disclosure requirements for data breaches (see, for example, Miller and Tucker 2009, 2011).

Assessing the appropriateness of different policy responses to data security requires empirical information about the relative costs to firms and consumers of data breach incidents and their prevention. This chapter reports some preliminary estimates of the costs to firms and consumers from disclosed data loss incidents, suggesting that costs are at least twice as large for consumers. Specifically, the chapter cites an estimated range out-of-pocket cost to consumers from each data breach of $400 to $700 from a report by Javelin Strategy and Research, and an estimated range of average costs to businesses per record lost of about $100 to $200 from a report by the Ponemon Institute. These initial estimates suggest that data disclosure requirements are not sufficient to cause firms to fully internalize even the costs of disclosed breaches, which suggests a role for greater intervention beyond disclosure rules to increase investment in data security.

However, uncertainty about these values, and the fact that they only reflect average costs, means that more reliable and extensive information could either support or overturn this initial conclusion. Furthermore, the actual costs of data loss incidents are likely to change over time as a result of evolving policies outside of data security. As discussed in the chapter, the costs to businesses from breaches should be expected to increase in the future if the legal environment evolves in such a way that consumers gain access to more recourse options to sue companies for breaches even without showing direct harm. The basis for these claims would be negligence for failing to meet industry standards for data protection or breach of contract for violations of privacy or security provisions. These legal options would make disclosure a more powerful tool for encouraging security investments, though enforcement would impose costs on consumers and lead to uncertain outcomes, which might be avoided with a more direct regulatory approach, such as penalties for breaches.

It is important for policymakers to recognize that the level of business investment in data security is not the only factor that affects the frequency or cost of data breaches. Consumer behavior, such as deciding what information to share and with what companies, as well as their reactions to disclosed breaches (involving their own data or not), can affect data loss and may itself respond to changes in public and corporate policies. For example, the cost of breaches may be low if consumers limit or distort the information they provide to firms. If improved data security at the firm level makes consumers more willing to share personal information, or less careful about protecting themselves from theft (by actively monitoring their financial accounts for fraud and checking credit reports for possible identity theft), the incremental cost from successful breaches could increase. The cost of breaches could also increase with better data security if the breaches that are least costly to prevent involve information that is least valuable to thieves and least harmful to consumers. Finally, the costs of data breaches are also affected by public and private efforts to prevent, detect, and penalize attempts to *use* lost or stolen data. For example, careful monitoring of credit card charges, financial transfers, and insurance claims by companies that process these transactions can prevent thieves from making use of the data. On the public policy side, data theft is already illegal, as are most fraudulent and malicious uses of lost or stolen data. However, enforcing these rules requires that resources be devoted to law enforcement for investigating crimes and developing new tools to address new threats. The ideal combination of data hoarding, data protection, consumer and firm efforts to detect fraud, and government efforts to investigate and punish fraud and theft, will depend on the costs of these efforts and their effects on the frequencies and costs of data loss.

In summary, this chapter about data loss introduces an important topic to the research agenda on the economics of digitization. It raises many questions for researchers and policymakers to consider and summarizes some of the initial empirical information on the topic. This is a research area with many open questions and opportunities for contributions by economists.

References

Ayres, Ian, and Steven D. Levitt. 1998. "Measuring Positive Externalities from Unobservable Victim Precaution: An Empirical Analysis of Lojack." *Quarterly Journal of Economics* 113 (1): 43–77.

Hirsch, Dennis D. 2006. "Protecting the Inner Environment: What Privacy Regulation Can Learn from Environmental Law." *Georgia Law Review* 41 (1): 1–63.

Miller, Amalia R., and Catherine Tucker. 2009. "Privacy Protection and Technology Diffusion: The Case of Electronic Medical Records." *Management Science* 57 (7): 1077–93.

———. 2011. "Encryption and the Loss of Patient Data." *Journal of Policy Analysis and Management* 30 (3): 534–56.

12

Copyright and the Profitability of Authorship
Evidence from Payments to Writers in the Romantic Period

Megan MacGarvie and Petra Moser

To encourage creativity, copyright creates intellectual property rights for "original works of authorship" in literature and music, computer software, web content, and many other important sectors of the digital economy.[1] Extensions in the length of copyright have emerged as a key policy lever by which national governments attempt to strengthen property rights in ideas. For example, the US Copyright Act of 1998 and the UK Copyright Act of 2011 extended the length of copyright protection for music from "life of author" plus fifty years to "life of author" plus seventy years. Proponents of longer copyrights argue that such shifts encourage creativity by increasing expected profits from writing (Liebowitz and Margolis 2005). Scott Turow, president of the American Authors' Guild warned that regimes that weaken copyright, such as digital piracy may cause the "slow death of the American author" (Turow 2013). Empirical analyses of file sharing, however, reveal no significant effects on the quantity or quality of recorded music (Oberholzer-Gee and Strumpf 2007; Waldfogel 2012, [chapter 14, this volume]), which suggests that the importance of copyright protection may be overstated.

Systematic evidence on the effects of stronger copyrights on the profit-

Megan MacGarvie is associate professor of markets, public policy, and law at Boston University and a faculty research fellow of the National Bureau of Economic Research. Petra Moser is assistant professor of economics at Stanford University and a faculty research fellow of the National Bureau of Economic Research.

We wish to thank Xing Li, Hoan Nguyen, and Alex Pitzer for excellent research assistance, and Stanford's Second-Year Graduate Research Program, the NBER Program on the Economics of Digitization, the Kauffman Foundation, and the National Science Foundation through CAREER Grant 1151180 for financial support. For acknowledgments, sources of research support, and disclosure of the authors' material financial relationships, if any, please see http://www.nber.org/chapters/c12997.ack.

1. Title 17, US Code 2011.

ability of authors, however, is scarce because data on payments to authors is typically not available to the public.[2] Evidence from a sample of 93 payments between 1746 and 1800 to authors of the Scottish Enlightenment indicates that payments to authors increased independently of the establishment of temporary monopoly rights for authors in 1774 (Sher 2010 258). Case studies of European composers Giuseppe Verdi (1813–1901) and Robert Schumann (1810–1856), however, indicate that composers of operas and songs benefited financially from the introduction of copyright protection for music. Scherer (2008 11) argues that, after copyright was introduced in parts of northern Italy in 1837, Verdi "saw the possibilities of copyright and exploited them to the full" to amass a fortune and reduce his efforts at the "exhausting drudgery" of composing operas.[3] The most systematic evidence comes from DiCola's (2013) survey of 5,000 US musicians, including composers, performers, and teachers. In this survey, the average respondent reported drawing 12 percent of their revenue from copyright-related sources.

This chapter adds to existing evidence by introducing a new, systematic data set on payments that publishers made to writers in Romantic Period Britain. These data include payments for 207 works of fiction to 105 authors by 11 publishers between 1800 and 1829. We have collected these data from digitized excerpts of ledgers of transaction, correspondence, and other types of archival materials for nineteenth-century publishing houses in Britain made available in the online database British Fiction 1800–1829: A Database of Production, Circulation, and Reception.[4] Longman & Co. of London, one of the largest publishing houses in Romantic Period England, published 133 of these titles, by 68 authors. Competing publishers include John Murray, Archibald Constable & Co., Cadell & Co., William Blackwood, and Oliver & Boyd.

This data collection is part of a broader research agenda, which examines the role of copyright as well as contractual agreements between authors and publishers on the creation of literary works. Once complete, a new quantitative data set for Romantic Period writers will include information on counts of physical copies, production costs, price, revenue, and publishers' advertising efforts. A complementary data set, which we collect from the cor-

---

2. For example, a recent study of the movie industry notes, "One of the reasons that IP contracts have not attracted much academic attention is the lack of adequate data" (Harris, Ravid, and Basuroy 2013, 2).

3. Scherer (2008, 11) reports a reduction in Verdi's count of operas per decade from fourteen in the 1840s, seven in the 1850s, two in the 1860s, and one in each of the succeeding three decades. Verdi, however, produced more influential operas later in his career, and may have used his wealth to produce a smaller number of high quality works. With the exception of *Nabucco* (1842), Verdi composed his most influential operas after 1850, thirteen years after the introduction of copyright: *Rigoletto* (1851), *La Traviata* (1853), *Simon Boccanegra* (1857; second version in 1881), and *Aida* (1871).

4. Garside, P. D., J. E. Belanger, and S. A. Ragaz. British Fiction, 1800–1829: A Database of Production, Circulation & Reception, designer A. A. Mandal. http://www.british-fiction.cf.ac.uk.

respondence of publishers and authors, will include information on contract negotiations and other interactions between publishers and authors.

In this chapter we examine changes in payments to authors after a substantial increase in the strength of copyrights in 1814, starting from low levels of protection. Intended to clarify a requirement to deposit copies of all new books with research libraries, the UK Copyright Act of 1814 also increased the length of copyright from twenty-eight years to the remainder of the author's life, and from fourteen to twenty-eight years for dead authors. Li, MacGarvie, and Moser (2014) exploit the fact that this change created a differential increase in the length of copyright for *dead* authors as a result of the Act to identify the effects of stronger copyright terms on price.[5] Difference-in-differences analyses of a new data set of book prices between 1790 and 1840 reveal a large and robust increase in price in response to longer copyright terms. Historical evidence suggests that publishers exploited the extension in copyright to practice intertemporal price discrimination, thereby increasing the average price of books.

Our research for this chapter exploits the fact that extensions in copyright terms under the 1814 Act allowed authors to sell a longer stream of expected revenues to publishers to examine whether—starting from low levels of existing protection—stronger copyright terms may in fact increase payments to authors. Data on payments to authors for 207 titles between 1800 and 1829 confirm that payments to authors increased significantly after 1814. Payments to the author of the median title increased by nearly 100 percent from 83.81 pounds between 1800 and 1814 (*l*, converted to 1800 real terms) to 166.48*l* between 1815 and 1829. On average, payments to authors almost tripled, with an increase from 163.59*l* for sixty-five titles until 1814 to 493.54*l* for 142 titles after 1814. Some of this increase was driven by high payments to the successful poet Sir Walter Scott, whose first novel was published in 1814. Excluding sixteen titles by Scott, payments to the author of the median title increased by 59 percent from 83.0*l* to 131.6*l* after 1814, and payments to the average author nearly doubled from 155.0*l* for sixty-four titles until 1814 to 248.21*l* for 127 titles after 1814.

Our data also make it possible to distinguish lump sum payments and income from profit sharing. These data show that the increase in payments was driven primarily by an increase in lump sum payments to authors. A total of 108 observations are for lump sum payments, thirteen include both types of payments, and eighty-six include income from profit sharing only.

---

5. Existing empirical analyses have found no effects of copyright on price or documented counterintuitive correlations (Khan 2005; Heald 2008). For example, price data for the US publisher Ticknor and Fields indicate that pirated books by European authors sold for a higher price than copyrighted books by US authors between 1832 and 1858 (Khan 2005, 252). Similarly, books that were bestsellers in the United States between 1913 and 1932 sold for roughly the same price in 2006, regardless of their copyright status, possibly because books that are in print seventy-four years after the initial date of publication are a heavily selected sample (Heald 2008).

Lump sum payments for the median title, including thirteen titles with income from profit sharing, more than tripled from 111.91*l* to 361.73*l* after 1814. For the average author, lump sum payments increased from 175.81*l* to 670.40*l*. Excluding Scott, lump sum payments increased from 110.58*l* to 304.99*l* for the median, and from 173.54*l* to 370.71*l* for the average author.

12.1 Copyright in Romantic Period Britain

Copyright was first formalized in Britain's Act for the Encouragement of Learning of 1710, commonly known as the Statute of Anne. The statute granted publishers of new books fourteen years of exclusive rights, with an extension to twenty-eight years if the author was alive at the end of the first fourteen years.[6] In return for exclusivity, publishers were required to register all new books with the Stationers' Company and deposit copies with the British library and eight university libraries in England and Scotland:

> Enacted that nine Copyes [sic] of each book or books upon the best paper that from and after the tenth day of April One thousand seven hundred and ten shall be printed and published as aforesaid or Reprinted and published with additions shall by the printer and printers thereof be delivered to the Warehouse Keeper of the said Company of Stationers for the time being at the hall of the said Company before such publication made for the use of the Royal Library the Libraryes [sic] of the Universities of Oxford and Cambridge the Librarys [sic] of the four Universities in Scotland the Library of Sion College in London and the Library commonly called the Library belonging to the Faculty of Advocates at Edinburgh respectively Which said Warehousekeeper [sic] is hereby required within ten days after demand. (Statute of Anne 1710)

When the first copyrighted books approached the end of their twenty-eight-year term, booksellers who had purchased copyrights sought injunctions from the Court of Chancery to stop competing publishers from printing copies of books that came off copyright. Their argument was that, as a "natural right of the author," copyright was a perpetual common law property right (Patterson 1986, 153; Feather 1988, 79). A decision in the House of Lords in *Donaldson v. Becket* in 1774 ended this "Battle of the Booksellers" (1743–1774; Patterson 1986, 153) and established that, unlike other types of property rights, copyright was limited to a certain number of years, defined by the duration of the copyright term. During these years, infringement was punishable by substantial fines. In 1801, for example, a printer who had violated copyright lost all infringing copies and paid a fine of 3d per sheet, "half to the crown, and half to whoever sued for it" (Seville

---

6. Booksellers had pushed for the Act, and "Except in the preamble, authors were not mentioned at all . . . the Act was a booksellers' act" (Feather 1988, 74–76). For books that had been published before the Act, booksellers received exclusive rights for twenty-one years starting in 1710 (Statute of Anne, §2, London, 1710).

1999, 239). Printers who imported infringing books were fined £10 (Seville 1999, 239), roughly twenty times the average weekly wage of working-class men in the early 1800s (Bautz 2007, 12).[7]

In 1798, a decision in *Beckford v. Hood* (1798, 7 D. & E. 620) called into question the deposit requirement as it established that books were eligible for infringement damages even if they had not been registered with the Stationers' Company. As a result of this decision, the number of book deposits per year fell by 40 percent between 1793 and 1803 (Deazley 2007, 816).

12.1.1   Extensions in the Length of UK Copyright in 1814

On July 29, 1814, to reaffirm the deposit requirement, Britain's Parliament passed

A Bill [as recommended on third re-commitment] to Amend the several Acts for the Encouragement of Learning, by securing the Copies and Copyright, of printed Books, to the Authors of such Books, or their Assigns

It required that—in order to be protected by copyright—publishers had to deposit copies with the British Museum and ten university libraries within twelve months of publication (§2). It also extended the length of copyright to twenty-eight years or the remaining length of the author's life, if the author was alive at the end of the twenty-eight-year term. For books within fourteen years from the first edition by authors who had died within the first fourteen years after first publication, this change implied an increase in the length of copyright from fourteen years under the Statute of Anne to twenty-eight years.

12.2   Data

The main data for the current analysis consist of payments to 105 authors by eleven publishers for 207 works of fiction published in Britain between 1800 and 1829. We have collected these data from a digital depository of archival records in British Fiction 1800–1829: A Database of Production, Circulation, and Reception.[8] These data include information on publishing for 441 titles, drawn from the records for nineteenth-century publishing houses Longman & Co (from the Special Collection of Reading University Library), William Blackwood, Cadell & Co., Constable & Co., John Murray II, and Oliver & Boyd (from the National Library of Scotland), as well as authors' correspondence and historical accounts of Britain's publishing industry.

To extract information on payments to authors from these sources, we first

---

7. In continental Europe and the United States, however, UK copyrights were not respected. To prevent the importation of pirated copies into Britain, excise officers were instructed to search luggage for books that may have been intended for resale (St. Clair 2004, 200).

8. Available at http://www.british-fiction.cf.ac.uk/, accessed January–March 2013.

performed an automatic search for keywords for "payment to author," "paid to author," "half profits to author," "cash," "interest," "pounds," "guineas," "copyright," and other terms connected with payments to authors. This algorithm identifies payments for 203 of 441 titles; we read these records individually to collect information on types, amounts, and dates of payments for each of these titles. We also examine the remaining 238 titles to search for payment and accounting information, which an automatic search may miss.[9]

For example, Longman's entries for Amelia Opie's *Tales of Real Life* (1813) read:

> Divide Ledger Entry, Longman & Co.
> 10 June 1813. The impression consisted of 2000 copies.
> . . .
> Jan 1814. By this date, 1693 copies had been sold, for a total of 973. 9. 6.
> [Jan 1814]. Half profits to author, 272. 8. 9; half profits to Longman & Co, 272. 8. 9.
> . . .
> Jan 1815. A further 172 copies had been sold by this date, for a total of 98. 18. 0.
> Jan 1815. Half profits to author, 43. 15. 8; half profits to Longman & Co, 43. 15. 7.
> . . .
> [Jan 1816]. The remaining 120 copies had been sold by this date, for a total of 69. 0. 0.
> [Jan 1816]. Half profits to author, 34. 9. 5; half profits to Longman & Co, 34. 9. 4.
> . . .
> [June] 1820. Half profits to author, 10. 12. 4; half profits to Longman & Co, 10. 12. 3.[10]

A careful reading of these entries allowed us to identify four additional observations with payment data. Detailed accounting data are available for ninety-eight additional titles. For eleven of these ninety-eight titles, accounting data report a loss for the publisher and no payment to authors. We exclude six titles for which payment is to a translator of a volume of a collected work rather than to the original author.

We then check the genre for all 207 titles; 206 of 207 titles are novels. The remaining title is John Banim's *Revelations of the Dead-Alive*, a collection of fictional essays (published in 1824 by Simpkin & Marshall).

Each of these observations covers a single book, and the large majority are for first editions (200 of 207). Three of the remaining seven observations

---

9. Out of 320 titles with dated information, records for an additional 69 titles include no information on payments to authors or other information on revenue and expenses. Thirty-three records for Oliver & Boyd include detailed data on advertising, which we plan to explore in future work.

10. Longman Divide Ledger 1D, p. 300, and Longman Divide Ledger 2D, 214.

are for first editions of new *volumes*. For example, an agreement between the author Charlotte Smith and the publisher Longman in 1802 covers volumes 4 and 5 of *The Letters of a Solitary Wanderer: Containing Narratives of Various Description* (both published in 1802).

Lags between payments and years of first editions occurred when publishers reviewed draft copies of a new book and agreed to purchase the rights to that book. For example, Longman wrote in a December 3, 1812, letter to Amelia Opie, concerning the author's *Tales*:

> We sent you a parcel by Coach on Tuesday which we hope you have received ere this. In the parcel we put a note informing you that we had paid the £4. 10. 0 agreeable to your request. // Your title pleases us; & we shall be happy to see the MS as soon as you can favor us with a perusal of it. (Longman Archives, Longman I, 97, no. 383)

And two days later, on December 5 of the same year, warning the author:

> We have certainly been playing somewhat at cross purposes. Perhaps your first note was not quite as clear as it ought to be to the weak capacities of booksellers; & they, by conning it frequently over, rendered the subject less clear to their comprehension. However now we understand that you have finished one of the *series* of Tales, & that the others are not written; on consideration, we would not advise you to put any part of the collection into the hands of the printer till you have written the whole that are to be published at one time; as, in this case, you would be harrased [*sic*] out of your life both with writing & correcting the proof sheets. (Longman Archives, Longman I, 97, no. 387)

In addition to the editors' own reviews, editors also asked other authors to comment on new manuscripts. For example, Longman writes to Amelia Opie on October 11, 1813, in reference to Elizabeth Benger's *The Heart and the Fancy* (published in 1813 by Longman):

> pray accept our best thanks for your remarks on the Heart & the Fancy (Longman Archives, Longman I, 98, no. 75).

The median payment to an author is made in the year in which the first edition of a book is published; fifty-five payments are made in the year before the first edition, and five payments are made two years in advance.

For most titles, publishers submitted payments to authors for a decade or less; for some titles, however, payments to authors span up to thirty-five years for profit-sharing payments. For example, in June 1836, Longman recorded a payment of 1.23*l* to Amelia Opie for *The Father and Daughter*, which was first published in 1801 (Longman Divide Ledger 3D, 259.) In June 1840, Opie received a payment of 2.41*l* from Longman for her novel *Temper* (published in 1812; Longman Divide Ledger 3D, 261*)*.

Among 207 titles, 133 include the publisher Longman; another eighteen include both publishers Blackwood and Cadell & Co., and three titles each include Blackwood and Cadell & Co. alone. Constable is a copublisher on six of Longman's titles, including three with Sir Walter Scott, and Colburn is a copublisher of one title with Longman.

Sixty-nine of 105 authors appear only once as an author in the data set. Six authors publish more than five books. Among them, Anna Maria Porter (1780–1832) accounts for nine novels, including the popular love story *The Hungarian Brothers* (published in 1807 by Longman, set in the French Revolutionary Wars). Porter collaborated with her sister Jane Porter on two volumes of stories *Coming Out* and *The Field of the Forty Footsteps* (published by Longman in 1828) and *Tales Round a Winter Hearth* (published in 1826 by Longman).[11]

The data include two books that were first published after the death of the authors. For William Williams's (d. 1791) *Journal of Llewellin Penrose* (published in 1815 by Murray), Murray paid a lump sum of 200*l* in 1814 to the author's estate (173.27 in year 1800 pounds), and published *Journal* in 1815.[12] For Joseph Strutt's (d. 1802) *Queenhoo-Hall*, published in 1808, Murray records a payment of 25.03*l* to Strutt's son.[13] Strutt died before the novel's completion, and the final chapter of the novel was written by Walter Scott.[14]

To calculate lump sum payments to authors and income from profit sharing, we tally individual entries from the ledgers of publishers. For example, Longman's archives record a lump sum payment to Opie of 400*l* for the copyright of her *Simple Tales* on April 23, 1806: "Payment to author: 400. 0. 0. Longman. Impression Book No. 3, fol. 53." Revenues from profit sharing are recorded in publishers ledgers, such as:

> Jan 1814. By this date, 1693 copies had been sold, for a total of 973. 9. 6 . . . [June 1834]. By this date, the remaining 8 copies had been sold as follows: 4 sold at 0. 3. 0 each, for a total of 0. 12. 0; 4 sold at 0. 11. 6 each, for a total of 2. 6. 0. Total sum from the sale of these 8 copies: 2. 18. 0. (Longman Divide Ledger 1D, 300; Longman Divide Ledger 2D, 214)

the total of which adds to nominal income from profit sharing of 413.27*l* for Amelia Opie from the *Tales of Real Life*. Nearly all profits are shared equally between authors and publishers. The exceptions are William Godwin's *Mandeville* (published in 1817 by Longman), which earned its author

---

11. In addition to the two books by the Porter sisters, three remaining titles were coauthored: *Coquetry*, by Charlotte Champion Pascoe and Jane Louisa Willyams; *Body and Soul*, by George Wilkins and William Shepherd; and *Tales and Legends*, by Marion and Margaret Corbett. One additional title may have been coauthored by a male and female author within the same family, *The Hebrew: A Sketch in the Nineteenth Century: With the Dream of Saint Kenya* (1828; by Charles William Chaklen and/or Miss Chaklen [E, MS 4016, fol. 170]).

12. Divide Ledger Entry, John Murray II, 15 Aug 1814, MS letter, Murray archives.

13. Murray Archives, Divide Ledger A, 45.

14. MS letter (copy), Murray Archives, Letter Book (Mar. 1803–Sept. 1823), pp. 200–01.

25 percent of profits (in addition to a lump sum payment of 453.41*l*), and twelve titles published on commission—the author was responsible for the costs of the edition and received all the profits after the publisher took a 10 percent commission on the book's sales (St. Clair 2004, 165).

To control for inflation, we convert all amounts into real single unit pounds using Clark's (2013) Retail Price Index with 1800 as the base year. One single unit pound (*l*) equals 20 shillings (s) or 240 pence (d). To calculate income from profit sharing, we convert each payment to year 1800 pounds, using the year of the payment as the base unit for the conversion, and then add the converted amounts to calculate the authors' total income from profit sharing for that title. For example, Opie's nominal income of 413.27*l* is equivalent to 374.19 year 1800 pounds.[15]

To normalize payments to authors by the size of books, we collect information on the length of each title, measured by the total number of pages. These data are available for all 207 titles. The median author earns a total income of 15.17*l* for 100 pages, with an average of 40.74*l* and a standard deviation of 77.86.

To examine whether the 1814 Act may have created a differential increase in payments for authors in different age brackets, we collect data on birth and death years of authors from the *Oxford Dictionary of National Biography* and online sources if no information is available from the latter source. Demographic data are available for sixty of 105 authors (or 152 of 207 titles).[16]

12.3 Lump Sum Payments to Authors

In a lump sum contract, publishers assume all risk and pay for the entire costs of printing and distribution. In return, authors give up any claims on future profits, and transfer copyright to the publisher (St. Clair 2004, 161). For example, Longman & Co. assert their property rights in Jane Porter's historical novel *The Scottish Chiefs* (published in 1810) in a letter to Mr. Barclay on August 12, 1824:

---

15. Available at http://measuringworth.com/ukearncpi/. Accessed on April 24, 2013. An 1820 contract between Scott and his publisher Archibald Constable covered four separate titles: *Ivanhoe, the Monastery, The Abbot*, and *Kenilworth* together were paid an amount of 5,000 guineas for copyright as part of Constable's plan to issue the four novels as part of an octavo set (Letter from Archibald Constable to Scott, 3 Nov 1821, Grierson, VII, 13).

16. The share of authors for which demographic data are available is roughly equal across time periods and across different types of payments. Demographic data are available for twenty-seven authors of forty-six titles until 1814, including twenty authors of twenty-eight titles with lump sum payments only, nine authors of sixteen titles with profit sharing only, and two authors of two titles with both types of payments. Demographic data are available for forty-six authors of 106 titles *after* 1814, including thirty authors of sixty-one titles with lump sum payments only, nineteen authors of thirty-six titles with profit sharing only, and seventy-six authors of nine titles with both types of payments.

The Copyright of the Scottish Chiefs is our property, we having purchased it of Miss Porter, as we have done all her other writings: and we consider it of so much value, that we should not be disposed to deligate [sic] the right of printing an edition to any one. We should however have no objection to sell you an edition of 1000 or 2000 copies. (Longman Archives, Longman I, 101, no. 459B)

Representatives of Longman continue to assert their rights for 21 years in another letter on the 9th of March 1831 (Longman Archives, Longman I, 102, no. 165A).[17]

Across all years, authors of 108 titles receive lump sum payments only, eighty-six receive only income from profit-sharing agreements (without a lump sum payment) and thirteen receive both types of payments.[18] The share of titles with profit-sharing agreements remains roughly constant over time. Until 1814, authors of thirty-eight in sixty-five titles received a lump sum payment; after 1814, authors of eighty-three in 142 total titles received a lump sum payment.[19]

The author of the median title (George Wilkins, *Body and Soul*, published in 1822 by Longman & Co.) received a lump sum payment of 224.45*l*.[20] The average lump sum payment across 121 titles with lump sum payments is 515.07*l*, with a standard deviation of 866.61*l*.[21] By comparison, a working-class male earned a nominal 23.58*l* in 1800 and 32.26*l* in 1829 (35.16 in year 1800 pounds).[22] The smallest lump sum payment is 4.23*l*, for Margaret Hurry's *Artless Tales* (published in 1808 by Longman);[23] the largest lump sum payment is 5928.08*l* for Walter Scott's *The Pirate* (published in 1822 in Edinburgh by Constable & Co. and in London by Hurst, Robinson & Co.).[24]

17. By comparison, copyright for less than one-third of 144 titles by Scottish Enlightenment authors between 1746 and 1800 remained registered in the name of the author (Sher 2006, 243). Registered titles may, however, be more valuable titles; only 40 percent of 360 titles in Sher (2006) were registered.

18. Three in thirteen titles with both types of payments are by Barbara Hofland: *Integrity* (1823), *Decision, A Tale* (1824), and *Self-Denial* (1827). The other ten titles are: Jane Porter's *Thaddeus of Warsaw* (1803), Miss M. G. T. Crumpe's *Isabel St. Albe* (1823), Orton Smith's *Sketches of Character* (1808), Robert Mudie's *Glenfergus* (1820), Scott's *Rob Roy* (1818), William Godwin's *The Seventeenth Century in England* (1817), George Wilkins' *Body and Soul* (1822), James Justinian Morier's *The Adventures of Hajji Baba, of Ispahan* (1824), William Henry Pyne's *Wine and Walnuts* (1823), and Scott's *Waverley* (1814).

19. The share of titles with lump sum payments only also remains roughly constant, with thirty-five of sixty-five titles until 1814 and seventy-three of 142 titles with lump sum payments after 1814.

20. Letter from James Fenimore Cooper to Francis Moore, August 10, 1827.

21. The average lump sum payment across 108 titles with lump sum payments only is 552.75*l*, with a standard deviation of 899.98*l*.

22. Bautz (2007, 12) reports that the typical wage of a working man was between nine and, very exceptionally, forty shillings. If a typical wage was 10s, and workers were able to work fifty weeks per year (which will probably lead us to overestimate total wage), a typical annual wage may have been 500s or 25*l*.

23. Longman Impression Book No. 3, fol. 111.

24. Letter from Joseph Ogle Robinson to Archibald Constable, National Library of Scotland, MS 326, fol.92.

Data on lump sum payments reveal a substantial increase in payments for the median author after 1814. Among thirty-eight titles with lump sum payments between 1800 and 1814, the median payment was 111.91*l* (between Robert Charles Dallas, *Percival*, 1801, and Charlotte Smith, *Letters of a Solitary Wanderer*, 1800, both published by Longman & Co.). Among eighty-three titles with lump sum payments between 1815 and 1829, publishers paid a lump sum of 361.73*l* to the author of the median book (Anna Maria Porter, *The Fast of St. Magdalen,* published in 1808 by Longman), more than three times the median payment between 1800 and 1814. Normalized by page counts, payments to the median author increased from 11.40*l* per 100 pages until 1814 to 32.22*l* per 100 pages afterward (with an average of 16.91*l* per 100 pages and a standard deviation of 16.27 until 1814, and an average of 71.96*l* per 100 pages and a standard deviation of 102.63 after 1814).[25]

The data also indicate that the increase in lump sum payments was heavily skewed toward a small number of authors (figure 12.1). On average, publishers paid authors 175.81*l* in fixed payments until 1814 (with a standard deviation of 221.33, table 12.1) and 670.40*l* after 1814 (with a much larger standard deviation of 999.59). Sir Walter Scott received the largest lump sum payments after 1814, with an average of 2,443.53*l*, 6.60 times the lump sum payments of 370.71*l* for other authors.

This differential change is consistent with survey data for US musicians in a 2011 (DiCola 2013) survey of US musicians, which suggests that more successful musicians draw a larger share of their revenues from copyright-related sources. For example, composers in the top income bracket reported drawing 68 percent of their revenue from copyright-related sources, compared with 12 percent for all musicians (including music teachers, as well as performers).

Even excluding Scott, lump sum payment to authors increase by more than 100 percent from an average of 173.53*l* for thirty-seven titles until 1814 to 370.71*l* for seventy-one titles afterward and from a median of 110.58*l* to 305*l*. Until 1814, the highest lump sum payments are 1,270.41*l* (Frances D'Arblay, *The Wanderer*, published in 1814 by Longman) and 579.56*l* (Sydney Owenson, *Woman: or, Ida of Athens*, published in 1808 by Longman). After 1814, the highest lump sum payments are 1,716.61*l* (Washington Irving, *Tales of a Traveller*, published in 1824 by Murray) and 1,501.15*l* (Sydney Owenson, *The O'Briens and the O'Flahertys*, published in 1827 by Colburn).

---

25. Among thirty-five titles with lump sum payments only between 1800 and 1814, the median payment was 110.58*l* (Smith's *Solitary Wanderer*). Among seventy-three titles with lump sum payments only between 1815 and 1829, publishers paid a lump sum of 396.01*l* to the author of the median book (Amelia Opie, *Tales of the Heart*, published by Longman in 1820), nearly four times larger than the median payment between 1800 and 1814. Normalized by page counts, payments to the median author increased from 11.19*l* per 100 pages until 1814 to 37.08*l* per 100 pages afterward.

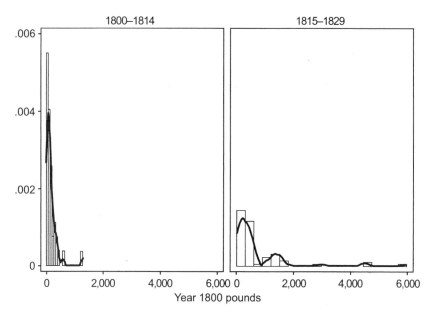

Fig. 12.1 Lump sum payments to authors

Notes: Histogram with Epanechnikov kernel density of lump sum payments per title in year 1800 unit pounds before and after the UK Copyright Act of 1814. The 1814 Act extended the length of copyright from twenty-eight years to life of the author for books whose authors survived more than fourteen years after first publication, and from fourteen to twenty-eight years for books whose authors died within fourteen years of first publication. Data include payments for 121 titles from eleven publishers and sixty-five authors. We have collected these data from archival records, including bookkeeping entries in publishers' ledgers and personal letters from P. D. Garside, J. E. Belanger, and S. A. Ragaz, British Fiction, 1800–1829: A Database of Production, Circulation & Reception, designer A. A. Mandal.

There is a clear shift in the distribution of lump sum payments to authors after 1814 when we exclude Scott (figure 12.2). Overall, we see a movement toward higher lump sum pay, with an increase in the standard deviation from 229.93 to 370.71 and a reduction in the share of small payments. Until 1814, 43.2 percent of the sample earned 100*l* or less; after 1814, 23.9 percent earned 100*l* or less.

12.3.1 Differential Changes in Payments to Younger Authors after 1814

Considering the life expectancy of Romantic Period writers, the 1814 Copyright Act implied a larger increase in copyright for younger compared with older authors. The author of the average title in our data set was 43.1 years old at the time of publication, and the author of the median title was 43 years old. The Act extended the length of copyright from twenty-eight years to "life of author" for living authors, but even based on optimistic calculations, a forty-two-year-old writer could only expect to live another

Table 12.1 Lump sum payments and income from profit sharing

		1800–1814	1815–1829	Diff.
Lump sum payments	Average	175.81	670.40	494.59
		(221.33)	(999.59)	(164.31)
	per 100 pages	16.91	71.96	55.05
		(16.27)	(102.63)	(16.78)
	N	38	83	
Income from profit sharing only	Average	124.49	180.68	56.19
		(182.02)	(487.14)	(105.66)
	per 100 page	17.19	18.09	0.90
		(25.30)	(40.90)	(8.55)
	N	27	59	
Total payments	Average	163.59	493.54	329.94
		(216.82)	(914.02)	(114.96)
	per 100 page	17.88	52.65	34.77
		(21.13)	(92.16)	(11.58)
	N	65	142	

Note: In year 1800 unit pounds. Data on lump sum payments include 108 titles with lump sum payments only and 13thirteen titles with both types of payments. Data on profit sharing are for 86eighty-six titles with profit sharing only. Total payments equal the sum of lump sum and profit-sharing payments. Collected from bookkeeping entries in publishers' ledgers, letters, and other types of archival sources for nineteenth-century publishing houses.

twenty-nine years in 1814.[26] Younger authors, however, could expect to live additional years, and therefore benefited more from the extension to "life of author." At the opposite extreme, authors above sixty-five years benefited more from the extension for books by dead authors from fourteen to twenty-eight years, which allowed them to sell a longer revenue stream to publishers. Only four titles in the data, however, are by authors above sixty-five, so we cannot credibly estimate a differential effect for older authors.

Consistent with a differential increase in the length of copyright, payments to authors below the age of thirty increased by a factor of four after 1814, from an average of 85.08*l* for five titles until 1814 to 426.99*l* for five titles after 1814 (table 12.2). These titles include only lump sum payments. Payments to the median author under age thirty (Francis Lathom, *Very Strange, but Very True!*, published in 1803 by Longman)—increased by a factor of 4.5 from 67.86*l* until 1814 to 304.99*l* after 1814.[27]

By comparison, lump sum payments to authors thirty years of age or

---

26. Based on calculations of life tables in Li, MacGarvie, and Moser (2014), which estimate years of remaining life conditional on living conditions in five-year intervals and on the authors' survival to a five-year age bracket. Forty-two is also the age of the average author at the year of the first edition in a data set of 1,072 book titles with information on price and other characteristics in Li, MacGarvie, and Moser (2014).

27. The median lump payment after 1814 is 304.99*l* (Mary Shelley Wollstonecraft, *The Last Man*, published in 1826 by Colburn).

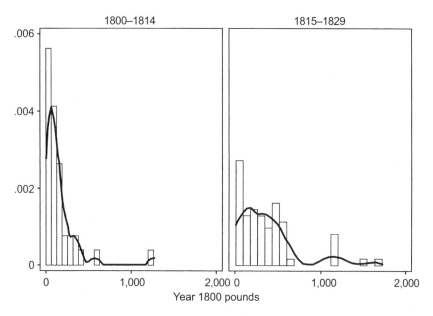

Fig. 12.2 Lump sum to authors, excluding Scott

Notes: Histogram with Epanechnikov kernel density of lump sum payments per title in year 1800 unit pounds before and after the UK Copyright Act of 1814. The 1814 Act extended the length of copyright from twenty-eight years to life of the author for books whose authors survived more than fourteen years after first publication, and from fourteen to twenty-eight years for books whose authors died within fourteen years of first publication. Data include payments for 108 titles from ten publishers and sixty-four authors. We have collected these data from archival records, including bookkeeping entries in publishers' ledgers and personal letters from P. D. Garside, J. E. Belanger, and S. A. Ragaz, British Fiction, 1800–1829: A Database of Production, Circulation & Reception, designer A. A. Mandal.

above increased by roughly a factor of 3.29 from an average of 226.48*l* for twenty-five titles before 1815 to an average of 746.30*l* on average for sixty-five titles after 1814. Payments to the author of the median title increased from 173.24*l* (Jane West, *The Loyalists*, published in 1812 by Longman) to 381.47*l* (John Galt, *Rothelan*, published in 1824 by Oliver and Boyd).

The increase in payments to older authors was in large measure driven by lump sum payments to Scott, who was forty-three years old in 1814, and published fifteen novels after 1814. Excluding Scott, lump sum payments to the average authors above twenty-nine years of age increased by 69 percent from 225.09*l* for twenty-four titles until 1814 to 362.02*l* for fifty-three titles after 1814. Payments to the median author, excluding Scott, increased from 152.01*l* (between Robert Charles Dallas's *Aubrey*, published in 1804 by Longman & Co. and West's *The Loyalists*) until 1814 to 316.76*l* (John Galt, *Sir Andrew Wylie*, published in 1822 by Oliver & Boyd).

Table 12.2   Payments to authors by authors' age

	Author age	1800–1814	1815–1829	Diff.
Lump sum payments				
All authors	Under 30	85.08	426.99	341.91
		(39.82)	(472.33)	(211.98)
	Thirty and above	226.48	746.30	519.82
		(256.14)	(1,090.57)	(221.13)
Excluding Scott	Under 30	85.08	426.99	341.91
		(39.82)	(472.33)	(211.98)
	Thirty and above	225.09	362.02	136.93
		(254.28)	(305.17)	(72.50)
Total payments				
All authors	Under 30	74.21	309.51	235.30
		(38.36)	(434.77)	(153.56)
	Thirty and above	238.59	621.84	383.24
		(254.52)	(1045.05)	(171.81)
Excluding Scott	Under 30	74.21	309.51	235.30
		(38.36)	(434.77)	(153.56)
	Thirty and above	225.70	273.84	48.14
		(245.13)	(285.17)	(54.00)

Note: Lump sum payments for ten titles with authors below age thirty and for ninety titles with authors age thirty and above. Total payments, including lump sum payments and profit sharing for fifteen titles with authors below age thirty and for 137 titles with authors age thirty and above. Data for all authors include information on one title by Sir Walter Scott, first published in 1814, when Scott was forty-three years old, and fifteen titles first published *after* 1814. Data on the age of authors are collected from the *Dictionary of Literary Biography*, the *Oxford Dictionary of National Biography*, and online sources. Total payments to authors calculated from bookkeeping entries in publishers' ledgers, letters, and other types of archival sources for nineteenth-century publishing houses.

12.4 Income from Profit Sharing

For eighty-six of 207 observations on payments to authors, authors only receive income from profit sharing, without lump sum payment; almost all of these authors receive 50 percent of profits.[28] For example, Longman's ledgers list a series of payments for Opie's *Tales of Real Life*:

Jan 1814. Half profits to author, 272. 8. 9; half profits to Longman & Co, 272. 8. 9 . . .
June 1834. Half profits to author, 1. 9. 0; half profits to Longman & Co, 1. 9. 0.

To calculate income that is purely from profit sharing, we convert each of these to year 1800 pound units and sum all payments in year 1800 pounds.

28. St. Clair (2004, 164) explains that profit-sharing arrangements allowed authors and publishers to share profits "either by half or in some other proportion, after all the costs of publishing had been met."

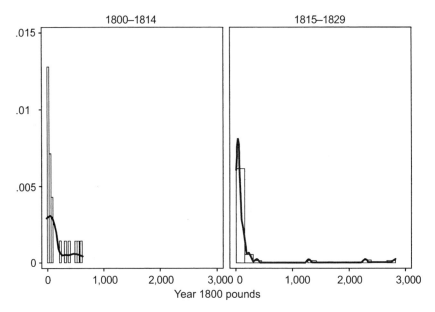

Fig. 12.3 Income from profit sharing

Note: Histogram with Epanechnikov kernel density of authors' income from profit sharing for titles without lump sum payments in year 1800 unit pounds before and after the UK Copyright Act of 1814. The 1814 Act extended the length of copyright from twenty-eight years to life of the author for books whose authors survived more than fourteen years after first publication, and from fourteen to twenty-eight years for books whose authors died within fourteen years of first publication. Data include payments for eighty-six titles from six publishers and fifty-two authors. We have collected these data from archival records, including bookkeeping entries in publishers' ledgers and personal letters from P. D. Garside, J. E. Belanger, and S. A. Ragaz, British Fiction, 1800–1829: A Database of Production, Circulation & Reception, designer A. A. Mandal.

For Opie's *Tales*, this adds to 374.19*l*.[29] Across all eighty-six titles with positive income from profit sharing, the median title earned 46.74*l* (Jane West's *Ringrove*, published in 1827 by Longman & Co.);[30] the average title earned 163.04*l*, with a standard deviation of 415.63.[31]

Income for the average title increased by 45.14 percent from 124.49*l* (for twenty-seven titles, with a standard deviation of 182.02) until 1814, to 180.68*l* (for fifty-nine titles with a standard deviation of 487.14). *Per page*, however, income from profit-sharing payments increased by only 13.5 percent from an average of 17.19*l* per 100 pages (with a standard deviation of

---

29. Longman Divide Ledger Entry 1D, Longman Co., 300 and Longman Divide Ledger 2D, 214.
30. Longman Divide Ledger 2D, 48, 301.
31. The smallest amount of income from profit sharing is 2.17*l* for Elizabeth Ogilvy Benger's *The Heart and the Fancy, or Valsinore* (published 1813 by Longman; Longman Divide Ledger Entry 1D, 296).

25.30) to 18.09*l* per 100 pages (with a standard deviation of 40.90). Payments to the median title declined from 47.65*l* (Margaret Roberts's *Duty*, published in 1814 by Longman)[32] to 46.49*l* (Barbara Hofland, *Patience*, published in 1824 by Longman).

A potential explanation for the lower increase in payments for titles with profit sharing is that they had more uncertain revenue streams, and therefore benefited less from the extension. For example, Longman's Owen Rees writes to Anna Bray on September 26, 1827:

> We very much regret that the sale of [your previous work] *De Foix* has not been such as to warrant our purchasing the copyright of your new work [*White Hood*]; but we would with pleasure undertake it on the plan of dividing the profits.[33]

Then, payments from profit sharing may have failed to increase after 1814, because expected benefits from additional years of exclusivity were small.

12.5 Total Income, Payments to Sir Walter Scott, and Titles without Income

To calculate total income, we add lump sum payments and income from profit sharing for all authors. The median total income—including lump sum payments *and* profit sharing is 130.53*l* (William Henry Pine, *Wine and Walnuts*, published in 1823 by Longman & Co.).[34] The largest total income is 5,928.08*l* (Walter Scott, *The Pirate*, published in 1822 by Constable & Co.) and the smallest total income is 2.17*l* (Elizabeth Benger, *The Heart and the Fancy*, published in 1813 by Longman). The observed increase in profit-sharing payments is heavily skewed toward a small number of titles (figure 12.4). Excluding Scott, however, the distribution is substantially less skewed (figure 12.5).

12.5.1 Sir Walter Scott

Four titles earned Scott more than 4,000*l* each in total income (including lump sum payments and profit sharing): *Rob Roy* (1818; 4,417.028*l* in total payments), *The Pirate* (1822; 5,928.08*l*), *Chronicles of the Canongate*, vol. II (1828; 4,503.44*l*), and *Anne of Geierstein* (1829; 4,455.31*l*). Total payments for Scott's other titles are nearly seven times greater compared with the average 127 titles by other authors after 1814: *The Monastery* (1820; 1,385.81*l*), *Ivanhoe* (1820; 1,385.81*l*), *The Abbott* (1820; 1385.81*l*), *Kenilworth* (1821; 1,385.81*l*), *Peveril of the Peak* (1822; 1,472.97*l*), *The Fortunes of Nigel* (1822;

---

32. Longman Divide Ledger 1D, 73.
33. Longman Archives, Longman I, 102, no. 52B. Bray earned 26.37*l* in profit-sharing income for *De Foix* (1826, by Longman & Co) and 14.92*l* for *The White Hoods* (1828, by Longman & Co).
34. Longman Divide Ledger 2D, 224.

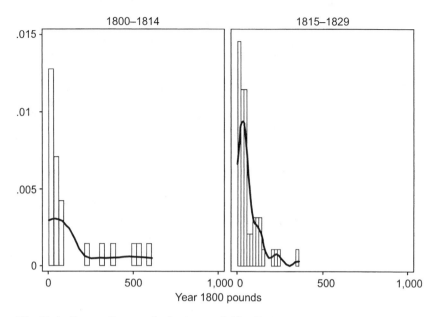

Fig. 12.4 Income from profit sharing, excluding Scott

Note: Histogram with Epanechnikov kernel density of authors' income from profit sharing for titles without lump sum payments in year 1800 unit pounds before and after the UK Copyright Act of 1814. The 1814 Act extended the length of copyright from twenty-eight years to life of the author for books whose authors survived more than fourteen years after first publication, and from fourteen to twenty-eight years for books whose authors died within fourteen years of first publication. Data include payments for eighty-three titles from six publishers and fifty-one authors (excluding Scott). We have collected these data from archival records, including bookkeeping entries in publishers' ledgers and personal letters from P. D. Garside, J. E. Belanger, and S. A. Ragaz, British Fiction, 1800–1829: A Database of Production, Circulation & Reception, designer A. A. Mandal.

1,472.97*l*), *Quentin Durward* (1823; 1,472.97*l*), and *Chronicles of the Canongate*, vol. I (1827; 2931.66*l*).[35]

A celebrated author of poems, such as *The Lay of the Last Minstrel* (1805) and *The Lady of the Lake* (1810), Sir Walter Scott's first novel was published in 1814, with the anonymous publication of *Waverley*. After 1814, the British Fiction data include fifteen novels by Scott, for which he earned an average of 2,570.60*l*.

Constable had initially offered Scott a lump sum payment of 700*l* for the copyright for *Waverley*, but Scott declined Constable's offer, allegedly arguing that Constable's proposed payment was "too much" (Lockhart 1838, 255). Instead, Scott and Constable agreed to a profit-sharing agreement for

---

35. In 1821, Scott sold the copyrights of four novels—*Ivanhoe, The Abbot, Kenilworth*, and *The Monastery*—to Constable for 5,000 guineas, equivalent to 5543.22 year 1800 pounds. Constable also purchased the remaining copyrights of *The Pirate, The Fortunes of Nigel, Peveril of the Peaks*, and *Quentin Durward*, for 5,000 guineas in 1821 (Lockhart 1838, 168).

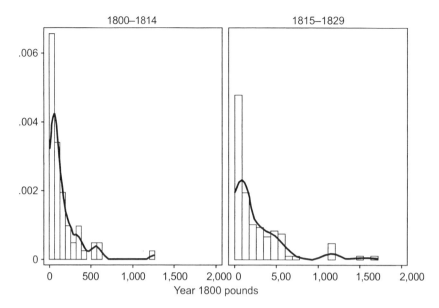

Fig. 12.5 Total payments to authors, excluding Scott

Notes: Histogram with Epanechnikov kernel density of total payments to authors in year 1800 unit pounds before and after the UK Copyright Act of 1814. The 1814 Act extended the length of copyright from twenty-eight years to life of the author for books whose authors survived more than fourteen years after first publication, and from fourteen to twenty-eight years for books whose authors died within fourteen years of first publication. Total payments equal the sum of lump sum and profit-sharing payments. Data include payments for 191 titles from ten publishers and 104 authors (excluding Scott). We have collected these data from archival records, including bookkeeping entries in publishers' ledgers and personal letters from P. D. Garside, J. E. Belanger, and S. A. Ragaz, British Fiction, 1800–1829: A Database of Production, Circulation & Reception, designer A. A. Mandal.

the first edition of *Waverley*, earning the author 455.72*l* in profit sharing for the seventh edition alone.[36] After the *Waverley* novels proved successful, Scott received large lump sum advances with additional income from profit sharing:

> For most of the novels after *Waverley* the method adopted was somewhat different. Scott sold to Constable and Co. the right to print two thirds of the first impression of 10,000 (in some cases 12,000) books for a fixed sum. Until 1822 or thereabouts the price of the two thirds was £3,000, but it seems to have been thereafter reduced to £2,500. The remaining one third was reserved for James Ballantyne, but in regard to one half of this third James acted as Trustee for Sir Walter. (Grierson 1938, 146)

---

36. The 455.72*l* for the seventh edition is the only payment for *Waverley* in the British Fiction data. St. Clair (2004, 245) reports "When a ship bringing the first copies of the latest *Waverley* novel from Edinburgh docked in London, the books would be distributed by noon the next day, even breaking the rules against working on the Sabbath."

Scott's experience, however, was unusual. For one, Scott was able to use an inheritance in 1805 (Grierson 1938, 33) to purchase a third share of Ballantyne & Company, a publishing house that was owned by Scott's childhood friend James Ballantyne and James's brother, John Ballantyne (Ballantyne 1838, 17). Following this purchase, many of Scott's works were copublished by Constable and Ballantyne, leaving Ballantyne in control of the production (Kelley 2010, 13).

Scott's novels were also extremely long-lived and frequently earned Scott substantial amounts of additional payments for later editions. For example, *Guy Mannering* (published in 1815 by Longman and Constable, printed by Ballantyne) was published in eleven editions (Garside 1999, 391). The British fiction data include payments in half-profits between March 1815 and November 1817 for the first through fourth edition; Scott received 1,278.08*l* for these editions.[37] For *Rob Roy*, Longman paid Scott 2,280.00*l* for the first edition in 1817, and 848.00*l* for the second edition in 1818. For *Tales of my Landlord*, copublished by Murray and Blackwood in 1816, Scott received 2,805.60*l* in profit sharing.[38]

12.5.2 Novels without Payments to Authors

Ten titles by Longman & Co. record a loss and no payments to the author. For example, Longman reports capital outlays, sales, and other expenses for Mary Anne Neri's gothic romance *The Hour of Trial: A Tale* (published in 1808 by Longman) without any references to payments to the author:

> [June 1808]. The impression consisted of 750 copies.
> 21 June–Dec 1808. Total outlay (paper, printing and misc. expenses): 155. 0. 0
> June 1808. To advertising: 17. 5. 0.
> . . .
> [Feb–July 1811]. To further advertising: 1. 2. 0.
> [Feb–July 1811]. To boarding 39 copies: 1. 19. 0.
> [n.d.]. Loss on the production of this novel: 0. 6. 1.[39]

Anecdotal evidence suggests that authors of books without payments were less popular and unfavorably reviewed. For example, *The AntiJacobin Review and Magazine* (1808; 192) describes Neri's *Hour of Trial* as

---

37. A sixth edition appeared in 1820, published by Constable alone (Garside 1999, 391). There are no records of a sixth edition, but the fifth edition was published in two parts (Garside 1999, 400).

38. Murray Archives, Ledger B, pp. 37–38 and Copy Ledger 1809–47 (part publishing), pp. 167–68.

39. Longman Divide Ledger 1D, p. 95, June 1808. Data on expenses are most detailed for Longman. There are two titles by other publishers with losses to publishers and positive payments to authors: *My Grandfather's Farm*, by Gabriel Alexander (paid 21.22*l*), published 1829 by Oliver and Boyd, and *St. Aubin*, by Janet Stewart (paid 8.72*l*), published 1821 by Oliver and Boyd.

rather calculated to deaden the energies, and excite desponding thoughts in the minds of youth, than to offer them the amusement for which they turn the pages of a Novel.

Four years earlier, *The Monthly Review of November* 1804 (315) had described Neri's *Eve of San Pietro* (published in 1804 by Cadell & Co.) as "a work of imitation . . . in many respects inferior to the original" (*The Monthly Review* 1804, 315).

Six of ten titles with negative profits and no payment to author were first published between 1800 and 1814, four were published after 1814. The average loss was 20.72*l*, with a standard deviation of 13.44, a maximum loss of 41.25*l* (Edward Trevor Anwyl, *Tales of Welsh Society and Scenery*, published in 1827 by Longman) and a minimum loss of 3.39*l*. The median loss is 19.98*l*.

12.6 Conclusions and Directions for Future Work

This chapter presents a new historical data set on revenues to publishers and payments to authors, which we have collected from archival sources, including ledgers of transactions, as well as letters between publishers and authors. Comparisons of publishers' payments to authors before and after 1814 indicate that payments to authors increased after the 1814 Copyright Act, which increased the length of copyright protection for authors. The data also show that younger authors, who benefited more from the extension in copyright from twenty-eight years to life of author, experienced a larger increase in payments compared with older authors.

Although our findings are primarily descriptive and cannot establish a *causal* effect of copyright, they are consistent with the view that *in principle* shifts toward stronger copyright laws can help to strengthen the economic incentives for creativity. It is important to keep in mind that the 1814 Act increased the length of copyright starting from a low base of preexisting rights at fourteen and twenty-eight years. By comparison, modern changes increase the length of copyright starting from a high base of preexisting rights, at fifty years or more beyond the death of authors. At extremely high levels of preexisting rights, the incentive effects of an additional year are likely to be small. The costs of stronger copyrights in terms of limiting diffusion, however, may be substantial. Diffusion effects may be as critical as incentive effects in determining the welfare implications of copyright, making them an important topic for future research.

Among all writers in Britain's Romantic Period, Sir Walter Scott received the largest payments. On average, Scott earned 10.3 times as much for fifteen novels after 1814, compared with 127 novels by other authors after 1814. Scott's works, such as *Waverley* and *Rob Roy* were particularly long lived, and the creation of long-lived copyright terms for these works allowed Scott's publishers to charge higher prices for an additional number of years

(Li, MacGarvie, and Moser 2014). Data on payments to Romantic Period authors suggest that Scott and other authors were able to extract some of the additional revenue stream from publishers. Other authors may have been inspired by Scott's example to invest in creative work. In fact, preliminary results of a related project on the gender and social background of new authors indicate a significant shift toward male authors, who may have been attracted by the increased profitability of writing. Some of these new entrants may have been overly optimistic in assessing their chance of emulating Scott's success, but this is a topic for future research. Additional data are needed to examine whether an increase in the profitability of writing helped to encourage the creation of additional books and higher quality books. Such analysis will investigate variation in creative output across genres as well as across quality levels.

The data also show that publishers used different payment schemes to strengthen authors' incentives to support the sales of their books, and we observe a substantial amount of variation in the timing, as well as in the size and in the types of payments across different types of authors and books. Exploring this variation requires additional data collection; once the data are complete, we hope to examine how publishers varied payment schemes to create incentives to create new works.

References

Ballantyne, John Alexander. 1838. *Refutation of the Mistatements and Calumnies Contained in Mr. Lockhart's Life of Sir Walter Scott, Respecting the Messrs. Ballantyne.* Boston: J. Munroe and Company.

Bautz, Annika. 2007. *The Reception of Jane Austen and Walter Scott: A Comparative Longitudinal Study.* London: Continuum.

Clark, Gregory. 2013. "What Were the British Earnings and Prices Then? (New Series)." MeasuringWorth. http://www.measuringworth.com/ukearncpi/.

Deazley, Ronan. 2007. "The Life of an Author: Samuel Egerton Brydges and the Copyright Act 1814." *Georgia State University Law Review* 23:809–46.

DiCola, Peter. 2013. "Money from Music: Survey Evidence on Musicians' Revenue and Lessons about Copyright Incentives." *Arizona Law Review* 55:301–43.

Feather, John. 1988. *A History of British Publishing.* London: Routledge.

Garside, P. D. (ed.). 1999. *The Edinburgh Edition of the Waverley Novels: Guy Mannering.* Edinburgh: Edinburgh University Press.

Grierson, Herbert John Clifford. 1938. *Sir Walter Scott, Bart.* New York: Haskell House Publishers.

Harris, Milton, S. Abraham Ravid, and Suman Basuroy. 2012. "Intellectual Property Contracts: Theory and Evidence from Screenplay Sales." Working Paper, University of Chicago.

Heald, Paul J. 2008. "Property Rights and the Efficient Exploitation of Copyrighted Works: An Empirical Analysis of Public Domain and Copyrighted Fiction Bestsellers." *Minnesota Law Review 2007–2008* Issue 4 (April): 1031–63.

Kelley, Stuart. 2010. *Scott-Land: The Man who Invented a Nation*. Edinburgh: Polygon.
Khan, B. Zorina. 2005. *The Democratization of Invention: Patents and Copyrights in American Economic Development, 1790–1920*. Cambridge, Cambridge University Press.
Li, Xing, Megan MacGarvie, and Petra Moser. 2014. "Dead Poets' Property: How Does Copyright Influence Price?" http://dx.doi.org/10.2139/ssrn.2170447.
Liebowitz, Stan J., and Stephen Margolis. 2005. "Seventeen Famous Economists Weigh in on Copyright: the Role of Theory, Empirics, and Network Effects." *Harvard Journal of Law & Technology* 18 (2): 435–57.
Lockhart, John Gibson. 1838. *Memoirs of the Life of Sir Walter Scott*, vol. 3. Paris: Baudry's European Library.
The Monthly Review; or, Literary Journal. 1804. London: T. Beckett.
Oberholzer-Gee, Felix, and Koleman Strumpf. 2007. "The Effect of File Sharing on Record Sales: An Empirical Analysis." *Journal of Political Economy* 155 (1): 1–42.
Patterson, Lyman. 1968. *Copyright in Historical Perspective*. Nashville, TN: Vanderbilt University Press.
Scherer, Frederic M. 2008. "The Emergence of Musical Copyright in Europe from 1709 to 1850." *Review of Economic Research on Copyright Issues* 5 (2): 3–18.
Seville, Catherine. 1999. *Literary Copyright Reform in Early Victorian England: The Framing of the 1842 Copyright Act*. Cambridge: Cambridge University Press.
Sher, Richard. (2006) 2010. *The Enlightenment and the Book: Scottish Authors and Their Publishers in Eighteenth-Century Britain, Ireland, and America*. Chicago: University of Chicago Press.
Statute of Anne, London. 1710. Primary Sources on Copyright (1450–1900), edited by L. Bently and M. Kretschmer. www.copyrighthistory.org.
St. Clair, William. 2004. *The Reading Nation in the Romantic Period*. Cambridge: Cambridge University Press.
Turow, Scott. 2013. "The Slow Death of the American Author." *New York Times*, April 7.
Waldfogel, Joel. 2012. "Copyright Protection, Technological Change, and the Quality of New Products: Evidence from Recorded Music since Napster." *Journal of Law and Economics* 55 (4): 715–40.

Comment   Koleman Strumpf

It is often stated that intellectual property (IP) protection is essential for the production of creative works. The argument is that artists have incentives to produce only if there is an initial period during which they have exclusive control over the sale of their books, music, or similar products. Quantifying how important such incentives are is necessary for setting appropriate IP policy, since the monopoly sale period can potentially result in lower consumer surplus as many potential buyers are priced out of the market (it

---

Koleman Strumpf is the Koch Professor of Economics at the University of Kansas School of Business.

For acknowledgments, sources of research support, and disclosure of the author's material financial relationships, if any, please see http://www.nber.org/chapters/c13026.ack.

could also result in less output because there are fewer opportunities to build on public domain work). However, measuring the incentive effect is hard to do, since changes in IP protection are infrequent and often involve periods long after the work was created.

It is this challenging empirical topic that the MacGarvie and Moser chapter addresses. The authors focus on the first step in the innovation process, namely whether copyright policy has an impact on remuneration to artists. The answer is not obvious, since such changes can influence the set of competing products (preexisting work, which might receive additional protection) and much of the returns may flow instead to intermediaries (such as publishers and distributors). Greater payments to artists is fundamental to the incentives argument, but it is typically hard to observe such payments because they are governed by nonpublic contracts.

While such information would be virtually impossible to collect in the current period, the authors assemble a rich data set of early nineteenth-century contracts between authors and British publishers. The contracts involve over one hundred authors and nineteen publishers over a thirty-year period. The data include the contract form (whether authors are paid via profit sharing or lump sum), information on the flow of payments to authors from publishers, as well as information about the authors.

These data from the dawn of IP protection are used to investigate how an expansion in the copyright period impacted book authors. In early nineteenth-century Britain, copyright protection was far shorter than in the current day. The 1814 Copyright Act significantly expanded the copyright length; figure 12C.1 summarizes the changes. The increased copyright length was particularly beneficial to younger authors for whom the "rest of life" provision was a significant increase beyond the twenty-eight year copyright period that previously existed. The main result of the chapter is that cumulative payments to authors rose significantly following the implementation of the Act, and that these payments disproportionately went to younger authors.

The empirical results are convincing, and I have little to add to the authors' excellent exposition. Instead, in the remainder of this commentary I will focus on some additional topics that could be explored with the data here, some puzzles in the results, and some implications and directions for future work.

The unique data that the authors assemble almost provides an embarrassment of riches. The rich level of detail allows the exploration of many questions in addition to the IP-related ones considered. For concreteness I will focus on one, the choice of contract form. Publishers paid authors using either a lump sum (essentially paying for the right to sell the book) or profit sharing (splitting the earnings from book sales). From the author's perspective profit sharing is riskier, but also involves a greater upside. Clearly the

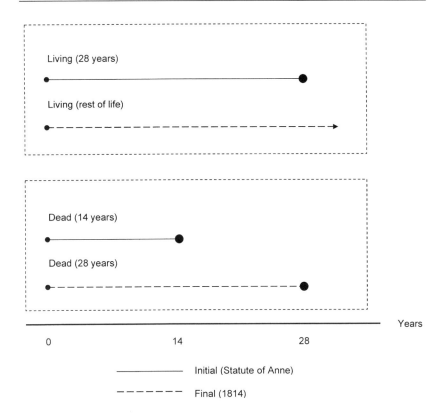

Fig. 12C.1 1814 Copyright Act

contract form will play an important role in the incentives for authors, so it is important to understand under what conditions each type will predominate.

Figure 12C.2 provides a simple conceptual framework for the contract choice for authors and publishers. The author has a book with uncertain future profits. Both publisher and author have expectations about how well it will sell and would like to maximize their own expected payments. Under a lump-sum contract, the Nash bargaining outcome is that the author will receive a payment that is some fraction of the average beliefs about sales. The publisher will keep the future book profits minus the lump sum payments. Under a profit-sharing contract they will again bargain, but here it is to determine what share of the uncertain future profits the author will receive with the publisher keeping the residual.

In this framework, there is no disagreement about the contract choice. If the author is sufficiently more optimistic about the books prospects, they both prefer profit sharing. If the publisher is sufficiently more optimistic, then both prefer a lump sum. The intuition is that when the author is more

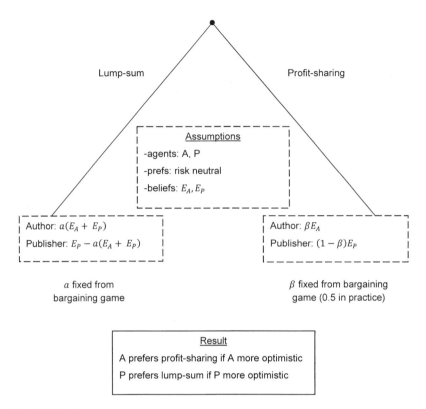

Fig. 12C.2   Contract choice

optimistic, then the upside potential of profit sharing is attractive to him. The publisher, who is less positive about the book, also prefers profit sharing since the author will demand a relatively large payment under the lump sum. The converse reasoning holds when the publisher is more optimistic.

This framework can be used to help better understand the behavior of the agents, but also suggests some puzzles. First, did books tend to be more profitable under profit-sharing contracts? Since these contracts should be used when authors are relatively more optimistic, this could be consistent with the notion that authors are relatively good at forecasting their future bookselling success. Such a condition would seem to be a natural precondition for the pro-IP protection incentives argument. Alternatively, if books are less profitable under profit sharing then a reexamination of this argument might be needed. Second, the copyright expansion of the 1814 Act should have changed the attractiveness of the two contract forms. In addition to increasing the mean profitability (which does not influence the contract choice), it also created more uncertainty (how well would copyrighted books sell long after their creation?) and disproportionately benefited certain aged authors. As such, one might expect there to be a change in the use of these contracts. But the chapter shows that the share of each contract form was roughly the same in the pre- and post-Act periods. Resolving this puzzle would be important in understanding author behavior and thus to understanding the implications of IP protection in this case.

The data also present additional puzzles related to the contractual form. One question is related to large increases in author income following copyright expansion. Recall that the 1814 copyright extension primarily benefited young authors whose work would now be protected for the remainder of their lives rather than the next twenty-eight years. While only a very small number of books would sell in marked quantities over twenty-eight years after they are first published, payments to the typical young author more than tripled in real terms following the 1814 Act. Particularly puzzling is that this same pattern also holds for lump sum payments, which presumably were made prior to the book even being published, so it is not just that these books are unexpectedly successful. This suggests other factors may have been in play, such as publishers paying an efficiency wage in the hope of publishing the author's later works. Other contractual solutions, such as multiple book deals, seem like a more direct way of addressing this, so further explanations might be needed.

A second issue relates to the superstar phenomenon. The 1814 Act would seem to be particularly beneficial to the very best-selling authors who would be the only ones to sell a significant number of copies in the additional period of copyright protection. While sales totals are not presented in this chapter, the figures indicate a significant lengthening of the right tail of payments in the post-1814 period. In fact, much of this effect is due to a single author, Sir Walter Scott. But if greater rents will accrue to the work of a smaller number of authors, publishers should have engaged in long-term contracts or devised other ways to ensure a continued relationship with the superstars. No such contractual innovations seem to have occurred.

A final issue is the difference between books published under lump sum and profit-sharing contracts. The copyright extension did not seem to be very beneficial to authors under a profit-sharing contract. The average profit-sharing payments per page actually declined post-1814. It also appears that the disproportionate increase in payments to young authors did not occur with profit sharing. Whether these differences are due to the issues highlighted in the conceptual framework or some other factors is clearly important to understanding the implications of greater IP protection.

The last few sections have highlighted a few topics that can be explored in future work, but this should not distract from the notable contributions of the chapter. It exemplifies how historical data can be employed to shed light on questions of great policy and academic concern. In fact, it would be extremely difficult to collect data this rich from modern sources, so this may very well be the only way to closely examine how changes in copyright impacts payments to artists (and eventually their creative output).

In future work the data here could be employed to address a variety of other IP-related questions. Just to pick one example, it would be interesting to see the impact of the copyright extension on piracy. In the current day, a spirited debate has centered on to what extent the Internet facilitates illicit consumption of copyrighted material. Critics of this view have argued that much digital piracy is fueled by copyright laws, which give creators control over first sale even decades after their creation. Under this reasoning, an unintended consequence of the 1814 Act could be an increase in book piracy. During this period, there was a thriving business of printers in Ireland and elsewhere reprinting copyrighted books and surreptitiously exporting them back to England. Such reprinting of British books later became a large part of the US book business as IP of noncitizens was not protected until 1891. Whether the copyright expansion studied here played a role in fueling this piracy is an exciting avenue for future research, and the answers would make a significant contribution to both the policy debate and the academic literature.

A final note in conclusion. The authors are careful about limiting the implications one can draw from their results. It is worth emphasizing that readers should do likewise. While it might be tempting to connect the flourishing of literature in the Romance period to the increased IP protection discussed here, the connection is not clear (not the least because some of the most notable Romance authors were German, and there was a near absence of copyright law in German states through the early nineteenth century). The empirical evidence here does not imply that greater copyright length increases creative output, since we do not know how responsive authors are to payments (both on the intensive margin by preexisting authors and the extensive margin involving entry/exit of authors). Also, there is only a relatively short period of data here, and there might be differences in the long term. For example, the growing stock of books with copyright protection might induce entry (through increasing the price of existing books) or hinder it (by decreasing the available public domain to build upon). And, finally, it is worth reemphasizing the differences from current copyright debates that involve extensions long after the art's creation, and so may have very different impacts on payment flows to artists as well as incentives for new production.

13
Understanding Media Markets in the Digital Age
Economics and Methodology

Brett Danaher, Samita Dhanasobhon,
Michael D. Smith, and Rahul Telang

13.1 Introduction

Digital distribution channels have created opportunities that have transformed the delivery of information, opening new ways for firms to add value to media and entertainment products. However, these new opportunities can create tension for firms struggling to adapt their business models to new markets and new competitors. The availability of pirated digital content only exacerbates this conflict, making it even harder for firms to develop viable digital business models. Piracy also raises issues for governments seeking to adapt established copyright practices to the unique realities of digital markets. Our intent in this chapter is to provide a tutorial for applying modern empirical methodologies to the abundance of natural experiments brought about by discrete changes in the media distribution market, thereby helping firms and governments adapt their practices based on data and empirical evidence as opposed to dogma and conventional wisdom.

Our position in this chapter is that empirical research using modern methods for causal identification are called for in order to determine the optimal

---

Brett Danaher is assistant professor of economics at Wellesley College. Samita Dhanasobhon is a PhD student at the H. John Heinz III School of Public Policy and Management at Carnegie Mellon University. Michael D. Smith is professor of information technology and marketing at the H. John Heinz III School of Public Policy and Management at Carnegie Mellon University. Rahul Telang is professor of information systems and PhD program chair at the H. John Heinz III School of Public Policy and Management at Carnegie Mellon University.

The authors thank the editors of this volume as well as Heidi Williams for helpful comments on this research. This research was conducted as part of Carnegie Mellon University's Initiative for Digital Entertainment Analytics (IDEA). Danaher acknowledges financial support from an Economics of Digitization Research Grant from the National Bureau of Economic Research. For acknowledgments, sources of research support, and disclosure of the authors' material financial relationships, if any, please see http://www.nber.org/chapters/c12999.ack.

copyright and business policies in the digital era. Having written several papers on these subjects, we hope to provide a roadmap for future research to apply econometric methods for causal inference to answer the many managerial and policy questions raised by digital markets. The research we discuss in this chapter addresses these questions by exploring factors that influence demand for media content across various distribution channels and how consumers respond to changes in these channels resulting from firm strategy or government action.[1] Our research to date has shown the following: First, that a graduated-response antipiracy law in France causally increased digital music sales by 22–25 percent following widespread awareness of the law. Second, that the shutdown of the popular file-sharing cyberlocker Megaupload.com causally increased revenues from digital movies by 6–10 percent. Third, that the removal of NBC's video content from the iTunes store caused piracy levels of that content to increase by 11 percent but had no impact on DVD sales of the same content, implying that digital distribution of media may mitigate piracy without necessarily cannibalizing physical channel sales in the short run. Finally, new research in this chapter demonstrates that distribution of television through online streaming (in this case, Hulu.com) can decrease piracy of that content by 15–20 percent. In short, our research seems to suggest that firms can compete against "free" pirated content by either making legitimate digital content easier to consume, or by making pirated content harder to consume. This implies that both firm strategy and government intervention may play a role in managing the disruption caused by digitization.

The remainder of our chapter proceeds as follows: In section 13.2 we summarize three of our prior studies pertaining to digital media, with a particular focus on the methodologies employed and other questions those methodologies might be used to answer. In section 13.3 we present new research on the impact of legal online streaming on demand for piracy. Finally, in section 13.4 we discuss the results presented in the chapter and set the agenda for future research.

13.2 Three Categories of Natural Experiments

In order to better understand the impact that a government intervention or a new firm strategy has on outcome variables such as sales or piracy levels, one must have a means to isolate and identify the causal impact of the event on the outcome. For example, if a government were to pass a policy aimed at reducing piracy, simply examining piracy levels before and after implementation of the policy would be insufficient to identify the impact

---

1. This chapter focuses on examples from our own work in order to describe various empirical methods. We are not the only ones to use such methods to explore questions related to the digitization of the media industries. For a broader summary of research and findings related to these issues, see Danaher, Smith, and Telang (2014).

of that policy change as piracy levels may have risen or fallen at that time for reasons unrelated to the policy. In the words of a common adage in the social sciences, "correlation doesn't establish causation."

To establish causation in such an environment, economists and social scientists often use a difference-in-difference strategy. The basic idea of a diff-in-diff approach is to identify a "control" group of individuals, regions, or products that can aid in estimating the counterfactual of what would have happened to the "treated" group if the treatment had not happened. The difference between this counterfactual and what we observe indicates the actual effect of the treatment, assuming that the control group can accurately predict the counterfactual. Thus, the selection of the control group is of paramount importance. The "gold standard" of causal inference in such research is randomized controlled trials (RCTs), whereby a random set of individuals or products are treated with a shock and the others are not. Such trials may not be out of reach—in our experience, firms in the media industries have been willing to randomly select some products to "treat" with availability on a new channel, shorter release windows, or variation in prices. When selection is truly random, many of the usual concerns about endogeneity are less salient, as unobserved characteristics will be similar on average across the control and treatment groups. Such experiments can be of value to both firms and researchers. However, when RCTs are not available, sometimes a natural or quasi-experiment can be found in which the selection of subjects into the treatment group may not be random, but may be random with respect to the outcome variables of interest. In this section, we give three examples of natural experiments and methodologies that can be used to analyze the causal impact of a treatment using a difference-in-difference methodology, but where each case involves a different type of variation in the data and thus a different manner of applying the methodology.

13.2.1 Case 1: The Effect of a Graduated Response Antipiracy Law on Digital Music Sales[2]

In the spring of 2009, the French government passed an antipiracy law known as HADOPI, establishing the HADOPI administrative authority and giving it the power to monitor online copyright infringement and to act against pirates based on information submitted by rights holders. The HADOPI authority had a number of responsibilities, including promoting and educating consumers about legal sales channels, but the most widely known program under HADOPI was the strikes and penalty system. Under this system, individuals would receive a warning for their first and second observed instances of copyright infringement, and upon the third they could be taken to court and potentially penalized with monetary fines or suspension of their Internet access for up to one month. This law was controversial

---

2. See Danaher et al. (2014).

and received a great deal of publicity, causing consumers to be very aware of the new policy and potentially affecting their behavior by migrating potential file sharers to legal purchasing channels. To analyze the impact of the HADOPI law on French consumers' digital music purchases, we obtained a panel of weekly iTunes digital music sales data from the four largest music labels for nearly three years surrounding the passage of HADOPI.

In this instance, the policy shock—the passage of HADOPI—was limited to one geographic region (France), and there was little reason to think it would have direct impact outside the boundaries of that country. Most other European countries had not experienced any relevant policy shocks at this time, and so our goal was to find a set of control countries whose sales trends over time closely matched France's prior to HADOPI, expecting that such a control group should have continued to trend similarly to France if not for the policy shock. We considered several control groups that in theory might have such a trend, examining only the pre-HADOPI sales trends to find the group that most closely matched France's trend.[3] The group of countries that best matched France's sales trends in the preperiod of our data was Spain, Germany, Italy, Belgium, and the United Kingdom. Notably these were also the five countries, other than France, with highest digital sales levels among European Union (EU) countries.

Before running a diff-in-diff model, another challenge that arose was selection of the "treatment date" that we would use in our model. Sometimes this is clear—if a government were to one day simply block all access to pirated material, that day would be the most obvious treatment date for analysis. However, the HADOPI bill was debated for over six months in the French government, even being passed by one government body only to be rejected and then subsequently accepted by another. With such confusion as to whether the law was in effect or not, we chose to consider the peak level of awareness of HADOPI as the effective treatment date. Google Trends data is a useful tool for measuring awareness of a law or policy, as it measures the number of searches over time for a given search term (as well as the number of articles containing the search term) for a given geographic area. Thus we used Google Trends to augment our data set and determine the effective treatment date of HADOPI.

The following Figure 13.1, reproduced from our paper, shows the results from an ordinary least squares (OLS) model predicting the natural log of iTunes song sales for France and the control group plotted against the Google Trends index of searches in France for the term "HADOPI."

---

3. In this stage, examining only the pre-HADOPI period is important. If one were to examine the entire period, one might be guilty of a form of "data mining," searching for a control group against which France would appear to increase or decrease after HADOPI. By only examining the preperiod to find the best-fitting control group, one remains agnostic as to the effect of the treatment and thus the diff-in-diff test that follows is valid.

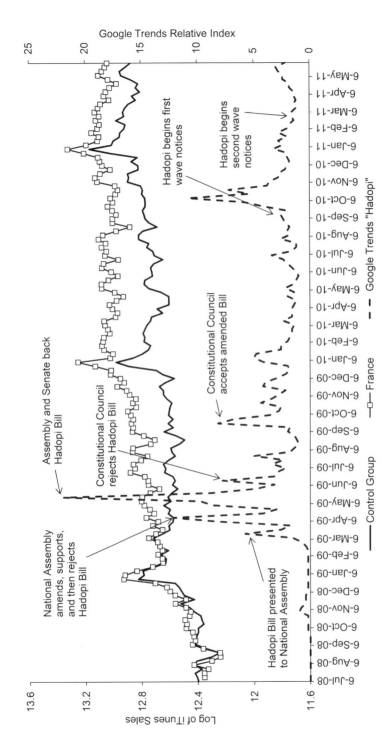

Fig. 13.1 iTunes song unit sales trends, France versus control group

Two important facts are clear in this picture. First, weekly sales trends of the control group match closely to sales trends in France prior to widespread awareness of HADOPI (moreover, a formal statistical test of joint differences between the control and treatment groups before treatment cannot reject that the two trends are the same during this period at a 95 percent confidence level). Second, increased awareness of the HADOPI law (proxied by Google search intensity) coincides with the persistent rise in the French sales trend above the control group.[4] Thus, these results suggest that awareness of the HADOPI law in France had a positive causal impact on iTunes sales in France, and that laws like this may migrate consumers from illegal file sharing to legal digital channels.

To provide further evidence that the effect we found was indeed causal, we added another level of difference to the model showing that the diff-in-diff increase in French sales was larger for more heavily pirated genres of music (and thus genres that should be more significantly impacted by the law) and smaller for less pirated genres. The logic here is that more heavily pirated genres should have a larger number of customers "treated" by the antipiracy intervention than less heavily pirated genres do.

The more general point about this paper is that when a government passes a policy or a firm implements a strategy in one region and when other regions could be expected to be unaffected by that change, a diff-in-diff strategy can provide useful evidence as to the policy's impact when a suitable control group can be found. This is not always easy. The iTunes store had been open in each of these countries for similar periods of time and so development of the market was reasonably stable across these countries. However, we found it difficult to study the impact of HADOPI on users of legal music streaming services like Deezer or Spotify, as these services were at very different levels of development across countries, and thus we could find no group of countries whose sales/subscription trends were following a pattern similar to France's. Despite this limitation, we believe that policy variation across countries (coupled with additional differences across attributes like genre) will be a powerful tool to analyze the impact of other government interventions like the Digital Economy Act in the United Kingdom and the Copyright Amendment Act of 2011 in New Zealand, as well as industry-led interventions like the Copyright Alert System put in place by US Internet Service Providers.

---

4. A point worth making about studies such as this is that the traditional standard error clustering approach (Bertrand, Duflo, and Mullainathan 2004) does not generate correct standard errors for the treated group in the posttreatment period, partly due to the low number of countries in the study, but also due to the fact that there is only one treated group. Our paper outlines a manner in which robust standard errors can be calculated in such a situation through permutational inference.

13.2.2 Case 2: The Effect of the Megaupload Shutdown on Digital Movie Sales[5]

In January 2012, the US Department of Justice secured an indictment against the popular cyberlocker Megaupload.com, allowing them to raid Mcgaupload's offices and shut down Megaupload's Internet presence. Prior to this, Megaupload was an online cloud storage service and the thirteenth most visited site on the Internet according to Alexa.com. However, according to the injunction, the vast majority of the content stored on Megaupload was copyright infringing and Megaupload's policies (such as not requiring passwords for storage accounts or providing incentives to upload popular content) encouraged rampant file sharing. The shutdown was controversial on many fronts, and opponents of the shutdown claimed that in spite of all of the costs of this government intervention, it would have little impact on consumer behavior as the content that had been available on Megaupload was available through other piracy channels (a conjecture aligned with empirical evidence presented by Lauinger et al. [2013]).

From an empirical perspective, what was notable about the shutdown was that it occurred all over the world on the same date and thus, unlike in our HADOPI study, there was no geographic region that could be considered a "control" area for estimating how sales would have changed in the absence of the shutdown. This challenge also arises with other policies or strategies that are taken worldwide all at once, or when there is a shock to a country but the only appropriate variation to study is within that country. In situations like this, no clear control group exists and so the simplest form of difference-in-difference may not be adequate to estimate the causal impact of the shock.

Fortunately, another way of implementing a diff-in-diff approach is to model the first difference as post- versus pretreatment but to use a more continuous variable as the second difference, where the continuous variable is a measure of how intensely each individual, region, or unit in the data was treated. In the Megaupload example, even though Megaupload was shut down in every country on the same date, each country had different preshutdown usage levels of Megaupload. To measure this variation, we gathered data on the number of unique visitors to Megaupload.com by country for the month prior to the shutdown, as well as data on the number of Internet users in each country at the end of the same month. Dividing the former by the latter, we imputed each country's Megaupload Penetration Ratio (MPR), or the percent of Internet account holders who visited Megaupload at least once in the month prior to the shutdown. With respect to the shutdown, the MPR can be seen as a measure of treatment intensity, as countries with higher MPR received a stronger "shock" from the shutdown

---

5. See Danaher and Smith (2014).

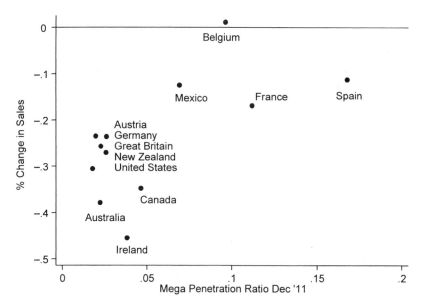

Fig. 13.2 Post-shutdown change in digital movie sales versus MPR (three weeks before and after shutdown)

and thus, if the shutdown actually boosted media sales, the post-shutdown sales growth should be larger in high MPR countries relative to low MPR countries.

Combining the MPR data with weekly digital movie sales data from two of the major motion picture studios, we showed that prior to the shutdown, the sales trends of high MPR countries were relatively similar to the sales trends of low MPR countries.[6] But immediately after the shutdown, high MPR countries experienced larger growth (or smaller declines from December to January sales levels) than low MPR countries do. Figure 13.2 presents a scatterplot that demonstrates this relationship, but in the paper we display results from OLS regression models that more precisely show the sales trends and more strongly support our inference that the shutdown of Megaupload caused an increase in digital movie sales.

One thing that stands out about this scatterplot is the positive relationship between increased MPR (x-axis) and increased relative sales change between December and January (y-axis). This positive relationship is the basis for the rest of the statistical evidence we provide in the paper that the shutdown of Megaupload caused an increase in digital movie sales. Another key takeaway is the importance of the diff-in-diff methodology here: sales in

---

6. The exception is during the Christmas holiday. In the paper we discuss how we deal with this anomaly in the preshutdown period.

nearly all of the countries were actually decreasing after the shutdown, but this is due to a seasonal decline from Christmas highs that happen every year in January. Simply examining average sales before and after the shutdown would show a decrease following the shutdown, but our diff-in-diff evidence indicates that the natural seasonal declines were mitigated by the closure of Megaupload, thereby causing revenues to be higher than they would have been if not for the closure.

It is worth nothing that in studies like this with a small number of clusters or "experiments" (countries), one might worry that preexisting trends could drive the results if high MPR countries were already growing faster than low MPR countries. In our paper we provide evidence from the preperiod indicating that this does not appear to be a driving factor. However, a better solution in situations like this is to add in country-specific trends to the diff-in-diff regression. Essentially this means modeling each country's specific week-to-week time trend based on some functional form (linear, quadratic, etc.), adding these terms into the regression, and asking if post-shutdown deviations from these modeled trends are larger in high MPR (high treatment intensity) countries. In Danaher and Smith (2014), we showed that the addition of these trends actually increased the magnitude of our coefficient of interest and did not impact its sign or significance.

As an additional test of causal inference, we tested whether the relationship between MPR and sales changes was unique to 2011–2012 (when Megaupload was shutdown) or whether this same sales change pattern was common during this time of year. Indeed, in event studies such as these, a placebo test of a similar time period at some point (or in some location) where there was no treatment can help to verify causal inference. Accordingly, we showed that there was no statistically significant relationship between the December 2011 MPR and the percent change in digital movie sales after January 19, 2013.

Finally, from a policy perspective, one might ask how a model like this, one that uses variation in treatment intensity across regions, can be interpreted and explained to someone without training in econometrics. Essentially, what the model does is to model the linear relationship (or any functional form one considers appropriate) between pre-shutdown MPR and post-shutdown changes in sales. This relationship can then be extrapolated to estimate what would have been the post-shutdown sales change in a country with zero Megaupload usage, which is akin to asking what would have happened to sales in a country unaffected by the shutdown. In this manner a control "counterfactual" is estimated, allowing one to then estimate how much lower sales would have been in each country if not for the shutdown. An analogy could be made to a form of medical trial—the experiment is like giving one group of sick patients a pill that is 20 percent medicine and 80 percent sugar (placebo), giving another group a pill in a 40/60 percent ratio, and still another group an 80/20 percent pill, and then asking whether the groups given a higher concentration of medicine began to recover faster after the treatment than the groups given lower concentrations.

We suggest that the type of event study we conducted with Megaupload might also be useful for examining the effects of shocks when there is no clear control group. For example, the shutdown of Limewire in 2010 was similar to Megaupload, and its effect on sales of recorded music should be of interest to policymakers. Or, in 2009, Youtube.com chose to stop allowing individuals in the United Kingdom access to all premium music videos on their site due to a breakdown in negotiations with the British Performing Right Society. If there existed some geographic variance across the United Kingdom in pre-blackout usage of YouTube for music video watching, then this shock could be used to determine the effect of streaming music content (on YouTube) on sales or piracy of that content—a question that is currently of great interest to many parties involved in the music industry.

13.2.3 Case 3: The Effect of Digital Distribution of Television on Piracy and DVD Sales[7]

Considerable debate exists within the media industries around the use of new digital distribution channels such as paid download stores like iTunes and subscription streaming services like Spotify or Hulu. Proponents argue that such channels will more readily compete with illegal file sharing by offering consumers a more convenient legal means of acquiring content that includes a revenue stream to rights holders. Critics worry that such channels—often delivering lower profit margins—will cannibalize preexisting channels with higher profit margins. With each potential channel the answers to these questions may be different, and yet they remain critical to determining the profitability of such channels or, in some cases, the size and direction of royalties that should be paid for the delivery of content.[8] But often these new channels are opened or closed with little evidence as to their effects on other channels.

Fortunately these questions can sometimes be answered, not using variance at the geographic level as above, but rather using variance at the product or firm level. Whether or not certain products are offered on these new channels is often based not on the piracy or sales levels of those products, but on contractual negotiations between rights holders and delivery channels.

For example, in early 2007 around 40 percent of all video content on the iTunes store was provided by NBCUniversal. Due to contract disputes related to iTunes pricing policies, NBC chose not to renew their contract

---

7. See Danaher et al. (2010).
8. For example, if users listening to a subscription music streaming service buy more music from existing channels, then perhaps royalties are unnecessary. But if these users buy less music, substituting streaming for purchasing, then the rate of sales displacement resulting from the service might be one determinant of the size of royalties that the streaming service should pay to rights holders.

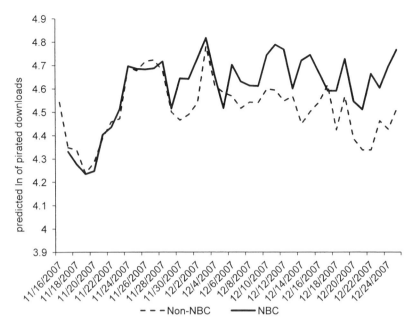

Fig. 13.3 NBC versus non-NBC piracy surrounding December 1, 2007

with iTunes and on November 30, 2007, they removed all of their television content from the iTunes store. However, similar networks (Fox, CBS, and ABC) continued to offer their content, providing a potential control group for NBC content. We used this product-level variation[9] and the NBC shock to determine the impact that selling television content on iTunes has on both piracy levels of that content and on physical DVD box set sales. Similarly, we used the return of NBC content to iTunes the following year to verify and provide additional insights into our results.

While the full results can be found in our paper, figure 13.3 highlights an example of the results from a diff-in-diff model comparing piracy of NBC content to a control group of ABC, CBS, and Fox content.

Similar to the results in our HADOPI paper, we show that the average pirated downloads of NBC episodes trended similarly to the average of control group episodes prior to iTunes removal,[10] but that immediately following the removal of NBC content from iTunes, piracy of those episodes spiked above the control group and remained above the control group during the

---

9. Technically this variation was at the network level, not the product level. But in the paper we argue that each television series was a unique experiment and treat standard errors accordingly.

10. An appropriate means of testing this is to ask whether a Wald test of joint significance for the difference between NBC and non-NBC content for all dates prior to the shock can be rejected at a specified significance level.

period covered by our data. Thus, we demonstrate that removing content from iTunes caused an increase in piracy, and by extension, that selling digitally on iTunes mitigates piracy. In the same paper, and using the same methodology, we showed that removal of NBC content from iTunes did not cause any increase in DVD sales of that content on iTunes, representing the reverse of the digital distribution question.

We believe that this approach has broad application to questions in the media industries in the age of digitization.

The negotiations between rights holders and content delivery platforms may create a plethora of natural or quasi-experiments where some rights holders come to terms with the platform (or do not come to terms) for reasons that can be shown to be unrelated to the dependent variables of interest. For example, on music streaming services, one label may choose to initiate or discontinue availability of its artists' albums while other labels make no changes to the status quo, and this might allow researchers to study the impact of music streaming on piracy, paid downloads, or CD sales. Our NBC paper provides a straightforward example of how to use such product-level variation to tease out the impacts of such strategies.

The focus of our descriptions of these three papers has been on the generalizability of these methodologies for a vast array of questions and experiments in the media industries following digitization. Specifically, our review establishes a set of methodologies and provides examples of how to impute causal impact across a variety of regularly occurring natural experiments—discrete changes at a country level (e.g., France and HADOPI), at a site level (e.g., Megaupload), or at a product or firm level (e.g., NBC and iTunes)—on variables of interest. Given the large number of these sorts of "natural experiments" driven by changes in how firms and governments respond to digital markets for entertainment, these methodologies could find wide application, and could help firms and governments understand the drivers of consumer behavior and the impact of such changes.

To demonstrate this, in the final section of this chapter we provide a proof-of-concept that these methodologies are generalizable to other settings by adapting the strategy from our NBC paper to study the effect of streaming television content on Hulu.com (a popular streaming site) on piracy of that content. Unlike the prior three examples where we provided high-level analysis, we now present precise details on data and methodology.

13.3 The Effect of Television Streaming on Piracy

Copyright holders have approached new digital distribution channels with a great deal of caution, despite the prevailing view that the vast majority of future sales inevitably will come through digital distribution, and the prevailing view that smart management should conduct experiments in advance of that arrival to understand the impact of these channels. Their concern about embracing new digital distribution channels seems to be driven by three main factors. First, digital distribution channels may substitute for sales in (more profitable) physical distribution channels. For example, Jeff Zucker, CEO of NBCUniversal, has been quoted as saying that the number one challenge for the motion picture industry in approaching digital channels is to avoid "trading analog dollars for digital pennies." Second, the use of digital distribution channels may accelerate the reduction in revenue from downstream channels, reducing the future profitability of present downstream channel partners. For example, it has been widely reported that Walmart forcefully protested Disney's distribution of its movies through iTunes by returning boxes and boxes of DVDs to Disney and by threatening to significantly reduce their future stock of Disney content. Finally, rights holders may be concerned that digital distribution channels are not commercially viable given the availability of "free" pirated content online. The concern here is that firms will have to significantly lower their prices today to compete with free pirated content and that this may reduce consumers' willingness to pay in the future. In short, competing with free pirated content today could have long-term impacts on the overall profitability of the industry in the future.

One managerial decision where these arguments have come into play is the decision of whether to allow television content to be shown on Internet websites for streaming video. Streaming video channels could be seen as low-margin competitors to the higher margin established broadcast of physical sales channels. On the other hand, allowing consumers to view television content through streaming channels may increase interest in the show and may decrease demand for digital piracy of this content. A legitimate streaming channel may also give copyright holders a great deal of flexibility in terms of assembling content and numerous opportunities to differentiate this content from physical DVDs, opening up new and untapped consumer markets and advertising revenues without significantly impacting demand in existing physical channels. In this more optimistic view, the firm who first figures out a viable streaming approach could improve its competitive position relative to its rivals, generating a strong incentive to experiment with these sorts of channels. Such a firm may also take a leadership position in creating platforms and infrastructure for digital distribution and streaming, thereby giving it a powerful position in the market.

Given these factors, it is notable that television and movie studios have begun to explore content distribution through many new digital distribution channels in recent years. These changes in distribution policies create a unique series of natural experiments in which to analyze the impact of free digital distribution on demand through physical channels and on demand for pirated content.

In our analysis below we analyze the impact of free streaming video websites on demand for digital piracy, and we also suggest that a similar approach could be used in the future to analyze the effect of streaming on physical sales or broadcast television. To analyze this question, we use a quasi-experiment that occurred on July 6, 2009, when ABC started streaming their television content on Hulu.com. Hulu.com is an advertising-supported Internet portal for streaming video. Interestingly, television networks themselves took leadership in creating this platform, and it was launched to the public in March 2008 as a joint venture between Fox and NBC. In April 2009, ABC reached an agreement to take a partial ownership position in Hulu.com and add its content to the site. This timing is important—Hulu had already existed for a year with content from two major networks, such that when ABC added their content to Hulu, the site already had a large existing user base and public awareness. As such, the addition of ABC represents a discrete shock to available content on a major delivery platform. The data suggests that this shock was exogenous with respect to piracy trends, as the timing was based on a series of contractual negotiations versus expectations of future piracy or sales.

In that sense, this experiment looks much like the one in our paper on NBC and iTunes in that when ABC added its content to Hulu.com on July 6, 2009, there were no shocks to content on other networks (NBC, CBS, CW, and Fox). Thus, television series on these four networks may serve as a control group for the treated ABC content, allowing us to identify the causal effect of Hulu.com streaming availability on levels of piracy. This differs from our prior paper on NBC in that we are studying a digital streaming service rather than a download service and we are studying the addition of content to a distribution channel rather than its removal from one.

Background and theory: Hulu.com was created as an attempt to give consumers a convenient, readily available platform on which to watch television content online on their own time. Unlike peer-to-peer file-sharing piracy, Hulu is a streaming service and requires no download time before one can watch episodes of a show. However, also unlike piracy, Hulu is supported by short, fifteen- to thirty-second advertisements inserted into the programs. And so despite the convenience and reliability of Hulu, it is not clear whether consumers will consider this service to be an attractive alternative to piracy.

During the timeframe covered by our data set, Hulu only offered the most recent five episodes of each television series, and all episodes and seasons before that were unavailable on Hulu.[11] Despite the fact that pirated copies of a television episode are often available through torrent sites the day after the episode airs, the owners of some series choose to delay availability of an episode on Hulu for several days after airing on television. This was not a factor in our study as the shock to availability occurred between seasons, so we study piracy of episodes of television that had aired at least a month prior to the beginning of our study. Nevertheless, it remains a question whether

---

11. Today, one can get access to all episodes of a number of series by paying to subscribe to Hulu Plus. However, Hulu Plus did not exist during the time period of our study.

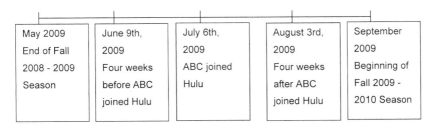

Fig. 13.4 Time line of events during period of study

consumers who would otherwise pirate will be attracted to the convenience (and legality) of Hulu enough to convert to consumption through legal streaming.

Finally, it is worth noting that television networks and their partners (like cable companies or downstream DVD sellers) may be worried that streaming would cannibalize DVD box set sales or over-the-air television viewing, where the profit margins are currently significantly higher than they are on streaming channels. In this study we will not analyze such potential cannibalization, but we believe one could undertake such analysis in the future with proper data on DVD sales, data on over-the-air audience viewing audience levels, and with a similar methodology to that employed here.

Data: To address the research question, we collected a panel of data on consumption of pirated television content through the BitTorrent tracker site Mininova.org. From these data, we analyzed all television series (excluding reality shows and live programming) that were available on the five major television networks (ABC, CBS, CW, Fox, and NBC) starting in the fall of 2008 and extending through the fall of 2009. This encompasses a total of seventy-one television series. We describe these data in more detail below.

Figure 13.4 displays the time line of events in our study. It shows that ABC added its content to Hulu on July 6, 2009, a date after the end of the fall 2008 to spring 2009 television season and before the start of the fall 2009 to spring 2010 television season. As a result, we focus our analysis on episodes of television programs from the fall 2008 to spring 2009 season, and our analysis period covers the four weeks before and after ABC added its content to Hulu (with robustness checks for different window lengths). We also include only episodes that have at least ten downloads on each date to increase the signal-to-noise ratio of our tests.

Table 13.1 summarizes, by network, the seventy-one television series in our data and whether they were available on Hulu.com during the fall 2008 season. As noted in the table, of the seventy-one television series active in the fall 2008 to spring 2009 television season, twenty-seven of these series had their most recent five episodes available on Hulu.

In terms of what changed, note that prior to July 6, 2009, there were no ABC series available on Hulu, while after July 6, 2009, nine ABC television

Table 13.1 Hulu availability for each network's series, fall 2008–spring 2009 season

	Not on Hulu	On Hulu	Total
ABC	16	0	16
CBS	19	0	19
CW	6	2	8
FOX	6	8	14
NBC	6	8	14
Total	53	18	71

series became available on Hulu. These are the only changes in availability during this time frame—of the remaining sixty-two series, the forty-four that were not available on Hulu prior to July 6, 2009, remained unavailable after July 6, 2009, and the eighteen that were available on Hulu prior to July 6, remained available on Hulu after July 6. As such, from these television programs, we use the nine ABC television series that were made available on Hulu on July 6, 2009, as our treatment group and the remaining sixty-two series whose status on Hulu did not change as the control group.

Following Smith and Telang (2009) and Danaher et al. (2010), we use BitTorrent piracy measured by Mininova.org as a proxy for overall video piracy for the television content in our sample. We selected Mininova because it was the most popular BitTorrent tracker site listed by Alexa.com during our study period.[12] A further advantage of Mininova is that it provided the number of cumulative downloads for each tracker listed on its site, allowing us to calculate the number of daily downloads for each piece of content in our sample. The process for gathering these data and coding them are described in more detail in our NBC/iTunes paper.

To study the effect of the addition of ABC video content to Hulu, we focus our analysis on the four-week period before and after the July 6, 2009, launch date. This allows us to calculate the change in piracy for ABC content after its addition to Hulu.com, and to compare this change to the change in the control group. We focus our analysis on the four-week before and after period because we want to see the immediate impact of the policy and we want to exclude unrelated factors that might affect consumption over a longer time frame. We also test whether the change in piracy observed below is typical of other time frames by conducting the same analysis described here on the period one year prior to our study (the four-week period before and after July 6, 2008) as a further counterfactual reference point for how ABC piracy would have changed if it had not been added to Hulu. Importantly, we limit our piracy analysis to just the most recent five episodes of each series in our data, as these are the only episodes of any series (treatment or control)

---

12. See http://www.alexa.com/browse/general/?&CategoryID=1316737.

Table 13.2   Daily number of downloads

Pirated downloads		Mean	Std. dev.	Percent change
Treatment	Before 7/6/09	353.8	428.2	
	After 7/6/09	209.4	302.5	−40.80
Control	Before 7/6/09	388.4	558.5	
	After 7/6/09	301	437.7	−22.50

that were on Hulu.[13] Table 13.2 provides summary statistics of piracy data during the four-week period before and after July 6, 2009.

We use a balanced panel of episodes that were available both before and after ABC joined Hulu in these summary statistics and in our regression analysis. Table 13.2 reports the mean of the daily download numbers for the most recent five episodes of each series in both the control and treatment group. We found that the average number of daily downloads is consistent with the previous literature (Danaher et al. 2010), showing between 200 and 400 downloads per episode per day.

During the four-week period before and after the addition of ABC content to Hulu, the average number of daily pirated downloads for the last five episodes in the treatment group decreased by 40 percent, whereas the average number of daily pirated episodes for the control group decreased by 23 percent. We note that we would expect the number of downloads to decrease over time given that episode popularity will decline following an initial surge of interest immediately after broadcast. However, the relative sizes of these summary statistics suggest that there was a larger decrease in piracy for those series that were added to Hulu than there was for series where there was no change in their Hulu availability. We explore this result more formally in our regression analysis.

Results: Before comparing changes in the treatment and control groups after the introduction of ABC content to Hulu, we gather evidence as to whether piracy of the control group can be expected to trend similarly to piracy in the treated group if not for the shock. We use equation (1) to compare the time trend of piracy levels in the control and treatment groups prior to July 6, 2009. If the control group trends similarly to the treated group prior to the shock, then one might reasonably expect it to provide a good estimate of the counterfactual for the treated group after the shock.

---

13. It would certainly be interesting to consider the impact that having five episodes on Hulu would have on piracy of the entire series. However, sometimes individuals download a torrent containing all episodes from a season or series, and because of the nature of our observational data, we cannot determine whether the download of a season is because the downloading individual wanted just two to three of the most recent episodes, and downloaded the season torrent to get them, or actually wanted the entire season. Any analysis on piracy of episodes other than the five most recent would be subject to this data limitation.

(1) $\ln Downloads_{it} = \beta_0 + \beta_1^t D_t + \beta_2^t D_t * ABCHulu_i + \mu_i + e_{it}.$

In equation (1) above, $Downloads_{it}$ is the total number of pirated downloads of episode i on day t, D_t is a vector of date fixed effects for each day, $ABCHulu_i$ is an indicator variable equal to one if episode i is broadcast on ABC and was made available on Hulu on July 6, 2009 (and is equal to 0 for all episodes on other networks and untreated episodes on ABC), and μ is a vector of episode fixed effects. In this model, vector β_1 captures the day-to-day piracy trend for the control group, and β_2 represents how this differs for piracy of the treated group. Rather than displaying eight weeks worth of coefficients, we plot the predicted value from the resulting coefficients in figure 13.5 using $\beta_0 + \beta_1$ as the predicted log piracy of the control group and $\beta_0 + \beta_1 + \beta_2$ as the predicted log piracy of the treated group.

While figure 13.5 demonstrates that piracy trends of the treatment and control groups were not quite the same prior to the experiment, they were quite close. However, after treated ABC series were added to Hulu on July 6, 2009, there is an immediate break in piracy levels of the last five episodes of each of these series in the treated group that is much larger than any drop/change in piracy of the control group. Based on the timing of this relative drop and the lack of a similar drop before the experiment, we believe the

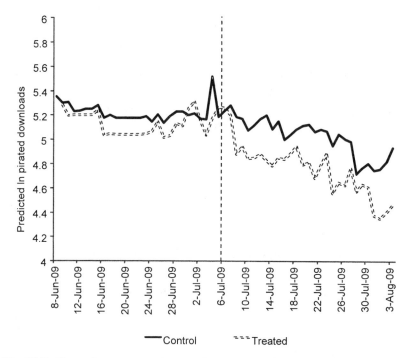

Fig. 13.5   Treated versus control group piracy surrounding July 6, 2009

most logical explanation is that people pirated ABC content less once it was added to Hulu.

In addition to this break in the treated group's piracy relative to levels in the control group, one also notes a break in the control group's piracy levels relative to historical norms. Because the other networks made no major policy changes on this date, this break might suggest a spillover effect: If new viewers of ABC content on Hulu discovered the other shows they like on Hulu, they may have stopped pirating those shows or they may have substituted from non-Hulu shows (which they previously pirated) toward newly discovered shows on Hulu. While we do not have a suitable identification strategy to formally test for these effects, we note that such a spillover effect result would be consistent with similar results in Danaher et al. (2010). They found that when NBC removed their television content from iTunes, in addition to an increase in demand for NBC piracy relative to the control group (ABC, CBS, FOX), there was also an increase in demand for piracy of the control group. Finally, we note that if there was a spillover effect in our present Hulu context, then our control group was partially impacted by the treatment and our reported results will underestimate the effect of adding content to Hulu on piracy of that content.

In order to obtain a statistical estimate of the size of the impact that the streaming channel had on piracy of ABC treated content, we adapt equation (1) as follows:

(2) $\ln Downloads_{it} = \beta_0 + \beta_1 After_t + \beta_2 After_t * ABCHulu_i + \mu_i + e_{it}$.

The variables in equation (2) are the same as in equation (1), except that here *After* is an indicator variable equal to one for all dates after and including July 6, 2009. Variable β_2 thus measures the average difference between treatment and control group in the period after ABC was added to Hulu, compared to any difference beforehand. Under the assumption that the treated group would have trended similarly to the control if not for the experiment, β_2 measures the effect that adding ABC content to Hulu had on piracy of that content.[14] Because there could exist correlation between downloads of different episodes of the same season or even series, we cluster our standard errors at the series level, treating each series in our data as a unique experiment.

Estimating equation (2) through OLS, β_2 is –0.19 (in the eight-week window specification), indicating that the postexperiment decrease in pirated downloads was 18 percent larger for treated ABC content than it was for

14. We ran a more flexible model with a full vector of date fixed effects that produced nearly identical estimates and standard errors for the coefficient of interest. But in this model the "after" variable (for the control group) is subsumed by these fixed effects and so we present the results from the less flexible specification in the table so that the reader may compare the change in the treatment group to the change in the control group.

Table 13.3   OLS of log-pirated downloads

	Eight-week window	Four-week window	Two-week window
After 7-6-2009	−0.194***	−0.072	−0.067
	(0.053)	(0.054)	(0.048)
After 7-6-2009 * ABC	−0.190	−0.169*	−0.164*
	(0.121)	(0.098)	(0.088)
Constant	5.214***	5.218***	5.232***
	(0.026)	(0.025)	(0.024)
Observations	14,132	7,121	3,886
No. of Series	71	71	71
R-squared	0.139	0.071	0.074

Note: Robust standard errors clustered at series level appear in parentheses.
***Significant at the 1 percent level.
**Significant at the 5 percent level.
*Significant at the 10 percent level.

control content (see table 13.3). The p-value for this coefficient is 0.13, so we cannot reject the null hypothesis that changes in ABC piracy were the same as for the control group. This may be due to lack of power in the test: when we conservatively cluster standard errors at the series level, there are only nine treated clusters in the data. However, if we shorten the experimental window to either one or two weeks before and after the treatment (thereby reducing random variance from other unrelated factors), we find similar coefficients but with p-values less than 0.1, allowing us to reject the null hypothesis at a 10 percent significance level or lower.

As further evidence, we estimated equation (2) for the same dates in 2008 (using content from the fall 2007 season), expecting no diff-in-diff change for ABC content as there was no shock to content in this period. Indeed, β_2 for the 2008 period is estimated as −0.02 with a standard error of 0.04, indicating that the change in piracy of ABC content was economically and statistically insignificant relative to the change in piracy of the control group content in this placebo test.

While the significance levels are somewhat low due to small sample size, the magnitude of the estimate is fairly large. Thus our point estimates and our placebo test indicate a pattern in which the addition of ABC content to Hulu caused a nearly 20 percent drop in pirated downloads of the added content, and we interpret this result similarly to the results in our paper on NBC and iTunes. That is, delivering television content in more convenient, readily available channels can cause a substantial number of pirates to turn from illegal file-sharing channels to legal channels. Future research might explore the coding of the torrent data differently in an attempt to determine whether the addition of the most recent five episodes of a series to Hulu reduces pirated consumption of just those five episodes (our finding) or pirated consumption of the entire series.

13.4 Discussion

We began this chapter by pointing out a variety of questions that have arisen in the media industries as a result of the digitization of content and of the resulting weakening of intellectual property due to file sharing. The goal of this chapter was to point researchers to a number of topics that we believe to be interesting and of managerial or regulatory importance, and then to highlight the importance of using natural experiments that arise in the context of rapidly changing media markets as a way of addressing these and other related questions.

To this end, we have shown how several of our papers address these topics through the analysis of natural experiments and through exploiting different types of variance in the data. We have given suggestions of other government interventions or firm strategies that are not well understood and that could be studied with one of the methodologies from our prior work.

Finally, as proof of concept, we applied the difference-in-difference model from our paper on distribution through the iTunes channel to a completely different data set and event: the streaming of television content to consumers on Hulu.com. As file sharing continues to be a commonly chosen consumption channel and as firms continue to innovate through new platforms or strategies for delivering content, the ability to understand the interactions between these channels and the impact that government policies can have on digital markets will only increase in importance. We hope that this chapter serves as a basis for new research to paint a clearer, more complete picture of the complex interplay between media firms' strategies, government policy, and consumer behavior.

References

Bertrand, Marianne, Esther Duflo, and Sendhil Mullainathan. 2004. "How Much Should We Trust Differences-In-Differences Estimates? *Quarterly Journal of Economics* 119 (1): 249–75.

Danaher, Brett, Samita Dhanasobhon, Michael D. Smith, and Rahul Telang. 2010. "Converting Pirates without Cannibalizing Purchasers: The Impact of Digital Distribution on Physical Sales and Internet Piracy." *Marketing Science* 29 (6): 1138–51.

Danaher, Brett, and Michael D. Smith. 2014. "Gone in 60 Seconds: The Impact of the Megaupload Shutdown on Digital Movie Sales." *International Journal of Industrial Organization* 33:1–8. http://ssrn.com/abstract=2229349.

Danaher, Brett, Michael D. Smith, and Rahul Telang. 2014. "Piracy and Copyright Enforcement Mechanisms." In *Innovation Policy and the Economy*, vol. 14, edited by Josh Lerner and Scott Stern, 31–67. Chicago: University of Chicago Press.

Danaher, Brett, Michael D. Smith, Rahul Telang, and Siwen Chen. 2014. "The Effect of Graduated Response Anti-Piracy Laws on Music Sales: Evidence from an Event

Study in France." *Journal of Industrial Economics* 62 (3): 543–53. http://ssrn.com/abstract=1989240.

Lauinger, Tobias, Martin Szydlowski, Kaan Onarlioglu, Gilbert Wondracek, Engin Kirda, and Christopher Kruegel. 2013. "Clickonomics: Determining the Effect of Anti-Piracy Measures for One-Click Hosting." Working Paper, Northeastern University.

Smith, Michael, and Rahul Telang. 2009. "Competing with Free: The Impact of Movie Broadcasts on DVD Sales and Internet Privacy." *Management Information Systems Quarterly* 33 (2): 312–38.

14
Digitization and the Quality of New Media Products
The Case of Music

Joel Waldfogel

Much of economists' research on the effects of digitization on media industries has been focused on harmful impacts of new technology—in particular, file sharing—on revenue. The recorded music industry was the first of the creative industries to face these challenges, and it has provided a leading case study. A large and still growing body of work has sought to establish that Napster and related technologies weakened the excludability of digital products and have reduced the ability of sellers to appropriate value. In the ensuing dozen years, recording industry revenue fell by about a third.[1] Because much of the recorded music industry has traditionally been investment-intensive—spending roughly a sixth of its revenue on artist development (including advances) and another sixth on music promotion—vitiated intellectual property rights prompted serious concern that consumers would see a diminished flow of new recorded music products.[2]

Rather than studying effects of technological change on the availability of new products, research focused only on the narrower question of whether the file-sharing aspect of digitization had reduced revenue on the implicit assumption that revenue reduction would reduce the surplus of both producers and consumers. It is perhaps surprising, then, that the volume of new

---

Joel Waldfogel holds the Frederick R Kappel Chair in Applied Economics at the Carlson School of Management, University of Minnesota, and is a research associate of the National Bureau of Economic Research.

For acknowledgments, sources of research support, and disclosure of the author's material financial relationships, if any, please see http://www.nber.org/chapters/c12996.ack.

1. A large literature explores the impact of file sharing on recorded music revenue. See Oberholzer-Gee and Strumpf (2007), Blackburn (2004), Rob and Waldfogel (2006), Liebowitz (2006), and Zentner (2006), to name a few. Most observers conclude that file sharing is largely responsible for the reduction in recorded music sales.

2. See IFPI (2010) for a discussion of the magnitude of investment by the major record labels.

media products—in music, books, and movies—has not decreased, but has instead increased. Moreover, the evidence on recorded music, which is most studied by virtue of having experienced effects of digitization first, shows that consumers have experienced no reduction in the volume of high quality recorded music products and may indeed have experienced an increase in the service flow from new work. Waldfogel (2012) documents that, based on critics' retrospective best lists, the volume of high quality music did not decline following Napster, and based on sales and airplay data by music vintage, the apparent quality of music vintages rose substantially following 2000.[3]

Continued development of new products in the face of weakened copyright protection is at first blush a puzzle, particularly in an industry with high investment: with less revenue available, record labels have less ability to invest in new products and new artists. Yet, digitization entails both new technologies that reduce demand as well as other new technologies that reduce the costs of bringing new works to market. Recognition of this possibility suggests a research agenda on the effects of reduced costs on the number of new products as well as the realized value of those products to buyers and sellers. The goal of this chapter is to begin that research agenda using recorded music as a context.

Tervio (2009) presents a theoretical framework that is useful for thinking about the product selection problem in the recorded music industry. The marketability of an artist is only known after consumers have been exposed to the product which, in turn, only happens after a label's traditionally large investment in production, promotion, and distribution activities. It is difficult to predict which artists will succeed, and only a small minority of artists whose albums are released—perhaps 10 percent—are profitable. Unpredictability means both that many released albums turn out unsuccessful and that many unreleased albums would be successful if released. The key to discovering more marketable artists to market is more "experimentation," that is, exposing more products to consumers.

This framework, along with some institutional features of the recording industry, may explain the puzzle of increased music quality following Napster. The major record labels that dominate the recorded music industry each have access to all aspects of the traditional processes for bringing music to market: recording, production, promotion, and distribution. These firms employ a high-cost strategy for experimentation, involving substantial expenditures for artist cash advances, professional recording, tours, and costly promotion of music on traditional radio stations. Alongside the majors is a large fringe of "independent" record labels, employing lower-cost methods for or bringing music to market. Notably, they do not typically incur the costs needed to get their artists' songs on the radio. Because of their limited resources in undertaking promotional activities, independent labels

---

3. See Waldfogel (2011, 2012).

(and artists releasing their own music) have traditionally faced difficulty in achieving substantial sales for their albums.

In the past few decades, changes in communication technology have made it possible for recording firms to undertake broader experimentation with less investment. Digitization has had obvious effects on the costs of producing and distributing recorded music. Low-cost equipment and software have reduced recording costs, and the Internet enables low-cost digital distribution; but success also requires the promotion of new products. Perhaps less obvious are digitization's impacts on promotion. Consumers can now be made aware of a wider range of new music more easily and through channels other than the traditional bottleneck of radio. Notable new avenues of promotion include online listening opportunities (Internet radio) as well as a growing cadre of online music reviewers.

Effective reduction in the cost of bringing new work to market raises the possibility that despite piracy's depressing impact on revenue, more music may be finding its way to market, allowing consumers to discover better music. This chapter seeks to systematically explore this possibility. To this end I assemble data on all album releases 1980–2010 (including label type), along with airplay information that I am able to assemble on album sales and airplay on both traditional radio (since 1990) and Internet radio (2006–2011), as well as the availability of reviews for albums at Metacritic since 2001. Using these data I address the following questions: First, how have the number of releases from major and independent labels, as well as self-released album, evolved over time? Second, have sales become concentrated in fewer, or in more, albums over time? Third, has promotion via airplay and album reviews changed over time? Fourth, how have the apparent pathways to commercial success changed over time? In particular, *how* are they achieving success—using radio airplay versus other means of reaching consumers? And finally, *who* is achieving success over time (majors or indies)?

The experience of Arcade Fire's album *The Suburbs* illustrates the mechanisms the chapter seeks to explore. The 2011 winner of the Grammy award for best album, *The Suburbs* provides a prominent example of promotion— and both commercial and critical success—without much traditional airplay. The album was released by the independent label Merge Records on August 3, 2010,[4] and received a Metascore of 87 at Metacritic, putting its rating in the top 5 percent of album scores. Despite critical acclaim for this and their previous albums (Metascores of 90 and 87, respectively, for 2004's *Funeral* and 2007's *Neon Bible*), their new album received little or no airplay. Neither it nor its predecessors ever appeared among the top 75 weekly songs on Billboard's airplay chart. Yet, its exposure on Internet radio was substan-

---

4. According to Amazon.com: http://www.amazon.com/The-Suburbs-Arcade-Fire/dp/B003O85W3A/.

tial. In its third week after release, the song "Ready to Start" had over 40,000 weekly listeners at Last.fm, and its listening remained at roughly 20,000 per week through February, 2010. The album won the Grammy for best album, and the album was certified Gold by the Recording Industry Association of America (RIAA), indicating sales of 0.5 million, on October 19, 2011.

Systematic analysis of the data paints the following picture, which provides a plausible explanation for the apparent increase in music quality over the past decade. First, there has been a substantial growth in independent releases and self-released works of music relative to major-label releases. Despite an absolute decline in major-label releases, the overall number of new works brought annually to market has increased by 50 percent since 2000. Second, there has been substantial growth in information channels by which consumers can learn about new music. Where traditional radio used to be the main institution for learning about new music, the past decade has seen the emergence and growth in alternative institutions, including Internet radio (with highly customized playlists able to air a wider variety of music) and online music criticism. New information channels are changing the pathways to commercial success. While 60 percent of the artists appearing among the weekly top 25 albums on the Billboard 200 during 1991 received substantial airplay during the year, the share has fallen steadily since. In 2010, only 30 percent of the Billboard top 25 artists had received substantial airplay during the year. Other modes of acquainting consumers with new music other than radio airplay are playing a larger role. A large share of the Billboard 200 artists not receiving airplay had instead been covered in the growing Web media: by 2010, 38 percent had recently been reviewed by at least three critical outlets covered in Metacritic.

This disintermediation of the traditional roles of the major record labels has given rise to a rather substantial change in the types of record companies achieving commercial success, as well as the channels by which consumers learn about the music that they ultimately purchase. Independent labels accounted for 13 percent of the artists appearing in the Billboard 200 in 2001, and this has risen steadily to 35 percent in 2010. Digitization has created divergence between the interests of the major recording labels that have traditionally dominated the market and smaller, independent labels. Major labels, represented by the Recording Industry Association of America,[5] have been vocal in advocating a governmental response to stem piracy. While the smaller, independent labels also face revenue losses from file sharing, their response has been different. They have responded to technological change by taking advantage of the new opportunities to release music at lower cost, and much of this new music is popular with consumers.

The chapter proceeds in six sections. Section 14.1 provides some institu-

5. See http://www.riaa.com/physicalpiracy.php?content_selector=What-is-Online-Piracy.

tional background on the recorded music industry, as well as a simple model in the spirit of Tervio (2009) for organizing ideas about the possible impact of digitization on the quality of music that markets provide to consumers. Section 14.2 describes the various data sources used in the study. Section 14.3 discusses our method for estimating sales from a combination of Billboard album sales ranks and Recording Industry Association of America (RIAA) sales certification data. Section 14.4 describes the changed information environment by contrasting the role of traditional airplay with the new environment of Internet radio and online music criticism. Section 14.5 then turns to results. First, I document the evolution of the number of album releases over time, overall, and by type of music label. Second, I document that the growth in the number of available new products has brought about a fragmentation of demand, particularly since 2000. While roughly 500 artists appeared on the Billboard 200 rankings during 2000, over 1,000 separate artists appeared on the Billboard 200 weekly rankings during 2010. This evidence is interesting in itself; it also provides an instructive contrast with other media markets that remain concentrated even as markets expand in relation to entry costs, as in Sutton (1991). Third, I present evidence on the changing composition of promotional channels for commercially successful artists. I document that a declining share of successful artists have traditional airplay, while a growing share are covered by online radio and critics. Fourth, I ask whether the formerly suppressed products now brought to market have substantial ex post value, in particular whether a growing share of commercially successful albums are released by independent labels. The conclusion provides some discussion of the results, in particular a discussion of factors that would lead to an increase in the number of available products to bring about fragmentation. I also discuss directions for further research.

14.1 Background: Digitization and Bringing Music to Market

14.1.1 Industry Background

Bringing new music to market relies broadly on four activities. First, a label must discover talent. Second, the label can invest in artists, both in the form of cash advances and the creation of professional-quality recordings of music that embody the quality they have discovered and nurtured. Third, they promote the music that they have recorded through both advertising and campaigns to get music on the radio. Finally, they produce and distribute physical recordings to consumers, via retailers. The major record labels have traditionally maintained all of these capabilities, and these activities are costly.

Major labels give artists cash advances. While these advances are recoupable from an artist's sales, they are "not recouped if sales do not reach certain levels. Thus it is the record company that bears the risk of the investment."[6] The International Federation of the Phonographic Industry (IFPI 2010) cites $200,000 as a typical advance for a new pop act and $1,500,000 as a typical advance for a superstar.

Recording itself has also been expensive. Recording an album has traditionally required an investment in studio time. Labels undertook this investment by lending artists money against future revenue from the resulting albums. Vogel (2007, 243) reports that, "[p]roduction costs for popular albums are generally budgeted for at least $200,000, and, if much studio time is used, costs can soar well past $350,000." The IFPI (2010) cites $200,000 as the recording cost for a typical new pop act and $400,000 for a superstar.

Marketing and promotion campaigns—involving concert tours, cooperative advertisers with local retailers, and radio and television ads—are also expensive. According to Vogel (2007, 244): "[m]arketing costs can often reach $100,000 for a fairly standard release and in excess of $500,000 for one by a major artist." The IFPI (2010) cites $300,000 as a typical cost of promotion and marketing for a new pop act and $2,300,000 for a superstar. Music videos and tour support add separate costs, totaling $300,000 for a typical new pop act and $450,000 for a typical superstar.

A major goal of these promotional campaigns is to get new music played on the radio. Space on radio station playlists has traditionally been scarce. As Vogel (2007, 244) puts it, "With popular-music stations able to add at most three or four new cuts per week to their lists, competition for airplay is intense: Every year an estimated 11,000 (nonclassical) major-label albums averaging some ten cuts per album is released, but it is now unusual for more than around 120 of these to sell more than 500,000 units in the physical (i.e., CD) format." It is perhaps not surprising, given the incentives to get music aired in conjunction with playlist scarcity, that the cost of promoting a hit single record was "about $150,000" in the 1980s (Caves 2000).

Distribution is also costly and is subject to scale economies. Because most successful records are in demand only briefly, "it is essential that retailers located over a wide geographic swath have their inventories quickly replenished."[7] As a result, "[m]ost records are thus distributed by large organizations with sufficient capital to stock and ship hundreds of thousands of units on a moment's notice."[8]

Incurring the costs associated with production, promotion, and distribution is by no means a guarantee of success. Vogel (2007, 244) reports that "perhaps as little as 10 percent of new material must make a profit large enough to offset losses on the majority of releases. . . . Labels will encourage

---

6. See IFPI (2010, 10).
7. Vogel (2007, 245).
8. Ibid.

the production of more material than can possibly succeed, in essence diversifying their portfolio of bets on new releases." Caves, quoting screenwriter William Goldman, (2000, 61) makes a similar point: "The payout is highly uncertain, however. *Nobody knows*: casual estimates suggest that roughly 80 percent of albums and 85 percent of single records fail to cover their costs."

New technologies have enabled disintermediation of the majors' traditional functions, that is, less expensive alternatives to the major labels' traditional method. Production is now far less expensive. An artist can create a recording with a few hundred dollars worth of software rather than hundreds of thousands of dollars of studio time. It is also possible to promote new music with neither expensive advertising nor traditional radio airplay. Instead, an artist can post music to YouTube, or an independent label can make an artist known through Internet radio. Major outlets include Pandora, Last.fm, rdio, and a multitude of others.

At an extreme, some highly successful artists have been discovered entirely without labels. Perhaps the best known example is Justin Bieber, who was discovered on YouTube.

> Bieber was discovered in 2008 by Scooter Braun, who happened to come across Bieber's videos on YouTube and later became his manager. Braun arranged for him to meet with Usher in Atlanta, Georgia, and Bieber was soon signed to Raymond Braun Media Group (RBMG), a joint venture between Braun and Usher, and then to a recording contract with Island Records offered by L. A. Reid. His debut single, "One Time," released worldwide in 2009, peaked in the top ten in Canada and charted in the top thirty in several international markets. His debut release, *My World*, followed on November 17, 2009, and was eventually certified platinum in the United States. He became the first artist to have seven songs from a debut album chart on the *Billboard* Hot 100.[9]

Bieber's story, while perhaps atypical, is not unique. Elliott (2011) provides accounts of 15 artists discovered on YouTube.[10]

Short of this extreme example are other possible new routes to success without the major labels' high investment. While there is a great deal of variation among independent labels, it is surely accurate to say that they employ lower-cost strategies. According to *Agenda Magazine*, "If there is an advance offered, it will not be as large as one from a major label." And, "an Indie label cannot usually allot quite as much money for marketing and

---

9. See http://en.wikipedia.org/wiki/Justin_Bieber. Accessed August 3, 2010. See also Desriee Adib, "Pop Star Justin Bieber Is on the Brink of Superstardom." Nov. 14, 2009. Good Morning America (http://abcnews.go.com/GMA/Weekend/teen-pop-star-justin-bieber-discovered-youtube/story?id=9068403), accessed August 3, 2011.

10. See Amy-Mae Elliott, "15 Aspiring Musicians Who Found Fame Through YouTube." Mashable.com, January 23, 2011 (http://mashable.com/2011/01/23/found-fame-youtube/#Jk5L0–SIceg, accessed August 3, 2011).

tour support as a major, so it might take longer to gain as much exposure as with a major label."[11] According to one source, "independents typically spend much less on marketing and promotion than major labels."[12]

Internet, rather than traditional terrestrial radio is part of the strategy. "For indie record labels, internet broadcasting as well as podcasting, represent a way to get (independent) music heard." According to the CEO of Magnatune (an independent music company), "Ever since Big Radio began being a pay-to-play (aka payola) system, indie labels have not had a way to reach their fans over the airwaves. And of course, fans of non-mass-media music would like diversity and quality in the radio offerings they can access. Indie labels want internet radio to survive and prosper: that is how we reach and build a fan base."[13]

Leeds (2005) provides additional evidence on the importance of the Internet for artists on independent labels: "no factor is more significant than the Internet, which has shaken up industry sales patterns and, perhaps more important, upended the traditional hierarchy of outlets that can promote music. Buzz about an underground act can spread like a virus, allowing a band to capture national acclaim before it even has a recording contract, as was the case this year with Clap Your Hands Say Yeah, an indie rock band."

Because independent record labels incur lower costs making each album, they can break even with far lower sales than a major label requires. "Unlike the majors, independent labels typically do not allocate money to producing slick videos or marketing songs to radio stations. An established independent like Matador Records—home to acts including Pretty Girls Make Graves and Belle and Sebastian—can turn a profit after selling roughly 25,000 copies of an album; success on a major label release sometimes doesn't kick in until sales of half a million" (Leeds 2005). "'No one's trying to sell six million records; we're trying to sell as many as we can,' said Chris Lombardi, Matador's founder. 'We're working with realistic success.'"

Summarizing the potentially transformative effects of new technologies and new communication channels, Knopper (2009, 246) describes artists' "newfound independence from major record labels" as:

> a shocking, liberating new world. They began their careers when labels had just about every bit of leverage possible in the star-making process. An artist who wanted to make a record needed studio time—and that cost money, which meant a sizable loan from the label. An artist who wanted to get a single onto a radio playlist needed connections—and that usually meant a label executive who had the money to hire an independent promoter. An artist who wanted to sell millions of copies of a

---

11. See http://www.agendamag.com/sept09/majors-vs-indie.html.
12. See http://en.wikipedia.org/wiki/Independent_music, accessed August 24, 2011.
13. See Vern Seward, "Internet Radio and the CRB: A View from Indie Labels." The Mac Observer. June 13, 2007. http://www.macobserver.com/tmo/article/Internet_Radio_And_The_CRB_A_View_From_Indie_Labels/.

record needed a big-time distributor with the clout to push CDs into big stores like Best Buy or Target—and that meant one of the major labels' own subsidiaries, like WEA or CEMA. Today, it's not necessary to hook up with a label to do all these things. An artist can make a record cheaply, and professionally, using software like Pro Tools. An artist can forgo the radio, building buzz and exposure online via do-it-yourself websites like MySpace, viral videos on YouTube, or any number of social networking services from Facebook to Garageband.com. As for distribution, who needs crates, trucks, warehouses, stores, or even the discs themselves? Artists can follow Radiohead's example and simply distribute the music essentially free online.

Many artists express enthusiasm for the new situation. Moby, a US artist with an album that has sold over a million copies, argues, "There was a time when the music business was incredibly monolithic and there were only two ways to get your music heard: sign to a major label, get your music played on MTV and get it played by big radio stations" (Sandstoe 2011). James Mercer (of the Shins, who have produced two albums that have each sold over half a million copies in the United States, quoted in Knopper 2009, 246): "You see these articles about the disaster in the music business. . . . It's now more likely I'll be able to start my own label, release my work, profit from it, and have a more lucrative career. For a band at our level, it's all a bowl of cherries."

These accounts stand in contrast to the trends in recorded music revenue, raising the question of whether they withstand more systematic inquiry.

14.2 Model

This section presents a simple model in the spirit of Tervio (2009) to illustrate the possible effects of technological change on the realized quality of music that consumers experience.[14] The model is meant to embody the idea that music is an experienced good whose quality and marketability are difficult to predict at the time of the investment decision. Instead, true quality is revealed only by the expensive process of bringing the product to market. In the model, music labels act as gatekeepers that finance recorded music products based on their ex ante promise. If the product is brought to market, firms and consumers discover and realize the ex post value of the product. Because of endemic unpredictability, ex ante promise is a poor predictor of ex post success.

Define q_i as an index of the quality of product i. Quality here should be

---

14. Tervio's model predicts a bias toward mediocrity: Labels could finance the adequate experimentation only if they could strike long-term contracts with artists, allowing them to finance the failed experiments with the proceeds from rare successes; but long-term contracts are not feasible. Hence, there is insufficient experimentation and an overreliance on predictably profitable but mediocre artists.

interpreted as an index related to both marketability and consumer welfare. Financiers and consumers cannot learn the true quality of the product prior to release. Instead, they form an estimate of ex ante promise of marketability: $q'_i = q_i + \varepsilon_i$, where ε is a mean-zero error.

Bringing a product to market has the substantial costs described above, and the product must be brought to market in order for buyers and sellers to learn the true quality of the product. Producers are risk-neutral, and they bring a new product to market if expected revenues cover costs, or if $q'_i > T_0$, where T_0 is a quality/marketability threshold such that products brought to market are expected to cover costs.

Technological change then brings two shocks to the market. First, piracy makes it more difficult to generate revenue, which raises the entry threshold T. But concurrent technological changes make it possible to record music and make it available to the public (and to learn its true quality) at lower cost. This allows firms to operate with a reduced T, which we refer to as T_1 when they use the lower-cost mode of production, promotion, and distribution.

If artist marketability were perfectly predictable at the time of investment, then all artists with true (realized) quality above the threshold ($q > T$) would be brought to market. If technological change fell from T_0 to T_1, then additional products with less ex ante promise would be brought to market. This would perforce benefit consumers, but the benefit would be relatively small, since all of the newly available products would have quality between T_0 and T_1. But as noted above, artist marketability is very unpredictable, so a relaxation of the entry threshold can raise the number of products that are highly marketable ex post, not just the number of products with ex post value between T_0 and T_1. Under the lower threshold, a product is launched when ex ante promise exceeds T_1, which occurs when $q_i > T_1 - \varepsilon_i$. Provided that ex post success is sufficiently unpredictable—var(ε) is sufficiently large—the lower-cost entry condition will give rise to additional entry of products with ex post marketability in excess of T_0. In short, provided that $T_1 < T_0$ and artist marketability is unpredictable, we can expect an increase in the quantity of high-quality products brought to market when T declines.

This framework, while simple, puts some structure on our inquiry. The first question is whether, in light of both piracy and potential cost reductions, the effective threshold has risen or fallen (and, by extension, whether more or fewer products come to market). Given an affirmative answer to the first question, a second question is whether the new products with less ex ante promise—and which previously would have been less likely to be launched—add substantially to the welfare delivered by available products. This is a difficult question, but we can certainly ask whether products launched by independent labels—and using low-cost methods of production, promotion, and distribution—grow more likely to become commercially successful. These questions, along with evidence about mechanism, occupy most of the rest of the study.

14.2.1 Data

I develop two basic data sets for this study using data from nine underlying sources. The first data set is a list of albums released in the United States from 1980 to 2010, where for each album I attempt to classify its label (major, independent, self-released) and its format (physical versus digital). The second basic data set is a list of commercially successful albums based on their inclusion on weekly top-selling album lists, along with my estimates of the albums' actual sales. These albums are then linked with measures of traditional radio airplay, promotion on Internet radio, coverage by music critics, and a designation of whether the album is on an independent record label.

The nine underlying data sources for this study may be grouped into six components. First, I have weekly rankings of US album sales, from three separate weekly Billboard charts. First among these charts is the Billboard 200 (from 1990 to 2011), which lists the top 200 bestselling albums of the week, based on Soundscan data.[15] Second, I observe the Heatseekers chart (2000–2011), which shows the weekly top 50 albums among artists who have never appeared in the top 100 of the Billboard 200, nor have they ever appeared in the top 10 of the more specialized Billboard charts.[16] Heatseeker artists can be viewed as artists emerging as commercially successful. Finally, I also observe the Billboard Independent chart, which shows the week's top-selling albums from independent music labels. I observe this for 2001–2011.[17] All of the Billboard charts are obtained from Billboard.biz.

Second, I observe two measures of traditional US airplay, from the Billboard Hot 100 airplay chart which, ironically, lists the 75 most aired songs of the week in the United States and from USA Top 200, which lists "the top 200 songs on US radio" each week. The Billboard chart lists "the week's most popular songs across all genres, ranked by radio airplay audience impressions measured from Nielsen BDS." Spins are weighted by numbers of apparent listeners.[18] I observe this for 1990–2011, again from Billboard.biz. Because I observe the top 75 songs of each week and not the entire universe of songs aired on the radio, I refer to the songs on the airplay charts as songs with "substantial airplay." I have a separate measure of airplay, the USA Airplay Top 200 ("The most played tracks on USA radio stations") between February 2009 and the end of 2011.[19] The latter source has the

---

15. The underlying data include 272,000 entries from weekly top-200 album sales charts, 1990–2011.
16. The underlying data include 31,775 entries from weekly top-50 album charts, 2000–2011.
17. The underlying data include 28,775 entries from weekly top-50 independent album charts, 2001–2011.
18. http://www.billboard.com/charts/radio-songs#/charts/radio-songs.
19. See http://www.charly1300.com/usaairplay.htm, accessed June 15, 2012.

advantage of covering nearly three times as many songs per week. Because airplay data cover songs while my sales data described albums, I aggregate both to the artist-year for linking and analysis.

Third, I observe critical assessments of new albums from Metacritic. Metacritic reports an assessment of each album on a 100-point scale. They report a review of at least three of over-100 underlying critical sites reports a review on an album. Metacritic appeared in 2000, so these reviews cover the period 2000–2011, and the coverage grows over the decade. There are 485 reviews in 2000, 867 in 2005, and 1,037 in 2010. According to Metacritic,

> We try to include as many new releases as possible, in a variety of genres. Generally, major pop, rock, rap and alternative releases will be included. We also try to include many indie and electronic artists, as well as major releases in other categories (country, etc.). Occasionally, we will also include import-only items (generally, UK releases) if it appears that they will not be released in the United States in the foreseeable future (otherwise, we will typically wait for the US release). Remember, if an album does not show up in at least 3 of the publications we use, it probably will not be included on the site.[20]

Fourth, I have data on the weekly rankings of songs aired at Internet radio site Last.fm from April 3, 2005 to May 29, 2011. While Pandora is the largest and most prominent Internet radio site, I lack Pandora listening data.[21] However, listening data on Last.fm are more readily available. According to Alexa.com, Pandora was the 308th ranked global site, and the fifty-fifth US site, on June 11, 2012. Last.fm is lower ranked: 766 globally and 549 in the United States. Last.fm reports the top 420 songs, according to the number of listeners, for each week.

Fifth, I observe RIAA data on total album shipments by year (1989–2011) as well as gold (0.5 million), platinum (1.0 million), and multiplatinum album certifications, 1958–2011. As I detail in section 14.3, I use the certification data in conjunction with Billboard sales rankings to construct weekly estimates of album sales, by album.

Sixth, I have a list of works of new recorded music, from Discogs.com. Discogs is a user-generated data set that bills itself as "the largest and most accurate music database . . . containing information on artists, labels, and their recordings." Using Discogs, I created a data set consisting of every US album released from 1980 to 2010. This is a total of 203,258 separate releases. (I aggregate versions on different media, e.g., CD, vinyl, file, into a single release.) My focus is albums, so I exclude singles.

There are 38,634 distinct labels among my Discogs data, and classifying

---

20. From "How do you determine what albums to include on the site?", at https://metacritic.custhelp.com/app/answers/detail/a_id/1518/session/L3Nuby8wL3NpZC9DOFVxQkczaw==, published June 10, 2010.

21. See http://www.edisonresearch.com/wp-content/uploads/2013/04/Edison_Research_Arbitron_Infinite_Dial_2013.pdf.

labels as major versus independents turns out to be challenging. Major labels are generally understood to be those labels owned by three underlying firms: Universal, Sony/BMG, Warner, and until recently, EMI. Unfortunately, for the purpose of identifying them in the data, labels operate with many imprints as the tallies above suggest. While published sources document the histories of some the major imprints (e.g., Southall 2003), such published sources cover only a small fraction of the labels in these data.

Fortunately, I can rely on a few other approaches to identify many labels that are either definitely major or definitely independent. First, a recent study by Thomson (2010) attempts to calculate the share of music on the radio released by independent record labels. For this purpose she needed to classify thousands of underlying albums' labels as major or independent. She enlisted the help of the American Association of Independent Music (A2IM) to create a list of major and independent record labels. Her list includes 6,358 labels, of which all but 688 could be coded as major or independent.[22] I begin with her classification. I also classify as major a label whose name includes the name of a major label (e.g., Warner, EMI, etc.). Finally, I classify as independent any label that Discogs refers to as "underground," "independent," "experimental," "minor," or "not a real label."

Despite all of these efforts, matching is incomplete. Of the works in Discogs, 26 percent can be identified as being on major labels. Another 20 percent of works can be identified as independent-label releases, and 3 percent are self-released. This leaves the label types for 51 percent of the albums in the database unidentified. That said, there is reason to believe that the releases on unknown labels are not from major record labels. Of the releases on unknown labels, 40 percent are on labels that release albums by no more than five artists. In some calculations below, I treat the unclassified labels as nonmajor labels.

14.3 Inferring Sales Quantities from Sales Ranks and Album Certifications

We would like to have data on the quantities sold for all albums, by album, but such data are unfortunately expensive to obtain. Fortunately, we can use the data at hand to construct reasonable estimates of sales for almost all albums. We have data on the weekly sales ranks of the top 200 selling albums, as well as sales milestones (0.5 million and multiples of one million) for high-selling albums. In addition, we have data on the total sales of all albums by year.

It is usual to assume that sales distributions follow power laws (see Chevalier and Goolsbee 2003; Brynjolfsson, Smith, and Hu 2003). That is, sales

---

22. A small number of additional labels have the classifications Disney and legacy, respectively.

quantities are believed to bear simple relationships with sales ranks. To be specific, $s_{it} = \alpha r_{it}^{\beta}$, where s_{it} is sales of album i in week t, r_{it} is the sales rank of album i in week t, and α and β are parameters. Because we observe when sales pass various thresholds, say, 0.5 million at gold certification, we can econometrically estimate α and β. Define the cumulative sales for album i in period τ as $S_{i\tau}$. Thus, $S_{i\tau} = \sum_{t=0}^{\tau} \alpha r_{it}^{\beta}$. If we include an additive error, we can estimate the parameters via nonlinear least squares. The coefficients have the following interpretation: α provides an estimate of the weekly sales of a number one-ranked album. The parameter β describes how quickly sales fall in ranks.

A few adjustments are needed for realism. Because the size of the market is changing over time, the parameters are not necessarily constant. We have data on thousands of album certifications across many years, so we can be flexible about the parameters. Given estimates of the parameters, we can construct estimated sales of each album in each week (or each year). We can use these data to calculate, say, the share of sales attributable to independent-label albums. We can also calculate the extent to which sales are concentrated in each year.

Data on certification-based sales provide some guidance on parameter stability. We can calculate the sales for the top-selling albums of the 1970s, 1980s, 1990s, and the first decade of the twenty-first century. We can then compare the log sales-log rank relationships across decades. (To be clear, these are not the Billboard weekly sales ranks referred to as r_{it} above; rather, these are ranks based on total sales ever from RIAA certification data.) Table 14.1 presents a regression of log sales on log ranks, where the constant and slope coefficients are allowed to vary across releases from the different decades, 1970–2010. Not surprisingly, the constant term varies substantially

Table 14.1   Log sales and log rank using certification data

	Coef.	Std. err.
Alpha		
1970	Omitted	
1980	0.8232	0.0649
1990	1.2295	0.0596
2000	0.1156	0.0610
Beta		
1970	−0.6717	0.0093
1980	−0.7547	0.0063
1990	−0.7376	0.0043
2000	−0.6105	0.0048
Constant	3.8853	0.0515

Note: Regression of the log certification-based sales of albums released 1970–2010 on their log sales rank within the decade.

across decades, reflecting the differing sales levels in the different decades. The constant term rises from the 1970s to the 1990s, then falls substantially in the first decade of the twenty-first century. (The exponentiated constants provide estimates of the sales of the top-ranked album of each decade.) The slope coefficient varies less across decades. In particular, it rises in absolute value from 0.65 in the 1970s to 0.75 during the 1980s and 1990s. The coefficient then falls in the first decade of the twenty-first century back to its level in the 1970s. A lower slope coefficient indicates that sales fall off less in ranks. The recent decline in the slope coefficient indicates that recent sales are less concentrated among the highest-ranked albums. These results indicate that we will want to allow the constant term to vary over time.

We implement the nonlinear least squares estimation with 3,272 albums receiving certification, released between 1986 and 2010. There is an apparent bunching of certifications of particular albums. That is, the gold and platinum certifications sometimes appear on the same date. Hence, I use only the sales associated with the highest certification for each album, and I assume that the sales associated with the accumulated certifications level of sales has occurred by the time of the last certification. Table 14.2 reports results. The first column reports a restrictive specification that holds both α and β constant over time. The second specification relaxes the constancy of α. Regardless of the method used, the β estimate is roughly 0.6. The α term varies over time with overall album sales. The rise in α in 2010 arises because the certification data end in 2010. Hence, the coefficient reflects the relationship between BB200 weekly ranks and the selected sample of albums that quickly achieve sales certification. Putting the 2010 coefficient aside, the pattern of α coefficients tracks overall sales trends, peaking around 1999 and falling thereafter. Figure 14.1 plots coefficients against total annual album shipments, both normalized to 1 in 1999, and the correspondence is close.

One shortcoming of the above approach is that it does not incorporate information about annual aggregate album sales. That is, nothing constrains the sum of simulated sales across albums to equal total reported shipments for the year. If we were to assume that the sales of albums that never appear on the Billboard weekly top 200 are negligible—in effect, that only about 500–1,000 albums per year had nonzero sales—then we would expect the sum of the implied sales across weeks in a year to equal the year's aggregate sales. That is, if we define σ_y as the aggregate album sales in year y, then: $\sum_{i=1}^{T} \sum_{t=0}^{52} \alpha r_{it}^{\beta} = \sigma_y$. This can be rewritten as $\alpha = \sigma_y / (\sum_{i=1}^{T} \sum_{t=0}^{52} r_{it}^{\beta})$. That is, once we have an estimate of β that we wish to apply to year y, we can infer α for that year as well. The sum of the simulated sales of the albums appearing in the Billboard 200 at some point during the year then equals the actual aggregate sales. I use this approach, which causes the sales tabulations of Billboard 200 albums to equal total shipments.

Table 14.2 Nonlinear least squares estimates of the relationship between RIAA certification-based sales and weekly Billboard album sales ranks

	(1)	(2)
Alpha	0.3422	
Beta	0.60063	0.61577
Alpha		
1986		0.3495
1987		0.04438
1988		0.3216
1989		0.3928
1990		0.30106
1991		0.23195
1992		0.31962
1993		0.4321
1994		0.58778
1995		0.44124
1996		0.46895
1997		0.42882
1998		0.4038
1999		0.53432
2000		0.45097
2001		0.48995
2002		0.40985
2003		0.32757
2004		0.4351
2005		0.2871
2006		0.20662
2007		0.24924
2008		0.23785
2009		0.15882
2010		0.82928

Notes: Estimates calculated using amoeba search algorithm. Standard errors to follow via bootstrapping.

14.4 The Changing Information Environment for Consumers

14.4.1 Internet versus Traditional Radio

Traditional radio operates in a relatively small number of predefined programming formats (top 40, adult contemporary, and so on), providing venues for the promotion of a relatively small share of new music. Major-label music dominates airplay on traditional radio. Thomson (2010) documents that between 2005 and 2008, music from independent labels accounted for 12–13 percent of US airplay.

Three recent developments hold the possibility of changing the number of new music products of which consumers are cognizant: Internet radio, expanded online criticism, as well as social media. While traditional radio

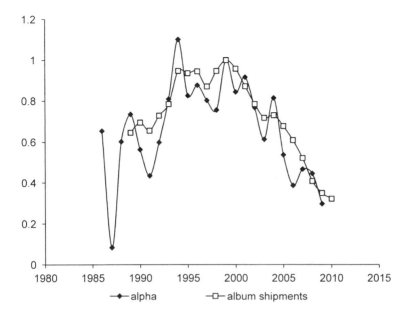

Fig. 14.1 Alpha and album shipments

stations have publicized a small number of artists in preordained formats, Internet radio allows listeners to tailor stations narrowly to their tastes. At Pandora, for example, users "seed" their stations with songs or artists that they like. Pandora then presents other songs that are similar. Last.fm operates similarly. While this personalization need not lead to a greater variety of artists receiving airplay—it would be possible for all listeners to seed their stations with the same songs or artists—in practice, personalization provides promotion for artists not receiving substantial traditional airplay.

To explore Internet radio listening patterns, I obtained song-listening statistics from Last.fm's weekly song chart, Feb. 2005–July 2011. Each week Last.fm reports the number of listeners for each of the top 420 songs at Last.fm. Figure 14.2 provides a characterization of listener volumes as a function of song rank on Last.fm. In 2010, a top-ranked song (according to volume of listeners) had about 38,000 weekly listeners. The 100th-ranked song had about 13,000, and the 400th song had roughly 8,000. I then compare the artists on Last.fm with those on traditional radio airplay charts.

Unfortunately, both of my airplay data sources are incomplete. Thomson (2010) documents that, over the course of a year (between 2005 and 2008), the top 100 songs accounted for about 11 percent of airplay, the top 1,000 songs accounted for almost 40 percent, and the top 10,000 accounted for nearly 90 percent. While the Billboard airplay data include 3,900 (75 × 52) song listings per year because songs persist on the charts, the total number of songs making the Billboard airplay charts is about 330 per year. The USA

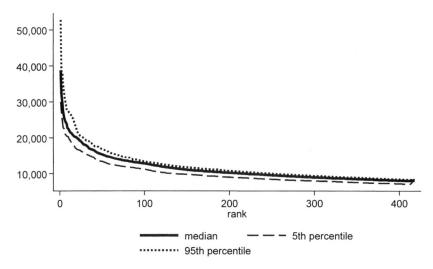

Fig. 14.2 Listening rank and weekly listeners, 2010

Airplay data go deeper. In 2010, the chart included 10,400 entries and 662 distinct songs. While I am missing more than half of the songs on the radio, I can still document stark differences between radio airplay and Internet radio artist coverage.

Despite the differences in list depth, both the Billboard airplay charts and Last.fm's song chart include roughly the same number of artists per year. In 2006 (with the first full year of data on Last.fm), Billboard's weekly top 75 lists included a total of 253 artists across the year. Last.fm's weekly songs lists included a total of 183 artists. Only thirty-three artists appeared on both lists. The overlap is quite similar in subsequent years. The degree of overlap by listening is somewhat larger than the overlap by artists: of the 2006 listening at Last.fm, 26 percent was to artists also on the Billboard airplay charts. Figures for 2007–2010 are similar. While this leaves open the possibility that the Last.fm songs are nevertheless on the radio, the degree of overlap with the longer USA Top 200 Airplay list is similarly low. In 2010, nearly 70 percent of the songs on Last.fm are not among those on the USA Top 200 list.

We see other indications that airplay patterns differ between traditional and Internet radio. I can construct crude indices of song listening from rank data as the reciprocal of the weekly rank, summed across weeks in the year. The correlation between this measure of listening across the two traditional airplay data sets is 0.75. The correlation between the airplay index from the Top 200 data and the Last.fm listening measure is 0.15. These results indicate that the majority of Last.fm listening appears to be for music not widely played on traditional radio and that Internet radio provides promotion for music that is less heavily promoted on commercial radio.

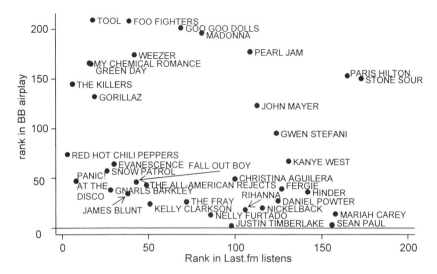

Fig. 14.3 Ranks in 2006 among artists on both

Among the songs on BB airplay and Last.fm lists, the correlation of airplay frequency is low (see figure 14.3 for scatter plot). There is other evidence that the two kinds of outlets allow the promotion of different sorts of artists. Tables 14.3 and 14.4, respectively, provide lists of the most heavily played artists on Last.fm not appearing on the BB list, and vice versa. Comparison of the lists shows clearly that Last.fm is comparatively skewed toward independent-label artists. Despite the shortcomings of the available airplay data, it seems clear that traditional and Internet radio provide promotional opportunities for different kinds of artists.

14.4.2 Growing Online Criticism

Critical assessments also substantively expand the set of artists promoted to consumers. Along with many other effects of digitization, the Internet has led to an explosion of outlets providing critical assessment of new music. Since 1995 the number of outlets reviewing new music—and the number of reviews produced per year—has doubled. These reviews are moreover made available freely on the Web (through sites like Metacritic and Pitchfork). These information sources hold the possibility of challenging radio's centrality in influencing musical discovery.

Of course, music criticism predates the Internet, but the growth of the Internet has been accompanied by a substantial growth in outlets offering music criticism. Metacritic.com is a website offering distilled numerical ratings of new music. They have operated since 2000 and they draw from over 100 sources of professional music criticism. Metacritic reports a "Metascore" for an album—a translation of reviews into a numerical score

Table 14.3   Top artists on Last.fm in 2006 without BB airplay

Artist	Listeners
Death Cab for Cutie	5,200,000
Coldplay	5,200,000
Radiohead	4,700,000
Muse	3,900,000
Arctic Monkeys	3,000,000
The Postal Service	2,800,000
The Beatles	2,400,000
System of a Down	2,300,000
Bloc Party	2,100,000
Nirvana	1,900,000
The Arcade Fire	1,900,000
Franz Ferdinand	1,700,000
Pink Floyd	1,400,000
The Strokes	1,300,000
The Shins	1,100,000
Interpol	1,100,000
Metallica	1,000,000
Linkin Park	973,630
Placebo	914,018
Thom Yorke	860,097
Jack Johnson	823,208
The White Stripes	806,304
Oasis	759,511
Yeah Yeah Yeahs	685,532
Sufjan Stevens	674,766

Note: "Listeners" is the sum of weekly listeners for each of the artists' songs appearing on the weekly top song lists across all weeks in the year. Included artists are those not appearing on the Billboard airplay list during the year.

between 0 and 100—if at least three of its underlying sources review an album. Underlying sources include originally offline magazines such as *Rolling Stone*, as well as newspapers. But many sources, such as Pitchfork, came into existence with, or since, the Internet. Of the reviews in Metacritic for albums released since 2000, over half are from sources founded since 1995. (See figure 14.4.) If these outlets can inform consumers about music, they may supplant the traditional role of radio. The number of albums reviewed at Metacritic has grown from 222 in 2000 to 835 in 2010, as table 14.5 shows. The vast majority of these albums are by artists who do not receive substantial airplay on traditional radio stations.

I also note that social media are likely having significant effects on consumers' awareness of music and other media products. Pew (2012) documents that across twenty countries, the median share of respondents "using social networking sites to share their views about music and movies" was 67 percent. An emerging body of evidence examines links between user-generated content and the success of new media products (see, e.g., Dellarocas, Awad, and Zhang 2007; Dewan and Ramaprasad 2012). The evidence

Table 14.4   Top 2006 airplay artists not on Last.fm weekly top 420

Artist	BB airplay index
Mary J. Blige	14.3111
Beyonce	12.01077
Ne-Yo	10.25575
Cassie	9.814961
Chris Brown	9.78202
Yung Joc	8.242962
Shakira	6.865558
Ludacris	6.041351
Chamillionaire	5.734164
Akon	5.227035
Chingy	4.291855
The Pussycat Dolls	3.868749
T.I.	3.838763
Nelly	3.655194
Dem Franchize Boyz	3.337012
Field Mob	3.009316
Lil Jon	2.825482
Jamie Foxx	2.409102
Natasha Bedingfield	2.189499
E-40	2.088703
Rascal Flatts	1.898755
Cherish	1.891394
Bow Wow	1.870972
Ciara	1.863268
T-Pain	1.803415

Note: BB airplay index is the sum of (1/rank) across airplay chart entries for the artist within a year. Included artists are those not appearing on the Last.fm weekly top song lists during the year.

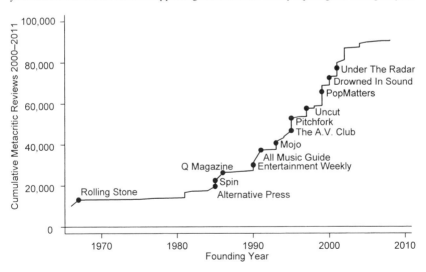

Fig. 14.4   Growth in reviews, sources founded since 1980 with over 2,000 reviews in Metacritic

Table 14.5 Number of artists appearing annually on lists

Year	Discogs releases	BB airplay	Metacritic	BB 200	Last.fm
1990	2,534	88		575	
1991	2,742	244		507	
1992	3,008	237		474	
1993	3,425	238		530	
1994	3,893	211		514	
1995	4,532	204		532	
1996	3,880	197		570	
1997	5,029	220		598	
1998	5,198	217		599	
1999	5,482	194	17	605	
2000	5,586	216	222	661	
2001	5,709	206	306	723	
2002	5,768	213	353	737	
2003	6,057	202	419	781	
2004	6,566	220	448	800	
2005	7,118	202	462	810	175
2006	7,862	211	492	877	183
2007	8,707	195	484	927	182
2008	9,191	206	798	1,021	197
2009	8,875	198	954	1,101	208
2010	8,226	178	835	1,018	229

presented above on Internet radio and criticism almost surely understates the growth in the richness of the information environment surrounding new media products.

14.5 Results

We are now in a position to evaluate the net effect of piracy and cost reduction, in conjunction with the changed information environment, on the volume and quality of new work brought to market. Do we see a greater volume of releases by artists with less ex ante promise? And do these artists' music contribute substantially to the products with ex post success?

14.5.1 Volumes of Major- and Independent-Label Releases

The first question is how the number and mix of new products has evolved. Have the majors reduced the number of new releases? Have the independent labels increased their volume of releases? I have access to two broad measures of the numbers of albums released each year in the United States. The first is an aggregate time series of album releases from the Nielsen Soundscan database. To appear among those data, an album must sell at least one copy during the year. According to Nielsen, the number of new albums released annually was 36,000 in 2000, grew to 106,000 in 2008, and

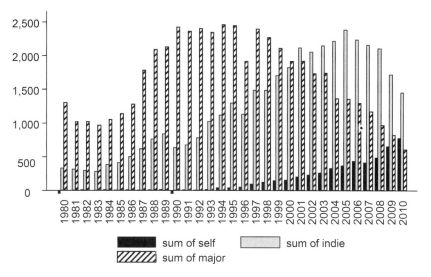

Fig. 14.5 Major, indie, and self-releases, excluding unknowns

has since fallen to about 75,000.[23] It is quite clear, as Oberholzer-Gee and Strumpf (2010) have pointed out, that there has been substantial growth in the number of albums released annually since 2000.[24] Because I lack access to the underlying Nielsen data, I cannot classify those releases by label type.

The Discogs data, while they cover only about a tenth of the total releases in Soundscan, contain album-level info along with label type. It is difficult to know how the Discogs and Soundscan samples relate to one another. Soundscan includes all music genres, while the Discogs figure here include only rock music. Inclusion in Discogs is not mechanically driven by sales; rather, albums are included because users contribute information. It is nevertheless encouraging that the total numbers of albums released according to respective data sources follow similar trends, rising from 2000 to 2009, then falling.

With the caveat about representativeness in mind, we can use the Discogs data to see how releases evolve over time by label type. Figure 14.5 provides a description based on only the identifiable label observations. Releases from major labels far outnumber independent releases between 1980 and roughly 2001. Since then, major-label releases have declined by more than half. The numbers of identifiable independent-label releases and self-released albums show a different pattern. While independent releases were a fraction of major-label releases between 1980 and 1995, they surpassed major-label

23. Data for 2000, 2008–2010 are reported at http://www.digitalmusicnews.com/stories/021811albums. Data for 2011 are reported at http://www.businesswire.com/news/home/20120105005547/en/Nielsen-Company-Billboard%E2%80%99s-2011-Music-Industry-Report.

24. See also Handke (2012).

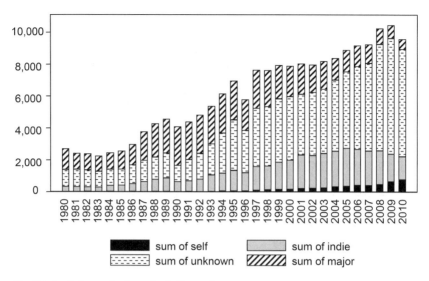

Fig. 14.6 Releases by type, including unknowns

releases in 2001. In 2010 identifiable independent-label releases outnumber major-label releases by a factor of two. Self-released recordings have also increased sharply, from a few hundred in the year 2000 to over a thousand in 2010.[25] Figure 14.6 aggregates independent releases, self-releases, and the releases on unknown labels (which we suspect generally to be independent of the majors). While major-label releases are, again, declining, it is clear that overall releases are increasing.

We have argued that the growth in new releases is driven by changed technologies for production and distribution. We see some direct evidence for this in a breakdown of new releases by whether they are physical or digital, in figure 14.7. I classify as "digital" the releases available only as digital files. Interestingly, there is a fairly substantial decline in the number of releases that include a physical version, but there is a rather substantial growth in digital-only releases, which by their nature have lower distribution costs.[26]

While major-label releases have declined sharply over the past decade, releases of independent and self-released albums have increased even more, driven in part by growth in purely digital products. The number of new

---

25. A curious feature of the data is that the number of releases—both independent and major—appears to have fallen recently. Annual major label releases peak in 1999; annual independent label releases peak in 2007. It is not clear whether the decline is real—it may be an artifact of the user-contributed nature of Discogs. Perhaps it takes a few years for users to fill-in recent years. Regardless of these timing issues, the number of major-label releases has fallen relative to the number of independent-label releases. This is a rather significant change relative to earlier periods covered in these data.

26. I include only multisong compilations in the data; that is, singles are excluded.

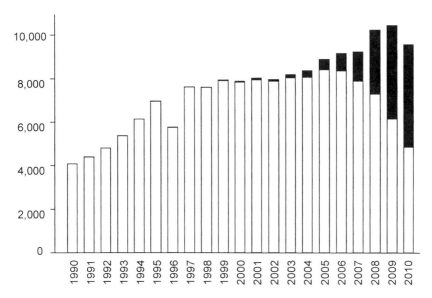

Fig. 14.7 **Physical and digital releases**

products coming into existence has continued to grow over time despite the collapse in revenue.

While growth in releases, as indicated by both Soundscan and Discogs, is consistent with growth in the number of products that consumers might discover to be appealing, neither the Soundscan nor the Discogs lists provide a direct measure of what we would like to observe. The story I am advancing here depends on digitization allowing more pieces of new music to get tested in the market. More releases may be a piece of this, but more releases do not by themselves indicate more "experimentation." Determining whether a product has appeal requires some substantial subset of consumers to listen and decide whether they find it appealing. Prior to digitization there was a relatively bright line between releases promoted on the radio and others. In the digital era, releases that are not promoted on the radio can nevertheless get exposure with consumers. Quantifying the extent of experimentation is challenging, if not impossible. At one extreme it is clear that the number of products that consumers can evaluate has risen. But even in the new digital world, it seems implausible to think that all 75,000 (or 100,000) new releases can be vetted to determine whether they are appealing to consumers. Still, in the language of the model, more products, including those with less ex ante promise, are now coming to market.[27]

---

27. The growth in the releases echoes a growth in the number of record labels than Handke (2012) documents operating in Germany.

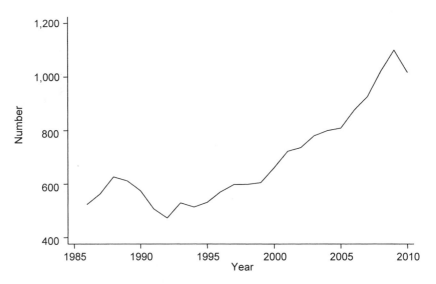

Fig. 14.8 Distinct artists on the BB 200

14.5.2 Sales Concentration

A growth in the available number of products tends generally to effect a combination of market expansion and business stealing, as new options draw some people to consumption and others from existing to new products. The spread of music piracy after 1999 (and the attendant reduction in music sales) obscures any market-expanding impacts of appealing new products. What we can study, instead, is whether new kinds of products (e.g., those that would not previously have been released) take market share from traditional types of products. We begin this inquiry in this section by documenting the evolution of sales concentration over the past few decades.

By construction, the number of weekly Billboard 200 listings is 10,400 per year (52 × 200). The number of distinct artists on the list, by contrast, depends on the number of distinct albums per artist (typically only one) and the length of time an album remains on the list. If albums remained on the list for only one week, and if each artist had only one album per year, then 10,400 artists would appear on the list during the year. At the other extreme, if albums remained on the list all year, then with one album per artist, 200 artists would appear on the list during a year. Because albums tend to remain on the list for a long time, the actual number of artists appearing on the weekly Billboard 200 in a year is far closer to 200 than 10,000. After fluctuating around 600 between 1986 and 1999, the number of distinct artists has grown steadily from 600 to 1,000 at the end of the decade (see figure 14.8).

We can explore sales concentration more directly with our simulated sales

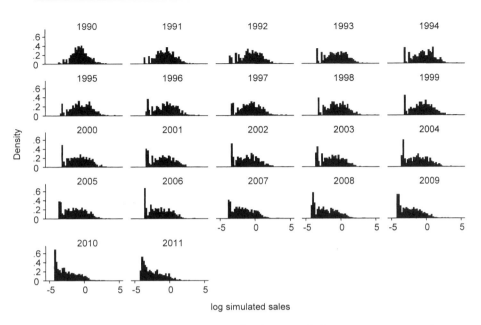

Fig. 14.9 Simulated album log sales distributions, graphs by year

data. To this end, we predict weekly sales for each album, then aggregate these sales across weeks and artists to produce annual sales by artist. Figure 14.9 shows the distributions of log sales across artists for each year, 1990–2010. In the early years, the log sales distributions are single peaked, with a peak near zero, meaning that the central tendency is for albums to have nearly one million in sales. As time goes on, mass in the distribution shifts left as a growing share of artists make shorter appearances on the chart (and a growing share of sales is accounted for by artists making short chart appearances).

This figures make it clear that sales are becoming less concentrated in a handful of artists. To say this another way, the increase in the number of available products seems to be manifested in a growth in the number of products achieving commercial success. This fact is interesting in itself, as it indicates a shift toward consumption of a broader array of music. It is also interesting as an example of a more general phenomenon. Entry, resulting from a reduction in entry costs relative to market size, need not reduce the concentration of consumption. Sutton (1991) describes contexts where quality is produced with fixed costs and consumers agree on quality. Some media products, including daily newspapers and motion pictures, conform to these conditions very well (see Berry and Waldfogel 2010; Ferreira, Petrin, and Waldfogel 2012). Music provides a contrast. Here, growth in the number

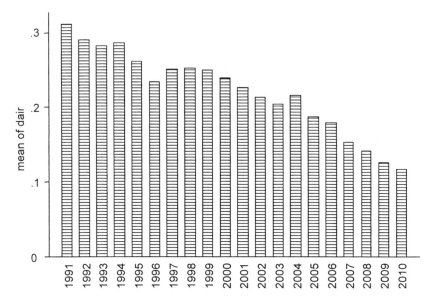

Fig. 14.10A Share of BB 200 with Billboard airplay

of products reaching consumers draws consumption to a wider array.[28] This begs the question of how consumers are becoming aware of the growing number of new products.

14.5.3 Success and Promotional Channels

Airplay has traditionally been an important element of albums' commercial success. Of the artists appearing in the Billboard 200 in 1991, just over 30 percent experienced substantial radio airplay. The top 200 includes albums selling both large and moderate quantities. If we restrict attention to the top 25 albums on the weekly Billboard 200, we see that 60 percent of BB top 25 artists also appeared on the BB airplay charts in 1991. While the share of BB top 25 artists receiving airplay fluctuated somewhat over the decade, it averaged about 50 percent and remained as high as 50 percent in 2001. In the past decade, the share of the BB top 25 with BB airplay has fallen steadily and now stands at about 28 percent. See figures 14.10A and 14.10B. Because Heatseekers are by definition not yet widely successful artists, we would expect less airplay, and we see this. But we also see a reduction in their airplay between 2000 and 2010. The share of Heatseeker artists with airplay falls from 8 percent to about 1 percent. See figure 14.11.

---

28. This suggests that horizontal differentiation is more important in music than in movies or newspapers, a finding reinforced in another study on the effect of market enlargement on music consumption. In Ferreria and Waldfogel (2013), a growth in world music trade promotes greater consumption of local music.

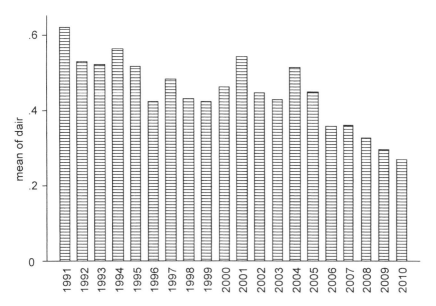

Fig. 14.10B   Share of BB 25 with Billboard airplay

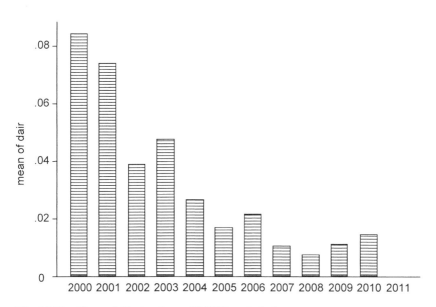

Fig. 14.11   Share of Heatseekers with Billboard airplay

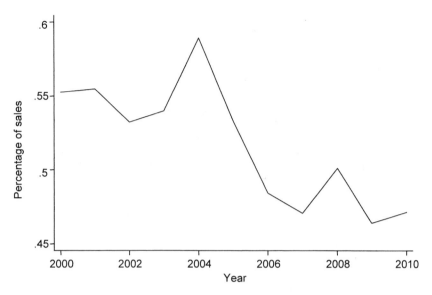

Fig. 14.12 Share of BB 200 sales in albums with Billboard airplay

Using our simulated sales data, we can also calculate the share of sales attributable to albums with substantial airplay. Figure 14.12 shows that the share of sales for artists with concurrent radio airplay fell from about 55 percent of sales in 2000 to about 45 in 2010.

While the share of artists with airplay declines, the share covered in Metacritic instead rises. The share of the Billboard 200 artists with contemporary (same-year) Metacrtic coverage rises from 15 to 35 percent between 2000 and 2010 (see figure 14.13) while the share of Heatseeker artists with Metacritic coverage rises from 6 to 30 percent (see figure 14.14). We observe Last.fm airplay for the limited period between 2005 and 2011, but during this period one-fifth of Billboard 200 artists receive substantial Last.fm play.

Thus far, we see (a) that there are more products, (b) more products achieve success, and (c) that a growing share of products achieve success without substantial airplay. An important remaining question is whether a wider variety of new products, including those lacking major-label backing and substantial airplay (i.e., those with less ex ante promise), can achieve success.

14.5.4 Whose Albums Achieve Success? (Independent vs. Major)

We have seen that independent labels account for a large and growing share of new music releases. If this wider-scale experimentation is responsible for the sustained flow of high-quality music since Napster, then at a minimum it must be true that these albums with less ex ante promise make up a growing share of the albums that ultimately become successful with

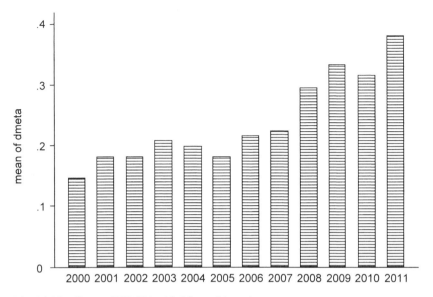

Fig. 14.13 Share of BB 200 with Metacritic reviews

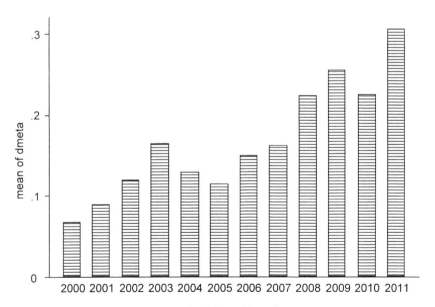

Fig. 14.14 Share of Heatseekers with Metacritic reviews

consumers. To examine this we ask whether albums from independent labels account for a growing share of top-selling albums.

Before turning to data on this question, we note that there is a substantial amount of controversy in the measurement of the volume of independent-record sales. Nielsen reports the volume of independent-record sales in its year-end music sales report. These reports are available online for the past decade, and they show that independent-record labels have sold a roughly constant 15 percent of overall music sales. However, Nielsen calculates the independent share according to the entity distributing a record rather than the entity producing the recording. The different methodologies produce very different results. While Nielsen reported an independent share of just under 13 percent for the first half of 2011, the American Association of Independent Music (A2IM) advocates a different methodology that produces an independent share of nearly one-third. As they put it, "Ownership of master recordings, not distribution, should be used to calculate market share. . . . But Billboard reports market share based on distributor and as a result sales from [independent labels] are embedded within the major-label market share totals."[29]

We take a conservative approach, calculating the independent share among commercially successful albums by merging the list of artists appearing on the weekly Billboard 200 each year (during any week of the year) with the artists appearing on the Billboard independent ranking during the year. Figure 14.15 shows results. The upper-left panel shows that the independent share among the full Billboard 200 rises from 14 percent in 2001 to 35 percent in 2010. We get a similar increase, albeit at a lower level, in the independent share among albums appearing in the weekly top 100, top 50, or top 25 among the Billboard 200. The independent share among artists appearing in the Billboard 25 rises from 6 percent in 2001 to 19 percent in 2010. We see a similar pattern in sales terms. As figure 14.16 shows, the share of BB 200 sales of albums from independent labels rises from 12 percent to about 24 percent between 2000 and 2011.

The growth in the independent-label role among the commercially successful artists confirms that products with less ex ante promise are not only coming to market, they also appear among the products generating commercial success and, therefore, welfare benefit.

14.6 Discussion and Conclusion

The growth in file sharing in the past dozen years has created a tumultuous period for the recorded music industry, presenting an enormous chal-

---

29. See Ed Christman, "What Exactly is an Independent Label? Differing Definitions, Differing Market Shares." Billboard, July 18, 2011; and Rich Bengloff, "A2IM Disputes Billboard/SoundScan's Label Market-Share Methodology—What Do You Think?" Billboard, March 3, 2011.

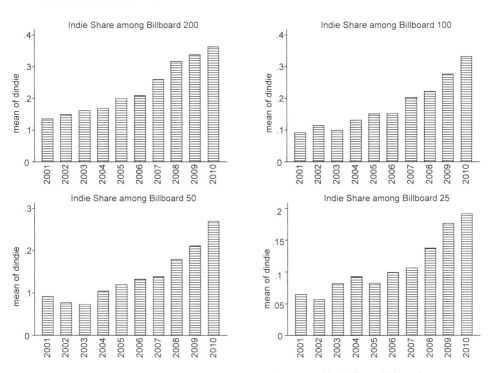

Fig. 14.15 Indie share among Billboard 200, Billboard 100, Billboard 50, and Billboard 25

lenge to the business model of traditional major music labels, leading to a great deal of research on the sales-displacing impacts of file sharing on revenue. Yet cost-reducing technological change in production and distribution, along with a digitally enabled growth in music criticism, have allowed smaller music labels (and individuals) to both release more music and bring it to consumers' attention.

Much of the music originating in the low-cost sector is succeeding commercially. Music from independent labels now accounts for over one-third of the artists appearing on the Billboard 200 each year. In effect, consumers are exposed to much more music each year. In the past consumers would not have been exposed to the independent-label music, and the majors would dominate commercial success. The growing presence of independent-label music in the Billboard 200 means that, when exposed to this broader slate of new music, consumers find much of the independent music to be more appealing than much of the diminished major-label fare. While the usual caveat that more research is needed probably applies, these results nevertheless provide a possible resolution of the puzzling increase in music quality documented elsewhere.

Beyond a possible explanation of continued music quality, the findings

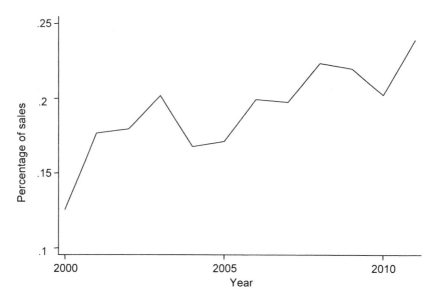

Fig. 14.16 Independent share of BB 200 sales

from this exercise may have some implications for the effects of digitization on product markets generally. Digitization, with its attendant reductions in entry costs relative to market size, was supposed to bring about both frictionless commerce and a proliferation of product varieties to serve niche tastes. In many contexts, the increase in market size along with reductions in fixed costs have not produced this sort of fragmentation. Sutton (1991) outlines circumstances in which an increase in market size need not give rise to fragmentation, in particular, that product quality is produced with fixed costs and that consumers largely agree on which products are better (i.e., competition is vertical). The first of these conditions clearly holds for recorded music. Quality is produced entirely with investments in fixed costs. Whether consumers agree on quality is less clear. Results here suggest that consumers do not agree—that competition has an important horizontal component. Hence, an increase in the number of products available leads to fragmentation of consumption. This feature of music provides a sharp contrast with some other media products, such as daily newspapers and motion pictures, where competition has more important vertical aspects. Music appears to be one product, however, where digitization leads to fragmentation and perhaps the satisfaction of niche tastes. Other contexts where these effects predominate remain to be documented.

The mechanism explored in this chapter is not limited to recorded music products. Further research could fruitfully explore the impacts of digitization on both the creation of new books, movies, and video games, to name a few creative products, as well as the effect of new products on buyers and sellers.

References

Berry, Steven T., and Joel Waldfogel. 2010. "Product Quality and Market Size." *Journal of Industrial Economics* 58:1–31.
Blackburn, David. 2004. "On-line Piracy and Recorded Music Sales." Unpublished manuscript, Harvard University. December.
Brynjolfsson, Erik, Michael D. Smith, and Yu (Jeffrey) Hu. 2003. "Consumer Surplus in the Digital Economy: Estimating the Value of Increased Product Variety at Online Booksellers." *Management Science* 49 (11): 1580–96.
Caves, Richard E. 2000. *Creative Industries: Contracts between Art and Commerce*. Cambridge, MA: Harvard University Press.
Chevalier, Judith, and Austan Goolsbee. 2003. "Measuring Prices and Price Competition Online: Amazon vs. Barnes and Noble." *Quantitative Marketing and Economics 1* 2:203–22.
Dellarocas, C., N. Awad, and X. Zhang. 2007. "Exploring the Value of Online Product Reviews in Forecasting Sales: The Case of Motion Pictures." *Journal of Interactive Marketing* 21 (4): 23–45.
Dewan, S., and J. Ramaprasad. 2012. "Music Blogging, Online Sampling, and the Long Tail." *Information Systems Research* 23 (3, part 2): 1056–67.
Ferreira, Ferando, Amil Petrin, and Joel Waldfogel. 2012. "Trade and Welfare in Motion Pictures." Unpublished manuscript, University of Minnesota.
Ferreira, F., and J. Waldfogel. 2013. "Pop Internationalism: Has Half a Century of World Music Trade Displaced Local Culture?" *Economic Journal* 123:634–64. doi: 10.1111/ecoj.12003.
Handke, Christian. 2012. "Digital Copying and the Supply of Sound Recordings." *Information Economics and Policy* 24:15–29.
International Federation of the Phonographic Industry (IFPI). 2010. "Investing in Music." London. http://www.ifpi.org/content/library/investing_in_music.pdf.
Knopper, Steve. 2009. *Appetite for Self-Destruction: The Spectacular Crash of the Record Industry in the Digital Age*. New York: Free Press.
Leeds, Jeff. 2005. "The Net is a Boon for Indie Labels." *New York Times*, December 27.
Liebowitz, Stan J. 2006. "File Sharing: Creative Destruction or Just Plain Destruction?" *Journal of Law and Economics* 49 (1): 1–28.
Oberholzer-Gee, Felix, and Koleman Strumpf. 2007. "The Effect of File Sharing on Record Sales: An Empirical Analysis." *Journal of Political Economy* 115 (1): 1–42.
———. 2010. "File Sharing and Copyright." In *Innovation Policy and the Economy*, vol. 10, edited by Josh Lerner and Scott Stern, 19–55. Chicago: University of Chicago Press.
Pew Research Center. 2012. "Social Networking Popular across Globe." Washington, DC. http://www.pewglobal.org/files/2012/12/Pew-Global-Attitudes-Project-Technology-Report-FINAL-December-12-2012.pdf.
Rob, Rafael, and Joel Waldfogel. 2006. "Piracy on the High C's: Music Downloading, Sales Displacement, and Social Welfare in a Sample of College Students." *Journal of Law and Economics* 49 (1): 29–62.

Sandstoe, Jeff. 2011. "Moby: 'Major Labels Should Just Die.'" The Hollywood Reporter. February 28. http://www.hollywoodreporter.com/news/moby-major-labels-should-just-162685.
Southall, Brian. 2003. *The A-Z of Record Labels*. London: Sanctuary Publishing.
Sutton, John. 1991. *Sunk Costs and Market Structure*. Cambridge, MA: MIT Press.
Tervio, Marko. 2009. "Superstars and Mediocrities: Market Failure in the Discovery of Talent." *Review of Economic Studies* 72 (2): 829–50.
Thomson, Kristin. 2010. "Same Old Song: An Analysis of Radio Playlists in a Post-FCC Consent Decree World." Future of Music Coalition. http://futureofmusic.org/feature/same-old-song-analysis-radio-playlists-post-fcc-consent-decree-world.
Vogel, Harold. 2007. *Entertainment Industry Economics*, 7th ed. Cambridge: Cambridge University Press.
Waldfogel, Joel. 2011. "Bye, Bye, Miss American Pie? The Supply of New Recorded Music Since Napster." NBER Working Paper no. 16882, Cambridge, MA.
———. 2012. "Copyright Protection, Technological Change, and the Quality of New Products: Evidence from Recorded Music since Napster." *Journal of Law and Economics* 55 (4): 715–40.
Zentner, Alejandro. 2006. "Measuring the Effect of File Sharing on Music Purchases." *Journal of Law and Economics* 49 (1): 63–90.

15
The Nature and Incidence of Software Piracy
Evidence from Windows

Susan Athey and Scott Stern

15.1 Introduction

In the summer of 2009, Microsoft planned to release a new version of its flagship operating system, Windows 7. Relative to Windows Vista, Windows 7 offered significant improvements for consumers, including "driver support to multitouch groundwork for the future, from better battery management to the most easy-to-use interface Microsoft has ever had" (CNET 2009b). The redesign of the core operating system, as well as the development of bundled applications and features, represented a significant investment on the part of Microsoft, with approximately 2,500 developers, testers, and program managers engaged on the project for multiple years. Perhaps more than any other Microsoft product before it, Windows 7 was designed with a global market in mind (Microsoft 2009). Microsoft explicitly included a large number of features aimed at serving this global market, including the Multilingual User Interface included in Windows Ultimate and creating a

---

Susan Athey is the Economics of Technology Professor and a professor of economics at the Graduate School of Business, Stanford University, and a research associate and codirector of the Market Design Working Group at the National Bureau of Economic Research. Scott Stern is the David Sarnoff Professor of Management of Technology and Chair of the Technological Innovation, Entrepreneurship, and Strategic Management Group at the MIT Sloan School of Management and a research associate and director of the Innovation Policy Working Group at the National Bureau of Economic Research.

This research was conducted while both researchers were Consulting Researchers to Microsoft Research. This chapter has benefited greatly from seminar comments at the NBER Economics of Digitization conference, Microsoft Research, the MIT Microeconomics at Sloan conference, and by Ashish Arora, Shane Greenstein, Markus Mobius, and Pierre Azoulay. Exceptional research assistance was provided by Bryan Callaway and Ishita Chordia. For acknowledgments, sources of research support, and disclosure of the authors' material financial relationships, if any, please see http://www.nber.org/chapters/c13002.ack.

low-priced version, Windows Home Basic, which was targeted specifically at emerging markets.

However, just weeks after the release of the final version of the software and individualized product "keys" to original equipment manufacturers (OEMs), a number of websites reported that one of the original equipment manufacturer master product keys issued to Lenovo had been hacked and released onto the Internet (CNET 2009a). Websites quickly assembled step-by-step instructions on how to gain access to a prerelease, pirated version of Windows 7, and developed tools and protocols that allowed users to install an essentially complete version of Windows 7 Ultimate in a small number of transparent steps. While Microsoft chose to discontinue the leaked product key for OEM installation (they issued a new key for legitimate use by Lenovo), users were allowed to activate Windows 7 with the leaked key. In addition, though they did receive a modest functionality downgrade, users of the leaked Lenovo key were able to receive regularized product support and updates for their system. Microsoft argues that this approach ensures that they can "protect users from becoming unknowing victims, because customers who use pirated software are at greater risk of being exposed to malware as well as identity theft" (CNET 2009b). Over the course of 2009, a number of additional leaked keys and methods for pirating Windows 7 appeared on the Internet, and, by 2012, there were a large number of country-specific unauthorized Windows installation web pages, often tailored to specific languages or countries.

By and large, most discussions of digital piracy—the use of the Internet to enable the unauthorized (and unpaid) replication of digital media including music, movie, and software—are based on specific instances of piracy, discussions of specific file-sharing websites (such as the Pirate Bay), or are closely tied to specific advocacy efforts. As emphasized by a recent National Academies study, the policy debate over piracy and the appropriate level of copyright enforcement is hampered by the lack of direct empirical evidence about the prevalence of piracy or the impact of enforcement efforts (Merrill and Raduchel 2013). This empirical vacuum is particularly important insofar as appropriate policy over piracy requires the consideration of both benefits and costs of particular policies. For example, the case for aggressive enforcement against piracy is strongest when piracy results from a simple lack of enforcement (or the absence of a legal framework for enforcing software copyright), while the argument for piracy tolerance is strongest when the primary impact of piracy is to provide access to low-income consumers whose alternative is nonconsumption. The development of appropriate policy, therefore, depends on an empirical assessment of the form that piracy takes in key settings.

This chapter addresses this need by undertaking a systematic empirical examination of the nature, relative incidence, and drivers of software piracy.

We focus specifically on a product—Windows 7—which was unambiguously associated with a significant level of private-sector investment by a private sector company. The key to our approach is the use of a novel type of data that allows us to undertake a direct observational approach to the measurement of piracy. Specifically, we take advantage of telemetry data that is generated passively by users during the process of Windows Automatic Update (WAU) and is maintained in an anonymized fashion by Microsoft. For machines in a given geographic area, we are able to observe the product license keys that were used to initially authenticate Windows, as well as machine characteristics (such as the model and manufacturer). We are able to use these data to construct a conservative definition of piracy, and then calculate the rate of piracy for a specific geographic region.[1] The primary focus of our empirical analysis is then to assess how the rate and nature of that piracy varies across different economic, institutional, and technological environments.

We document a range of novel findings. First, we characterize the nature of "simple" software piracy. While software piracy has, of course, always existed, our examination of Windows 7 suggests that the global diffusion of broadband and peer-to-peer systems such as Pirate Bay has given rise to a distinctive type of software piracy: the potential for global reuse of individual product keys, with sophisticated and active user communities that develop easy-to-follow instructions and protocols. While the use of peer-to-peer networking sites has been associated for more than a decade with piracy for smaller products such as music or video, there is now a relatively direct way that any broadband user can access a fully functional version of Windows for free through the Internet. In particular, we document that a very small number of abused product keys are responsible for the vast bulk of all observed piracy, and that the vast majority of piracy is associated with the most advanced version of Windows (Windows Ultimate). This finding suggests that one proposed type of antipiracy initiative—offering a "bare-bones" version at a greatly reduced price—may be of limited value, since such efforts will have no direct impact on the availability of a fully featured version of Windows for free (and may be considered a poor substitute). We are also able to detect a distinctive industrial organization to piracy: piracy rates are much higher for machines where the OEM does not install Windows during the production process, and the rate of piracy is much lower for machines produced by leading OEMs.

Third, we are able to evaluate how software piracy varies across differ-

1. In constructing a novel and direct observational measure of piracy, our work complements but also offers an alternative to the small prior literature on software piracy that has used a more indirect measure of piracy that *infers* the rate of piracy from the "gap" between the stock of sales/licenses allocated to a particular region/segment and audits of the "software load" for typical devices for users within that region/segment (Business Software Alliance 2011).

ent economic, institutional, and technology environments. In addition to traditional economic measures such as gross domestic product (GDP) per capita (and more nuanced measures, such as the level of income inequality), we also gather data characterizing the overall quality of the institutional environment (e.g., using measures such as the World Bank Rule of Law Index or the Foundational Competitiveness Index; Delgado et al. [2012]), the ability of individuals within a country to take advantage of broadband, and the innovation orientation of a country. Our results suggest that the level of piracy is closely associated with the institutional and infrastructure environment of a country. In particular, the level of piracy is negatively associated with measures of the quality of institutions in a given country, including commonly used aggregate indices of institutional quality as well as more granular measures that capture the role of specific institutions such as property rights. At the same time, piracy has a positive association with the accessibility and speed of broadband connections (as faster broadband reduces the time required for pirating) and is declining in the innovation intensity of a country. Most importantly, after controlling for a small number of measures for institutional quality and broadband infrastructure, the most natural candidate driver of piracy—GDP per capita—has no significant impact on the observed piracy rate. In other words, while the pairwise correlation between piracy and GDP per capita is strongly negative, there is no direct effect from GDP per capita. Poorer countries tend to have weaker institutional environments (Hall and Jones [1997], among many others), and it is the environment rather than income per se that seems to be correlated with the observed level of piracy. Importantly, this finding stands in contrast to prior research, which has not effectively disentangled the role of institutions from the role of income per se.

Finally, we take advantage of time-series variation in our data to directly investigate the impact of the most notable antipiracy enforcement efforts on the contemporaneous rate of Windows 7 piracy. Specifically, during the course of our 2011 and 2012 sample period, a number of individual countries imposed bans on the Pirate Bay website, the single-largest source of pirated digital media on the Internet. Though such policy interventions are endogenous (the bans arise in response to broad concerns about piracy), the precise timing of the intervention is reasonably independent of Windows 7 piracy in particular, and so it is instructive to examine how a change in the level of enforcement against piracy impacts the rate of Windows 7 software piracy. Over a range of different antipiracy enforcement efforts, we find no evidence for the impact of enforcement efforts on observed piracy rates. Overall, this chapter offers the first large-scale observational study of software piracy. Our analysis highlights the value of emerging forms of passively created data such as the Windows telemetry data, and also the role of both institutions and infrastructure in shaping the overall level of piracy.

15.2 The Economics of Software Piracy

The economics of piracy and the role of intellectual property in software is a long-debated topic (Landes and Posner 1989; Merrill and Raduchel 2013; Danaher, Smith, and Telang 2013). Like other forms of intellectual property such as patents, the copyright system has the objective of enhancing incentives for creative work and technological innovation by discouraging precise copying of expression, and is a particularly important form of intellectual property for software. In the case of global software products such as Windows, uneven copyright enforcement across different countries can result in a reduction in incentives to innovation and a distortion in the level of country-specific investment (e.g., companies may limit investment in language and character support in countries with high rates of piracy). The impact on regional investment would be of particular concern if the underlying driver of variation in piracy was the result of simple differences in legal institutions (such as the strength and respect for property rights) rather than the result of income differences (in which case there might also be a low willingness-to-pay for such value-added services). Piracy also has the potential to impose direct incremental costs on both software producers and purchasers of valid and updated software by facilitating the diffusion of viruses and other forms of malware. Because of the potential for a negative externality from the diffusion of pirated software, many software companies (including Microsoft) provide security updates (and some number of functionality updates) for pirated software. More generally, because software production is characterized by high fixed costs and near-zero replication costs, piracy redistributes the burden of funding the fixed costs of production onto a smaller share of the user population.

Interestingly, the main argument against strict copyright enforcement is also grounded in the structure of production costs. With near-zero costs of replication, enhancing access to a broader user base (whether or not they are paying or not) increases the social return of software (even as it limits private incentives to incur the initial sunk costs). This argument is particularly salient to the extent that there is a limited impact of piracy (or the level of copyright enforcement) on the level of creative expression or innovation (Waldfogel 2011). However, many of the most widely diffused software products are produced by profit-oriented firms in which product development is the single most important component of overall costs.

It is also possible that the main impact of piracy arises not simply from enhancing access, but from facilitating implicit price discrimination (Meurer 1997; Gopal and Sanders 1998). If there is a strong negative relationship between price sensitivity and willingness to incur the "costs" of piracy (e.g., time, potential for functionality downgrades), then tolerance of piracy may facilitate a segmentation of the market, in which suppliers charge the monopoly price to the price-insensitive segment, and allow the price-sensitive segment to incur a higher level of transaction costs or a lower level of product quality. This argument is reinforced when the underlying product also exhibits significant network effects, so that even the price-insensitive consumers benefit from more widespread diffusion (Conner and Rumelt 1991; Oz and Thisse 1999). Importantly, the role that piracy plays in facilitating price discrimination depends on whether the segmentation that results between pirates and paying users reflects the type of consumer heterogeneity emphasized in these models. For example, the price discrimination rationale is more pertinent to the extent that piracy is concentrated among low willingness-to-pay consumers (e.g., consumers with a low level of income).

Both the benefits and costs to piracy may be evolving over time with the increasing diffusion of the Internet and broadband connectivity. During the era of desktop computing, software piracy required physical access to at least one copy of the software media (such as a disk or CD), the bulk of piracy involved a limited degree of informal sharing among end users, and so the level of piracy was likely to have been roughly proportional with the level of commercial sales (Peace, Galletta, and Thong 2003). However, the Internet has significantly increased the potential for digital piracy, since a single digital copy can now, in principle, be shared among an almost limitless number of users (and there is no requirement that pirates have any prior or subsequent social or professional contact with each other). Internet-enabled piracy is likely to have increased over the last decade with the diffusion of broadband and the rise of download speeds. Since the middle of the first decade of the twenty-first century, there has been a very significant increase in the diffusion of broadband to mainstream consumers in the United States and abroad (Greenstein and Prince 2006), which has reduced the cost of large-scale software piracy. For example, a pirated version of Windows 7 requires downloading a ~ 10 GB file; it is likely that the extent and nature of piracy are qualitatively different when download times are at most a few hours as opposed to a few days. With the rise of the Internet and ubiquitous broadband connections, the potential for software piracy for large software product has become divorced from local sales of physical media.[2]

Despite the potential growing importance of software piracy, and the development of a rapidly emerging and even abundant literature examining the incidence of piracy and the role of copyright enforcement on digital mass media entertainment goods such as music, movies, and books (Oberhozer-Gee and Strumpf 2010; Merrill and Raduchel 2013; Danaher, Smith, and Telang 2013), systematic empirical research on software piracy is at an early

2. The rise of the Internet and broadband has also reshaped the interaction between users and software producers. During the desktop era, a software product was essentially static, and users received only limited updates or software fixes. With the rise of the Internet and broadband, software authorization and distribution is routinely achieved through an online connection, and users receive regular security and functionality updates to their software.

stage. Nearly all prior studies of software piracy depend on a single data source, the Business Software Alliance (BSA). The BSA measure is calculated based on an indirect auditing methodology (see BSA [2011], for a more complete discussion of the BSA methodology). In particular, the BSA undertakes an inventory of the "software load" for typical devices within a particular region (broken down by particular types of software), and then compares the level of installed software with observed shipments and payments to software suppliers through authorized channels. In other words, the BSA *infers* the rate of piracy as the "residual" between the level of measured software and paid software in a given country and for particular software segment. Taken at face value, the BSA data suggests that software piracy is a highly significant phenomena; the BSA estimates that the annual "lost sales" due to piracy are worth more than 60 billion USD as of 2011, and that the rate of software piracy is well above 50 percent of all software in many regions around the world, including Latin America, Asia, and Eastern Europe (North America registers the lowest level of piracy as a region). Though the BSA methodology for inferring piracy is imperfect, this approach has the advantage of offering a consistent measurement of piracy across countries, software product segments, and over time. However, as it is an inherently indirect measure, such data cannot be utilized for the types of observational studies that have sharpened our understanding of piracy in the context of areas such as music and movies.

A small literature exploits the BSA data to evaluate the extent of software piracy and the relationship between software piracy and the economic, institutional, and technology environment. The most common focus of this literature is to examine the relationship between piracy and the level of economic development (Burke 1996; Marron and Steele 2000; Silva and Ramello 2000; Gopal and Sanders 1998, 2000). Over time, this literature has been extended to also include more nuanced measures of the institutional environment and the level of technology infrastructure (such as Banerjee, Khalid, and Strum 2005; Bezmen and Depken 2006). For example, Goel and Nelson (2009) focus on a broad cross-sectional examination of the determinants of the BSA piracy rate, including not only GDP per capita, but also measures of institutional "quality" such as the Heritage Foundation Property Rights and Economic Freedom Index. Goel and Nelson also include a number of measures of technology infrastructure. Among other findings, they discover that countries with higher prices for telephone service have a lower rate of piracy (i.e., reduced telecommunications access limits piracy). Finally, this literature suggests that measures of variation within the population, such as income inequality, may also promote piracy; with a higher level of income inequality, the monopoly price for paying customers will be sufficiently high that a higher share of individuals will select into incurring the transactions costs associated with piracy (Andres 2006).

Overall, our understanding of software piracy is still in a relatively embryonic state. On the one hand, similar to other debates about intellectual property enforcement, theory provides little concrete guidance about optimal policy in the absence of direct empirical evidence. The need for empirical evidence is particularly important given the likelihood that the nature and extent of piracy is changing as the result of the global diffusion of broadband infrastructure. At the same time, the extant empirical literature usefully highlights a number of broad correlations in the data, but has been limited by reliance on an indirect measure of piracy and a loose connection to the theoretical literature.

Three key issues stand out. First, while the prior literature emphasizes both the role of GDP per capita as well as the role of the institutional environment in shaping piracy, the policy debate suggests that it is important to disentangle the relative role of each. For example, if the primary driver of piracy is poverty (i.e., a negative association with GDP per capita), then the case for aggressive antipiracy enforcement efforts is limited, as piracy is likely serving to simply enhance access to software but is not likely to be a source of significant lost sales. In contrast, if piracy is the result of a low-quality institutional environment, then any observed correlation with GDP per capita may be spurious; instead, the lack of strong legal and property rights institutions may be contributing to a low level of economic development as well as a high level of piracy. In that case, antipiracy enforcement actions may have a salutary effect by directly enhancing the institutional quality and property rights environment of a given location. Second, the global diffusion of broadband may have changed the nature of piracy. To the extent that piracy is facilitated by broadband diffusion, the rate of piracy should be higher for countries and regions where broadband infrastructure is more prevalent (e.g., where there are higher access speeds and/or lower prices for broadband service). To the extent that changes in "frictions" like the cost of downloading have a nontrivial effect on piracy, it suggests that there are a fair number of individuals "at the margin" between pirating and not pirating, and that piracy can be influenced through institutional changes or frictions imposed by regulation or product design features that make piracy more challenging. Finally, existing studies have not been able to isolate the impact of antipiracy enforcement efforts on software piracy. Consistent with recent studies of enforcement efforts in music and movies, an observational study of software piracy alongside shifts over time in the level of enforcement may be able to offer direct evidence about the efficacy of such efforts in restricting the unauthorized distribution of software.

15.3 The Nature of Software Piracy: A Window onto Windows Piracy

In our initial investigation of software piracy, we found relatively little systematic information within the research literature about how software piracy actually works as a phenomena: How does one actually pirate a piece of software? How hard is piracy, and how does that depend on the type of software that one seeks to pirate, and the type of telecommunications infrastructure that you have access to? How does pirated software actually work (i.e., are there significant restrictions in terms of functionality or updates)? What are the main "routes" to piracy?

15.3.1 The Organization of Windows 7 Distribution Channels

To understand the nature of digital software piracy (and how we will measure piracy with our data set), we first describe how users are able to receive, authenticate, and validate a legitimate copy of Windows, focusing in particular on the practices associated with individual copies of Windows 7. We then examine the nature of software piracy within that environment.

To authenticate a valid version of Windows requires a Product License Key, a code that allows Microsoft to confirm that the specific copy of Windows that is being installed on a given machine reflects the license that has been purchased for that machine. Product License Keys are acquired as part of the process of acquiring Windows software, which occurs through three primary distribution channels: the OEM channel, the retail channel, and the volume licensing program.

The OEM Channel

By far, the most common (legal) way to acquire a copy of Windows is through an OEM. The OEMs install Windows as part of the process of building and distributing computers, and the vast majority of OEM-built computers include a copy of Windows. To facilitate the authentication of Windows licenses, each OEM receives a number of specialized Product License Keys (referred to as OEM SLP keys), which they can use during this OEM-installed process. In other words, while OEM SLP keys may be used multiple times, legal use of these keys can only occur on machines that (a) are from that specific OEM, and (b) for machines where Windows was preinstalled. Users with OEM-installed Windows have the option to enroll in Windows Automatic Update, which provides security and functionality updates over time.

The Retail Channel

A second channel to legally acquire Windows is through a retail store (which can either be an online store or bricks-and-mortar establishment). The retail channel primarily serves two types of customers: users who are upgrading their version of Windows (e.g., from Windows XP or Vista), and users who purchased a "naked" machine (i.e., a computer that did not have a preinstalled operating system). Each retail copy comes with a unique Retail Product Key, which is valid for use for a limited number of installations (usually ten). Retail Product Keys should therefore be observed only a small number of times. Users with a Retail Product Key have the option to enroll in Windows Automatic Update, which provides security and functionality updates over time.

The Enterprise Channel

The final way to acquire Windows is through a contractual arrangement between an organization and Microsoft. For large institutional customers (particularly those that want to preinstall other software for employees), Microsoft maintains a direct customer relationship with the user organization, and issues that organization a Volume License Key Server, which allows the organization to create a specific number of copies of Windows for the organization. While each Volume License Key is unique, most Windows Enterprise customers receive updates through the servers and IT infrastructure of their organization, rather than being enrolled directly in programs such as Windows Automatic Update.

In each distribution channel, each legal Windows user undergoes a process of authenticating their copy of Windows. In the case of OEM-installed Windows or the retail channel, that authentication process occurs directly with Microsoft. In the case of Windows Enterprise, that authentication occurs via the server system that is established as part of the contract between Microsoft and the volume license customer.

15.3.2   The Routes to Windows Piracy

We define software piracy as the "unauthorized use or reproduction of copyrighted software" (American Heritage Dictionary 2000). While software piracy has always been an inherent element of software distribution (and has often closely been associated with hacker culture), the nature of piracy changes over time and reflects the particular ways in which users are able to access software without authorization or payment. There seem to be three primary "routes" to piracy of a mass-market, large-format software product such as Windows: local product key abuse, sophisticated hacking, and distributed product key abuse.

Local Product Key Abuse

Since the development of software with imperfect version copying, individual users have occasionally engaged in the unauthorized "local" replication of software from a single legal version. Indeed, the ability to replicate a single copy of Windows across multiple computers is explicitly recognized in the Windows retail licensing contract, which allows users up to ten authorized replications. Abuse of that license can involve significant replication of the software among social or business networks, or deployment within an organization well beyond the level that is specified in a retail license or reported through a volume license key server. Most users who engage in local product key abuse will continue to anticipate receiving software updates from the software vendor. A useful observation is that, when a certain limited number of copies is to be expected (e.g., less than 100), the seller can simply set a price to reflect the scalability of each piece of software once it is deployed in the field.

Sophisticated Hacking

A second route to piracy involves far more active involvement and engagement on the part of users and involves an explicit attempt to "hack" software in order to disable any authentication and validation protocols that are built into the software. Though this does not seem to be the primary type of piracy that occurs in the context of a mainstream software product such as Windows, it is nonetheless the case that the ability to measure such piracy (particularly using the type of passively generated data that is at the heart of our empirical work) is extremely difficult.

Distributed Product Key Abuse

The third route to piracy is arguably the most "novel" and follows the evolution of piracy for smaller-sized digital products such as music or even movies. In distributed peer-to-peer unauthorized sharing, users access a software copy of Windows through a peer-to-peer torrent site such as the Pirate Bay (a ~ 10 GB file), and then separately download a valid/usable product license key from the Internet. Users then misrepresent that the key was obtained through legal means during the authentication and validation process. In our preliminary investigation of this more novel type of piracy, we found the "ecosystem" for peer-to-peer sharing to be very well developed, with a significant level of focus in online forums and sites on pirating a few quite specific keys. To get a sense of how piracy occurs, and the role of globally distributed abused product keys in that process, it is useful to consider a small number of "dossiers" that we developed for a select number of such keys:

The Lenovo Key (Lenny). Approximately three months prior to the commercial launch of Windows 7, Microsoft issued a limited number of OEM System Lock Pre-Installation (SLP) keys to leading OEMs such as Lenovo, Dell, HP, and Asus. Issuing these keys allowed these OEMs to begin their preparations to preinstall Windows on machines for the retail market. Within several days of the release of these keys to the OEMs, the Lenovo key for Windows 7 Ultimate was released onto the Internet (REFS). This widely reported leak led Microsoft to issue a separate key to Lenovo for the same product (i.e., so that all "legitimate" Lenovo computers would have a different product key than the key that was available on the Internet.) Also, Microsoft imposed a functionality downgrade on users who authenticated Windows 7 with the Lenovo key; a message would appear every thirty minutes informing the user that their product key was invalid, and the desktop would be defaulted to an unchangeable black background. Within a few weeks (and still well before the commercial introduction of Windows 7), a number of websites had been established that provided step-by-step instructions about how to download a clean "image" of Windows 7 from a site such as the Pirate Bay or Morpheus and how to not only authenticate Windows with "Lenny" (the Lenovo product key) but also how to disable the limited functionality losses that Microsoft imposed on users that authenticated with the Lenovo key (Reddit 2013; My Digital Life 2013).[3] It is useful to emphasize that the Lenovo key leak allowed unauthorized users to gain access to a fully functional version of Windows 7 prior to its launch date and also receive functional and security updates on a regular basis. As of April, 2013, Google reports more than 127,000 hits for a search on the product key associated with Lenny, and both the Windows 7 software image and the Lenovo product key are widely available through sites such as the Pirate Bay.

The Dell Key (Sarah). Though the Lenovo key received the highest level of media and online attention (likely because it seemed to be the "first" leaked OEM key associated with Windows 7), the Dell OEM SLP key for Windows 7 was also released onto the Internet within weeks after its transmission to Dell, and months before the commercial introduction of Windows 7. Similar to Lenny, a large number of websites were established providing step-by-step instructions about how to download an image of Windows that would work with the Sarah product key, and instructions about how to use the leaked product key and disable the minor functionality downgrades that Microsoft imposed on users with this key. In contrast to the Lenovo key, the Dell key was never discontinued for use by Dell itself; as a result, there are literally millions of legitimate copies of Windows 7 that employ this key. However, by design, this key should never be observed on a non-Dell machine, or even a Dell machine that was shipped "naked" from the factory (i.e., a Dell computer that was shipped without a preinstalled operating system). For computers that validate with this key, a simple (and conservative) test of piracy is an observation with Sarah as the product key on a non-Dell machine or a Dell machine that was shipped "naked" (a characteristic also observable in our telemetry data).

The Toshiba Key (Billy). Not all OEM SLP Windows keys are associated with a high level of piracy. For example, the Toshiba Windows Home Premium Key is associated with a much lower level of piracy. This key was not released onto the Internet until just after the commercial launch of Windows 7 (October 2009), and there are fewer Google or Bing hits associated

---

3. This latter reference is but one of many making claims such as the following: "This is the loader application that's used by millions of people worldwide, well-known for passing Microsoft's WAT (Windows Activation Technologies) and is arguably the safest Windows activation exploit ever created. The application itself injects a SLIC (System Licensed Internal Code) into your system before Windows boots; this is what fools Windows into thinking it's genuine" (My Digital Life 2013). That post is associated with more than 7,000 "thank yous" from users.

with this product key (less than 10 percent of the number of hits associated with the Lenovo and Dell keys described above). In other words, while this version of Windows could be pirated at a much more intensive level if other copies (including all copies of Windows Ultimate) were unavailable, the Windows piracy community seems to focus their primary attention on a small number of keys, with a significant focus on leading OEM SLP Ultimate keys.

Overall, these short dossiers of the primary ways in which retail Windows 7 software piracy has actually been realized offer some insight into the nature of Windows piracy as a phenomena, and guidance as to the relative effectiveness of different types of enforcement actions either by government or by Microsoft. First, while discussions of software piracy that predates widespread broadband access emphasizes the relatively local nature of software piracy (e.g., sharing of physical media by friends and neighbors, instantiating excess copies of a volume license beyond what is reported to a vendor such as Microsoft), Windows 7 seems to have been associated with a high level of digital piracy associated with a small number of digital point sources. In our empirical work, we will explicitly examine how concentrated piracy is in terms of the number of product keys that are associated with the vast bulk of piracy. Second, the globally distributed nature of the ways to access a pirated version of Windows suggests that it may be difficult to meaningfully impact the piracy rate simply by targeting a small number of websites or even product keys. Based on the voluminous material and documentation publicly available on the Internet (and reachable through traditional search engines), it is likely that small changes in the supply of pirated software might have little impact on the realized level of piracy.

15.4 Data

The remainder of this chapter undertakes a systematic empirical examination of the nature and incidence of software piracy. Specifically, we take advantage of a novel data set that allows us to observe statistics related to a large sample of machines that install Windows on a global basis that receive regular security and functionality updates from Microsoft. Though these data have important limitations (which we discuss below), they offer the opportunity to undertake a direct observational study of software, and in particular the ability to identify whether machines in a given region are employing a valid or pirated version of Windows. We combine this regional measure of piracy with measures of other attributes of machines, as well as regional variables describing the institutional, economic, and technology environment to evaluate the nature and relative incidence of piracy.

15.4.1 Windows 7 Telemetry Data

Our estimates of the piracy rates of Windows 7 are computed by drawing on a data set that captures information about machines (including "hashed" data providing their regional location) that enroll in a voluntary security update program known as Windows Automatic Updates (WAU). When a machine enrolls in the program, a low-level telemetry control, formally known as Windows Activation Technologies (WAT), is installed, which performs periodic validations of the machine's Windows 7 license. During each of these validations, which occur every ninety days by default, data is passively generated about a machine's current hardware, operating system configuration, and basic geographic information. This information is transmitted to Microsoft and maintained in a hashed manner consistent with the privacy protocols established by Microsoft.[4] More than 400 million individual machines transmitted telemetry information to Microsoft during 2011 and 2012, the period of our sample.

We make use of a research data set consisting of an anonymized sample of 10 million machines, where, for a given machine, the data set includes the history of validation attempts for that machine over time. For each of these validation episodes, the data set includes information on the broad geolocation of the machine at the time of validation,[5] the product key used to activate Windows 7, the version of Windows 7 installed, and a set of machine characteristics including the manufacturer (OEM) and the machine model, the PC architecture, and whether an OEM installed a version of Windows during the manufacturing process.

Though the Windows telemetry data offers a unique data source for observing software in the field, users face a choice about whether to enroll in the WAU program. Self-selection into Windows Automatic Update engenders two distinct challenges for our data. First, Windows Enterprise customers and others that employ volume licensing contracts with Microsoft primarily opt out of WAU and instead manage updating Windows through their own IT departments (a process which allows them, for example, to also include organization-specific updates as well). While we do observe a small number of machines that report a volume license key, we exclude this population entirely from our analysis in order to condition the analysis on users who attempt to validate with either an OEM SLP or retail product key license.[6] In that sense, our empirical analysis can be interpreted as an examination of piracy by individual users and organizations without any

---

[4]. During the validation process, no personal information that could be used to identify an individual user is collected. For more details, see http://www.microsoft.com/privacy/default.aspx.

[5]. The geographical location of a machine during its WAT validation attempt is constructed based on the Internet Protocol (IP) address that was used to establish a connection with Microsoft in order to undergo validation. In order to preserve anonymity, only the city and country from which the IP address originates is recorded in our data set.

[6]. There are number of reasons for doing this, most notably the fact that due to the highly idiosyncratic nature of VL agreements, it is extremely difficult to determine what constitutes an abused VL product key.

direct contract with Microsoft. Second, users with pirated versions of Windows may be less likely to enroll in the automatic update program. As such, conditional on being within the sample of users who validate with an OEM SLP or retail product key, we are likely estimating a lower bound on the rate of piracy within the entire population of machines.

15.4.2 Defining Piracy

Using the system information recorded by the Windows telemetry data, we are able to check for the presence of key indicators that provide unambiguous evidence for piracy. We take a conservative approach to defining each of these in order to ensure that our overall definition of piracy captures only machines consistently possessing what we believe are unambiguous indicators of piracy. Consistent with the discussion in section 15.3, we therefore identify a machine as noncompliant for a given validation check if it meets one or more of the following criteria:

- For those validating with an OEM key:
  a. Machines associated with known leaked and/or abused keys in *and* in which there is a mismatch between the OEM associated with the key and the OEM of the machine.
  b. Machines with an unambiguous mismatch between the product key and other machine-level characteristics.
- For those validating with a retail key:
  a. Known leaked and/or abused retail product keys with more than 100 observed copies within the machine-level WAT population data set.

This definition captures the key cases that we highlighted in section 15.3. For example, all machines that validate with the "leaked" Lenovo product key, Lenny, will be included in this definition, since this a known leaked key that should not be matched with any machine. This also captures all uses of the Dell OEM SLP key (Sarah) in which validation is attempted on a non-Dell machine or a Dell machine that also reports having been shipped naked from the factory (in both of these cases, there would be no legal way to receive a valid version of the Dell OEM SLP key). Similarly, any machine that was exclusively designed for Windows XP or Vista (so that no OEM key for Windows 7 was ever legally installed on that machine) but reports an OEM SLP Windows 7 key will be measured as an instance of noncompliancy.

Because we observe the full history of validation attempts for any given machine (though the data for each machine is anonymized beyond its broad regional location), we are able to define piracy as the persistence of noncompliance across all validation attempts by a given machine. In other words, if a machine originally uses a noncompliant version of Windows but then reauthorizes with a valid license key, we define that machine as being in "compliance" in terms of our overall definition. We therefore define a machine as a pirate if, for each of the validation attempts associated with that machine, it satisfies one of the unambiguous noncompliant criteria stated above.

We then construct our key measure, PIRACY RATE, as the aggregation of piracy across the machines within the sample within a given region divided by the number of machines we observe within that region (see table 15.1). Overall, weighted by the number of machines per country, the overall piracy rate is just over 25 percent; if each of the 95 countries in our sample is treated as a separate observation, the average country-level piracy rate is just under 40 percent.

15.4.3 Machine Characteristics

We are able to observe and then aggregate a number of additional characteristics of machines within a given country. While the decision of whether to pirate Windows and other hardware and vendor choices is clearly endogenous, we nonetheless believe that it is informative to understand what types of machines tend to be associated with pirated software (or not). Specifically, we define four measures that we believe usefully characterize key machine attributes and in which it is useful to compare how the rate of piracy varies depending on machine characteristics:

- Frontier Model: An indicator equal to one for machine models that were exclusively built following the launch of Windows 7.
- Leading Manufacturer: An indicator for whether a machine was produced by one of the leading twenty OEMs, as determined by their market share within the telemetry population.
- Frontier Architecture: An indicator equal to one for machines with a 64-bit CPU instruction set (also known as an x86-64 processor). Approximately 63 percent of the machines in our sample are equipped with an x86-64 processor.
- Windows Home Premium/Professional/Ultimate: An indicator for whether the installed version of Windows 7 on a machine is Windows Home Premium, Professional, or Ultimate, respectively.

15.4.4 Economic, Institutional, and Infrastructure Variables

Once we have classified each of the machines in our sample, we construct a measure of the incidence of piracy for each of the ninety-five countries in our sample, which we then incorporate into a data set of country-level economic, institutional, and technology infrastructure variables. Our data on country-level characteristics can be classified into three broad categories: (a) economic and demographic factors, (b) institutional quality, and (c) technology and innovative capacity. The variable names, definitions, and means and standard deviations are in table 15.1. For our basic economic and demographic measures, such as GDP per capita, the current rate of infla-

Table 15.1 **Summary statistics**

		Country level $N = 95$	Country level weighted by machines $N = 95$
Dependent variable			
Piracy rate	Share of noncompliant (i.e., pirated) machines	.38	.25
Machine characteristics			
Frontier model	Windows 7 ready model	.57 (.09)	.63 (.48)
Leading manufacturer	Indicator for whether machine is produced by one of 20 top manufacturers (by market share)	.75 (.12)	.80 (.40)
Frontier architecture	Indicator for 64-bit CPU architecture	.50 (.16)	.63 (.48)
Windows Ultimate	Indicator for whether machine is Windows Ultimate	.40 (.20)	.25 (.43)
Windows Professional	Indicator for whether machine is Windows Professional	.19 (.06)	.18 (.38)
Windows Home Premium	Indicator for whether machine is Windows Home Premium	.41 (.19)	.58 (.49)
Economic, institutional, and demographic indicators			
GDP per capita	GDP per capita (IMF)	22,215.42 (17,898.45)	32,498.37 (15,628.68)
Foundational Competitiveness Index	Competitiveness Index score (Delgado et al. 2012)	.22 (.78)	.55 (.76)
WB Rule of Law	World Bank Rule of Law Index	.36 (.97)	.75 (.99)
Settler mortality	European settler mortality (Acemoglu et. al. 2001)	111.96 (298.43)	39.12 (107.39)
Property rights	Heritage Foundation Property Rights Index	53.66 (24.99)	63.47 (26.64)
Gini coefficient	Gini coefficient for income inequality (Central Intelligence Agency 2007)	38.3 (10.18)	39.57 (8.58)
Lending rate	Lending interest rate (EIU)	8.83 (5.93)	7.38 (7.72)
Inflation	Annual (%) change in CPI (IMF)	4.63 (3.66)	3.53 (5.77)
Population (in millions)	Total population (IMF)	61.32 (189.35)	167.52 (219.43)
Population density	People per sq. KM (WDI)	301.25 (1,021.36)	188.29 (696.51)
Measures of innovative & technological capacity			
Patents per capita	USPTO-filed patents per one million inhabitants (USPTO)	34.5 (70.09)	118.37 (116.96)
Broadband speed	Wired broadband speed per 100 Mbit/sec (ICT/ITU)	4.96 (12.84)	6.73 (16.98)
Broadband monthly rate	Wired broadband monthly subscription charge (USD) (ICT/ITU)	24.15 (11.47)	24.12 (10.07)
Computer	Percent of households with a computer (ICT/ITU)	54.07 (27.30)	66.94 (22.08)
Internet	Internet users (%) of population (ICT/ITU)	52.21 (23.99)	65.72 (20.74)

Note: With exception to the CIA Factbook's Gini coefficient, which was computed in 2008, we take the average of all indicators over our sample period (2011–2012), unless otherwise indicated.

tion and population, we use standard data from the International Monetary Fund (IMF) for the most current year (2012 in nearly all cases). The Gini coefficient for each country is drawn from the CIA World Factbook, and a measure of the lending interest rate is drawn from the Economist Intelligence Unit.

We then incorporate four different measures of overall "institutional quality" of a country. Our first measure, foundational competitiveness, is drawn from Delgado et al. (2012), who develop a multiattribute measure that captures a wide range of factors that contribute to the baseline quality of the microeconomic environment, as well as the quality of social and political institutions within a given country. Foundational competitiveness incorporates a wide range of prior research findings on the long-term drivers of country-level institutional quality, and reflects differences across countries in their institutional environment in a way that is distinguishable from simply the observed level of GDP per capita (Delgado et al. 2012). We also include two additional contemporary measures of institutional quality, including the Rule of Law measure developed as a part of the World Bank Doing Business Indicators (Kaufmann, Kraay, and Mastruzzi 2009), and a Property Rights Index developed by the Heritage Foundation. Finally, building on Acemoglu, Johnson, and Robinson (2001), we use settler mortality (as measured in the early nineteenth century) as a proxy for the historical origins of long-term institutional quality. Environments where European settler mortality was low led to more investment in setting up more inclusive institutions, resulting in a historical path leading to more favorable institutions over time. We will therefore be able to examine how the historical conditions giving rise to institutions in a given location impacts the rate of piracy today. It is important to note that all of these measures are highly correlated with each other, and our objective is not to discriminate among them in terms of their impact on piracy. Instead, we will evaluate how each of these measures relates to piracy, and in particular consider whether their inclusion reduces the relative salience of contemporary economic measures such as GDP per capita or the Gini coefficient.

Finally, we use a number of measures of the technological and innovative capacity of a country. In terms of telecommunications infrastructure, we use two different measures (from the International Telecommunications Union) of broadband infrastructure, including broadband speed and broadband monthly rate. We also investigate alternative measures of the information technology and Internet infrastructure, including the percentage of households with a computer and the percentage of the population with access to an Internet connection. Interestingly, for the purpose of evaluating the incidence of operating systems piracy, we believe that measures associated with broadband connectivity are likely to be particularly important, since low-cost and rapid broadband connection would be required for downloading the large files that are required for Windows 7 piracy. Finally, though we experimented with a wide range of measures, we use the number of USPTO-filed patents per capita as our measure of the innovation orientation of an economy (other measures lead to similar findings).

15.5 Empirical Results

Our analysis proceeds in several steps. First, we examine some broad patterns in the data, highlighting both the nature and distribution of Windows 7 piracy around the world. We then examine the impact of the economic and institutional environment on piracy, both looking at cross-country comparisons, and a more detailed examinations of cities within and across countries. We also briefly consider how the rate of piracy varies with particular populations of machines and computer characteristics, in order to surface some of the potential mechanisms that are underlying differences in piracy across different environments and among individuals within a given environment. Finally, we undertake a preliminary exercise to assess the causal short-term impact of the primary antipiracy enforcement effort—the blocking of websites such as Pirate Bay—on observed piracy rates in our data.

15.5.1 The Nature and Incidence of Piracy

We begin in figure 15.1, where we consider how piracy is promulgated, focusing on the incidence of individual product keys within the population of pirated machines. The results are striking. Consistent with our qualitative discussion in section 15.3, the vast bulk of observable piracy is associated with a relatively small number of product keys. The top five keys each account for more than 10 percent of observed piracy in our data, and more than 90 percent of piracy is accounted for by the top twelve product

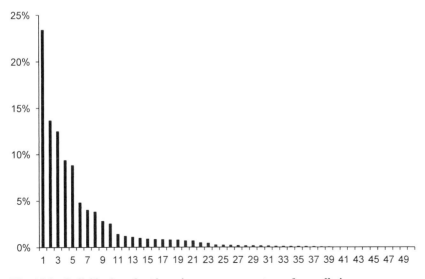

Fig. 15.1 Individual product key piracy as a percentage of overall piracy

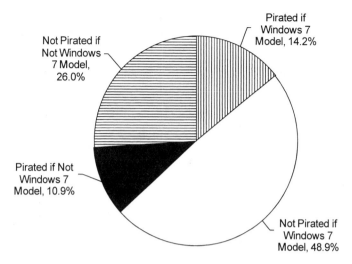

Fig. 15.2A Piracy and Windows 7 models: Share of machines

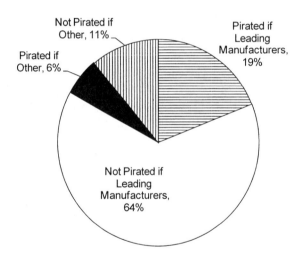

Fig. 15.2B Piracy and leading manufacturers: Share of machines

keys. At least in part, this extreme concentration is consistent with the idea that global piracy is associated with user communities that provide easy-to-follow instructions associated with individual product keys, and so there is similarity across users in their precise "route" to piracy. Of course, it is likely that enforcement efforts that focused on individual keys would likely simply shift potential pirates to other potential keys (and websites would spring up to facilitate that process).

We continue our descriptive overview in figures 15.2A and 15.2B, where

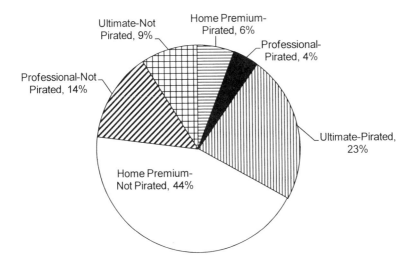

Fig. 15.3   Piracy and Windows 7 version: Share of machines

we break out the rate of piracy by the type of OEM and the type of machine. In figure 15.2B, we examine how the rate of piracy varies by whether the machine is associated with a leading OEM or not. On the one hand, the rate of piracy is much higher among machines that are shipped from "fringe" rather than leading OEMs. However, this is only a small share of the entire sample (less than 20 percent). In other words, while the incidence of piracy is much lower among machines produced by leading OEMs, the bulk of piracy is nonetheless associated with machines from leading OEMs. Similarly, figure 15.2B describes how the rate of piracy varies depending on whether a particular computer model was introduced before or after the debut of Windows 7. Just over a third of observed copies of Windows 7 are associated with machines that were produced prior to the introduction of Windows 7, and so are likely machines that are "upgrading" from Windows Vista (or an even earlier version of Windows). Interestingly, the rate of piracy for machines associated with clear upgrades is only slightly higher than for machines produced after the introduction of Windows 7 (29 versus 22 percent).

Finally, there is striking variation across the *version* of Windows installed. While the piracy rate associated with Home Premium is quite modest, more than 70 percent of all piracy is of Windows Ultimate, and, amazingly, nearly 70 percent of all observed copies of Windows Ultimate are pirated (figure 15.3). Windows piracy is associated with machines that, by and large, are not produced by leading manufacturers, and, conditional on choosing to pirate, users choose to install the most advanced version of Windows software.

15.5.2 The Economic, Institutional, and Technological Determinants of Software Piracy

We now turn to a more systematic examination of how the rate of piracy varies by region (the drivers of which are the main focus of our regression analysis in the next section). Figures 15.4A and 15.4B highlight a very wide range of variation across regions and countries. While the observed piracy rate in Japan is less than 3 percent, Latin America registers an average piracy

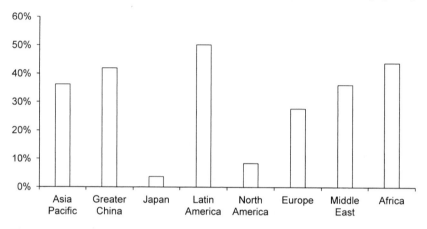

Fig. 15.4A Piracy rate by region

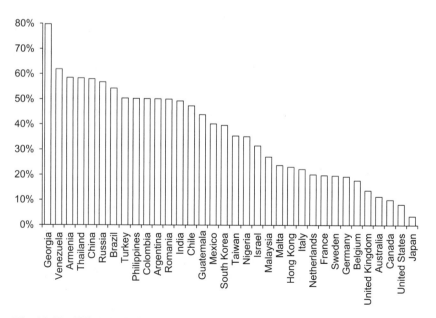

Fig. 15.4B Windows 7 piracy rate by country

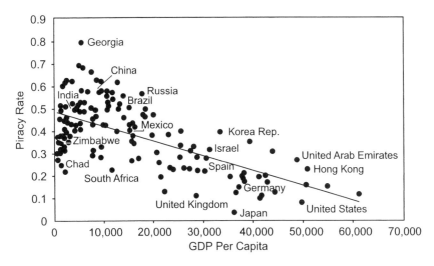

Fig. 15.5 GDP per capita versus country-level piracy rates

rate of 50 percent. Interestingly, after Japan, there is a group of advanced English-speaking countries—the United States, Canada, Australia, and the United Kingdom—which register the lowest rates of piracy across the globe. At the other extreme is Georgia, where the observed piracy rate reaches nearly 80 percent. Perhaps more importantly, a number of large emerging countries such as Russia, Brazil, and China are each recorded at nearly 60 percent. Finally, it is useful to note that a number of reasonably "wealthy" countries (e.g., South Korea, Taiwan, and Israel) boast piracy rates between 30 and 40 percent. As emphasized in figure 15.5 (which simply plots the country-level piracy rate versus GDP per capita), there is a negative but noisy relationship between piracy and overall prosperity.

These broad correlations provide the foundation for the more systematic examination we begin in table 15.2. We begin with table 15.2, column (1), a simple regression that documents the relationship illustrated in figure 15.5—there is a negative correlation between piracy and GDP per capita. However, as we discussed in section 15.3, the relationship between piracy and GDP per capita is subtle: Is this relationship driven by the fact that poor countries tend to have poor institutional environments (and so are likely to engage in more piracy), or does this reflect differences in opportunity cost or price sensitivity? To disentangle these effects, we include a simple set of measures associated with country-level institutional quality. In table 15.2, column (2), we include foundational competitiveness (Delgado et al. 2012) as an overall index that aggregates many different facets of the institutional environment, and in table 15.2, column (3), we focus on a more straightforward (but perhaps more blunt) measure of institutional quality, the World

Table 15.2 Software piracy and the economic, institutional, and infrastructure environment

	Windows 7 piracy rate			
	1	2	3	4
Ln GDP per capita	−.151***	−.082***	−.061***	−.026
	(.014)	(.021)	(.018)	(.02)
Competition index		−.096***		−.039**
		(.017)		(.019)
WB Rule of Law			−.097***	
			(.014)	
Ln Patents per capita[a]				−.023***
				(.007)
Ln broadband download speed				.008
				(.009)
Ln broadband monthly rate				−.087***
				(.026)
Lending rate				.005***
				(.001)
Observations	95	95	95	95
R-Squared	.599	.674	.708	.762

Note: Robust standard errors in parentheses.
[a]Ln patents per capita is defined as Ln(1 + patents per capita).
***Significant at the 1 percent level.
**Significant at the 5 percent level.
*Significant at the 10 percent level.

Bank Rule of Law Index. In both cases, the coefficient on GDP per capita declines by half, and is only marginally significantly different from zero.

We investigate this further in table 15.2, column (4), where we include a small number of additional controls for the quality of the telecom infrastructure and the degree of innovation orientation of the economy. On the one hand, consistent with earlier studies emphasizing the importance of the telecommunications infrastructure in piracy (Goel and Nelson 2009), piracy is declining in the price of broadband access and (not significantly) increasing in average broadband speed. The relative significance of these two coefficients depends on the precise specification (and they are always jointly significantly different from zero); the overall pattern suggests that piracy is sensitive to the ability to download and manage large files, consistent with the hypothesis that broadband downloads of pirated content is a primary channel through which Windows piracy occurs. The piracy rate is also declining in patents per capita—the rate of piracy by consumers and businesses is lower in countries with a higher rate and orientation toward innovation. In unreported regressions, we found that a number of alternative measures of the "innovation environment" (e.g., measures of the overall

R&D budget, as well as various indices of innovative capacity) had a negative association with piracy. However, we were unable to disentangle the separate effect of these broader measures of the innovation orientation of a region and a simpler measure such as patents per capita. Finally, computer purchasing and procurement is a capital good; in countries with a higher lending rate, the observed rate of piracy is higher (and this result is robust to the use of the real rather than nominal lending rate as well). Perhaps most importantly, once controlling for these direct effects on the piracy rate (and across a wide variety of specifications including only a subset or variant of these types of measures), GDP per capita is both small and insignificant.

Rather than income per se, the results from table 15.2 provide suggestive evidence that piracy rates are driven by the institutional and technological attributes of a given country, including, most importantly, whether they have institutions that support property rights and innovation. Poorer countries tend to have weaker institutional environments (Hall and Jones [1997], among many others), and it is the environment rather than income per se that seems to be correlated with the observed level of piracy. We explore the robustness of this core finding in table 15.3, where we examine several alternative ways of capturing the baseline institutional environment of a country and evaluate the impact of GDP per capita on piracy once such measures are included. In table 15.3, columns (1) and (2), we simply replace the Foundational Competitiveness Index with the World Bank Rule of Law measure and the Heritage Foundation Property Rights Index, respectively. In both cases, the broad pattern of results remains the same, and the coefficient on GDP per capita remains very small and statistically insignificant. In table 15.3, columns (3) and (4), we extend this analysis by focusing on the subset of countries highlighted in the important work of Acemoglu, Johnson, and Robinson (2001). Acemoglu, Johnson, and Robinson argue that the colonial origins of individual countries have had a long-term impact on institutional quality, and they specifically highlight a measure of settler mortality (from the mid-1800s) as a proxy for the "deep" origins of contemporary institutional quality. We build on this idea by directly including their measure of settler mortality. Though the sample size is much reduced (we are left with only forty-three country-level observations), the overall pattern of results is maintained, and there is some (noisy) evidence that settler mortality itself is positively associated with piracy (i.e., since a high level of settler mortality is associated with long-term weakness in the institutional environment); most notably, in both columns (3) and (4) of table 15.3, the coefficient on GDP per capita remains small and insignificant.

We further explore these ideas by looking at a few case studies, examples of city pairs that share roughly the same income level but are located in countries with wide variation in their institutional environment. Drawing on city-specific GDP per capita data from the Brookings Global Metro Monitor Project, we identify four city-pairs with similar income levels but

Table 15.3   Alternative measure of institutional quality

	Windows 7 piracy rate			
	1	2	3	4
Ln GDP per capita	−.015	−.018	−.019	−.006
	(.018)	(.017)	(.039)	(.039)
WB Rule of Law	−.074***			
	(.021)			
Ln patents per capita[a]	−.013	−.016**	−.022	−.023
	(.009)	(.008)	(.014)	(.01)
Ln broadband download speed	.013	.014	4e-4	.005
	(.009)	(.009)	(.015)	(.014)
Ln broadband monthly rate	−.087	−.076***	−.106**	−.122***
	(.025)	(.024)	(.045)	(.045)
Lending rate	.005***	.005***		.005***
	(.001)	(.001)		(.002)
Prop. rights		−.003***		
		(.001)		
Ln settler mortality			.045*	.04
			(.026)	(.027)
Observations	95	93	43	43
R-Squared	.786	.79	.664	.694

Note: Robust standard errors in parentheses.
[a]Ln patents per capita is defined as Ln(1 + patents per capita).
***Significant at the 1 percent level.
**Significant at the 5 percent level.
*Significant at the 10 percent level.

wide variation in measured institutional quality (as measured by the World Bank Rule of Law Index) (see table 15.4). The results are striking. While Johannesburg and Beijing have roughly the same GDP per capita, the piracy rate in Beijing is recorded to be more than twice as high as Johannesburg (a similar comparison can be made between Shenzhen, China, and Berlin, Germany). A particularly striking example can be drawn between Moscow, Russia, and Sydney, Australia, where relatively modest differences in "prosperity" cannot explain a nearly fourfold difference in the observed piracy rate. While these suggestive examples are simply meant to reinforce our more systematic regression findings, we believe that this approach—where one exploits variation within and across countries in both GDP and institutions through regional analyses—offers a promising approach going forward in terms of evaluating the drivers of piracy in a more nuanced way.

Figure 15.6 sharpens this analysis by plotting the actual piracy rate versus the predicted piracy rate (as estimated from table 15.2, column [4]). Several notable countries with high piracy rates and intense public attention on the issue (such as China and Brazil) have an observed piracy rate

Table 15.4 City-pair comparisons: Rule of law and GDP per capita comparisons by piracy rate

Pair	City	Country	GDP per capita (thousands [$], PPP rates)	Rule of Law Index (WB)	Piracy rate
1	Johannesburg	South Africa	17.4	0.10	0.24
1	Beijing	China	20.3	−0.45	0.55
2	Kuala Lumpur	Malaysia	23.9	0.51	0.29
2	São Paulo	Brazil	23.7	0.013	0.55
3	Moscow	Russia	44.8	−0.78	0.56
3	Sydney	Australia	45.4	1.77	0.15
4	Shenzhen	China	28	−0.45	0.44
4	Berlin	Germany	33.3	1.69	0.24

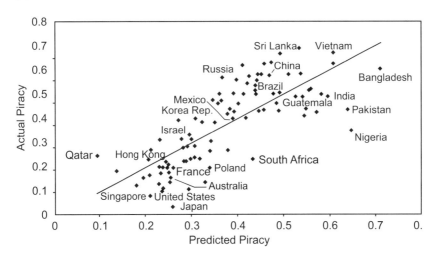

Fig. 15.6 Predicted versus actual piracy rate

only slightly above that which would be predicted by their "fundamentals." The leading English-speaking countries and Japan have low piracy rates, but those are even lower than predicted by the model. Finally, it is useful to highlight some of the most notable outliers: New Zealand registers a piracy rate far below that which would be predicted by observable factors, and South Korea realizes a level of piracy well above that which would be predicted by observables. Overall, our results suggest that the wide variation of piracy observed across countries reflects a combination of systematic and idiosyncratic factors.

Finally, in table 15.5, we examine a number of other potential drivers of piracy that have been discussed in the prior literature. For example, in

Table 15.5 Other potential drivers of piracy

	Windows 7 piracy rate				
	1	2	3	4	5
Ln GDP per capita	−.025	−.028	−.026	−.012	−.025
	(.02)	(.02)	(.026)	(.024)	(.02)
Competition Index	−.039**	−.034*	−.052**	−.032	−.036*
	(.019)	(.02)	(.022)	(.021)	(.019)
Ln broadband download speed	.008	.01	.009	.01	.008
	(.009)	(.009)	(.01)	(.009)	(.009)
Ln broadband monthly rate	−.087***	−.094***	−.09***	−.087***	−.087***
	(.026)	(.027)	(.027)	(.025)	(.026)
Ln patents per capita[a]	−.023***	−.024***	−.02*	−.022***	−.023***
	(.007)	(.007)	(.01)	(.007)	(.007)
Lending rate	.005***	.005***	.005***	.005***	.005***
	(.001)	(.001)	(.002)	(.001)	(.002)
Ln population	3e-4				
	(.007)				
Ln population density		−.009			
		(.006)			
Gini coefficient			2e-4		
			(.001)		
Internet				−.001	
				(.001)	
Inflation					.002
					(.003)
Observations	95	95	85	95	95
R-Squared	.762	.767	.769	.764	.762

Note: Robust standard errors in parentheses.

[a]Ln patents per capita is defined as Ln(1 + patents per capita).

***Significant at the 1 percent level.
**Significant at the 5 percent level.
*Significant at the 10 percent level.

table 15.5, columns (1) and (2), we include measures of population and population density, while in table 15.5, column (3), we include a measure of country-level income inequality. The inclusion of these measures does not have a material effect on our earlier findings, and are estimated to have a small and insignificant impact. Similar patterns are observed when we include a measure of overall Internet penetration, or a measure of inflation. While the small size of our country-level data set precludes use from drawing firm conclusions about the relative importance of these additional factors, our overall pattern of results suggests that software piracy is closely associated with fundamental features of the institutional and technological environment, rather than being primarily driven by measures of income or income inequality.

15.5.3 The Relationship between Piracy and Machine Characteristics

While the primary focus of the analysis in this chapter has been on the impact of the broader economic, institutional, and technological environment on country-level piracy, it is also useful to explore the composition of piracy *within* a country, and specifically examine the relationship between piracy and other elements of the machines that users are purchasing and/or upgrading. To do so, we reorganize our data set to capture the level of piracy within a given country for a certain "type" of machine (e.g., the rate of piracy for computers that are produced by a leading OEM after Windows 7 was introduced). We are therefore able to examine how the rate of piracy varies among different populations of machines; we control for country-level differences in the overall rate of piracy by including country-level fixed effects in our specifications, as well. We weight the regressions so that each country is weighted equally, but we weight each machine type within a country according to its share within the country-level population. The results are presented in table 15.6. First, consistent with the global averages we presented in figures 15.2A and 15.2B, table 15.6, columns (1) and (2), document that the rate of piracy is much higher for machines that are produced by fringe manufacturers or assemblers, and is modestly higher among machines that are unambiguously receiving an upgrade (i.e., from

Table 15.6   **Piracy and machine characteristics**

	Windows 7 piracy rate			
	1	2	3	4
OEM leading manufacturer	−.391***		−.274***	−.234***
	(.011)		(.011)	(.009)
Windows 7 model		−.227***	.003	−.005
		(.008)	(.011)	(.008)
OEM leading[a] Windows 7 model			−.180***	−.047***
			(.013)	(.009)
Frontier architecture				−.094***
				(.005)
Windows Professional				.048***
				(.008)
Windows Ultimate				.426***
				(.07)
Observations	4,518	4,518	4,518	4,518
R-Squared	.487	.360	.534	.862

Note: Robust standard errors in parentheses.

[a]Ln patents per capita is defined as Ln(1 + patents per capita).

***Significant at the 1 percent level.
**Significant at the 5 percent level.
*Significant at the 10 percent level.

Windows Vista) as the machine was not produced after Windows 7 was launched. Perhaps more interestingly, there is a very strong interaction effect between these two machine characteristics. Essentially, the highest rate of piracy is observed among older machines (i.e., not Windows 7 models) that are produced by fringe manufacturers or assemblers. This core pattern of interaction is robust to the inclusion or exclusion of a variety of controls, including a control for whether the machine has frontier hardware (i.e., a 64-bit versus 32-bit microprocessor) and also if one accounts for the precise version of Windows that is installed. Also consistent with our earlier descriptive statistics, it is useful to note that the rate of piracy is much higher for machines with Windows Pro and Windows Ultimate; given the global availability of all versions of Windows, it is not surprising that pirates choose to install the highest level of software available.

15.5.4 The Impact of Antipiracy Enforcement Efforts on Software Piracy

Finally, we take advantage of time-series variation in our data to directly investigate the impact of the most notable antipiracy enforcement efforts on the contemporaneous rate of Windows 7 piracy. Specifically, during the course of our 2011 and 2012 sample period, a number of individual countries imposed bans on the Pirate Bay website, the single largest source of pirated digital media on the Internet. Though such policy interventions are broadly endogenous (the bans arise in response to broad concerns about piracy), the precise timing of the intervention is arguably independent of changes over time in Windows 7 piracy in particular, and so it is instructive to examine how a change in the level of enforcement against piracy impacts the rate of Windows 7 software piracy.

We examine three interventions: the ban of Pirate Bay by the United Kingdom in June 2012, by India in May 2012, and by Finland in May 2011. For each country, we define a "control group" of peer countries that can be used as a comparison both in terms of the preintervention level of piracy as well as having enough geographic/cultural similarity that any unobserved shocks are likely common to both the treatment and control countries. For the United Kingdom, the control group is composed of France and Ireland; for India, we include both geographically proximate countries such as Bangladesh and Pakistan, as well as the other BRIC countries (Brazil, Russia, India, and China); and for Finland, we use the remainder of Scandinavia. For each country and for each month before and after the intervention, we calculate the rate of piracy among machines that are first observed within the telemetry data for that month. As such, we are able to track the rate of "new" pirates within each country over time. If restrictions on the Pirate Bay were salient for software piracy, we should observe a decline in the rate of new piracy for those countries impacted by the restriction (relative to the trend in the control countries), at least on a temporary basis. Figures 15.7A, 15.7B, and 15.7C present the results. Across all three interventions,

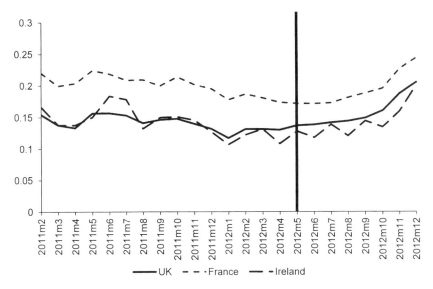

Fig. 15.7A UK piracy rate (effective ban date, June 2012)

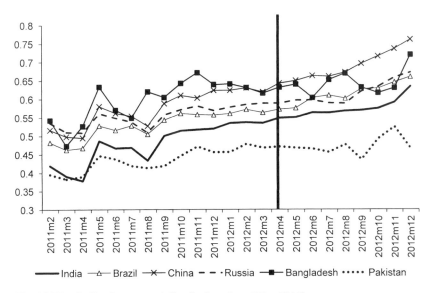

Fig. 15.7B India piracy rate (effective ban date, May 2012)

there does not seem to be a meaningful decline in the rate of piracy after the Pirate Bay restriction, either on an absolute basis or relative to the trend followed by the control countries. We were unable to find a quantitatively or statistically significant difference that resulted from these interventions. This "nonfinding" suggests that, at least for operating system piracy, the main focus on supply-side enforcement effects may be having a relatively

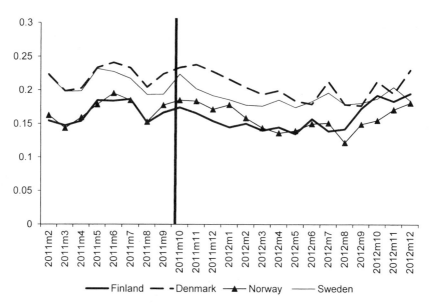

Fig. 15.7C Finland piracy rate (effective ban date, November 2011)

small impact; there may simply be too many alternative sources of pirated Windows, and the pirate-user community may be sufficiently pervasive so as to provide potential pirates with new routes to piracy in the face of supply-side enforcement efforts.

15.6 Conclusions

The primary contribution of this chapter has been to conduct the first large-scale observational study of software piracy. By construction, this is an exploratory exercise, and even our most robust empirical findings are limited to considering the specific domain of piracy of Windows 7. With that said, we have established a number of novel findings that should be of interest to researchers in digitization and piracy going forward.

First, our research underscores the global nature of software piracy, and the role of large-scale global sharing of software and piracy protocols. Relative to the pre-Internet era where piracy may indeed have been pervasive but its diffusion was local (almost by definition), the diffusion of the Internet, the widespread availability of broadband, and the rise of user communities that specifically provide guidance about how and what to pirate have changed the nature of contemporary software piracy.

Second, though the type of data that we use are novel, the bulk of our analysis builds on a small but important literature that has linked the rate of piracy to the economic, institutional, and technological environment. At one level, our findings using observational data are broadly consistent with that prior literature; however, our analysis has allowed us to clarify a key empirical distinction: at least in the context that we examined, it is the quality of the institutional environment, rather than income per se, which is more closely linked with piracy. This finding is particularly salient, since a key argument against copyright enforcement depends on income-based price discrimination. Clarifying the distinction between the quality of institutions and income can be seen in a particularly sharp way by comparing cities that have similar income levels, but are located in countries with different institutional environments. Though we only undertake a small number of comparisons of this type, our exploratory work looking at cities suggests a future direction of research that can sharpen our identification argument: Do cities that are at different levels of income but share the same institutions behave more similarly than cities with the same level of income but with different institutions? Finally, our observational data allows us to directly assess the impact of the most high-profile enforcement efforts against piracy—the choices by individual countries to restrict access to the Pirate Bay over the last several years. Over a number of different experiments, and examining a number of alternative control groups, we are not able to identify a meaningful impact of these enforcement efforts on the observed rate of Windows 7 piracy. While such enforcement efforts may be having a meaningful effect on other types of piracy (e.g., movies or music), supply-side enforcement initiatives have not yet meaningfully deterred large-scale operating systems piracy.

More generally, our analysis highlights the potential value of exploiting new types of data that passively capture user behavior in a direct way. By observing the actual choices that users make about what types of software to install (and where and in conjunction with what types of machine configurations), our analysis offers new insight into both the nature and incidence of software piracy. By and large, our results are consistent with prior measures such as those produced by the Business Software Alliance that suggest that the rate of software piracy is a large and meaningful economic phenomenon. Our results suggest that those earlier findings are not simply the result of the BSA methodology, but reflect the underlying phenomena. This is particularly important since the rate of piracy is extremely low in the United States, and so claims about piracy are often met with some skepticism. Our direct observational approach not only reinforces those earlier findings, but has allowed us to document both the nature and drivers of piracy in a way that may be instructive for policy and practice going forward.

References

Acemoglu, D., S. Johnson, and J. Robinson. 2001. "The Colonial Origins of Comparative Development: An Empirical Investigation." *American Economic Review* 91 (5): 1369–401.

American Heritage Dictionary, 4th Ed. 2000. "Software Piracy." Boston: Houghton Mifflin.
Andres, A. R. 2006. "Software Piracy and Income Inequality." *Applied Economics Letters* 13:101–05.
Banerjee, D., A. M. Khalid, and J. E. Strum. 2005. "Socio-Economic Development and Software Piracy: An Empirical Assessment." *Applied Economics* 37:2091–97.
Bezmen, T. L., and C. A. Depken. 2006. "Influences on Software Piracy: Evidence from Various United States." *Economics Letters* 90:356–61.
Burke, A. E. 1996. "How Effective are International Copyright Conventions in the Music Industry?" *Journal of Cultural Economics* 20:51–66.
Business Software Alliance (BSA). 2011. "Ninth Annual BSA Global Software 2011 Piracy Study." http://globalstudy.bsa.org/2011/.
Central Intelligence Agency. 2007. *The World Factbook 2008*. New York: Skyhorse Publishing.
CNET. 2009a. "Microsoft Acknowledges Windows 7 Activation Leak." News by Dong Ngo. http://news.cnet.com/8301–10805_3–10300857–75.html.
———. 2009b. "Microsoft Windows 7." Online Professional Review. http://reviews.cnet.com/windows/microsoft-windows-7-professional/4505–3672_7–33704140–2.html.
Conner, K. R., and R. P. Rumelt. 1991. "Software Piracy: An Analysis of Protection Strategies." *Management Science* 37 (2): 125–37.
Danaher, B., M. D. Smith, and R. Telang. 2014. "Piracy and Copyright Enforcement Mechanisms." In *Innovation Policy and the Economy*, vol. 14, edited Josh Lerner and Scott Stern, 24–61. Chicago: University of Chicago Press.
Delgado, M., C. Ketels, E. Porter, and S. Stern. 2012. "The Determinants of National Competitiveness." NBER Working Paper no. 18249, Cambridge, MA.
Goel, Rajeev, and M. Nelson. 2009. "Determinants of Software Piracy: Economics, Institutions, and Technology." *Journal of Technology Transfer* 34 (6): 637–58.
Gopal, R. D., and G. L. Sanders. 1998. "International Software Piracy: Analysis of Key Issues and Impacts." *Information Systems Research* 9 (4): 380–97.
———. 2000. "Global Software Piracy: You Can't Get Blood Out of a Turnip." *Communications of the ACM* 43 (9): 82–89.
Greenstein, S., and J. Prince. 2006. "The Diffusion of the Internet and the Geography of the Digital Divide in the United States." NBER Working Paper no. 12182, Cambridge, MA.
Hall, Robert E., and Charles I. Jones. 1997. "Levels of Economic Activity across Countries." *American Economic Review* 87 (2): 173–77.
Kaufmann, D., A. Kraay, and M. Mastruzzi. 2009. "Governance Matters VIII: Aggregate and Individual Governance Indicators, 1996–2008." World Bank Policy Research Working Paper no. 4978, World Bank.
Landes, W. M. and R. A. Posner. 1989. "An Economic Analysis of Copyright Law." *Journal of Legal Studies* 18:325–66.
Marron, D. B., and D. G. Steel. 2000. "Which Countries Protect Intellectual Property? The Case of Software Piracy." *Economic Inquiry* 38:159–74.
Merrill, S., and W. Raduchel. 2013. *Copyright in the Digital Era: Building Evidence for Policy*. Washington, DC: National Academic Press.
Meurer, M. J. 1997. "Price Discrimination, Personal Use and Piracy: Copyright Protection of Digital Works." *Buffalo Law Review*. https://ssrn.com/abstract=49097.
Microsoft. 2009. "Announcing the Windows 7 Upgrade Option Program & Windows 7 Pricing- Bring on GA!" Windows 7 Blog by Brandon LeBlanc. http://blogs.windows.com/windows/archive/b/windows7/archive/2009/06/25/announcing-the-windows-7–upgrade-option-program-amp-windows-7–pricing-bring-on-ga.aspx.

My Digital Life. 2013. "Windows Loader: Current Release Information." Forum. http://forums.mydigitallife.info/threads/24901-Windows-Loader-Current-release-information.

Oberholzer-Gee, F., and K. Strumpf. 2010. "File Sharing and Copyright." In *Innovation Policy and the Economy*, vol. 10, edited by Josh Lerner and Scott Stern, 19–55. Chicago: University of Chicago Press.

Oz, S., and J. F. Thisse. 1999. "A Strategic Approach to Software Protection." *Journal of Economics and Management Strategy* 8 (2): 163–90.

Peace, A. G., D. F. Galletta, and J. Y. L. Thong. 2003. "Software Piracy in the Workplace: A Model and Empirical Test." *Journal of Management Information Systems* 20 (1): 153–77.

Reddit. 2013. "Is Anyone Using a Pirated Copy of Windows 7 or 8?" Reddit Thread. http://www.reddit.com/r/Piracy/comments/1baus9/is_anyone_using_a_pirated_copy_of_windows_7_or_8/.

Silva, F., and G. B. Ramello. 2000. "Sound Recording Market: The Ambiguous Case of Copyright and Piracy." *Industrial and Corporate Change* 9:415–42.

Waldfogel, J. 2011. "Bye, Bye, Miss American Pie? The Supply of New Recorded Music since Napster." NBER Working Paper no. 15882, Cambridge, MA.

Comment   Ashish Arora

The growth of the digital economy has also increased interest in the unauthorized use of digital goods. The existing literature has tended to focus either on the issue of whether a particular instance of piracy—unauthorized use—is a net social "bad" (e.g., whether it is a form of de facto price discrimination), or the efficacy of specific types of enforcement efforts. Some studies do provide estimates of the extent of piracy, but the results are not credible because the studies are linked to advocacy efforts and suffer from weaknesses in methods and implausible assumptions. The question has become more salient with the rise of broadband technologies that have apparently made it easier to distribute digital products, including pirated products. Athey and Stern have done an important service by providing a reasonable measure of the problem for an important product.

An important contribution of the chapter is its careful attention to measurement. Even with the new technology that allows Microsoft to discern whether the product use is based on an authorized key, matters are not straightforward. For instance, I know from personal experience that unless laptops are regularly connected to the network of the institution that purchased the license to the software, Microsoft policy is to incorrectly treat that use as unauthorized. Athey and Stern get around this problem by focusing

---

Ashish Arora is the Rex D. Adams Professor of Business Administration at the Fuqua School of Business at Duke University and a research associate of the National Bureau of Economic Research.

For acknowledgments, sources of research support, and disclosure of the author's or authors' material financial relationships, if any, please see http://www.nber.org/chapters/c13127.ack.

on specific keys, and by attending to whether the machine eventually reauthorizes with a valid key.

Given the conservatism of the estimates, the results give one pause. The scale of the problem is large. Over a quarter of all copies of Windows 7 are unauthorized with significant variation across countries. My "back-of-the-envelope" calculations indicate that a 25 percent piracy rate for Windows alone implies $6.1 billion in lost revenue and $3.8 billion in lost operating income for Microsoft. These are consistent with the large estimates of losses due to piracy reported by advocacy organizations such as the BSA, but they assume a direct correspondence between the extent of piracy and the extent of the loss. One needs better estimates of the demand (for the authorized product and for the pirated one) to assess the validity of such estimates.

Premium versions of the software are more prone to the problem, implying that this is not a case of de facto price discrimination. Put differently, a common prescription in both IT and pharmaceuticals for combating piracy is for manufacturers to introduce lower-priced versions in poorer countries. The Athey-Stern results suggest that this prescription will not work.

They note another interesting result, albeit without comment. Although machines from smaller manufacturers tend to have a higher percentage of pirated software, the bulk of the pirated software is in computers produced by the leading manufacturers (OEMs). Further, these are also the manufacturers responsible for the keys that allow for unauthorized installations of Windows 7. Some obvious questions arise. Are Microsoft's contracts, or the enforcement of those contracts, with these OEMs at fault? Are the OEMs contriving to reduce their payments to Microsoft by shipping machines without Windows? What liability do OEMs face when a key given to them is leaked?

Athey and Stern instead focus on relating observed levels of piracy to country-specific institutions. They conclude that institutions associated with a greater respect for private property reduce piracy, even after controlling for how rich the country is. In plain words, the incidence of piracy is greatest in middle-income countries afflicted with corrupt governments or weaker capitalist institutions, or both. This finding could reflect greater moral acceptance on the part of buyers of pirated products or a greater profitability (for a given level of demand for pirated products) of supplying pirated products (or both). It appears that this is mostly a demand-side explanation because greater enforcement (e.g., shutting down Pirate Bay) appears to have little effect on the measured rate of piracy. More precisely, greater enforcement against suppliers of pirated products appears to be ineffective in reducing piracy.

If so, then producers of digital goods face an uncomfortable decision, namely, to coerce their customers to use authorized products only. Indeed, Microsoft appears to have moved in this direction, forcing users to regularly authenticate their software, and imposing modest downgrades of product functionality. It appears that this is not enough to dissuade a significant number of buyers from choosing the pirated products, which are cheaper or perhaps even free.

Two sets of research questions arise. The first relates to pricing. In effect, countries with higher rates of piracy have a lower willingness to pay for the authentic product. If so, might the problem lie in how the authentic product is priced? It would be interesting to know if Microsoft has experimented with discounts and other ways of tweaking its price and what this tells us about the implied willingness to pay for pirated products. It may well be that Microsoft is already pricing optimally, given the ineffectiveness of supply-side enforcement efforts.

A second, and related, question is whether customers should be induced to eschew pirated products by downgrading the functionality of pirated products by denying updates and patches. Such a strategy may also be costly because some legitimate users may be incorrectly classified as using unauthorized software. Other possible costs include greater security risks for legitimate users (a larger fraction of unauthorized users may have compromised machines), legal liability, and reputation costs.

It is obvious that such an exercise requires estimates for the willingness to pay for the authentic product as well as the willingness to pay for the pirated product. More generally, sensible estimates of the demand would also help inform us about the magnitude of the lost revenue and profits. It is striking, though perhaps not surprising, that the chapter is silent on the issue. However, any such exercise must also take into account competitive conditions. It may well suit a dominant producer to have its product crowd out a possible competitor, be it an alternative operating system product (Linux) or a competing platform (Apple). Tolerating or even encouraging some level of piracy may be a way to keep competitors at bay. Thus, it would be interesting to explore whether countries with high rates of piracy also have higher shares of Microsoft Windows relative to alternate operating systems.

Regardless, this study makes an important contribution by carefully documenting the incidence of piracy across the world, and correlating it with the level of institutional development of the country.

Contributors

Ajay Agrawal
Rotman School of Management
University of Toronto
105 St. George Street
Toronto, ON M5S 3E6 Canada

Ashish Arora
Fuqua School of Business
Duke University
Box 90120
Durham, NC 27708-0120

Susan Athey
Graduate School of Business
Stanford University
655 Knight Way
Stanford, CA 94305

Michael R. Baye
Department of Business Economics
 and Public Policy
Kelley School of Business
Indiana University
Bloomington, IN 47405

Timothy F. Bresnahan
SIEPR
Landau Economics Building, Room 325
579 Serra Mall
Stanford, CA 94305-6072

Erik Brynjolfsson
MIT Sloan School of Management
100 Main Street, E62-414
Cambridge, MA 02142

Brett Danaher
Department of Economics
Wellesley College
Wellesley, MA 02481

Babur De los Santos
Department of Business Economics
 and Public Policy
Kelley School of Business
Indiana University
Bloomington, IN 47405

Samita Dhanasobhon
School of Information Systems and
 Management
Heinz College
Carnegie Mellon University
Pittsburgh, PA 15213

Chris Forman
Georgia Institute of Technology
Scheller College of Business
800 West Peachtree Street, NW
Atlanta, GA 30308

Contributors

Joshua S. Gans
Rotman School of Management
University of Toronto
105 St. George Street
Toronto ON M5S 3E6 Canada

Matthew Gentzkow
University of Chicago
Booth School of Business
5807 South Woodlawn Avenue
Chicago, IL 60637

Avi Goldfarb
Rotman School of Management
University of Toronto
105 St. George Street
Toronto, ON M5S 3E6 Canada

Shane M. Greenstein
Kellogg School of Management
Northwestern University
2001 Sheridan Road
Evanston, IL 60208-2013

Hanna Halaburda
Bank of Canada
234 Laurier Avenue West
Ottawa, ON, K1A 0G9 Canada

John Horton
Stern School of Business
New York University
44 West Fourth Street, 8-81
New York, NY 10012

Tatiana Komarova
Department Of Economics
London School of Economics and
 Political Science
Houghton Street
London, WC2A 2AE England

Nicola Lacetera
University of Toronto
105 St. George Street
Toronto, ON M5S 2E9 Canada

Randall Lewis
Google, Inc.
1600 Amphitheatre Parkway
Mountain View, CA 94043

Elizabeth Lyons
IR/PS
UC San Diego
9500 Gilman Drive, MC 0519
La Jolla, CA 92093-0519

Megan MacGarvie
Boston University
School of Management
595 Commonwealth Avenue, Room
 522H
Boston, MA 02215

Catherine L. Mann
International Business School
Brandeis University
Waltham, MA 02453

Amalia R. Miller
Department of Economics
University of Virginia
P. O. Box 400182
Charlottesville, VA 22904

Petra Moser
Department of Economics
Stanford University
579 Serra Mall
Stanford, CA 94305-6072

Denis Nekipelov
Monroe Hall, Room 254
University of Virginia
P.O. Box 400182
Charlottesville, VA 22904

Justin M. Rao
Microsoft Research
641 Avenue of the Americas, 7th Floor
New York, NY 10011

David H. Reiley
Google, Inc.
1600 Amphitheatre Parkway
Mountain View, CA 94043

Marc Rysman
Department of Economics
Boston University
270 Bay State Road
Boston, MA 02215

Steven L. Scott
Google, Inc.
1600 Amphitheatre Parkway
Mountain View, CA 94043

Jesse M. Shapiro
University of Chicago
Booth School of Business
5807 S. Woodlawn Avenue
Chicago, IL 60637

Timothy Simcoe
Boston University
School of Management
595 Commonwealth Avenue
Boston, MA 02215

Michael D. Smith
School of Information Systems and
  Management
Heinz College
Carnegie Mellon University
Pittsburgh, PA 15213

Christopher Stanton
University of Utah
David Eccles School of Business
1655 East Campus Center Drive
Salt Lake City, UT 84112

Scott Stern
MIT Sloan School of Management
100 Main Street, E62-476
Cambridge, MA 02142

Koleman Strumpf
University of Kansas
School of Business
Summerfield Hall
1300 Sunnyside Avenue
Lawrence, KS 66045-7601

Rahul Telang
School of Information Systems and
  Management
Heinz College
Carnegie Mellon University
Pittsburgh, PA 15213

Catherine E. Tucker
MIT Sloan School of Management
100 Main Street, E62-533
Cambridge, MA 02142

Hal R. Varian
Google, Inc.
1600 Amphitheatre Parkway
Mountain View, CA 94043

Joel Waldfogel
3-177 Carlson School of Management
University of Minnesota
321 19th Avenue South
Minneapolis, MN 55455

Scott Wallsten
Technology Policy Institute
Suite 520
1099 New York Ave., NW
Washington, DC 20001

Matthijs R. Wildenbeest
Department of Business Economics
  and Public Policy
Kelley School of Business
Indiana University
Bloomington, IN 47405

Lynn Wu
University of Pennsylvania
The Wharton School
JMHH 561
3730 Walnut Street
Philadelphia, PA 19104

Evgeny Yakovlev
New Economic School
Nakhimovsky pr., 47, off. 905
Moscow 117418, Russia

Author Index

Abhishek, V., 163n25
Abowd, J., 283
Abraham, M., 199, 203
Abramovsky, L., 239
Abrams, S. J., 171
Acemoglu, D., 460, 467
Acquisti, A., 284, 285, 315, 317, 335, 344
Agarwal, D., 212
Aggarwal, G., 283
Agrawal, A., 11, 12, 222, 239, 241, 244, 250
Akerlof, G. A., 244
Alloway, T., 313n2
Ambrus, A., 176, 179
Anderson, C., 172, 236
Anderson, H. E., 314n3
Anderson, R., 318
Anderson, S. P., 176, 179
Andres, A. R., 449
Antras, P., 239
Appleton-Young, L., 91
Armstrong, M., 176, 179, 229, 258n2
Arola, C., 119
Arora, A., 12, 344n28, 345
Arrow, K. J., 93, 312
Arthur, W. B., 24n3
Athey, S., 176, 179
August, T., 345
Autor, D. H., 10, 228, 229, 244
Awad, N., 426
Ayres, I., 353

Bachlechner, D., 341n18
Bagwell, K., 192
Bajari, P., 38n23
Bakos, J., 9
Balasubramanian, S., 9
Baldwin, C. Y., 23, 25, 31, 34
Ballantyne, J. A., 376
Bamberger, K. A., 343n26
Banerjee, D., 449
Bar-Isaac, H., 10, 238
Basuroy, S., 358n2
Bautz, A., 361, 366n22
Baye, M., 9, 139n4, 139n5, 143n11, 143n12, 149
Becker, G. S., 23, 191
Berners-Lee, T., 27
Berry, S. T., 176, 433
Bertrand, M., 390n4
Bezmen, T. L., 449
Bhagwati, J., 245
Blackburn, D., 407n1
Blake, T., 192, 193, 200, 200n15, 246
Bloom, N., 229n3, 254
Blum, B. S., 9, 12
Boardman, A., 57
Bojanc, R., 344n28
Bradley, C., 280n1
Brecht, M., 341n18
Bresnahan, T. F., 5, 21n1, 24, 26, 49n1, 50, 52n3
Broder, A., 211

Brodersen, K., 128
Brooks, F., 24n5
Brynjolfsson, E., 8, 9, 10, 57, 84, 91, 93, 114, 139, 147, 237, 239, 419
Bucklin, R. E., 194
Burke, A. E., 449
Burks, S., 252n1

Cabral, L., 10, 230
Calvano, E., 176, 179
Calzolari, G., 285
Campagnoli, P., 120
Campbell, K., 340
Card, D., 198
Carlin, J., 198n13
Carrière-Swallow, Y., 119
Carter, C. K., 132
Carty, M., 344n28
Caruana, G., 10, 238
Case, K. E., 94, 106
Castells, M., 13
Castle, J. L., 120
Catalini, C., 11, 12
Caves, R. E., 412, 413
Chakrabarti, D., 212
Chan, D., 200
Chevalier, J., 10, 139, 419
Chipman, H., 122
Choi, H., 93, 113, 119, 129, 152n19, 246
Chown, T., 343n26
Ciriani, V., 283
Clark, D. D., 30
Clark, K. B., 23, 25, 31, 34
Clay, K., 139
Clyde, M. A., 133
Coles, P., 243
Colfer, L., 31
Conner, K. R., 448
Cuñat, V., 10, 238
Cutler, D. M., 174

D'Amuri, F., 152n19
Danaher, B., 386n1, 387n2, 391n5, 394n7, 400, 447, 448
Davenport, T. H., 93
David, P. A., 21n2, 24n3
Deazley, R., 361
Debreu, G., 312
De Jong, P., 132
Delgado, M., 446, 460, 465
Dellarocas, C., 229n2, 426
DellaVigna, S., 169

De los Santos, B., 139n5, 140, 143n11, 143n12, 144n13, 149
Demetz, L., 341n18
Demsetz, H., 191
Deng, A., 194n4, 215
Depken, C. A., 449
Dettling, L. L., 228, 245
Dewan, S., 426
DeWitt, D., 283
Diamond, P., 9
Dickie, M., 200
DiCola, P., 358, 367
Dover, Y., 10
Dranove, D., 21n2
Duflo, E., 390n4
Duncan, G., 283
Durbin, J., 120, 132
Dutcher, E. G., 229n3
Dwork, C., 283

Eckert, S. E., 341
Edmonds, R., 169
Einav, L., 8
Elberse, A., 172, 236
Ellison, G., 9
Ellison, S. F., 9
Evans, D. S., 259

Fader, P. S., 92
Farrell, J., 24n3, 25, 25n6
Fawcett, N. W. P., 120
Feather, J., 360
Ferreira, F., 433, 434n28
Fienberg, S., 283
Fiorina, M. P., 171
Fischetti, M., 27
Fisher, A., 200
Fleder, D., 10
Fogel, R. W., 55
Forman, C., 9, 83, 139
Foros, Ø., 176, 179
Fradkin, A., 11
Francois, J., 245
Frankel, A. S., 274
Friedman, A., 285
Frühwirth-Schnatter, S., 132
Fryer, H., 343n26

Galan, E., 119
Galletta, D. F., 448
Gans, J. S., 176, 179, 258n1, 258n2
Garicano, L., 10, 254

Garside, P. D., 376, 376n37
Gelman, A., 133, 198n13
Gentzkow, M., 83, 84, 169, 170, 171, 172, 173, 174, 175, 180
George, E. I., 121, 133
Gerking, S., 200
Geva, T., 114
Ghani, E., 223, 244, 250
Ghose, A., 9, 83, 139
Ghosh, J., 133, 246
Ginsberg, J., 93, 152n19
Glaeser, E. L., 94, 174
Goel, R., 449, 466
Goldfarb, A., 8, 9, 10, 11, 12, 66, 83, 84, 140, 192, 200, 285, 315
Gonen, R., 192, 202
Goolsbee, A., 12, 57, 59, 139, 310, 419
Gopal, R. D., 447, 449
Gordon, L. A., 344n28
Greene, W. H., 177
Greenstein, S. M., 5, 6, 11, 24, 37, 49n1, 50, 58, 310, 448
Grierson, H. G. C., 365n15, 375, 376
Griffith, R., 239
Gross, R., 285
Grossklags, J., 285
Grossman, G. M., 239
Guzmán, G., 152n19
Gyourko, J., 94

Hall, R. E., 446, 467
Han, L., 94
Handke, C., 429n24, 431n27
Hann, I.-H., 315
Harris, M., 358n2
Harvey, A., 120
Heald, P. J., 359n5
Heaton, P., 10
Hellerstein, R., 119
Helpman, E., 239
Henderson, R., 31, 50
Hendry, D. F., 120
Hirsch, D. D., 314, 353
Hitt, L. M., 8, 239
Hoekman, B., 245
Hoffman, D. A., 344
Holley, R. P., 141n6
Homer, N., 282
Hong, H., 139
Hong, S.-H., 13
Horowitz, J., 283
Horrigan, J. B., 91

Hortaçsu, A., 10, 140, 230
Horton, J. J., 219, 223, 242, 244, 245, 246, 250, 253
Hosanagar, K., 10
Hu, Y. J., 10, 91, 139, 147, 159, 192n3, 248, 314, 419

Ioannidis, C., 314
Israel, M., 77n14

Jabs Saral, Krista, 229n3
Jeon, G. Y., 310
Jerath, K., 163n25
Jerman-Blazic, B., 344n28
Jin, G. Z., 10
Johnson, G., 200, 204, 214n26
Johnson, J., 163n25
Johnson, M. E., 344
Johnson, S., 460, 467
Jones, B. F., 23
Jones, C. I., 446, 467
Jullien, B., 52n2

Kahn, L., 252n1
Kaplan, E., 169
Karagodsky, I., 324n12, 340
Kato, A., 10
Katz, M., 77n14
Kaufmann, D., 460
Kaya, C., 237
Kee, K. F., 78n15
Kelley, S., 376
Kerr, W. R., 223, 244, 250
Kessides, I. N., 191
Khalid, A. M., 449
Khan, B. Z., 359n5
Kim, H. H., 8
Kim, Y.-M., 310
Kind, H. J., 176, 179
King, S. P., 258n1, 258n2
Klenow, P. J., 57, 59, 310
Knight, S. C., 341
Knopper, S., 414, 415
Kohavi, R., 194n4, 215
Kohn, R., 132
Komarova, T., 295
Koopman, S. J., 120, 132
Korolova, A., 284
Kraay, A., 460
Krieger, A. M., 192n3
Krishnan, R., 139
Krugman, P., 90

Ksiazek, T. B., 172
Kuhn, P., 252n2
Kumar, D., 200
Kuruzovich, J., 93
Kwon, J., 344

Labbé, F., 119
Lacetera, N., 222, 239, 241, 244, 250
Lambert, D., 283, 296
Lambrecht, A., 205n20
Landes, W. M., 447
Langlois, R., 24
Lauinger, T., 391
Lazear, E. P., 245
Lazer, D. A., 93
Leeds, J., 414
LeFevre, K., 283
Levin, J. D., 8
Levitt, S. D., 353
Lewis, R. A., 193, 194, 196, 200, 201, 202, 202n19, 204, 205, 214n26, 246
Li, X., 359, 369n26, 378
Liebowitz, S. J., 77n14, 357, 407n1
Liu, P., 11, 129
Lockhart, J. G., 374, 374n35
Lodish, L., 192n1, 192n3
Loeb, M. P., 344n28
Lovell, M., 197
Lyons, E., 222, 239, 241, 244, 245, 250, 254n4

MacCarthy, M., 332
MacCormack, A., 34
MacGarvie, M., 359, 369n26, 378
MacKie-Mason, J., 25n6
Madigan, D. M., 121, 123
Magnac, T., 283
Mahoney, J. T., 31
Manley, L., 141n6
Mann, C. L., 324n12, 340, 341
Manski, C., 283
Mansour, H., 252n2
Marcucci, J., 152n19
Margolis, S., 357
Marron, D. B., 449
Mastruzzi, M., 460
Maurin, E., 283
Mayzlin, D., 10, 139
McAfee, A., 93, 246
McCarty, N., 171
McCulloch, R. E., 121, 133

McDevitt, R., 6, 58, 310
McLaren, N., 119
Merrill, S., 447, 448
Meurer, M. J., 447
Middeldorp, M., 119
Milgrom, P., 240
Mill, R., 222, 244, 250
Miller, A. R., 12, 285, 353, 355
Mincer, J., 198
Moe, W. W., 92
Moffitt, R., 282
Molinari, F., 284
Moore, R., 343n26
Moraga-González, J. L., 144n14
Moreau, F., 237
Morgan, J., 9, 139n4
Morton, F. S., 310
Moser, P., 359, 369n26, 378
Mowery, D., 5
Mukherjee, S., 283
Mullainathan, S., 170, 172, 390n4
Mulligan, D. K., 343n26
Murphy, J., 200
Murphy, K. M., 23, 191

Nandkumar, A., 345
Narayanan, A., 282
Nekipelov, D., 295
Nelson, M., 449, 466
Netz, J., 25n6
Nguyen, D. T., 194, 201
Nissim, K., 283
Nosko, C., 192, 193, 200, 200n15, 215, 246
Nowey, T., 341n18

Oberholzer-Gee, F., 12, 13, 236, 357, 407n1, 429, 448
Oh, J. H., 57, 84
Olston, C., 192, 202
Orr, M., 341
Oussayef, K. Z., 341
Oz, S., 448

Pallais, A., 220, 239, 241, 243, 244, 250, 252n1
Panagariya, A., 245
Pandey, S. D., 192, 202, 212
Park, N., 78n15
Patterson, L., 360
Pavan, A., 285
Pavlov, E., 192, 202

Peace, A. G., 448
Pearson, R., 283
Peitz, M., 3
Peltier, S., 237
Pentland, A. S., 90
Peranson, E., 240
Petrin, A., 433
Petris, G., 120
Petrone, S., 120
Petrongolo, B., 244
Pimont, V., 344n28
Pissarides, C. A., 244
Poole, K. T., 171
Posner, R. A., 447
Prince, J., 66, 84, 448
Prior, M., 171
Pym, D., 314

Qin, X., 120

Raduchel, W., 447, 448
Raftery, A. E., 121, 123
Rahman, M. S., 91
Ramakrishnan, R., 283
Ramaprasad, J., 426
Ramello, G. B., 449
Rao, J. M., 193, 196, 205
Ravid, S. A., 358n2
Reed, D. P., 30
Reed, W. R., 120
Reichman, S., 114
Reiley, D., 193, 200, 201, 202, 202n19, 204, 205, 214n26, 246
Reisinger, M., 176, 179
Resnick, P., 230
Retzer, K., 335
Ridder, G., 282
Rigbi, O., 11
Rob, R., 12, 13, 407n1
Roberds, W., 314n3
Robinson, J., 56n1, 460, 467
Rochet, J.-C., 258n1, 258n2
Rockoff, H., 274n23
Romanosky, S., 317, 335, 344
Rosen, S., 235
Rosenthal, H., 171
Rossi-Hansberg, E., 239
Rosston, G., 6, 59
Roth, A. E., 240
Rue, H., 132
Rumelt, R. P., 448

Rusnak, J., 34
Russell, A., 26n7, 29
Rutz, O. J., 194
Rysman, M., 37, 42, 52n2, 142n10, 229

Saloner, G., 24n3
Saltzer, J. H., 30
Sanchez, R., 31
Sanders, G. L., 447, 449
Sands, E., 252n1
Sandstoe, J., 415
Savage, S. J., 6, 59
Scherer, F. M., 358, 358n3
Schmid, D. W., 344n28
Scholten, P., 9, 139n4
Schreft, S., 314n3
Schreiner, T., 201
Scott, S. L., 123, 130
Shaked, A., 176
Shanbhoge, R., 119
Shapiro, J.M., 169, 170, 171, 172, 173, 174, 175, 180
Sharp, R., 335
Shepard, N., 132
Sher, R., 358, 366n17
Sherwin, R., 23
Shiller, R. J., 94, 106
Shleifer, A., 170, 172
Shmatikov, V., 282
Shum, M., 139
Silva, F., 449
Simcoe, T., 5, 25, 26n7, 27n9, 38, 42
Simester, D., 237
Simon, H. A., 23, 90, 111
Sinai, T., 9, 85
Singer, N., 316n4
Sinkinson, M., 169
Smarati, P., 283
Smith, A., 23
Smith, M. D., 9, 10, 139, 159, 237, 314, 386n1, 391n5, 400, 419, 447, 448
Smith, V. C., 274n23
Srinivasan, T. N., 245
St. Clair, W., 361n7, 365, 371n28, 375n36
Stanton, C. T., 222, 223, 229, 244, 250, 253
Steele, D. G., 449
Stigler, G. J., 9, 23, 139, 244
Strum, J. E., 449
Strumpf, K., 12, 13, 357, 407n1, 429, 448
Suhoy, T., 119
Sullivan, R. J., 332

Sunstein, C., 9, 170, 171
Sutton, J., 176, 411, 433, 440
Sweeney, L., 282, 283

Tadelis, S., 192, 193, 200, 200n15, 215, 246
Tang, Z., 314
Taylor, C., 285
Telang, R., 285, 335, 345, 386n1, 400, 447, 448
Tervio, M., 408, 411, 415
Thisse, J. F., 448
Thomas, C., 222, 229, 244, 250, 253
Thomas, R. C., 318
Thomson, K., 419, 423
Thong, J. Y. L., 448
Tirole, J., 52n2, 258n1, 258n2
Trajtenberg, M., 26, 52n3
Tucker, C. E., 8, 9, 10, 12, 192, 200, 205n20, 236, 285, 315, 353, 355
Tunca, T. I., 345
Turow, S., 357

Valenzuela, S., 78n15
Vanham, P., 219
Van Reenen, J., 254
Varian, H. R., 9, 13, 93, 113, 119, 123, 130, 152n19, 246, 284, 285
Vigdor, J. L., 174
Vilhuber, L., 283
Vogel, H., 412, 412n7
Volinsky, C., 123

Waldfogel, J., 3, 9, 12, 13, 85, 176, 357, 407n1, 408, 408n3, 433, 434n28, 447
Waldman, D. M., 6, 59
Walker, T., 194n4, 215
Webster, J. G., 172
Wellman, B., 78n15, 79
Weyl, E. G., 52n2, 258n2
Wheeler, C. H., 244
White, M. J., 174
Wilde, L. L., 244
Wildenbeest, M. R., 139n5, 140, 143n11, 143n12, 144n13, 144n14, 149
Williams, J., 314
Wolff, E., 139
Woodcock, S., 283
Wright, G., 280n1
Wu, L., 92

Xu, Y., 194n4, 215

Yakovlev, E., 295, 301
Yan, C., 310
Yglesias, M., 259
Yildiz, T., 200

Zeckhauser, R., 230
Zentner, A., 77n14, 237, 407
Zhang, J., 11, 236
Zhang, X., 11, 426
Zhang, Z. J., 163n25
Zhu, F., 11

Subject Index

Page numbers followed by *f* or *t* refer to figures or tables, respectively.

Activity bias, 205–9
Acxiom, 316
Adam Smith marketplace, 311–12
Ad exchanges, 201
Advertising, 191; activity bias and, 205–9; case study of large-scale experiment, 202–5; challenges in measuring, 192–95; computational, advances in, 211–13; computational methods for improving effectiveness of, 195–99; evolution of metrics for, 199–202; measuring long-run returns to, 209–11; study of online, 10; targeted, 3, 195, 199; untargeted, 199n14. *See also* Digital advertising
Agency model, Apple's, 160
Airbnb, 11
Amazon, 140, 316
Amazon Coins, 257
American Time Use Survey (ATUS), 7, 56, 59–71; computer use for leisure, 61–62, 62t; demographics of online leisure time, 65–70; ways Americans spend their time, 62–63, 63f, 64f, 65f
Antipiracy enforcement efforts, impact of, 472–74
Apple: agency model, 160; iBookstore, 160; platform-specific currencies of, 259
Appliances, home, predicting demand for, 100–101

Arrow-Debreu "complete" market, 312
Attribution problem, 201–2
ATUS. *See* American Time Use Survey (ATUS)
Authors, payments to, 357–60; data, 361–65; income from profit sharing, 371–73; lump sum, 365–71; total income to, 373–77. *See also* Copyrights
Automated targeting, 195, 199

Barnes & Noble, 140, 141; top search terms leading users to, 145–47, 146t
Barnesandnoble.com, 140
Basic structural model, 120–21
Bayesian model averaging, 123. *See also* Variable selection
Bayesian Structural Time Series (BSTS), 120, 124, 129, 130
Beckford v. Hood, 361
Berners-Lee, Tim, 27
Bitcoin, 258, 259, 272
Book industry, 138–39; current retail, 140; data sets for, 143–44; overview of, 140–44
Book industry, online: literature on, 139–40; price dispersion and, 139
Book-oriented platforms, search activity on, 150–51, 152t
Book-related searches: combining data from comScore and Google Trends, 152–55;

491

Book-related searches (*cont.*)
  dynamics of, 151–52; for specific titles, 155–59
Books: booksellers' sites for finding, 148–49; online sales of, 137–38; online searching for, 144–51; price comparison sites for, 144. *See also* E-books; Print books
Books, searching for, 144–51
Book searches, 9
Booksellers, searching for, 144–51
Booksellers' sites: activities of searchers after visiting, 149–50, 149t; for finding books, 148–49
Bookstores, online, for book searches, 144
Bookstores, revenue of leading, 143, 143t
Borders, 140
Boundaries, firm, online contract labor markets and, 239–40
Brick-and-mortar books stores: retail sales of, 142–43, 142f
BSTS. *See* Bayesian Structural Time Series (BSTS)
Business Software Alliance (BSA), 449

Case-Shiller index, 91–92
Cerf, Vint, 26
CERN. *See* European Organization for Nuclear Research (CERN)
ChoicePoint, 316
Clark, David, 26
Click-through rate (CTR), 192, 199–200
Communications costs, effect of low, 2
Complementaries, between display and search advertising, 201–2
Complete-markets framework, 311–12; atomistic interaction among players and, 316–17; frictionless markets and, 315; full information and, 315; trade-offs and, 315; violating, 312–14
Computational advertising, advances in, 211–13. *See also* Advertising
"Computer use for leisure," 62–63, 64f
Computing market segments: platforms and, 5
comScore, 152–55
Consumer research behavior, literature on, 139
Consumer sentiment: nowcasting, 124–27; University of Michigan monthly survey of, 124
Contract labor, demand for, 228

Contract labor markets: influence of information frictions on matching outcomes in, 220–23; introduction to, 219–22; patterns of trade in, 220
Contract labor markets, online: boundaries of the firm and, 239–40; demand for contract labor in, 228; design of, 240–43; digitization and, 11; economics of, 226–30; geographic distribution of work and, 230–35; growth in, 221–22; income distribution and, 235–39; labor supply and, 227–28; platforms and, 229–30, 240–43; social welfare implications of, 243–45
Copyrights, 357; data for analysis of, 361–65; digitization and, 13–14; evidence on effects of stronger, 357–58; example of Sir Walter Scott, 373–77; income from profit sharing and, 371–73; lump sum payments to authors and, 365–71; in romantic period Britain, 360–61
CTR. *See* Click-through rate (CTR)
Currencies: platform-specific, 258–59; private, 11. *See also* Private digital currencies
Customer acquisition, 200–201

Data, online, potential of, 8
Data breaches: cross-border, 330–33; discipline by equity markets and, 339–41; discipline by equity markets and, literature review of, 347; disclosure of, 317; frameworks for analyzing, 310–20; probability distribution of, 318–19; at Target, 318n8; trends in business costs of, 335–39. *See also* Information loss
Data holders, 316
Data security, digitization and, 12–13
Data subjects, 316
Dell key (Sarah), 454
Digital advertising, 191–92; data reporting for, 192. *See also* Advertising
Digital books. *See* E-books
Digital currencies. *See* Private digital currencies
Digital information: challenges of privacy and security and, 2
Digital media, studies of: case 1: effect of graduated response antipiracy law on digital music sales, 387–90; case 2: effect of Megaupload shutdown on dig-

ital movie sales, 391–94; case 3: effect of digital distribution of television on piracy and DVD sales, 394–96

Digital movie sales, effect of Megaupload shutdown on, 391–94

Digital music sales, effect of graduated response antipiracy law on, 387–90

Digital news. *See* News, online

Digital piracy, 357; defined, 444

Digital Rights Management (DRM), 141–42

Digital technology, 1; demand for, 6; role of growth of digital communication in rise of, 1–2; search costs and, 8–9

Digitization: economic impact of, 1; economic transactions and, 7–8; frictions and, 11; government policy and, 12–15; markets changed by, 10; markets enabled by, 10–11; online labor markets and, 11; online sales and, 137; personal information and, 3; private currencies and, 11; ways markets function and, 8–9

Digitization Agenda, 309, 310

Digitization research, 2–3

Digitized money transfer systems, 258; platforms and, 258

Disclosure, of data breaches, 317, 334–35

Distribution, near-zero marginal costs of, 9–10, 12

Donaldson v. Becket, 360–61

DRM. *See* Digital Rights Management (DRM)

eBay, 11

E-books, 138, 139, 141; prices of, 159–62; sales of, vs. print books, 141t; searching for, 144–45; shift to, 140–41. *See also* Print books

Economic transactions: digitization and, 7–8

Economic trends, predicting, 92–94

ePub format, 141

Equity markets, discipline by, and data breaches, 339–41; literature review of, 347

E-readers: definition of, 141; formats for, 141–42; Kindle, 9, 141; Nook, 9, 141; Sony LIBRIé, 140–41

European Organization for Nuclear Research (CERN), 27

European Union (EU) Privacy Directive, 316

Facebook, privacy breaches and, 284

Facebook Credits (FB Credits), 257, 259, 260; case study of, 260–62

Financial Crimes Enforcement Network (FinCEN), 272

Forecasting, traditional, 89. *See also* Nowcasting; Predictions

Frictions, digitization and, 11

General purpose technology (GPT), 21–22

Genome-wide association studies (GWAS), 282

Gold farming, 259

Google, 316

Google Correlate, 119

Google Trends, 95–96, 115, 119, 124, 152–55

Government policy, digitization and, 12–15

GWAS. *See* Genome-wide association studies (GWAS)

Hacking, 321; origins, 331

HADOPI, 387–90

HapMap data, 282

Hart, Michael, 140

Home appliances, predicting demand for, 100–111

Household behavior, 6–7

Housing market, 90–92; empirical results of models, 100–111; implications of advances in information technology for, 111–14; indicators, 96–97; literature review of for predicting, 92–94; modeling methods for predicting, 97–100. *See also* Predictions

Housing price index (HPI), 92, 96, 100–101, 102, 104, 105, 106–9

Housing trends, predicting, 93

Hulu.com, 398–404

Hypertext Markup Language (HTML), 27

Hypertext Transfer Protocol (HTTP), 27

IAB. *See* Internet Architecture Board (IAB)

iBookstore, 160

IEEE. *See* Institute for Electrical and Electronics Engineers (IEEE)

Income distribution, online contract labor markets and, 235–39

Individual disclosure, 282; modern medical databases and, 282–83
Information, personal, digitization and, 3
Information aggregation, 314; literature on benefits vs. costs, 316–18; value of personal, 315
Information flows, applying pollution model to, 314–15
Information loss: amounts, 320–22, 321f; costs of, 317–18; costs of increased security and, 344–45; creating insurance markets and products for, 344; cross-border, 330–33; data needs and analysis for, 346; differences by sector, 324–30; disclosure of, 317; legal recourses, 343–43; legislative approaches to reducing harm from, 317; market discipline vs. nonmarket regulatory/legal discipline and, 333–45; market value of, 339; methods, 320–22, 321f; policy interventions for, 341–43; trends, 320–33; types of, 322–24; in US, 333. *See also* Data breaches; Information marketplaces
Information marketplaces, 312–14; balancing benefits and costs of, 319–20; challenges to pricing and, 319–20; conceptual framework for, 345; frameworks for analyzing, 310–20; international jurisdiction and, 346; pollution model of, 314–15. *See also* Information loss
Information stewardship, 314–15
Information technology, implications of advances in, for housing market, 111–14
Insider fraud, 321
Institute for Electrical and Electronics Engineers (IEEE), 5
Intellectual property, 13. *See also* Copyrights
Internet, 2, 4–5; digital piracy and, 448; estimating value of, 55–56; evolution of protocol stack, 32f; existing research on economic value of, 57–59; housing market and, 91–92; online sales and, 137; standardization of, 26–30; supply and demand, 4–7
Internet Architecture Board (IAB), 26
Internet data, potential of, 8.
Internet Engineering Task Force (IETF), 5, 22, 26–30; linear probability models of, 39–40, 40t; major participants, 36–41, 37t; most cited standards, 29–30, 30t, 31t; protocol stack and, 31–33; summary statistics, 39, 39t

Kalman filters, 120–21
k-anonymity approach, 283
Kindle, 9, 141

Labor, division of, Internet modularity and, 36–41
Labor markets. *See* Contract labor markets
Labor supply, online contract labor markets and, 227–28
"Last click" rule, 201
Leisure time: ways Americans spend their, 62–63, 63f, 64f
Leisure time, online: computer use for, 61–62; demographics of, 65–70; items crowded out by, 71–80; opportunity cost of, 56; times people engage in, 70–71
Lenovo Key (Lenny), 453–54
Liberty Exchange, 258
LIBRIé e-book reader, Sony, 140–41
Linden dollars, 258
Linkage attacks, 282, 283, 284
Lump sum payments, to authors, 365–71

MAE. *See* Mean absolute error (MAE)
Market-making platforms, 229–30
Marketplace: Adam Smith's, 311–12; complete, 312; information, 312–14
Markov Chain Monte Carlo (MCMC) technique, 123, 131–33
Mean absolute error (MAE), 100, 100n10, 103–5
Mean squared error (MSE), 100n10
Media, polarization and, 171–72. *See also* News, online
Medical databases, individual disclosure and, 282–83
Megaupload, 391–94
Megaupload Penetration Ratio (MPR), 391–94
Metrics, advertising, evolution of, 199–202
Microsoft, 443–44; platform-specific currencies of, 258–59
Microsoft Points, 257
Mirroring hypothesis, 31
Models, 40t; Apple's agency model, 160; basic structural, 120–21; Bayesian model averaging, 123; linear probability

models of IETF, 39–40; platform, 262–72; pollution model of information marketplaces, 314–15; for predicting housing market, 97–100; of production and consumption of online news, 170–71, 175–81; structural time series models, 130–31; structural time series modes, 120–21; theoretical, of recorded music industry, 415–17; of treatment effects, 285–90

Modular design, virtues of, 24

Modularity, Internet, 23–25; age profiles for RFC-to-RFC citations, 42–43, 43t; age profiles for RFC-to-RFC citations and US patent-to-RFC citations, 44, 44t; decomposability and, 33–35; distribution of citations to RFCs over time, 41–44; division of labor and, 36–41; protocol stack and, 30–33; setting standards and, 25–26

Modular system architecture, 22

Monster, 11

Movies, online sales of, 137–38

M-Pesa, 258

MPR. *See* Megaupload Penetration Ratio (MPR)

MSE. *See* Mean squared error (MSE)

Music, online sales of, 137–38

Music industry. *See* Recorded music industry

Nanoeconomics, 93

Napster, 407, 408

National Association of Realtors (NAR), 100–101, 106

National Instant Criminal Background Check (NICS), 128

Network effects, 285

News, online, 169; data sources for, 173–74; descriptive features of consumption of, 174–75; discussion of model's results, 184–88; estimation and results of model of, 181–84; model of production and consumption of, 170–71, 175–81; politics and, 169–70; segregation of consumption of, 174–75, 175f. *See also* Media

Nintendo, platform-specific currencies of, 258

Nook, 9, 141

Nowcasting, 8, 119; consumer sentiment, 124–27; gun sales, 128

oDesk, 11, 219–20; users of, 240; work process on, 226–30

Online currencies. *See* Currencies; Private digital currencies

Partial disclosure: occurrence of, 296; statistical, 305–6; threat of, 283, 284

Payment Card Industry Data Security Standards, 317

Payments, to authors, 357–60; data, 361–65; income from profit sharing, 371–73; lump sum, 365–71; total income to, 373–77. *See also* Copyrights

PayPal, 258

Personal information, digitization and, 3

Piracy, 385; effect of television streaming on, 396–404. *See also* Digital piracy; Recorded music industry; Software piracy

Platforms, 5; competition between, 6; computing market segments and, 5; defined, 5, 258; digitized money transfer systems and, 258; literature, 258; market-making, 229–30; model, 262–72; online contract labor markets, 240–43; private digital currencies and, 258; pure information goods and, 10. *See also* Private digital currencies

Platform-specific currencies, 258–59

Polarization: media and, 171–72; rising US, 171

Policy, government, digitization and, 12–15

Pollution model, applying, to information flows, 314–15

Predictions: for demand for home appliances, 100–101; economic, 90–91; empirical methods for, 97–100; information technology revolution and, 89–90; literature review, 92–97; social science research and, 90. *See also* Housing market

Price comparison sites, for books, 144

Price dispersion, 139

Print books, 141; prices of, 159–62; sales of, vs. e-books, 141t. *See also* E-books

Priors, 123–24

Privacy: challenges of, and digital information, 2; digitization and, 12; role of disclosure protection and, 285; security vs., 284–85

Privacy Rights Clearinghouse (PRC) data, 320–21, 324

Private digital currencies, 11, 257; vs. digitization of state-issued currencies, 257–58; economic model of, 262–72; future directions for, 273–75; platforms and, 258, 262–72; regulatory issues, 272–73
Productivity, 4
Product License Keys, 451
Product searches, online, 138
Project Gutenberg, 140
Prosper, 11
Protocol stack, 30–33; citations in, 35f; evolution of, 32–33, 32f; TCP/IP, 31
"Purchasing intent" surveys, 192

Q-coin, 273
qSearch database, 150–51
Query technology, 89–90

Real estate economics, 94
Real estate market. *See* Housing market
Recorded music industry, 407–8; background of, 411–15; data used for study of, 417–19; effective cost reduction for new work and piracy in, 409–10; inferring sales quantities from sales ranks and album certifications for, 419–22; Internet vs. traditional radio and, 422–25; online criticism and, 425–28; results of net effect of piracy and cost reduction in, 428–38; systematic data analysis of, 410; theoretical framework for production selection problem in, 408–9; theoretical model of, 415–17
Requests for Comments (RFCs), 26, 29, 30t
Russian Longitudinal Monitoring Survey (RLMS), 281–82, 300–305

Sales, online, 137
Scott, Sir Walter, 373–77
Search costs: digital technology and, 8–9
Search engine optimization (SEO) market, 242
Search engines: book-related searches on, 145–48; real estate agents, 91; using, for books, 144
Search engine technology, 90
Searches, online, 9
Search Planner, 145–48, 146t
Search terms, top twenty-five Google, leading users to Barnes & Noble, 145–47, 146t
Security: challenges of privacy and security and, 2; costs of, and information loss, 344–45; data, digitization and, 12–13; privacy vs., 284–85
Selective prediction, 171–72
Social science research, predictions and, 90
Social trends, predicting, 92–94
Software piracy, 14–15, 444–46; defined, 452, 457–58; economic, institutional, and infrastructure variables of, 458–61; economics of, 447–50; machines associated with, 458; methods, 450–55; results between machine characteristics and, 471–72, 471t; results for nature and incidence of, 461–63; results of economic, institutional, and technological determinants of, 464–71; results of impact of antipiracy enforcement efforts on, 472–74; routes to, 452–55; summary statistics, 459t. *See also* Windows 7
Solow Paradox, 4
Sony: LIBRIé e-book reader, 140–41; platform-specific currencies of, 259
Spike-and-slab variable selection, 121–23
Standards, setting, modularity and, 25–26
Standard-setting organizations (SSOs), Internet, 22
State-issued currencies, digitization of, 257–58
Statistical partial disclosure, 305–6
Stock market, discipline by, and data breaches, 339–41
Streaming, television, effect of, on piracy, 396–404
Structural time series models, 130–31; for variable selection, 120–21
Synthetic data, 283

Target data breach, 318n8
Targeted advertising, 3, 195, 199
TCP/IP. *See* Transmission Control Protocol/Internet Protocol (TCP/IP)
Television streaming, effect of, on piracy, 396–404
Time series forecasting, 120–21
Toshiba key (Billy), 454–55
Transmission Control Protocol/Internet Protocol (TCP/IP), 6, 22, 29; protocol stack, 31
Treatment effects, 280–85; case study of religious affiliation and parent's decision on childhood vaccination and medical checkups, 299–305; identification of,

from combined data, 290–95; inference of propensity score and average, 296–99; models of, 285–90

UK Copyright Act of 1814, 359; extensions in length of, 361
UK Copyright Act of 2011, 357
Untargeted advertising, 199n14
US Copyright Act of 1998, 357

Variable selection: approaches to, 120–23; Bayesian model averaging, 123; spike-and-slab, 121–23; structural time series for, 120–21
Visa, 316

Walmart, 140
Windows 7: authenticating valid version of, 451; data for estimating piracy rates of, 455–57; legal ways of acquiring, 451–52; routes to pirating, 452–55. *See also* Software piracy
Work, geographic distribution of, online contract labor markets and, 230–35
World of Warcraft (WoW) Gold, 259
World Wide Web Consortium (W3C), 5, 22, 27–30; protocol stack and, 31–33; publications, 28–29, 28f

Zellner's g-prior, 122